D1130742

SOVIET
EDUCATION
for
SCIENCE
and
TECHNOLOGY

TECHNOLOGY PRESS BOOKS
IN THE SOCIAL SCIENCES

SOVIET
EDUCATION
—————————————— for ——
SCIENCE
and
TECHNOLOGY

ALEXANDER G. KOROL

Published jointly by

The Technology Press of

Massachusetts Institute of Technology

and

John Wiley & Sons, Inc., New York

Chapman & Hall, Ltd., London

Library of Congress Catalog Card Number: 57-13446

Printed in the United States of America

FOREWORD

In recent years the attention of the nation has been drawn with increasing frequency to the accomplishments, presumed and real, of the Soviet educational system; interest has focused in particular on the apparent Soviet success in training large numbers of scientists, engineers, and technicians. Government officials responsible for the conduct of the cold war have pointed with apprehension to the lead which Soviet Russia appears to have acquired over the United States in the preparation of the specialists vital to modern war and industry; educators and scientists, concerned on cultural as well as national security grounds, have adduced the Soviet case as proof of the need for alterations of priorities in American education.

Characteristic of many of these statements is the slim evidence on which they are based. Comparisons between the Soviet and the American trained-manpower potential, for instance, often rest on estimates of numbers of students enrolled and graduated in various fields. Such quantitative evaluations, even when derived from reliable statistics, do not tell us very much if they fail to take adequate account of the many relevant factors which go into determining the quality of Soviet education. It is the object of Mr. Korol's book to examine the organization and effectiveness of the Soviet formal training process in science and technology and to bring out implications for the over-all quality of Soviet-trained scientists and engineers.

Certainly the most obvious method of getting at the quality of an educational system is by judging its products. But in the Soviet case it is precisely these products, the scientists and the engineers, who are the unknown quantities. Our interest, moreover, is not historical as much as predictive; we want to know how the present and future generations are likely to turn out.

This study has relied on two techniques for measuring the quality of Soviet education. The more direct approach has been to gather together materials used in Soviet schools and submit them for evaluation to American educators in the relevant fields. Analysis of the content of Soviet textbooks, examinations, syllabi, and curricula at different levels of the educational system has permitted inferences to be drawn regarding the breadth and depth of the Soviet student's knowledge and skill. This intensive investigation has concentrated on the two representative fields of physics and mechanical engineering.

The quality of education in the Soviet Union has been measured also in a less direct way, by means of an examination of the characteristics of the educational system as a whole. Specialized training for science and engineering cannot be intelligently viewed without an understanding of the philosophy and organization of the system of higher education and of the general and specialized education which precedes it. How many and what kinds of students are being given a higher education, and how are they drawn into the special fields of particular interest to the Soviet state? Are there at various levels shortages of school facilities or of appropriately trained teachers which will affect the quality of Soviet education for science and technology? How are Soviet educational philosophy and practice evolving to meet the rapidly changing requirements of an industrialized society? In an effort to point to the specific factors influencing the quality of scientific education, the author of this book undertakes a careful analysis of the entire Soviet system of higher education.

In his final chapter Mr. Korol ventures some comments on the implications of the Soviet educational system for educational policy in the United States. These comments will be a helpful corrective to the prevalent generalization that our central problem is to win the race for numbers of scientists and engineers graduated. As this study of the aims and characteristics of education in Soviet Russia makes clear, communist purposes are both different from and narrower than ours. Such recent evidences of Soviet technical achievement as the launching of a satellite are less to be explained by the numbers of Soviet technicians who have degrees than by the capability of a totalitarian system to allocate its best brains by direction to the solution of a problem which is given effective top priority by the rulers of the system. The central issue on which our security depends is not whether we can graduate more engineers and scientists than the Soviets. It is whether we can improve still further the quality of our scientific training. It is whether we can find better methods consistent with our democratic principles for focusing the attention of our best scientific minds on the technical problems critical to our security.

It is whether we can effectively administer our research and development effort.

While not minimizing the seriousness of the threat to us of Soviet accomplishments in training people to serve Soviet ends, Mr. Korol makes it clear that our concept of the functions of education in a democracy is and should be very different from theirs, and that we would do ourselves a great disservice by accepting the criteria they apply. We owe him a debt of gratitude for outlining in so painstaking and thorough a fashion what it is the Soviets are trying to do and how they are going about it. Only against the background of this kind of study can we penetrate behind numerical comparisons to the qualitative factors with which we should be most concerned.

The project from which this book is derived was begun by the Center for International Studies in 1953 as a continuation of the work on Soviet society which has been part of the Center's research program since its origin six years ago. The work was continued after 1955 under a grant from the Carnegie Corporation of New York. The views set forth in this book are naturally those of the author and may not be taken as representing the position of the Center for International Studies or of the Massachusetts Institute of Technology.

MAX F. MILLIKAN
Director, Center for International Studies
Massachusetts Institute of Technology

Cambridge, Massachusetts
October 18, 1957

PREFACE

An examination of the educational process within a given society can provide both important clues to an understanding of the moral and intellectual climate in which its people live and significant data for an estimate of the direction of its progress. Its present educational endeavor, perhaps more effectively than any other common process, can serve as a barometer of tomorrow's social climate.

Under the impact of revolutionary advances in physical science and because of the urgent tasks which face contemporary man, now committed to economic development on a world-wide scale, scientific and engineering education have acquired unprecedented importance. The trends in these two fields provide a sound basis for estimating the present and future technological and industrial capabilities of any one nation or group of nations, and potentially of mankind as a whole.

Unfortunately, progress toward the ideal of universality of science and, by extension, of economic development has been greatly impeded by the withdrawal of the Soviet Union and other countries dominated by the Soviet Union from the common tasks of international cooperation. Soviet science and technology have been mobilized to challenge and to compete—not to cooperate—with the rest of the world. They are a vital force in the development of the military and economic capabilities of totalitarian government. At present these capabilities represent a threat to the survival of individual and national integrity throughout the world.

It is critically important, therefore, for us to examine Soviet education, especially in the fields of science and technology.

In this book my aim has been twofold: to present a general outline of the entire educational system of the Soviet Union from elementary through graduate school and selectively to illustrate in some detail Soviet training in physics and mechanical engineering. The present volume derives directly from research on Soviet education which was carried out at the Center for International Studies, Massachusetts Institute of Technology. The original study and the present volume cover Soviet education up to 1957. I have attempted also to indicate some of the major trends which seem likely to influence Soviet educational efforts in the years immediately ahead.

The reader should be forewarned that this is not a comparative study although, in order to illustrate contrasts or similarities, some direct references to American educational data have been given. In citing American examples my only purpose was to provide an occasional frame of reference—a yardstick by which the scale of the Soviet educational scene could be concretely appreciated. In no case were such comparisons meant to suggest the relative merit or lack of merit of either system.

The first chapter considers the Soviet organization of general education through the secondary level and touches upon the major alternatives to academic advancement, such as labor and vocational training programs. Chapters 2 and 3 examine the ten-year school, the Soviet counterpart of the American twelve grade system from elementary through high school. Chapter 4 deals with a sector of the Soviet system which includes many so-called technicums and other specialized schools which train students for work in a great variety of fields at the subprofessional level. The major part of the book, Chapters 5 through 10, is devoted to Soviet undergraduate higher education, with Soviet curricula in physics and a typical major in mechanical engineering shown in detail and compared with the most nearly equivalent curricula at the Massachusetts Institute of Technology. Chapter 11 comments on the organization and conduct of Soviet graduate training. In the concluding chapter I have attempted a necessarily speculative type of inquiry, seeking to convey my view of Soviet education in the context of its goals and contrasting these with the goals of American education.

The scope of material here presented is necessarily limited. I am aware that many aspects of Soviet education not specifically discussed here or only barely indicated, including sociological factors, would be of interest to the general reader and the specialist alike. A more detailed presentation and analysis of technical material on curricula, textbooks, and teaching methods would perhaps be desired by an educator. A social scientist would wish to examine statistical data and trends in a more comprehensive manner. Nevertheless, I have endeavored to present as balanced an array of facts, including the latest available official Soviet statistics, as could be synthesized from the usually scattered, highly selective, and unrepresentative official pronouncements and gross statistics. It is perhaps unnecessary to emphasize that no useful judgment can be derived from any uncritical acceptance of such undifferentiated data and sweeping generalities on education in the Soviet Union as are being distributed by the Soviets for foreign consumption.

It is my hope that this book may usefully contribute to the growing store of American knowledge of Soviet education and thus help in developing a better understanding of its social and political implications.

ALEXANDER G. KOROL

Cambridge, Massachusetts
June 6, 1957

ACKNOWLEDGMENTS

In the preparation of the manuscript and in seeing it through to book form I have incurred an indebtedness which can never be adequately acknowledged. I am grateful first to the Center for International Studies and its director, Max F. Millikan, and to the Center's parent organization, the Massachusetts Institute of Technology. They made it possible for me to undertake the writing of this book. More specifically, I am indebted to the Center for International Studies for the privileges afforded me in the preparation of this work—the use of source material, data, translations, research memoranda, reports, and papers developed in the course of the Center project on Soviet education. My indebtedness, therefore, extends to all who contributed to that original study.

During the pilot stage of the project, conducted during the summers of 1953 and 1954, Stanislaw Kownacki and Eleanor M. Rowell contributed original research and a number of papers. In its final stages the burden of research was shared by Leon Trilling, Assistant Professor of Aeronautical Engineering, MIT, and Grace Kennan, Center research assistant. Dr. Trilling, whose general contribution included a number of interviews and an extensive examination and analysis of documentary material, is the author of the major project paper, *Soviet Education in Aeronautics: A Case Study*. Miss Kennan was responsible for a large part of the study, translation, abstracting, and analysis of original material, as well as the preparation of source memoranda which were used in evaluations by members of the MIT faculty and the writing of interim research papers and analyses. George B. Baldwin participated in all stages of research in his capacity as a senior consultant for the project.

Ruth Carson and later Margaretta Clapp, as secretaries for the project, carried the main responsibility for the technical chores of research, including the preparation of a large number of interim papers. Jean P. S. Clark edited and arranged for the distribution of all the major papers produced under this project.

In addition to the staff of the Center, research and other contributions were made by Taras V. Butoff, Nicholas DeWitt, Boris I. Gorokhoff, Raymond F. Scott, and Barbara Tschirwa. Homer L. Dodge and Norton T. Dodge made a very important contribution by preparing for the Center for International Studies a series of notes on the observations made by them during visits to a number of educational institutions in the Soviet Union in 1955 and by making available much documentary material on Soviet education.

A number of MIT faculty members, including those specifically mentioned in the text of this book, volunteered their indispensable expert help in an advisory capacity and in the evaluation of Soviet textbooks and other documentary material.

All of the above and many other individuals, including staff members of the Center for International Studies, contributed in countless ways toward the realization of the objectives of the original project for which I served as director. To all those who have helped me in the preparation of the manuscript for this publication, I offer my sincere thanks.

The following individuals have read and commented on selected chapters of the first draft: H. Russell Beatty, Michael B. Bever, John Chipman, Norman C. Dahl, David A. Dudley, Nathaniel H. Frank, Philip Franklin, John A. Hrones, Malcolm G. Kispert, Mildred Lamson, Frank A. McClintock, Walter McKay, Philip M. Morse, John T. Norton, George W. Pratt, Jr., Ascher H. Shapiro, Milton C. Shaw, Alan H. Stenning, B. Alden Thresher, Leon Trilling, Victor F. Weisskopf, and Jerome Wiesner.

Among those who have read the entire first draft of Chapters 1 through 11, I am particularly indebted for their criticism and comments to Secor D. Browne, Morris D. Friedman, Beatrice L. Korol, and C. Richard Soderberg.

Finally, I acknowledge with affection and gratitude the collaboration in the preparation and final editing of this work of my colleagues at the Center for International Studies, Camilla D. Hodgen, Donald L. M. Blackmer, and Richard W. Hatch.

Although this book would not have appeared but for the contributions here acknowledged, the author alone bears the responsibility for the material, conclusions, and views here expressed.

CONTENTS

Contents

LIST OF CHARTS AND TABLES

LIST OF ABBREVIATIONS

SOVIET
EDUCATION
for
SCIENCE
and
TECHNOLOGY

THE SOVIET SYSTEM OF MASS EDUCATION

1. Soviet Schools of General Education

The Ten-Year School

The nearest Soviet counterpart of the twelve grades comprising elementary and secondary education in the United States is the so-called ten-year school, with ten grades, age 7 to 17, divided into 4-3-3 progressive stages very roughly corresponding to the 6-3-3 division of the elementary, junior high, and (college preparatory) senior high school grades in the American system. In terms of the Soviet 4-3-3 grade divisions an individual school may have only the first four grades (elementary school), or seven grades ("incomplete secondary" or "seven-year school"), or all ten grades ("complete secondary" or "ten-year school"), each corresponding grade being identical as to content and level of instruction in all such schools.*

Beyond the fact that both the twelve-grade schools in the United States and the Soviet ten-year school provide mass education up to the college level and that both are coeducational there are no significant similarities. On the contrary, as will be discussed in the following chapters, in every essential aspect the two systems stand in sharp contrast. For the present we need to note only one of the most distinguishing characteristics of the Soviet ten-year school: the uniformity of its curricula, textbooks, and methods of instruction, grade for grade, with only minor regional variations throughout the Soviet Union. In Moscow or Irkutsk, Russians or Buryats, boys or girls in corresponding grades follow the same curriculum prescribed by the Ministry of Public Education and study identical subjects, following uniform syllabi and, except for the language in which they are written, identical "approved"

---

* Georgian and Lithuanian schools have an 11-year course of instruction; Latvia and Estonia have both ten- and eleven-year schools.

textbooks. Thus, in theory, each intermediate level (elementary, after 4 years, at age 11; "incomplete secondary," after 3 more years, at age 14) and the terminal level, after graduation from the tenth grade at age 17, are all clearly definable as to the scope and subjects of instruction they imply.

In reality, the uniformity is purely formal. There are significant qualitative differences between the city and rural schools of general education, those in the densely populated areas and in remote localities, those in the predominantly Russian communities and in the national minority regions. Furthermore, not all Soviet children attend regular (full-time) ten-year schools; there are also part-time schools for "working youth" (grades V through X) and part-time evening schools for (usually over-age) "rural youth" (grades I through VII). Although the subjects, as well as the scope of instruction, in these schools are identical on paper with those provided in the curricula of the regular schools, these part-time schools are qualitatively distinct. There is also an unknown but relatively small number of military schools of secondary education with a curriculum in general subjects comparable or identical to that in the corresponding grades of the regular ten-year school. Moreover, beginning with the 1956–1957 academic year, still another type, the widely commented upon boarding schools designed to place Soviet secondary education under completely controlled conditions, have been opened in limited numbers. These schools are briefly discussed in Chapter 2, but it will be some years before their relation to higher education will become apparent.

The Universal and Compulsory Minimum

In tsarist Russia, according to historian George Vernadsky, just prior to World War I the number of pupils in the primary schools was 8 million, somewhat over half the number of children of school age. The educational committee of the Duma estimated that universal education through the primary grades would be reached in 1922.[1] As history would have it, that year, after the virtual destruction of the pre-Revolutionary (state and private) school system during the civil war, witnessed the very nadir of public education in the by then 5-year-old Soviet Russia. Not until 1930 was legislation passed prescribing 3 years of education (age 8 through 10) as a universal and compulsory minimum for 1930–1931, to be expanded to 4 years (age 8 through 11) by the following year;* and not until c. 1934 was 4-year elementary education established on a basis anywhere nearly approach-

* 16th Congress of the Communist Party, June–July 1930.

ing universality. Nonetheless, the Party's 17th Congress, held in January 1934, proclaimed for a universal 7-year base, an objective which only recently has been realized.

The history of the intervening years is worth noting. The 18th Congress (1939) prescribed the achievement during the third Five Year Plan (1938–1942) of universal *secondary education* (10 years, age 8 through 18) in the cities and "the final achievement" of universal 7-year education. Whatever progress in that direction may have been made from 1939 to 1941 was reversed by the war. In 1949 it was decreed that compulsory 7-year education must be made universal within 3 years. On August 13, 1950, *Pravda* stated that "since last year our country has everywhere passed on to universal compulsory seven-year education." *Pravda's* claim was premature. Since c. 1954, however, with some substantial lapses here and there, most Soviet children have continued on at least through the seventh grade (age 7 through 14);* and in 1956 the Constitution of the USSR was amended to state in its article on education that in the Soviet Union a 7-year education is universal and compulsory.†

It is the Soviets' intention that 10 years of education shall be the minimum by 1960. Judging by past progress toward universality of 7-year education, it is doubtful that this objective will be fully met. As late as 1955 it was said:

> Year after year the national plan in regard to universally compulsory education is not fulfilled. Many children still receive no instruction, and the number of children who leave school is still extremely large.[2]

In the meantime, however, the changes made in the definition of objectives and a continued expansion of part-time schools and of vocational training facilities in the Soviet Union should materially help to raise the proportion of students with 10 years of education of one type or another. As originally formulated by the Party's 19th Congress (1952), the minimum was to be a *ten-year school* education—in urban

---

* The entering age for the first grade was changed to 7 by a decree dated September 8, 1943.

† Article 121, as amended July 14, 1956:

"The citizens of the USSR have the right to education.

"This right is secured by universal compulsory seven-year education, by the widespread development of secondary education; by [the fact] that education of all types—whether secondary or higher education—is free; by a system of state scholarships for college and university students who distinguish themselves; by the conduct of school instruction in the native language [of the student]; and by the provision for industrial, technical, and agronomic free training of workers at factories, state farms, machine-tractor stations, and collective farms."

(*Narodnoye obrazovaniye*, No. 9, September 1956.)

areas by 1955, and throughout the Soviet Union by 1960. The 20th Congress, however, in 1956 somewhat modified the original formulation of the 1960 goal; its directive prescribes "essentially to achieve" universal 10-year education which need not be ten-year school education but 10 *years* of education and thus may include 7 years of general education and 3 years of technical or vocational training; and the 7 years of general education may include education obtained on a part-time basis.

Part-Time Schools of General Education

We have already mentioned the schools for "working youth" and for "rural youth." Although first organized as emergency war measures to provide a modicum of education for the adolescent girls and boys employed in industry and in agriculture whose normal education was interrupted or who had no previous education, both have apparently become permanent fixtures in the Soviet educational system.

The schools for working youth were organized in 1943, their aim, according to the regulations issued in the following year, being to provide general education corresponding to the scope of the seven- and ten-year schools and "to nurture the youth in the spirit of unconditional love of the Motherland and devotion to the Soviet rule." The establishment of these schools is the responsibility of the councils (soviets) in each of the fifteen political subdivisions ("states") of the Soviet Union and of their prototypes at the lower levels of administration, down to the city councils. Academic supervision and authority, as with all other schools of general education below the university level (except the "technicums," see Chapter 4), rest with the ministries of public instruction in each of the constituent "states" of the Soviet Union. Each school for working youth by definition is attached to one or more of the industrial enterprises in a given locality, it being the responsibility of these industrial units to provide the necessary space and equipment and to see that the work schedule of the employed juveniles does not interfere with the established school hours. The pupils enrolled in schools for working youth may be divided into as many groups as there are work shifts in a given plant, each group attending 3 hours of morning, afternoon, or evening classes 3 days a week for 48 weeks per year.

There are two types of schools for working youth: the 7-year level, with grades V through VII, and the 10-year level, with grades V through X. Although a prior completion of grades I through IV was assumed, the regulations of 1944 provided for the organization of preparatory groups for those who had not completed elementary education. Soviet statistics show that, at least since 1950, the per cent of over-age students at the elementary level has been dropping. In the fall of 1950, when the total registration in these schools was 838,000, some 86,000 were to be enrolled in grades I through IV; in 1955 the comparable figure was reported at 54,000 in the total working youth school registration of 1.4 million.[3] Fall registration statistics for working youth schools from 1950 through 1955 are shown in Table 1. The steadily growing registration for the three upper grades of these part-time schools suggests that, in addition to the promoted working youth pupils, the senior grade ranks include a substantial number of pupils transferred from schools of general education.

TABLE 1. FALL REGISTRATION IN PART-TIME SCHOOLS FOR WORKING YOUTH
1950–1955
USSR

Year	Total Registration (thousands)	Registration by Grades		
		I–IV (thousands)	V–VII (thousands)	VIII–X (thousands)
1950	838.3	85.6	460.4	292.3
1951	1,001.8	91.6	527.1	383.1
1952	1,126.3	80.5	558.8	487.0
1953	1,352.9	79.0	628.1	645.8
1954	1,416.6	72.8	589.9	753.9
1955	1,387.1	54.0	533.9	799.2

Source: Kul'turnoye stroitel'stvo SSSR, statisticheskii sbornik (Cultural Progress of the USSR, a Statistical Compilation), Moscow: State Statistical Publications, 1956 (hereafter referred to as Kul'turnoye stroitel'stvo SSSR, 1956), pp. 156–157.

No direct statistics are available on either the actual *attendance* or the number *completing* a given grade in working youth schools. Nevertheless, one source specifically stated that in 1952 (when, we would add, the supply of ten-year school graduates was low relative to the quota for college freshman enrollment) 16,000 graduates of the schools for working youth entered institutions of higher education.[4] The fact that qualitatively the graduates of the working youth schools are rated below the graduates of the full-time, regular schools is clear from numerous Soviet references. In 1954, for example, the RSFSR Deputy Minister of Education wrote:

Many institutions of higher technical education refer to the graduates of the working youth schools with alarm. The graduates of the working youth schools possess solid work-experience, are distinguished by considerable purposefulness, application and persistence in studying; and those among them who enter [that is, are admitted to] institutions of higher education give promise of becoming valuable workers. But they lag behind the pupils of the regular schools in theoretical preparation; they frequently fail to qualify in the competitive admission examinations; and those who are admitted show indifferent achievement in higher mathematics and, as a result, a poorer mastery of all other scientific and engineering subjects.[5]

It would be a safe assumption that a very large proportion, if not all, of the working youth school graduates who qualify for admission to schools of higher education enter either as correspondence or evening students on a part-time basis combined with full-time employment.

The schools for rural youth, "for the purpose of instructing the rural youth and adolescents [14 years of age and older] without a disruption of agricultural work," were established in 1944. These are evening schools originally planned to conduct classes 4 hours per day, 5 days per week from November 1 through March. Two types are recognized: the elementary, with grades I through IV, and the seven-year, with grades I through VII. In many cases a "school" for rural youth is simply a group of over-age peasant children enrolled in special evening classes at the regular schools. In the fall of 1950 only 511.7 thousand children were registered in some 15,564 "schools"—an average of fewer than thirty-three pupils per unit. In 1955 the total registration was

TABLE 2. FALL REGISTRATION IN PART-TIME SCHOOLS FOR RURAL YOUTH
1950–1955
USSR

Year	Total Registration (thousands)	Registration by Grades		
		I–IV (thousands)	V–VII (thousands)	VIII–X (thousands)
1950	511.7	259.8	248.3	3.6
1951	481.1	210.6	268.1	2.4
1952	455.2	144.5	308.2	2.5
1953	479.2	109.8	364.7	4.7
1954	395.8	68.0	320.4	7.4
1955	345.4	44.1	277.8	23.5

Source: Kul'turnoye stroitel'stvo SSSR, 1956, pp. 156–157.

345.4 thousand for 10,772 "schools"—about thirty-two students per school. Although originally these schools were limited to seven grades, Soviet statistics since c. 1950 have shown a small registration for the upper grades—for the tenth grade, for instance, 0.3 thousand in 1950, 1.9 thousand in 1954, and 5.1 thousand in 1955. A summary of the rural youth school registration statistics is given in Table 2. In contrast with the comparable figures for the working youth schools, the total registration in the rural youth schools has been declining.

Judging by many indications—among them, the irregularity of attendance, high drop-out rates, part-time teachers, and lack of facilities—both the efficiency and the quality of these schools are lower than in the working youth schools.

No high claims are made for either type even in the most patriotic Soviet accounts. On the contrary, a typical comment runs something like the following:

> The educational process in schools for working and rural youth is badly organized. Many schools are not fully staffed. Lessons are conducted at hours which are not suitable for the employed youngsters—hence the poor attendance and low level of achievement.[6]

The Russian Republic (RSFSR) Minister of Higher Education in 1955 implied that these part-time schools are not expected to maintain regular standards when he emphasized that "hoodlums and pupils who do not respond to correction" should be expelled from the regular schools and added that "such people would not be denied the opportunity for the education they need for the future [inasmuch as they can study] in schools for young industrial and agricultural workers."[7]

The peak of registration, if not of actual enrollment, may have been reached for the agricultural youth schools in 1950, with a 512,000 registration, and in the industrial schools perhaps in 1954, with over 1.4 million on the rolls. Since these dates, the registration in both categories has been declining; but in 1955, some 11 years after these emergency schools were first established, they still accounted for 1.7 million pupils—roughly, 6 per cent of the number enrolled in the regular schools. Apparently, their enrollment is again expected to increase. E. I. Afanasenko, the RSFSR Minister of Education, as reported in *Uchitel'skaya gazeta* of May 16, 1956, stated that in the RSFSR alone (which accounts for approximately 55.2 per cent of the USSR population) by 1960 there should be 1.15 million enrolled in the working youth schools and 0.23 million in the rural part-time schools. Whatever the future rate of growth and particular role of these part-time schools, they have not in the past figured significantly in the education of future scientists and engineers, and no more needs to be said about them for our purpose.

2. Special Schools of Secondary Education

Military Schools

In tsarist Russia the schools of secondary education included gymnasiums (classical schools preparing students mainly for the universities), the Russian counterpart of the German *Oberrealschule* (intended largely for the future students of engineering schools), commercial secondary schools (with programs generally intended as preparation for professional schools), and the so-called cadet corps schools which combined secondary education (more or less of the *Oberrealschule* type) with military upbringing and which were designed largely to prepare students for officers' training and careers in the tsarist armed forces. Under the Soviets, gymnasiums and other civilian types of pre-Revolutionary schools were reorganized and eventually integrated within the uniform network of the ten-year schools; the cadet corps schools were categorically abolished in 1918. But some 26 years later, during the last war, a system of conceptually identical schools was organized— tsarist-type uniforms and all—as the Suvorov and the Nakhimov schools, named after General A. V. Suvorov (1730–1800) and Admiral P. S. Nakhimov (1802–1855), respectively. These are Soviet preparatory schools for the Soviet counterparts of the United States Military, Naval, and Air Academies.

The training of the future Soviet officers starts early. According to one émigré source, the entrance age for the Suvorov and Nakhimov schools was originally set at 8 years of age, but, he added:

> Experience has shown that little boys who have just left home were unbearably lonesome away from the family and were unable all at once to immerse themselves in the intricacies of the military science prescribed [by the USSR Ministry of Defense] for the first-graders.[8]

A Soviet encyclopedia* states that instruction at the Suvorov schools starts with the fourth grade (age 11) and at the Nakhimov schools with grade VI. Both types of schools give the equivalent of the ten-year school general education plus a great deal of military training, including summer camping, exercises, and training cruises. No statistics as to the enrollment, graduation, or disposition of Suvorov and Nakhimov graduates are available. The same source (2nd Ed., Vol. 29) states that "there are Nakhimov schools in Baku and Leningrad"; perhaps there

---

* *Bolshaya sovetskaya entsiklopediya* (hereafter referred to as *BSE*), 2nd Ed., Vol. 29, 1954, and Vol. 41, 1956.

are only two of these pre-naval training schools in the Soviet Union. The number of Suvorov schools is not known to this writer.

Whatever their number, it is certain that these pre-officer training schools enjoy a highly privileged position and that their students are given extraordinary care and attention. Not only is the instruction in these schools free, but in every other respect the boys selected for training are cared for wholly by the state. All references suggest that no costs are spared to provide the best of facilities, teaching personnel, and physical living conditions—perhaps by way of compensation for the extremely rigorous regime and discipline. Judging by all accounts, the students of these establishments are likely to be extremely well conditioned, thoroughly indoctrinated, and otherwise fully prepared for Soviet officer training and future careers in the Soviet armed forces.

Specialized Secondary Education

A very important Soviet alternative, and, since 1952, a supplement, to the regular ten-year school education is provided by a large network of schools usually called technicums or more generally "schools of specialized secondary education." These schools combine general education with a program of vocational training at the subprofessional level. They accept, on a competitive basis, seven-year school graduates (age 14) for the normal course of instruction of 4 years and ten-year school graduates for an accelerated course of from 2 to 2½ years training for all kinds of occupations, including those in engineering and other technical fields.

The technicums, with a total enrollment in 1955–1956 of nearly 2 million, of whom 1.7 million were full-time resident students, play a vital role in the formation and growth of the all-important subprofessional specialists in every imaginable occupational category. Because of their importance for the industrial and the economic mechanism of the Soviet Union generally, they are discussed separately in Chapter 4.

Here it may be noted that no one category of American institutions for subprofessional education can be properly equated to the Soviet technicums as a group. Even in the Soviet system they occupy a unique administrative and functional position. Whereas all civilian schools of general education in the Soviet Union are under the complete jurisdiction of the ministries of public education, the technicums are under a dual control. Academically, they are supervised by the Ministry of *Higher* Education; in all other respects each technicum is operated by, and exclusively for, an industrial or other operational ministry or agency of the state or for a single plant under their control. Thus, although in terms of general education technicums are formally equated with the ten-year school, they are outside the basic network of general schools of public education; and, although technicums are under the control of the Soviet Ministry of Higher Education, they are not rated as higher educational institutions.

3. THE USSR "STATE LABOR RESERVE" AND ITS TRAINING PROGRAMS

Some hundreds of thousands of teen-age Soviet boys and girls are drafted each year for training in the schools of the USSR "State Labor Reserve," a very important, centrally controlled adjunct of Soviet industry.

The original decree of October 2, 1940, "On the State Labor Reserves of the USSR," authorized an annual draft of from 800,000 to 1,000,000 males 14 to 17 years of age for training, the term of which was to vary from 6 months to 2 years, and for a subsequent compulsory work duty of 4 years "at regular wages" during which period they were deferred from military service. The decree obligated every rural community (collective farm) to provide each year two males, 14 to 17, either volunteers or draftees, per one hundred of the community's total population between the ages of 14 and 55. The urban quotas were to be established yearly by the Council of Ministers and filled by the city councils (soviets). During the war the labor draft was extended to girls from 16 to 18 years old; and in 1947 it was extended to include girls from age 15 to 18 and young males up to 19 years of age.

The quotas authorized by the 1940 labor draft decree have not been filled every year. An article published in *Pravda* on August 20, 1956 stated that more than 8 million State Labor Reserve workers had been trained since the inauguration of the plan in 1940, and that during the 1955–1960 period the labor reserve schools must train "three and a half million such workers for industry, transportation, construction, and agriculture."

Scholastically and occupationally these schools are a dead end. It is plainly evident that their chief function has been to provide a pool of cheap mobile labor under the guise of an educational procedure. An article in *Pravda*, February 15, 1948, for instance, reported that in 1947 "pupils in labor schools produced 2 million tons of coal and 270,000 tons of ore, overhauled and repaired 2,000 locomotives and 17,000 freight cars, built 2,000 metalworking machines, and made 60 million rubles' worth of spare parts for agricultural machinery." As to mobility, in 1947 and 1948, for instance, to meet the shortage of workers in the coal industry, Soviet labor reserve schools "trained and sent about 690,000 young workers" to the coal mines.[9] The implications of such official statements are clear; the fraudulence of the Soviet stand against child labor is evident.

Vital as these schools are for the Soviet economy, only a brief further mention needs to be made here of the several types of schools operated within the Soviet labor reserve system. We shall refer to them later only as Soviet alternatives to the more advanced training with which we are mainly concerned.*

The FZO Schools

At the lowest level stand the Soviet labor reserve schools of "FZO"—"factory and plant instruction." These schools recruit and train young workers, male and female, largely for coal and ore mining, metallurgical and oil industries, and the building trades—all of which together represent numerically the largest category of labor reserve workers. The normal age of enrollment is 16 to 19; and the course of instruction varies from the originally prescribed 6 months up to 1 year in certain trades. FZO training is supposed to include 100 hours of classroom instruction along with direct work training in shops or plants. No prior education seems to have been required of pupils recruited for training in these schools. It is not clear how the short term of instruction in FZO schools will be reconciled with the plan to achieve universal 10-year education by 1960 unless at least 9 years of prior education should be made the entrance requirement. As shown in Table 3, since 1940, and through 1955, these schools have recruited 5.1 million young workers, of whom 990,000 were trained during the fifth Five Year Plan (1951–1955).

Trade, Railroad, and Mining Schools

A 2-year term was originally prescribed for training in semi-skilled industrial, maintenance, and service occupations in schools (usually called uchilishcha) such as Labor Reserve Railroad Schools and others. The entrance age for these 2-year schools is 14 for boys and 15 for girls, but only elementary prior education is required to qualify for enrollment. Now that the 7-year general education has been officially declared to be the universal minimum throughout the Soviet Union, the educational base of pupils enrolled in these schools is likely to be raised accordingly. Furthermore, inasmuch as 10 years of education

* For a brief but highly informative account and analysis of the USSR labor reserve system see Solomon M. Schwarz, *Labor in the Soviet Union*, New York: Praeger, 1952, pp. 77–83.

is to be the minimum by 1960, the term of instruction in these schools will probably be increased at least by one year in order to eliminate the obvious discrepancy.

The 2-year course of training in the labor reserve trade schools is structured on a 7-hour per day basis (2 hours of classwork, 5 hours of job training), 6 days per week, September through June. In July there are no classes but job training of 3 hours per day continues; August is the vacation month.[10] The total scheduled hours of the course are distributed between job training (about 52 per cent) and other types of instruction, including drafting, mathematics, physics, and the Russian language (about 17 per cent in all), technical subjects (about 12 per cent), physical education, and "political classes." Since 1940, when they were first organized in their present form, and through 1955, these schools trained a total of 2.4 million workers.

Technical Trades Schools

As will be more fully discussed elsewhere, in recent years (since c. 1953) the yearly Soviet crop of ten-year school graduates has been running far in excess of the planned rate of admission to the universities and other types of institutions for higher education. This situation has posed a problem, since the last three grades of the 10-grade undifferentiated Soviet system of general education have been traditionally conceived and conducted as college preparatory grades. The training of the ten-year school graduate, like that of the American high school graduate of 50 years ago, has been aimed to qualify him for college.

As one of the means for channeling the surplus of the 10-year graduates into the labor-hungry Soviet industry and agriculture, there was created in 1954 a new type of short-term training school, the technical trades school, to be operated within the State Labor Reserve system. Some 250 of these schools were established in that year at industrial plants, mines, machine-tractor stations, and other state enterprises. The term of instruction was set at one year for most trades, with a 2-year maximum. The schools were to give training in some 98 occupational categories—such as machinery operators, mechanics, plumbers, estimators, draftsmen, inspectors, and other skilled and junior supervisory occupations—in several industrial fields and in agriculture.* In 1955, after both the number of schools and the number of training programs had been increased, some 280 trades were taught in these schools. As of April 1956 there were 439 technical trades schools with a total

---

* A detailed summary and analysis of the training programs and other information on technical trades schools is included in Cenis Source Memorandum No. 31.

enrollment of approximately 117,000.[11] In the meantime, as of November 1, 1955, the training period was dropped to only 6 months in some categories, a 10-month term was prescribed for others, and the original 1-year and 2-year courses were retained for certain occupations.[12] The shorter term of training has already been criticized by the Deputy Director of the USSR Labor Reserve, who in August 1956 wrote:

> One should recognize it was an error to shorten the term of training at the technical trades schools; the trainees of the previous graduating classes, before the term of instruction was shortened, were better prepared to start productive work.[13]

The technical trades schools of the State Labor Reserve have not been in existence long enough to permit a categorical appraisal of their relationship to other types of vocational training, let alone of their potential role in preparing young ten-year school graduates for engineering training. According to the regulations, the trainees who distinguish themselves by graduating with "excellent" grades need only to *pass* the required entrance examinations, without having to compete on the basis of grades, to gain admission to the extension, that is, part-time, schools of higher education. In general, it appears that all these trade schools are decidedly of the terminal type conceived more or less on a crash basis to alleviate the shortage of qualified workers in industry and agriculture and to help wean the reluctant ten-year school

TABLE 3. NUMBER OF YOUNG WORKERS TRAINED IN LABOR RESERVE SCHOOLS OF THE SOVIET UNION, BY FIVE-YEAR PERIODS, 1941–1955
(In Thousands of Workers)

Kind of School*	1941–1945	1946–1950	1951–1955	1941–1955
FZO	1,790	2,368	990	5,148
Trade	685	1,024	719	2,428
Technical	. . .	. . .	27	27
All three	2,475	3,392	1,736	7,603

Source: The National Economy of the USSR, 1956, p. 203.

* FZO—"Factory, Plant [and Mine] Training" schools. Course of training: 6 months.

Trade—railroad, mining, and other trade schools with a 2-year course of instruction.

Technical—technical trades schools, *tekhnicheskiye uchilishcha*, established in 1954 to train (1 to 2 years) ten-year school graduates in manual (technical) skills.

graduate from his visions of the privileged status which in the Soviet Union is firmly identified with higher education. It is quite certain that in their first 2 years of operation the technical trades schools have not been popular with the students. It is also likely that the drop-out rate has been fairly high; for instance, it was reported that 60,000 students were enrolled at the outset in 1954 but, as shown in Table 3, only 27,000 were graduated in 1955. A substantial proportion of these students apparently enter employment without having completed the course.

4. SCHOOLS OF MECHANIZATION IN AGRICULTURE

Schools for the training of agricultural machinery and tractor mechanics in the Soviet Union have been operated by the Ministries of Agriculture and of State Farms. In 1954 the Ministry of Agriculture was accused of having failed to provide instructors, textbooks, equipment, and other facilities for the mechanization of agriculture schools in its jurisdiction. Consequently, according to *Pravda,* January 5, 1954, all such schools were transferred to the Ministry of Culture; and later, when *this* ministry was reorganized, in March 1954, the Main Administration of the Labor Reserves assumed control over most of them.

The schools of mechanization in agriculture train mechanics and operators of tractors, combines, and other agricultural machinery. The minimum entering age is 17 for both males and females; a prior 10-year secondary education is preferred but not required.[14] In 1954 the labor reserve agricultural mechanization schools accounted for about 44 per cent of the mechanics so trained and for nearly 50 per cent (of a smaller total) in 1955, as follows (in thousands):

Trained in:	1954	1955
Labor Reserve Schools	344	284
Other schools	436	294
Total	780	578

One wonders if there are enough tractors and other agricultural machines in the Soviet Union to keep all these mechanics busy, considering the fact that the total number trained in 6 years (1950–1955) has been reported at 3,764,000.

5. THE ROAD TO HIGHER EDUCATION

Although statistics are lacking, it is certain that since the expansion of the upper grades enrollment of the ten-year school the resident freshmen of Soviet universities and colleges have been almost exclusively recent or former graduates of the ten-year schools. Only a small number of successful applicants comes from other types of Soviet schools, notably from technicums—under the rule whereby the best 5 per cent of the technicum graduates are permitted to apply for admission to the institutions of higher education.   The extension (evening and correspondence) facilities at the university level are somewhat less selective, operating under less stringent rules of admission, but the student's choice of part-time programs is as a rule limited to the immediate field of his regular employment.

A schematic representation of Soviet school enrollment in major categories below the university level is shown on Chart 1 at the end of this chapter.   The chart shows, approximately to scale, the number of students enrolled during the 1955–1956 school year by grades in accordance with the documented and in some cases estimated statistics given in Table 4.   The chart, whatever its possible inaccuracies in distributing Soviet school enrollment by grades, is reliable enough, we believe, to illustrate a number of points of major significance, including the following:

1. The magnitude of Soviet efforts to provide some education for all.

2. The relatively small number of students admitted to resident status in institutions of higher education—in itself suggesting a high degree of selection.

3. The small number of school-age individuals who receive formal vocational training relative to the enrollment in the largely undifferentiated ten-year school of general education.

4. The "inverted pyramid" distribution of pupils in grades IV through VII—a reflection of the wartime birth deficit.

The last two factors have been particularly instrumental, it appears, in bringing about a number of highly significant developments in the field of basic ten-year school education since c. 1953, above all, the expansion of upper-grade enrollment and the curricular changes in the ten-year school which lead away from the former college preparatory orientation toward a vocational emphasis.   These and other changes will be considered in the following chapter.

16   **Soviet Education**

CHART 1. PROGRESSION TO HIGHER EDUCATION IN THE SOVIET UNION. (*Source:* Table 4.)

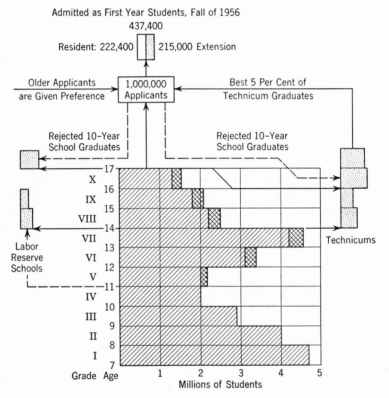

Admitted as First Year Students, Fall of 1956
437,400
Resident: 222,400   215,000 Extension

Older Applicants are Given Preference   1,000,000 Applicants   Best 5 Per Cent of Technicum Graduates

Rejected 10-Year School Graduates   Rejected 10-Year School Graduates

Labor Reserve Schools

Technicums

Grade Age   1   2   3   4   5
Millions of Students

Ten Grades in Schools of General Education
Regular Schools   Part-Time Schools

TABLE 4. SOVIET SCHOOL ENROLLMENT, PROGRESSION TO HIGHER
EDUCATION AND ALTERNATIVE
(Data Used for Chart 1)

1. Schools of General Education, enrollment by grades, 1955–1956, in millions

Grade	Estimated		Soviet Figures
X	1.3		1.3
IX	1.8	5.25	
VIII	2.2		
VII	4.2		
VI	3.1	9.3	
V	2.0		
IV	2.0		
III	2.9		
II	4.0	13.6	
I	4.7		
Total enrollment	28.2 millions		28.15 millions

2. Schools for Working and Rural Youth, 1955–1956

Enrollment by Grades	X	VIII–X	V–VII	I–IV	Total
Working youth	223	799	534	54	1,387
Rural youth	5	24	278	44	346
Total (thousands)	228	823	812	98	1,733

Estimated distribution of total enrollment by grades (approximately in proportion to the regular ten-year school enrollment):

Grade	Millions	Grade	Millions
X	0.23	V	0.17
IX	0.27	IV	
VIII	0.32	III	negli-
VII	0.37	II	gible
VI	0.27	I	

3. Labor Reserve schools, 1956 enrollment

	Estimated
FZO, 6-month course*	100,000
Trade Schools, 2-year course	300,000
Mechanization of Agriculture, 1-year course	250,000
Technical Trades School, 1-year course (average)	120,000
Total for Labor Reserve schools	770,000

4. Technicums (*Pravda*, April 25, 1956, p. 3, reported total technicum enrollmen at 1,959,000. *Kul'turnoye stroitel'stvo SSSR, 1956*, on p. 231 gives 1,960.4 thousand.)

TABLE 4 (continued)

Estimated Distribution by Years

Fourth	570
Third	640
Second	350
First	400
Total	1,960 thousand

5. College Admissions Data, fall of 1956†

Resident full-time students	222,400
Part-time, evening and correspondence students‡	215,000
Total college admissions, fall of 1956	437,400

Source: (except as noted) *The National Economy of the USSR, 1956*, pp. 229 and 230.

* *Izvestia*, December 11, 1955, states 100,000 were to be enrolled.

† *Trud*, August 31, 1956.

‡ In 1955 the number was 176,000.

NOTES TO CHAPTER 1

1 George Vernadsky, *A History of Russia*, 3rd revised Ed., New Haven: Yale University Press, 1951, p. 195.

2 *Uchitel'skaya gazeta*, November 30, 1955, p. 4; in *The Current Digest of the Soviet Press* (hereafter referred to as *CDSP*), Vol. VII, No. 50, p. 32.

3 *The National Economy of the USSR, a Statistical Compilation*, issued by the Central Statistical Administration, Council of Ministers USSR, Moscow, 1956. Mimeographed translation (272 pp.) published by the U. S. Government, p. 230 (hereafter referred to as *The National Economy of the USSR, 1956*).

4 A. Shtyl'ko, *Pod'em kul'turno-tekhnicheskovo urovnya trudyashchikhsya* (The Rise in the Cultural and Technical Level of the Toilers), Moscow: Goskul'prosvet, 1953, pp. 44–46.

5 *Sovetskaya pedagogika*, No. 5, 1954, p. 121.

6 K. Mikhailov in *Sovetskaya Latviya*, March 20, 1954.

7 "Train Younger Generations to Be Alert and Disciplined," *Pravda*, October 13, 1955, p. 2; in *CDSP*, Vol. VII, No. 41, p. 26.

8 N. Aksakov, "Suvorovtsy i nakhimovtsy," *Svoboda* (Munich), No. 15, August 1953, p. 5.

9 A. Bordadyn (Deputy Director of the USSR Council of Ministers' Chief Administration of the Labor Reserves), "Nazrevshiye voprosy podgotovki trudovykh rezervov" (The Urgent Questions in the Training for Labor Reserves), *Pravda*, August 20, 1956, p. 2.

10 E. N. Medynskii, *Narodnoye obrazovaniye v SSSR* (Public Education in the USSR), Moscow: RSFSR Academy of Pedagogical Sciences, 1952, p. 145 (hereafter referred to as E. N. Medynskii, *Narodnoye obrazovaniye v SSSR*).

11 *BSE*, 2nd Ed., Vol. 42, 1956, p. 392.

12 "Povysit' kachestvo raboty tekhnicheskikh uchilishch" (Raise the Quality of

Work at the Technical Trades Schools), *Professional'no-technicheskoye obrazovaniye,* No. 10, October 1955, pp. 1 f.

[13] A. Bordadyn, *op. cit.*

[14] *Spravochnik dlya okonchivshikh sredniye shkoly* (Reference Book for Those Who Have Completed Secondary Schools), Moscow: Uchpedgiz, 1955, p. 44.

THE TEN–YEAR SCHOOL:

ORGANIZATION AND CURRICULUM

The ten-year school had become established in approximately its present form by 1934, ending an experiment in public education begun in 1918, when the so-called Unified Labor School was conceived and introduced as the only form of pre-university education.

The Unified Labor School included two levels: the first with a 5-year course, age 8 through 12, and the second with a 4-year course terminating at age 17. Students were organized in coeducational groups partly by age and partly by levels of achievement. Under the 1918 plan the teaching process, superficially derived from the concept of progressive education, emphasized group activities; textbooks were all but abolished; and there was no compulsory homework of any kind. All examinations—entrance, promotional, and final—were abolished; the schools were forbidden to take any disciplinary action against students; the internal management of each school was entrusted to the school council, which included one student representative of each age group of pupils 13 years of age and older. "Beginning with its elementary form," the directive on the Unified Labor School stated, "self-management of children [hereby] introduced is gradually to develop into a harmonious formalized organization."[1]

All accounts agree that the result of the early Soviet experimentation with the school system was educational chaos. A return to traditional practices was resorted to in the early 1930's, and a 1934 decree prescribed the still-existing grade ("class") system, leading progressively to elementary (4-year), incomplete secondary (7-year), and secondary (10-year) education. Strict discipline, standardized and centrally approved textbooks, a fixed school calendar, promotional and final examinations, the pre-Revolutionary system of grading from "1" (total failure) to "5" (excellent), and even school uniforms were all restored.*

In 1936 a directive of the Central Committee of the Communist Party put an abrupt stop to the growing preoccupation of Soviet educators with practices based on child study—pedology—which were derived largely from American developments in the use of school-child psychology, psychometrics, intelligence and aptitude testing, and the educational concepts and theory of guidance.[2] The Central Committee of the Party condemned the entire concept of pedology, stating that its application resulted in directing a large number of children to remedial classes or special schools, and that the number of such special schools was growing rapidly—"contrary to a direct stipulation" of the Central Committee and Soviet government, "on the opening of [only] two or three schools for defective children or those pupils who disorganize the school regime." The Central Committee ordered the Ministry of Public Instruction to "liquidate" the position of school pedologists, to "extract" books on pedology from circulation, to remove pedology from the normal school curriculum, and to subject all the theoretical writings of the pedologists to "damning criticism in the press." From then on, environment alone was assumed to matter in the making of a Soviet man.

One consequence of this directive was to deprive Soviet educators of any opportunity to develop objective aptitude testing techniques. A related fact is that the oral examination at all levels of education remains the prevailing method for testing achievement in the Soviet school system even though with the greatly expanded school enrollment oral examinations consume a large part of the school calendar. In any event, the rationale of the 1934 directive has been sustained and reasserted as recently as 1955, as for instance in a Soviet encyclopedia which defines pedology as "a reactionary bourgeois pseudo-science of the child based on the assumption of a fatalistic predestination of the child's fate by biological and social factors, by the influence of inheritance and unchanging environment."[3] The encyclopedia article goes on to quote from the 1934 directive that the aim of pedology is "to prove special giftedness and a special right to life of the exploiting classes and of 'superior races' while on the other hand [to rationalize] the physical and spiritual doom of the working classes and 'inferior races.' "

* The introduction of uniforms was decreed in 1936—"to be first effected in Moscow, Leningrad, Kiev, Kharkov, and Minsk"—but was not achieved even in the largest cities until recently because no uniforms could be produced in sufficient quantities. All recent pictures of Soviet schoolrooms show pupils wearing uniforms.

The 1934 directive ordered a survey of enrollment in special and remedial classes and the transfer of a majority of children enrolled in them to ordinary schools. Three years later the Council of Commissars declared against the other end in the school spectrum—the model schools, which, it was said, the Ministry of Public Instruction had been gradually developing to the detriment of its basic duty, the raising of standards uniformly throughout the school system. The model school was condemned; thereafter all schools were to be the "usual, normal schools." Thus, by 1937, at least in principle, the moulding of the Soviet school system into a homogeneous pattern was completed; and the ten-year school, aside from wartime dislocations, remained essentially uniform throughout the Soviet Union until the 1950's.

1. Enrollment and the Population Factor

As noted at the end of Chapter 1, certain other than ideological pressures have combined strongly to influence the course of Soviet educational policy in recent years. One of them, the pressure of numbers, is particularly significant and warrants a brief statistical detour.

The expansion of Soviet school enrollment from its abysmal decline in 1922 to its present very large size (relative to the general status of the Soviet economy) has been most impressive in spite of the fact that it has consistently trailed behind official promises. The peak was reached just before World War II, with a total school enrollment of 34.5 million in 1940–1941. In the postwar years, beginning with 1949–1950, the size of the school-age population has declined because of the wartime deficit in the birthrate. As far as the school enrollment is concerned, the deficit, which naturally asserted itself first at the lowest grade and progressed upward each year, resulted in the 1955–1956 school year in a relative shortage in grades IV and V and an inverted pyramid distribution for grades IV through VII, approximately as shown on Chart 1.

In a move which may not have been entirely unrelated to the demographic cave-in, the 19th Party Congress in 1952 reopened the drive to achieve 10-year universal education. The task of carrying out this objective fell primarily upon the ten-year school, more specifically upon its "high school" component, grades VIII through X. Since the *total* school enrollment was falling, it became that much easier to expand the upper-grade enrollment and greatly to increase the number of graduates from the tenth, the terminal, grade without a proportional increase in plant and facilities. In 1950–1951 the total school enrollment stood at 33.2 million, of which number only some 290,000, or less than 1 per cent, were enrolled in the tenth grade. In 1955–1956 the total enrollment fell to 28.1 million, but the tenth-grade pupils numbered 1.3 million, or 4.6 per cent of the total.* The enrollment figures for these and other selected years are recorded in Table 5 and shown graphically on Chart 2, where the pattern of change can be seen at a glance.

TABLE 5. ENROLLMENT IN SOVIET REGULAR SCHOOLS OF GENERAL EDUCATION IN SELECTED YEARS, TOTAL AND BY GRADE LEVELS

(In Millions of Pupils)

YEAR AND CATEGORY		TOTAL	I–IV	V–VII	VIII–X	X
1940–1941	Rural	23.8	16.0	6.8	1.0	
	Urban	10.7	5.4	4.0	1.3	
	All schools	34.5	21.4	10.8	2.3	0.45
1950–1951	Rural	21.5	13.5	7.4	0.6	
	Urban	11.7	6.2	4.6	0.9	
	All schools	33.2	19.7	12.0	1.5	0.29
1954–1955	Rural	17.1	7.6	7.3	2.2	
	Urban	12.3	5.1	4.3	2.9	
	All schools	29.4	12.7	11.6	5.1	1.1
1955–1956	Rural	16.1	7.9	5.8	2.4	
	Urban	12.0	5.7	3.5	2.8	
	All schools	28.1	13.6	9.3	5.2	1.3

Source: The National Economy of the USSR, 1956, p. 229. (Some of the figures cited here are rounded and adjusted to the totals.)

Complete data on school enrollment, 1922–1923 to 1955–1956 (except for World War II years), are also given in *Kul'turnoye stroitel'stvo SSSR, 1956*, pp. 122 and 123.

* The decline in the total enrollment was wholly at the expense of the rural population, as can be seen by comparing 1940–1941 and 1955–1956 rural school enrollment figures given in Table 5. Note particularly the fall in the rural component of the elementary grades—from 16 million in 1940–1941 down to 7.6 million in 1954–1955. This phenomenon reflects partly the continued urbanization in the Soviet Union and partly the disproportionate World War II losses among the rural male population, as can be surmised from the following statistics:

	Urban	Rural
1940 population (millions)	60.6	131.1
Grade I–IV enrollment (millions)	5.4	16.0
Per cent of population	8.9	12.2
1956 population (millions)	87.0	113.2
Grade I–IV enrollment (millions)	5.7	7.9
Per cent of population	6.5	7.0

Source: Same as for Table 5.

CHART 2. ENROLLMENT IN SOVIET REGULAR SCHOOLS OF GENERAL EDUCATION IN SELECTED YEARS.   (*Source:* Table 5.)

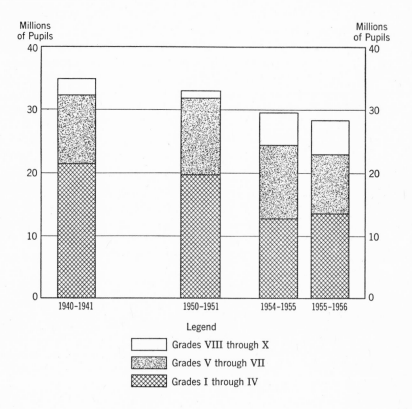

Legend

☐ Grades VIII through X

▓ Grades V through VII

▨ Grades I through IV

The rapid growth of the tenth-grade enrollment is especially significant in light of the fact that for some years (prior to 1952) the number of new ten-year school graduates closely paralleled the number of resident (full-time) college freshmen matriculated in the fall of the corresponding year. In 1951, for example, there were approximately 290,000 new ten-year school graduates; in the fall of that year approximately 250,000 resident freshmen were matriculated. Since then the number of pupils graduating from the tenth grade has kept rapidly increasing—to 440,000 in 1953, 1.1 million in 1955, and 1.3 million in 1956; but the rate of matriculation for resident instruction at Soviet universities has remained fairly constant, with considerably less than 300,000 resident freshmen being admitted each year (Table 6). It is evident, therefore, that just on the basis of these figures the ten-year school is no longer mainly a college preparatory school and that an increasing number of ten-year school graduates find it impossible to go on to higher education.

TABLE 6. SOVIET TENTH-GRADE SCHOOL ENROLLMENT AND NUMBER OF
FRESHMEN ADMITTED TO INSTITUTIONS OF HIGHER EDUCATION
FOR RESIDENT INSTRUCTION,* IN SELECTED YEARS
(In Millions of Students)

Year†	Tenth Grade	Freshmen‡
1950	0.22	0.24
1951	0.29	0.25
1952	0.32	0.24
1953	0.44	not available
1954	0.88	0.30
1955	1.1	0.29
1956	1.3	0.22

Sources: 1. Kul'turnoye stroitel'stvo SSSR, 1956, p. 213.
2. The National Economy of the USSR, 1956, pp. 229, 234.
3. Nicholas DeWitt, Soviet Professional Manpower, Washington, D.C.:
National Science Foundation, 1955, pp. 273, 298, and 299 (rounded).
4. Table 5.

* Resident freshmen include evening students; in 1955 the total number of freshmen and their distribution were as follows:

Admitted to full-time resident instruction	257,173
Admitted to part-time evening instruction	28,453
Admitted to correspondence study	175,818
Total admissions	461,444

† School enrollment for the school year ending in the given year and freshmen admitted in the fall of that year.
‡ Excluding Communist Party schools.

The very rapid expansion of the upper-grade enrollment has naturally called for a series of measures by the Soviet government to increase
correspondingly the supply of teachers, textbooks, and teaching aids
for grades VIII through X. The sharp increase in the number of "high
school" graduates has led, as was noted in Chapter 1, to the development of new means—such as the technical trades schools and the
shortened technicum courses—for the channeling of graduates who
cannot be absorbed in the universities into industry and agriculture.
Finally, the changing role of the ten-year school has brought about a
number of significant alterations in the curriculum, especially since
1952, when the Party revived the perennial but previously ineffectual
campaigns for the "polytechnization" of the educational process
throughout the school system.

It is clear that recent developments in the Soviet ten-year school
system have already brought about a considerable degree of differentiation within the heretofore rigid structure of secondary education.
The new boarding schools and the various recent changes in the ten-
year school curricula, both of which will be discussed elsewhere in this
chapter, exemplify current Soviet efforts to solve the problems related
to the statistical pattern outlined in this section: a surplus of college-
preparatory graduates relative to the number of freshman vacancies
in Soviet universities. With a substantial advance toward universal
education to age 17, the Soviet school has entered a phase in some
respects not unlike that experienced by the American educational
system in the last half century when high school enrollment increased
rapidly relative to the total population of the corresponding age group.
In 1900 only 7 per cent of the population 14 to 17 years of age in the
United States attended high school; in 1950 the comparable figure was
75 per cent.[4] The Soviet Union, with about one-third of the appropriate age group enrolled in grades VIII through X of its ten-year
school, stands today in this respect where the United States was
approximately 35 years ago. As Dr. James Bryant Conant has pointed
out, a fundamental dilemma developed in the United States:

> . . . an inherent difficulty is our desire on the one hand to give a
> general education on a democratic basis for *all* American youth,
> and on the other, to give the best specialized professional training
> for a certain selected few.[5]

The aims and methods of public education in the Soviet Union
are not identical with those in the United States, but in many respects
the Soviet problem of numbers is not dissimilar from our own—except
that in the United States relatively larger numbers are likely to be
involved in the immediate years ahead, with an anticipated increase

in the high school enrollment (grades IX through XII) of more than 50 per cent in the next 10 years, from 7.7 million in 1956–1957 to 11.9 million by 1966–1967.[6] We have already mentioned Soviet efforts to expand vocational training as one of the measures in meeting the problem of advancing universal education to age 17. It remains now to examine the effect of the recent developments on the curriculum of the ten-year school, the major component of general education in the Soviet Union.

2. POLYTECHNIC INSTRUCTION

"Polytechnic instruction" and "polytechnic education" are two terms which have persisted since the earliest days of the Soviet regime in Soviet writings on education. When first enunciated, no doubt by Lenin, the word "polytechnic" was only vaguely defined and was used presumably to designate a type of teaching referred to by Marx and Engels which "familiarizes one with the basic principles of all productive processes and at the same time gives the child or the adolescent the skill of using the simplest tools employed in every branch of production."[7]

"Polytechnic" education for all up to age 17 was in 1919 proclaimed by the Communist Party as the objective and method of the Soviet school.[8] The stand on "polytechnization" was confirmed in 1921, when, because of the generally desperate economic and social conditions following the civil war, the upper age limit even on paper was lowered to 15.[9] Whatever the influence of the Party's directive upon the actual process of education, in 1931 the Central Committee observed that the schools had failed to prepare "fully literate persons who have a good mastery of scientific fundamentals (in physics, chemistry, mathematics, native language, geography and other subjects)."[10] That this unsatisfactory development was related in the Committee's mind to the original approach toward "polytechnization" of schools is clear from the Committee's further statement:

> Every attempt to disassociate polytechnization of the school from a systematic and firm mastery of science—especially of physics, chemistry, and mathematics, the teaching of which must be based upon rigorously defined and carefully worked out syllabi and curricula and carried out in accordance with a firmly established school calendar—represents a most fundamental perversion of the concept of the polytechnic school.[11]

Thereafter less was said about "polytechnization," and school discipline, uniform and traditionally academic curricula, and conventional methods of instruction were rapidly reintroduced throughout the school system. Although the Party plan for 1933–1937 (second Five Year Plan) confirmed the objective of a "universal compulsory poly-technic education" within the scope of the seven-year school, the slogan by then had apparently ceased to have any operational meaning, and the vision of a "polytechnic" education for all had apparently joined the limbo of other early Soviet declarations, there to remain dormant for some 20 years.

In 1952, when the 19th Party Congress passed a resolution "proposing to undertake the realization of polytechnic instruction throughout the secondary schools"[12] and declared for a gradual estab-lishment of 10-year education on a universal basis, the question of polytechnization was vigorously revived. Since then, "polytechniza-tion" has been the dominant theme of official directives, Soviet writings on education, discussions at conferences, and editorial comments on the schools. In 1953 the RSFSR Academy of Pedagogical Sciences, the highest Soviet authority on educational theory and methodology, pub-lished a book entitled *Polytechnic Instruction in Schools of General Education,* a joint work of five authors.[13] In the introductory chapter the authors defined the concept of "polytechnic preparation" in the words of Marx, Engels, Lenin, and, of course, Stalin, who wrote:

> What would be the consequence if not only separate groups of workers but the majority of workers should raise their cultural-technical level to the level of engineering-technician personnel? Our industry would be lifted to a height beyond the reach of the industries of other countries.[14]

The second chapter of the book discusses the relationship between general education and "polytechnic" instruction. The latter term emerges to mean simply that theory and application are interde-pendent and must be equally emphasized and developed. To be truly "polytechnic," a course of instruction must include vocational training:

> If the students are to be given only theoretical knowledge of scientific principles on which productive processes are based at the neglect of inculcating work skills, then the polytechnic instruction will have an abstractly-theoretical character and will have poorly prepared [the students] for work. If only the work skills are incul-cated without the theoretical knowledge of productive processes, then the instruction will not be a polytechnic instruction but a sterile training in trades—"technicianism."[15]

The authors of *Polytechnic Instruction in Schools of General Edu-cation* point out that, to achieve the ideals of "polytechnic" instruction, knowledge, abilities, and skills must be developed in equal measure. In physics, for instance, "polytechnic" knowledge should include the most important applications of physics in engineering and technology, such as metal fabrication, power generation and distribution, automation, radio, and railroad, automotive, and air transport. The abilities and skills which must be developed in conjunction with the study of physics include the mastery of measuring techniques—determination of weight, specific gravity, pressure, velocities, efficiency of machines, temperatures, specific heat, electric current characteristics, light and illumination intensities, and others—and the development of certain manual skills. A question naturally arises as to just what comprised the laboratory work in Soviet secondary school physics before the 1952 rediscovery of polytechnic instruction.

The authors of the text imply that in mathematics, similarly, polytechnic instruction should impart knowledge in applied mathematics, mentioning specifically the systems of coordinates, elementary functions, linear equations, orthographic projection, geometric similarities, and the derivative as it expresses the rate of processes. The abilities and skills to be emphasized in a polytechnic approach to instruction in mathematics are comprehensively and minutely listed, including the following:

> . . . rapid mental and written computation; ability to round-off numbers and to check results of operations; ability to use tables, handbooks, abacus, and slide rule; ability, in reading formulas, to understand the direction of change in its numerical value with a given change in its component parts; ability readily to plot points corresponding to the given coordinates and to write coordinates of given points and otherwise to use graph paper; ability to use scales, measuring tapes and chains, compass, calipers, triangles and squares, protractor, and simple geodetical instruments; ability to take field measurements and to make field layouts, compute areas and volumes by direct measurements or from maps and drawings, to lay out plots of land of given sizes, to determine elevations and contours, to make diagrams and sketches; the skill of analyzing and synthesizing spacial forms; ability to formulate and solve equations in working out various technical and economic problems; ability to carry out bookkeeping, budgetary, and cost computations—[16]

"and so forth," the text concludes, the authors realizing perhaps that such a list of applications can be continued *ad infinitum*. The major part of the book, over 200 pages, is devoted to the means of achieving polytechnic objectives in schools of general education. The headings obviously include every known phase, method, and element of the teaching process, and the text throughout exemplifies opportunities for relating theory to practical ends, including industrial application.

Following the appearance of the book we have just described, a veritable flood of both theoretical and practical discussions on polytechnization of instruction inundated the pages of the Soviet educational press. The theoretical discussions emphasized the ideologic importance of "the polytechnic approach"—for instance, in mathematics, in demonstrating that "The concepts of both the numbers and the [geometric] figures have been derived exclusively from physical reality and have not emerged as intellectual concepts within the mind."[17] Consequently, one Soviet educator visualized mathematical excursions to the countryside as the best means for presenting fifth or sixth grade mathematics in a polytechnic light:

> Think of the many straight and broken lines, of angles and triangles, trapezoids and parallelograms, cones and cylinders, parallelepipeds and pyramids that pupils will see in nature itself![18]

At the practical level the discussions and plans have concentrated largely on the need to improve school laboratory facilities, to reduce the time allotted to book learning in favor of instruction by doing, to provide shop training facilities in all schools, and to make manual training a regular part of the school curriculum.

Although from the time of the 1952 resolution polytechnization was to be the point of departure for all subsequent changes in teacher training, revisions of curricula and syllabi, and development of new teaching methods, the central authorities did not propose a sudden metamorphosis of the entire secondary school system.

One reason why no precipitate action could be taken was the lack of shop equipment—and school shops were considered indispensable for the realization of polytechnic objectives. Even after the introduction of manual training in the school curriculum, *Moscow Pravda* (August 25, 1955) reported that only 209 of the total 627 schools in Moscow had workshops. Another reason for the slow rate of transition to the new plan was the lack of teachers possessing the so-called "polytechnic outlook" and skills. Retraining courses were organized, practical craftsmen were drawn from industry to supervise school shops, and the curricula of the teacher training institutions (including universities) were altered to include some manual training and instruction in craft techniques; but the supply of qualified teachers could not catch up with the demand. An article published in the *Literary Gazette* (December 29, 1955, p. 2), for instance, observed:

> Not infrequently the polytechnization of instruction is realized [only] in a formal sense. Many schools have no shops and no study rooms

equipped for instruction in machinery and electrotechnics; the pupils have no textbooks for these subjects, and the teachers lack methodological guidance. But—most important—there is a shortage of [qualified] individuals; the individuals who could make polytechnization a reality are not at hand.

Both of these, however, seem to be superficial explanations of the fact that, despite all efforts, classroom academic instruction has changed slowly, if at all. The fundamental reason seems to be that no one, not even the teachers, has clearly understood just what is expected.

In 1954 a group of Soviet engineers, in an article published in the *Literary Gazette,* suggested that "it was time" for the Ministry of Public Education to decide upon "concrete forms of polytechnic instruction. The fact," commented the authors, among them two university officials, "that so far the teachers talk about polytechnic instruction instead of carrying it out cannot but be a matter of concern."[19] A conference on polytechnic instruction which was held a year later, in December 1955, concluded that the RSFSR Academy of Pedagogical Sciences and the Ministry of Education "have not yet become real organizers of the new experiment [sic] and do not study and generalize the achievements of leading schools to a sufficient extent."[20] The achievements referred to by the conference seem to have been not so much the introduction of vocational and manual training in schools as simply the assignment of school children to work under the so-called "polytechnic contracts"—apparently a recently coined term for a long familiar Soviet practice. In 1955 V. Petrov, a school inspector, wrote:

> The polytechnic contract has acquired a particular importance in attracting the pupils to take part in agricultural work on the collective and state farms. A polytechnic contract obligates the school and farm administrators in advance to apportion the work of different types by grades and to utilize the pupils' labor to the greatest possible advantage of the farm and of the labor and polytechnic training of the school students.[21]

The theme of labor training appears to have become definitely associated with the slogan "polytechnization of schools"; and it is also clear that the experiment aims to curb the stirrings of nonconformity, challenging attitudes, problems of delinquency, and the distinct aversion to physical labor under Soviet conditions which appears to prevail in the mood of Soviet students aspiring to higher education. "The most responsible and important questions for us," said I. A. Kairov, the RSFSR Minister of Higher Education, in 1954, "are the moral nurture of children, their upbringing in labor and their training for labor activities." Pointing out the new role of the school, Kairov added:

The school is now faced with the responsible task of uniquely re-educating the pupil's psychology. Up to the present time the school only prepared them for the institutions of higher education. Now, when a considerable portion of those finishing school will go directly into life, our task is to nurture young people right from the beginning in the habits of work, in the love of work, and in respect for laboring people.[22]

And in 1956, at the 20th Party Congress, Khrushchev spoke of "a certain rift between our schools and life" and of unpreparedness of the graduates for work. He also added that many teachers and members of the RSFSR Academy of Pedagogical Sciences "are still engaged in general talk on the usefulness of polytechnic education but are doing nothing for its practical realization."[23]

As to the influence of the "polytechnic approach" on the methods of academic instruction, there appears to have been relatively little change, pending further development of new syllabi, textbooks, and methodological instructions and the expansion of shop and laboratory facilities. Such changes as have already been made in the ten-year school curriculum will be discussed elsewhere in this chapter, where it will become clear that under the pressure of polytechnization the Soviet ten-year school has already moved away from its former college preparatory position toward a distinctly vocational orientation.

In February 1956, at the 20th Congress of the Communist Party, Khrushchev announced the intention to establish, side by side with the regular ten-year school system, a network of boarding schools of general education for children up to age 17. At the time of his surprising announcement, it would have been logical to conclude that what Khrushchev had in mind was eventually to delegate the college preparatory functions to the new boarding schools while, by "polytechnization" and other means, gradually transforming the regular ten-year school into one huge system for vocational education and training. Whatever ultimate relationship between the new boarding schools and the regular ten-year schools may develop, it appears that in their first year of operation (1956–1957) the new schools are also conceived as schools of "polytechnic" education.

3. THE BOARDING SCHOOL

We have previously made brief references to the new boarding schools in the Soviet Union which were opened in the fall of 1956. The 1956 fall enrollment of these schools was probably not larger than 75,000 (and may have been as low as 60,000) and was limited to grades I through VII. Consequently, whatever their eventual role, they cannot affect the Soviet supply of engineers and scientists until possibly 1964. From that standpoint, no further discussion of these schools would be warranted at this time. Nevertheless, since the emergence of these boarding schools provides an excellent illustration not only of Soviet control of school policies and current educational objectives but also of the Soviet social process generally, it is relevant to set down here a brief summary of the way these schools—an important step toward differentiation within the 10-year system of education—came into being.

The point of departure in Khrushchev's argument in favor of his proposal to establish the boarding schools was "the problem of creating the spiritual prerequisites for completing . . . the transition from the lower stage of communism to its higher stage"[24]—that is, the problem of properly conditioning the coming generation for the presumably known climate of the future stage. He continued the argument by pointing out that children of war widows and children of working parents "find themselves left in the care of relatives or neighbors and sometimes without supervision at all." In the Soviet Union, it should be noted, families in which both parents are employed are the rule.* Khrushchev proposed that the state assume a larger role in the nurture and upbringing of children. Referring to the tsarist schools for the children of privileged classes, such as the Pages and Cadet Corps and Institutes for Girls of Noble Birth, in which he said "the children received a thoroughly aristocratic upbringing," he said that the task of the Soviet state is to bring up the "builders of a new society, individuals of great spirit and lofty ideals, wholeheartedly serving their people who are marching in the vanguard of all progressive mankind." It was to advance these Soviet objectives that he proposed that the building of boarding schools be undertaken forthwith "in the suburbs, in the countryside, in healthful wooded areas." He further outlined some details on the organization and functioning of the new schools: good equipment and facilities must be provided and conditions created "for the rounded physical and mental development of young citizens of the Soviet land"; good teachers ("engineers of the souls") must be selected for these schools; children should be enrolled only at the request of their parents; parents could visit on holidays, during vacations, or after school hours; tuition and maintenance cost to be charged on the ability-to-pay basis, in certain cases the state bearing the entire cost.

* On the Soviet family problems see, e.g., Naum Yasnyi, "Razrusheniye sem'i i drugiye problemy naseleniya" (The Break-up of the Family and Other Population Problems), *Sotsialisticheskii vestnik*, No. 7–8, July–August 1956, pp. 144–146.

Such, in all essential detail, was the blueprint for the new schools as first presented. The then Minister of Public Education, A. I. Kairov, speaking at the same congress a few days later, stated that Soviet teachers, education officials, and parents greeted Khrushchev's proposal "with satisfaction and gratitude." He said that to organize these boarding schools would be a prime task of his ministry, but he did not elaborate on Khrushchev's plans.[25]

Some of the features mentioned by Khrushchev in connection with the new schools were not as novel as they may have appeared from his announcement. Both the Suvorov and Nakhimov (military) schools, for instance, established in 1943 and 1944, respectively, are patterned clearly after the tsarist Cadet Corps. A number of other special schools for children of such privileged groups as the secret police and schools for the training of talented children in arts have been distinctly in the category of elite schools. Furthermore, state-operated boarding establishments for children, notably various types of Homes for Children and institutions operated by the NKVD-MVD (detention cells, receiving and distribution centers, and labor colonies for children), have been a Soviet phenomenon ever since the civil war, continuing through the collectivization of peasants, the purges of the 1930's, World War II, and the postwar purges—each major "advance" in Soviet history having left in its wake hundreds of thousands of orphans and homeless children.* It is not surprising, therefore, that at what was apparently the first organizational conference on the proposed schools, held by the Central Committee of the Communist Party in May 1956, those with experience in operating Homes for Children were represented.[26] The MVD may also have directly participated in the conference inasmuch as its present head, N. P. Dudorov, in June 1956 was reportedly quoted on the subject of boarding schools in the *Evening Moscow*.[27]

The May 1956 conference, in which Khrushchev and other members of the Central Committee participated, worked out some details and defined the organization and purposes of the boarding schools in somewhat more specific terms than those given by Khrushchev in February.

---

* 1928 On the Procedure and Rules for the Placement of Inmates of Homes for Children and Other Juveniles with the Toilers in Urban Areas and Labor Settlements

1935 On the Liquidation of Homelessness of Children

1942 On the Placement of Children Who Find Themselves Without Parents

1943 On the Improvement of Homes for Children

This list is by no means inclusive; it gives the titles of only those selected decrees the text of which appears in *Direktivy VKP(b) i postanovleniya sovetskovo pravitel'stva o narodnom obrazovanii za 1917–1947 gg.*, Vol. I, pp. 228–271.

Before the beginning of the school year on September 1, 1956, a number of particulars had been announced, some officially, some speculatively. In June of 1956, for instance, a long article significantly entitled "On the New System of Social Upbringing" was published in *Soviet Pedagogy,* an official organ of the RSFSR Academy of Pedagogical Sciences.[28] It referred to the new schools as *internat*-schools, that is, as boarding schools,* and defined the boarding school, in combination with nurseries and kindergartens, as being intended to complete the organization of the system for the upbringing, education, and training of children by the state. The author of the article, N. A. Petrov, continued with a comment on what he considered the groundless concern "of certain educators and parents" that the new system may lead to the abridgment of parental rights and obligations and prove to be detrimental "to a further strengthening of the Soviet family." He also suggested that distinctly new schools are needed because the regular schools have failed to measure up to their tasks:

> Day by day it becomes more and more evident that the existing system of upbringing [by parents and in regular schools] cannot fully cope with the [task] of creating broadly developed builders of the communist society among the new generation.

Petrov emphasized the fact that far more was involved than just the distinction between boarding and day schools, noting:

> Certain workers of the public educational system take the position . . . that it is enough to add a dormitory to a regular school of general education or to change the "Home for Children" sign to a sign reading "Boarding School" in order to solve the problem.

He then went on to outline some of the concrete provisions which should or could be incorporated in the organization and practices of the new schools.

Simultaneously with or shortly after the publication of N. A. Petrov's article in *Soviet Pedagogy* many other articles were published amplifying or modifying the earlier announcements. The RSFSR Academy of Pedagogical Sciences and the Ministry of Public Education were given the task of working out regulations for the new schools to be submitted to the Council of Ministers for approval. Apparently, no formal regulations were issued until after the beginning of the 1956 school year, although in the meantime, according to *Pravda* (September 23, 1956), some 300 boarding schools were duly opened.

---

* A Soviet dictionary (*Tolkovyi slovar' russkovo yazyka,* D. N. Ushakov, editor, Vol. I, 1935) defines the word "internat" as "(1) School dormitory for pupils (obsolete); (2) a boarding school (obsolete); (3) internship."

We have not seen the formally approved statute. Nevertheless, it is possible roughly to summarize the official interpretation of Khrushchev's directives and some of the actual steps taken to open a few boarding schools on September 1, 1956. Only the major elements suggestive of the possible trend need be mentioned.[29]

Most important, the new boarding school is visualized as a model for future developments in Soviet education. The basic idea of boarding schools, according to *Pravda* (June 28, 1956), is that in boarding schools "the educational influence of teachers embraces the entire life of children from early childhood, when they no longer need direct maternal care, until maturity." Although they admit that it will be some years before the ideal can be achieved, and that the present plan visualizes an enrollment in the boarding schools of only approximately a million students by 1960, Soviet authorities say that the boarding school principle must be eventually extended to the entire school system.[30]

For the present, the same type of formal education as is provided in the regular ten-year schools—including the "polytechnic outlook"—will be aimed at in the boarding schools, plus labor training combined with "production work." *Pravda* (September 23, 1956) stated:

> The boarding schools must be closely connected with industrial enterprises, Machine Tractor Stations, collective and state farms where the pupils of the senior grades will gain experience in production. The income derived from [the operation of] workshops and of auxiliary enterprises [such as farms] of the boarding schools will be used to improve the food, living and cultural services provided for the students, and also to expand the workshop and other [productive] facilities of the schools.

The students, it is planned, will eventually be able to specialize in various arts, crafts, and skills, the following examples having been specifically mentioned: lathe operator, milling machine operator, electrician, plant laboratory assistant, field expert, livestock specialist, horticulturist, farm machine operator, stenographer, and typist. It has also been indicated that eventually the upper-grades curriculum will have three options: physics-technological, chemistry-agronomical, and humanities.

In the early stages of discussion it was said that admission preference was to be given to those children "whose parents cannot provide the necessary conditions for a good upbringing"—later, more specifically, to "orphans, children of poor parents, children of war and labor invalids, single mothers [widows and unmarried], and of working parents (both father and mother employed)." On that basis, it would seem that many millions of Soviet children would qualify for admission on a preferential basis. What criteria are actually being used by the local admissions committees (representing Party, government, and public organizations) is not clear. It was reported that some 15,000 applications were made in the Leningrad "county," with only 2,100 vacancies in the ten boarding schools opened there for 1956–1957. Originally it was understood that only boarding students would be enrolled in these schools, but the latest regulations provide also for the enrollment of children who live with their parents.

Although *Pravda* (June 28, 1956) stated that in the initial stages "efforts should be focused on sending children age 7 to 17—the most impressionable age," no boarding schools so far have been mentioned with grades higher than the seventh; and the majority of schools in the fall of 1956 apparently opened with only grades I through IV or V. Some suggestions have been made on the desirability of eventually expanding the course of instruction by one year over the ten-year school term, especially in areas where Russian is not the language of instruction; but age 17 appears generally intended to be the normal age for graduation from the boarding schools, as it is in the regular ten-year schools.

What is more significant is that the plans call for the eventual inclusion of kindergartens within the boarding school system and of *nurseries*—apparently in hopes of somehow achieving better results than in the boarding nurseries operated up to now. According to I. A. Kairov (*Sovetskaya pedagogika*, No. 7, July 1956), investigations have shown that in the Soviet nurseries "children remain absolutely helpless to age two, and neither speak nor play at age two and a half." It is not clear why the new system is expected to overcome the basic handicaps of the institutional care of infants. Equally puzzling is *Pravda's* assertion (September 23, 1956) that ". . . the boarding schools are called upon to assist in the further strengthening of the Soviet family, in a still greater enlistment of women-mothers in active public service."

Khrushchev stipulated that boarding schools should be located in healthful wooded areas. *Pravda* (July 1, 1956) reported that in coming years special buildings would be constructed for the boarding schools following designs which were being developed. For the time being, however, existing buildings, not necessarily in wooded areas (including buildings previously occupied by ordinary schools or Homes for Children), were being remodeled. It was intended, however, in all cases to provide suitable laboratory shops and recreational facilities for all boarding schools. Furthermore, according to the announcements, only the best and most experienced teachers and supervisors were to be appointed to boarding schools, and special refresher courses were given to the selected teachers. Whatever the intentions, it is quite clear that neither the teaching personnel nor even the housing and needed equipment had been fully organized in time for the opening of these schools except on a makeshift basis and then largely only at the expense of the regular schools in the same localities.*

One way or another, 300 boarding schools of some kind started operations 6 months after Khrushchev "proposed" their establishment. Whether such schools ever assume the form he visualized remains to be seen. In the meantime, the official promulgation of the boarding school theories clearly indicates the failure of the previously accepted plan of one kind of education for all. As one Soviet commentator recently admitted, the Soviet ten-year school "gives the same haircut to everybody."[31] The curricula variations visualized for the boarding schools for a few years hence provide a clear indication of the new trend which will be further examined in the last section of this chapter.

4. SCHOOL PLANT AND FACILITIES

In the 1950–1951 school year, according to Soviet statistics, there were 201.6 thousand elementary seven- and ten-year schools in the Soviet Union. Since then, widely publicized but relatively modest school building programs have continued from year to year, some 11,000 new schools having been reported as constructed in the 1951–1955 period (about one half of them at and by the collective farms).† But the total number of schools in operation at the end of this period was about 195,000, reflecting, apparently, the abandonment of some 28,000 schools during the same period in consequence of consolidation and through obsolescence.

Recently published statistics show that during the entire 27-year period under the Five Year Plans, from 1929 through 1955, a total of

* For a description of one boarding school in operation see *Sovetskaya Kirgiziya,* October 12, 1956.

† Not all of the collective farm schools perhaps should be included in this total, or in the computation which follows. Most of these schools are likely to be part-time schools for rural youth rather than regular schools. Official statistics show:

State-constructed schools including reconstructed schools, 1929–1955	55,634
Schools built on the initiative and funds of the collective farms	
1946–1950	14,193
1951–1955	5,771
Total	75,598

The National Economy of the USSR, 1956, pp. 171–172.

approximately 75,000 schools were built (counting in that total the reconstructed schools which were damaged during the war). On that basis it would appear that perhaps half of the 195,000 schools operating in 1955–1956 were inadequate. Further direct and indirect evidence indicates also that such school buildings as are available are poorly distributed and in some localities much too small. Operating schools on a two-shift basis is quite common in the Soviet Union; and in many localities, particularly in the more recently settled areas, three shifts have been resorted to for many years. Since, on the *average,* if Soviet statistics are to be taken at face value, there were only 144 pupils per school in 1955–1956,* the multiple-shift operation of schools must be due primarily to the poor geographic distribution of school buildings. And it also follows that many Soviet schools are quite small, since typical ten-year schools and most of the urban schools have a normal enrollment of about 500 pupils, and some of *these* schools operate on two shifts, taking care of twice that number of students.†

Recently published statistics (*Kul'turnoye stroitel'stvo SSSR, 1956,* pp. 168–169) show that over 100,000 schools, that is, two-thirds of the total number, began the 1955–1956 school year on a two-shift basis but only 1,393 schools opened with a three-shift schedule.‡ Although these figures show that the third shift has been practically eliminated, it is nevertheless clear that at the recently maintained rate of school construction it will be many years before the present shortage of school buildings in the Soviet Union is eliminated. In 1956, according to standardized plans, "more than 1,000" school buildings were to be constructed in the RSFSR: in densely populated areas, 3- and 4-story schools, designed for 800 and 960 pupils, respectively, and in rural locations either 1- or 2-story buildings, for enrollments of 160 and 400 pupils. It remains to be seen how many of these schools actually have been completed. For many years new school construction in the Soviet Union has consistently lagged behind the planned rate. Judging by such evidence, for instance, as letters to the editors in the Soviet press, interminable delays occur in the course of school construction and

---

* For comparison, in 1951–1952 (before the rapid increase in school enrollment had set in) the total enrollment in the 161.5 thousand public and private schools of the United States was 26.6 million, or 165 pupils per school.

† The average enrollment in schools having all ten grades under one roof in 1955–1956, according to the data given in *The National Economy of the USSR, 1956,* p. 228, is approximately 560 pupils.

‡ The per cent of pupils by shifts was reported as follows:

First shift	63.0
Second shift	36.5
Third shift	0.5

many years may elapse between the time the funds are appropriated and the time a school is ready for occupancy.[32] In fact, the principal complaint has been not that appropriations for school buildings are lacking, but that, because of bureaucratic divisions of responsibility, lack of concern on the part of the various agencies involved, and, more tangibly, shortage of materials, actual construction drags even when, willingly or otherwise, the local Soviet citizens volunteer their spare-time labor to build schools.

In February 1956 Kairov, then RSFSR Minister of Public Education, in his speech to the 20th Party Congress stated that approximately 7,000 schools with a total capacity for 2.5 million students would be built under the sixth Five Year Plan (1956–1960) in the RSFSR. The building of these schools, Kairov said:

> . . . will make it possible to ensure universal education, to eliminate completely the three-shift system which prevails in some schools, and to move schools from bad and unsuitable buildings.[33]

Since 1952, when the emphasis on vocational training (under the omnibus slogan, "polytechnization of instruction") was last revived, much attention has been given to plans for improvement of school laboratories, experimental plots of ground for agricultural instruction, and shops of various kinds for manual training. An architectural competition on school designs was held in 1956. The plans selected for school construction scheduled to begin in 1957 were reported in *Pravda* (August 21, 1956) to include shops and other facilities for manual training. In connection with the introduction of manual training (beginning with the 1954–1955 school year) efforts have been made to obtain or to improvise some shop facilities and tools. A list of the recommended shop equipment issued by the RSFSR Ministry of Public Education is given in Appendix A. Judging by recent Soviet press reports, relatively few schools even a year later were able to assemble all the needed equipment, modest as the recommended selection and quantities of tools listed by the Ministry may seem by American standards.

There are special departments within the ministries of public education concerned with the procurement and distribution of teaching aids, projection equipment, laboratory apparatus, and supplies. In the RSFSR the Ministry has two such departments, one in charge of school supplies generally (Glavsnabpros) and the other in charge of laboratory and technical apparatus (Glavuchtekhprom). Scientific school equipment displays and stores are maintained in the larger cities. Such a store in Leningrad was visited in April 1955 by an American physicist and educator, Dr. Homer L. Dodge, and his son, Dr. Norton T. Dodge, an economist, to whom we are indebted for much information on the educational and other institutions they visited in the Soviet Union. They reported that the equipment they saw at the Leningrad store looked "just like the equipment advertised in the catalogue of the Central Scientific Company or any one of the other [American] companies catering especially to high schools."

Among the institutions visited by the Dodges was a ten-year school in Moscow (School No. 201), which is apparently shown to all foreign visitors who desire to visit a school. Teaching aids, apparatus, and demonstration equipment in Soviet schools are assembled for instruction to the upper grades in special rooms for mathematics, physics, chemistry, and biology. In the particular school visited by the Dodges equipment was adequate, but, in comparison to similar equipment in a good urban high school in the United States, neither as good nor plentiful enough to permit very many students to perform simultaneously the same experiment either individually or in small groups. Judging by references in the Soviet press, the laboratory equipment of the urban schools is considerably better and more plentiful than in the rural areas. Although in the postwar years school equipment and supplies have become increasingly available, there are still frequent complaints about the difficulties and delays in obtaining needed equipment. Specific shortages are frequently pointed to in the Soviet press, one consequence being the continuing emphasis on improvisation in school laboratory and shop apparatus, teacher- and student-made equipment, and the adoption of discarded industrial equipment for school use.

5. Tuition

Until 1940 no tuition was charged at any level of the Soviet educational system. In October of that year, retroactively to September 1, tuition was introduced in all universities and other institutions of higher education, in technicums (but not in labor reserve schools), and in the last three grades, the college-preparatory grades, of the ten-year school. Tuition in these grades (VIII through X) was set at 200 rubles per year in large cities and 150 rubles elsewhere. At that time the average monthly wage of an industrial worker in the Soviet Union was approximately 380 rubles.[34] Moderate as the tuition figure may appear, it was sufficiently high to diminish considerably the enrollment in these grades—perhaps much more than the planners anticipated. In any case, immediately after the introduction of tuition many exceptions on a regional basis and otherwise were made in order, apparently, to reduce the rate of withdrawal from school.* Although the 1952 declaration for a universal ten-year school education made tuition anomalous, the provision was not formally abolished until June 6, 1956.[35]

The economic effect of abolishing tuition cannot have been very significant. In the first place, the tuition of 150 to 200 rubles per year had remained unchanged since it was first introduced in 1940, but wages and salaries had considerably increased. In 1956, therefore, relative to the average industrial worker's income, the yearly tuition—if in fact charged—may not have amounted to much more than 2 per cent of annual money income. Secondly, from the accounts of recent visitors to the Soviet Union it appears that since 1952 the tuition requirements were in fact suspended progressively, city by city and area by area, as facilities for the mass enrollment in grades VIII through X were organized. The universal elimination of tuition throughout the Soviet Union beginning with the 1956–1957 school year is likely to be of economic benefit to some rural families. However, in many agricultural communities and in sparsely populated regions generally, it is not tuition which has kept children from attending classes but the lack of schools nearby or of transportation and dormitory facilities.

6. SUPPLY AND QUALIFICATION OF TEACHERS

The continuous efforts at expansion and development in the Soviet school system have embraced an interdependent large-scale effort to train qualified teachers at a rate which would anticipate growing needs. The results of the teacher training effort have not been perfect either qualitatively or quantitatively, as Soviet official statements for foreign consumption would indicate. Nevertheless, the gains have been impressive. Throughout the 1930's, according to Soviet statistics, the pre-Revolution (1914–1915) pupil-teacher ratio of approximately 34 to 1 was maintained notwithstanding the rapidly growing enrollment; and by 1940–1941 the pupil-teacher ratio in schools of general education had decreased to 28.6 to 1. The war decimated the ranks of Soviet school teachers, military draft and assignment of teachers to war work being among the principal factors. However, the postwar effort to increase the number of teachers, which included emergency appointments followed by compulsory extension training and the expansion of the regular teacher training facilities, is reported to have resulted by the 1950–1951 school year in a pupil-teacher ratio of 23.3 to 1.[36]

* For additional comments on tuition see Chapter 6.

Since c. 1950 three major factors have greatly influenced Soviet teacher training policies: (1) the temporary *drop* in total school enrollment; (2) the disproportional and rapid expansion of the *upper* grades enrollment; and (3) the 1952 revival of the "polytechnic approach" to general education. These factors in combination have resulted, on the one hand, in an over-all abundance of teachers relative to the decreased enrollment and, on the other, in acute specific shortages relative to the rapidly changed pattern of demand. For the 1955–1956 school year Soviet statistics show an enrollment of 28.1 million pupils and 1,655,000 teachers in the regular schools of general education, or a pupil-teacher ratio of approximately 17 to 1.

In comparison with the ratios obtaining in the educational systems of other countries this is a very low figure. In the United States, for instance, in 1951–1952 the ratio was approximately 26.7 to 1.* It should be noted, however, that a direct comparison of the pupil-teacher ratios for the Soviet and American school systems can be misleading. If one considers the student *class hours per week* per teacher, the comparison appears in a somewhat different light; for in Soviet schools, it will be remembered, students in the last three grades average 33 class hours per week as against, perhaps, not more than 25 class hours of scheduled instruction—if that many—for a typical American high school student. The fact remains that, assuming Soviet official statistics to be correct, the number of school teachers actually engaged in teaching in 1955–1956 was considerably larger in the Soviet Union than it was in the United States—both relative to the enrollment and in absolute terms.†

Table 7 shows the fall 1955 Soviet teacher statistics by categories. Excluding teachers of singing, drawing, and other nonacademic subjects, and excluding principals and supervisors in charge of instruction, there were 1,270,000 regular teachers—of whom, incidentally, 78 per cent were women. Counting the regular teachers only, the pupil-teacher ratio for the 1955–1956 registration was still a very low 22 to 1.

* Other examples (limited to the *primary* schools only) from UNESCO, *World Survey of Education, Handbook of Educational Organizations and Statistics, 1955:*

England and Wales	30.7 to 1
France (public schools only)	45.1 to 1
Sweden (1951)	22.1 to 1

† In the United States "a possible supply reservoir lies in the large number of certified teachers who are not teaching. Nobody knows the exact size of this group but it is estimated to number around one million." Hamilton Herman, *The Critical Period for American Education*, Massachusetts Institute of Technology, 1956, p. 4.

The ratio was least favorable at the elementary school level (30 to 1); in grades V through VII the ratio was approximately 17 to 1, and in the upper grades, VIII through X, approximately 20 to 1. It is to be noted, however, that more than one third of the grade VIII through X teachers have had less than 5 years of experience and that a large number of them must have been upgraded recently in order to take care of the expanded upper-grade enrollment. Thus in 1950 there were only 80,000 regular teachers for these grades; by the fall of 1955 there were 267,000, an increase of 187,000 in 5 years. The additional fact that Soviet published sources, in spite of this large increase, complain not only of specific but also of general teacher shortages suggests that the distribution of the teacher force—by level of training and by fields, especially in recent years—has been considerably out of accord with the stated needs.

In 1955 the Deputy RSFSR Minister of Education, Mrs. A. N. Malysheva, stated:

> . . . [despite the fact that] every year teacher training institutions graduate tens of thousands of young specialists, there are more than 150 thousand [about 18 per cent of the total number for the RSFSR] individuals engaged in teaching who do not possess the necessary pedagogical education. One-seventh of the directors of the ten-year schools and the majority of the seven-year school directors do not have higher education.[37]

Official statistics published in 1956 (*Kul'turnoye stroitel'stvo SSSR, 1956*, p. 179) confirmed Mrs. Malysheva's statement and gave information on the level of training for teachers in all the categories listed in Table 7. The data generally show an improvement since 1950. Nevertheless, in the fall of 1955 the formal qualifications of many teachers were below the established standard. The number and per cent of the total in each category with a substandard formal training were as follows:

Teachers in Grades	Thousands	Per Cent of Total in This Category
I–IV	9.4	2.1
V–VII	162.0	29.1
VIII–X	87.1	32.6
Total	258.5	20.4*

More important, however, is that the supply of teachers, in spite of central planning of teacher training, greatly varies from field to field.

---

* A similarly computed per cent of regular teachers (excluding teachers of singing, drawing, music, drafting, and physical education and supervisory personnel) with substandard education in the fall of 1950 was 21.7.

TABLE 7. TOTAL NUMBER AND DISTRIBUTION OF ELEMENTARY, SEVEN-YEAR, AND TEN-YEAR SCHOOL TEACHERS BY GRADES AND, IN PER CENT, BY SEX AND TEACHING EXPERIENCE

Fall of 1955

USSR

(In Thousands)

Categories	Total Number (100 per cent)	Per Cent Distribution		
		Women	Teaching Experience	
			Up to 5 Years	25 Years and More
Elementary, grades I–IV	446.7	86.5	18.3	10.1
Grades V–VII	556.8	74.4	29.3	6.9
Grades VIII–X	267.1	70.0	34.6	9.6
Teachers of Music, Singing, Drawing, Drafting, and Physical Education	101.4	29.6	43.0	2.9
Principals, Elementary School	108.6	69.4	10.0	10.0
Principals, Seven-Year School	58.6	22.5	12.1	8.6
Principals, Ten-Year School	26.8	21.3	10.2	17.9
Supervisors,* Seven-Year School	26.0	50.2	19.2	6.7
Supervisors,* Ten-Year School	32.6	52.0	14.4	13.7
All categories	1,624.6	70.2	25.3	8.5

Source: Kul'turnoye stroitel'stvo SSSR, 1956, pp. 178–179.

* In charge of instruction.

At a national USSR conference on public education held in August 1955 the planning of teacher training and allocation practices of the Ministry in the postwar period was one item of discussion. One "county supervisor" of education, Nikolaev, reported in part as follows:

> We ask for 17 teachers of the French language but they send us 44. We do not know what to do with all the history and the Russian language teachers for grades V through VII.

Teacher training is a specialized process. Under the Soviet system such sudden shifts from above in educational policies and school organization as "polytechnization" and the new boarding school principles must throw the entire educational process, including the training of teachers, out of gear. There is no evidence to show that even the rapid expansion of the upper-grade enrollment after 1952 was clearly enough anticipated by the Soviet planners to be reflected in suitable provisions for the training of additional teachers qualified to teach upper-grade subjects. It should certainly have been evident that, with the temporary drop in the school enrollment after 1953, the need of the Soviet school system was not so much to train more new teachers as to raise the qualifications of existing teachers. In this connection, the 1952 decision to move toward universality of ten-year school education is significant. One source states that, whereas the total enrollment in all three upper grades (VIII through X) in 1950–1951 was about 1.5 million for the entire USSR, in the RSFSR alone more than 1.1 million students entered the eighth grade in the fall of 1953.[38] To meet this sudden jump in the "high school" enrollment it became necessary to increase the teaching load of the regular teachers and to upgrade a large number of teachers lacking sufficient training. Steps were also taken through the Ministry of Higher Education and other organizations to modify the rate of training, composition, and allocation of the currently graduating and forthcoming graduates from the teacher training establishments.

There are four major sources of teacher supply in the Soviet Union. The minimum level of formal training which qualifies a person to teach in the elementary grades (I through IV) is provided by the so-called Pedagogical Schools, which require a 7-year general education for admission. Until 1947 the term of instruction in these schools was 3 years; in 1947 it was extended to 4 years. Thus the minimum age at graduation for the elementary school teachers is 18, only one year beyond the ten-year school. Since c. 1954 a modified 2-year course of training has also been organized in the Pedagogical Schools for the ten-year school graduates. The majority of these schools (c. 1948 there were about 700 of them) train teachers for grades I through IV, but some also prepare kindergarten teachers, Pioneer (Soviet "boy and girl scouts") leaders, and others.

The 4-year teacher training curriculum of the Pedagogical School (see Table 8) averages about 1,150 class hours of instruction. The curriculum emphasizes mathematics (14 per cent of total hours) and sciences: physics (5.5 per cent), chemistry (2.4 per cent), and natural science, including botany, anatomy, physiology, zoology, and, of course, the Foundations of Darwinism (5.9 per cent). About 20 per cent of the class time which is given to the academic subjects taught in the elementary schools (Russian language, arithmetic, history, geography, and biology) is spent on the study of teaching methods. It may be noted that, although elementary school mathematics does not go beyond simple arithmetic, the elementary school teachers study algebra (144 hours) and geometry (182 hours). They also study physics and chemistry although these subjects are not taught at the elementary school level.

TABLE 8.   SUBJECTS OF INSTRUCTION AND CLASS HOURS IN THE FOUR-YEAR
CURRICULUM (BEYOND SEVEN YEARS OF GENERAL EDUCATION) FOR THE
TRAINING OF ELEMENTARY SCHOOL TEACHERS IN THE SOVIET UNION
c. 1952–1953

Subject of Instruction	Class Hours	Per Cent
Russian Language	447	9.7
Literature	389	8.4
Mathematics (Arithmetic, Algebra, Geometry)	647	14.0
Physics	254	5.5
Chemistry and Mineralogy	110	2.4
Natural Science	274	5.9
Geography	289	6.3
History	399	8.7
History of the Communist Party	92	2.0
USSR Constitution	51	1.1
Psychology	57	1.2
Pedagogy	190	4.1
History of Pedagogy	64	1.4
Logic	54	1.2
School Hygiene	36	0.8
Penmanship	108	2.3
Drawing	245	5.3
Singing	209	4.5
Physical Education	280	6.1
Practical Work (Shop and Agricultural)	205	4.5
Teaching Observation and Practice	212	4.6
Total Hours in 4 Years	4,612	100.0

Source: E. N. Medynskii, *Narodnoye obrazovaniye v SSSR* (Public Education in
the USSR), Moscow: RSFSR Academy of Pedagogical Sciences, 1952, pp. 191 f.
(hereafter referred to as E. N. Medynskii, *Narodnoye obrazovaniye v SSSR*).

To qualify for teaching in grades V through VII the minimum
requirements in the Soviet Union have been (since c. 1935), first, completion of a ten-year school general education and, second, graduation
from the so-called Teachers' Institute,* an institution of higher education with a 2-year course of specialized instruction. Thus the minimum
age at which one may qualify for teaching the middle grades is 19.

Teachers' Institutes, which provide differentiated training for teaching one subject or a set of subjects in the grades V through VII
curriculum, have the following departments: physics-mathematics, natural science, geography, history, and Russian language and literature.
In c. 1946 there were some 196 Teachers' Institutes functioning in the
Soviet Union, with an enrollment of 43,000 students. With the 1952
declaration for a universal ten-year school education, the limited type

* *Uchitel'skii institut.*

of training given at the Teachers' Institutes conflicted with the then planned integration and continuity of the ten-year school curriculum. Beginning with 1953 the number of these institutions, therefore, started to decline, and by 1955 there were only 52 Teachers' Institutes remaining, with perhaps fewer than 10,000 students. A number of the former Teachers' Institutes have been converted, by expanding their term of study to 4 years, into the so-called Pedagogical Institutes, specialized schools of higher education which, prior to c. 1954, trained school teachers exclusively for grades VIII through X—the "high school teachers."

In 1946 there were 120 Pedagogical Institutes (versus 196 Teachers' Institutes) with an enrollment of approximately 79,000. By 1955 the number of Pedagogical Institutes had increased to 225, of which number 19 specialized exclusively in the preparation of foreign language teachers for the secondary schools and 4 gave instruction only by correspondence. The post-1953 enrollment in these institutes is likely to have had an even greater proportionate increase since the admissions quota for teacher training has been raised by 45 per cent.

The organization of Pedagogical Institutes is similar to that of other Soviet schools of higher education, the structure and functioning of which is discussed in Chapters 5 through 7. Thus the 4-year institutes are organized by departments (faculties) corresponding to the categories of subjects taught in the secondary schools: Russian language and literature, history, geography, natural sciences, physics-mathematics, pedagogy, and, in some, foreign languages. Each department conducts distinct courses in accordance with the centrally approved standard curricula and class schedules. To take an example, the physics-mathematics departments in all Pedagogical Institutes throughout the Soviet Union, with only minor variations in the national minority areas, follow a uniform compulsory curriculum, using identical syllabi and textbooks approved by the Ministry of Higher Education for the training of teachers of either physics or mathematics, or both, in the secondary schools. Since 1954 the tendency has been to introduce even greater specialization. Separate curricula beginning with the *first year* of study have been introduced for the training of teachers of physics and mathematics. The mathematics curriculum of a Pedagogical Institute is included in Chapter 8, where the reader will find additional comments on Soviet teacher training. Here it should be noted that the former single course for training teachers of natural science (botany, zoology, human anatomy and physiology, Darwinism, and organic and inorganic chemistry) has in some Pedagogical Institutes been divided into separate chemistry and natural science options. This separation seems likely to become standard for all Pedagogical Institutes.

The most recent series of changes in the curricula of these institutes derives from the injunctions on education issued by the 1952 (19th) Communist Party Congress, one of them on the "polytechnization of schools." We have already briefly reviewed the early effects of the new drive at the school level. The effects were also felt at the teacher training level, but concrete changes here came about even more slowly than in the schools themselves. For the first 2 years following the 1952 directive the curricula remained unchanged, but a greater emphasis on applications in teaching physics, other sciences, and mathematics was apparently attempted. Leningrad and Kirov Pedagogical Institutes reported that in the lectures on general physics such topics as heat engines of different types, modern hydro-turbines, high-voltage transmission, and technical uses of X-rays, ultraviolet rays, and gamma rays were treated in considerable detail. The courses in theoretical mechanics, the institutes reported, were adjusted to consider such topics as the technical aspects of friction, the influence of resonance on the performance of machines, and the kinematics and dynamics of crank drive mechanisms. In teaching elementary mathematics, calculating skills were emphasized, graphic solutions of equations and inequalities demonstrated, and the topic of nomograms added.[39] These and similar presumably novel elements of instruction obviously could not have gone very far toward achieving the objectives set by the 19th Party Congress.

Since the term "polytechnic instruction" implied an increasing emphasis on vocational and manual training, proposals were made to include in teacher training courses practical instruction in making visual teaching aids, demonstration equipment, and laboratory apparatus. It was held that the foremost need of the Pedagogical Institutes was to improve laboratory facilities, to equip training shops, and to introduce courses in manual training and technology.

It is apparent from the following comment that, despite the reported early experimentations in training "polytechnically oriented" school teachers, no basic changes in the curricula were made until 1954.

> Over two years have passed since the 19th Party Congress' directive to "begin to carry out polytechnic training in the secondary school," and only in the 1954–1955 school year have new curricula been introduced that to a certain degree make provision for training teachers according to this directive.[40]

The 1954 revised curricula demonstrate the Soviet theory that, although the polytechnic outlook must influence the teaching of every subject, the teaching of physics, chemistry, natural science, mathematics, and geography is especially subject to polytechnic reorientation. The 1954 physics teacher training curriculum, now a wholly distinct requirement, reduced the number of hours for the study of mathematics from 1,064 hours to 650, a reduction of nearly 40 per cent; increased the hours allotted to physics courses; and added a few new subjects, among them methods of mathematical physics and history of physics. The syllabi for all subjects were to be progressively revised to emphasize the technical and applied aspects of each discipline.

To whatever extent the 1954 revised curricula permitted the adjustment of teacher training to polytechnic ends, one aspect of the former curricula, the total load of the student, was not changed. The pre-1954 pedagogic institute curricula (in seven subject specializations) averaged 4,479 class hours of scheduled and compulsory attendance; the new curricula, as approved by the Ministry of Higher Education in June 1954, averaged 4,506 hours (including teacher observation and practice and summer Pioneer Camp practice); and the new curriculum in natural science provided for an increase from 4,825 to 5,175 hours.

The question of student overload and the excessive hours of class or otherwise compulsory attendance in the Soviet schools of higher education will be more fully discussed in Chapters 7 and 8; we mention these data here principally to illustrate the problems of Soviet planning. At the end of August 1954, approximately two months after the approval of the new curricula, which were to become effective on September 1, the Communist Party's Central Committee and the USSR Council of Ministers passed a decree (to which we shall make many references in the following chapters) entitled "On Improvement of Training, Assignment, and Use of Specialists with Higher and Secondary Specialized [e.g., technicum] Education." One of the major provisions of this decree was a directive to reduce the students' scheduled load "in order to increase their time for independent work."[41] We have no information as to what changes may have been made in the composition of the teacher training curricula since then, but it was recently announced that beginning with the 1956–1957 school year *the term of instruction at the Pedagogical Institutes is to be 5 years* instead of 4.

The last major source of "high school" teachers in the Soviet Union to be considered here is the universities. Soviet universities are discussed at greater length in the chapters dealing with higher education. Here we shall mention only the fact that a definite proportion of the approximately 20,000 university graduates per year are directed to teach in secondary schools. Sixty per cent of the physics and mathematics university majors—perhaps up to 3,000 graduates—were so assigned in 1955. It may also be noted in passing that our general impression, gained from numerous firsthand and other sources, is that, qualitatively, it is the lower end of the university graduate rostrum that gets assigned to teach in schools. But it is also our definite impression that any university-trained school teacher in the Soviet Union ranks very much higher than the graduate of a Pedagogical Institute. The recent extension of pedagogical training to 5 years should eventually reduce the present pronounced qualitative differences between the university-trained and pedagogical-institute-trained Soviet school teachers.

Before going on to the curriculum of the ten-year school and the subjects which Soviet teachers are called upon to teach after they complete training in one of the four institutions described above, we would also briefly comment on the composition and status of the teachers as a group. According to Soviet statistics the proportion of women among school teachers is growing, and in 1955–1956 women accounted for 70 per cent of the total number. We have no statistics to cite, but our considered impression is that Soviet school teachers, especially male teachers, form two rather distinct age groups, the older of which, including some with pre-Revolutionary teaching experience, being in the minority; and the much younger postwar graduates, with relatively short experience, forming the great majority.

A Soviet official spokesman on education, E. N. Medynskii, contrasted the position of teachers in the USSR with that of teachers in "capitalist countries," where the teacher, according to Medynskii, is "beaten down, lacks public respect, and receives a pittance for his labor." He buttressed his argument by quoting the following testimony:

By Lenin—Our public teacher must be placed at a level higher than he has ever been, or is now, or can be in a bourgeois society. . . .
By Stalin—The regiments of public teachers are among the most important components of our great army of workers building a new life on the foundations of socialism. . . .
By Kalinin—stating that he "repeatedly spoke and wrote about the teacher warmly."

Even before the war, Medynskii adds, more than 4,000 teachers were decorated with medals; 5,228 teachers were similarly honored in 1944; and since 1948 medals have been given to teachers on the basis of years of teaching, a decoration after the first 10 years and every 5 years thereafter.[42]

"In the Soviet land," stated an article published in *Pravda* (May 10,

1953), "the work of the people's teacher is surrounded by the greatest respect and care. With us, the people's teacher has been placed in a position of such eminence as he has never occupied before, as he does not and cannot occupy in any capitalist country." To the extent that the "eminent position" of a Soviet teacher is reflected by his money income, the available information fails to substantiate these constantly repeated claims. At the time *Pravda's* comment was published the teachers' monthly salary schedule (in rubles) was as follows:[43]

In Grades	Urban	Rural
I–IV	520–690	490–635
V–VII (approx. average)	700	665
VIII–X	690–850	635–765

At that time the range of from 520 rubles to 850 rubles per month represented roughly the equivalent of from about two to possibly three and a half times the earnings of the lowest paid common labor— for instance, women street cleaners in Moscow. The considerably lower salary scale of rural teachers suggests that for at least 60 per cent of the Soviet teachers the average earning per month was less than 600 rubles—hardly an enviable income by any standard. It is true, however, that rural communities are obligated to furnish lodging, light, and fuel without cost to the teachers. The standards of these perquisites vary, judging by the accounts, from deplorable to, by Soviet measure, good. The depressed financial status of Soviet primary and secondary teachers stands in a very sharp contrast to the relatively very high standing of college and university teachers—with a ratio of incomes of approximately 1 to 5. Since 1952 the Soviet teachers' salaries have apparently been raised—but so have salaries and wages generally, and the ratio still stands approximately as before.

7. THE TEN-YEAR SCHOOL CURRICULUM

Two principal facts must be borne in mind in any examination of the Soviet ten-year school curriculum. First, the curriculum of the ten-year school is structured more or less in two stages, the first 7 years being designed to provide the total general education available to the great majority of pupils, and the additional 3 years, at least until recently, to prepare relatively few for professional training. Second, there has been a continuous process of change in the ten-year schools since 1952, when the transition to a universal ten-year school education was initiated, and the Party's directive calling for the "polytechniza-tion" of the ten-year school was issued. Moreover, that process has by no means come to the end of a cycle. In 1954 the RSFSR Ministry of

Public Education estimated that the reconstruction of the ten-year school of general education into a polytechnic pattern might take "up to three years."[44] It will probably take considerably longer. In 1956, for instance, a newly revised curriculum was introduced by the RSFSR Ministry *experimentally* at only 500 schools in the RSFSR. Although details of the latest version are not available, it is clear that the direction of change is definitely along the trend originated in 1952.

It is our purpose to examine the ten-year school curriculum both in terms of its two-part structure and in the context of the whole process of change over the last 4 years.

The division of the ten-year school into two stages results in some duplications at the upper level. For example, physics is taught in grades VI (2 hours per week) and VII (3 hours per week) as an elementary but fairly representative survey of basic physical phenomena in mechanics, heat, electricity, and light. Naturally, at this level the topics are presented in their simplest and almost purely descriptive form. The course is repeated in a more extensive and detailed manner in grades VIII through X, now with a considerable emphasis on quantitative relationships. Other subjects in the Soviet curriculum above the elementary level are somewhat similarly structured in two cycles. Although there has been some tendency since 1952 toward greater unification of and continuity in the curriculum, the pattern of individual subjects has not materially changed inasmuch as the seven-year school has in no sense been abandoned and is not likely to be soon discontinued as a terminal school of *general* education. The important observable changes have been in the composition and content of the ten-year school curriculum, the latest information available to us being that for the 1955–1956 school year.

It is too soon to know all the effects of the new curriculum; and, as noted, further changes have already been made and introduced on a limited basis in 1956–1957. In the course of what appears to be a continued search for one curriculum ideally suited for Soviet mass education, a growing tendency toward differentiation within the ten-year schools can be discerned. Although the curriculum as here described still applies almost universally throughout the system, there are some significant exceptions. In the non-Russian speaking area classes are conducted in the native language, with Russian given as an additional subject from the second grade on. Experimental courses have occasionally been tried in selected schools; thus, for instance, shorthand was introduced in some fifty schools in 1947, and Latin was taught in thirty-two schools of the RSFSR starting in 1952. Another development took place recently in the Ukraine—ostensibly a version of "polytechnic" instruction, but clearly designed to prepare students for factory work. Under the Ukrainian plan, called "industrial educa-tion," selected classes in designated schools went through the regular but shortened curriculum 5 days per week, spending the sixth day at factories—2 hours at lectures and 4 hours in actual job training or work.[45] Still another type of experimental school is the special lan-guage school where the regular curriculum is followed but instruction is in a foreign language.

The recent experimentation with and departures from the prevail-ing curriculum and method of instruction may eventually lead to the development of several distinct types of 10-year education, only one of which would retain the present college preparatory character of the ten-year school. For the time being, however, the relative number of atypical schools and their combined enrollment remains small. Con-sequently, for our purposes the curriculum of the ten-year school will be taken as a uniform Soviet curriculum. But within this uniform curriculum significant changes have taken place since 1952.

The details of the progressively introduced changes need not be gone into here. A direct comparison between the 1955–1956 curriculum and the one which was in force in the 1952–1953 school year is sufficient to show their effect. We have therefore included for detailed exami-nation the curricula shown in Tables 9, 10, 11, and 12—two tables for each year so as to show the hours of instruction separately for the first seven and for the last three grades. The direction of change both in the first 7 years and in the last 3 is fairly clear at a glance.

The 1955–1956 seven-year curriculum shown in Table 9 provides for only an insignificant reduction in the total number of school hours in comparison with its 1952–1953 predecessor, the new total being 6,402 hours versus 6,435. But the distribution of class hours has been changed materially, as can be seen from the following tabulation:

Subject of Instruction	1952–1953 Class Hours	1955–1956 Class Hours	
		Added	Subtracted
Russian Language and Literature	2,508	...	165
Mathematics	1,518	...	132
History	314	...	50
USSR Constitution	66	...	66
Geography	347	...	50
Biology	313	...	16
Chemistry	82	...	16
Physical Culture	396	66	...
Singing	132	66	...
Manual Training	...	330	...
Total	5,676	462	495

TABLE 9. SEVEN-YEAR SCHOOL CURRICULUM, 1955–1956

Hours of Instruction per Week by Subjects in Each Grade and Total Hours for Grades I through VII, in Class Hours of 45 Minutes Each and in Per Cent

Subject	Hours per Week*							Total, Seven Grades	
	I	II	III	IV	V	VI	VII	Hours	Per Cent
Russian Language and Literature	13	13	13	9	9	8	6	2,343	36.6
Mathematics†	6	6	6	6	6	6	6	1,386	21.7
History	...	...	...	2	2	2	2	264	4.1
USSR Constitution	...	...	...	...	...	...	...	...	...
Geography	...	...	...	2	3	2	2	297	4.6
Biology	...	...	...	2	2	2	3	297	4.6
Physics	...	...	...	...	...	2	3	165	2.6
Astronomy	...	...	...	...	...	...	...	...	...
Chemistry	...	...	...	...	...	...	2	66	1.0
Psychology	...	...	...	...	...	...	...	...	...
Logic	...	...	...	...	...	...	...	...	...
Foreign Language‡	...	...	...	...	4	4	3	363	5.7
Physical Culture	2	2	2	2	2	2	2	462	7.2
Drawing (Art)	1	1	1	1	1	1	...	198	3.1
Drafting (Engineering)	...	...	...	...	...	...	1	33	0.5
Singing	1	1	1	1	1	1	...	198	3.1
Manual Training	1	1	1	1	2	2	2	330	5.2
Shop Work	...	...	...	...	...	...	...	...	...
Total	24	24	24	26	32	32	32	6,402	100.0

Source: Narodnoye obrazovaniye, No. 7, July 1955, p. 4.

* Classes are held 6 days a week. In grades I, II, III there are 33 school weeks in the year; in grades IV through VII there are 34 school weeks in the year. The extra week in grades IV through VII is for field trips.

† Arithmetic, grades I through VI; Algebra and Geometry, grades VI through VII.

‡ English, German, or French, depending on availability of teachers.

TABLE 10.   SEVEN-YEAR SCHOOL CURRICULUM, 1952–1953

Hours of Instruction per Week by Subjects in Each Grade and Total Hours for Grades I through VII, in Class Hours of 45 Minutes Each and in Per Cent

Subject	Hours per Week*							Total, Seven Grades	
	I	II	III	IV	V	VI	VII	Hours	Per Cent
Russian Language and Literature	15	14	15	8	10	8	6	2,508	39.0
Mathematics†	6	7	6	7	7	7	6	1,518	23.6
History	...	...	...	3	2	2.5	2	313.5	4.9
USSR Constitution	...	...	...	...	...	...	2	66	1.0
Geography	...	...	...	2.5	3	2.5	2.5	346.5	5.4
Biology	...	...	...	2.5	2	3	2	313.5	4.9
Physics	...	...	...	...	...	2	3	165	2.6
Astronomy	...	...	...	...	...	...	...	...	...
Chemistry	...	...	...	...	...	...	2.5	82.5	1.3
Psychology	...	...	...	...	...	...	...	...	...
Logic	...	...	...	...	...	...	...	...	...
Foreign Language‡	...	...	...	...	4	4	3	363	5.6
Physical Culture	1	1	2	2	2	2	2	396	6.1
Drawing (Art)	1	1	1	1	1	1	...	198	3.1
Drafting (Engineering)	...	...	...	...	...	...	1	33	0.5
Singing	1	1	1	1	...	...	...	132	2.0
Manual Training	...	...	...	...	...	...	...	...	...
Shop Work	...	...	...	...	...	...	...	...	...
Total	24	24	25	27	31	32	32	6,435	100.0

Source: E. N. Medynskii, *Narodnoye obrazovaniye v SSSR*, pp. 74 and 86.

* Classes are held 6 days a week, 33 weeks a year.
† Arithmetic, grades I through VI; Algebra and Geometry, grades VI and VII.
‡ English, German, or French, depending on availability of teachers.
Note: Fractional figures show the average of two semesters.

TABLE 11. TEN-YEAR SCHOOL CURRICULUM, 1955–1956

Total Hours of Instruction by Subject for the First Seven Grades, Hours per Week, Total Hours for Grades VIII through X, and Total for Grades I through X, in Class Hours of 45 Minutes Each and in Per Cent

Subject	Hours I–VII	Hours per Week*			Total Hours and Per Cent			
					VIII–X		I–X	
		VIII	IX	X	Hours	Per Cent	Hours	Per Cent
Russian Language and Literature	2,343	5.5	4	4	445.5	13.6	2,788.5	28.8
Mathematics†	1,386	6	6	6	594	18.2	1,980	20.5
History	264	4	4	4	396	12.1	660	6.8
USSR Constitution	...	...	...	1	33	1.0	33	0.3
Geography	297	2.5	3	...	181.5	5.6	478.5	5.0
Biology	297	2	1	...	99	3.0	396	4.1
Physics	165	3	4	4.5	379.5	11.6	544.5	5.6
Astronomy	...	...	...	1	33	1.0	33	0.3
Chemistry	66	2	3	3.5	280.5	8.6	346.5	3.6
Psychology	...	...	...	1	33	1.0	33	0.3
Logic	...	...	...	...	...	...	...	...
Foreign Language‡	363	3	3	3	297	9.1	660	6.8
Physical Culture	462	2	2	2	198	6.1	660	6.8
Drawing (Art)	198	...	...	...	...	...	198	2.1
Drafting (Engnrg.)	33	1	1	1	99	3.0	132	1.4
Singing	198	...	...	...	...	...	198	2.1
Manual Training	330	...	...	...	...	...	330	3.4
Shop Work	...	2	2	2	198	6.1	198	2.1
Total	6,402	33	33	33	3,267	100.0	9,669	100.0

Source: Narodnoye obrazovaniye, No. 7, July 1955, p. 4, and Table 9.

* Classes are held 6 days a week, 33 weeks a year.

† Algebra and Geometry, grades VI through X; Trigonometry, grades IX and X.

‡ English, German, or French, depending on availability of teachers.

Note: Fractional figures show the average of two semesters.

TABLE 12.   TEN-YEAR SCHOOL CURRICULUM, 1952–1953

Total Hours of Instruction by Subject for the First Seven Grades, Hours per
Week, Total Hours for Grades VIII through X, and Total for Grades I
through X, in Class Hours of 45 Minutes Each and in Per Cent

Subject	Hours I–VII	Hours per Week*			Total Hours and Per Cent			
					VIII–X		I–X	
		VIII	IX	X	Hours	Per Cent	Hours	Per Cent
Russian Language								
and Literature	2,508	5.5	6	5	544.5	16.8	3,052.5	31.6
Mathematics†	1,518	6	6	6	594	18.4	2,112	21.8
History	313.5	4	4	4	396	12.3	709.5	7.3
USSR Constitution	66	. . .	. . .	. . .	. . .	. . .	66	0.7
Geography	346.5	3	2.5	. . .	181.5	5.6	528	5.5
Biology	313.5	2	2	. . .	132	4.1	445.5	4.6
Physics	165	3	2	4.5	313.5	9.7	478.5	5.0
Astronomy	. . .	. . .	. . .	1	33	1.0	33	0.3
Chemistry	82.5	2	2	3.5	247.5	7.7	330	3.4
Psychology	. . .	. . .	2	. . .	66	2.0	66	0.7
Logic	. . .	. . .	. . .	2	66	2.0	66	0.7
Foreign Language‡	363	3.5	3.5	4	363	11.2	726	7.5
Physical Culture	396	2	2	2	198	6.1	594	6.1
Drawing (Art)	198	. . .	. . .	. . .	. . .	. . .	198	2.0
Drafting (Engnrg.)	33	1	1	1	99	3.1	132	1.4
Singing	132	. . .	. . .	. . .	. . .	. . .	132	1.4
Manual Training	. . .	. . .	. . .	. . .	. . .	. . .	. . .	. . .
Shop Work	. . .	. . .	. . .	. . .	. . .	. . .	. . .	. . .
Total	6,435	32	33	33	3,234	100.0	9,669	100.0

Source: E. N. Medynskii, *Narodnoye obrazovaniye v SSSR*, pp. 74 and 86, and
Table 10.

* Classes are held 6 days a week, 33 weeks a year.
† Algebra and Geometry, grades VI through X; Trigonometry, grades IX
and X.
‡ English, German, or French, depending on availability of teachers.
Note: Fractional figures show the average of two semesters.

No change has been made in the allocation of hours for the study of physics (165 hours), foreign language (363 hours), art drawing (198 hours), and engineering drafting (33 hours). The study of the USSR Constitution has not been eliminated from the curriculum of the ten-year school as the foregoing tabulation might suggest; it has been shifted to grade X and reduced from 66 to 33 hours.

With 7-year education in the Soviet Union having become established on a universal basis, the 1955–1956 curriculum as shown in Table 9 outlines the areas and the minimum extent of instruction to which for all practical purposes every 14-year-old youngster in the Soviet Union is now exposed.

The direction of changes made in the three upper grades generally has been also in favor of science and shop training at the expense of humanities, as follows:

Subject of Instruction	1952–1953 Class Hours	1955–1956 Class Hours	
		Added	Subtracted
Russian Language and Literature	545	...	99
Biology	132	...	33
Psychology	66	...	33
Logic	66	...	66
Foreign Language	363	...	66
USSR Constitution	...	33	...
Physics	313	66	...
Chemistry	248	33	...
Shop Work	...	198	...
Total	1,733	330	297

No change has been made in the hours given to the study of mathematics (594 hours), history (396 hours), geography (181 hours), astronomy (33 hours), physical culture (198 hours), and engineering drafting (99 hours).

The resultant net shift in the distribution of class hours for the ten-year school curriculum as a whole is summarized in Table 13. The allotment for "academic" subjects (humanities, science, and mathematics) has been reduced by 660 hours—mainly at the expense of humanities, with a corresponding increase of time given to "nonacademic" subjects—largely to manual and shop training. The academic subjects for which the hours have been reduced are Russian language and literature, mathematics, history, Constitution of the USSR, geography, biology, foreign language, psychology, and logic.

In fact, logic as a separate subject has been dropped. The nonacademic courses for which the class time has been increased are singing and physical education; new courses in manual and shop work training have been added.

TABLE 13.   DISTRIBUTION OF CLASS HOURS BY CATEGORIES OF SUBJECTS
IN THE TEN-YEAR SCHOOL CURRICULUM
1952–1953 and 1955–1956
USSR

	1952–1953		1955–1956	
Type of Subject	Hours	Per Cent	Hours	Per Cent
Humanities	5,214	53.9	4,653	48.1
Science and Mathematics	3,399	35.2	3,300	34.2
Academic, subtotal	8,613	89.1	7,953	82.3
"Skill" subjects*	462	4.8	1,056	10.9
Physical Education	594	6.1	660	6.8
Nonacademic, subtotal	1,056	10.9	1,716	17.7
Total Hours	9,669	100.0	9,669	100.0

Source: Tables 11 and 12.

* Includes Singing, Drafting, Art Drawing, and (for 1955–1956) Manual Training and Shop Work which were introduced in 1954–1955.

A first general conclusion, then, is that the curricular changes in the last four years have perceptibly shifted the Soviet ten-year school educational process away from the areas of intellectual inquiry and toward the cultivation of manual skills; away from humanities and toward science and technology; away from academic efforts toward trades and vocational endeavors. Secondly, the 1955–1956 ten-year school curriculum provides for a somewhat smaller academic load than formerly—no doubt a highly beneficial factor as far as the student is concerned, particularly since the syllabi of the individual subjects have also been somewhat scaled down. *Pravda* (August 27, 1955),[46] in an editorial comment on the radical changes in the school curriculum, pointed out that one of the tasks had been

. . . to cut the programs [syllabi] fundamentally in order to make the school courses easier for the pupils and to ensure that their knowledge is deep and lasting.

It seems to us that the greatest significance of the present Soviet ten-year school curriculum is seen in comparison to American requirements. Even the 1955–1956 watered-down Soviet curriculum of college

preparatory type in science, mathematics, and—leaving content aside—
in humanities appears to be nearly as demanding as the curricula maintained by only relatively few among the best American schools.

It is beyond the scope of our examination to compare rigorously the
fixed ten-year school Soviet curriculum with the flexible, decentralized,
and loose organization of subjects and course offerings in the American
system of public and private school education as a whole. Nevertheless, a random illustration may help to bring out the profound
contrast in which the two curricular systems stand. For this purpose
the hours given in the last *four* years (grades VII through X) of the
Soviet ten-year school (4,355 class hours) have been graphically compared with three selected examples of American high school (4-year)
curricula on Chart 3. The 4-year totals are subdivided into subtotals
under categories of science, mathematics, humanities, physical education, and "skill" subjects. Three American examples are given, marked
A, *B*, and *C*.

The curriculum and composition of subject categories under example
A are representative of the outstanding college preparatory technical
high schools, such as Brooklyn Technical High School, Baltimore Polytechnic Institute, and others. The total number of class hours in example *A* (approximately 4,700) is larger than the total for the last four
grades of the Soviet ten-year school, primarily because the allotment
of time for shop training given in the American *technical* high schools
is about three times as much as the Soviet school provides. The mathematics allotment in American technical or science high schools exemplified in the diagram under *A* is somewhat larger than that of the
Soviet ten-year school curriculum, and some of the American high
schools offer an introduction to calculus. The Soviet mathematics
curriculum does not include calculus as such, but some elements of
the limit theory, functions, and derivatives are introduced in algebra,
geometry, and trigonometry.

Example *B* shows typical *minimum* high school requirements for
admission to an accredited American school of engineering. At the
Massachusetts Institute of Technology, for instance, specific minimum
requirements in mathematics include algebra (3 units),* plane geom-
try (1 unit), and trigonometry (½ unit)—a total usually involving about
630 class hours of instruction. The Soviet ten-year school provides
798 class hours—with solid geometry included. In science the minimum
American requirement is one unit of physics—approximately 180 class

---

* A "unit" is a full year's study in a secondary school subject taken four or
five times a week. Here a unit is taken as being equivalent to 180 class hours
of work.

CHART 3. DISTRIBUTION OF CLASS HOURS BY CATEGORIES IN THE LAST FOUR YEARS OF SECONDARY SCHOOLS. (*Source:* See text.)

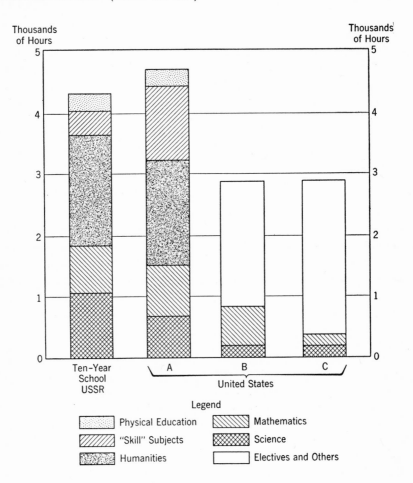

Legend

Physical Education   Mathematics

"Skill" Subjects   Science

Humanities   Electives and Others

hours. The Soviet science allotment is 1,064 hours in the last four grades. The total minimum "unit" requirement for admission to MIT is 15 units (4 years of English counting for 3 units) which roughly corresponds to a total of 2,880 class hours in 4 years of high school. There are 4,355 class hours in the Soviet fixed curriculum in grades VII through X.

Example C represents typical *minimum* requirements to graduate from American high schools in many states, calling for only one year of mathematics and of science.

The word "minimum" must be emphasized in the last two references because both the science and mathematics content and the total hours shown in these examples do not represent any actual averages, which of course can be and are very much higher in individual cases. The chart suffices to show, nevertheless, the great fluctuation in the science and mathematics requirements and in total hours of instruction among American high schools as compared with the uniformly demanding, universal curriculum of the Soviet counterpart.

Every boy and girl in the Soviet Union who completes the ten-year school course (1.3 million in 1956) has had, roughly, the equivalent of 4.4 high school years of mathematics and 5.9 high school years of science.* In contrast, it has been estimated that in 1954 about 23 per cent of American *public* high schools offered neither physics nor chemistry (but these schools accounted only for 5.8 per cent of the twelfth grade enrollment);† only 1 out of 5 American public high school students takes physics, and only two-thirds take any algebra.[47] More specifically, in mathematics the enrollment in intermediate algebra equalled 28.5 per cent of the number of pupils in the eleventh grade; in trigonometry and solid geometry approximately 13 per cent of the number enrolled in the twelfth grade.[48] In science, nearly 73 per cent of those enrolled in the tenth grade take biology, but only 32 per cent of the eleventh grade pupils take chemistry; and in the twelfth grade only 23.5 per cent take physics.[49]

All these figures refer to American *public* high school offerings and enrollment. They do not indicate the average level of preparedness among American high school graduates who continue on to college, but they do show that a very large number of American boys and girls are not even exposed to the content, method, and concepts of

* Assuming one high school year at 180 hours of instruction per subject, 5 hours per week, 36 weeks per school year.

† In 1956–1957 the total number of high school seniors in the United States was approximately 1.6 million; therefore, as many as nearly 100,000 American seniors may not have had even the opportunity to study either physics or chemistry.

mathematics and science except in their rudimentary and diluted forms. Moreover, the figures cited, according to the source from which they are taken, are from data which "do not differentiate among the types of science and mathematics courses, whether descriptive and narrative or whether analytic and basic—i.e., standard college preparatory."[50]

The sharp contrast between the Soviet ten-year school curriculum and American high school curricula reflects the general difference between European and American education rather than a feature unique to the Soviet Union. There are considerable similarities, for instance, between the Soviet ten-year school and the German primary school, which is universal, plus the *Oberrealschule,* which is a secondary school emphasizing science and mathematics. Both curricula are set; neither the Soviet nor the German provide for elective subjects. Compared with the great majority of American schools, the German curriculum also includes more science and mathematics: 13 years of mathematics (including arithmetic), 9 years of biology, 6 years of physics, and 5 years of chemistry are required. However, unlike the Soviet ten-year school, the *Oberrealschule* is only one of three basic types of German schools for those planning to go on to higher education (the other two being the classical gymnasium and the modern language gymnasium). Thus, although there are no electives in the *Oberrealschule,* the students who have chosen this type of school may be assumed to have an interest, inclination, and aptitude for science.* The Soviet ten-year school is for all practical purposes the only school of general education in the Soviet Union; and every Soviet child enrolled in the ten-year school is exposed in equal measure to the challenge of its science- and mathematics-oriented curriculum.

* It should also be noted that there are significant differences between the curricula of *Oberrealschule* and that of the ten-year school. The *Oberrealschule* curriculum spans 13 years instead of 10 years. Judging by the curriculum the *Oberrealschule* graduate attains a considerably higher level of knowledge than the ten-year school graduate; that is why the course at the *technische Hochschule* (for which the *Oberrealschule* normally is the preparatory school) last only 3 years while the course at a Soviet higher school of engineering lasts 5 years.

NOTES TO CHAPTER 2

1 Charter of the Unified Labor Schools approved on December 18, 1923, cited in *Direktivy VKP(b) i postanovleniya sovetskovo pravitel'stva o narodnom obrazovanii; sbornik dokumentov za 1917–1947 gg*. (Directives of the Communist Party and Acts of the Soviet Government on Public Education; a Collection of Documents from 1917–1947), Vol. I, Moscow-Leningrad: RSFSR Academy of Pedagogical Sciences, 1947, pp. 128–134 (hereafter referred to as *Direktivy VKP(b) i postanovleniya sovetskovo pravitel'stva o narodnom obrazovanii za 1917–1947 gg.*).

2 "O pedologicheskikh izvrashcheniyakh v sisteme narkomporsov" (On the Pedological Perversions in the Public Education System), *Pravda*, July 5, 1936, cited in *Direktivy VKP (b) i postanovleniya sovetskovo pravitel'stva o narodnom obrazovanii za 1917–1947 gg.*, Vol. I, pp. 191 ff.

3 *BSE*, 2nd Ed., Vol. 32, 1955, p. 279.

4 *Vitalizing Secondary Education*, Report of the First Commission on Life Adjustment Education for Youth, U. S. Department of Health, Education, and Welfare, Bulletin 1951, No. 3, reprinted 1954, p. 4.

5 *Education in a Divided World*, 1948, p. 65.

6 *The Impending Tidal Wave of Students*, a report of the Committee on Special Projects, the American Association of Collegiate Registrars and Admissions Officers. Prepared by Ronald B. Thompson, The Ohio State University. Pp. 12–13.

7 K. Marx and F. Engels, *Sochineniya* (Works), Russian Ed., Vol. 13, Part One, p. 199.

8 Eighth Congress, March 1919, cited in *Directivy VKP (b) i postanovleniya sovetskovo pravitel'stva o narodnom obrazovanii za 1917–1947 gg.*, Vol. I, p. 8.

9 *Ibid.*, pp. 26–27.

10 "O nachal'noi i srednei shkole" (On the Elementary and Secondary School), September 5, 1931, cited in *Directivy VKP(b) i postanovleniya sovetskovo pravitel'stva o narodnom obrazovanii za 1917–1947 gg.*, Vol. I, p. 151.

11 *Ibid.*

12 *BSE*, 2nd Ed., Vol. 33, p. 556.

13 *Politekhnicheskoye obucheniye v obshcheobrazovatel'noi shkole* (Polytechnic Instruction in Schools of General Education), M. A. Mel'nikov and M. N. Skatkin, editors. Moscow: RSFSR Academy of Pedagogical Sciences, 1953.

14 *Ibid.*, p. 6, citing I. V. Stalin, *Ekonomicheskiye problemy sotsializma v SSSR* (Economic Problems of Socialism in the USSR), Moscow, Gospolitizdat, 1952, p. 28.

15 *Ibid.*, p. 16.

16 *Ibid.*, p. 17.

17 F. Engels, *Anti-Dühring*, Ogiz, 1948, p. 35.

18 A. I. Mozhayev, "Vneklassnaya rabota kak sredstvo rasshireniya politekhni cheskovo krugozora uchashchikhsya" (Extracurricular Work as a Means for Broad ening the Pupil's Polytechnic Horizon), in *Matematika v shkole*.

19 *Literaturnaya gazeta*, November 18, 1954, p. 2.

20 *Izvestia*, December 21, 1955, p. 2; in *CDSP*, Vol. VII, No. 51, February 1, 1956, pp. 29–30.

21 "Pravil'no reshat' zadachu politekhnicheskovo obucheniya" (Correctly to Solve the Task of Polytechnic Instruction), *Sovestskaya Kirgiziya*, October 16, 1955, p. 3. For other examples of the apparently similar arrangements see *Uchitel'skaya gazeta*, May 25, 1955; also June 25, 1956.

[22] *Komsomol'skaya pravda,* August 11, 1954.

[23] *Pravda,* February 15, 1956.

[24] *Ibid.* For the complete translation of Khrushchev's speech, see *CDSP,* Vol. VIII, Nos. 4 and 5. The passage dealing with the boarding schools is in No. 5, March 14, 1956, p. 11.

[25] *Pravda,* February 25, 1956, p. 11; in *CDSP,* Vol. VIII, No. 19, June 20, 1956, p. 19.

[26] *Pravda,* June 28, 1956, p. 1; in *CDSP,* Vol. VIII, No. 27, August 15, 1956, p. 5.

[27] *Novoye Russkoye Slovo* (New York), September 9, 1956.

[28] *Sovetskaya pedagogika,* No. 6, June 1956, pp. 3–12.

[29] The following sources were used in making the summary:

Pravda, June 28, 1956, p. 1; July 1, 1956, p. 3; July 9, 1956, p. 2; August 13, 1956, p. 1; September 23, 1956

Uchitel'skaya gazeta, June 9, 1956, pp. 3–4; June 27, 1956, p. 2

Pravda vostoka, July 4, 1956

Kommunist Armenii, May 19, 1956

Sovetskaya Rossiya, September 23, 1956, p. 1

Trud, July 27, 1956

Kazakhstanskaya pravda, July 22, 1956, p. 3

Sovetskaya pedagogika, No. 7, July 1956, pp. 1–16

Komsomol'skaya pravda, August 3, 1956, p. 1

Leninskaya pravda, July 26, 1956, p. 1; August 18, 1956, p. 2

Sovetskaya Kirgiziya, October 12, 1956

Leningradskaya pravda, August 16, 1956, p. 2

Turkmenskaya iskra, July 24, 1956, p. 2; August 10, 1956, p. 2

Many of the articles here listed can be found in *CDSP,* Vol. VIII, No. 27 (August 15, 1956) and No. 32 (September 19, 1956).

[30] E.g., *Pravda,* June 28, 1956, p. 1 (an editorial); in *CDSP,* Vol. VIII, No. 27, p. 5.

[31] N. A. Petrov, *Sovetskaya pedagogika,* No. 6, June 1956, pp. 3–12.

[32] E.g., *Pravda,* June 23, 1956, p. 2.

[33] *Pravda,* February 25, 1956, p. 11; in *CDSP,* Vol. VIII, No. 19, p. 19. In March 1956 I. A. Kairov was made president of the RSFSR Academy of Pedagogical Sciences and E. I. Afanasenko appointed minister of the RSFSR Ministry of Public Education (*Pravda,* March 29, 1956).

[34] *Gosudarstvennyi plan razvitiya narodnovo khozyaistva SSSR na 1941 god* (State Plan for the Development of the USSR Economy in 1941), American Council of Learned Societies Reprints: Russian Series No. 30, p. 513.

[35] *Pravda,* June 10, 1956, p. 1.

[36] *The National Economy of the USSR, 1956,* p. 228.

[37] *Narodnoye obrazovaniye,* No. 10, 1955, p. 77.

[38] *Sovetskaya pedagogika,* No. 7, July 1953, p. 4. No. 10, November 1953 (p. 3), of the same journal states that the RSFSR enrollment in grades VIII through X increased by 500,000 but confirms 1.1 million students admitted to grade VIII (p. 4).

[39] A. M. Arsen'ev (Deputy Minister of Education, RSFSR), "Podgotovka studentov fiziko-matematicheskikh fakul'tetov k osushchestvleniyu politekhnicheskovo obucheniya v shkole" (The Preparation of Students of the Physics-Mathematics Faculties for the Realization of Polytechnic Instruction in the Schools), *Sovetskaya pedagogika,* No. 5, 1954, p. 115.

[40] N. P. Suvorov, "New Curricula of Pedagogical Institutes," *Sovetskaya pedagogika,* No. 3, March 1955, pp. 85–95; in *CDSP,* Vol. VII, No. 23, p. 6.

[41] *Ibid.*

[42] E. N. Medynskii, *Narodnoye obrazovaniye v SSSR*, pp. 155–156.

[43] *Ibid.*, p. 158.

[44] *Sovetskaya pedagogika*, No. 7, 1954, p. 4.

[45] E.g., *Literaturnaya gazeta*, November 20, 1955, p. 2.

[46] In *CDSP*, Vol. VII, No. 34, p. 29.

[47] *Offerings and Enrollments in Science and Mathematics in Public High Schools*, U. S. Department of Health, Education, and Welfare, Office of Education, Pamphlet No. 118, 1956, pp. 2 ff.

[48] *Ibid.*, p. 2.

[49] *Ibid.*

[50] *Ibid.*

— 3

THE TEN–YEAR SCHOOL:

INSTRUCTION, TEXTBOOKS, AND EXAMINATIONS

1. SCHOOL SYLLABI

As we have already noted in Chapter 2, first steps toward rigid centralized control of the Soviet school system were taken in the early 1930's. Since then, Soviet central planning has affected all elements of the teaching process, including the content of instruction, textbooks, and the grading and examination procedures—the topics to be commented upon in this chapter. It can certainly be said that no school generation in the Soviet Union has progressed through the 10 years from the first grade to graduation without witnessing major changes in the curriculum, content of courses, and school rules.

In September 1931 the Central Committee of the Party, noting that the school theretofore had failed to produce "fully literate persons," ordered the introduction of syllabi with a "precisely delineated scope of systematic knowledge [in] the native language, mathematics, physics, chemistry, geography, and history."[1] A year later the Committee attacked the new syllabi, criticizing, among other faults, the excessive scope of material included for individual subjects and the lack of integration among subjects (e.g., parts of geometry needed for the fifth-year drafting course were not given until the sixth year). The Committee issued a number of specific instructions, referring as follows to the syllabi in sciences:

> The missing elements of statics, the concept of force, and Newton's laws must be introduced in the physics syllabus; in biology—the knowledge of cell and cell structure of organisms; in chemistry the syllabus must be more systematically structured to assure the mastery of elementary concepts in chemistry.[2]

No details were spelled out, but the directive urged that more time be given to the study of mathematics so as to prepare the student for "the transition to successive [higher] levels of professional-technical education."

The same Committee report noted that no syllabus for history had been worked out—foreshadowing a perennial Soviet difficulty. History syllabi and textbooks in the Soviet Union have been particularly short-lived; following the 20th (de-Stalinization) Congress in 1956, for the *n*th time the schools were for a period operating without a syllabus or a textbook in modern history. New syllabi and history textbooks for grades IX and X, however, were issued apparently in time for the 1956–1957 school year.[3]

Soviet school syllabi are worked out by the RSFSR Ministry of Education, usually in cooperation with the Academy of Pedagogical Sciences, and printed by the Ministry's publishing establishment (Uchpedgiz). These syllabi issued by the Ministry are compulsory for all schools. It is apparently the practice to print a new syllabus in booklet form for each subject every year. Each successive syllabus in substance is usually merely a reprint with only minor or no changes—except in history; but following any major shift in educational policies some alterations in the arrangement and sequence of topics, if not necessarily in content, are made in all syllabi. In general the practice appears to be: first, to set the curriculum in line with the latest Party directive; second, to adjust the syllabi to the curriculum; and third, to rearrange, edit, and in some cases—such as in revisions of history— to rewrite textbooks to suit the syllabi. The entire process of shaping the content, emphasis, and organization of school instruction moves distinctly in one direction, from the top down, the teacher's job being merely to carry out the assignments.

A syllabus typically consists of two parts: the first, called Explanatory Note, states the objectives of the course and gives suggestions and instructions to the teachers; the second, the syllabus proper, lists in detail the topics to be covered, indicates the number of class hours for each major group of topics, and may also give an estimate of hours normally required for homework.

The introductory parts of the explanatory notes are apparently changed or revised at each printing in order, no doubt, to give as nearly up-to-date an ideological orientation to the teachers as possible. The 1948 physics syllabus, for example, stated that

. . . the cultivation of Soviet patriotism and of Soviet national pride . . . is one of the tasks of the physics teacher. . . .
The priority of our [Soviet] scientists in one or another branch

of science and engineering must be developed for the pupils with exhaustive clarity. Corresponding directions are given in the syllabus. . . .

The note appended to the 1952 syllabus in mathematics somewhat similarly emphasized that

> . . . while teaching mathematics, the teachers should realize the general goals of a communist upbringing—the formation of a Marxist-Leninist world outlook, inculcation of Soviet patriotism and Soviet national pride, and the development of will power and character.

The more recent statements on the ancillary objectives of teaching science and mathematics are less broad and less chauvinistic but reflect the "polytechnic outlook." Instead of the paragraph we have just quoted, the notes on the 1955–1956 mathematics syllabus include the following statement:

> The teaching of mathematics serves the general objectives of the communist upbringing of pupils and must assure a certain degree of readiness on the part of pupils for their future practical activity. . . .

More important, however, the explanatory notes include a number of directions on how certain topics should be presented. These sections of the notes, so far as can be judged from the limited number of syllabi we have seen, are apparently repeated year after year without variation. Although they are no doubt helpful to the teacher, the majority appear to encourage or to invite stereotyped presentation. The following, for example, is typical:

> In the Xth grade, in studying the volume of pyramids the teacher may elect one of the two methods of presenting the topic described in the geometry textbooks by A. P. Kiselev and by N. A. Glagolev.

The syllabus proper lists the major topics and subtopics much as they would appear in a highly detailed table of contents in a textbook and briefly outlines the type of problems, exercises, or demonstrations to be used in connection with each major topic.

The most stable syllabi in content and organization appear to be those in mathematics. Some changes have been made in the mathematics programs since 1954, when the ten-year school curriculum was reorganized, with the announced objective of simplifying the mathematics course. By 1955–1956, however, only the arithmetic syllabi for grades V and VI and the algebra syllabus for grade VI actually were revised. Compared with the 1952 syllabus previously in effect, the principal substantive change in arithmetic was to shift the section on percentage from the fifth grade to the sixth grade. In algebra, according to a prefatory statement in the Ministry's pamphlet, the topic on factoring, formerly the last topic of grade VI algebra, has been transferred to the seventh grade. In fact, this topic seems to have disappeared from the formal syllabus since it is not mentioned in the copy of the 1955–1956 mathematics syllabus examined by this writer, a summary of which for the fifth through seventh grades is given in Appendix B. Although in large part the new syllabus is identical with the 1952 syllabus, it contains one new topic, "Practical Studies," for which six class hours are allotted in fifth grade (age 11 to 12) arithmetic, and which, reflecting the new more practical orientation, lists the following field exercises:

> Marking the points and plotting straight lines on a location. Measuring distances by using measuring chain or tape, field compass, and by pacing. Estimating distances by sight. Learning the uses of the *ekker* [a hand instrument for sighting 90° and 45° angles]. Laying out a rectangular plot of ground and computing its area. Computing the area of quadrangular plots.

As a rule, for each major topic listed in the official syllabus there is a corresponding section in the textbook of the course in question. Thus the frequent changes in syllabi require similar changes in Soviet textbooks, which are periodically revised if only to match the chapter headings of the same old material to a new syllabus—although for many years the Ministry of Education has been striving to develop standard, lasting textbooks.

2. Soviet School Textbooks

A decisive step toward regularization of the teaching process was taken in February 1933, when the Central Committee denounced the 1918 principle whereby "textbooks as such must be banished from the school" and ordered forthwith the preparation of "stabilized textbooks designed to remain suitable for a large number of years" in all school subjects, all such textbooks to be ready by July 15, 1933. At the same time the Committee enunciated a policy which survives until the present time. Its directive stated that "For each separate subject there must be a single compulsory textbook approved by the RSFSR Commissariat of Education and published by Uchpedgiz."[4]

Although that objective, however doubtful its educational value may be, has been more or less achieved and maintained until recent years, the problem of supply and distribution has been a continuing one; and the Soviet school system has found it increasingly difficult in recent years to provide textbooks—as was intended—for every single student. As late as 1946 the number of published textbooks (18 million in 1945 and 50 million in 1946) was sufficient, statistically speaking, to provide:

> . . . one copy of every title for every two pupils in the elementary school and one for every three to four pupils enrolled in the secondary [grades V through X] school.[5]

But in reality, the pupils were not supplied with textbooks quite to that extent, for a 1946 comment stated:

> . . . a check has shown that, as a result of extreme neglect in distribution and delivery, not more than half the number of published textbooks has reached the schools.[6]

It is apparent that shortages have continued even though the rate of textbook production has been increasing. In 1954 *Pravda* (November 30) stated that there were "without doubt, sufficient textbooks to supply every pupil," but:

> Facts show, however, that the textbook trade is poorly organized in many cities and villages. Millions of textbooks lie in warehouses, stores, and shops . . . when at the same time there is a shortage of them at many schools.

And in May 1955 an article published in the *Literary Gazette,* to cite only one of many similar articles, stated that pupils in Odessa cannot purchase textbooks, but:

> At the same time tons of textbooks are sitting in a damp warehouse at the Odessa railroad station. Many textbooks have remained there for years.[7]

Soviet students purchase their textbooks at official prices which are very low even by Soviet standards, a paper-bound set of ten-year school algebra books (two textbooks and two collections of problems) costing 5.70 rubles—that is, at a realistic dollar equivalent, about $0.50 for the four books.[8] Because of the shortage, however, Soviet schoolbooks are often mentioned as one of the items traded illegally at black market prices.

The supply and frequently the quality of schoolbooks are especially poor in the areas where instruction is in some other language than Russian, part of the difficulty arising simply from delays in getting the Russian text translated and in obtaining the necessary paper and cardboard for the local printing establishments.[9]

More important perhaps than lack of materials and poor distribution as a cause for shortages has been the necessity for frequent, sometimes trivial, revisions. In 1953 *Pravda,* blaming the ministries of education, stated:

> Instead of replacing obsolete textbooks with new, high quality textbooks which would serve schools for many years, the ministries of education constantly make all kinds of changes in them and add supplements, a practice which grossly violates the stability principle.[10]

Since the enunciation of the "polytechnic approach" to general education in October 1952 and also the later directives to lighten the academic burden of pupils, plans have been mentioned to revise or to rewrite practically all secondary school textbooks. In August 1956 the RSFSR Minister of Education, E. I. Afanasenko, stated:

> The RSFSR Ministry of Education, jointly with the Academy of Pedagogical Sciences, continues the work of perfecting and of further lightening the school syllabi and textbooks.
>
> . . . . .
>
> Some instructions as to additional deletions in the syllabi and textbooks for grades V–X in the Russian language, literature, physics, chemistry, and other subjects have been issued.[11]

In the same article Afanasenko touched upon the major reason— re-rewriting of history—why once again millions of Soviet textbooks have become obsolete since the last (February 1956) Communist Party Congress. He said:

> One must admit that the cult of J. V. Stalin's personality has negatively influenced the content of educational and upbringing work of the school. It has widely penetrated the school syllabi, especially those in the history of the USSR, general history and literature, the textbooks—from the primers and readers for the first-graders through the textbooks of the normal schools, and also reference texts published for the schools, instructions for the teachers, and educational journals.[12]

At this point we would emphasize that the particular problem to which Afanasenko referred, and which involves something more than just rewriting books, does not directly affect the status of Soviet schoolbooks in science and mathematics. Soviet mathematics textbooks, especially, are quite free of any ideological slant; and, relatively speaking, so are schoolbooks on science except for their preoccupation with the Russian priority in everything. In fact, only the science and mathematics textbooks have been referred to—and with considerable justification—by Soviet educators as having been "stabilized." The textbooks in physics by Professor I. I. Sokolov, for instance, have been published in three parts and reprinted many times apparently

without any changes.*   In 1948, when for the first time the topic
"Structure of the Atom" was added to the tenth grade physics syllabus
(3 class hours), the explanatory note pointed out that the topic did
not appear in the "latest editions of the stabilized textbook" and
suggested that teachers should make use of the popular science literature for its presentation.[13]   Similarly, Soviet school mathematics
textbooks can indeed be called stable—if not ossified.   For example,
N. Rybkin's *Plane Trigonometry* was first published in 1894 and has
survived its thirty-second (1954) edition—not quite in its original form,
to be sure, because there have been some revisions, or at least additions:[14] the twenty-fifth-edition textbook had 104 pages, and the 1954
edition, 114 pages.†

The most widely used algebra textbook in the Soviet Union is
A. P. Kiselev's *Algebra,* first published in 1888.   It too has had a few
minor rearrangements, revisions, and additions.   Kiselev's *Algebra* has
been normally published in two parts: Part I for grades VI and VII,
and Part II for grades IX and X;[15] but other subdivisions by parts
have also been printed for some reason.   The latest editions of Kiselev's
Algebra examined by us overlap by one grade: Part I covers grades
VI through VIII in the 1954 (28th) edition, and Part II covers grades
VIII through X in the 1956 (33rd) edition.   The overlapping sections,
for grade VIII, however, do not match, and Part I does not contain
all the material called for by the 1955–1956 sylllabus.   Why they do
not publish one complete volume, allowing the order of presentation
to be determined by the syllabus, is not clear.   A Soviet specialist on
mathematics teaching, V. M. Bradis, in the third (1954) edition of his
textbook *Methods of Teaching Secondary Mathematics,* stated that
". . . on the whole the book [Kiselev's *Algebra*] fails fully to reflect
modern science."   He also stated that an experimental algebra textbook written by P. S. Alexandrov and A. N. Kolmogorov (both outstanding Soviet mathematicians) was published in 1940 and was
intended eventually to replace Kiselev's classic.   As of 1956, however,
Kiselev's textbooks were apparently still being used not only in algebra
but also in arithmetic and geometry.   Kiselev's *Geometry* was first

---

* The copies to which we had reference were: *Kurs fiziki* (Course in Physics).
Part I: *Mechanics* (for the seventh grade), 9th Ed., 1948.

Part II: *Oscillations and Waves—Heat* (for the ninth grade), 11th Ed., 1950.

Part III: *Electricity—Optics* (for the tenth grade), 8th Ed., 1947; also 11th Ed.,
1950. The eleventh edition of this textbook includes a chapter entitled "Structure
of the Atom" (pp. 348–380), a topic which was added sometime after 1948.

† It is possible that Rybkin's text was replaced in 1956 by a new textbook: S. I.
Novoselov, *Trigonometry.*

published in 1882, and until the Revolution it had been the standard text in all Russian schools. Kiselev's *Geometry* was resurrected in 1938 although at the time, as Bradis states, "it was already recognized that the secondary school needed a new textbook in geometry."[16]

During the war N. A. Glagolev's *Elementary Geometry* was published, but it has not apparently gained wide use. In the meantime still another geometry textbook (Part I, plane geometry for grades VI through IX) has appeared among textbooks mentioned in the 1956 references.* We have not seen this latest text. Heretofore Soviet schoolbooks on mathematics and science have been distinguished by the formality, directness, and economy of the text, emphasizing theoretical concepts and using only a limited number of examples, largely of abstract rather than applied nature. As one American physicist commented to this writer, "A Soviet algebra textbook *is* algebra, not some version of 'consumer mathematics' with pictures." In appearance Soviet textbooks are austere if not drab, unrelieved by illustrations except in the form of old-fashioned line sketches of 1900 vintage. It is a likely assumption that new Soviet texts in mathematics (also in science) will attempt to relate theory closer to practical implications.

A list of selected textbooks recently or currently in use in Soviet secondary schools is given in Appendix C.

3. Grading System and "Percentomania"

In 1935, when several specific measures were taken toward a further centralization of control over the Soviet school system, the Party Central Committee decreed the introduction of a single school curriculum throughout the Soviet Union.[17] At the same time a uniform school calendar was introduced; the number of class hours (up to 6 class hours of 45 minutes each, 6 days per week) was fixed for every school grade by law; school uniforms were prescribed; a formal grading system ("very poor," "poor," "fair," "good," and "very good") was introduced after a lapse of some 18 years.

Along with such changes, a major step was taken toward formalizing promotion and graduation procedures; for the first time in the Soviet school system formal examination procedures were instituted. The 1935 decree ordered schools to discontinue the "incorrect practice of using 'individual questionnaires' under which the teacher, ahead of time, designates certain questions individually for each student, and correspondingly prepares the student to answer these questions."

* N. N. Nikitin and A. I. Fetisov, *Geometriya* (listed more fully in Appendix C).

Henceforth, the directive stated, the promotion and graduation tests were to provide "verification of the student's knowledge in various sections of the course"; and the School Section of the Central Committee was instructed to work out "standards for the evaluation of achievement, such standards to be uniform for the USSR and to be so designed that a given level of knowledge would be identically evaluated in every school."[18]

With the introduction of a formal grading system and with solidification of state control, the school system fell victim to an endemic Soviet disease called "percentomania": not only the pupils but also the teachers and schools were now "rated" according to the percentage of successful students. Inevitably, administrative and political pressures forced the teachers to reduce the number of failures by the simple mechanism of upgrading evaluations in the spirit of "socialist competition."* The Soviet government, which of course was itself responsible for the condition, nevertheless reacted to the developing tendencies by passing numerous decrees condemning:

> . . . the intolerable practice of chasing after bloated percentages of success (the so-called "percentomania," which leads to falsification of results), a practice which profanes and perverts the perfectly proper and admirable slogan of the advanced Soviet teachers: to give firm and deep knowledge to all pupils, to have no repeaters [that is, pupils left in the same grade for another year].[19]

The order from which we have just quoted included several specific directives intended to assure the elimination of "percentomania," among them an order whereby the ranking of individual schools, school districts, and cities on the per-cent-of-success basis was "categorically prohibited." The government, however, found it necessary to issue a number of reminders in subsequent years. In 1941 the authorities in charge of public education were again enjoined against evaluating "the work of schools and of teachers solely on the basis of the student

---

* The Soviet *Encyclopedic Dictionary* (Vol. III, Moscow, 1955, p. 271) defines "socialist competition" in an article, the opening sentence of which reads as follows: "Socialist competition [is] a method of increasing labor productivity and of perfecting production on the basis of maximal activity of the working masses." Former Soviet citizens speak of "socialist competition" in sarcastic terms as a social pressure promoted with a great show of enthusiasm by ambitious Party leaders—to force workers to pledge bigger and better efforts to "fulfill and overfulfill" the stepped-up production and other statistically expressible plans.

Under "socialist competitions" teachers, pupils, and school administrators would jointly and separately enter into compacts publicly pledging to achieve "100 per cent passing grades," with proportions of "A's" and "B's" agreed upon in advance. (*Spravochnik direktora shkoly* [A Handbook for the School Director], Moscow, 1954, p. 78.)

success ratios."[20] In 1943 school administrators and inspectors were made answerable for passing on to the central authorities "unverified data on the pupils' success"; and both the higher administrative officers of the school system and the school directors were "categorically forbidden, in summing up results and in evaluating the work done by schools, to rank the teachers and the school on the basis of the students' success ratios alone."[21] In 1944 an order was issued prohibiting "the practice of socialist competition in schools, among the pupils and teachers, with respect to academic work";[22] and "the incorrect and harmful practice of evaluating the work of a school and of a teacher on the basis of the students' average success ratios" was once again forbidden. Furthermore, pointing at the real virus of "percentomania," the directive ordered school administrators "decisively to eliminate any kind of pressure upon the teacher in [his] evaluation of progress made by the pupils." And yet 11 years later an editorial on school education in *The Baku Worker* (January 12, 1955) included the following comment:

> Not infrequently the work of the schools is judged on the per-cent-of-success basis. "Percentomania" leads to an artificial raising of marks.

In the meantime the rules for testing the pupils' achievement have also been elaborated and strengthened. In January 1944 the system of verbal grading, introduced 10 years earlier, was abandoned in favor of the pre-Revolutionary numerical system of marks (from "5" down to "1," with "3" being the lowest passing mark). The Minister of Education stated that the change was aimed at "a more distinct and accurate evaluation of the pupils' achievement and at a higher level of demand as to the quality of the pupils' knowledge." In what manner the new designations could help the achievement of these purposes he did not say. A month later, however, the Minister issued a set of instructions on the criteria to be used in grading numerically the student's work and conduct.[23] We quote the officially stated criteria for the highest mark ("5") and the lowest passing mark ("3"):

> The mark "5" is given in the event the pupil exhaustively knows, excellently understands, and has firmly mastered all the syllabic material. He answers correctly the questions (within the scope of the syllabus) with comprehension and assurance. He knows how to use the acquired knowledge independently for various practical tasks. In oral answers and in written work he uses literate, correct language and does not commit errors.
> The mark "3" is given in the event the pupil reveals the knowledge of the basic material in the syllabus. He experiences certain difficulties in applying knowledge to practical ends but overcomes such difficulties with only modest help from the teacher. He makes

errors in the exposition of material and in speech when replying to oral questions. He makes errors in his written work.

4. FINAL AND PROMOTIONAL EXAMINATIONS

During the summer following the introduction of the new grading system in January 1944, the central governing body of the Soviet Union issued a law prescribing formal final examinations for graduation at all three levels of the ten-year school: elementary, after grade IV, age 11; seven-year, age 14; and the decisive secondary school finals at the end of the tenth year, the make or break of the student's future chances of obtaining higher education. Beginning with 1945 those satisfactorily passing the ten-year school finals (Russian language, literature, mathematics, physics, chemistry, history, and foreign language) were to be issued, as in the tsarist days, the so-called Certificate of Maturity. Only the holders of such certificates were henceforth to be permitted to apply for admission to the institutions of higher education.*

Since 1945, those graduates who have had a final grade of "5" in all subjects of instruction (what we would call straight-A graduates) have been awarded gold medals in addition to the certificate, and those who have received a "5" in all the final examination subjects and a "4" in not more than three other subjects have received silver medals. The award of medals, another example of tsarist practice resurrected by the Soviets, has served both as a psychological incentive and as a device to single out individuals especially well qualified for advanced study in institutions of higher education. Until recently medal holders were entitled to enter universities and colleges without having to take a set of competitive entrance examinations.

The first Certificate of Maturity examinations were held in May–June 1945, and perhaps the majority of new certificate holders entered institutions of higher education as freshmen in the fall of that year. In December the RSFSR Commissar of Education summarized the first experience with the certificate examinations as follows:

> Many graduates of the secondary schools, especially of the schools in the rural areas, have shown poor knowledge of the Russian language and of national literature. Rubber-stamp-like phrases in the written compositions and in oral answers testify to the still insufficient attention given by the schools to the cultivation of the pupils' spoken language and to their general development.
> In the area of mathematics, the absence of sufficient skill in making rational and rapid arithmetic and algebraic calculations is

---

* In December 1946 rules were also published for the holding of Certificate of Maturity examinations for persons older than 17 and for those who had not previously attended a secondary school or had dropped out prior to completion.

typical of the secondary school graduates, as is also the weakness in three-dimensional visualizing and an insufficient development of mathematical thinking.

The graduates know historical facts and the most important chronological dates included in the syllabi but do not always demonstrate the necessary understanding of the significance of the individual historical events.

The freshmen entering institutions of higher education still reveal an insufficient ability to apply their knowledge in physics and chemistry for the solution of practical problems and for the explanation of the various physical and chemical processes.[24]

The official criticism attributed all the enumerated shortcomings of secondary education to "formalism in teaching and in the pupils' knowledge"—that is, as we would translate it, teaching by rules and learning by rote.

Such accounts of the conduct of class lessons as are cited in the Soviet educational press would indicate that time-consuming and old-fashioned methods of instruction in fact prevail; and firsthand descriptions by former students bear witness to the rigid, authoritarian pattern of Soviet teaching methods. The accounts of many German students who studied in the Soviet Union after the war agree in stating that, in a typical class lesson, the teacher would start the class by calling on two or three students to repeat the material of the previous lesson almost verbatim, and that the second half of the class hour would be occupied by the teacher delivering the next section of the textbook, again following the text almost or actually verbatim.

Under the Soviet political climate literal adherence to the text is inevitably forced upon both teacher and student alike in the humanities—Soviet "civics," literature, and history. Even the most cautious Soviet comments on the teaching of literature, for example, deplore "memorized-by-rote phrases from the textbook on the image of one or another literary hero."[25] But there are apparently no comparable ideological pressures on the teacher of physics or mathematics; and from all available evidence we would conclude that, as anywhere else, the quality of teaching in these disciplines in Soviet schools varies largely with the teacher. It would also seem that the fixed syllabus, standardized textbooks, and formalized methods of presentation provide a definite lower limit for the kind of instruction in science and mathematics a Soviet pupil may get. He may not necessarily gain imaginative understanding of everything he learns; but, if he survives to graduation, he will have gained at least a very thorough grounding in rules, techniques, and definitions.

Whether or not "formalism" limits Soviet teaching in mathematics and science, the general overloading of students with compulsory work, including excessive homework assignments, especially in mathematics, has no doubt been an important factor in lowering the average quality of achievement among the secondary school pupils. The introduction of final examinations in 1945 served to increase the already great pressure upon students.

In 1946, in a further effort to tighten up the selection process, the Ministry of Education issued extensive regulations on promotion examinations.[26] Under these regulations progression of pupils up to grade IV was governed by marks received during the year. A resulting mark of "2" or lower for a single subject, unless the deficiency was made up during the summer, meant remaining in the same grade for another year. In higher grades (V, VI, VIII, and IX) a year-average mark of "2" in more than two subjects (except drawing, drafting, and military-physical training) automatically kept the student for a second year. Otherwise, whatever the grades received during the year, the students of intermediate grades took year-end promotion examinations.

As first established, the schedule (beginning with 1946) called for the following examinations:

At the End of Grade	Oral	Written	Total
IV (Elementary "final") Russian Language and Arithmetic, Written and Oral	2	2	4
V (Promotion) Russian Language and Arithmetic, Written and Oral	2	2	4
VI (Promotion) Russian Language (Written and Oral), Algebra (Written), History, Biology, and Geography (Oral)	4	2	6
VII (Seven-year "final") Russian Language and Literature (Two Written and One Oral), Algebra and Arithmetic (Written), Geometry, History, Constitution of the USSR, Geography, Physics, Zoology, and a Foreign Language (Oral)	8	3	11
VIII (Promotion) Literature (Written and Oral), Algebra (Written), Geometry, History, Biology, Physics, and a Foreign Language (Oral)	6	2	8
IX (Promotion) Literature (Written and Oral), Algebra (Written), Geometry, History, Geography, Biology, and a Foreign Language (Oral)	6	2	8
X (Certificate of Maturity, final examinations) Russian Language, Literature, Mathematics (Algebra, Geometry, and Trigonometry)—Written and Oral; Physics, Chemistry, History (History of the USSR and Modern History)—Oral only.	8	3	11
Total number of examinations	36	16	52

It should be noted that until recently all school examinations in the Soviet Union were made up not by the teachers themselves, or even by the school or school district authorities, but by the respective ministries of education.

The pattern of promotion and final examinations established by the Soviet Ministry of Education in 1946 culminated its efforts to combat "percentomania," to assure promotion and graduation on merit, and to improve the quality of school instruction. As already suggested, one result of the new requirements was a great increase in the work load of the pupils. To drill for examinations became the major concern of both students and teachers.

Since most of the examinations, as the reader will have observed, are oral, it is of interest to note how Soviet oral examinations are conducted. The subject matter of each course is divided into about sixty or more topics. Two or more of such topics, briefly identified or structured in the form of questions, plus a problem (in such subjects as physics, mathematics, and chemistry) constitute one of approximately thirty "examination tickets."* At the time of examination all "tickets" are placed face down upon the examiners' table. As each student is called, he draws one of the tickets lottery fashion; or, at the price of lowering his mark by one grade, he may gamble and draw a second choice. Having drawn his ticket, the student has 15 to 20 minutes to organize his answers or recitation (and any blackboard work) before facing the examiners. The important point, however, is that the entire set of tickets with their questions *is distributed weeks in advance.*† The last weeks of each year, therefore, are spent in review and drill by *tickets* and specific questions. Many of the questions, furthermore, are repeated year after year in different combinations.

Since its introduction the examination schedule has been repeatedly modified and reduced. In April 1954, for example, some weeks before the examinations were to start, it was announced:

> Starting with the 1953–1954 school year the number of promotion and final examinations . . . is to be drastically reduced—*to eliminate overloading the pupils with studies* [our emphasis].[27]

In 1955 another change was made whereby each school was permitted to draw up its own examination tickets for the promotion tests (for students in grades V, VI, VIII, and IX).[28] In September 1956

* The Russian term *"bilet"* or "ticket" more specifically refers also to the slip of paper on which a given set of examination questions is printed or written.

† No actual problems, such as in mathematics, are known in advance, but the *type* of problem which may be a part of a given ticket is clearly identified by reference to a standard collection of school problems.

the Ministry of Education announced that all promotion examinations (and the fourth grade "finals") were to be abolished forthwith.

It is clear that the possession of a Certificate of Maturity with or without a school medal has not proved to be a reliable enough index of preparedness and aptitude for college work. As will be more fully discussed in Chapter 6, medals no longer assure admission to higher schools; even the gold medal from a ten-year school no longer guarantees an automatic admission to every Soviet school of higher education.

In any case, in the face of experience, and with the changed role of the ten-year school, the scope and severity of the final examinations (the seven-year and the Certificate of Maturity ten-year finals) have been scaled down. Beginning with 1957, seven-year finals were to include only 3 (instead of 11) examinations, an oral and a written in Russian language and a written examination in mathematics (arithmetic and algebra). According to a recent announcement, the Certificate of Maturity final examinations will call for only the following 7 examinations: a written examination in literature and oral examinations in algebra, geometry, physics, chemistry, history, and one foreign language. The new schedule thus represents a further reduction in requirements which have been gradually lowered from the 11 examinations originally specified in 1946. Moreover, the scope of the student's responsibility has been gradually reduced. Whereas in former years the students were examined in the entire course of a given subject, the final examinations held in 1955 were based largely on the material covered in the tenth grade and only "the most essential topics and questions from the material covered in the earlier years of study."[29]

The remaining part of this chapter will outline the procedure followed in conducting the Certificate of Maturity examinations, present the content of examinations in mathematics and physics in detail, and summarize a comparative analysis of the questions in mathematics and physics which was made by the Evaluation and Advisory Staff of the Educational Testing Service, Princeton, New Jersey, at the request of the Center for International Studies.*

5. Ten-Year School Final Examinations

Although, as already noted, individual schools were authorized in 1955 to draw up promotion examinations, the preparation of questions

* Permission to include the Educational Testing Service analysis in this study was kindly given by Dr. Warren G. Findley, Director, Evaluation and Advisory Service, and is hereby gratefully acknowledged with thanks to Dr. Findley and to the members of his staff who participated in making the analysis.

and topics for the final examinations remains in the hands of the Ministry of Education. The Ministry continues to publish the examination material in pamphlet form well in advance of the examinations. According to the publication data shown on the examination pamphlet, the material for the 1955 examinations was "approved for printing" in January 1955 for a run of 1,200,000 copies—1,000,000 copies for sale at 40 kopeks and 200,000 copies for free distribution.[30]

The examination pamphlet contains a brief explanatory note and a set of questions, arranged by "tickets," for the oral examinations in literature, algebra, history, physics, and chemistry.* The tickets in the final examinations are used exactly in the same manner as was outlined in the preceding section. In the 1955 example the number of tickets in one subject varied from 40 (in history) to 21 (in algebra) with 2 or 3 questions or topics on each ticket, as follows:

Subject	No. of Tickets		No. of Questions or Topics per Ticket
Literature	31	2	
History	40	2	
Algebra	21	3	(including one problem)
Physics	33	3	(including one problem)
Chemistry	28	3	(including one problem)

The problems in algebra (one for each ticket) are not specified in the official tickets, each school (teacher) designating a problem of his own choice for each ticket. "In selecting a problem," the instructions read, "the teacher should consider the difficulty, extent, and content of the theoretical material specified in the same ticket." The problems in physics, one for each ticket, may be either formulated by the teacher or selected by him from a published collection—in accordance, however, with the type of problem specified by the Ministry. Similarly,

* The written tests are also made up by the Ministry but not distributed in advance. In 1955, in addition to the five oral examinations listed above, there were also presumably two written tests, in Russian language and literature and in geometry and trigonometry. We have not seen the written tests in these subjects.

In 1952–1954 the regulations called for a total of nine examinations, as follows:

1. Russian Language and Literature (Written Composition).
2. Russian Language and Literature (Oral).
3. Algebra (Oral).
4. Geometry and Trigonometry (Written).
5. Geometry (Oral).
6. Physics (Oral).
7. Chemistry (Oral).
8. History of the USSR, grades VIII through X (Oral).
9. Foreign Language (Oral).

the problems in chemistry are identified as to type in the official tickets, but the teacher selects a suitable specific formulation.

The problems so selected are limited in number to the number of tickets and approved by the school director at least 10 days in advance of the examinations. It is to be expected that the selected problems are identical in type with those used during the school year and during the intense review period preceding the final examinations. Thus a student contemplating the forthcoming finals knows from the official pamphlet that he will be responsible for 306 specific questions or topics in the five subjects and that of that total he will draw ten questions—two in each subject—at the examination. He also knows that he will be asked in his oral examinations to solve on the blackboard one problem in algebra, one in chemistry, and one in physics.

The final examinations are spaced a few days apart during a period of about 30 days following the middle of May. Only those students whose yearly record in all subjects is a "3" or better (and not less than a "5" in conduct) are normally permitted to take them. The examinations are conducted by the school examining committee, of which the director of the school is the chairman. The members of the committee sitting on a given examination include the teacher of the subject, two or three other teachers, and a representative of the "county" office of the Ministry of Education. The grading, according to regulations, is done by the examining committee, with the final grade in case of disagreement arrived at by majority vote. There are numerous indications, however, that the grade given by the teacher is as a rule concurred in by other members of the commission.

The student's Certificate of Maturity shows final grades for every subject of instruction. Grades for the subjects in which examinations are held reflect both the yearly record and the grades received in examinations; all other final grades are posted in the certificate on the basis of the yearly grades only. A pupil who fails to earn a final grade of at least "3" in all subjects (and a "5" in conduct) is not given a Certificate of Maturity—a document which he must have to apply for admission to an institution of higher education. Thus an unknown number who complete a ten-year school but fail to earn a Certificate of Maturity are barred from higher education of any type. This number includes both those who fail in one or more finals and those who have been previously disqualified on the basis of yearly grades. No statistics have been encountered by this writer on the per cent of ten-year graduates ending up without the all-important Certificate of Maturity.

Before we examine the content of Soviet "high school" final tests, it is important to emphasize the circumstances described above under which these tests are administered, especially the fact that examination questions are known months in advance, and that, with very few exceptions, the questions are repeated year after year in the same or only slightly different combinations.* It is not without significance that year after year the Ministry advises that

> In order to avoid mechanical memorization, review of the material should be conducted not in accordance with the "tickets" but following the regular syllabi. . . .[31]

It is a foregone conclusion that in practice the pupils review and drill on the tickets and thus necessarily rely largely on memorization. Nevertheless, important as is the qualification of advance knowledge, the scope of the final examination questions is comprehensive and demands a thorough preparation and review—whether by rote or otherwise.†

Examination in Algebra

We invite the reader now to take the Soviet "high school" test in algebra, drawing any one of the following twenty-one tickets which— face down—confronted Soviet graduating pupils in June 1955 and 1956. In addition to the topics for oral presentation, each ticket calls for a problem or example to be worked out on the blackboard.

I. (1) Groupings and their types. Number of ways of arranging m elements in groups of n. Number of permutations of m elements.
(2) Problem or example.
(3) Quadratic equations. Complete and incomplete quadratic equations. Solution of quadratic equations of the type: (i) $x^2 + px + q = 0$ and (ii) $ax^2 + bx + c = 0$.
II. (1) Combinations. Number of combinations of m elements in groups of n. Equality: $C_m^n = C_m^{m-n}$.
(2) Problem or example.

* For example, the 1956 questions in algebra are identical with those used in 1955.
† The text of the Soviet 1955 examination questions in physics appears to have impressed one team of American writers strongly enough for them to arrive at what is surely a highly erroneous conclusion:
"Judging by the last year's Soviet equivalent of a college-entrance examination [we are assuming the authors refer to the examinations reviewed in the remaining part of this chapter] in physics, Russian boys *know* [our emphasis] about as much physics by the end of their last year in high school as the physics majors [*sic!*] at the Massachusetts Institute of Technology have learned by the end of their sophomore year."
Joseph and Stewart Alsop, "The Race We Are Losing to Russia," *The Saturday Evening Post,* April 28, 1956.

(3) Analyzing the roots of a quadratic equation by discriminant and coefficients.

III. (1) Product of binomials, which differ only in their second terms.

(2) Problem or example.

(3) Finding a certain percentage of a given number and the reverse problem.

IV. (1) Newton's binomial theorem (derivation of formula).

(2) Problem or example.

(3) Expressing the sums and products of the roots of a quadratic equation through its coefficients.

V. (1) Equality of coefficients of the terms equidistant from each end of the binomial expansion. General term of the formula in Newton's binomial. Sum of binomial coefficients.

(2) Problem or example.

(3) Expressing a second degree trinomial in the form of linear factors.

VI. (1) Imaginary number. Complex number. Imaginary unit of a complex number. Conditions which make a complex number equal to zero. Conditions of equality of two complex numbers.

(2) Problem or example.

(3) Exponential function. Properties of exponential function and its graph.

VII. (1) Addition and subtraction of complex numbers written in algebraic form.

(2) Problem or example.

(3) Logarithmic function, its properties and graph.

VIII. (1) Multiplication and division of complex numbers in algebraic form.

(2) Problem or example.

(3) Arithmetic progression. Summation formula for the terms of an arithmetic progression.

IX. (1) Geometrical interpretation of complex numbers. Trigonometric form of a complex number.

(2) Problem or example.

(3) Finding per cent ratio of one number to another.

X. (1) Analysis of the quadratic trinomial (discriminant of the trinomial being a positive number).

(2) Problem or example.

(3) Logarithm of a product.

XI. (1) Inequality. Basic properties of inequalities. Addition and subtraction of inequalities.

(2) Problem or example.

(3) Logarithm of a quotient.

XII. (1) Inequalities of the same and of opposite sense. Theorem about the sense of inequalities when the same number is added to each side of the inequality. Consequences of this theorem.

(2) Problem or example.

(3) Logarithm of the power and the root.

XIII. (1) Theorem on the sense of inequalities when both parts are either divided or multiplied by a positive or a negative number.
(2) Problem or example.
(3) Common logarithms and their properties.

XIV. (1) Solution of a first degree inequality with one unknown. Solution of a system of such inequalities with one unknown.
(2) Problem or example.
(3) Linear function and its graph.

XV. (1) Analysis of linear equations with one unknown.
(2) Problem or example.
(3) Formula for any term of an arithmetic progression.

XVI. (1) Analysis of a system of two linear equations with two unknowns.
(2) Problem or example.
(3) Direct proportional relationship and its graph.

XVII. (1) Analysis of a quadratic trinomial (with the discriminant of the trinomial being a negative number or equal to zero).
(2) Problem or example.
(3) Proportion. Basic property of proportion. Finding of the unknown member of a proportion.

XVIII. (1) Solution of a second degree inequality with one unknown.
(2) Problem or example.
(3) Ratio of two numbers. Substitution of a ratio of fractions by a ratio of whole numbers.

XIX. (1) Bézout's theorem and its implications.
(2) Problem or example.
(3) Inverse proportionality and its graph.

XX. (1) Solution of binomial equations of the third, fourth, and sixth degrees.
(2) Problem or example.
(3) Geometric progression. Formula for any term of a geometric progression.

XXI. (1) Solution of trinomial equations.
(2) Problem or example.
(3) Sum of the terms of a geometric progression.

As mentioned in an earlier section, the Center for International Studies submitted these examination tickets to the Educational Testing Service, whose Evaluation and Advisory Staff analyzed the questions and compared them with the College Entrance Examination Board mathematics examinations. The resulting conclusions were prefaced by a set of important precautions:

Any comparison of these [Soviet examination] questions in algebra with questions in College Board mathematics examinations is extremely difficult and must be interpreted with caution. There are several reasons for care in analysis and interpretation, among which are the following:

(1) The questions are vaguely stated, and there is very little indication as to the kind of response required in order to achieve a good score.

(2) Nothing is known about the score distribution or the difficulties of individual questions.

(3) Even if one did know something about the scoring technique, the responses required, and the resulting score distribution, there is no way of determining whether responses were the result of rote memorization or cramming. That is to say, the questions and accompanying material give little insight into the kind of mathematical instruction given. Also, although the indicated test administration provides for security, opportunity is given for cramming.

The Educational Testing Service analysis, made with these precautions and reservations in mind, emphasized that any interpretive reading of the conclusions should be done with similar precautions. We quote the conclusions on the Soviet mathematics test in full:*

1. All 42 questions given in the 21 tickets are based on algebraic topics. Considering all 21 tickets at once, there is an excellent distribution of such topics, one which, with the exceptions given below, United States students largely cover in taking the 2½ years of algebra that is a part of the four-year sequence in high school mathematics upon which the College Board Advanced Mathematics Examination is based.

Exceptions:

(1) Among the more important topics not in the 21 tickets which U.S. students taking the Advanced Mathematics Examination should know something about are the following: (a) coordinate geometry, (b) limits, (c) statistics, (d) probability, and (e) absolute value. However, these topics are given *little* emphasis in the Advanced Math test, and students are not expected to know much about them.

(2) Among the topics which receive little or no emphasis in the Advanced Math test but received considerable attention in the 21 tickets are the following: (a) solution of inequality relationships, (b) equations of degree greater than two, and (c) logarithmic and exponential functions. These topics are normally a part of U.S. college freshman courses, although some high school students do receive a minimum amount of instruction in such topics and they are a fundamental part of the College Advanced Placement Examinations. (The Advanced Placement Examination should not be confused with the Advanced Math Examination.)

2. The 21 tickets, considered as a whole, sample subject matter in algebra that is roughly equivalent to that in the College Board Advanced Mathematics examination. Of course, about 50% of the Advanced Math test consists of questions in trigonometry and solid

---

* The analysis which led to these conclusions includes a brief description of all College Board mathematics tests. It is given in Appendix D.

geometry. These U.S.S.R. questions give little evidence of how much trigonometry and solid geometry Russian students have studied and when.*

In the opinion of most curriculum groups undertaking revision of the traditional high school mathematics program (e.g., the Commission on Mathematics of the College Entrance Examination Board), most topics listed in the above exceptions should be a part of the high school mathematics course of study.

3. Because of the lottery-type system used for these tickets, it seems appropriate to speculate that all Russian students who take this examination have studied all of the topics involved in all 21 tickets. If the average U.S.S.R. student starts the 10-year school at age 7, as has been previously indicated, it *might* be the case that those Russian students who take the examination in question are one year ahead age-wise, in algebraic training, of those U.S. students who take the Advanced Math test.

4. A statement of *speculation:* the nature and phrasing of each question in all tickets open up the possibility that the Russian examinee is expected to give a much more complete and somewhat more theoretical answer than is expected of the student taking the College Board Advanced Mathematics Examination. If this were the case, and if there had been no emphasis upon rote memorization of subject matter, then one would have to conclude that the Russian examination demands a more advanced and theoretical concept of algebra than the Advanced Math test and, possibly, U.S. teaching.

5. In conclusion, considering the 21 tickets as a whole, there is the possibility that this Russian examination represents the climax to a good high school algebra course of study. However, except for the speculation in (4) above, the examination is not truly advanced in subject matter over the College Board Advanced Math test.† (Note

---

* No information on the ten-year school geometry and trigonometry was available to the evaluator at the time this analysis was made. The reader will have noted that the Soviet school curriculum includes 5 years of geometry and 2 years of trigonometry (but in class hours the equivalent of approximately 2 high school years of geometry and 1 of trigonometry). Total hours for mathematics in the ten-year school curriculum are shown in Table 11 (Chapter 2), and a detailed breakdown of class hours for arithmetic, algebra, geometry, and trigonometry is given in Appendix B.

The exact nature of the ten-year school final examination in geometry and trigonometry (one written test for both) is not known to this writer. From a detailed inspection of the Soviet syllabi and textbooks for these two subjects, however, and from the fact that 4 hours is the normal time allotted to this test, this writer's conclusion is that the preparation for the ten-year school final examination in geometry and trigonometry would be equally as demanding and must be as thorough as that required to pass the algebra examination here analyzed.

† "Compare this with the fact that a member of the ETS staff who was largely responsible for this analysis reports this fact: an examination given in 1955 to twelfth grade students in Norway contains topics in algebra, coordinate and solid geometry, and trigonometry which are definitely at least a half year beyond the material covered in the Advanced Mathematics Examination."

that no comparison in level of response is made here, for reasons given before.)

Certainly the U.S.S.R. test does not involve any of the more modern ideas of mathematics—e.g., set concept, modern algebra, symbolic logic, probability, statistics. It seems pertinent to point out here that the College Board has appointed a Commission on Mathematics to investigate desirable revisions of the high school mathematics curriculum that will probably result in inclusion of these modern mathematical ideas in the course of study. Consequently, changes in College Board examinations to reflect this possible revised curriculum seem likely to occur. What is the likelihood that such changes can and will occur in the U.S.S.R.?

No categorical answer to this question can be given; the recent trend has been, as we have seen, under the pressure of "polytechnization" somewhat to lighten the mathematics share in the ten-year school curriculum; but whatever future revisions are made by the Soviet Ministry—whether to introduce certain modern mathematical ideas or further to reduce the student's load—will apply throughout the school system unless in the meantime a distinct category of college preparatory school should emerge in the Soviet Union from the current experimentation with the schools of general education.

Examination in Physics

The 1955 Soviet "high school" physics examination questions were arranged in thirty-three tickets. Each ticket included two topics (each consisting of several related items) for oral presentation and either a problem or a laboratory demonstration of a standard set-up experiment. Again, we list verbatim the two topics on each ticket and, when called for, the *sample* problem. The reader is reminded that the problems given below are not the actual problems given at the examinations but those which are cited by the Ministry as prototypes to be followed by the teachers in selecting actually designated problems. The prototypes are taken (as designated by number in the official pamphlet) from a standard Soviet collection of physics problems, P. A. Znamenskii and others, *Sbornik voprosov i zadach po fizike* (Collection of Questions and Problems in Physics), for grades VIII through X of the secondary school (4th Ed., Moscow: Uchpedgiz, 1952). The thirty-three tickets for the 1955 Soviet "high school" examination in physics, including 25 problems and 8 laboratory demonstrations, were as follows:

> I. (1) Electric charge. Electric field. Coulomb's Law. Units of quantity of electricity.
> (2) Motion with constant acceleration. Acceleration. Ve-

locity of motion with constant acceleration. Velocity graph. Derivation of the path equation for motion with constant acceleration.

(3) A steam hammer weighing 10 tons falls through a distance of 25 m. upon an iron block weighing 200 kg. How many blows of the hammer will be required to raise the temperature of the iron block by 40 degrees? 60 per cent of the heat generated by the impact goes into the heating of the iron block.

II. (1) Intensity of the electric field. Lines of force. Homogeneous field.

(2) Newton's first law. Examples from engineering.

(3) A kerosene burner ["Primus"] burns 3 g. of kerosene per minute with 40 per cent efficiency. How long will it take to heat on this burner 1.5 liters of water from ten degrees to the boiling point (100 degrees)?

III. (1) Conductors and dielectrics in an electric field. Dielectric constant.

(2) Newton's second law. Examples from engineering.

(3) A cylindrical oil tank is 8 m. high and has a base of 5 m. radius. The level of stored oil at a temperature of minus 5 degrees is 20 cm. below the top of the tank. If the temperature is raised to plus 30 degrees will the oil spill? The expansion of the tank is to be neglected.

IV. (1) The work of a charge transfer in a homogeneous electrical field. Difference of potentials. Units of the difference of potentials.

(2) Newton's third law and its application in engineering.

(3) Laboratory problem: experimental check of the Boyle-Mariotte law.

V. (1) Capacitance. Units of capacitance. Condensers and their uses.

(2) The law of universal gravitation.

(3) A metal bottle of 40 lb. capacity contains 8 kg. of compressed oxygen at a temperature of 15 degrees. What is the pressure?

VI. (1) Cathode rays. Emission of electrons by heated bodies. Electron tubes.

(2) Free fall of bodies.

(3) Laboratory demonstration: determination of the surface tension coefficient of water.

VII. (1) Electrolysis. Faraday's law. Industrial applications of electrolysis.

(2) Motion of a body projected at an angle to the horizon.

(3) What quantity of firewood would be required to melt 1 m. [sic] of snow to water when the air temperature is minus 8 degrees and the water level in the snow melting box [snegotop] has the temperature of plus 3 degrees? The efficiency of snegotop is 30 per cent.

VIII. (1) Conductors connected in series. Derivation of formula for the total resistance of series-connected conductors. Additional resistance in voltmeters.

(2) Circular motion of a body. Centripetal acceleration (without derivation of the formula). Centripetal force. Centrifugal mechanisms and their application in industry and agriculture.

(3) A vessel contains 500 g. of water and the same quantity of ice at zero temperature. What quantity of steam at 100 degrees must be introduced into the water to melt the ice and to bring the temperature of the water to 30 degrees? The specific heat of the vessel is 40 calories per degree.

IX. (1) Conductors connected in parallel. Derivation of the formula for total resistance of a circuit with parallel-connected conductors. Shunts for ammeters. Parallel connections in engineering applications.

(2) Addition of nonparallel forces. Resolution of a force into components, acting at an angle. Examples from engineering.

(3) Two lights of 50 candle power each hang at a distance of 1 m. above a table. The distance between the lights is 1 m. 40 cm. Find the level of illumination on the table (i) under each lamp and (ii) at a point equidistant from both lights.

X. (1) E.M.F. of the current source. Ohm's law for the entire circuit.

(2) Equilibrium of forces acting on a solid body which has an axis of rotation. Moment of force; examples of application in engineering.

(3) Laboratory demonstration: determination of the index of refraction of a substance.

XI. (1) Work done by an electric current. Joule-Lenz law. Arc-welding.

(2) Center of gravity. Forms of equilibria of bodies (the recitation should be illustrated by examples from engineering).

(3) Laboratory demonstration: determination of the optical power of a lens.

XII. (1) Magnetic field of a direct current and of a coil carrying current. Effect of a magnetic field on current. Intensity of a magnetic field. Magnetic flux.

(2) Vibrations in an elastic medium and the formation of waves (transverse and longitudinal); wave length.

(3) A converging lens gives an image of an object which is located 30 cm. away on the other side of the lens at a distance of 60 cm. What is the principal focal length of the lens and its optical power? Construct the image of the object.

XIII. (1) Iron in a magnetic field. Electromagnet. Electromagnetic field.

(2) Oscillating motion (as exemplified by the mathematical pendulum). Amplitude, period, frequency. Laws of the pendulum. The uses of the pendulum.
(3) The objective of a slide projector has a power of 8 diopters. At what distance from the screen should the projector be located in order to give 1 to 25 magnification?

XIV. (1) Oscillograph. Microphone and telephone. Loudspeaker.
(2) Kinetic and potential energy. Derivation of the kinetic energy formula. Expression for the magnitude of potential energy of a raised body.
(3) Floating in kerosene an object is submerged by 0.75 of its volume. What is the specific gravity of the object? What part of its volume would be submerged in water?

XV. (1) Electromagnetic induction. Conditions determining the magnitude of the induced e.m.f. Lenz law.
(2) The generation and propagation of sound. Velocity of sound. Utilization of sound in engineering applications.
(3) Laboratory demonstration: determination of the specific weight of a substance by hydrostatic weighing.

XVI. (1) Generation of alternating current. Period, frequency, phase of an alternating current. A.C. generators.
(2) Pressure in a moving liquid and gas. The lifting force of a plane. Importance of N. E. Zhukovskii's work in the field of aviation.
(3) A block of wood weighing 500 g. slides upon a horizontal surface being set into motion by a weight of 300 g. suspended by a string which passes over a sheave to the block. The coefficient of friction is equal to 0.2. With what acceleration will the block move and what is the tension of the string? The sheave friction is to be disregarded.

XVII. (1) The principle of a three-phase current. Working principle of a three-phase motor.
(2) Pascal's law. Hydraulic press.
(3) To both ends of a string passing over a sheave are attached weights of 95 g. each. Additional weights are added: 7.5 g. to the weight on the left and 2.5 g. to the weight on the right side. What will be the distance travelled by the weight on the left side in 2 seconds?

XVIII. (1) Rectification of an alternating current. Electron tube as a rectifier. D.C. generator.
(2) Bases of the molecular-kinetic theory. Diffusion and Brownian motion.
(3) A bullet leaves the muzzle at a velocity of 865 m./sec. What is the velocity of the rifle if its mass is 470 times greater than the mass of the bullet? Why is it recommended that in shooting the rifle be firmly held against the shoulder?

XIX. (1) Transformation of current. Transmission and distribution of electrical energy. Progress in electrification of the USSR. The use of electric motors in industry, agriculture, and transportation.
(2) Thermal expansion of bodies. Coefficients of linear and volumetric expansion. Consideration of thermal expansion in some engineering problems.
(3) An automobile weighing 5 tons including the load travels upon an arched bridge at 21.6 km./hour. What is the force of pressure upon the bridge if the radius of its curvature is 50 m.?

XX. (1) Oscillatory circuit. Transformation of energy in an oscillatory circuit. Generation of undamped oscillations. Electrical resonance.
(2) Thermal expansion of gases. Guy-Lussac law. Absolute temperature.
(3) A truck weighing 3 tons travels at a speed of 36 km./hour. What is the magnitude of the braking force which would be required to bring the truck to a stop within a distance of 50 m.?

XXI. (1) Invention of the radio by Popov. Principle of radio-telephone transmission (A.M.). Diagram of a crystal and of the simplest tube-type radio receiver.
(2) Gas pressure in light of the molecular-kinetic theory. Boyle-Mariotte law.
(3) Find the center of gravity of a dumbbell-like arrangement with unequal spheres as follows: one sphere, 3 cm. radius, 1.5 kg. in weight; the other sphere 6 cm. radius, 12 kg. in weight. The two spheres are connected by a rod 50 cm. long weighing 2 kg.

XXII. (1) The stream of light, power of light, and illumination. Laws of illumination. Photometer.
(2) Combined law of Boyle-Mariotte and Guy-Lussac.
(3) A scale 1 m. in length is placed on the table with one quarter of its length overhanging the edge. If a weight of 250 g. is attached to the overhanging edge the entire pressure is at the edge of the table. What is the weight of the scale? What portion of the scale must overhang the edge of the table if a weight of 125 g. is attached?

XXIII. (1) Phenomena of reflection and refraction of light. Refraction index. Total internal reflection of light.
(2) Surface tension in liquids.
(3) Laboratory demonstration: determination of efficiency of a simple mechanism.

XXIV. (1) Lenses. Derivation of the lens formula. Optical power of a lens. Forming an image with the aid of a lens.
(2) Moistening phenomena. Capillary phenomena, their importance in everyday life and in agriculture.
(3) A horse is pulling uphill a cart of 500 kg. The length of the incline is equal to 1.5 km. and the height to 100 m.

Determine the work done by the horse against the force of gravity and the force of friction. What is the efficiency if the coefficient of friction is equal to 0.06?

XXV. (1) Optical instruments and their importance. Path of light rays in a microscope and a telescope.
(2) Elasticity of a solid. Hooke's law.
(3) Two identical small spheres, one carrying a charge of plus 20 units C.G.S.E. and the other minus 14 units C.G.S.E. are brought together and separated again to a distance of 2 cm. Find the force of interaction between them.

XXVI. (1) Concept of interference and diffraction of light. Wave length of light.
(2) Mechanical equivalent of heat. Law of conversion and conservation of energy.
(3) Laboratory demonstration: determination of the unit resistance of a conductor.

XXVII. (1) Dispersion of light. Visible, infra-red, and ultraviolet parts of the spectrum.
(2) Melting and its explanation on the basis of the molecular-kinetic theory.
(3) Laboratory demonstration: determination of internal resistance in a source of current.

XXVIII. (1) Continuous and line spectra. Absorption spectrum Spectral analysis and its application.
(2) Boiling. The dependence of boiling temperature and pressure. Engineering applications.
(3) Determine the potential at the terminals of a two-volt battery with an internal resistance of 0.8 ohms if the terminals are connected by a nickel conductor 210 cm. long with a cross-section of 0.2 mm.^{2}

XXIX. (1) X-rays. Use of X-rays in medicine and engineering.
(2) Vaporization. Explanation of vaporization on the basis of the molecular-kinetic theory.
(3) An arc lamp at 50 volts consumes 500 watts. What is the quantity of heat generated in the wires during the interval of ten minutes if the distance between the generator and the arc lamp is 100 m. and the wires are made of copper with 2 mm.^{2} cross-sections?

XXX. (1) Photoelectric effect. Stoletov's work on the photoelectric effect. The concept of quanta. Photoelectric cells and their application.
(2) Saturated and unsaturated steam. Relation between the volume and pressure of steam at constant temperature.
(3) A current generator with an electromotive force of 150 volts and an internal resistance of 0.4 ohms supplies current for 10 lights of 240 ohms resistance each and 5 lights of 145 ohms resistance each connected in parallel. The resistance of the wiring is 2.5 ohms. Find the voltage supplied to the lights.

XXXI.   (1) Photoluminescence and its application. The pressure of light.
(2) Absolute and relative humidity. (Psychrometer.)
(3) An elevator weighing 1.2 tons travels upward at the rate of 15 m./0.5 min. The voltage at the motor terminals is 220 volts and its efficiency is 90 per cent. Find (i) power consumed by the motor in kw., (ii) intensity of current in the motor, (iii) energy required for one trip, (iv) the cost of one trip on the basis of 0.04 R./1 kw. hr.

XXXII. (1) Structure of an atom—electron shells and nucleus. Emission and absorption of energy by an atom.
(2) Conditions necessary for the functioning of heat engines. Efficiency of heat engines.
(3) Through a coil submerged in 314.2 g. of kerosene contained in an aluminum calorimeter which has a mass of 55.5 g. a current of 1.1 ampere and of 8 volts intensity is passed for 20 minutes. As a result the temperature of the kerosene went up from 13 degrees C. to 27.5 degrees C. Determine the heat equivalent of work.

XXXIII. (1) Structure of atomic nucleus. Uranium nucleus fission. Chain reaction. Release of energy in nuclear distintegration.
(2) Methods of increasing the efficiency of heat engines (steam engine, internal combustion engine).
(3) In an electrolysis of $ZnSO_4$ solution 10 kw. hr. of work were expended. Determine the quantity of zinc produced if the potential at the terminals was 4 volts.

A description of two analyses of the Soviet physics tickets made by the Educational Testing Service is given in Appendix E, to which the reader is referred for detailed comments. Here we shall cite only the major observations. In comparison with the College Board physics examinations (specifically identified in Appendix E) the per cent of distribution of subject matter areas covered in the Soviet questions is broadly about the same, with possibly greater emphasis in the Soviet test on electricity and modern physics. On the basis of the average number of lines required to reach a solution (the same person, the author of the Educational Testing Service analysis, taking the compared tests) the analyst observed:

. . . [some of the Soviet problems] in regard to average length of computation are close to the [College Board] Advanced Placement Test, though subjectively it is thought that they [the Soviet problems] are not quite so difficult.

One of the unknown factors with reference to the Soviet problems is whether the constants, properties, coefficients, and units needed to solve Soviet examination problems are given to the pupil or are expected to be known by him from memory. In the College Board tests all such outside data are usually stated in the questions.

The distribution of topics mentioned in the Soviet examination tickets was judged to be good, roughly corresponding with most of what is taught in American schools and, in addition, containing a number of topics not usually taught in most American schools. The reader is again referred to the full text of the analysis (Appendix E); but we cite here the observation that some of the thirty-two such topics not taught in United States schools but included in the Soviet tickets "are regarded as more difficult concepts to grasp than the other topics which are taught in the United States." Included among these thirty-two topics we would note four which "the American student would not be expected to know"—one of them "Invention of the radio by Popov." The analysis also revealed that Soviet examination questions suggest a strong emphasis on application of physics principles in engineering and particularly to the generation of heat from various kinds of fuel oil, kerosene, and firewood, such as in the snow melting problem in "Ticket No. VII."

To sum up, we have sampled the scope and coverage of topics in algebra and physics in the qualifying examinations given to the majority of, if not all, Soviet "high school" students. A comparison with a number of College Board tests suggests, with the reservations indicated above, that in algebra Soviet "high school" graduates (1,300,000 in 1956) would be expected fully to match the level of achievement on which the College Board Advanced Mathematics Examination is predicated; in the United States, however, only about 10 per cent of the twelfth grade students take mathematics at the level on which this College Board test is based.[32] This means that in 1953 perhaps not more than 150,000 new high school graduates in the United States were qualified to take the College Board Advanced Mathematics Examination.*

The analysis of the Soviet examination topics in physics shows a thorough coverage, including some conceptually more difficult topics not usually taught in the American high schools. The problems included in the Soviet physics examination are of comparable difficulty with those given in the Advanced Placement College Board tests; but

---

* American high school seniors and total fall enrollment (grades 1 through 12) as given in *Statistical Abstract*, 1956, p. 108:

	1952	1956 (projection)
Total enrollment	29,058,000	34,623,000
Seniors	1,503,000	1,652,000

again, whereas all or nearly all Soviet "high school" graduates confront these or similar problems in their final examination, the College Board Advanced Placement tests are taken only by the select few American high school graduates desiring to qualify for an *advanced* (sophomore) standing in college physics. The Advanced Placement test is a recent formulation; as of 1955 the number of American high school graduates taking this test may not have exceeded 2 per cent of those taking the standard achievement physics test. That is indeed a very small per cent of the total number of high school graduates in 1955; as we have noted in Chapter 2, only 23.5 per cent of all twelfth grade high school students (as of 1954) studied physics.

It is no doubt true that the College Board examination technique, requiring the examinee to respond to a large number of questions and problems not published beforehand, demands a surer and a broader knowledge than does a comparable response to the Soviet tests. For the sake of argument, however, whatever the differences in favor of one or the other type of training or testing, and allowing for the fact that we cannot know what level of knowledge is required *to pass* Soviet examinations, this central fact stands: *all Soviet ten-year school graduates,* whatever their average achievement, are exposed to and study topics in mathematics and science up to a level reached by very few American young men and women with high school education.

The reader will recall that the Soviet ten-year school science curriculum (summarized in Table 11, Chapter 2), in addition to physics, includes chemistry, biology, and astronomy, these four science subjects taking up nearly 20 per cent of class time in grades V through X—the Soviet counterpart of American junior high and high school. During the same 6-year period mathematics takes up over 14 per cent. The 34 per cent of school time allotted to science and mathematics comes to 2,168 class hours, or to approximately 12 high school "units": 5.1 in mathematics and 6.9 in science. As was shown in the preceding chapter, the majority of American public high schools require for graduation (Example C on Chart 3) only one unit of science and one in mathematics; in 1953 fewer than 4 per cent of American schools required either trigonometry or solid geometry even of *college preparatory* pupils.[33]

NOTES TO CHAPTER 3

[1] *Narodnoye obrazovaniye* (Public Education), Basic Decisions, Orders, and Instructions, compiled by A. M. Danev, Moscow: Uchpedgiz, 1948, pp. 42 ff. (hereafter referred to as *Narodnoye obrazovaniye,* compiled by A. M. Danev).

2 *Ibid.*, p. 69.

3 E. I. Afanasenko (the RSFSR Minister of Education), in *Uchitel'skaya gazeta,* August 15, 1956, p. 2.

4 *Narodnoye obrazovaniye,* compiled by A. M. Danev, p. 71.

5 *Kul'tura i zhizn',* No. 19, December 31, 1946, quoted in *ibid.*

6 *Ibid.*

7 I. Pikarevich, "Uchebniki valyayutsya v pakgauzakh" (Textbooks Are Lying Around in Warehouses), *Literaturnaya gazeta,* May 26, 1955, p. 2.

8 See Appendix C for additional examples.

9 On the problems of textbooks for the national minority schools see, e.g., *Uchitel'skaya gazeta,* January 22, 1955, or *CDSP,* Vol. VII, No. 5, March 16, 1955, pp. 37–38.

10 July 6, 1953, p. 1.

11 *Uchitel'skaya gazeta,* August 15, 1956, p. 3.

12 *Ibid.*

13 *Programmy srednei shkoly. Fizika. Astronomiya* (Physics, Astronomy), Uchpedgiz, 1948, pp. 7 and 19. The topic "Structure of the Atom" was further outlined as follows: The structure of the atom: nucleus and the electron shell. The composition of an atomic nucleus—protons and neutrons. Fission of the atomic nucleus by neutrons. Atomic energy.

14 V. M. Bradis, *Metodika prepodavaniya matematiki v srednei shkole* (Methods of Teaching Mathematics in the Secondary Schools), 3rd Ed., Moscow: Uchpedgiz, 1954, p. 407.

15 *Ibid.*, p. 211.

16 *Ibid.*, p. 336.

17 *Direktivy VKP(b) i postanovleniya sovetskovo pravitel'stva o narodnom obrazovanii za 1917–1947 gg.,* Vol. I, p. 179.

18 *Ibid.*, p. 180.

19 From an order of the RSFSR Commissariat of Education, September 4, 1939, in *Narodnoye obrazovaniye,* compiled by A. M. Danev, p. 93.

20 *Ibid.*, p. 96.

21 *Ibid.*, p. 97.

22 *Ibid.*, p. 100.

23 Instructions dated February 29, 1944, cited in *ibid.,* p. 98.

24 *Ibid.*, p. 101.

25 *Vestnik vysshei shkoly,* No. 4, April 1954, p. 29.

26 *Narodnoye obrazovaniye,* compiled by A. M. Danev, pp. 102 ff.

27 *Pravda,* April 21, 1954, p. 3; "On Reducing the Number of Examinations in Schools," *CDSP,* Vol. VI, No. 16, June 2, 1954, p. 32.

28 *Kommunist,* May 20, 1955, p. 3; *Pravda,* May 24, 1955 (leading editorial).

29 *Bilety dlya ekzamenov na attestat zrelosti za kurs srednei shkoly na 1954–1955 uchebnyi god* (Sets of Questions for Examinations Leading to the Certificate of Maturity upon Graduation from the Secondary School in the 1954–1955 School Year), Uchpedgiz, 1955.

Complete text (except for omissions as noted) of this pamphlet listing the official examination questions has been translated by the Center for International Studies (Cenis Translation Series 55–12). All the foregoing citations and factual material on the Certificate of Maturity examinations are based on or quoted from the Cenis Translation.

30 Cenis Translation Series 55–12.

The 1956 Soviet examination material, it may be noted in passing, was approved for printing even earlier (December 1, 1955) for a run of 1,000,000 copies (800,000 at 35 kopeks and 200,000 free).

[31] *Bilety dlya ekzamenov na attestat zrelosti za kurs srednei shkoly* (Tickets for the Secondary School Certificate of Maturity Examinations), 1955–1956 school year, Moscow: Uchpedgiz, 1956.

[32] Kenneth E. Brown, *Mathematics in Public High Schools*, Bulletin 1953, No. 5, Washington, D.C.: Office of Education, 1953, p. 23 (cited in Appendix D).

[33] *Ibid.*, p. 27.

THE SECONDARY ENGINEERING
(INDUSTRIAL) TECHNICAL SCHOOLS

The alternative to college training in engineering and technology in the Soviet Union is provided by schools for subprofessional training called *tekhnikumy* or, more generally, "specialized secondary schools." Until recently nearly all technicums had a 4-year course of instruction. Seven years of general schooling (seven-year school or its equivalent) is the required minimum for admission to technicums; the minimum age of students entering technicums is 14, and the minimum age at graduation is 18. Thus the lowest chronological span of technicum training corresponds to that of our high school. However, since persons up to 30 years of age are admitted to technicums and no maximum age is set for those entering evening and correspondence courses, the *average* age of the technicum student is considerably higher than that of an American high school student.

In c. 1952, shortened courses of instruction were experimentally organized in a few technicums for the graduates of ten-year schools; and in 1954 the plan was expanded to introduce similar programs throughout the technicum system. In 1955 more than 50 per cent of the students starting technicum training were reportedly graduates of the ten-year school.[1] The current policy is to give preference to applicants who have had not less than 2 years of practical experience (employment) following completion of the ten-year school. World War II veterans are also given preference. Although, like any other applicants, they are required to pass prescribed entrance examinations satisfactorily, their grades are not competitively ranked with those of other applicants in filling the planned matriculation quotas. A higher ratio of older students, bringing to the technicum their practical experience, should make for more effective vocational training, but perhaps only at the expense of the *average* achievement in theoretical and professionally-oriented courses.

If all technicums were to shift to a 2-year curriculum for ten-year school graduates, the age composition of the student body would tend to become stabilized within a range comparable to that of the American junior (2-year) colleges. It is not likely, however, that all technicums will be converted to the new plan in the immediate future. What, in effect, may happen is that the heretofore more or less uniform system will become differentiated, with the 2-year technicums becoming similar to our terminal type junior colleges and the 4-year technicums similar to our specialized (vocational) high schools. As of 1955, however, judging by the information included in a handbook *(Spravochnik)* on Moscow Oblast' technicums, the majority have parallel courses: the regular 4-year programs and special programs (2 to 2½ years) for the graduates of ten-year schools.

1. Types of Technicums

Not every technicum is a "technical" school in the sense of training engineering technicians, engineering aids, and junior engineers. An official handbook defines technicums in the various categories as follows:[2]

> Industrial [and construction] technicums train mining technicians, technician-metallurgists, technologists, mechanics, electricians, electro-mechanics, constructors, heat-technicians, chemists, radio technicians, builders, hydro-technicians, and other specialists for the various branches of industry and construction.
>
> The transport technicums train technician-mechanics, electricians, operating technicians, track technicians, boat mechanics, quartermasters, automotive mechanics, and other specialists for railroad, automotive, marine, and river transport.
>
> The communications technicums train electrical technicians for wire communications, radio technicians, and technicians for postal services.

Other categories of technicums (economic, agricultural and forestry, pedagogical, library, medical, and art) are similarly described.

Out of 3,425 specialized secondary schools listed in a 1948 Soviet handbook (shown by categories in Table 14), only 994 (29 per cent) fall more or less clearly within the fields of industrial training. Undifferentiated references to technicums and to the technicum graduates can therefore be extremely misleading. A 1954 article in the *New York Times* stated:

... the Soviet Union has built a vast network of intermediate technical training schools. As nearly as can be estimated there are 3,700 such schools with an enrollment of 1,600,000 students. In the United States there are approximately 1,000* 2-year technical schools with an enrollment slightly under 50,000.[3]

TABLE 14. THE NUMBER OF SPECIALIZED SECONDARY SCHOOLS (TECHNICUMS)
FOR TRAINING IN INDUSTRIAL AND OTHER FIELDS

USSR
1948

Industry or Field	Number of Schools
Fuel	96
Metallurgy	58
Power and electrotechnics	42
Machine and instrument construction	128
Chemical and rubber industry	35
Light and textile industry	56
Food industry	111
Pulp and paper industry	53
Technicums of the Labor Reserve	21
Polygraphic production [printing and graphic arts]	4
Construction, construction materials and communal economy [trade and services]	151
Transport	148
Communications	19
Geology, geodesy, meteorology	21
Industrial technicums, various	51
Subtotal, industrial	994
Agriculture	551
Forestry	22
Economy and law	229
Education	701
Cultural enlightenment	73
Art	197
Public health	615
Physical culture and sports	43
Subtotal, other than industrial	2,431
Total number of specialized secondary schools	3,425*

Sources: (1) *Sredniye spetsial'nye uchebnye zavedeniya SSSR* (*tekhnikumy, uchilishcha, shkoly*), Moscow, 1948. Information given in this handbook is summarized in Cenis Source Memorandum No. 28.

(2) *Kul'turnoye stroitel'stvo SSSR, 1956*, p. 231.

* In 1956 the total number of technicums including 41 correspondence schools was 3,753.

* The Third Annual Engineering Technician Survey of Enrollments and Graduates, made by the American Society for Engineering Education under the chairmanship of Donald C. Metz, shows for 1954–1955 a total of 148 institutions with technical institute programs with a total enrollment of 57,398. See Appendix G.

From this statement one is likely to gain an impression that in 1954 the Soviet Union was training some thirty-two times as many engineering technicians as were comparably trained in American (2-year) technical institutes. It is obvious that the true American counterpart of the total enrollment of the various Soviet technicums would include not only the students enrolled in American *technical institutes* but also many thousands enrolled in some of the junior colleges generally, in business schools, correspondence schools, certain vocational training programs, schools of nursing, some of the high schools with specialized terminal-type of vocational training, the vast system of technical training in the armed forces, and so on. This chapter is concerned only with the "technical" technicums, that is, those training engineering technicians and similarly qualified industrial personnel. The term "engineering technician" is used here provisionally for the Russian designation *"tekhnik"* and more specifically for the categories of specialists of the subprofessional *(tekhnik)* level employed in engineering, technological, and servicing processes in industry and physical plants of the economy. Correspondingly, in Soviet terminology the word *"tekhnik"* is usually qualified as to (a) the type of function (e.g., design, production, construction, or servicing); (b) the branch of industry (e.g., machine building); and (c) the particular kind of technology (e.g., fabrication of metal by cutting tools). Soviet-trained technicians in any one branch of the machine building industry, for instance, would include such categories as:

tekhnik-konstruktor, technician-designer (e.g., ". . . of metal-cutting equipment")

tekhnik-tekhnolog, technician-technologist (e.g., ". . . in fabrication of metals by cutting")

tekhnik-mekhanik, technician-mechanic (e.g., ". . . installation and maintenance of equipment in machine building plants").*

2. Engineering (Industrial) Technicums and Their Enrollment

Soviet statistics on the matriculation, enrollment, and graduation from technicums for 1940, 1950, and 1955 are shown in Tables 15, 16, and 17, respectively. Table 18 lists the number of technicum graduates by fields of specialization in 1950 and 1955. The figures cited in these tables are of utmost significance. They clearly demonstrate

* Cenis Source Memorandum No. 28, which is a summary of the data given in an official 1948 handbook on technicums, includes a list of some 285 major areas of specialization (but not the subdivisions which are recognized in each area).

the magnitude of the Soviet effort to expand technicum training and the direction in which this effort has been applied since the end of World War II.

In 1940–1941 the total enrollment in technicums and similar Soviet schools of specialized secondary education was 975,000; this figure for 1955–1956 was 1.96 million—twice the prewar enrollment. In the meantime, however, the enrollment in *industrial* (and construction) technicums has expanded even more; in 1955–1956 it stood at *four and a half times* the 1940–1941 enrollment (843,000 versus the prewar 187,000). The upward trend established in 1945 continues. It can be best illustrated by comparing the admissions to industrial and construction technicums with the total admissions to all technicums in the same year. The per cent share of the industrial and construction technicum admissions shows an unmistakable trend.

Admissions

Year	All Technicums (Thousands)	Industrial and Construction	
		Thousands	Per Cent of All
1940	382.9	80.2	20.9
1945	387.6	108.1	27.9
1950	426.3	142.2	33.3
1954	594.8	245.3	41.2
1955	587.6	245.5	41.8

The nearly identical figures for 1954 and 1955 no doubt reflect the stepped up quota established after the 19th Party Congress (1952). It may be assumed that at least 75 per cent of those who enter technicum training will have graduated 4 years later.* At the 1954 rate of admission, Soviet industrial technicums, therefore, could graduate in 1958 and annually thereafter approximately 180,000 students. The available graduation statistics show that the number of industrial and construction technicum graduates has been rapidly increasing.

Graduations

Year	All Technicums (Thousands)	Industrial and Construction	
		Thousands	Per Cent of All
1940	236.8	21.7	9.2
1945	118.1	16.0	13.5
1950	313.7	85.4	27.2
1954	332.3	108.3	32.6
1955	387.8	140.8	36.3

* E.g., industrial and construction technicums admitted 142.2 thousand in 1950 and graduated 108.3 thousand (76 per cent) in 1954.

It should be noted that the recent expansion of the total technicum enrollment, and particularly in the industrial and construction technicums, is partly accounted for by an increase in part-time evening enrollment and in the number of correspondence students. In 1945 there were few evening technicums, and only five technicums gave instruction by correspondence. Fewer than 9 per cent of all the technicum students admitted in 1945 were enrolled in correspondence technicums, and fewer than 1,000 of these in industrial and construction courses by correspondence. In contrast, of the total 245.5 thousand matriculated at industrial and construction technicums in 1955, 48.6 thousand (20 per cent) were part-time evening students, and 36.2 thousand (15 per cent) enrolled for study by correspondence.

TABLE 15. ADMISSIONS TO TECHNICUMS AND OTHER SCHOOLS OF SPECIALIZED SECONDARY EDUCATION BY CATEGORIES OF SCHOOLS

USSR

1940, 1950, and 1955

Admissions	1940		1950		1955	
	Thousands	%	Thousands	%	Thousands	%
Students admitted, total	382.9	100.0	426.3	100.0	587.5	100.0
Resident*	331.2	86.5	365.1	85.6	478.7	81.5
Correspondence	51.7	13.5	61.2	14.4	108.8	18.5
Industrial and construction	80.2	21.0	142.2	33.3	245.5	41.8
Transport and communications	22.9	6.0	28.0	6.6	48.5	8.3
Agriculture	48.1	12.5	59.3	13.9	98.2	16.7
Economy and law	18.6	4.9	34.8	8.2	51.7	8.8
Education	117.4	30.6	105.8	24.8	51.7	8.8
Health, physical education, and sports	85.5	22.3	48.3	11.3	81.2	13.8
Arts and motion pictures	10.2	2.7	7.9	1.9	10.7	1.8

Source: Kul'turnoye stroitel'stvo SSSR, 1956, pp. 236–237. (The source gives these data also for 1945 and 1954.)

* Includes part-time evening students. In 1955, 54.8 thousand students (9.8 per cent of the total number) matriculated for part-time evening study.

The slower rate of training on a part-time basis and by correspondence would no doubt delay by 2 or 3 years the achievement of the annual graduation rate we have indicated—180,000 or more, for the industrial and construction technicums. Nevertheless, with the introduction in 1954 of short-term courses for the ten-year school graduates, the number of technicum graduates has probably sharply risen

TABLE 16. ENROLLMENT IN TECHNICUMS AND OTHER SCHOOLS OF SPECIALIZED
SECONDARY EDUCATION BY CATEGORIES OF SCHOOLS

USSR

1940–1941, 1950–1951, 1955–1956

Enrollment	1940–1941		1950–1951		1955–1956	
	Thousands	%	Thousands	%	Thousands	%
Total enrollment	974.8	100.0	1,297.6	100.0	1,960.4	100.0
Resident*	819.5	84.1	1,116.9	86.1	1,673.9	85.4
Correspondence	155.3	15.9	180.7	13.9	286.5	14.6
Industrial and construction	187.5	19.2	449.9	34.7	843.1	43.0
Transport and communications	54.4	5.6	88.6	6.8	150.3	7.7
Agriculture	114.7	11.8	162.0	12.5	337.8	17.2
Economy and law	43.1	4.4	93.4	7.2	134.6	6.9
Education	345.3	35.4	347.5	26.8	247.2	12.6
Health, physical education, and sports	204.4	21.0	126.0	9.7	215.9	11.0
Arts and motion pictures	25.4	2.6	30.2	2.3	31.5	1.6

Source: Kul'turnoye stroitel'stvo SSSR, 1956, pp. 230 ff. (The source gives these
data for 1945–1946 and for 1954–1955.)

* Including part-time evening students.

TABLE 17. GRADUATION FROM TECHNICUMS AND OTHER SCHOOLS OF SPECIALIZED
SECONDARY EDUCATION BY CATEGORIES OF SCHOOLS

USSR

1940, 1950, and 1955

Graduates	1940		1950		1955	
	Thousands	%	Thousands	%	Thousands	%
All technicums	236.8	100.0	313.7	100.0	387.8	100.0
Resident*	207.8	87.8	283.7	90.4	361.1	93.1
Correspondence	29.0	12.2	30.0	9.6	26.7	6.9
Industrial and construction	21.7	9.2	85.4	27.2	140.8	36.3
Transport and communications	8.3	3.5	18.9	6.0	23.9	6.2
Agriculture	21.5	9.1	48.7	15.5	57.8	14.9
Economy and law	7.2	3.0	24.9	8.0	30.5	7.9
Education	85.8	36.2	76.6	24.4	73.5	19.0
Health, physical education, and sports	90.3	38.2	54.2	17.3	56.3	14.5
Arts and motion pictures	2.0	0.8	5.0	1.6	5.0	1.2

Source: Kul'turnoye stroitel'stvo SSSR, 1956, pp. 238–239. (The source gives
these data also for 1945 and 1954.)

* Includes part-time evening students. In 1955, 16.0 thousand graduates (4.1
per cent of the total number) were in that category.

TABLE 18.   DISTRIBUTION OF TECHNICUM GRADUATES
BY FIELD OF SPECIALIZATION
USSR
1950 and 1955

Field of Training	1950		1955	
	Thousands	%	Thousands	%
Geology and exploration of deposits	1.8	0.6	5.6	1.4
Development of geological deposits	6.0	1.9	13.0	3.4
Power industry	7.7	2.4	12.7	3.3
Metallurgy	4.9	1.6	4.5	1.2
Machine and instrument construction	26.6	8.5	34.9	9.0
Electrical machines and instrument construction	2.4	0.8	4.8	1.2
Radio engineering and communications	5.2	1.7	11.9	3.1
Chemical technology	4.4	1.4	7.2	1.9
Wood, pulp, and paper technology	2.4	0.8	5.1	1.3
Construction	14.6	4.6	32.4	8.3
Transportation	11.1	3.5	12.6	3.2
Consumer food products technology	4.9	1.5	5.7	1.5
Consumer goods technology	5.0	1.6	5.9	1.5
Geodesy and cartography	0.8	0.3	1.4	0.4
Hydrology and meteorology	0.6	0.2	1.1	0.3
Subtotal: industry, technology, transport, communications, and construction	98.4	31.4	158.8	41.0
Agriculture	46.6	14.9	50.4	13.0
Economy [trade and services]	26.3	8.4	41.6	10.7
Legal	4.2	1.3	1.3	0.3
Health and physical culture	54.2	17.3	59.6	15.4
Education	76.7	24.4	70.2	18.1
Arts	5.0	1.6	4.2	1.1
Unspecified	2.3	0.7	1.7	0.4
Total number of graduates	313.7	100.0	387.8	100.0

Source: Kul'turnoye stroitel'stvo SSSR, 1956, pp. 241–242.

in 1957 and theoretically may have reached approximately 600,000—
including as many as 250,000 graduates of the industrial and construction technicums alone.*

* An article published in *Izvestiya* (July 17, 1954, p. 1) anticipated that about
165,000 ten-year school graduates would enter technicums (of all types) in the
specially organized 2-year and 2½-year courses ("Specialized School Network
Grows," *CDSP*, Vol. VI, No. 29, September 1954). It may be assumed that about
70,000 (42 per cent) of these special students entered industrial and construction
technicums for a 2½-year course, thus swelling the ranks of the "1957 class."

At their present rate of matriculation (245,000 per year), and assuming that about one-third of their students are ten-year school graduates enrolling for 2½-year courses, the industrial and construction technicums should reach their peak—possibly more than 250,000 graduates per year—in 1958. Thereafter the rate of output will, of course, level off to something like 200,000 per year unless the training policy or the rate of admissions is changed. Apparently it is the intention to continue the present policy. In July 1955 the Plenum of the Central Committee resolved "to increase the number of specialists being trained on the secondary school base."[4]

3. SHORTAGE OF ENGINEERING TECHNICIANS

The almost certain increase in number (and perhaps in quality) of technicians within the next few years is an important factor in assessing Soviet industrial capabilities. There has apparently been a chronic relative shortage of technicians, partly inherited from the pre-Revolutionary industrial organization and perpetuated doubtless by rigid planning. One of the aims of the first Five Year (1928–1932) Plan was to expand the training of technicians so as to have, by 1933, not fewer than 1½ technicians for every engineer.[5] This ratio seems to have been established as a guide for planning the number to be trained in the respective categories. Although there have been persistent complaints on the relative shortage of technicians, this plan was apparently maintained for 15 years. As shown in Table 19, the ratio of new industrial technicum graduates to new engineers for 1929 through 1932 was approximately 1.5 to 1; during the postwar (fourth 1946–1950) Five Year period the ratio of the output of technicians to engineers was planned at approximately 2.9 to 1.* Nevertheless, as late as October 1954 *Pravda* complained that the ratio of technicians to engineers was still 1 to 1; and in November of that year the Minister of Higher Education, V. P. Yelutin, cited a "recent" decision of the

* As follows:

Field	Technicians	Engineers	Ratio T/E
Industry and construction	347,000	120,000	2.9 to 1
Transportation and communications	74,000	24,000	3.1 to 1
Total, industrial	421,000	144,000	2.9 to 1

Source: S. V. Kaftanov, *Report to the Supreme Soviet on March 16, 1946;* quoted by Boris I. Gorokhoff, "Materials for the Study of Soviet Specialized Education," unpublished manuscript, National Research Council, 1952, p. 164. From another source (*Vestnik vysshei shkoly,* 1946, No. 10, pp. 3–4) Gorokhoff quotes 2.6 to 1 and 2.5 to 1 planned ratios for 1950 (p. 165).

Council of Ministers to increase the ratio of technicians to engineers by training "for each specialist of higher qualification not fewer than two to four specialists of medium qualification."[6]

TABLE 19. NUMBER OF ENGINEERS AND TECHNICIANS GRADUATED
UNDER THE FIRST, SECOND, AND THIRD FIVE YEAR PLANS
USSR
1929–1940

Period	Engineers* (thousands)	Technicians* (thousands)	Ratio Technicians/Engineers
1929–1932	67.7	98.6	1.5 to 1
1933–1937	134.4	213.2	1.6 to 1
1938–1940	89.0	(112.0)	1.3 to 1
15-year prewar	291.1	423.8	1.5 to 1

Source: Nicholas DeWitt, *Soviet Professional Manpower*, Washington, D.C.: National Science Foundation, 1955, Table B–1, pp. 350–351. Figure shown in parentheses is estimated.

* Industry, construction, transportation, and communications.

The Soviet effort to train a sufficient number of technicians is not handicapped by the unwillingness of the students to enter technicums. There appear to be many more applicants than there are "planned vacancies." From the standpoint of the student, and presumably his parents, the technicum apparently provides a thoroughly acceptable compromise as compared with professional engineering training. In some essential ways the technicum graduates are seen to be better off than engineers; their responsibilities are less demanding, and their rate of pay is relatively satisfactory. To have a son graduate from a technicum is a great achievement for a family of modest background. Anyone who is accepted at a technicum receives a state scholarship which, in some fields, compares favorably with those available at the universities and engineering institutes. The stipends vary from field to field (providing an incentive to enter the fields of training with the highest price tag), from year to year, and with the level of achievement attained by the student in the preceding semester. A few examples of the technicum monthly stipends are shown in Table 20. In comparison with the prevailing wages the 1954–1955 scholarships, ranging from 185 to as high as 490 rubles, are substantial. The starting salary of a technicum *teacher,* for instance, is reported to be between 1,300 and 1,400 rubles per month; laboratory technicians employed at the universities are paid, depending on their grade, from 600 to 900 rubles per month; and the starting wage of a technicum *graduate* is not likely to average much more than 1,000 rubles per month.

TABLE 20. STIPENDS PAID TO THE STUDENTS OF TECHNICUMS
USSR
1943 scale, 1954 actual, and 1955 reported
(in rubles per month)

Kind of Technicum	Year of Instruction			
	I	II	III	IV
1943 Official rates:*				
Category A	80	100	120	140
Category B	125	150	175	200
Category C	225	255	300	330
1954 Published rates:				
2 yr. 10 mo. School of Aerial Photography	260	285	310	...
Metallurgical†	185	?	?	487
Chemico-mechanical‡	185	?	?	320
Nonferrous metallurgy	185	?	?	285
Electro-mechanical	185	210	235	260
1955 Coal Mining Technicum:§				
Mining technology	...	...	360	490
Construction	...	...	235	390

Sources: 1943 official rates from *Vysshaya shkola* (The Higher School), Basic Regulations, Orders, and Instructions, compiled by M. I. Movshovich, Moscow: "Sovetskaya Nauka," 1945, pp. 73 ff. (hereafter referred to as *Vysshaya shkola*, compiled by M. I. Movshovich). Examples for 1954 from a Handbook (*Spravochnik dlya postupayushchikh v tekhnikumy*) for Moscow and Moscow Oblast'.

* Category A includes all technicums except industrial and transportation technicums which are listed in categories B and C. Category B includes technicums of the ministries of the following industries: aviation, oil, coal, power plants, ferrous metal, nonferrous metal, chemical, tank, armament, military supplies, transportation, construction, mine ordnance (*narkomminvooruzheniya*). Category C is comprised of those technicums in category B which train for the following branches of production: coal mining, ore mining, construction of mines, underground electro-mechanics, mining survey, blast furnace smelting, steel production, electro-metallurgical, rolled products, nonferrous and precious metals, crude oil, oil processing, forging and casting, synthetic fuels, noxious chemicals, boilers, and geology.

† "From 185 to 487 rubles, depending on the year, the specialty [field], and on the student's level of achievement."

‡ "Depending on the year and the students' level of achievement."

§ *Kiyevskii gornyi tekhnikum* (Kiev Mining Technicum) since 1954–1955 has accepted only ten-year school graduates for a 2-year course of training.

4. Enrollment in American Technical Institutes
and in Soviet Technicums

Technicum training in engineering and technology, that is, in
industrial, construction, communications, and transport technicums,
is most nearly comparable to the training given in our 2-year technical institutes. It should be noted, however, that, whereas in the
Soviet Union technicums are the sole source of supply of new technicians, in the United States the technical institutes are only one of
several sources. With that qualification, it is nevertheless significant
that our current enrollment in the technical institutes is very small
in comparison with that in the Soviet industrial technicums.

As shown in Table 21, the total 1954–1955 enrollment in such state,
municipal, privately endowed, and proprietary schools, and in extension divisions of colleges and universities, including part-time students,
in the United States was 60,747.[7] This enrollment implies a potential
graduation rate of 10,000 to 13,000 full-time students and perhaps a
total of 20,000 or more if part-time students are included. H. Russell

TABLE 21.   Enrollment in Technical Institutes
United States
1954–1955

Institutions		Enrollment		
Type	Number	Full-time	Part-time	Total
State and municipal	22	11,255	10,451	21,706
Privately endowed	12	4,624	8,503	13,127
Extension divisions*	14	4,608	11,319	15,927
Proprietary	19	6,153	2,800	8,953
YMCA schools	2	126	908	1,034
Total	69	26,766	33,981	60,747

Source: Table I, "Annual Survey of Technical Institutes 1954–1955," prepared
by Leo F. Smith, Dean of Instruction, Rochester Institute of Technology, *Technical Education News*, Vol. VIX, No. 4 (July–August 1955).

* Of colleges and universities.

Beatty, President of Wentworth Institute, has stated that, depending on how a technician is defined, our current rate of graduation
(full-time students) is between 9,000 and 14,000 per year. In his opinion we ought to train about 90,000 technicians to meet adequately the
growing need for technical manpower both in the rapidly expanding
new industries and for the introduction of new processes in existing
industries.[8] A recent article by Karl O. Werwath, President of the

Milwaukee School of Engineering, puts the case in more urgent terms, pointing out that an engineer is part of a team which includes *five* engineering technicians. The author concludes that we are graduating only one-eighth the needed number of engineering technicians at the present time, and that to retain our position we must increase the rate at which new technicians are trained to ten times the current rate.[9] C. S. Jones, President of the Academy of Aeronautics, has commented on the size of enrollment in technical institutes (51,228 in 1953–1954 and 60,747 in 1954–1955):

> Though these figures are impressive and represent a steady growth, they are a far cry from the suggested 3 to 1 ratio when compared with the 160,000 enrolled in engineering colleges. Several hundred thousand would be more in line.[10]

The Soviets, as we have shown, may now have nearly a million students enrolled in industrial technicums; by 1957, and for 2 or 3 years thereafter, they may graduate as many as 250,000 industrial and construction technicians per year.* It is important to note, however, that not all of the potential Soviet graduates will be *engineering* technicians, and that it is impossible to equate the quality, content, and level of their training to any one definable category of American-trained technicians.

5. Destinations of Technicum Graduates

Technicum training is mainly terminal. It is not designed as preparation for further higher education, and only a small proportion of technicum graduates become students in engineering institutes.

In the first place, only the top 5 per cent in each technicum graduating class are *permitted* to apply for admission to an engineering school; and the extra year of study at the technicum (as compared with the last three grades of the ten-year school) does not give the technicum graduate an advanced standing in the institutes. We have seen no statistics showing how many of the top 5 per cent of the technicum graduates actually apply for admission to engineering institutes right after graduation from the technicum or how many of those who do apply are accepted. But, although in the 1930's many of the technicum

---

* An article published in *Vestnik vysshei shkoly*, No. 4, April 1948, pp. 12–17, estimated that by c. 1955 industrial and construction technicums (not including transportation and communications) would graduate 90,000 to 100,000 annually. See Boris I. Gorokhoff, "Materials for the Study of Soviet Specialized Education," unpublished mimeographed report, Washington, D.C.: National Research Council, Office of Scientific Personnel, 1952 (hereafter referred to as Boris I. Gorokhoff, "Materials for the Study of Soviet Specialized Education"), pp. 156 ff. and p. 205, where the author summarizes this important article and comments on its salient points.

graduates continued their education at the institutes, it is not likely that with the current relative oversupply of ten-year school graduates any significant number of the technicum students in the top 5 per cent can qualify immediately upon graduation for admission to engineering institutes.* Secondly, all other technicum graduates are legally permitted to apply for admission to an engineering school only after completing 3 years of employment assigned to them by the ministry; and, because of the many restrictive conditions of employment and the relative shortage of technicians, it is doubtful if at the present time and in the immediate future many of the technicum-trained technicians can take advantage of this provision.

One exception should be noted. There have been instances when technicum graduates were encouraged, if not drafted, to enter engineering institutes for training in a number of designated fields. Such drives have probably been occasioned by the perennially developing discrepancies between the planned and subsequently existing demand for technicians, between the planned and the actual output of men trained for a certain set of specific duties. Thus, for instance, the Ministry of Transportation in 1951 listed seven fields of specialization in which technicum graduates with a minimum of *five* years of experience were offered engineering training in a number of designated institutes.

Thus at least 95 per cent, if not more, of all technicum graduates are forthwith assigned by their respective ministries to a job, as often as not at the plant associated with a particular technicum or elsewhere within the industrial organization of the ministry. The individual preference of the graduates as to one or another location appears to have little bearing on the destination specified in the "travel orders" (the inevitable and indispensable *putevka* of every professional and subprofessional employee in the Soviet Union) which are issued to them. No recent data are available on the distribution of technicum graduates by type of work within industries. A 1940 survey made by the Communist Party reported the following distribution of 164,000 technicians:[11]

Type of Duty	Number	Per Cent
Administrative	41,000	25
Managerial	41,000	25
Production	82,000	50
Total	164,000	100

* The 1954–1955 enrollment in the last three grades (VIII through X) of the ten-year schools was four times the 1950 enrollment (Zverev's speech, *Pravda Ukrainy,* February 4, 1955, p. 1:6).

6. Administration and Control of Technicums

Although it may be convenient to compare Soviet industrial (or engineering) technicums with American technical institutes, there are essential differences between them—even if one disregards the all-important, fundamental difference in the political and sociological climates in which they operate.

Soviet technicums are controlled jointly by the Ministry of Higher Education, which has academic and general jurisdiction over the entire network of these schools, and by the various industrial ministries (state trusts), each ministry having jurisdiction over a group of technicums in which to train its future junior supervisory, research, and operating personnel. Whereas in 1946 most of the engineering institutes (up to that time similarly attached to a given industrial ministry) were transferred to the exclusive jurisdiction of the Ministry of Higher Education, the technicums have remained within the various, vertically integrated industrial complexes. The respective industrial ministries finance and administer their technicums, but the Ministry of Higher Education exercises control over admission policies, curricula, and academic standards through its department of specialized secondary education. The exact boundaries of academic control are not entirely clear. It appears that the Ministry of Higher Education controls the over-all organization of curricula (allocation of time among political, general science, and specialized courses) and syllabi for all but some of the specialized subjects which are geared to the specific needs of one or another occupational field within a specific ministry.*

In general, it may be assumed that the control functions of the

---

* Thus, for instance, certain textbooks used in technicums are approved by the Ministry of Higher Education, others by the industrial ministries, as the following examples show:

Approved by the Ministry of Higher Education:
  Mathematics (e.g., N. P. Tarasov, *Course of Higher Mathematics for Technicums;* P. P. Andreev, *Course in Elementary Geometry*)
  Chemistry (e.g., L. M. Smorgonskii, *Textbook on Organic Chemistry;* G. I. Klyukovskii and L. A. Manuilov, *Physical Chemistry and Chemistry of Silicon*)
  Mechanics (e.g., I. N. Veselovskii, *Course in Mechanics for Technicums*)
  Machine Design (e.g., Ya. M. Pavlov, *Machine Details*)
Approved by Industrial Ministries:
  Ministry of Machine Tool Construction (e.g., A. L. Chestnov, *Technology of Fabrication of Measuring Tools and Devices*)
  Ministry of Defense Industry (e.g., S. O. Dobrogurskii and V. K. Titov, *Computing-Solving Mechanisms*).

Ministry of Higher Education with reference to technicums are identical or similar to those which were officially prescribed in 1943 for its predecessor, the Sovnarkom (Council of Ministers) Committee on Higher Schools. They were as follows:[12]

(a) To study and develop and to submit for the consideration of the USSR Council of Ministers questions on the development of technicums.

(b) To compile over-all plans for the enrollment of students in technicums with reference to the requirements of the different ministries (agencies) and to submit such plans for the approval of the USSR Council of Ministers.

(c) To establish the composition of technicum fields of study and the list (and nomenclature) of specialties in which technicum students are trained.

(d) To issue directives with reference to the enrollment and the graduation of technicum students.

(e) To establish academic schedules and curricula.

(f) To approve syllabi and textbooks for all general subjects.

The distribution of technicums by major *industries* (fuel, metallurgy, and others) has already been noted (Table 14). Within each industrial grouping, however, there are subdivisions corresponding to the various ministries in control of the specific schools within each industrial category. Thus, for instance, the 96 fuel industry technicums in 1948 were allocated among eleven ministries or administrations; and the 128 technicums in the category designated "Machine and Apparatus Construction" included 11 groups of schools, each group controlled by a different ministry or administration. The complex division of responsibilities between the Ministry of Higher Education and the industrial ministries on the one hand, and, on the other, among the several ministries, each concerned with training technicians for its own specific needs rather than technicians of given general qualifications, is unquestionably detrimental to the effectiveness and quality of technicum training. For example, some thirty-four ministries, each in its own network of many technicums, train technicians specializing in "industrial and public construction."[13] Because of the vertical integration of industrial responsibilities (including the training of personnel) each ministry attempts to train not only in skills uniquely related to its needs but also in basic skills.

Matters have gone so far, for example, that the USSR Ministry of the Metallurgical Industry trains specialists in forestry and railroad operations, the Ministry of Power Plants and Electric Industry in telephone communications, and the Ministry of Building Materials in the foundry production of ferrous metals, forestry, and architecture.[14]

Ever since the organization of the vertically integrated industrial trusts for rapid development of key industries under the Five Year Plans, the horizontally distributed functional needs of the growing industrial economy and the vertically assigned managerial responsibilities for industrial performance have been in conflict. The weaknesses of the technicum training system, as it has been organized, reflect the basic characteristics of Soviet industrial management generally and illustrate the fact that the Soviet economy has been unable to achieve a satisfactory balance between horizontal and vertical integration of its industrial organization. In the spring of 1957 the Soviet government under Khrushchev initiated a vast plan to decentralize its system of control over industry and to shift from the heretofore vertical control of each specific industry toward a horizontal integration of industrial activities generally on a regional basis. Any changes made in that direction will necessarily affect the organizational structure of technicum training and may in time eliminate some of the defects in technicum education of which the Soviet press has been complaining.

7. Soviet Comments on Technicums

With all the prominence of educational themes in the Soviet daily press, journals, and foreign-language propaganda pamphlets, very little of substance is said about specialized secondary education.* The press publishes in lengthy detail the regular secondary school statistics, curricula, syllabi, methodology, and teaching experience, but only undifferentiated crude statistics and general qualitative statements—largely unfavorable and critical—on the technicums. Here are a few comments selected at random from recent Soviet articles:

The required laboratories and shops are absent. In Siberia, the

---

* In the 1930's and earlier the RSFSR Commissariat (Ministry) of Public Education published a journal entitled *Proftekhnicheskoye obrazovaniye* dealing with the problems of engineering, technical, and vocational training. The latest copy we were able to find was for August–September (No. 8–9) 1930.

In December 1954 the Ministry of Higher Education started publishing *Sredneye spetsial'noye obrazovaniye* (Secondary Specialized Education), a journal dealing with methodology and other questions of technicum training. (*Vestnik vysshei shkoly*, January 1955, p. 53.)

Far East, Central Asia, and Kazakhstan the number of secondary specialized schools is insufficient.[15]
The Minsk Technicum of Light Industry has 780 sq. m. [8,396 sq. ft. of floor space] for 500 students [16.6 sq. ft. per student]. This space comprises nine classrooms, a tailoring shop, a club, a library, and consultation offices of a correspondence light industry technicum course in which 150 students are enrolled.[16]
Our trouble is that many of the departments [ministries] which have been allocated funds to build technicums do not build them, or do not equip them properly.[17]
By 1960 the school floor area [presumably average for all technicums in the USSR] ought to be brought up to 4 to 5 sq. m. [43 to 54 sq. ft.] per student.[18]

Typical comments on the textbooks complain of "acute shortage" of textbooks and visual aids[19] and complete lack of textbooks "for the majority of specialized subjects."[20] In consequence ". . . students do not read texts but prepare themselves [for examinations] on the basis of condensed summaries [konspekty]." And the same author states that the teachers, in the absence of teaching aids, spend much time "having to draw sketches of machines and of machine details in chalk on the blackboards."[21]

Because of the frequent and sudden changes in curricula and syllabi, textbooks rapidly become obsolete. There are many complaints that the agencies responsible for the production of up-to-date textbooks fail to keep up with the requirements.

Often the [secondary school] textbooks follow in a condensed form the syllabi of the same courses at the institutions of higher learning.[22]
Lately one observes the resumption of a method whereby whole sections of a course are dictated. This practice arises from the fact that textbooks do not correspond to the [required] syllabi. Furthermore, the textbook suffers from the absence of unity between theory and practice.[23]
Plans for publishing textbooks for technicums are not fulfilled year after year. In 1952, for example, only 111 out of 194 textbooks provided by the plans . . . were published.[24]

The organization of curricula is also frequently criticized: "In some technicums, for example, the courses on the repair of farm machinery are given before the courses on the farm machinery, and courses on the mechanization of animal husbandry before the courses on electrical equipment."[25]
The frequent comments on the teaching staff as a rule point out that technicums use mostly part-time teachers.[26]
It has been recently reported in the Soviet press that the present

number of technicums is c. 4,000 and the enrollment (full-time students) c. 1,500,000. On the average, therefore, the present technicum may have about 350 students; but there are apparently many technicums with an enrollment of 2,000 or more.* Consequently, there must be a significant number of very small technicums. Considering the fact that there are four grades (years) in a technicum curriculum, which includes all the subjects taught in the last 3 years of the ten-year school *plus* a large number of general and specialized technical subjects, *plus* shop and industrial practice, it is not likely that satisfactory standards of instruction are uniformly maintained except in the larger technicums.

8. Recent Observations by Visitors

Two Americans, Homer L. and Norton Dodge, visited one of the large technicums (Coal Mining Industry, in Kiev) in May 1955. This particular technicum in Kiev (founded in 1947) represents perhaps the best of its kind. It may or may not be an accident that a number of recent visitors (among them Columbia students in 1954 and William Benton, the publisher of the *Encyclopedia Britannica,* in 1955) when in Kiev were taken to see this particular school. The coal mining technicums generally, it should be noted, have been singled out in the Soviet press as an example for other ministries to follow.[27] Although we cannot take this technicum as a typical example of some 1,000 industrial (engineering) intermediate schools in the Soviet Union, the observations made by the Dodges on the visit to this technicum in part are applicable to technicums generally. From the Dodges' account as it was given to this writer we single out for comment a few details which indicate the possible changes in policy governing the technicums and thus the trend of their development.

1. "The number of courses (specialties) has been reduced from four to two."

The Dodges were told that the technicum conducts (apparently beginning with 1954–1955) only two courses. This change must have been made on relatively short notice. In a handbook for that year, published in March 1954, *five* courses were listed for this technicum, as follows:[28]

Open workings of coal deposits.
Mining electro-mechanics.
Mine construction.
Industrial and civil constructions.
Construction and utilization of automotive roads and bridges.

* The average enrollment per engineering technicum in 1939 was 377.

The two courses, which are the only ones now offered, were identified to the Dodges as:
[Coal?] mining technology.
[Mine?] construction and auxiliary facilities.
The new courses deal directly and specifically with coal mines and coal mining technology. This one example may indicate a more generally exerted effort to eliminate duplication of training facilities.

2. "The Kiev mining technicum is now accepting only ten-year school graduates."

This appears to be one of perhaps very few technicums to change over to a shortened (now 2½ years) post-secondary school curriculum. We have not attempted to make a detailed check, but, as we mentioned earlier, the typical arrangement at the present time is to enroll the ten-year graduates in a special group while continuing to accept seven-year graduates for the usual 4-year course.[29] It may be assumed, however, that in 1956–1957 additional technicums changed to the new basis, discontinuing the 4-year program altogether.

3. "It is planned that all technicums, except the cultural technicums, will be reorganized to accept only ten-year school graduates."

Such a plan would of course be consistent with the plan to extend universal *ten-year school* general education throughout the Soviet Union by 1960. If that plan were actually to be achieved, not only the 4-year technicum would have to be abolished, but also the entire network of Labor Reserve trade, vocational, and industrial schools mentioned in Chapter 1. Furthermore, the postwar "emergency" schools (for rural and for working youth, also mentioned in Chapter 1) logically should die off or be converted to a regular ten-year school curriculum of an appropriate level. The early pronouncements on the gradual expansion of universal 10-year education almost invariably added parenthetically "*(desyatiletka)*"—the colloquial but officially used term for the ten-year school.[30] Later references tended to be somewhat ambiguous; it was not clear whether 10 years of education *of any kind* or a *ten-year school* education is to become universal by 1960.

The recently published directive of the Central Committee of the Communist Party reads as follows: "Essentially to achieve [*osushchestvit' v osnovnom*] *Universal Secondary Education* in cities and rural localities by means of teaching children and youths in secondary schools of general education (*desyatiletka*) and in secondary specialized educational institutions."[31] In the light of this considerably toned-down version of the earlier directive, it does not appear probable that all technicums will be rapidly converted to 2½- or 2-year junior colleges. As we have already stated, it seems more likely that some will continue to operate on a 4-year basis alongside the regular ten-year schools. The net effect will be to advance the process of differentiation among the heretofore uniform schools. The recent introduction of industrial (*promyshlennye*) classes in regular ten-year schools is another sign of differentiation in education at high school level.[32]

4. "Last year [1954] there were four to five applicants for each opening [at Kiev coal mining technicum]."

The number of new students to be admitted each year for different types of training is predetermined and set by the plan. With the current great expansion of enrollment in the upper classes of the ten-year schools, the number of ten-year school graduates who desire to continue their education is many times larger than the planned freshman enrollment in higher schools and in technicums, leading possibly to a more stringent selection of new students.*

5. "The technicum teaches approximately the same subjects as a mining institute but with more emphasis on practice, less on theory."

This comment confirms our view that with the introduction of a 2-year course for the ten-year school graduates Soviet technicums will become similar to the American 2-year technical institutes. The reformed technicums should at least in theory eventually be able to produce more broadly trained subprofessional specialists than those trained on a 7-year base. We say "in theory" because very little specific and qualitatively significant information on technicum training (especially with reference to the new short courses) is available.

9. THE TECHNICUM CURRICULA

The only complete curriculum of a 4-year technicum that we have located is a *proposed* curriculum for a mining technicum.[33] Nevertheless, a few observations indicative of the composition and academic level of the technicum curricula can be made. One clue, of course, is provided by the admissions requirements.

A Soviet seven-year school graduate (age 14) will have had 7 years of mathematics, 4 years of biology, 2 years of physics, 1 year of chemistry, 3 years of foreign language, and 1 year of mechanical drawing. Thus, although we may have reservations on the quality of Soviet secondary school teaching, the Soviet seven-year graduates at age 14 have probably had a greater exposure to the subject matter directly relevant to a future technicum education than the majority of American high school graduates (but not those in science or technical courses). In mathematics, for instance, the Soviet seven-year graduate will have studied:

1. Arithmetic—6 years; 6 or 7 hours per week for the first 5 years of school and 2 hours per week in the sixth class (grade).

2. Algebra—2 years; 3 hours per week in his sixth class and the first semester of the seventh class and 4 hours per week in the last semester.

3. Plane Geometry—2 years; 2 hours per week in his sixth year and $2\frac{1}{2}$ hours (average of two semesters) per week in the seventh year.[34]

---

* The 1954 rules of admission to technicums note that ". . . acceptance of applications may be terminated earlier than the designated date [July 31] if there are more than five applications for each vacancy."

Admission to technicums is selective, the choice among applicants being made largely on the basis of grades received in the entrance examinations. Until 1955, the (7-year base) applicants were examined in four subjects:

1. USSR Constitution (Oral).
2. Russian Language (Written, dictated text).
3. Russian Language and Literature Readings (Oral).
4. Mathematics (Written and Oral).*

The syllabus for the oral examination in mathematics has included the following topics:

Arithmetic:
    Whole numbers.
    Laws of operations and properties (associative, commutative, and distributive).
    Divisibility of numbers.
    Common fractions.
    Metric system of measures.
    Decimal fractions.
    Ratio and proportions.
    Percentage.
Algebra (more or less equivalent to high school Algebra I):
    Literal expressions.
    Relative numbers.
    Monomials and polynomials.
    Factoring of polynomials.
    Algebraic fractions.
    Equations of the first order with one unknown.
    Systems of equations of the first order.
    Extraction of square roots.
Geometry (more or less equivalent to high school Geometry I):
    Basic concepts.
    Angles.
    Triangles.
    Basic construction problems.
    Parallel lines.
    Polygons.
    Quadrilaterals.
    Geometric location of points.
    Circumference and circle.
    Measurement of angles.
    Inscribed and circumscribed triangles.

This background in mathematics of the 14-year old applicant to a

* In 1955 the rules were amended, reducing the number of examinations to the following: Russian Language (Written Composition), Mathematics (Oral only).

Soviet technicum appears to be only slightly short (Algebra II) of that expected in American 2-year technical institutes from *high school-*educated applicants. Wentworth Institute, for instance, requires of its applicants for training as engineering technicians satisfactory grades (but no entrance examination) in Algebra I and II and Plane Geometry. But in some American technical institutes requirements are apparently considerably lower. A report of the Physics Staff of Purdue University Technical Institute includes the following paragraph:

> Since high school graduation is the only prerequisite for admission to many technical institutes, no particular mathematics, science, or vocational subjects may be relied upon as a common background. Except for the common branch of arithmetic, little mathematical knowledge may be taken for granted.[35]

Thus some of the American technical-institute freshmen (at age 19) with 2 years of training ahead of them may not have as much formal mathematical background as a Soviet seven-year school graduate (at age 15) entering a technicum for a 4-year term.

The general part of a 4-year technicum education is referred to in Soviet literature as being comparable or even equivalent to that of the regular secondary school. If that were so, the technicum curricula in general subjects would be about the same as in the last three grades of the ten-year school. However, that is not quite the case. Table 22 shows a comparison in hours (and in per cent of total instruction time) of the curricular load in the last three grades of the ten-year school (actual, 1952–1953) and for the corresponding subjects in the (proposed) 1952–1953 technicum plan of instruction. The class hours of instruction allotted to these general subjects in grades VIII, IX, and X of the ten-year school and in the technicum curriculum are 2,755 and 1,851, respectively. Thus the technicum course gives only two-thirds as much time to general subjects as do the three upper grades of the ten-year school. It should be emphasized that our technicum data are restricted to only one proposed (rather than actual) curriculum out of many; and that considerable fluctuations in the allocation of time by subjects occur depending on the "profile" of a given technicum. From all available evidence, however, the proportion (and hours) of time allotted to general subjects in the aggregate as shown in Table 22 is typical of all industrial (engineering) technicums.

Table 23 summarizes the subjects included in the curriculum to which we have referred in the preceding pages (*proposed* curriculum of a mining technicum). Of the total 4,682 hours of scheduled instruction, some 36 per cent (1,685 hours) is allotted to lectures and the rest

TABLE 22. Class Hours of Instruction Allotted to Subjects Which Are
Common to Both the Last Three Grades of a Ten-Year School
and a Typical Four-Year Mining Technicum
USSR
c. 1952–1953

Subject	Ten-Year School Grades VIII–X		Mining Technicum 4 Years	
	Hours	Per Cent	Hours	Per Cent
Mathematics	594.0	18.4	400	8.5
Physics	313.5	9.7	228	4.9
Chemistry	247.5	7.7	98	2.1
Foreign Language	363.0	11.2	186	4.0
Drafting	99.0	3.1	172	3.7
Russian Language and Literature	544.5	16.8	316	6.6
History	396.0	12.2	265	5.7
Physical Culture	198.0	6.1	186	4.0
Subtotal	2,755.5	85.2	1,851*	39.5
All other subjects	478.5	14.8	2,831	60.5
Total hours	3,234.0	100.0	4,682	100.0
Average per year	1,078.0		1,170	

Sources: Ten-year school: Chapter 2; technicum: proposed curriculum, see text.

* 67.2 per cent of the corresponding subtotal for the ten-year school.

of the time to shop, laboratory, field, and group work.*   In addition to
the scheduled hours of instruction the curriculum provides from 26
to 30 weeks of obligatory summer employment, presumably related to
the field of specialization.

A conspicuous feature of the curriculum is its heavy concentration
on narrowly specialized vocational subjects.   Topics geared to the
requirements of a *specific job* take up 50 per cent of the time.   Although the available data do not permit any detailed comparison
with technical courses offered in American technical institutes, it is
interesting to note, for instance, that in a course "Machine Construction and Tool Design" at Wentworth Institute the highly specialized subjects ("Mechanical Design" and "Machine and Tool Design")

* For comparison, the 2-year course in machine construction and tool design at
Wentworth Institute, Boston (total scheduled hours 1,792 or 38.3 per cent of the
4-year technicum hours), is distributed as follows:

Recitation	816 hours	45.5 per cent
Laboratory and Shop	976 hours	54.5 per cent
Total	1,792 hours	100.0 per cent

TABLE 23. ASSUMED DISTRIBUTION OF TOTAL HOURS AND OF LECTURE HOURS
OF SCHEDULED INSTRUCTION IN A FOUR-YEAR INDUSTRIAL TECHNICUM
USSR
c. 1951

Category of Subjects	Four-Year Course		Lectures Only	
	Hours	Per Cent	Hours	Per Cent*
General (History, Russian, and Foreign Language)	767	16.4	301	39
Science (Mathematics, Physics, and Chemistry)	726	15.5	250	34
General Technical (Drawing, Mechanics, Electricity)	704	15.0	268	38
Specialized Technical	1,717	36.7	866	50
Shop and Field Work	582	12.4	...	...
Physical Culture	186	4.0	...	...
Total, in 4 years	4,682	100.0	1,685	36

Source: Proposed curriculum, Boris I. Gorokhoff, "Materials for the Study of
Soviet Specialized Education."

* Per cent of total scheduled hours of instruction for this category of subjects.

Note: In addition to scheduled instruction, technicum training includes from
c. 25 to 30 weeks of designated summer employment.

take up only 16.1 per cent of the time (288 hours), while more or less
general technical subjects (Drawing, Strength of Materials, Electricity,
Heat, etc.) are given 36.6 per cent of curricular time (656 hours).

10. THE NEW TWO-AND-A-HALF-YEAR COURSES

We can only guess at the curricular changes now being introduced
for the Soviet 2½-year technical course following graduation from the
ten-year school. Our impression is that there is much confusion and
uncertainty as to the new curricula. As late as January 1955 an article
written by a technicum teacher suggested some rather fundamental
changes:[36]

> . . . [The teaching of] physics, mathematics, and history ought to
> be eliminated for those entering technicums from the ten-year
> school, but the knowledge of engineering drafting ought to be rein-
> forced. Although the secondary school curriculum allots 132 class-
> hours for drafting, students learn it poorly.

And the director of a Moscow technicum has pointed out that the
methodological implications of changing from the 7-year to 10-year
base have not been considered. He puts the blame on the lack of

cooperation between the individual ministries and the Ministry of Higher Education. There are many other indications that the program was launched without advance preparation of suitable curricula, selection of textbooks, provision for additional physical facilities, and, most importantly, for augmenting the teaching staff for the groups of advanced students.

The problem of adjusting the curricular load to suit the new 2½-year course can be very approximately illustrated as follows:

Normal 4-year technicum course	4,682 hours
Less time allotted for those subjects which are given in grades VIII through X of regular school (Table 22)	1,851
Hours allotted to specialized technical subjects	2,831

The technicum school year provides for approximately 31 weeks of instruction with about 38 scheduled class hours per week, or a total of some 1,178 hours per year, 2,356 hours for 2 years. Considerable adjustment therefore will be required to fit in all the specialized technical courses plus the additional mathematics (introduction to calculus) and, possibly, additional technical drafting. Although the new course is actually of 2½ years' duration, it provides only for 2 academic years of instruction plus two 8-week sessions of summer employment (for which students are paid).*

11. In Conclusion

Until more details are known it is impossible either to form a clear view of the 2½-year curriculum or to estimate the change in the character of training of technicians which the new plan will bring about. In the immediate future the forced-draft expansion of the upper-grades contingent of technicum trainees is likely to aggravate some of the shortcomings which have persisted throughout the history of technicums and to tax the existing facilities. The new program for the training of ten-year graduates is certain to increase sharply the rate of graduation for the next 4 or 5 years. At the peak of the current program, perhaps in 1958, as many as 200,000 engineering technicians will be added to the Soviet pool of industrial manpower. The new program is also capable of gradually raising the average qualifications of future Soviet technicians. However, unless profound changes are made

---

* The 4-year course provided up to 30 weeks (3 summers, 10 weeks each) of similar (obligatory) employment in the field of training.

in the entire philosophy and objectives of the Soviet state and in the organization of its complex state machinery, which manipulates industrial trusts at the direction of the Communist Party, Soviet technicums will continue to train their students in very narrowly specialized skills for rigidly defined and limited vocational functions, many of which perhaps could be best learned on the job. The Soviet technicians so trained will nevertheless be nearly as well or as well qualified to handle their tasks *in the particular vocational slots to which they are likely to be assigned* as their nearest counterparts in the United States, the 2-year technical institute graduates—of whom we currently train perhaps not more than approximately 20,000 per year. By training at least ten times as many engineering technicians as are presently trained in American technical institutes, the Soviet Union, as regards the crucial engineering-technician ratio, may create conditions temporarily more favorable than those which now exist in the United States.

Notes to Chapter 4

[1] *Izvestiya,* June 2, 1955. An article published in January of that year (A. Puluz'yan, "O podgotovke kadrov so srednem spetsial'nym obrazovaniyem" [On the Training of Cadres with a Specialized Secondary Education], *Kommunist,* Armenian SSR, January 5, 1955) stated that 60 per cent of new technicum students in 1955 would be ten-year school graduates.

[2] *Spravochnik dlya postupayushchikh v sredniye spetsial'nye uchebnye zavedeniya (tekhnikumy, uchilishcha, shkoly) v 1954 g.,* Moscow: "Sovetskaya Nauka," 1954, p. 9.

[3] Benjamin Fine, "Russia Is Overtaking U.S. in Training of Technicians," *New York Times,* November 7, 1954.

[4] Resolution of Plenum of Central Committee of CPSU. Adopted on July 11, 1955 on N. A. Bulganin's report. *Pravda* and other papers, July 14, 1955.

[5] "On the Improvement of Training New Specialists," Resolution of the Plenum of the Central Committee VKP(b), July 12, 1928, *Kul'turnoye stroitel'stvo SSSR* (Cultural Development of the USSR), a statistical reference book, Moscow-Leningrad: Gosplanizdat, 1940, p. 109.

[6] V. P. Yelutin, "Sovershenstvovat' podgotovku spetsialistov" (To Perfect the Training of Specialists), *Pravda,* November 13, 1954, p. 2:1–6. Innumerable references to the 1954 decision of the Council of Ministers (and the Central Committee of the Communist Party) dealing with higher education appear in the Soviet press (e.g., *Vestnik vysshei shkoly,* No. 12, 1954, pp. 1–6; *Kommunist,* Armenian SSR, January 5, 1955, p. 3:1–4). See Appendix I.

[7] "Annual Survey of Technical Institutes 1954–1955," prepared by Leo F. Smith, Dean of Instruction, Rochester Institute of Technology, *Technical Education News,* Vol. XIV, No. 4 (July–August 1955).

[8] Statement made in an informal conversation and cited here with Mr. Beatty's permission.

9 Karl O. Werwath, P. E., "The Role of the Technician in Our Nation's Future," *American Engineer,* September 1955, p. 17. The author names 160,000 as being the desired annual rate.

10 C. S. Jones, "The Technical Institute and Some of Its Problems," *The Journal for Engineering Education,* Vol. 45, No. 2 (October 1954), p. 153.

11 Boris I. Gorokhoff, "Materials for the Study of Soviet Specialized Education," unpublished mimeographed report, Washington, D.C.: National Research Council, Office of Scientific Personnel, 1952, p. 171 (hereafter referred to as Boris I. Gorokhoff, "Materials for the Study of Soviet Specialized Education"), citing the figures given by G. M. Malenkov in *Bolshevik,* 1941, No. 3–4, pp. 28–29.

12 *Vysshaya shkola* (The Higher School), Basic Regulations, Orders, and Instructions, compiled by M. I. Movshovich, Moscow: "Sovetskaya Nauka," 1945, p. 22 (hereafter referred to as *Vysshaya shkola,* compiled by M. I. Movshovich).

13 N. Zalivakin, "Properly Organize the Basic Training of Specialists," *Pravda,* July 6, 1953; in *CDSP,* Vol. V, No. 27, pp. 35 ff.

14 *Ibid.*

15 V. Smernikov, "Important Questions of Training Specialists of Middle Qualification," *Pravda,* October 7, 1955, p. 2:3–4. It should be noted, however, that there are technicums attached to or operated in conjunction with industrial plants which provide shop facilities for training.

16 O. Semenova, "To Improve the Training of Technical Cadres," *Sovetskaya Byelorussiya,* March 10, 1955, p. 2:5–6.

17 "Expand and Improve Training of Specialists with Secondary Education," *Pravda,* September 15, 1954, p. 1; in *CDSP,* Vol. VI, No. 37, October 27, 1954.

18 A. Puluz'yan, *op. cit.*

19 "Expand and Improve Training of Specialists with Secondary Education," *Pravda,* September 15, 1954, p. 1.

20 V. Smernikov, *op. cit.*

21 A. Puluz'yan, *op. cit.*

22 Yu. A. Ber, in *Sovetskaya pedagogika,* No. 4, 1955, p. 118.

23 P. F. Bogushevskii, in *Sovetskaya pedagogika,* No. 4, 1955, p. 117.

24 N. Zalivakin, *op. cit.*

25 "Expand and Improve Training of Specialists with Secondary Education," *Pravda,* September 15, 1954, p. 1.

26 E.g., V. Smernikov, *op. cit.*

27 N. Zalivakin, *op. cit.*

28 *Spravochnik dlya postupayushchikh v sredniye spetsial'nye uchebnye zavedeniya (tekhnikumy, uchilishcha, shkoly) v 1954 g.,* Moscow: "Sovetskaya Nauka," 1954, p. 340.

29 *Spravochnik dlya postupayushchikh v tekhnikumy* (Moscow and Moscow Oblast'), 1954, *passim.* The admission rules (paragraph 3) also imply that in certain technicums the plan provides for the enrollment of ten-year school graduates in separate groups. (Translation of 1954 admission rules is included in Cenis Translation Series 55-42.)

30 "Complete by the end of the 5-year period (1951–1955) the transition from 7-year education to universal secondary education (*desyatiletka*) in the capital of the republics, cities . . . ," *Directives of the XIX Party Congress on the Five Year Plan for the Development of the USSR in 1951–1955,* quoted in *Spravochnik direktora shkoly* (School Director's Handbook), Moscow: RSFSR Ministry of Education, 1954.

31 *Pravda,* January 15, 1956, p. 4:4 (our translation). The Cominform's *For Lasting Peace, for a People's Democracy* (No. 3, January 20, 1956, p. 5) translates the opening of this paragraph as follows: "To complete in the main the introduction of universal secondary education. . . ."

See also the letter circulated by the RSFSR Minister of Education, No. 23-M, January 31, 1953, quoted in *Spravochnik direktora shkoly* (School Director's Handbook), Moscow, p. 145.

32 T. Palladiyeva, "Shkola i proizvodstvennoye obucheniye," *Literaturnaya gazeta,* November 1955, pp. 2:1–6; also, same paper, May 28, 1955, pp. 2:1–6.

33 I. M. Pugach, in *Ugol',* No. 8, 1951; quoted and commented on by Boris I. Gorokhoff, *op. cit.,* pp. 216 ff. Gorokhoff reconstructed the assumed actual 1950–1951 curriculum on the basis of the proposed changes. Both the reconstructed and the proposed curricula are included in Nicholas DeWitt, *Soviet Professional Manpower,* Washington, D.C.: National Science Foundation, 1955, pp. 290 and 291, and commented upon on p. 75. It should be noted that the total hours (6,122) include 1,440 hours (33 weeks at 48 hours) of (the required) summer employment, not of class or laboratory instruction. In our opinion the proposed curriculum does not materially depart from the then existing actual curriculum.

34 The examples cited here are based on the 1952 syllabi in secondary school mathematics *(Programmy srednei shkoly. Matematika,* Moscow: Uchpedgiz, 1952). A translation of these syllabi is given in Cenis Translation Series 56-1. For changes in the distribution of hours since 1952–1953 see Chapters 2 and 3.

35 "A Prescription for a Technical Institute Text in Basic Physics," *Technical Education News* (A McGraw-Hill Book Company, Inc. publication), Vol. XIV, No. 4 (July–August, 1955), p. 6.

36 A. Puluz'yan, *op. cit.*

CHAPTER
— 5

SOVIET HIGHER EDUCATION:
THE INSTITUTIONAL SYSTEM

1. The Schools and Their Enrollment

An Historical Note

The relatively vigorous growth of higher education in twentieth century pre-Revolutionary Russia was all but arrested during the latter years of World War I and the Revolution of 1917.[1] The general economic collapse which followed the overthrow of the Provisional Government in October of that year and the subsequent civil war brought educational processes almost to a standstill. By 1921 the higher schools for all practical purposes had ceased to function.

During the recovery period following the expedient and strategic shift from the excesses and open terror of "war communism" to the New Economic Policy, old universities and other schools of higher education gradually assumed their traditional role, although in a vastly different setting. Their students now were recruited on the basis of social origin and ideological reliability rather than academic qualifications; special faculties ("Workers' Faculties," or Rabfak) were organized at the order of the Communist Party to give accelerated college-preparatory training to workers having little or no formal education. "Party-Thousands" of politically qualified appointees were administratively enrolled *en masse* for higher training.* Compliance with the political and philosophical tenets of Bolshevism became the necessary minimum requirement for a teacher to remain on the faculty staff; and curricula of humanities and social science faculties,

---

* For a recent brief Soviet account of this early period see "Iz istorii stroitel'stva sovetskoi vysshei shkoly" (On the History of Development of the Soviet Higher School), *Vestnik vysshei shkoly*, No. 12, December 1955, pp. 55–60.

now controlled by the Party theoreticians, were purged of disciplines which conflicted with Party ideology. In addition to the still-existing regular schools of higher education, special schools, also officially rated as schools of higher education, were organized, among them Communist Schools of Higher Education (Kom VUZ), Communist Agricultural Schools of Higher Education (VKSKhS), and others, some of them surviving into the 1930's and later. But, aside from these special schools for training organizational specialists in communism, the number of regular schools, their general organizational structure, curricula, and the syllabi of scientific and technical subjects remained for a few years essentially as before, patterned largely on German prototypes. The ranks of educators were reduced by the flight of many teachers and scholars abroad and the elimination of many more through purges and exile. Nevertheless, to the extent that the Bolshevik government permitted them to express in action their devotion to the cause of education, those teachers who remained at their posts carried on in the old academic tradition, despite tremendous difficulties, until about the end of the 1920's.

With the inauguration in 1928 of the Five Year Plans for rapid industrialization, there followed a period of frantic experimentation with the educational system. Sweeping orders, decrees, and instructions followed one another in rapid succession. The objective was to mobilize, expand, and channel the capabilities of the educational system so as to make it serve exclusively the planned needs of a state committed to industrialization at any cost. Many of these early innovations and costly experiments have long since been abandoned; in many essential respects the educational system under Soviet rule has in fact reverted to pre-Revolutionary forms and practices.* Nevertheless, some of the fundamental changes introduced in the early 1930's (such as the integration of schools by fields of study into the corresponding industrial complexes of the state machinery) have basically altered the institutions and methods of higher education, especially in the training of engineers and technologists.

The Number of Schools of Higher Education and Their Enrollment

Prior to the Revolution there were 95 institutions of higher learning in Russia. The 1913–1914 enrollment was approximately 117,000 students, which would average about 8.3 persons per 10,000 of the total population. As of January 1955, the listed higher schools in the Soviet

* For Soviet references to the American system of higher technical education see Appendix J.

Union (not including military academies of various kinds) numbered 762; the enrollment in the 1955–1956 academic year, including part-time students, was reported at 1,865,000 or, relative to the population, somewhere between 90 and 93 persons per 10,000 of total population.*

This impressive growth in the number of schools and in enrollment has not been achieved gradually or consistently. The number of

TABLE 24. NUMBER OF SCHOOLS OF HIGHER EDUCATION, ENROLLMENT AND
AVERAGE NUMBER OF STUDENTS PER SCHOOL
USSR
1924–1929 and 1930–1935 and Selected Postwar Years

Year	Number of Schools	Students (thousands)*	Students per School
1924–1925	169	169.5	1,003
1925–1926	145	167.0	1,152
1926–1927	148	168.0	1,135
1927–1928	148	168.5	1,138
1928–1929	152	176.6	1,162
1924–1930 average	152	169.9	1,118
1930–1931	579	287.9	497
1931–1932	701	405.9	579
1932–1933	832	504.4	606
1933–1934	714	458.3	642
1934–1935	688	527.3	766
1930–1935 average	703	436.7	621
1945–1946	789	539.2	683
1950–1951	880	845.1	960
1953–1954	818	1,042.7	1,275
1954–1955	798	1,146.5	1,437
1955–1956	765	1,227.9	1,605

Source: Kul'turnoye stroitel'stvo SSSR, 1956, pp. 201–202.

* Not including correspondence students.

schools especially has been subject to great fluctuations. During the 1924–1929 period, that is, during the period of the New Economic Policy and before the industrialization drive under the first Five Year Plan had gained momentum, the number of schools and the enroll-

* In the United States the total resident college enrollment in 1951–1952 (in 1,854 schools of higher education, including 513 junior colleges) was approximately 2,302,000 or 152 persons per 10,000 of total population. The 1954 (fall) enrollment (reported by the United States Office of Education, quoted in *World Almanac 1956,* p. 481) was 2,499,750; the 1955 (fall) enrollment was approximately 2,721,000 (United States Department of Health, Education, and Welfare, Circular No. 460, December 1955) or 163 persons per 10,000 of the total population (estimated at 166,738,000; Census Bureau, *Current Population Report,* No. 131, February 1956).

ment was quite stable. There were then, on the average, approximately 150 schools in operation (including special communist schools) with an average total enrollment of about 170,000 students. The corresponding averages for 1930–1935 (see Table 24) show that in this period the number of schools increased to 4.6 times the earlier average number (703 schools versus 152)—most of the increase occurring in 1929–1930; the enrollment, however, rose only to 2.6 times the 1924–1929 average (from 170,000 to 436,700). In 1940–1941 the total enrollment at Soviet institutions of higher education was 811.7 thousand, including 226.7 thousand correspondence students and 585.0 thousand resident students. The average enrollment per school during the last 3 prewar years was approximately 456 resident students.

The Process of Growth

The phenomenal increase in the number of schools between the 1928–1929 and 1930–1931 academic years was achieved primarily by splitting up the existing schools of engineering and the university faculties into units confined to one particular narrow branch of technology and by reconstituting these units either singly or in combination with other similarly isolated parts into separate new schools.

The transformation of one of the oldest and best engineering schools may serve as an example of the process which was set in motion in 1929. The Moscow Higher Technical School (established in 1832), with its five departments, was split five ways:

1. The department of mechanical engineering was left to carry on as the parent organization but under a new name, Higher Mechanical-Machine Construction School (VMMU). In 1932–1933 it was renamed Moscow Mechanical Machine Construction School (MMMU), and finally, in 1937, it reverted to the original status of a department within the partly reconstituted parent organization which at the same time had regained its original name, Moscow Higher Technical School; its present full name is: "Moscow, Order of the Red Banner of Labor, Higher Technical School Named after N. E. Bauman."

2. The original department of chemical engineering was first reorganized under the name of Higher School of Chemical Technology (VKhTU). Later it became the major part of the Voroshilov Military Academy of Chemistry (VKhA), which, in turn, was renamed and is now known as VAKhZ, Military Academy of Chemical Defense Named after K. E. Voroshilov.

3. The department of aeronautical engineering became the nucleus of the present Moscow Aviation Institute (MAI).

4. The department of power engineering became a separate school under the name of Moscow Power Institute (MEI).

5. The civil engineering department became first the Higher School of Construction Engineering (VISU) and later (reinforced by the transfer of teaching personnel and facilities from other schools) the present Military Engineering Academy (VIA) Named after V. V. Kuibyshev.

It was by such a process that the number of schools was rapidly increased with the inauguration of the Five Year Plans. Thereafter, because of frequent reorganizations, reconsolidations, and regroupings, the number of schools, rising to the prewar peak of over 800, became less stable. In the meantime, the enrollment was slowly, but also unevenly, rising. In the last year before World War II, as we have noted, it reached the prewar peak of approximately 800,000 resident students, a number equal to about two-thirds the total college enrollment in the United States at that time.*

During World War II the system suffered greatly both from the general national crisis and from dislocation wrought by the war and the temporary loss of great territories occupied by the Germans. After the war the system of schools for higher education was rapidly restored more or less to its former size and the enrollment continued to expand.†
In 1951 the number of listed schools rose temporarily to 887 and the resident enrollment to over 900,000. Thereafter the number of schools dropped, but the enrollment continued to rise and by c. 1955 had expanded to approximately 1½ times the prewar peak. In consequence, the average resident enrollment by 1955–1956 had grown to nearly 3½ times the 1940–1941 average—1,605 students per school against 456.

The rapid postwar reconstruction of facilities and the sharply increased enrollment in the institutions of higher learning since 1950 illustrate the magnitude and the urgency of the effort exerted in Soviet Russia to enlarge the scale of training. These efforts have consistently been directed toward the training of *specialists,* of government servants possessing a set of specific skills and competency to fill, in accordance with the state plan, a predetermined number of jobs in the various predetermined categories of professional service. In comparison with

---

* Continental United States enrollment (fall, regular sessions):

1937–1938	1,220 thousand
1939–1940	1,365 thousand

† According to an article in a Soviet encyclopedia (*BSE,* Volume on the USSR, Col. 1236), 334 schools of higher education (with a prewar enrollment of 233,000) were wholly or partly destroyed in the course of war.

the educational systems of other countries, the most distinguishing characteristic of the Soviet system of higher education is its utilitarian and vocational orientation. The concept of education which guides the more than 700 liberal arts colleges in the United States dedicated to general education is wholly alien to the Soviet philosophy. In the Soviet Union everybody works for the state; the state planners attempt to anticipate the needs for workers of different categories and arrange to train them presumably in just the right numbers at each level of training in the various fields and for every designated *"spetsial'nost"* ("specialty") within each field. These facts are basic determinants of Soviet educational policies and of the organization and rate of growth of its system of higher education.

Two Basic Types of Institutions of Higher Education

Soviet civilian institutions of higher education include two general types: the universities, of which there were thirty-four in 1956, and the institutes—a general category embracing more than 700 schools (729 as of January 1955).*

The distinction between the two types rests mainly on the fact that courses of study in the universities are organized more or less horizontally within and around a given major field (e.g., physics, chemistry, mathematics), whereas those in all other types of schools (institutes) are geared to the specific requirements of a particular industry (e.g., mining, aviation, printing industry) or a well-defined vocation (e.g., high school teaching of mathematics, choir conducting, agronomy). The distinction between the universities and all other types of Soviet institutions of higher learning might be further indicated by the fact that it is only in the universities that each basic science, such as physics or chemistry or mathematics, constitutes a field of study ("specialty") *per se.*

Future Soviet physicists, chemists, and mathematicians receive their undergraduate training only at the universities; in the engineering schools (including the so-called polytechnic institutes) undergraduate physics, chemistry, and mathematics are given only as service courses. But even the universities of the Soviet Union are far more vocationally oriented than their counterparts outside the Soviet bloc. Beginning with 1955, for instance, all university graduates were to be certified as school teachers of their specialty (such as history, Russian language, or physics). The vocational bias of the Soviet university is also clearly reflected in the designations of majors ("specialties")

* The opening of the newest university, Yakutsk State University, was announced in *Pravda*, October 7, 1956.

offered at the undergraduate level. As will be shown later, several of the university majors of undergraduate instruction are also offered in a number of specialized schools of higher education generically referred to as institutes.

The Institutes

With a few exceptions, the schools categorized as "institutes" can be identified directly by their names, e.g., Moscow Engineering-Physics Institute. Others, however, are named "academies" (e.g., Leningrad Forestry Engineering Academy), or *"uchilishche"* (e.g., Moscow Higher Technical Uchilishche, i.e., school). Music conservatories are also included in the general category of "institutes." At the undergraduate level the institutes train for all types of employment; correspondingly, they fall into a number of more or less distinct and internally homogeneous groups of institutes such as pedagogical, medical, and arts. Table 25 lists all the major categories and subgroupings and gives the number of schools in each category included in the 1955 Soviet official handbook.*

The breakdown of schools by the type of instruction (in residence, by correspondence, and in the evening classes) as shown in Table 25 is as follows:

Type of Instruction	Number of Schools
In residence	737
By correspondence	22
Evening classes	3
Total	762

In addition to the 22 correspondence-type and 3 evening institutes

---

* The total number listed, including universities, is 762. As mentioned earlier, the number of schools has been fluctuating; for example:

Year	Schools
1941	789
1951	866
1954	791

The reduction in the total number of schools since 1951 is largely accounted for by the rapid elimination of the 2-year Teachers' Institutes (which train for secondary school teaching in grades V through VII) in consequence of the plan to achieve 10-year universal education by 1960.

An article by A. Nesmeyanov, President of the USSR Academy of Science, in *Kommunist*, No. 2, 1956, refers to 798 schools of higher education; his count may include the military schools.

TABLE 25. NUMBER OF INSTITUTIONS OF HIGHER EDUCATION LISTED BY
CATEGORIES AND TYPE OF INSTRUCTION
USSR
January 1955

Column E gives the number of resident schools which also have an evening department.
Column C gives the number of resident schools which also have a department for instruction by correspondence.

Categories and Subcategories	TOTAL	Resident Total	E	C	Evening only	Correspondence only
I. Universities	33	33	2	27	...	...
Institutes:						
II. Polytechnic and Industrial		23				
1. Polytechnic	20		15*	6	...	1
2. Industrial	5		4†	2	...	1
III. Power, Electrotechnical, Radio-technical, and Physicotechnical		7				
1. Power	3		1	...	...	1
2. Electrotechnical	2		2	...	...	...
3. Radiotechnical	2		2	...	...	...
4. Physicotechnical	1		...	...	...	...
IV. Machine Construction, Shipbuilding, Aviation, Polygraphic, and Motion Picture Engineering		26				
1. Machine construction; machine tools and tools; mechanical; and automotive	16		12†	...	1	1
2. Shipbuilding	2		2	...	...	...
3. Aviation	7		7	...	...	...
4. Polygraphic	3		1	...	...	1
5. Motion picture engineering	1		...	1	...	...
V. Geologic, Mining, Oil, Peat, and Metallurgical		24				
1. Geologic; mining; oil; and peat	15		8	2	...	...
2. Metallurgical and mining metallurgical	11		5	3	2	...
VI. Chemical technology	9	9	6	1	...	...
VII. Food and Fishing Industries		11				
1. Food industries	9		5	2	...	1
2. Fishing industries	4		...	...	...	1
VIII. Light Industries		7				
1. Light industry	3		2	1	...	1
2. Textile	5		5	...	...	...
IX. Engineering-Construction, Geodetic, and Automotive Highways		25				
1. Engineering-construction	19		10	8	...	1
2. Geodetic	2		...	1	...	...
3. Automotive highway	6		4	2	...	1
X. Hydrometeorological	2	2	...	2	...	...
XI. Transport and Communications		25				
1. Railroad transport	13		11	...	...	1

TABLE 25 (continued)

Categories and Subcategories	TOTAL	Resident Total	E	C	Evening only	Correspondence only
2. Water transport	4		1	4	...	...
3. Marine and navigation	4		...	3	...	...
4. Civil air fleet	1		...	1	...	...
5. Communications	5		2	3	...	1
XII. Agricultural and Forestry		106				
1. Agricultural	63		...	52	...	1
2. Zootechnical,‡ milk, and veterinary	21		...	7	...	...
3. Mechanization and electrification of agriculture	7		1	5	...	...
4. Hydromelioration§ and land management	6		...	4	...	...
5. Forest and forest technology	11		6	8	...	1
XIII. Economics		22				
1. Economics	8		7	...	...	1
2. Finance economics	9		6	...	...	1
3. Trade economics	5		3	...	...	1
4. Engineering economics	3		3	1	...	...
XIV. Law	6	5	...	5	...	1‖
XV. Art		46				
1. Architecture and industrial arts	3		...	...	...	...
2. Visual arts	9		...	1	...	...
3. Music conservatories	21		7	2	...	...
4. Theatre and motion pictures	13		...	1	...	...
XVI. Medical		75				
1. Medical	65		...	...	...	...
2. Stomatological	2		...	...	...	...
3. Pharmaceutical	8		...	4	...	...
XVII. Physical Culture	13	13		9	...	...
XVIII. Pedagogical, Historical Archives, and Library		278				
1. Pedagogical	206		31	173	...	4
2. Pedagogical, foreign languages	19		1	14	...	...
3. Library, literature, historical archives	5		3	4	...	...
4. Teachers' [2-year course]	52		...	17	...	...
Total	762	737	175	376	3	22

Source: Spravochnik dlya postupayushchikh v vysshiye uchebnye zavedeniya v 1955 godu, Moscow: "Sovetskaya Nauka," 1955.

* Of these, in addition to the regular evening courses, six also have an affiliated (*filial*) evening school in a different location.

† One has an affiliated evening school.

‡ Soviet term for animal husbandry.

§ Soviet term embracing irrigation, flood control, water conservation, and related branches of engineering.

‖ Has 14 affiliated branch institutes.

some of the resident schools also have similar facilities. As of January 1955, there were 376 correspondence and 175 evening departments maintained in conjunction with 737 schools of resident type.

Engineering Institutes

All the institutes listed in categories II through XI in Table 25 are schools of engineering, collectively referred to as "institutions of higher technical education," or VTUZY (plural). The institutes shown in categories XII (3, 4, and 5), XIII (4), and XV (1) are also rated as VTUZY.* Although the exact number of schools formally included in this category has not, to our knowledge, been published, it is easily estimated from Table 25. On this basis, 3 evening schools, 13 correspondence schools, and 188 schools of resident type would be counted (January 1955) as schools of higher technical education, VTUZY (see Table 26).† This count includes only the civilian schools of engineering. The Soviet Union also maintains military schools for training in engineering and applied science at advanced levels. These schools are not regularly mentioned in the Soviet handbooks and journals on higher education, but even the occasional references (in encyclopedias, the army newspaper, *Krasnaya Zvezda,* and other miscellaneous sources, including the recently published *Betrayal of an Ideal* by G. A. Tokaev, a former student of the Zhukovskii Military Air Academy) make it unmistakably clear that military schools of engineering occupy an extremely important and highly privileged place in the total Soviet plan for selecting and training the technical specialists needed to advance its efforts toward superiority in the weapons race and in technology generally. There has been available no direct information which would permit full evalua-

* This conclusion is based on a detailed comparison of the table on VUZY as of September 15, 1950, published in *BSE,* 2nd Ed., Vol. 9, p. 512 and the 1950 *Spravochnik* (handbook listing all institutions of higher education in the USSR).

† The number of active VTUZY may be somewhat larger; it has been reported, for instance, that in 1955 a polytechnic institute was opened at Komsomol'sk, a machine construction institute at Molotov, and a branch of the Moscow Evening Machine Construction Institute in Kolomna. (*Ezhenedel'nyi obzor,* No. 59, 1955 [Munich], p. 18.)

The Minister of Higher Education, V. P. Yelutin, speaking at a press conference on April 14, 1956, stated that there were 193 schools of higher technical education; it is not clear whether he meant only the resident-type schools or whether his number includes also the extension institutes—in which case his figure would suggest that some eleven schools have been eliminated, through consolidation or otherwise, since 1954–1955. *Pravda* (July 7, 1956, p. 2) named the following new night schools: Molotov Machine Construction Institute, Shcherbakovsk Aviation Technology Institute, and Komsomol'sk Polytechnic Institute.

tion of the scope and the type of training given in all the military schools of engineering. Nevertheless, enough evidence exists (such as textbooks used in these schools) to show the qualitative importance of these schools for Soviet science and technology. On the basis of indirect evidence, the role of the military air academies (and particularly of the Zhukovskii Military Air Academy in Moscow) in the total complex of training for and development of the Soviet Union aircraft industry

TABLE 26. NUMBER OF INSTITUTES OF HIGHER TECHNICAL EDUCATION (VTUZY)
USSR
1950 and 1955

Type of School	1950	1955
Polytechnic and industrial	20	23
Machine construction, mechanical, and shipbuilding	25	25
Power, electrotechnical, and communications	6	11
Mining-metallurgical	18	21
Oil	3	3
Chemical technology and food technology	20	20
Architectural and construction	25	28
Light industry	7	7
Forestry, technology and management	11	10
Transport (RR and river) and hydrometeorology	23	23
Mechanization and electrification of agriculture, and hydromelioration	12	13
Motion picture engineering	2	1
Engineering economics	3	3
Evening VTUZY	3	3
Correspondence VTUZY	10	13
Total number, VTUZY	188	204
Resident schools which also enroll:		
Evening students	47*	115
Correspondence students	49*	60

Sources: 1950 data (as of September 15) is from *BSE*, 2nd Ed., Vol. 9, 1951, p. 512; 1955 data from Table 25.

* As counted in 1950 *Spravochnik*.
Note: Other years (number of VTUZY):
1940   156 (*BSE*, 2nd Ed., Vol. 9, 1951, p. 512.)
1953   201 (*Entsiklopedicheskii slovar'*, Vol. I, Moscow, 1953, p. 369.)

has been described and evaluated by Dr. Leon Trilling, Assistant Professor of Aeronautical Engineering at the Massachusetts Institute of Technology, in his *Soviet Education in Aeronautics: A Case Study*.[2] It is a safe assumption that military schools devoted to other branches of engineering play a similarly important role in their respective fields of applied science. It should be noted that military schools of higher technical education have a long history in Russia. Many of the outstanding scientists and mathematicians of pre-Revolutionary Russia were educated in military schools. The Soviets have revived and expanded a system which traces its origin to the times of Peter the Great.

The following list of technical and other professional military schools includes some of the names encountered in the sources used for the study. Although the list is by no means complete, it shows the diversity of technical fields included in the military curricula:

1. Academy of Armored-Tank and Mechanized Troops Named after I. V. Stalin.[3 and 4]

2. Academy of Artillery Sciences.[3]

3. Armament Industrial Academy.

4. Higher Military-Engineering School [uchilishche] of Construction.[4]

5. Leningrad Military Air Academy.[4]

6. Military Academy of Chemical Defense Named after K. E. Voroshilov (VAKhZ).[4]

7. Military Air Engineering Academy Named after Professor N. E. Zhukovskii.[5]

8. Military-Artillery Academy Named after F. E. Dzherzhinskii.[6]

9. Military Electrotechnical Academy of Communications Named after S. M. Budennyi.[6 and 7]

10. Military Engineering Red Banner Academy Named after V. V. Kuibyshev (VIA).[8]

11. Military Medical Academy Named after S. M. Kirov.[8]

12. Molotov Military Academy of Administrative Services and Supply.[7]

13. Naval Academy of Shipbuilding and Armaments.[7]

14. Riga Military Air Engineering Institute.

In addition to the undergraduate 4- to 5-year courses of study, most of these and other specialized military schools have graduate programs and carry on extensive research.

Engineering Training in Evening Schools and by Correspondence

Besides providing day-time resident instruction, the majority of resident engineering schools maintain either correspondence divisions or evening departments or both. In 1950 there were 49 correspondence divisions and 47 evening departments listed in conjunction with the resident VTUZY. The 1955 Soviet handbook lists 60 of the former and 115 of the latter. This rapid increase in the extension facilities for technical training is significant. It reflects a conscious effort to increase the rate of training technical personnel to a higher level of competency without diminishing the current contribution of the technical labor pool. The emphasis has been particularly strong on the expansion of evening courses, and the numerically impressive recent increase in the total enrollment of engineering students is partly the result of this drive. As shown in Table 27, whereas the enrollment in engineering schools doubled in the 5-year period, the number of students in the evening schools increased nearly forty-two times.

TABLE 27.   ENROLLMENT IN SCHOOLS OF HIGHER TECHNICAL EDUCATION
BY TYPES OF INSTRUCTION
USSR
1950 and 1955

Type of Instruction	1950	1955 (estimated)	
	Thousands	Thousands	Per Cent of 1950
Resident, full-time	278.3	450.0	162
Resident, evenings	2.4	100.0	4,167
Subtotal	280.7	550.0	196
Correspondence	40.7	100.0	246
Total enrollment	321.4	650.0	202

Sources: 1950 data (fall enrollment as of September 15) are from *BSE*, 2nd Ed., Vol. 9, 1951, p. 512.   1955 data derived from the following statements:

1. Total enrollment and one figure ("more than 200,000") for correspondence and evening combined, "Inzhenernye kadry dlya narodnovo khozyaistva," *Pravda Ukrainy* (quoting V. P. Yelutin, the Minister of Higher Education), December 9, 1955, p. 1:3–4.

2. Correspondence ("more than 100,000"), "Aktivizirovat' nauchnuyu deyatel'-nost' zaochnykh vtuzov" (To Activate Research in the Correspondence Institutions of Higher Technical Education), *Vestnik vysshei shkoly*, No. 12, 1955, pp. 10–14.

Note: Total enrollment in other years:
Oct. 1940   176,800 (*BSE*, 2nd Ed., Vol. 9, 1951, p. 512.)
    1953   350,000 (*Entsiklopedicheskii slovar'*, Vol. I, Moscow, 1953, p. 369.)

Further expansion of facilities for training employed individuals on a part-time basis is definitely in the offing. Additional courses for instruction by correspondence have been organized since 1955 and additional evening programs introduced in a number of resident-type schools, among them Kiev Polytechnic, Don Industrial, Dnepropetrovsk Metallurgical, Dnepropetrovsk Engineering Construction, Krivoi Rog Mining, and Zaporozh'ye Agricultural Machinery Institutes.[9]   A 1954 editorial in a journal published by the Ministry of Higher Education stated that by 1960 the number of extension students in "technical specialties" is to be at least three times as great as it was in 1953.[10]

Current Expansion

The current phase of rapidly expanding enrollment, which has increased the average number of students per school to nearly three times that just before World War II, is also characterized by:

1. The relatively larger increase of the engineering school enrollment (nearly 35 per cent of the total enrollment in the 1955–1956 academic year versus about 26 per cent in 1950). The average number of engineering students per school in that year was nearly double (1.8 times) the number 5 years earlier.

2. The greatly increased proportion of students studying engineering by correspondence or in evening schools while holding full-time jobs (on a 6-day week basis, 8 hours per day). In 1955–1956 this category of students accounted for slightly more than 30 per cent of the total number enrolled in engineering courses; in 1950 the same category accounted for less than 14 per cent of the total engineering student enrollment.

The ratios of students in engineering schools to total enrollment in 1950 and 1955 are recapitulated in Table 28.

Both the very rapid increase in the total enrollment and the shift toward the extension type of instruction in engineering has unquestionably increased the strain on the educational system. From the nature of the various corrective measures which have been recently proposed, promised, or put into effect it is evident that the present expansion is taking place in a context of competing government priorities. Political expediency since Stalin's death has tended to encourage relaxation of control over the academic processes, but economic realities and commitments demand continued regimentation. Superimposed upon this dilemma of totalitarian rule is a more pressing problem—how to increase rapidly and simultaneously both the number and the quality of technical personnel.

Change is inherently difficult in any situation where only the central authority may introduce any shifts from previous policy. This difficulty is compounded in the Soviet Union both by the built-in political rigidities of the state system and by the fact that the institutional and policy controls over education are vested exclusively at the apex of the Communist Party power mechanism. These factors in the past have severely restricted, if not altogether precluded, the

TABLE 28. FALL ENROLLMENT IN ENGINEERING AND IN OTHER SCHOOLS OF
HIGHER EDUCATION LISTED BY TYPE OF INSTRUCTION
USSR
1950 and 1955

Kind of School and Type of Instruction	1950		1955	
	Thousands	Per Cent	Thousands	Per Cent
1. Daytime and evening				
Engineering (VTUZ)	281	33.3	550	44.8
Other	564	66.7	678	55.2
Total resident	845	100.0	1,228*	100.0
Index	100		145	
2. Correspondence				
Engineering (VTUZ)	41	10.2	100	15.6
Other	361	89.8	539	84.4
Total Correspondence	402	100.0	639*	100.0
Index	100		159	
3. Resident and correspondence				
Engineering (VTUZ)	322	25.8	650	34.8
Other	925	74.2	1,217	65.2
Total	1,247	100.0	1,867*	100.0
Index	100		150	

Sources: Total enrollment and correspondence subtotals are from *Kul'turnoye stroitel'stvo SSSR, 1956*, p. 207. Other figures for 1950 are either quoted directly (rounded to the nearest thousand) or derived as residuals from *BSE*, 2nd Ed., Vol. 9, pp. 512 and 515. 1955 figures are from Table 21 and residual.

* *Vestnik vysshei shkoly*, No. 3, March 1956, pp. 3 and 5, gives the following figures:

Total enrollment   1,865 thousand
Part-time   718 thousand

leaving only 1,147 thousand for 1955–1956 full-time, resident enrollment.

exercise of initiative by individual educators and institutions. All consequential decisions regarding educational philosophy, policies, and practices are formulated by the central authority, and proclaimed, usually in the name of the Central Committee of the Communist Party and/or the Council of Ministers, as directives uniformly applicable to all the relevant schools in the Soviet Union.

2. CENTRAL STATE ADMINISTRATION

The actual day-to-day administration, the carrying out and the enforcement of the directives issued by the central authority concerning higher education, is apportioned among many and various overt and covert agencies of the state, each with its specific area of responsibility to the central authority and, in some instances, with conflicting interests and mutually incompatible criteria of achievement.

Political indoctrination and discipline within the educational system are promoted directly through the Party units at all levels of academic organization or indirectly via the affiliated Communist Youth League (Komsomol) and the Soviet version of labor unions ("Professional Unions"), which are in a position to grant or withhold both material and intangible benefits. Political reliability is watched over by *spetsotdely,* "special departments" responsible to the secret police. A number of state industrial trusts (ministries) and other operating agencies of the state, through their departments of education (GUUZ),* administer funds appropriated for their schools in the state budget, handle all business and managerial affairs in the schools under their control, and, in varying degrees, participate in the formulation of academic policies. The most important agency controlling the academic life of the Soviet Union, however, is the USSR Ministry of Higher Education.† Although it was formed only a few years ago (in 1946), the institutions and functions now embodied in this very large and complex organization have a long history.

In the course of the drastic reorganization of higher schools c. 1929–1930, the newly formed engineering and other schools were apportioned among the various industrial and other operational agencies of the state. For a time there was no single agency empowered to exercise

* Main Administration of Schools—of a given industrial ministry.

† Formally a "Union-Republic" type of ministry (i.e., one which administers through identical ministries in each of the sixteen republics comprising the USSR), but actually no republican ministries of higher education were organized until 1955, when such a ministry was established for the Ukrainian SSR. The 1957 plan for decentralization of industrial authority may also eventually lead to the establishment of additional Ministries of Higher Education of republic jurisdiction—in Byelorussia, Georgia, and other political subdivisions of the Soviet Union. It is not likely, however, that the central administrative organ, the USSR Ministry of Education, would be abolished. A Corresponding Member of the USSR Academy of Sciences, N. M. Zhavoronkov, suggested, however, that the Ministry could be reconstituted and named, once again, Committee on the Higher School—the old VKVSh (*Pravda,* April 25, 1957, p. 2).

general control over academic standards and methods.*   Under the pressures exerted by the respective controlling agencies (ministries) to train men rapidly for particular jobs in construction and industry, the curricula and academic practices became totally disorganized. In 1932 the Central Executive Committee, appraising the results of the educational effort, accused the commissariats in charge of schools, and also the harassed school administrators directly, of "perversions" in carrying out "the decisions of the Party and of the government." They were accused of giving:

> . . . one-sided attention to increasing the number of schools and students while giving insufficient attention to questions of the quality of academic work; and also in excessive fractionalization of specialties in consequence of which certain VTUZY and VUZY frequently graduated specialists with the qualifications of a technician, not of an engineer.[11]

In the same declaration the Executive Committee pointed out that in a number of the VUZ and VTUZ (engineering) curricula such "important subjects as physics and chemistry were altogether absent." Among the many measures decreed by the document from which we have just quoted was an order to form (at the level of the central government) a special, continuously functioning committee (Committee on the Higher Technical School) to deal with the problems of higher technical education. Its purposes and powers in 1932 were defined as follows:

> . . . to authorize [*utverzhdat'*, to confirm, to establish, to approve] academic plans [curricula and academic calendars], syllabi, and methods of instruction at the specialized institutions of higher education; to authorize [the number, type, location, size, etc. of schools in] the network of these academic institutions; and to control the conduct of educational work at these institutions.[12]

In the course of time the exercise of central *academic* authority over the institutions of higher learning (as distinct from budgetary, managerial, and administrative controls) was expanded. In 1936 the Committee on the Higher Technical School was replaced by a new central supervisory body, the All-Union (i.e., for the USSR as a whole)

---

* The RSFSR Commissariat of Public Instruction had a section called *Glavprofobr* (for Main Administration of Professional Education) but its functions were diffuse. There was also an earlier attempt to coordinate the work of technical training; a committee of five, the Main Committee on Professional Technical Education, was organized in 1920 (replacing a similar former section in the Commissariat of Public Instruction) but it was wholly ineffective. At that time the emphasis was on *decentralization,* and the committee was instructed "under no condition to limit the initiative" of the various other agencies engaged in educational work.

Committee on the Higher School (VKVSh). Its jurisdiction was extended to include not only the technical but in time also all other types of higher schools.* The powers and scope of this Committee were further enlarged in subsequent legislation; by c. 1945 there remained no area in the life of a Soviet academic institution, nor any phase of the academic process, which was not controlled by VKVSh. The extensiveness of its jurisdiction and the multiplicity of its responsibilities can be perhaps most simply illustrated by listing the various operating units under this Committee. As of c. 1945, the Committee had a separate department (section, administration, bureau, commission, or office) for each group of schools or activities listed below.

A. Twelve departments corresponding to the various types of schools under its control:
   1. Universities
   2. Pedagogical
   3. Heavy Industry
   4. Defense Industry
   5. Military
   6. Light Industry and Food Industry
   7. Transport and Communications
   8. Agricultural
   9. Medical
   10. Economics and Law
   11. The Arts
   12. Foreign Language and the Teaching of Foreign Languages in Higher Schools

B. It had sixteen functional departments:
   13. Military Training and Schools of Physical Culture
   14. Textbooks
   15. Teaching of Marxism-Leninism
   16. Budgetary-Planning
   17. Cadres
   18. Distribution [assignment to jobs] of Young Specialists [i.e., graduates]
   19. Material and Living Conditions of Students
   20. *Spetsotdel* ["Special Department," in charge of internal political surveillance and of personal dossiers]
   21. Control and Inspection
   22. Administrative
   23. Legal

* Military schools of higher education and schools of the All-Union Committee on the Arts were at first exempt. In 1937 military schools were also placed under the "academic-methodological" guidance of VKVSh (SNK SSSR, September 29, 1937, No. 1716; quoted in *Vysshaya shkola*, compiled by M. I. Movshovich, p. 22). In 1943 the majority of the technicums (industrial, agricultural, economic, transport, and communications) were also placed under the academic supervision of VKVSh (SNK SSSR, July 2, 1943, No. 721; quoted in *Vysshaya shkola*, p. 22).

24. Secretariat
25. Central Accounting
26. Academic Institutions of the Committee [the department in charge of schools directly and completely operated by VKVSh]
27. Scientific Research Work at the Institutions of Higher Learning
28. Housing
C. The Committee also had a number of specialized operational units, among them the following five:
29. Lecture Bureau
30. Committee's Press, "Sovetskaya Nauka"
31. Library
32. All-Union Office "Uchpromtekhsnab" ["industrial-technical supply for instructional purposes"]
33. VAK, Higher Attestation [of academic degrees and titles] Commission

The functions prescribed for VKVSh originally and those added by subsequent legislation can be roughly classified as (1) staff functions of assembling information and making representations and recommendations to the central authority on the basis of data obtained from the various compartments of the educational system; and (2) executive functions involving (a) the carrying out of any specific order, plan, or program of the central authority with reference to education, and (b) the exercise of its authority to make certain administrative decisions—naturally in the spirit of the prevailing general Party line.

In its staff capacity the Committee was supposed to perform the following duties:

1. Draft and submit for consideration general plans for the development of higher education in the Soviet Union.

2. Consolidate the annual and the Five Year Plans for schools (including the size of the teaching staff) and submit the drafts of such plans for consideration.

3. Analyze the school budgets of the various agencies and submit its findings.

4. Submit proposals for the establishment of new schools and for consolidation or liquidation of the existing schools.

5. Analyze plans made by departments (industries) and by the various Soviet republics for the number of freshmen to be admitted to schools of various kinds, and to one or another area of specialization in each school; prepare consolidated plans for the enrollment of new students and submit for approval.

6. Compile and submit plans for the distribution of graduates among the various agencies of the state.

7. Analyze plans submitted to the central authority pertaining to the manufacture and distribution of laboratory equipment, and give its conclusions with reference to these plans.

8. Study the plans submitted by the various state units to the central authority on any foreign assignments proposed for the faculty members and give its conclusions with reference to such plans.

9. Submit its conclusions as to the proposals and plans for the importation of scientific and teaching-aid equipment and for procurement of foreign publications for schools of higher education.

10. Keep statistics on the teaching personnel in higher education.

In the exercise of executive authority delegated to it the Committee on the Higher School directly intervened in practically every sphere of academic life. In its executive capacity the committee was authorized to:

1. Confirm appointments of professorial and other teaching personnel and of the library workers at the institutions subject to its supervision (VUZY and technicums).

2. Establish the list of the various specialties taught at the institutions of higher learning and in technicums; the number, types, and groupings of schools in various categories; and the designations of faculties, sections, and areas of specialization in all schools and of the academic chairs (*kafedra*) comprising the faculties.

3. Grant individual charters to the institutions of higher education (such charters, it should be noted, except for name of the school and other minor details, follow to the letter a prescribed model charter which was approved in September 1938).

4. Exercise control over "correct utilization of young specialists"; that is, to see to it that a graduate engineer, for instance, is in fact assigned to an engineering duty.

5. Confirm the consolidated plans for the enrollment and training in graduate schools and for the job assignments of those who complete graduate work.

6. Issue general directives and instructions on the questions dealing with school admissions and graduations.

7. Establish complete academic plans (curricula and calendar) and syllabi of all the general academic subjects and of those among specialized subjects which are common to several curricula.

8. Provide guidance to the various agencies on the carrying out of academic plans and on the drafting of syllabi which are to be prescribed directly by the agency in question for such specialized subjects as may be designated by VKVSh.

9. Pass upon plans submitted for the publication of textbooks and reference books; authorize textbooks for all the general subjects and for those specialized subjects of instruction which are common to a number of schools under different agencies (ministries).

10. Prepare a consolidated plan of research to be carried on at the institutions of higher education.

11. Coordinate and direct research activities at the institutions of higher education under the various agencies.

12. Upon occasions initiated (*po predstavleniyu*) by the agencies of the USSR and of the Union Republics, appoint and release from office the school directors and the deputy directors in charge of academic work.

13. Upon occasions initiated through the appropriate agency by the school directors, confirm appointments of those in charge of the academic chairs (*kafedra*).

14. Confirm (*1*) the composition of the academic council at those schools which are authorized to confer (advanced) academic degrees and (*2*) the list of disciplines in which such degrees may be awarded in these schools.

15. Review and consider the plans submitted by the various agencies having schools under their jurisdiction for the training of teaching personnel and improving the qualifications of teachers; coordinate and direct activities of the various agencies in connection with such programs.

Finally, the Higher Attestation Commission (VAK) of the Committee was empowered "to deal with questions on the granting of academic degrees and titles." The decisions of the individual institutions with reference to such awards, it should be noted, are advisory or provisional and subject to an explicit or a tacit confirmation by VAK.

In March 1946 the chairman of VKVSh (S. V. Kaftanov) was made a member of the Council of Ministers. In April of the same year the status of the committee was changed to that of a ministry—the USSR Ministry of Higher Education. It inherited the organization and personnel of the former committee and all of its functions, including those enumerated above. Furthermore, with the establishment of the Ministry of Higher Education, a large number of schools was *removed* from the control of other (industrial) ministries and placed under direct and now complete control of the new ministry. By this jurisdictional shift a total of over 300 schools, including all universities, polytechnic institutes, and the majority of other engineering institutes, were assigned to the Ministry of Higher Education.[13] Since 1946 practically all the schools listed in categories I through X of Table 25 and those in categories XII through XIV (except 63—agricultural, 21—animal husbandry, and a few others) have been under its control. Thus with very few exceptions (such as the railroad institutes) all schools of engineering (VTUZY) and of science (universities) are now integrated into one huge bureaucratic system under unified academic, budgetary, and administrative supervision. The academic control of the Ministry, as we have already indicated, extends to all other schools, including presumably the military schools of engineering.

In comparison, it will be remembered that prior to 1936 *all schools* of one or another type of engineering were severally controlled and operated by and for the respective industries. The Ministry of Nonferrous Metals had its own network of schools, distinct from those of the Iron and Steel Ministry or of the Coal Ministry. Just before World War II, in 1941, one of the many Soviet "specialties" (majors) of mechanical engineering, "Machine Tools, Tools, and Mechanical Fabrication of Metals," was offered by twenty-seven schools (including two universities); these twenty-seven schools "belonged," in various numbers, to one or another of eleven distinct and separate agencies.* The consolidation of 1946 was hailed in the Soviet press as a reform of great significance. S. V. Kaftanov who became the Minister of Higher Education wrote:

> The concentration of the administration of the higher educational establishments in the Ministry of Higher Education leads to great advantages in the quality of preparation of specialists, the use of teaching personnel, and the strengthening of the material and technical base.[14]

Medynskii, the official spokesman of the Soviets on education, stated that:

> This total concentration of direction [or guidance] in the hands of the Ministry of Higher Education was undertaken for the purpose of improving the life and work of the higher educational establishments of nationwide importance, those which train the cadres of science, engineering, and agriculture.[15]

Whatever the initial reason for consolidating the control over these schools, it is clear that no substantive changes in the curricula and organization of engineering schools which were transferred to the Ministry have been made until very recent times. And even 10 years later, the great majority of the Soviet engineering schools, in com-

---

* Among them, commissariats (ministries) of General Machine Construction (2 schools), of Nonferrous Metals (1 school), of Heavy Industry (5 schools), of Medium Industry (4 schools), and of Electrical Industry (1 school).

parison with American counterparts, were rather narrowly specialized to meet the immediate needs of a given branch of industry. The current trend, however, is definitely toward broadening the base of undergraduate engineering training and eliminating excessively narrow undergraduate specialization.

As to "improving the life" of the educational establishments, there have been no changes made in the charter of the universities and institutes since a uniform charter was formalized in 1938; and there is no evidence that in consequence of consolidation individual schools, let alone individual educators, have gained any significant room in which to exercise their initiative. Since Stalin's death, however, there has been a general relaxation; many educators have advocated greater autonomy for the institutions of higher learning in internal management and the conduct of academic work. A revision of the charter has been under discussion,[16] but no changes in the structure of schools have been made, and in 1957 the administrative and academic arrangements still followed, with only minor variations, the pattern established in the mid-1930's.[17] In the spring of 1957, however, the Soviet government announced its plan to decentralize control of industries and to reorganize them horizontally on a regional basis, under regional Economic Councils. The dissolution of many industrial ministries necessarily involves changes in the budgetary and administrative control over the institutions of higher education. It was announced (*Sovetskaya Litva*, April 13, 1957, p. 2) that beginning with the 1957–1958 academic year the institutions of higher education of a given economic region would be assigned to the administrative and budgetary control of the regional Economic Councils.

3. Local Administration

Administrative Officers

The highest officer (rector in a university, director in an institute) is appointed, in the final analysis, by the Central Committee of the Communist Party, although formally the appointments are effected by the Ministry of Higher Education. As a rule the highest officer is himself a member of the Communist Party. Since 1936 only persons with higher education (including training in special Communist Party schools) are eligible for appointment to the post; prior to that time no particular academic or educational qualifications were stipulated for the directors. The director is responsible to the Ministry of Higher Education; in schools which administratively are under some other ministry (such as schools of railroad engineering) he is also responsible to the school administration of that ministry.

Direct responsibility for teaching and research work of every institution of higher learning falls upon the "deputy director in charge of scientific and educational matters." He is appointed by and holds office at the pleasure of the Ministry of Higher Education, presumably in applicable cases at the initiative of any other agency (ministry) which may be directly concerned with the administration of the school in question. The same *administrative* agency (or, in some cases, its counterpart at the Ministry of Higher Education itself) appoints and dismisses the executive officer ("director's assistant in charge of administration and plant management"), presumably at the initiative of the director. Although not provided for in any published rule or regulation, and not officially counted within the school administration, another very important officer is the inevitable director of the "special department" (*spetsotdel*), an overt office of the secret police, independent of any academic or industrial authority. Thus the administrative structure of universities and institutes embodies the usual Soviet pattern of organization, with multiple lines of limited authority and unlimited accountability which converge and can be resolved only at the highest level of the central government. Superficially, however, the academic administration within the individual institutions of higher learning follows the pre-Revolutionary pattern.

Faculties and Academic Chairs

The primary unit of academic organization in any institution of higher learning in the Soviet Union is the chair (*kafedra*) of a given academic discipline or of a group of related disciplines, for example:

Chair of Semiconductors and Dielectrics.
Chair of Mathematical Analysis.
Chair of Machine Tools.
Chair of Forging and Stamping Manufacture.

The professor in charge of the chair, whose appointment is subject to confirmation by the Ministry of Higher Education, directs both the academic and research work of the professors, docents, assistants, other personnel, and graduate students attached to the chair. Thus the chair (*kafedra*) is functionally comparable to a department in American institutions (e.g., physics department) in its undergraduate work of conducting service courses for other "departments" (e.g., mechanical engineering department, school of engineering) and, at the graduate level, in the supervision of research and of advanced training.

In Soviet schools graduate students are attached to a particular *chair,* but undergraduate students beginning with their freshman year are enrolled in one or another faculty *(fakul'tet)*, that is, an academic and administrative unit ("department," "school") which consolidates the work of a number of chairs for undergraduate and graduate instruction in a particular field. The name of the faculty more or less accurately designates its field, for example:

Physics-Mathematics Faculty.
Mechanics-Mathematics Faculty.
Mechanical Faculty.
Welding Faculty.

The field of study is not, however, designated in the names of the extension departments *(otdeleniya)* which many resident schools maintain, although they too are in some cases called "faculties," namely: Evening Faculty, Correspondence *(zaochnyi)* Faculty.*

Each faculty is headed by a dean *(dekan)* appointed by the Ministry of Higher Education. A Soviet institution of higher learning, depending on its type, has one or more faculties. In 1955 the universities, for instance, had on the average seven resident faculties; three of the largest universities (Moscow, Leningrad, and Kiev) had twelve each; three smaller universities (Gor'ki, Dnepropetrovsk, and Uzbek) had only four (see Table 29). Polytechnic institutes also have on the average seven resident faculties (see Table 32). Other engineering schools have, as a rule, fewer faculties; for instance, engineering institutes of the category defined as "Machine Construction, Machine Tools and Tools, Mechanical, and Automechanical Institutes" (listed in Table 34) have, typically, two to four resident faculties. The smaller number of faculties is the major organizational difference which distinguishes "polytechnic" and "industrial" institutes from all other schools of engineering.

A faculty conducts courses in a number of "specialties"—majors or options—which the student may select. For example, a student enrolled in the physics-mathematics faculty of a university may take as his "specialty" mathematics, mechanics, or physics. Furthermore, if, for example, his specialty is physics, toward the end of his undergraduate (5-year) course he will select one of the following ten "specializations" within his specialty:

---

* *Zaochnyi*—"in absentia"—faculty or school of instruction provides instruction by correspondence but also requires its students to attend a number of short sessions (laboratory work, diploma projects) in residence; examinations are also taken in person at the school.

Theoretical Physics.
Low-Temperature Physics.
Molecular Physics.
Optics.
X-Ray and Physics of Metal.
Magnetism.
Solid State Physics.
Electrophysics.
Structure of Matter.
Radio Physics.*

Similarly, an engineering student enrolled, for example, in the mining-geological faculty of the Georgian Polytechnic Institute (one of seven faculties at that school) will have a choice of eight specialties. Let us assume he selects "Geophysical Methods of Search and Prospecting for Deposits of Useful Minerals" as his specialty. He will eventually take as his (undergraduate) specialization one of the following: "Geophysical Methods of Prospecting for Ore and Non-Ore Deposits," or "Geophysical Methods of Prospecting for Oil, Gas, and Coal Deposits," or "Geophysical Methods for the Exploration of Wells."

In the early 1930's the number of "specialties" and of "sharply defined specialties" taught in the institutions of higher learning mushroomed to a fantastic number. By 1932 the total number was nearly 900, of which 330 were engineering specialties; at one time there were 111 specialties in just *one branch* of mechanical engineering, that of machine design. The qualitative consequences of training organized on this basis were catastrophic, and, beginning with 1932, there was introduced a series of measures designed to reverse the trends initiated c. 1929 and to reduce the number of specialties. In the regulations published in the fall of 1933 the number of formal categories of training was considerably reduced; nevertheless, the new list still prescribed 46 distinct specialties in machine design, among them, for instance, such course titles as Mechanical Engineer of Steam Locomotive Construction or Mechanical Engineer of Railroad Car Construction. Although extreme fragmentation in engineering training was eliminated by the reforms of the 1930's, the Soviet system of technical education continued to struggle with the problem of how to combine engineering education (of the kind demanded by the status of science and technology) with training for a specific technical job (as demanded by the ministry in charge of production). The arguments of the 1930's against

* The Russian terms here translated as "specialty" and "specialization" are *spetsial'nost'* and *spetsializatsiya,* respectively.

TABLE 29. NUMBER OF FACULTIES AND NUMBER OF "SPECIALTIES" TAUGHT IN
EACH OF THE THIRTY-THREE STATE UNIVERSITIES
USSR
1955

Ref. No.	Name [location]*	Faculties	"Specialties"
1	Azerbaidzhan [Baku]	7†	20
2	Byelorussian [Minsk]	7†	13
3	Vil'nyus	7†	18
4	Voronezh	6†	13
5	Gor'ki	4	8
6	Dnepropetrovsk	4†	8
7	Erevan	8†	20
8	Irkutsk	7†	14
9	Kazan'	7†	17
10	Kazakh [Alma-Ata]	7†	18
11	Karelo-Finnish [Petrozavodsk]	5†	9
12	Kiev	12†	22
13	Kirgiz [Frunze]	7†	14
14	Kishenev	6	13
15	Latvia [Riga]	8‡	24
16	Leningrad	12†	41
17	L'vov	11†	22
18	Molotov	7	14
19	Moscow	12†	36
20	Odessa	6†	10
21	Rostov-na-Donu	5†	13
22	Saratov	8†	13
23	Central Asia [Tashkent]	8	19
24	Tadzhik	5†	11
25	Tartu [Estonia]	5†	18
26	Tbilisi	10	26
27	Tomsk	7	14
28	Turkmen [Ashkhabad]	5‡	11
29	Uzhgorod	5†	9
30	Uzbek [Samarkand]	4†	7
31	Ural [Sverdlovsk]	6†	13
32	Kharkov	8†	15
33	Chernovtsy	6†	11
	Total number in 33 universities	232	534
	Average per faculty	...	2.3
	Average per university	7	16

Source: Spravochnik dlya postupayushchikh v vysshiye uchebnye zavedeniya SSSR v 1955 godu.

* "State University" omitted; also omitted are honorifics, such as "named after Lenin."

† Also has Correspondence (*zaochnyi*) Faculty.

‡ Also has Correspondence (*zaochnyi*) and Evening Faculties.

TABLE 30.   LIST AND NUMBER OF ALL FACULTIES WITHIN THE
THIRTY-THREE STATE UNIVERISTIES
USSR
1955

Faculty	Number
1. Physics	7
2. Physics-Mathematics	25
3. Mechanics-Mathematics	7
4. Natural Sciences-Mathematics	1
5. Natural Sciences	2
6. Chemistry	27
7. Biology	14
8. Biology-Chemistry	1
9. Biology-Soil	14
10. Geology	15
11. Geologic Exploration	1
12. Geology-Geography	8
13. Geography	15
14. Medical	3
15. Agricultural	1
16. Engineering Construction	1
17. Forestry Engineering	1
18. Mechanical	1
19. Technical	1
20. Economics	12
21. Journalism	3
22. History	16
23. History-Law	1
24. History-Philology	15
25. Law	14
26. Philology	18
27. Philosophy	3
28. Oriental	2
29. Foreign Languages	2
30. Foreign Languages and Literature	1
Total number of resident faculties	232
Evening faculties	2
Correspondence (*zaochnye*) faculties	27

Source: Compiled from *Spravochnik dlya postupayushchikh v vysshiye uchebnye zavedeniya SSSR v 1955 godu.*

Table 31. University Faculties Offering Courses in Mathematics, Physics, Mechanics, Astronomy, and Geophysics at Thirty-Three State Universities
USSR
1955

Faculties		Number of Faculties of a Given Name Offering:				
Name	No.	Math.	Physics	Mech.	Astronomy	Geophysics
Physics-Mathematics	25	25	25	8	. . .	. . .
Mechanics-Mathematics	7	7	. . .	6	3	. . .
Physics	7	. . .	7	. . .	. . .	2
Natural Science-Mathematics*	1	1	1	. . .	. . .	. . .
Total number	40	33	33	14	3	2

Source: Spravochnik dlya postupayushchikh v vysshiye uchebnye zavedeniya SSSR v 1955 godu.

* Tartu (Estonian SSR) University; this faculty also included chemistry, botany, zoology, physical geography, and economic geography.

Note: Chemistry is offered in all but four (Karelo-Finnish, Kirgiz, Tadzhik, and Uzbek) universities, usually as the only course of the chemistry faculty, except at Tartu University (see footnote above), at Latvia University (where the chemistry faculty also includes technology of silicates and chemical technology of wood pulp), and at Turkmen University (where botany, zoology, and chemistry are given under the faculty of biology-chemistry).

TABLE 32. NUMBER OF FACULTIES AND OF "SPECIALTIES" TAUGHT IN
POLYTECHNIC AND INDUSTRIAL INSTITUTES
USSR
1955

A. Nineteen Polytechnic Institutes

Ref. No.	Name [location]	Faculties	"Specialties"
1	Azerbaidzhan [Baku]	4*	12
2	Byelorussian [Minsk]	8*	21
3	Gor'ki	7*	16
4	Gruzinskii [Georgian, at Tbilisi]	7*†	36
5	Dal'nevostochnyi [Vladivostok]	7*	17
6	Erevan	6†	17
7	Kaunas	5*	18
8	Kiev	8†	22
9	Leningrad	9*	33
10	L'vov	9*	25
11	Novocherkassk	7*	19
12	Odessa	4*	7
13	Sredneaziatskii [Tashkent]	6	24
14	Tallin	5*†	15
15	Tomsk	12*†	29
16	Ural [Sverdlovsk]	10*†	32
17	Frunze	2	5
18	Kharkov	11*†	29
19	Chelyabinsk	5*	15
	Total for 19 Polytechnic Institutes	132	392
	Average per Institute	7	20.6

* Also has a division for evening classes.
† Also has a division for instruction by correspondence.

B. Four Industrial Institutes

Ref. No.	Name [location]	Faculties	"Specialties"
20	Azerbaidzhan [Baku]	6*†	13
21	Donetskii [Stalino]	6*†	13
22	Kuibyshev	4*	10
23	Penza	4*	5
	Total for 4 Industrial Institutes	20	41
	Average per Institute	5	10

* Also has a division for evening classes.
† Also has a division for instruction by correspondence.

C. Two Correspondence (*zaochnye*) Institutes

Ref. No.	Name [location]	Faculties	"Specialties"
24	Vsesoyuznyi Polytechnic [Moscow]	9	58
25	Leningrad Industrial	6	19
	Total for 2 Correspondence Institutes	15	77
	Average per Institute	7.5	37

TABLE 32 (continued)

D. Recapitulation for All Twenty-Five Institutes

Number of Schools	Type of Institute	Regular		Number of Schools with Special Departments	
		Faculties	"Specialties"	Correspondence	Evening
19	A. Polytechnic	132	392	7	15
4	B. Industrial	20	41	2	4
2	C. Extension	15	77	...	...
25	Total	167	510	9	19
	Average per Institute	6.7	20.4	...	...

Source: Compiled from *Spravochnik dlya postupayushchikh v vysshiye uchebnye zavedeniya SSSR v 1955 godu.*

TABLE 33. LIST OF FACULTIES OF POLYTECHNIC AND INDUSTRIAL INSTITUTES*
USSR
1955

Name of the Faculty	Number of Institutes
1. Automechanical [avtomekhanicheskii]	1
2. Automotive and Tractor [avtotraktornyi]	3
3. Chemical and Food Technology	1
4. Chemico-Technological	15
5. Concentration and Briquetting of Coal	1
6. Construction Materials	1
7. Construction [and] Power [energeticheskii]	1
8. Construction [stroitel'nyi]	13
9. Electric Machinery Construction	1
10. Electric Power [elektroenergeticheskii]	2
11. Electromechanical [elektromekhanicheskii]	2
12. Electrophysics [elektrofizicheskii]	1
13. Electrotechnical [elektrotekhnicheskii]	8
14. Engineering Construction	2
15. Engineering Economics	5
16. Engineering Physics	1
17. Forestry Engineering	1
18. Geologic Prospecting [-razvedochnyi]	6
19. Heat Engineering [teplotekhnicheskii]	1
20. Heat Power [teploenergeticheskii]	2
21. Hydromelioration [gidromeliorativnyi]	2
22. Hydrotechnical	6
23. Light Industry	1
24. Machine Construction [-stroitel'nyi]	2
25. Mechanical-Machine Construction	2
26. Mechanical [mekhanicheskii]	17

TABLE 33 (continued)

Name of the Faculty	Number of Institutes
27. Mechanico-Technological	1
28. Mechanization of Forest Industry	1
29. Metallurgical	9
30. Metallurgy of Ferrous Metals	1
31. Metallurgy of Nonferrous Metals	1
32. Mining	7
33. Mining-Chemical	2
34. Mining Construction	1
35. Mining-Geological	1
36. Mining-Mechanical	2
37. Mining-Operations [gornopromyslovyi]	1
38. Motion Picture Engineering	1
39. Oil [neflyannoi]	2
40. Oil Processing Mechanics [neflemekhanicheskii]	1
41. Oil Production [neflepromyslovoi]	1
42. Peat	1
43. Physico-Mechanical	1
44. Physico-Technical	1
45. Power [energeticheskii]	10
46. Power Machinery Construction	2
47. Precision [tochnaya] Mechanics	1
48. Radiotechnical	8
49. Railroad Transportation	1
50. Ship Repair	1
51. Shipbuilding	2
52. Silicates	4
53. Technological	1
54. Technology of Inorganic Substances	1
55. Technology of Organic Substances	1
56. Textile	1
57. Welding	1
Total number of faculties comprising 25 institutes	167

Source: Compiled from *Spravochnik dlya postupayushchikh v vysshiye uchebnye zavedeniya SSSR v 1955 godu.*

* This list includes the names of the faculties in the institutes enumerated in Table 26.

TABLE 34. NUMBER OF FACULTIES AND OF "SPECIALTIES" TAUGHT AT
SIXTEEN "MACHINE CONSTRUCTION, MACHINE TOOLS AND TOOLS,
MECHANICAL, AND AUTOMECHANICAL INSTITUTES"
USSR
1955

Ref. No.	Name [location] of the Institute*	Faculties	"Specialties"
1	Altai [Barnaul], Agricultural Machinery Construction	2‡	5
2	Bezhitsa, Transport Machinery Construction	2§	5
3	Zaporozh'ye, Agricult. Mach. Construction	3§	4
4	Izhevsk, Mechanical	1§	2
5	Leningrad, Mechanical†	?§	?
6	Leningrad, Precision Mechanics and Optics	3§	5
7	Moscow, Automechanical	2§	5
8	Moscow, Engineering-Physics	4	?
9	Moscow, Machine Tools and Tools	3§	4
10	Moscow, Higher Technical School	5	17
11	Omsk, Machine Construction	2§	3
12	Rostov, Agricult. Mach. Construction	2§	4
13	Stalingrad, Mechanical	4§	5
14	Tula, Mechanical	3§	3 (?)
	Subtotal, 13 resident institutes	36	62
15	All-Union [Moscow] Correspondence Machinery Construction	5	10
16	Moscow Evening Machine Construction	2	6
	Total, 15 schools	43	78

Source: Spravochnik dlya postupayushchikh v vysshiye uchebnye zavedeniya SSSR v 1955 godu, pp. 87–92.

* The word "institute" omitted.

† In 1955 name listed as "Leningrad Order of Red Banner Mechanical Institute." In the 1950 *Spravochnik*, it was listed as "Leningrad Order of Red Banner Military Institute"; in 1940 simply as "Military-Mechanical Institute." None of these listings gives any details except the address (1 First Krasnoarmeiskaya) and the fact that it has an evening department.

‡ Also an evening department and an affiliated evening program at Rubtsovsk.

§ Also an evening department.

too many specialties, too many faculties, too much "parallelism" in curricula, and a too narrow job orientation in engineering training continued to appear in educational literature, and the same arguments have been strongly revived since Stalin's death. Beginning with 1947–1948 (following the establishment of the Ministry of Higher Education in 1946) further revisions in the organization of specialties were introduced. By 1953–1954 there were altogether 295 engineering specialties taught in the institutions of higher learning.[18] For the purpose of planning, these specialties comprised 24 groups such as:

Group	Number of Specialties
Metallurgy	12
Machine and Apparatus Construction	
(a) Power Machinery	9
(b) General Machinery	26
(c) Apparatus	7
Electrical Machinery, Devices, and Apparatus Construction	9

The number of "specializations" within these and other specialties is not readily ascertainable from the available data.

Further efforts have recently been made to reduce the number of undergraduate specializations in Soviet engineering schools.[19] However, in view of the conditions created by the vertical integration of formal engineering training within specific industries, and by the extremely sharp differentiation in the ranking of these industries by the Soviet leaders as to their relative importance (e.g., the aviation industry vs. consumer goods industries), it is not likely that Soviet engineering education can wholly emancipate itself from the curricular and other constraints imposed upon it by central planning.

The Learned Council

Within the very limited area of self-government and discretion in which each individual school conducts its academic affairs, the highest academic authority of each institution is formally exercised by its Learned Council. Presided over by the director, the Council is composed of the deputy directors, deans of faculties, professors in charge of academic chairs, and representatives of the various nonacademic organizations, such as the Communist Party cells and the affiliated Komsomol sections and academic workers' unions which penetrate the student body and the faculty. Representatives "of the enterprises and establishments for which the educational institutions train specialists" may also sit on the Learned Councils.

The officially prescribed duties of these academic councils apparently have not changed since 1938; one of the more recent Soviet sources described them practically in the exact words of the 1938 charter:[20]

> The following are among the duties of the Learned Council: to discuss and consider the semester and annual plans and reports on the work of the institutions, its faculties, and chairs and to generalize their experience; to consider methodological questions of teaching and of topics for research; to discuss and propose individuals for the academic titles of docent and professor; to grant the academic title of *assistent* [lowest academic title] and to grant academic degrees of *kandidat* and of *doktor* of sciences.

That author properly amends his statement by pointing out that the award of the title of professor and the degree of *doktor* are subject to confirmation by the Higher Attestation Committee of the Ministry of Higher Education. As already mentioned, the composition of the Learned Council itself is controlled by the Ministry of Higher Education, whose Attestation Commission controls academic appointments and the awarding of academic degrees generally. Similarly, the composition of the academic body by faculties and chairs, the curricula and syllabi of the courses, the choice of approved textbooks, the number and the distribution by faculties and specialties of new students (both freshmen and graduates), and many other important parameters of institutional and academic life are established (and frequently changed on short notice or no notice at all) by orders from above.

It is quite evident that in the prevailing general system the potentialities of the Learned Council for improving the quality of education are severely limited by both institutional and ideological restrictions. This is not to say that individual institutions and educators play no role whatsoever in the formulation of educational policies; there are many channels for communication of opinion and ideas from the school level up to the Ministry. But the changes introduced by the Ministry from time to time (as a rule in fulfillment of previously announced over-all directives of the Central Committee of the Communist Party) usually embody in one sudden move a series of radical alterations which are prescribed across the board for all schools or for a group of schools within a given category. Thus an imaginary composite graph which would record educational development in the Soviet Union is to be visualized as distinctly a step function of decisions centrally made on a big scale, with conditions remaining more or less constant between one and another shift in central policies. One of these major shifts was the restoration of essentially traditional educational practices in the mid-1930's; another, involving considerable changes in the curricula, followed the establishment of the Ministry of Higher Education in 1946; finally, the decisions of the Central Committee in 1954 precipitated a number of changes in higher education, some of which we shall mention in later chapters.

NOTES TO CHAPTER 5

1 For a concise and informative account of higher education in Russia up to 1918, see "Universities and Higher Technical Schools" by Paul J. Novgorotsev, *Russian Schools and Universities in the World War*, New Haven: Yale University Press, 1929.

2 Leon Trilling, *Soviet Education in Aeronautics: A Case Study*, Cambridge: Center for International Studies, Massachusetts Institute of Technology, 1956 (mimeographed); also published in *Aviation Week*, a McGraw-Hill publication, in four installments beginning with the August 20, 1956 issue.

3 *Krasnaya zvezda* (Red Star), Soviet army newspaper, September 17, 1948.

4 *Vysshaya shkola*, compiled by M. I. Movshovich, p. 250.

5 *BSE*, 2nd Ed., Vol. 16, 1952, p. 228.

6 *Vysshaya shkola*, compiled by M. I. Movshovich, p. 250.

7 *Krasnaya zvezda*, September 17, 1948.

8 *BSE*, 2nd Ed., Vol. 8, 1951, p. 469.

9 B. Koval' (Minister of Higher Education, Ukrainian SSR), "Vazhneishiye zadachi vysshei shkoly" (The Most Important Tasks of the Higher School), *Pravda Ukrainy*, November 20, 1955, p. 3.

10 *Vestnik vysshei shkoly*, No. 10, October 1954, p. 5.

According to *Pravda*, December 5, 1953, there were nearly 500,000 correspondence students in that year; assuming that some 100,000 were taking engineering courses, the 1960 target would be 300,000 or approximately 50 per cent greater than the 1955–1956 correspondence enrollment in engineering (see Table 22).

11 Ordinance of the Central Executive Committee of the USSR, "On the Academic Programs and Regime in the Higher Schools and Technicums," September 19, 1932 (S. Z. USSR, 1932, No. 68, Art. 409), quoted in *Direktivy VKP(b) i postanovleniya sovetskovo pravitel'stva o narodnom obrazovanii za 1917–1947 gg.*, Vol. I, p. 78.

12 *Ibid.*, p. 89.

13 E. N. Medynskii, *Narodnoye obrazovaniye v SSSR*, p. 170; ". . . about 350":

In the reshuffle of command posts following Stalin's death, the Ministry was abolished (March 15, 1953) and its functions and role assumed by the Ministry of Culture; a year later (March 9, 1954) in another sudden reorganization the Ministry of Higher Education was resurrected. *BSE*, 2nd Ed., Vol. 27, 1954, p. 533.

14 *Vestnik vysshei shkoly*, No. 10, 1946, p. 5, quoted in Boris I. Gorokhoff, "Materials for the Study of Soviet Specialized Education," p. 11.

Prior to 1946 Kaftanov was chairman of the Committee on the Higher Schools; he was replaced by V. N. Stoletov in 1951.

15 E. N. Medynskii, *Narodnoye obrazovaniye v SSSR*, p. 171.

16 E.g., N. I. Nazarov, "Podgotovka proekta ustava vysshikh uchebnykh zavedenii" (Preparation for the Projected Charter for Higher Educational Establishments), *Vestnik vysshei shkoly*, No. 4, 1955, pp. 16–21.

17 The text of the charter, approved by the Council of Commissars (Ministers) on

September 5, 1938 (S. P. USSR, 1938, No. 41, p. 237), is given in *Vysshaya shkola,* compiled by M. I. Movshovich, pp. 26–34.

18 I. A. Lyasnikov, *Podgotovka spetsialistov promyshlennosti SSSR* (The Training of Specialists for the Industry of the USSR), Moscow: Gospolitizdat, 1954, p. 89.

19 Jakow Budanow, *Technical Institutes in the USSR,* Research Program on the USSR, Mimeographed Series No. 26, New York, 1952, p. 4.

20 S. Kaftanov, *Vyssheye obrazovaniye v SSSR* (Higher Education in the USSR), Moscow: UK Vlksm Molodaya "Gvardiya," 1950, p. 79.

SOVIET HIGHER EDUCATION:

SELECTION, ENROLLMENT,

AND GRADUATION

In 1954 the USSR Council of Ministers and the Central Committee of the Communist Party issued a set of apparently far-reaching instructions to the administrators of the educational system.* The text of this directive has not been published in the general press; and we have been unable to locate the text of the instructions which were subsequently issued (apparently on September 9, 1954) by the Ministry of Higher Education prescribing the specific changes within the school system which would, in the estimate of the Ministry, lead to the achievement of objectives stipulated by the central authority. Judging by the comments which have subsequently appeared in Soviet literature on education, the objective with reference to higher training in engineering and science was to improve the quality of the graduates. The 1954 directive appears to have indicated at least three dimensions in which the quality was to be improved. First, the students were to be trained more broadly; second, they were to be encouraged to do more independent work; third, they were to be trained for more rapid integration within industry and other fields of professional practice.

These three aspects of professional and especially of engineering training—broad preparation, ability to work independently, and immediate practical competency—have been repeatedly emphasized ever since the reforms of the 1930's. In the past, industrial and political expediency have militated against broad and comprehensive training,

* Decree dated August 30, 1954.

and the rigidly planned, extremely crowded curricula have left little time and given little encouragement for independent work by undergraduate students. It is not at all clear how far the current reforms will go toward eliminating those shortcomings of technical education which have been a perennial source of complaint by both the educators and users of professional skills. It is clear, however, that many aspects of the academic process—admissions policies, curricula, distribution of academic time, structure of faculties, and the range of options—have undergone considerable change since 1954.

Furthermore, the 20th Congress of the Communist Party held in February 1956 once again underscored the need for improvement in the quality of training.[1] The same directive stipulates continued numerical growth in the output of higher school graduates:

> During the sixth Five Year Plan [1956–1960] the number of higher school graduates shall be increased to 1.5 times [the number graduated during 1951–1955] and the number of those trained in heavy industry, construction, transport, and agricultural specialties shall be doubled.[2]

Thus Soviet schools of higher education are under the dual stress of rapidly increasing enrollment (particularly in the extension facilities) and a drive to improve the quality of instruction. The problem of functioning effectively under these pressures is compounded by other plans affecting the school system, such as the planned geographic dispersion of facilities and the utilization of school facilities for industrial research. Under the existing system of administration it will take many years for the Soviet school system to translate into action the broad directives issued in the name of the 20th Congress even if, as has been indicated, individual schools should be granted progressively increasing autonomy. In the meantime, of course, another shift of top-level policy could reverse or change the present course.

1. Admission Rules and Requirements

The metamorphosis of Soviet educational policies since the Revolution could be well illustrated by the successive changes in the rules of admission to the institutions of higher learning. Here, for the sake of brevity, we shall concentrate on the most recent changes and current practices. To set the admissions question in proper historical perspective, however, we must make one reference to the earliest Soviet formulation of the prerequisites for a higher education. In a gesture designed to outdo the most radical reforms previously proposed for higher education, the Council of Commissars in August 1918 annulled the already completed registration of students for the 1918–1919 academic year and prescribed new rules. The old academic qualifications were abandoned, and it was ordered that henceforth:

> Any person irrespective of citizenship or sex who has reached the age of sixteen may enroll as a student at any institution of higher learning without having to submit a diploma, certificate, or other evidence of completion of secondary or other schooling.[3]

This sweeping order specifically prohibited school authorities from requesting any other information except the age and identity of applicants. In practice, however, a number of restrictive qualifications were gradually introduced. A policy of discrimination on the basis of social origin continued in effect until 1935; in the early 1930's academic qualifications became a formal requirement. Today an applicant seeking admission to an institution of higher learning in the USSR is required to designate the faculty *and the specialty* in which he desires to receive instruction. The application must be accompanied by the following eight documents:

1. Autobiography.
2. The *original* copy of the certificate of graduation from a secondary school (a provision which precludes applying to more than one institution in any one year).
3. Passport (presented personally).
4. Three photographs.
5. Record of military service status.
6. Record of employment (if any).
7. Medical certificate.
8. Certificate of residence.

Applications for admission are accepted only between June 20 and July 31 each year, and (since 1936) new students are admitted only at the beginning of the academic year. Until 1955 the age limit for applicants was set between the ages of 17 and 35. The lower limit has now been eliminated, perhaps to accommodate those graduates of the ten-year school who may be a month or two short of their seventeenth birthday at the time they file the application—a situation which must frequently arise under the existing rules of admission to the ten-year schools, which require a youngster entering school to reach his seventh birthday by the beginning of the school year. It may be parenthetically noted, however, that we have found no evidence of any provisions for skipping a grade or other means for accelerated progression through the secondary schools in the Soviet Union.

All applicants who satisfy the requirements enumerated above and are not disqualified on medical or other grounds are grouped in categories on the basis of (1) their scholastic record in the secondary school and (2) certain factors in their own or their parents' status which entitle the applicant to preferential treatment as described below. These categories are as follows:

A. Applicants whose secondary school grades entitled them to enter without taking any entrance examination.

1. Ten-year school gold medal holders (straight A's in the ten-year school finals) are so admitted to any university or institute.

2. Ten-year school silver medal holders are similarly admitted to some schools.

3. A-students (*otlichniki*) among those technicum graduates (top 5 per cent) who are entitled to continue education (without first having to work in industry for 3 years) are also admitted by certain of the higher schools without entrance examinations.

B. Applicants who (for certain schools only) must take competitive entrance examinations in *one* subject (most nearly related to the field of study for which they apply, such as mathematics for engineering majors).

This category was introduced in the fall of 1955 with reference to applicants only to certain designated schools for which demand is greatest, such as in Moscow or other large cities. These schools now require silver medal holders and the best technicum graduates (categories A2 and A3 above) to take competitive examinations in one subject, whereas previously these applicants were admitted to any school without such examinations. Those in this category who fail in competition within the group may compete on general terms with those in the category described below.

C. Applicants who must take and satisfactorily pass entrance examinations in from three to five subjects (depending on the field of study applied for). This category consists of two groups:

1. Those who are admitted *noncompetitively*, provided that they receive a grade of "satisfactory" or better on all the required examinations. This subcategory includes:*

a. Veterans of World War II.

* In 1953, upon completion of the new building of the Moscow University, some 120 freshmen representing 45 national minorities within the USSR were locally selected by special committees and enrolled at the University of Moscow without undergoing competitive examinations. *Vestnik vysshei shkoly*, No. 9, September 1953, p. 19.

b. Children of officials and administrative employees of Ukhta Combine, Pechora coal mines, Dal'stroi, and all organizations in the Magadan Oblast' generally—that is, in the areas where forced labor camps are located in greatest concentrations.

c. Children of officials and employees of the various organizations and enterprises which were formerly under Dal'stroi, NKVD (but are now operated by other ministries), and also of employees in other remote areas where there are forced labor camps and industries oper ated by prisoners.

d. The graduates of Soviet schools in Liaotung Peninsula (China, Kwangtung Leased Territory).

2. Those (numerically the largest group) whose entrance examination grades are ranked competitively. The available (as prescribed by the Ministry) freshman vacancies are filled, following the examinations, from the top of the list down.

Under a 1955 directive, preference in granting entrance to the institutions of higher learning is given ("other things being equal") to those applicants who have had two or more years of work experience or have completed active military service following their graduation from a secondary school. This provision is probably aimed at two related objectives: first, to divert the recently increased number of ten-year school graduates to technicums, vocational schools, and directly to industry; second, to weight the composition of the student body in favor of the more mature students with practical experience and, presumably, with greater seriousness of purpose than the mass-produced graduates fresh from the ten-year school. The director of Kharkov State University, I. Bulankin, who was among those endorsing the change in admissions policies, wrote:

We, the teachers, remember with affection those students [i.e., older veterans] who were attending classes in the first years after the war.[4]

Under Soviet conditions the right of noncompetitive enrollment is a great privilege. Once admitted, the student has a very good chance of surviving to graduation, since the attrition rate in Soviet institutions of resident type, as will be shown, is relatively low. Furthermore, those who qualify for noncompetitive examinations are spared the anxiety and tension apparently created among applicants taking competitive examinations, who are aware that thousands of applicants who pass the examinations satisfactorily nevertheless fail of admission. In criticizing the established procedure, the director of a medical school, V. S. Yurov, pointed to the state of accentuated nervous tension among those taking the competitive entrance examinations and added:

Having observed this situation year after year, one necessarily asks the question: "Why do we organize the admissions procedure in such a manner as to inflict a severe trauma upon the many who pass the examinations but fail of enrollment on competitive grounds?"

In the absence of any systematically published data, it is impossible to estimate reliably the composition of the current enrollment by categories, to know, for instance, how many are enrolled noncompetitively on the basis of privilege, having made only a mediocre showing on the examinations. The presumption is, however, that this last-named category constitutes a minority. Furthermore, the degree of competition (and therefore the selectivity) must vary greatly from school to school and from faculty to faculty. As already noted, only certain schools (e.g., Moscow University) now require the silver medal holder to take an entrance examination in his key subject. It should be noted, however, that, although prior to 1955 medal holders had "an unquestionable right to be enrolled without any entrance examinations," some informal screening among them apparently has been practiced:

> . . . certain schools of higher education not only interfere with the rights of the medal holders and, under the guise of personal consultation, do in fact examine them, but they also assign for solution specially selected, complex problems in mathematics and physics, thus placing the medal holders at a disadvantage relative to those who take regular competitive examinations.[5]

There are no current statistics published on the number of applicants. It is, however, certain that in the last few years the number has been large enough to permit high selectivity in the fields of training most sought after by Soviet students—science and technology. The competitive positions—of one school against another, one faculty versus another in the same school, and even one "specialty" against another in the same faculty—vary a great deal, being inversely related to the number of authorized vacancies in each school, faculty, and specialty and directly related to the number of applicants. At the University of Kharkov as a whole, for example, there were (1954), on the average, three applicants for every vacancy, five applicants for every vacancy in the Physics Faculty, and fifteen applicants for every opening in the History Faculty. We do not know how many vacancies in these two faculties were provided for by the plan, but the presumption is that the number of vacancies in the physics course was the larger. In the fall of 1953 there were nearly 8,000 applicants for some 3,000 vacancies at the University of Moscow. The Physics, Chemistry, and Biology-Soil Faculties had, relatively, the largest number of applicants. *Izvestiya* (August 21, 1955) noted again "a great flood of applicants" with "two or three" contenders for every resident vacancy. At the University of Moscow, according to the article, there were 7,700 applicants in the fall of 1955, of whom 2,673 were admitted. Since the applicant may apply to only one school in any given year, the rejected applicant as a rule must either give up the idea of becoming a resident student or wait one year for another try. In some years, however, special arrangements have been made by the school administration for the transfer of some applicants rejected by one school for admission to another.

The annual quota of students to be admitted for training in various categories is set in accordance with the plan. If statistics were available on the number of vacancies versus the number of applicants by categories, the data could perhaps provide an illuminating comparison between the scale of priorities set by the planners and the relative desirability of the various fields of study in the minds of the young Soviet students. It appears that Soviet students are far less strongly motivated to enter a particular field of study than they are to achieve the status of a person with higher education, and that they have a general preference for the politically safe prestige fields of science. Many comments made by former Soviet citizens seem to illustrate this general attitude. One postwar defector, for instance,

> . . . had been advised against becoming a geologist because pure geology was a dying subject in the USSR since the Soviet rulers were interested mainly in applied geology. The source had wanted to go to the Timiryazev Academy and to become a plant geneticist. This was in 1938, before Lysenko had established his domination over agricultural science. However, the rector of the Timiryazev Academy had discouraged him, by pointing out that he would not have an opportunity to engage in pure scientific work. The rector had said that the academy was interested mainly in training agronomists. He then thought of studying medicine, a subject which had attracted him because he was fond of studying human psychology, but he abandoned this idea upon ascertaining that he would probably be sent to the provinces after graduation. So he decided to become a geologist. It was not easy to obtain admission to the . . . Geological Institute, for there were 5 to 10 times as many applicants as there were places in the Institute. This was true of all the best institutes, particularly scientific ones. People who failed to obtain admission to one of these better institutes usually went to a pedagogical institute or to a *tekhnikum*. They became secondary school teachers in most cases. There was not much interest in going to institutes specializing in history or the humanities because one could not do independent work in these fields but had to produce political propaganda.[6]

Many observers of the educational scene in the Soviet Union have concluded that the degree of selectivity is high and that it is based almost solely on academic merit. Eric Ashby, in "Soviet Science *Is* a Challenge to Us," has stated that in "proceeding to higher education, merit is the only test."[7] It is difficult to agree with this statement with-out qualifying it in many essential respects. It was not until 1936 that a wholly discriminatory denial of the opportunity to obtain higher education, based on the social origin *of parents,* was formally removed.[8]

Ample provisions for general discrimination on political and ideological grounds, including those specifically provided for in the criminal codes of the Soviet Union, have continued in full force; and it is quite clear that political reliability, or at least overt political submissiveness, has remained a significant element in judging the merit of those who wish to acquire the advantages of higher education. This is particularly noticeable in the existing practices of selection for graduate study.

There are other factors in the educational setting in the Soviet Union which also interfere with selection purely on academic merit. One of them arises from the extremely uneven geographic concentration of educational facilities. A third of the entire student population "study in Moscow, Leningrad, and Kiev."[9] If Kharkov, another large educational center, were to be added, the pattern of concentration would stand in even greater relief. These four cities accounted for 170 schools of higher education, including some of the oldest and best institutions, out of the total of 762 listed civilian schools as of 1955. The extreme concentration of higher schools in a few large centers works to the disadvantage of students from rural and remote areas if only because of the housing shortage in the large cities, which is but partly offset by facilities provided students by the school.

It should be noted also that the excessive and disproportionate concentration of educational resources in large cities conflicted with the Soviet government's economic plans. By 1957 the relative shortage of professionally qualified individuals in the new industrial areas away from the established metropolitan centers apparently had become acute. As one measure designed to force a dispersion of academic resources, it was announced (*Sovetskaya Litva,* April 13, 1957, p. 2) that the 1957–1958 admissions quotas of the institutions of higher education in Moscow, Leningrad, Kiev, and Kharkov would be cut by 25 per cent. At the same time, the admissions quotas of certain provincial institutions of higher education in other industrially strategic areas were to be correspondingly increased. The teaching staffs were presumably to be adjusted in proportion.

2. Tuition and Scholarships

Direct economic factors, contrary to Soviet propaganda assertions, have also worked against selectivity exclusively on merit. It was announced that beginning with the 1956–1957 academic year no tuition would be charged in any Soviet schools, including schools of higher education. The propaganda effect of this announcement is obvious; but it is too early for any realistic evaluation of the operational significance of this potentially important measure. Any assumed net effect—such as expansion of educational opportunity, improvement of the material status of students, or removal of economic factors from the selection process—may be enhanced, neutralized, or even negatively counterbalanced by other measures, such as the change in the system of scholarship and in the rules of admission.

Tuition varying from 300 to 500 rubles per year has been in effect since 1940: 400 rubles in schools of higher education located in Moscow, Leningrad, and fifteen other large cities; 300 rubles in schools located elsewhere, except higher schools of the arts where tuition was set at 500 rubles.*

We are inclined to view the introduction of tuition in 1940 and the concomitant expansion of the scholarship system as typical of the measures promulgated in that year to reinforce control over the allocation and distribution of manpower (and even perhaps to divert young people away from school into the labor pool) rather than as a means of "apportioning a part of the cost of education . . . to the toilers themselves."[10] It appears that the introduction of tuition promptly forced many students to drop out. In any event, there followed a large number of additional decrees, explanations, and instructions whereby various categories of students (or students in certain regions and of certain schools) were excused from paying the newly established tuition. Simultaneously with the various rulings on the application of tuition, provisions for scholarships were expanded.

In 1943 the Council of Commissars published a comprehensive schedule of scholarships to be granted to students in various categories. This schedule, with some modifications, appears to be still in effect. The amounts of scholarship vary with the year of study, the school attended, the faculty in which the student is enrolled, and, finally, with the grade standing of the student. For those attending "the most important industrial and transport" schools of higher education (87

* In 1940 the average industrial earnings per man were approximately 400 rubles per month.

schools listed in the decree) the scholarships start at 210 rubles per month during the first year and progressively increase each year, reaching 315 rubles a month during the last (fifth) year at school. The scholarships for students in training for certain enumerated specialties (a total of seventeen specialties in underground mining, heavy metallurgy, and in chemical industries) start at 315 and go up to 400 rubles per month in the last year of study. The scholarships in the remaining categories of schools (or courses of training), that is, in agricultural, pedagogical, medical, and other higher educational institutions, start at 140 rubles a month and reach 210 rubles a month by the last year.[11]

The amount of the scholarship paid during a given semester is increased by 25 per cent for all students who received grades of A in all subjects for the preceding semester. There are also available a number of special scholarships, named after Stalin, Molotov, Voroshilov, and others, to the "most outstanding A-students." These special scholarships, some of which are quite large, are awarded by the different ministries upon the recommendation of the Learned Council. The Stalin scholarships established in 1939 were set at 500 rubles per month for students in civilian schools and at 1,000 rubles for students of military schools of higher education—3,000 scholarships at 500 rubles per month and 1,000 military school scholarships.[12]

It appears that in the postwar period the amounts under the regular schedule of scholarships were increased by perhaps 80 rubles per month. There is also evidence that students in certain elite institutions receive higher than the basic amounts. In 1954 the regular scholarships at Moscow University ranged from 290 rubles per month for freshmen to 500 rubles for seniors. Just how extensive the system of scholarships is cannot be definitely ascertained from the available references. An article in *Vestnik vysshei shkoly* (No. 4, 1951, p. 9) stated that more than 75 per cent of resident students receive scholarships. Soviet officials seem to agree in telling foreign visitors that about 90 per cent of the students in Soviet higher educational institutions receive scholarships. It has been said that 97 per cent of the students attending Moscow University are on scholarship. Once granted (on the basis of grades received at the entrance examinations), the scholarship continues from semester to semester as long as the student maintains the required minimum level of achievement. It is not clear just what that minimum is, but, as is true of other variables in school life within the USSR, the practices evidently vary not only from school to school but among the different majors:

> . . . students of chemical, hydrotechnical, radiotechnical, and certain other specialties [at the Kaunas Polytechnic Institute] continue to receive a scholarship even if their grades include several

"satisfactory" grades [that is, C] whereas students in other specialties lose their scholarships if they have just one "C" [in any semester grades].[13]

We could obtain no comprehensive data on a student's budget which would permit us to pass categorical judgment on the adequacy of the scholarships. The monthly rent in a student dormitory is apparently low, about 15 rubles per month. The cost of books, although very low by American standards, is likely to be rather a substantial burden on a Soviet student's budget. For instance, a three-volume university reference text on general physics (S. E. Frish and A. V. Timoreva, *Kurs obshchei fiziki*) is priced at 49.05 rubles.* A prescribed textbook on thermodynamics for engineering students (A. S. Yastrzhembskii, *Tekhnicheskaya termodinamika*, 7th Ed., 1953) costs 16.55 rubles; a two-volume textbook in mathematical analysis also for engineering students (A. F. Bermant, *Kurs matematicheskovo analiza*, 7th Ed., 1953) is priced at 18 rubles. A basic textbook for machine construction engineering students on the theory of machines and mechanisms (I. I. Artobolevskii, *Teoriya mekhanizmov i mashin*, 3rd Ed., 1953), a volume of 712 pages, costs 14.60 rubles.

In addition to the tuition, the cost of books, and other normal maintenance costs (food, clothes, and personal services), there are apparently a number of other charges the students must meet, such as, until 1957, a compulsory subscription to the State loan (35 rubles a month) and a small tax on all scholarships over 260 rubles per month.[14]

There seems to be general agreement among observers that, on the average, scholarships in the Soviet Union at best cover subsistence costs and that some aid from parents or from part-time and vacation earnings is apparently indispensable in many or most cases. Eric Ashby states that in talking to students he

> . . . had the impression that they can just live on their state grants, but it needs self-denial and good luck to do so.[15]

A recent British source gives a less optimistic opinion:

> In view of the bare personal living wage of 700 rubles a month, these scholarships, offset by fees and other costs, are not sufficient to sustain life for a student without other means.[16]

It would seem, however, that these and many similar observations by recent visitors to the Soviet Union overstate the case and that, relative to the prevailing physical standards of living in the Soviet Union,

---

* At the official "rate of exchange" of 4 to 1 the price in this country would be $12.25 plus freight. The actual retail price of these three volumes at the Four-Continent Bookstore (Soviet agency) in 1955 was $5.25, that is, at the exchange ratio (disregarding freight) of 9.35 rubles to one dollar.

the students are not so badly off as the ruble size of their scholarships might indicate. Furthermore, the importance of physical standards should not be exaggerated. In pre-Revolutionary Russia students were proverbially impecunious,[17] and to rise above physical discomforts was a badge of honor. The fact that many more Soviet ten-year school graduates apply for admission to schools of higher education than there are vacancies is also a clear indication that the relative frugality of scholarships is not a deterrent strong enough to overcome other motivations. Nevertheless, economic considerations apparently have played a part in forcing the students who fail to qualify for scholarships in any one semester to drop out. It is for this reason, one may assume, that beginning with 1956–1957 a new procedure for granting scholarships was introduced to recognize not only the grades but also the need of the student.[18] In conclusion, then, it appears that under the Soviet system students who receive competitively qualifying grades on the entrance examinations (and thereafter maintain passing grades) have been financially provided for—if on a minimum basis. The anticipated cost of education, therefore, has not been an important factor in the Soviet Union in keeping qualified students from going on to higher education. What are important, however, are the remaining questions of whether the emphasis on the student's grades and the nature of the entrance examinations promote the most efficient selection of students with the best academic potential, and whether other than academic considerations affect the grading of examinations.

3. Entrance Examinations

Applicants to the majority of engineering institutes and to the science faculties of universities take entrance examinations in five subjects: Russian language and literature, mathematics, physics, chemistry, and foreign language (English, German, French, or Spanish).[19]

The scope of the examinations is defined each year by the Ministry of Higher Education several months in advance, permitting the applicants to review the required material during the summer. Examinations are conducted between August 1 and August 20 of each year. Separate institutions offer voluntary short-term refresher or preparatory courses prior to the examination period. There appears to be no uniform provision for these preparatory sessions. Thus Moscow University conducts during the entire month of July "consultations on all subjects included in the examinations." One source reports having taken a 4-month preparatory course at a medical institute;[20]

other sources indicate review sessions of about 2 months' duration. We do not know whether these courses are conducted as a general review of subjects or as a drill in specific questions likely to be asked at the forthcoming examinations.

Whereas the scope of the entrance examinations is prescribed by the Ministry of Higher Education, the actual questions are left to the examiners. It is obvious that the difficulty of questions and, even more important, the grading standards vary from institution to institution and from faculty to faculty.

Russian Language and Literature

Prior to the fall of 1955 both written and oral examinations (separately graded) were prescribed in Russian language and literature for all applicants, the written examination (c. 2 hours) being of essay type on one of three or four designated themes of "literary or socio-political" character.*

The syllabus of the oral examination includes phonetics, morphology and orthography, parts of speech and syntax of the Russian language, and other topics, such as, in the 1954 syllabus:

> Basic postulates of I. V. Stalin's teaching on the importance of language in the life of society, on the grammatical structure, word composition, and on fundamental vocabulary. . . .

The same topic in the 1955 syllabus, it should be noted, was described as "Marxist-Leninist teachings on the importance of language in the life of human society." Similarly, in weathercock fashion, a student may be called upon to comment (1950) on the Russian language "and its importance as the national language of the great Russian people," or (1954) "as one of the most important languages of the world," or (1955) "as the language of communication among the multi-national peoples of the USSR and one of the most important languages of the world." Generally speaking, examination questions in literature, history, and other subjects which by their nature lend themselves to a variety of interpretations are so structured as to leave no doubt in the student's mind as to the only currently acceptable tone of the answer.

In 1955 such examinations were eliminated except for students applying for training in philological subjects, journalism, and linguistics. All other applicants are given only the written test. Thus

---

* In schools where the language of instruction is other than Russian, the written examination may consist of simply writing down a dictated Russian theme or excerpt. Students applying to these schools must, however, pass an essay-type test in the language of instruction.

the entrance examination load of those applying to study engineering and physical sciences has been correspondingly lightened.

Mathematics

Most applicants for admission to schools of higher education must take an oral examination in mathematics, and applicants to engineering schools and science faculties of the universities take a written test also. Among those who do not have to take a test in mathematics are students applying for admission to courses within the following general fields: philology, philosophy, history, law, library science, pedagogy, psychology, biology, agronomy, medicine, physical culture, the arts, and a few others.

The syllabus of the entrance examination in mathematics includes three sections with subdivisions as follows:

1. Arithmetic and Algebra
   a. Real and complex numbers
   b. Transformation of algebraic expressions
   c. Equations; inequalities; functions and their graphs
   d. Progressions
   e. Logarithms
   f. Theory of permutations and combinations; binomial theorem
2. Geometry
   a. Plane geometry
   b. Solid geometry
3. Trigonometry
   a. Definitions and basic properties of trigonometric functions
   b. Transformation of trigonometric expressions and solution of trigonometric equations
   c. Solution of triangles[21]

The topics enumerated under each of the headings listed above cover the entire ten-year school curriculum in mathematics.

There is no solid basis for estimating how comprehensive and searching the oral examinations are in actual practice, what level of response is expected under various conditions of competition, and how severely and objectively the answers are graded. Indirect evidence leaves no doubt that standards vary considerably from institution to institution. Written tests in mathematics lend themselves to more nearly objective evaluation; and, if data on both the tests and the results were available, it would be possible to pass valid judgment on the level and quality of mathematical preparation needed to gain admission to Soviet institutions of higher education. Although a number of actual examination problems used at one time in different institutions can be found in Soviet educational literature, the performance data are lacking. One set of problems in mathematics used at the entrance examination to the Mechanics-Mathematics Faculty of Moscow University is reproduced in Appendix F. The Dean of this faculty, an outstanding Soviet mathematician, A. N. Kolmogorov, commented for the benefit of the applicants with reference to the entrance examinations in mathematics as follows:

> One should keep in mind that in order to be accepted to a university the first requirement is a firm knowledge of the [secondary] school course and an ability, on the basis of this knowledge, confidently and in a clear-cut manner to solve the more usual, so to speak, standard problems.[22]

The problems quoted in Appendix F are typical, according to Kolmogorov, of those encountered in the entrance examinations. In contrasting these problems with those given at the public mathematics competitions for students of the secondary schools,* he wrote:

> No special ingenuity of any kind is required to solve examination problems. In the majority of cases these problems can be solved by progressive application of the rules and techniques learned in school. Such independent thinking as may be required for the solution amounts to a systematic analysis of the question following a most natural sequence.[23]

However, the actual examples cited in connection with this article by Professor Kolmogorov suggest that he somewhat understated the case. The problems, on the whole, are much more challenging than his comment would imply. Dr. Philip Franklin, Professor of Mathematics at the Massachusetts Institute of Technology, analyzed the entire set of examination problems appended to Kolmogorov's article and summarized his conclusions as follows:

> One example in algebra plus one in geometry, in view of the fact that each consists of three or four problems, would make up a three-hour examination.†
> The material covered is comparable with the algebra, geometry, and trigonometry required for entrance to engineering schools in the United States. There is considerable emphasis on certain advanced topics of above average difficulty, such as simultaneous

---

* Nineteen examples of problems used at public competitions in ten-year school mathematics are given in Appendix F.

† One source, V. M. Bradis, *Metodika prepodavaniya matematiki v srednei shkole*, Moscow: Uchpedgiz, 1951, p. 85, states that Soviet written examinations in mathematics are "three or four hours or even longer."

quadratics, the theory of the quadratic, and maximum problems in algebra, construction problems in geometry, and identities in trigonometry. In this respect the coverage is more like that of the older American and British textbooks than our present-day ones, which minimize complicated techniques to make room for motivating applications.

Any student succeeding in solving two-thirds of the parts assigned to him would certainly have demonstrated a preparation and ability above the median of our freshman class.

Although certain fields and general ideas appear more than once, the problems do not fall into types. Thus the examination would not lend itself to special coaching or cramming. Most of the problems have a little twist that involves perceptive thinking on the part of the solver. Thus they test ingenuity, originality, and a thorough grasp of principles rather than memory.

These examinations are definitely more difficult than any we have used for entrance. They are more like those we [at MIT] have used in scholarship or prize competitions, and the prize competitions for high school students now organized in various parts of the United States. They may well indicate courses for the candidates more comparable with those of our few outstanding high schools of science and independent schools than the run-of-the-mill courses.

The question immediately arises as to how well Soviet applicants do in these examinations. No statistics are available, but some indication of the achievement level in the mathematics examinations at Moscow University is given in Kolmogorov's article, as follows:

> . . . one should not assume that universities accept only those who solve all the problems given at the examination. (At the entrance examinations for admission to the Moscow State University in 1953, only very few students solved all six problems; correct solution of four out of six problems was rated as a very good result; and only those who failed to solve at least two problems were unconditionally denied admission.)[24]

Physics and Chemistry

The entrance examinations in physics and in chemistry are oral. Like all entrance examinations, they are supposed to be conducted in accordance with the instructions and within the scope of a single syllabus prescribed by the Ministry of Higher Education for each subject, the same syllabus being equally applicable in all schools of higher education, whether universities, engineering institutes, or normal schools.

The syllabi in physics and in chemistry enumerate in considerable detail all the topics in these subjects which are included in the corresponding ten-year school syllabi and textbooks, but they give no meaningful indication as to the level of response required of the applicant to merit a passing grade. The 1955 syllabus for the entrance examination in physics, for instance, states that the purpose of the examination is:

> . . . to reveal the degree to which the student understands the nature of physical phenomena; the ability to interpret the physical meaning of magnitudes which appear in one or another formula; and also the ability to solve problems and appropriately to analyze the results and conclusions incidental thereto.[25]

The text of the syllabus, however, merely lists the various topics as they might be given in a table of contents of a textbook, and includes no reference as to the type of any problems which presumably may be given in the course of examination.

The following eight fields of physics are represented in the syllabus: mechanics (54 topics); oscillations, waves, and sound (17 topics); liquids and gases (22 topics); molecular-kinetic theory (6 topics); heat (38 topics); electricity (96 topics); optics and light (57 topics); the structure of the atom (8 topics). Broadly speaking, the distribution of topics (298 in all) corresponds to the distribution of topics taught in the physics course of the ten-year school and is quite similar, for instance, to the distribution of topics included in the example of the final tenth-grade examination in physics cited in Chapter 3. Some of the comments made in that chapter with reference to the contents of the final examination apply with even greater force to the more comprehensive syllabus of the entrance examination requirements. This syllabus contains a number of topics not usually taught in the majority of American high schools, among them such topics in modern physics as the concept of quanta and emission and absorption of energy by an atom. The observation previously made on the relatively heavy emphasis of the ten-year school curricula on the application of physics in engineering and technology is even more strongly exemplified in the syllabus of the entrance examination, which lists such topics as the working principles of reactive motors, hydraulic presses, steam engines, internal combustion engines, three-phase motors, and transformers; and refers to industrial installations of various types, such as power plants.

The 1955 syllabus also reflects the currently diminishing but still strong preoccupation with the priorities of Russian and Soviet contributions in the field of physics; among the topics devoted to this theme are these:

K. E. Tsiyolkovskii, the pioneer of jet propulsion theory
N. E. Zhukovskii and the world-wide importance of his work in the field of aviation

184 Soviet Education

M. V. Lomonosov, theory on the structure of matter
The inventor of steam engines, I. I. Polzunov
A. N. Lodygin's incandescent lamp
The discovery of the electric arc by Academician V. V. Petrov
The inventor of electric welding, N. G. Slavyanov
The invention of the transformer by P. N. Yablochkov
The invention of the radio by A. S. Popov.

The 1954 syllabus contained a specific injunction: "The student must be familiar with the discoveries in the field of physics made by the outstanding Russian scientists and inventors." Reflecting more recent attitudes, the 1955 syllabus stipulates familiarity with the discoveries made "by Russian, Soviet, and the leading foreign scientists and inventors."

The syllabus of the examination in chemistry is similarly constructed. It lists some 189 topics under twenty-two major headings, of which nine deal with fundamental theory (64 topics) and the other thirteen (125 topics) are largely descriptive, with topics on metallurgical processes, metals, and specific elements, including the following:

1. Hydrogen (7 topics).
2. Halogens (10 topics).
3. Oxygen (8 topics).
4. Sulphur (13 topics).
5. Nitrogen (12 topics).
6. Phosphorus (7 topics).
7. Carbon (32 topics).
8. Silicon (5 topics).
9. Metals, general properties (7 topics).
10. Alkali metals (5 topics).
11. Calcium (6 topics).
12. Aluminum (5 topics).
13. Iron (8 topics).

The sections dealing largely with the fundamentals of theory include the following:

1. Chemical and physical phenomena (4 topics).
2. Simple and compound substances (6 topics).
3. Fundamentals of atomic-molecular theory (10 topics).
4. Valence (6 topics).
5. Solutions (7 topics).
6. Oxides, bases, acids, and salts (15 topics).
7. Electrolytic dissociation (6 topics).
8. Periodic law (6 topics).
9. Radioactive substances and radioactive decay (4 topics).

Compared with the composition of American College Entrance Examination Board tests in chemistry, the distribution of topics (64 in fundamentals and 125 in largely descriptive and applied categories) suggests that on the whole the Soviet applicant is rated somewhat less on his knowledge of theory in chemistry than is his American counterpart.

Foreign Languages

With very few exceptions, the admission procedure in Soviet institutions of higher learning includes an oral test in one of the following foreign languages: English, German, French, or (since 1955) Spanish.* Thus, according to the published basic rules, all applicants to engineering schools and science faculties of the universities must take an entrance examination in a foreign language. However, in a supplement to the rules of admission for 1955 it is stated that all applicants to agricultural schools, including those selecting an engineering specialty, are excused from the entrance test in foreign language.[26] The same supplement also contains another informative provision: "Persons who, in their Certificate of Maturity, do not have a grade in a foreign language are excused from having to take an entrance examination in a foreign language. . . ." In theory all holders of the certificate of graduation from a ten-year school should have had the prescribed instruction in one foreign language (a total of 660 class hours over a period of 5 years, in grades V through X); it is evident, however, that not all schools have been able to provide language instruction.†

According to the published rules, those applicants who are required to take the language examination are expected to know how to read, to know the fundamentals of grammar including syntax, to possess a vocabulary "sufficient to understand foreign texts of medium diffi-

* The following categories of applicants are not required to take foreign language tests:
    Those applying to schools which train in "physical culture specialties"
    Applicants to the (2-year) Teachers' Institutes for training in other than foreign language courses
    Those applying for admission to certain accelerated courses of training in engineering and agricultural schools.
The rules also except from the foreign language test most of the applicants to those institutions of higher education in which the language of instruction is other than Russian. Also excused are applicants for admission to schools (or faculties) of animal husbandry and veterinary training.

† "It is well known that in many schools, particularly in the rural areas, foreign languages are not taught at all, and in a number of other schools this subject is taught by a nonspecialist as a sideline." *Izvestiya,* September 15, 1955, in a letter to the editor.

culty," to understand the spoken language, and to be able to respond orally to questions or to comment on a given text. The use of a dictionary is permitted in the oral translation test, which apparently constitutes the major part of the examination. Judging by the many laments in the Soviet educational literature on the low level of average achievement of the ten-year school graduates in foreign languages, the entrance requirements are probably not very high in absolute terms. In any event, foreign language instruction in Soviet institutions of higher education (compulsory in nearly all curricula) starts at the elementary level. Furthermore, a given student does not necessarily continue to study the language of his original choice; in some curricula a specific language, usually English, is prescribed. In general, it would seem that the Soviet entrance test in languages is not very demanding.

The most significant difference revealed in comparing entrance examinations in the Soviet Union with their nearest American counterpart, the College Board tests, is not in the topical content but in procedure. The written College Board tests, having a large number of questions of varying difficulty ranging broadly over the entire field of a subject, permit objective grading and statistical comparison of results. The oral examinations given in the Soviet institutions of higher learning (graded "excellent," "good," "satisfactory," and "unsatisfactory") naturally leave more to chance and to the individual propensities of the examiner; and evaluation of the level of achievement, both absolute and relative, is largely dependent on the examiner's attitude. Furthermore, the American College Board aptitude tests provide a basis for determining the field of study—humanities, arts, engineering, or science—most likely to be fruitful for a given student. In Soviet practice, "the results upon which the question of admission hinges frequently derive from a mechanical summation of grades obtained at the entrance examinations";[27] that is, whatever the prospective field of study, the grades received in different subjects have equal weight. The present system of competition fails to distinguish, for instance, between two students whose combined grades are the same, although one of the students received a low grade in mathematics and the other in foreign language. An oral test *can* provide the most effective means of ascertaining the scope, the level, and the quality of a student's knowledge. One questions whether the Soviet examiners, facing scores and hundreds of applicants progressively during the examination period (August 1 through August 20), are able to maintain the required level of thoroughness; and, even more importantly, whether the academic criterion is the only criterion employed by the individual examiners and the admissions committee.

4. Other Factors in the Selection Process

It is certain that in the past other than academic criteria—"proletarian origin," political reliability, Party endorsement—were given considerable weight in the selection process. Aside from such political or ideological considerations, which now may have been largely eliminated, there remains The Plan, perhaps the single most important parameter to which all variables of academic selection and quality must adjust themselves. We would emphasize again that the size of the freshman class in each faculty is predetermined for the country as a whole and for each school. The number of applicants for admission to a given faculty of a given institution may fall short of, equal, or greatly exceed the number which must finally be enrolled as freshmen—but the planned enrollment must be met. Therefore the admissions criteria, including the standards of examination, must necessarily vary from institution to institution, from faculty to faculty, and from year to year. The nature of the problem is well illustrated by a comment by Professor Kolmogorov in the article to which we referred earlier in this chapter:

> The quotas for admission to the freshman classes of our institutions of higher education at the present time [1952] are so large that even at the Moscow University the main concern of the admissions and of the examining committee is not to lose a single applicant who is sufficiently well prepared and is capable of serious work in a given faculty.[28]

Elsewhere the article states that the quota for freshmen in the mathematics faculties was increased in 1952 and points out how important it is that the expanded quota be filled by those who not only are sufficiently well prepared but also *like* mathematics.[29]

The case just cited illustrates the problem of a sudden increase in the academic load of one department. The opposite effect of the bureaucratically controlled allocation of school vacancies, that of a sudden decrease in the load, also presents major problems. For instance, the Lvov Polytechnic Institute had for some years enrolled 100 freshmen for training in the "Geology and Exploration of Oil and Gas Deposits." In 1955 the matriculation quota was cut to only 25 freshmen without prior adjustment in the size and composition of the teaching personnel of the faculty in question.[30] Still another variation of the same problem arises when a school is directed to admit students for training in some field for which it lacks either the teaching personnel or the laboratory facilities or both. For example, as reported by the director of the Kharkov Polytechnic Institute:

... in 1954 the plan was for our institute to matriculate a group of students to be trained in "Machinery and Apparatus of the Food Industries." The institute has neither the laboratory base nor the personnel for training engineers of this specialty.[31]

In the meantime, the author points out, the institute was in a position to expand its enrollment in the fields of hydraulic, turbine, and internal combustion engineering for which the institute has ample resources; but "in these specialties for some years now no plan has been made for us to expand the enrollment." It is clear that the existing Soviet method of allocating admissions quotas not only affects the standards of selection but also creates problems of under- and over-utilization of the academic resources of a given institution.

It is difficult to assess accurately the influence of the national quota system for admissions to the institutions of higher education, but there is no doubt that it is a major factor controlling the academic selection process. As previously noted, the ratio of the number of applicants to the number admitted as freshmen has been increasing in postwar years, largely because of a considerable increase in the number of new ten-year school graduates. According to a recent article in *Narodnoye obrazovaniye* (No. 3, 1956), the total number of ten-year school graduates during a 5-year period (1950–1955) was somewhat under 3,000,000; of these, the article states, only 1,380,000 or some 46 per cent were accepted for training at the institutions of higher education. This over-all ratio of better than two contenders for each vacancy (counting only the recent graduates of the ten-year schools alone) would imply an opportunity for careful selection; but it is clear that this opportunity is likely to be unevenly distributed between, for instance, Moscow University, outstanding in prestige, facilities, and teaching personnel, and a provincial normal school—a situation to be found in any educational system but which has special consequences for the Soviet student. It will be remembered that an applicant may file his application at only one school in a given year. If he fails one of the entrance examinations, or, having passed, still fails to qualify for admission according to the competitive system, in some cases he may nevertheless gain admission to another school where either the examination which he failed is not required or the competition is not so keen. But, apparently, this last-minute transfer of application and of examination grades can be made only by special arrangement, since the published rules contain no provision for the transfer of credentials by rejected candidates. It is likely that transfer practices vary, depending on the supply-demand ratio of applicants. In the 1954 Handbook of Moscow University, for instance, it was stated that a number of other institutions of higher learning were represented on its Committee to deal with the transfer of surplus applicants;[32] the 1955 edition of the Handbook does not mention alternative opportunities for applicants failing of admission to the institution of first choice.

Thus, inevitably the small number of elite institutions in the few larger educational centers such as Moscow, Leningrad, Kharkov, and Kiev find themselves in the advantageous position of having a large surplus of applicants from which they can select the academically most promising contingent to fill the quota; and the most advantageous position in this respect is occupied by those schools or faculties which train for the most highly rated occupations, presumably science and engineering. However, in the end, the selection process as it operates throughout the Soviet educational system is most strongly characterized by the nationally fixed quota on the one hand and, on the other, by the relative indifference and passivity of the average student as to his choice of *specific* field of higher education. As one Soviet educator recently stated:

> Experience has shown that not infrequently the applicants address themselves to those institutions where it is easier to pass examinations. Striving to gain admission to any school of higher education, they request, lest they lose a year, to be considered for admission to any one of the faculties [for which they may qualify].[33]

In the mind of a Soviet student a completed formal training at an advanced level is a necessary and sufficient requirement for an immediate advancement in his social and material standing and for a desirable subsequent career. It is clear that the relative indifference to the particular field of advanced training, coupled with the relatively large current supply of applicants, assures that the planned vacancies, even in the fields of training which intrinsically may be least desired by the average applicant, are competitively filled. It is equally clear that in this competition the ambition to get ahead is far stronger than motivations deriving from natural aptitudes or intellectual curiosity.

Comments by foreign observers on the social backgrounds of the student body suggest yet another set of factors which may play an important role in the selection process. Whereas in the early days of the Soviet rule much emphasis was placed on the growing percentage of students of worker and peasant origin (58 per cent in 1931),* no statistics showing social distribution have been published for many

---

* It may be noted, however, that this share was considerably short of the earlier targets; for instance, the Central Committee's resolution of November 16, 1929 directed that "the percentage be brought within a few years to not less than 70 per cent."

years. Indirect indications, including the testimony of several observers interviewed in connection with this study, strongly suggest that the student body has progressively become weighted in favor of children of Party officials, civil servants, officers of the armed forces, and other elite groups whose relatively privileged positions are linked to the maintenance and continuity of the present regime.

A French student who attended Moscow University in 1948 and a German student enrolled at Leningrad University in 1953 estimated that some 50 per cent of the student body were of such background, while well under 10 per cent were distinctly of working-class origin.[34] One returned German scientist reported a systematic policy of piling difficulties in the way of the admission of children with suspected anticommunist family backgrounds. When children of several German specialists applied for admission to the science faculties at Moscow and Leningrad they were shunted, with rather flimsy excuses, to the philology and foreign language faculties. Another German scientist interviewed in the course of our study stated that a number of vacancies at the institutions of higher learning are reserved for active Party members whose Party work takes up so much time that they cannot competitively qualify on the basis of academic achievement.

5. Mobility and Term of Study

For a variety of reasons, both institutional and personal, there is every probability that once a Soviet student is admitted to a particular faculty of an institution of higher learning he will remain in the same school and as a rule under the faculty of original designation for the rest of his undergraduate course. In effect, his choice of vocational opportunities or fields of professional activity is almost irrevocably and rather narrowly predetermined when as a freshman he enters a particular compartment of the system for training specialists. The lack of horizontal mobility between the universities and the specialized industrial engineering institutes is particularly significant, since, inasmuch as science and mathematics majors are offered only at the universities, it is difficult, if not impossible, for a young student to rectify what originally might have been a mistaken choice between science and engineering. It is doubtful that the average Soviet student attempts a shift even if the course to which he has been admitted is not his first choice.

On the other hand, administratively initiated transfers of students from one field of study to another occur frequently, most likely in response to discrepancies between yesterday's planned allocation by specialties and today's judgment of the anticipated need. For instance, at the beginning of the 1955–1956 academic year a considerable number of students in their second, third, and even fourth year of study were shifted from the courses of their original designation to other specialties. This move, it was explained, was made in order to "increase the output of specialists in electrification of industrial enterprises, in industrial and civil construction, in technology of machine construction, in accounting, and in other specialties."[35] Similarly, administrative transfers from one institution to another occur frequently, as when students are selected for training in the military schools or transferred for organizational reasons. A school may be closed, consolidated, or relocated on short notice. Such transfers may or may not be advantageous to a particular student, but they do not interrupt the continuity of his training.

For all practical purposes, resident students attending Soviet schools of higher education are not subject to military draft. Depending on the field of study, they are either deferred for the duration of the course or exempted from active military duty altogether—as are the majority of engineering students.[36] Once accepted, any Soviet student who maintains passing grades (provided he is able to finance himself in the event his grades fall below the minimum required for a scholarship) is likely to remain in an institution of higher learning for the prescribed term of instruction.

The term of instruction differs with the type of school, ranging from 2 years in the normal schools of junior-college type* to 6 years in medical schools, as the following examples show:

Type of School	Term of Instruction
Teachers' Institutes	2 years
Pedagogical [Normal] Institutes	4 years
Universities	5 years
Institutes	from 4 to 5.5 years
Medical schools	6 years

In the evening faculties and divisions of the regular schools and institutes the normal term of undergraduate instruction is from 5 years and 10 months to 6 years. Within the "institute" category, most of the resident engineering schools have a 4 year and 10 month term of instruction; a number of schools, however, have a 5 year and

* *Uchitel'skii institut* (Teachers' Institute) (category XVIII–4 in Table 25) is a type of school which will probably be discontinued; there were 196 such schools in 1946 but only 52 as of January 1955.

6 month term—Moscow (Bauman) Higher Technical School being one example.

It is important to note that, along with the normally scheduled terms of instruction listed above, some emergency, or accelerated, programs for the training of engineers have been revived. Thus, for instance, in 1953 the Minister of Culture, P. K. Ponamarenko, stated:

> During this year special faculties for training mechanical-engineers-for-agriculture in a two-year term of instruction must be organized in order to assist in raising the qualifications of the Machine-Tractor Station directors and chief engineers who have had specialized secondary education [technicum] and who have revealed themselves in a positive light in their work for a number of years. It is scheduled to establish these faculties at five institutes of Mechanization and Electrification of Agriculture . . . [and at two other schools] with a total yearly admissions quota of 700 students.[37]

Even more significant is the fact that both the 1954 and the 1955 general admission rules applicable to all higher schools provide for a distinct category of applicants as follows:[38]

> Those applying to the sections of accelerated preparation in institutions of higher technical training (2 years 4 months) which enroll persons who are graduates of a specialized secondary school and have had three years of work experience in their specialty and also persons who have incomplete higher education. . . .

At the White-Russia Polytechnic Institute, for instance, "one of the regular graduations from its department of accelerated training of engineers—in 2 years and 4 months"—was to take place in the fourth quarter of 1955.[39] It is not, however, ascertainable how numerous these abbreviated programs have become and how many of the emergency-trained individuals are included in the rapidly expanded current output of graduates classified as engineers—71.2 thousand in 1956.[40]

6. Attrition and the Rate of Graduation

Statistics on matriculation, enrollment, and graduation of resident students (including part-time evening students) in recent years are given in Table 35. For reasons shown on the preceding pages, the number of Soviet students who, once admitted, do not continue to graduation is made up largely of those who fail to meet the academic requirements. Consequently, the attrition rate or its complement, the rate of graduation, for the Soviet system should be highly indicative of the correspondence between the academic achievement of the students and the standards of academic performance maintained by the schools. Unfortunately, no direct and sufficiently detailed data are available to permit a comprehensive analysis of the graduation scores achieved by succeeding school generations of various categories. It is possible, however, roughly to establish by indirect methods the order of magnitude of academic casualties (from all causes) for the entire system of higher schools. Furthermore, the available data permit us to examine the record of the resident and extension components of the Soviet training effort separately.

TABLE 35.   RESIDENT SCHOOLS* OF HIGHER EDUCATION:
MATRICULATION, ENROLLMENT, AND GRADUATION
USSR
1944–1956

Year	Matriculated (thousands)	Enrollment (thousands)	Graduated (thousands)
1944–1945		(411.9)†	49.2
1945–1946	176.5	539.2	67.3
1946–1947	206.0	649.5	86.3
1947–1948	194.2	705.6	121.5
1948–1949	193.6	734.4	138.3
1949–1950	210.2	778.2	147.9
1950–1951	237.5	845.1	168.4
1951–1952	255.5	918.2	175.8
1952–1953	260.8	971.5	172.0
1953–1954	281.7	1,042.7	174.4
1954–1955	299.1	1,146.5	183.8
Ten years	2,315.1	Average: 833	1,435.7
1955–1956	285.6	1,227.9	
1956–1957			
1957–1958			

Source: Kul'turnoye stroitel'stvo SSSR, 1956, pp. 201–204.

* Including evening (part-time) schools; new students matriculated in 1955 included:

90 per cent full-time day students	257.2 thousand
10 per cent part-time evening students	28.4 thousand

† Estimated.

As a rough index of the academic mortality rate among the resident students the following computation, for instance, can be made (all figures are in thousands), as shown in Table 35:

	Thousands
1. 1944–1945 total resident enrollment (412 thousand) less spring 1945 graduating class (49 thousand)	363
2. Add: New students matriculated during the 10-year period, 1945–1954	2,315
	2,678
3. Deduct: Graduations, 1946–1955	1,436
	1,242
4. Add: Students matriculated in the fall of 1955	286
Hypothetical 1955–1956 enrollment assuming no dropouts	1,528
Actual 1955–1956 resident enrollment	1,228
Difference accumulated over the period of 10 years, thousands	300

Assuming that these official statistics correctly represent the actual progression of the school population, and, therefore, that the average enrollment was 833,000 for the 10-year period, the attrition of 30,000 students per year is 3.6 per cent of the yearly average enrollment—a remarkably low figure.

Assuming that the term of instruction in the resident schools of the Soviet Union is 5 years on the average, the data shown in Table 35 can be arranged to give another even more pertinent rough estimate— the per cent of a specific generation of first-time students surviving to graduation; that is, the number of students graduated during a 5-year period can be related to the number admitted during the preceding 5 years, as follows:

$$\text{"Success ratio"} = \frac{1951\text{--}1955 \text{ resident graduates } 874}{1946\text{--}1950 \text{ first-time students } 1,041} = 84 \text{ per cent}$$

In any direct comparison of the retention rate of the Soviet school system with a similarly computed percentage for colleges in the United States many factors would have to be considered before the respective two scores could be considered reasonably commensurable. Neverthe-less, we would note that the ratio of the number of graduates to the number of first-time students (taken with a 4-year lag) for the United States has been running in the neighborhood of only 60 per cent.[41] This crude index, it is interesting to note, corresponds rather closely with a number of other more refined estimates of the academic attrition rate in the United States. One estimate (current as of c. 1953) gave the following ratio:[42]

	Thousands	Per Cent
Number entering college	442	100.0
Number graduating	261	59.0

The National Manpower Council stated that "About two-fifths of those who start college—many with superior ability—do not graduate."[43] A few years ago the Department of Health, Education, and Welfare initiated a "Study of College Student Retention and Withdrawal." The tentative tabulation of its findings shows that of 12,643 unmarried, nonveteran students who entered schools in 1950 as first-time registrants 38.62 per cent graduated in 1954.[44] (It may be noted that in the privately controlled institutions 46.6 per cent of the students in the sample graduated in 1954—as against 32.5 per cent in the publicly controlled schools.)*

The score shows the per cent of students graduating in *4 calendar years*, whether at the institution of original registration or elsewhere, but it does not include those students who for various reasons (military duty, health, economic) may have dropped out but temporarily. Thus the "ultimate" graduation ratio of the sample may approach but can hardly be expected to exceed the previously indicated national average of approximately 60 per cent. As against this figure our rough estimate for the Soviet Union is 84 per cent.

It is difficult to believe that such a high score could normally be maintained against a set of rigidly enforced academic standards. It also seems extremely doubtful that *any method* of preselection could be so effective as to assure consistently the low rate of attrition which Soviet school statistics would imply; and, as has been shown, the Soviet admission procedures and standards, quite apart from the question of their methodological effectiveness, are neither uniform nor consistent.

To what extent the remarkable retention record in the Soviet institutions of higher education merely demonstrates the power of The Plan is a matter of conjecture. It would seem that the planners must use a certain predetermined coefficient in calculating the rate at which students are enrolled versus the required rate of graduation. Thus there are not only admission quotas but also, we may assume, quotas for graduations. Ample indirect evidence points to a compelling urge on the part of everyone concerned to promote from year to year and eventually to graduate every student, presumably in compliance with

* This unquestionably reflects the difference in the admission standards in the private versus the publicly controlled institutions. Similarly, for instance, at the Massachusetts Institute of Technology (one of the 147 schools participating in the study) 61 per cent of the students selected for the sample graduated in 1954, as against the average of 42.7 for all technological institutes included in the sample.

the quota rather than on the basis of achievement alone. A contrary assumption would be difficult to reconcile with the numerous separate cases and examples of poor scholarship cited in the Soviet press.

Almost 15 per cent of the students enrolled in the Physics Faculty and 10 per cent of those enrolled in the Radio-Physical Faculty of Tomsk University [after the 1953–1954 winter examinations] had academic indebtedness.

. . . in many cases the low level of achievement can be explained by the fact that students are overburdened by compulsory [scheduled] work.

. . . in this [Physics-Mathematics] faculty [of the Moscow Pedagogical Institute], with a total enrollment of 660 students, 136 have not fulfilled the academic plan; 26 received two unsatisfactory grades; 13 received three unsatisfactory [mid-year] grades.[45]

In the face of these and many similar comments it appears that, as is the case with the selection process, The Plan plays a considerable if not a decisive role in the maintenance of a very high ratio of promotions and graduations among resident students attending Soviet schools of higher education.

No direct admission of this fact is likely to be found in Soviet comments on the problems of education; but there have been many Soviet references to the examination and promotion practices which clearly show that the selection is far from being on merit alone. We cite here a few illustrative excerpts from one recent source.

An article in *Komsomol'skaya pravda* (November 23, 1956) points out that the number of potential freshmen (ten-year school graduates) has greatly increased in recent years. The writer of that article observes that although this development should facilitate the selection of "the most talented and diligent" individuals for higher education, the standards of training have been dropping. He attributes these phenomena to two basic factors:

. . . incorrect organization of entrance examinations and an artificially created atmosphere of guardianship over students during their years of training.

He goes on to say that regular teachers seldom serve as examiners:

Their place . . . is often taken by people who have no teaching experience. Frequently students are selected by people who do not teach in the given institution.

The examinations, he implies, are hurriedly conducted because the examiners are paid on piece-work basis—so much "per head."

Perhaps even more important, the author of this article states that, with the steadily increasing number of ten-year school graduates vis-à-vis a fixed number of vacancies, "crammers" have appeared. These tutors

... for fairly high payments "cram" young men and women who have just graduated [from the ten-year school]. Experience shows that such "cramming," which, naturally, cannot give real knowledge, proves to be a more reliable way of entering an institution of higher education than a thorough mastery of the school courses.

... under the existing system entrance examinations ... do not provide a reliable method of selecting the most able and most industrious young people for the institutions of higher education.

On the progression of students to graduation, the author of this article gives no detailed analysis but categorically states that:

The expulsion of a student from an institution of higher education is now an exceptional event. The entire work in the higher educational establishments is so organized as to avoid expulsions.

Correspondence Students' Graduation Rates

Table 36 gives matriculation, enrollment, and graduation statistics for the entire system of Soviet higher education by correspondence—special divisions of the regular schools and institutions which provide instruction exclusively by correspondence. In contrast with the low rate of attrition among the resident students, a very large per cent of the students enrolled in the Soviet extension courses drop out. Moreover, it is obvious that on the average those who continue to graduation take many more than the prescribed 6 years to complete the course. This conclusion rests on the fact that the number of extension training graduates relative to the enrollment is very low even if one allows for a high rate of attrition and a currently expanding enrollment. For instance, one extension engineering institute with an enrollment (1954–1955) of 6,500 students graduated only 503 students in 3 years, as follows:[46]

Year	Number Graduating
1952	141
1953	162
1954	200

In 1955 *Moscow Pravda* said that 19,000 students were enrolled in the All-Union Correspondence Polytechnic Institute. Another source said that in 1955 "more than 500 students" graduated from the same institute.[47] Even with a generous allowance for a possibly expanding enrollment, this number is extremely low considering that the nominal term

TABLE 36.   CORRESPONDENCE SCHOOLS OF HIGHER EDUCATION:
MATRICULATION, ENROLLMENT, AND GRADUATION
USSR
1944–1956

Year	Matriculated (thousands)	Enrollment (thousands)	Graduated (thousands)
1944–1945		(87.2)*	5.4
1945–1946	109.2	191.0	8.7
1946–1947	121.2	222.2	12.2
1947–1948	86.9	258.0	16.5
1948–1949	98.2	297.7	24.3
1949–1950	114.1	353.9	29.0
1950–1951	111.6	402.3	33.0
1951–1952	118.9	437.9	43.4
1952–1953	126.5	470.0	48.2
1953–1954	149.1	519.3	60.4
1954–1955	169.9	584.0	62.0
Ten years	1,205.6	Average: 373.6	337.7
1955–1956	175.8	639.1	
1956–1957			
1957–1958			

Source: *Kul'turnoye stroitel'stvo SSSR, 1956*, pp. 202–204.

* Estimated.

of instruction is 6 years. The relatively low rate of graduation and
relatively high attrition among the extension students of one institution
was reported by an American visitor to the Soviet Union in 1955:

> The Voroshilovgrad Pedagogical Institute . . . has 1,700 regular stu-
> dents and 3,000 correspondence students. This year they graduated
> something like 250 to 270 correspondence students . . . these figures
> suggest that not all correspondence students complete the six-year
> course.[48]

The attrition of extension students can be estimated more generally
and compared with the graduation score of the resident schools on the
basis of data in Table 36, as follows:

		Thousands
1.	1944–1945 total correspondence enrollment (87.2 thousand) less spring 1945 graduating class (5.4 thousand)	81.8
2.	Add: New students matriculated during the 10-year period, 1945–1954	1,205.6
		1,287.4

	Thousands
3. Deduct: Graduations, 1946–1955	337.7
	949.7
4. Add: Students matriculated in the fall of 1955	175.8
Hypothetical 1955–1956 enrollment assuming no dropouts	1,125.5
Actual 1955–1956 enrollment	639.1
Difference accumulated over the period of 10 years, thousands	486.4

This gives an average yearly attrition of 48.6 thousand or 13 per cent of the average enrollment of 374,000—nearly four times the comparable ratio for the resident schools, and some 40 per cent of the yearly average of new students (120,000) admitted during 1945–1954.*

The estimated "success ratio" for resident students showed that approximately 84 out of 100 freshmen entering a Soviet institution of higher education will graduate 5 years later. A lag of 6 years is more appropriate for the correspondence school students. On that basis, again using the data in Table 36, the "success ratio" of the correspondence students can be estimated as follows:

$$\frac{1951–1955 \text{ correspondence graduates } 247}{1945–1949 \text{ first-time students } 529.6} = 46.6 \text{ per cent}$$

It is evident, therefore, that the productivity of the Soviet system of training by correspondence is extremely low. Nevertheless, because of the large number involved in this type of training, some 35 per cent of the total college enrollment, the correspondence school graduates comprise a significant part of the yearly increment to the pool of trained Soviet manpower. In the 1946–1950 period correspondence school graduates accounted for only 14 per cent of the total number; in 1951–1955 (fifth Five Year Plan) more than 22 per cent of all higher school graduates came from the correspondence classes (Table 37). The announced plan for 1956–1960 sets as a target the graduation of 1,680,000 from institutions of higher learning in 5 years; if the present trend of an increasing reliance on the output of the correspondence facilities continues, about 35 per cent of the 1956–1960 total (or nearly 600,000) may be expected to be so trained.

Here we may note (as a postscript to Chapter 4 on the technicums) that correspondence training at the technicum level appears also to

* A director of an extension institute, commenting on the correspondence instruction, stated that attrition reaches "sometimes 20 and more per cent [base not specified]." *Vestnik vysshei shkoly,* No. 11, November 1954, p. 22.

TABLE 37. GRADUATIONS FROM INSTITUTIONS OF HIGHER EDUCATION BY
SELECTED CATEGORIES AND BY TYPES OF TRAINING
USSR
1946–1955 and 1956 Actual; 1956–1960 Plan
(Thousands of Graduates)

Category	1946–1950 Actual	1951–1955 Actual	1956–1960 Plan	1956 Actual
Engineering		255	510 (?)	71
Agriculture		92	184 (?)	26
Subtotal	174	347	694	97
Other	478	774	986	
Total	652	1,121	1,680	
of these:				
Resident schools	561	874		
Correspondence courses	91	247		

Sources: Tables 35 and 36 and *Vestnik vysshei shkoly*, No. 3, March 1956, pp. 3 and 4.

TABLE 38. NUMBER OF GRADUATES FROM INSTITUTIONS OF HIGHER EDUCATION
(VUZY) AND FROM SPECIALIZED SECONDARY SCHOOLS (TECHNICUMS AND
SIMILAR) TRAINED IN RESIDENT AND IN CORRESPONDENCE COURSES
DURING THE FOURTH AND FIFTH FIVE YEAR PLANS
USSR
1946–1950 and 1951–1955

Period	Level of Training	Resident	Corre-spondence	Total	
		Thousands	Thousands	Thousands	Per Cent
Five years 1946–1950	Technicum	1,156	122	1,278	66
	College (VUZ)	561	91	652	34
	Combined Per Cent	1,717 89.0	213 11.0	1,930 100.0	100
Five years 1951–1955	Technicum	1,436	124	1,560	58
	College (VUZ)	874	247	1,121	42
	Combined Per Cent	2,310 86.2	371 13.8	2,681 100.0	100
Ten years 1946–1955	Technicum	2,592	246	2,838	62
	College (VUZ)	1,435	338	1,773	38
	Combined Per Cent	4,027 87.3	584 12.7	4,611 100.0	100

Sources: Tables 35 and 36 and *The National Economy of the USSR, 1956,* p. 235.

suffer from a slow rate of progression, large attrition, and generally low efficiency. Table 38, in which resident and correspondence graduations for both the colleges and the technicums are given, shows, for instance, that in the 10-year period 1946–1955 out of 2,838,000 technicum graduates only 246,000 (approximately 8.7 per cent) were correspondence graduates.

7. SOME CONCLUSIONS FROM SOVIET STATISTICS

The graduating class of the Soviet resident schools of higher education in 1955 was larger than in any previous year: 183.8 thousand. It represented an increase of 80 per cent over the prewar peak of 102.2 thousand resident graduates in 1940.

Approximately 55 per cent of the 1955 graduates were women, who constituted about 40 per cent of the graduates of schools for industry, construction, transport, and communications and about 80 per cent of the graduates of schools for teacher training. More than 25 per cent of all 1955 graduates were trained as school teachers—the majority in the Pedagogical Institutes (4-year course) and some in the Teachers' Institutes (2-year course). Some 35 per cent were graduates of the engineering and technological schools, including 13,000 engineering graduates specializing in machine and instrument construction. About 10 per cent of all graduates completed a 5-year university course—more than half of them in science and nearly a quarter of them in physics and mathematics.

Soviet graduation statistics, whenever published, are usually arranged by general categories of schools associated with (1) industry and construction, (2) transport and communications, (3) agriculture, (4) economics and law, (5) education, (6) health, physical education, and sports, and (7) the arts and motion pictures. Another type of distribution gives the number of graduates by general fields of specialization. Graduation statistics for 1955 are shown in Table 39 by categories of schools and in Table 40 by broad fields of training. From these arrangements of Soviet statistics we can discern two significant trends.

First, the graduates from schools for industry, construction, transport, and communications in 1955 accounted for 26.8 per cent of the total graduating class—an increase over the average share of these graduates in the previous years. (For the 1946–1950 period—fourth Five Year Plan—the average was 20.6 per cent—134,000 out of a total of 652,000 graduates; for the 5-year period 1951–1955 it was 23.1.) That continuing emphasis is given to training specialists in this category is further indicated by the steadily increasing proportion of admissions to industrial, construction, transport, and communications schools. In 1945 the freshmen matriculated in these schools accounted for 21.7 per cent of the total number of new students; in 1950, for 24.6; in 1954, for 35.6; and in 1955, for 37.9 per cent.

Second, a continuing emphasis on training for basic and heavy industries is discernible from the listing of graduates by fields of specialization as shown in Table 40. For example, in 1950 the graduates trained in the fields of geology, exploration of useful mineral deposits, and development of deposits numbered 3,074; in 1955 the corresponding number was 9,266—an increase of 200 per cent. In machine and instrument construction the number of graduates increased from 9,101 to 15,736 in 1955. In contrast, the number of graduates trained in technology of food products decreased from 2,295 to 1,878.

TABLE 39. NUMBER OF GRADUATES BY TYPES OF SCHOOLS OF HIGHER EDUCATION AND BY TYPES OF TRAINING (RESIDENT AND CORRESPONDENCE)
USSR
1955

From Schools for:	All Graduates		Resident	Corre-spondence
	Thousands	Per Cent	Thousands	Thousands
Industry and construction	56.5	23.0	53.3	3.2
Transport and communications	9.5	3.8	9.1	0.4
Agriculture	24.1	9.8	23.0	1.1
Economics and law	15.6	6.4	9.1	6.5
Education*	120.8	49.2	70.6	50.2
Health, physical culture	16.8	6.8	16.3	0.5
Arts, motion pictures	2.5	1.0	2.4	0.1
All schools	245.8	100.0	183.8	62.0
Per cent	100.0		74.8	25.2

Source: Kul'turnoye stroitel'stvo SSSR, 1956, pp. 214 f.

* Includes university graduates and graduates of Pedagogical (4-year) and Teachers' (2-year) Institutes.

The statistics shown in Tables 39 and 40 tell us nothing about the composition of the *university*-trained graduates, that is, the composition of Soviet graduates in science; and there are no published data on the allocation of university students by science majors. However, the distribution of students by *faculties* has been given from time to time,* and such a distribution of the 115.6 thousand resident students enrolled

* See Table 30 for the list and number of university faculties.

TABLE 40. NUMBER OF GRADUATES BY FIELDS OF SPECIALIZATION IN RESIDENT
AND CORRESPONDENCE SCHOOLS OF HIGHER EDUCATION
USSR
1950 and 1955

	1950	1955	
Field of Training	Number	Number	% of 1950
Geology and exploration of deposits	1,721	3,976	231
Development of geological deposits	1,353	5,290	391
Power	2,380	4,957	208
Metallurgy	1,416	2,656	188
Machine and instrument construction	9,101	15,736	173
Electrical machines and instruments	1,433	2,981	208
Radio engineering and communications	1,427	2,950	207
Chemical technology	2,586	4,954	192
Lumber, pulp, cellulose, and paper	727	1,885	259
Technology of food products	2,295	1,878	82
Consumer goods technology	1,240	1,669	135
Construction	4,873	9,440	194
Geodesy and cartography	294	540	184
Hydrology and meteorology	379	628	166
Agriculture and forestry	12,859	24,563	191
Transportation	3,059	4,236	138
Economics	10,103	16,138	160
Law	5,648	8,126	144
Health and physical culture	20,747	16,943	82
Enlightenment [education]:			
Universities	12,323	15,560	126
Pedagogical and library institutes	78,529	98,249	125
Arts	2,376	2,491	105
All fields	176,869	245,846	139
In this total:			
Resident, full-time (day) students	145,817	179,229	123
Part-time evening students	2,029	4,603	227
Correspondence students	29,023	62,014	214

Source: Kul'turnoye stroitel'stvo SSSR, 1956, pp. 215, 217.

in the universities at the beginning of the 1955–1956 academic year is
shown in Table 41. The table shows that approximately 57 per cent
of the university students were enrolled in science faculties, 2 per cent
in technical faculties, and 41 per cent in all others. Among the science
faculties, physics and mathematics accounted for about 25 per cent of
the total enrollment.

We can conclude, then, if we assume the shown distribution to be
typical of the 1956 graduating class, that in 1956 Soviet university
graduates (see Table 42) included approximately 5,000 physicists and

TABLE 41. . University Enrollment by Faculties and Total for All
Thirty-Three Universities at the Beginning of the
1955–1956 Academic Year

USSR

Faculties		Enrollment	
Number	Name	Students	Per Cent
25	Physics-Mathematics	14,830	
6	Physics	6,254	
7	Mechanics-Mathematics	5,122	
2	Radio Physics	1,272	
1	Engineering Physics	1,362	
1	Natural Science-Mathematics	816	
	Subtotal	29,656	25.64
26	Chemistry	8,997	
1	Chemistry-Biology	399	
2	Natural Sciences	733	
13	Biology	3,241	
14	Biology-Soils	6,009	
1	Biology-Geography	233	
15	Geology	7,932	
1	Geology-Exploration	190	
9	Geology-Geography	4,137	
15	Geography	4,577	
	Subtotal	36,448	31.51
2	Engineering	481	
1	Construction Engineering	599	
1	Forestry Engineering	314	
1	Mechanical [Engineering]	750	
1	Radio Engineering and Communications	50	
	Subtotal	2,194	1.90
18	Law	6,946	
13	Economics	4,680	
1	Economics-Law	373	
4	Foreign Languages	1,514	
1	Foreign Languages and Literature	289	
2	Oriental Studies	125	
2	Oriental	367	
3	Journalism	1,588	
1	Agriculture	351	
3	Medical	1,864	
16	History	5,363	
18	Philology	13,130	
15	History-Philology	8,387	
1	History-Philosophy	656	
1	History-Law	452	
1	Physical Education	75	
2	Philosophy	618	
?	Faculties unspecified	576	
	Subtotal	47,354	40.95
247	Total enrollment	115,652	100.00

Source: Kul'turnoye stroitel'stvo SSSR, 1956, pp. 218–229.

TABLE 42. UNIVERSITY ENROLLMENT, RESIDENT STUDENTS, BY YEARS OF
THE COURSE AND TOTAL FOR ALL THIRTY-THREE UNIVERSITIES
AT THE BEGINNING OF THE 1955–1956 ACADEMIC YEAR
USSR

Year of the Course	Number of Students	Per Cent
First	22,779	19.7
Second	26,751	23.1
Third	24,752	21.4
Fourth	21,670	18.8
Fifth	19,700	17.0
Total	115,652	100.0

Source: Kul'turnoye stroitel'stvo, SSSR, 1956, pp. 218–229.
Note: The source also gives 1955–1956 total enrollment, first-year enrollment, and graduation in 1956 in figures which include *correspondence* students. Thus the number of correspondence students in these three categories can be determined as follows:

	Students, 1955–1956		
	Total Enrollment	First Year	Graduated
Resident and Correspondence	166,256	36,690	22,866
Resident only	115,652	22,779	19,700
Correspondence	50,604	13,911	3,166

mathematicians, not counting any correspondence school graduates who may also have been in these categories.

Looking ahead, and judging by the matriculation figures given in Table 36, the total number of graduates should continue to increase, reaching a new peak of approximately 250,000 in 1959, after which time and for some years the number is likely to decline considerably, partly because of the relative shortage of college-age population by 1960. Moreover, the fact that the number of resident students matriculated in the fall of 1955 showed a decrease of 5 per cent from the previous year while the number admitted to correspondence courses showed an increase of nearly 28 per cent suggests an increasing pressure forcing the Soviet government to channel the greatest possible number of the student-age population into the labor force.

NOTES TO CHAPTER 6

[1] V. P. Yelutin, "Vazhneishiye zadachi vysshei shkoly" (The Most Important Tasks of the Higher School), *Vestnik vysshei shkoly,* No. 3, March 1956, p. 3; also "Vdokhnovlyayushchiye perspektivy" (Inspiring Perspectives), *Vestnik vysshei shkoly,* No. 2, February 1956, p. 2.

[2] V. P. Yelutin, "Vazhneishiye zadachi vysshei shkoly," *op. cit.*, p. 4.

[3] Decree of the RSFSR Council of Commissars, August 2, 1918 (S. U. 1918, No. 57, Art. 632), quoted in *Direktivy VKP(b) i postanovleniya sovetskovo pravitel'stva o narodnom obrazovanii za 1917–1947 gg.*, Vol. II, p. 8.

[4] "Student i shkola zhizni" (Students and the School of Life), *Literaturnaya gazeta*, May 26, 1955, p. 2:1–2.

[5] V. I. Chernyshenko in *Vestnik vysshei shkoly*, No. 4, April 1954, p. 33.

[6] *Interview Report No. 5*, September 2, 1952, Department of State, Washington, D.C., p. 9.

[7] *New York Times*, April 18, 1954. Dr. Ashby is the author of *Scientist in Russia*, London: Penguin Books, Ltd., 1947, a pioneer study of outstanding value.

[8] Decree dated December 29, 1935. *Pravda*, December 30, 1935, No. 359 (6605), quoted in *Direktivy VKP(b) i postanovleniya sovetskovo pravitel'stva o narodnom obrazovanii za 1917–1947 gg.*, Vol. II, p. 89.

"To rescind . . . the limitations based on the social origin of persons entering these [higher schools and technicums] educational institutions, or on the limitation of rights of their parents."

[9] *Vestnik vysshei shkoly*, No. 4, April 1955, pp. 6–7.

[10] The decree passed on October 2, 1940 established tuition *retroactively* to September 1, that is, to the beginning of the academic year. (S.P. USSR, 1940, No. 27, Art. 637; quoted in *Vysshaya shkola*, compiled by M. I. Movshovich, p. 65.)

[11] *Ibid.*, pp. 73–78.

[12] *Ibid.*, p. 83.

[13] K. M. Barshauskas, "Prodolzhat' sovershenstvovaniye uchebnykh planov" (Continue Perfecting the Academic Plans), *Vestnik vysshei shkoly*, No. 2, February 1956.

[14] *Soviet Education*, n.p., September 1953, p. 17.

[15] Eric Ashby, *Scientist in Russia*, London: Penguin Books, Ltd., 1947, p. 74.

[16] *Soviet Education*, n.p., September 1953, p. 17.

[17] Paul J. Novgorotsev, *Russian Schools and Universities in the World War*, New Haven: Yale University Press, 1929, p. 141.

[18] *Vestnik vysshei shkoly*, No. 9, September 1956.

[19] *Pravila priema i programmy priemnykh ekzaminov dlya postupayushchikh v vysshiye uchebnye zavedeniya v 1955 g.* (Rules of Admission and Syllabi of Entrance Examinations for Those Entering Higher Educational Institutions in 1955), Moscow: "Sovetskaya Nauka," 1955.

Examinations in Russian language and literature are given to all applicants. Depending on the course of training applied for, other subjects than those listed above may be substituted (to make a total of not fewer than three and not more than five), such as: drafting and drawing (schools of architecture), history of the USSR, geography, and language of instruction (if other than Russian) in some schools.

[20] *Interview Report No. 9*, Department of State, Washington, D.C., p. 14.

[21] Summarized from *Pravila priema i programmy . . .* , *op. cit.*, pp. 20–24.

[22] A. N. Kolmogorov, *O professii matematika* (On the Profession of a Mathematician), 2nd Ed., enlarged, Ministry of Higher Education, Moscow: "Sovetskaya Nauka," 1954, p. 11.

[23] *Ibid.* Examination problems cited by Kolmogorov are given in Cenis Translation Series 55-43; one set of problems is given in Appendix H.

[24] *Ibid.*, p. 12.

[25] Complete texts of the physics syllabi for the entrance examinations in 1954 and in 1955 are given in Cenis Translation Series 55-40. The original text of these

and other syllabi can be found in any of the numerous Soviet school handbooks (*spravochniki*).

[26] *Spravochnik dlya postupayushchikh v moskovskii universitet v 1955 g.*, p. 99.

[27] V. S. Martynovskii, director of a technological institute, in *Vestnik vysshei shkoly*, No. 4, April 1954, p. 33.

[28] Kolmogorov, *op. cit.*, p. 12.

[29] *Ibid.*, p. 5.

[30] N. G. Maksimovich, "Pervoocherednye voprosy organizatsii issledovatel'skoi raboty" (The Foremost Questions in Organizing Research Work), *Vestnik vysshei shkoly*, No. 2, February 1956, p. 18.

[31] M. Semko, "Sovershenstvovat' deyatel'nost tekhnicheskikh vuzov" (To Continue Perfecting the Activities of Engineering Schools), *Pravda*, February 2, 1956, p. 4:1–3.

[32] *Spravochnik dlya postupayushchikh v moskovskii universitet v 1954 g.*, p. 61.

[33] E. Ya. Novik, "Bol'she vnimaniya uchebno-organizatsionnym voprosam" (For a Greater Attention to the Questions of Academic Organization), *Vestnik vysshei shkoly*, No. 11, November 1954, p. 21.

[34] Cenis Source Memorandum No. 29, pp. 4, 15, and 17.

[35] Ministry of Higher Education editorial in *Vestnik vysshei shkoly*, No. 7, July 1955, p. 2.

[36] The deferment practice apparently rests upon Art. 20 of the law *On Universal Military Obligation*, September 1, 1939, as amended to 1941 (*Pravda*, September 18, 1941). The article reads (in part): "No one shall be exempt from appearance for induction except persons receiving a deferment for completion of their education."

The exemption of students in most engineering and technological specialties was provided in the decree of September 15, 1943, entitled "On the Size of Scholarships, the Process of Awarding Scholarships in the Institutions of Higher Learning and in the Technicums and on the Exemption of Students from Induction into the Red Army." This decree lists 83 engineering schools in which students are automatically exempt and 13 categories of technicums (by ministerial jurisdiction). *Vysshaya shkola*, compiled by M. I. Movshovich, pp. 73 ff. For a discussion of the deferment practices see Nicholas DeWitt, *Soviet Professional Manpower*, Washington, D.C.: National Science Foundation, 1955, pp. 23–28.

[37] *Vestnik vysshei shkoly*, No. 11, November 1953, p. 8.

[38] *Spravochnik dlya postupayushchikh v moskovskii universitet v 1954 g.*, p. 84.

[39] *Sovetskaya Byelorussiya*, May 28, 1955, p. 2:5–6.

[40] Anticipated total of engineering graduates. *Vestnik vysshei shkoly*, No. 3, March 1956, p. 4. In addition to the graduates from accelerated courses, this total must include the extension-trained engineers.

[41] For instance, for the continental United States:

First-time Students		Bachelor's degrees awarded‖		
Fall of	Thousands	Spring of	Thousands	Per Cent¶
1945	475†	1949	365*	76.8
1947	619†	1951	383*	61.9
1949	594†	1953	305§	51.3
1950	517§	1954	293§	56.7
1951	472§	1955	287‡	60.8
Total	2,677	Total	1,633	61.0

208 Soviet Education

Sources:
* Biennial Survey of Education in the United States, Chapter 4, Section 1, *Statistics of Higher Education: Faculty, Students, and Degrees, 1950–1952*, Washington, D.C.: Office of Education, 1955, p. 37.
† *Ibid.*, p. 24.
‡ *New York Times*, December 9, 1955.
§ U. S. Office of Education (quoted in *The World Almanac*, 1953, p. 568).
‖ Including 1st professional degrees.
¶ Per cent of the corresponding number of first-time students.

42 *America's Resources of Specialized Talent*, prepared by Dael Wolfle, director, Commission on Human Resources and Advanced Training, New York: Harper & Brothers, 1954, Appendix G.2, p. 314.
43 *A Policy for Scientific and Professional Manpower*, New York: Columbia University Press, 1953, p. 19.
44 Paper presented by Robert E. Iffert, Specialist for Faculty and Facilities, on December 29, 1955, American Association for the Advancement of Science, Section Q, Atlanta, Georgia. Mimeographed reprint of the Department of Health, Education, and Welfare, Division of Higher Education. Table 6 Tentative. The sample (original quota 15,000 students) includes students of universities, technological schools, liberal arts colleges, teachers colleges, and junior colleges selected by sampling techniques.
45 *Vestnik vysshei shkoly*, No. 4, April 1954, pp. 1, 3.
46 *Vestnik vysshei shkoly*, No. 11, November 1954, p. 15.
47 *Spravochnik dlya postupayushchikh vo Vsesoyuznyi Zaochnyi Politekhnicheskii Institut*, Moscow: USSR Ministry of Higher Education, 1955, p. 27.
48 Stated to this author by Dr. Norton T. Dodge.
Many similar examples are to be found in Soviet publications; examples from *Vestnik vysshei shkoly*, No. 3, March 1953, and No. 7, July 1955; *Uchitel'skaya gazeta*, May 14, 1955, and others are cited in "Vyssheye zaochnoye i vecherneye obrazovaniye v SSSR," *Vestnik Instituta po izucheniyu SSSR* (Munich), No. 4, October–December 1955, pp. 94–108.

SOVIET HIGHER EDUCATION:

THE ACADEMIC PLAN

Central control of the education of specialists in the USSR is embodied in "academic plans" established by the Soviet Ministry of Higher Education for all the designated areas of specialization within the authorized fields of professional training. Thus a given academic plan (*uchebnyi plan*) presumably reflects the current judgment of the Ministry as to (1) the kind of training the specialist must have in order to satisfy the needs of the operating (industrial and other) ministries and (2) the most effective use of the available academic resources in the conduct of this training.

Since each academic plan prescribes the academic calendar, the curriculum, and the course schedule for the entire term of instruction and sets forth other course requirements in detail, *uchebnyi* plans obviously play a decisive role in shaping the entire academic process and the content and quality of instruction in the Soviet system of higher education. It is important, therefore, to outline the major characteristics of these centrally established plans under which Soviet institutions of higher education have operated, and to examine evidence on both the qualitative implications of this unique system of educational management and its impact on the academic process as a whole.

The basic structure of Soviet academic plans for professional training—training for a specific job—was first established in the early 1930's; and frequent and numerous changes, especially in curricular details, were made in subsequent years. The most recent and apparently far-reaching campaign calling for fundamental improvements in the entire academic process and involving a very considerable revision of both the university and engineering courses stems from the Party directives of 1954. Appendix I gives a translation of one of the most detailed single statements in the Soviet press on the specific content of instructions issued by the Minister of Higher Education in September 1954 to the ministerial agencies under his control.

With reference to the *uchebnyi* plans these instructions called for a prompt preparation of several procedural plans, among them, "within one month":

1. A plan for the revision of curricula and syllabi in accordance with the new list of specialties.
2. A plan for the broadening of the existing specializations within the specialties.
3. A plan for the establishment of a list of specialties in new technologies.
4. A plan ("within a four-month period") for the strengthening (*ukrupleniye*) of the academic chairs (*kafedry*) and faculties.

This chapter outlines and comments upon the major areas of the Soviet academic pattern, taking into consideration wherever sufficient evidence is available the changes projected in fulfillment of the 1954 Party directives.

1. The Formulation of Plans

In theory, the *uchebnyi* plans established by the Ministry represent a consensus of both the educators and the practicing members of the professions. At least it is invariably so asserted by the Ministry and the experts it employs. For instance, M. G. Uroyev, identified with the Ministry's administration in charge of universities, writes:

> The new [1955–1956] academic plans of the universities are the result of a large-scale collective work. The Main Administration ... has drawn into this work all the universities of the country and representatives of all the university specialties. The commissions created in the course of this work have examined and considered the proposals and comments received in the process of developing these plans from the members of the academic chairs collectively and from individual professors and teachers. The completed drafts of the plans were thoroughly discussed by many scientific-pedagogical groups and later by the collegium of the USSR Ministry of Higher Education and [only thereafter] formally adopted [so that they would serve] as the base—sufficiently well considered and approved by the scientific-pedagogical community—for the training of highly qualified specialists.[1]

In practice, judging by the past history of changes in the *uchebnyi* plans, there have been considerable difficulties in arriving at a consensus and in formulating programs "approved by the scientific-pedagogical community." Generally, the comments of the educators suggest that "every [new] *uchebnyi* plan, having been cleared of the defects of the former, contains new defects."[2] More specifically, it has been said that consensus on any one plan *as a whole* cannot be arrived at under the present system; that plans are hurriedly developed and frequently introduced with very short or no notice; that plans disregard individual differences in the institutions to which they apply; and in some cases, after all the conferences and consultations and recommendations, no fundamental changes are in fact made.

One Soviet professor of engineering wrote in 1951:

> Unfortunately, the *uchebnyi* plans for many of our specialties and the syllabi for separate course-subjects are organized not on the basis of scientific considerations of pedagogy but, as a rule, on a crash basis—after, so to speak, a poll of the "local people," those who head up the academic chairs.[3]

In 1953 a staff member of another engineering institute described in detail a large-scale project undertaken in 1951, involving the work of many commissions and much consultation and aimed at "a *radical* [our emphasis] re-examination of all the curricula and syllabi." The author stated that:

> The majority of the participants in the work of the commissions did not see eye to eye; every one of them—all specialists in various fields—exaggerated the importance of his own discipline for the shaping of a specialist of a given type and correspondingly demanded an increased number of hours in the curriculum.[4]

Inasmuch as "these demands could be neither reconciled nor satisfied," the Ministry then proposed for discussion the curricula already formulated by it. As to the final outcome of these discussions, the author concluded:

> The fact must be admitted that the curricula of 1951 differ in almost no respect from the curricula of 1945–1946, if one disregards an insignificant reduction in the number of hours (8 to 9 per cent) allotted to the basic educational disciplines.[5]

He also quotes a concrete example of the "before and after" distribution of curricular hours for one of the engineering specialties, "Industrial and Civilian Construction"—presumably a 5-year course:

Category of Subjects	Class Hours Allotted	
	1945	1951
"Social science"	394	396
General science subjects	1,298	1,192
General technical subjects	1,082	1,130
Specialized subjects	1,766	1,802
Total hours*	4,540	4,520

* Not including industrial practice and the preparation of the diploma project.

A recent comment suggests the organizational difficulty which may arise under the present system when significant changes are made and introduced on short notice:

> The revised and considerably changed *uchebnyi* plans were fixed by the Ministry of Higher Education in the middle of August [1954] and distributed to the institutes during the second part of August with an injunction to follow the new plans, beginning September 1, for students of the first three years of the course. It is difficult to visualize a successful transition to the new plans in such a hurry.[6]

Since a given *uchebnyi* plan, with few exceptions, applies to a number of schools wherever located and however different in academic resources, it is frequently impossible or impractical for some schools to meet its requirements adequately. The Ministry of Higher Education itself has pointed out that:

> ... all agricultural institutes conduct their work following one and the same *uchebnyi* plan and the same syllabi without taking into account the natural and economic peculiarities of the area in which a given institution operates.[7]

The failure of the plan to differentiate between individual institutions creates a variety of problems for a given school, of which the following is a typical example:

> Without a [prior] agreement with the [Tallin Polytechnic] Institute new specialties were introduced [by the Ministry of Higher Education in the Institute's *uchebnyi* plan], such as "Commercial Fisheries" and "Technology of Fish Products" with an annual quota of 25 new students, although neither specialty corresponds to the profile of the Institute nor does it have the required technical base and qualified teachers for these specialties.[8]

But perhaps the most significant comments, those raising the fundamental issue involved in the present system of formulating *uchebnyi* plans, and not until lately openly voiced, can be exemplified by a quotation from a recent article descriptively entitled, "For Greater Initiative and Independence":

> It would seem to us that the Ministry of Higher Education, having concentrated the development of curricula and syllabi in its Main Administrations, with the collective participation, to be sure, of the personnel of the separate departments, has nevertheless excessively centralized the formulation of these basic documents.[9]

The author is even more specific with reference to the syllabi:

> In our opinion, the Ministry of Higher Education should abandon the practice of centralized formulation of syllabi and, having allowed each institution of higher learning the right of composing the syllabi, retain for itself only the control function and the organization for the exchange of experience among the faculties of the [separate] institutions.

Thus the author hopefully suggests the type of control informally and voluntarily practiced among the colleges and universities in the United States via, for instance, such accrediting agencies of the professional engineering societies as the American Society for Engineering Education.

2. School Calendar

The term of instruction in Soviet institutions of higher education, as we have already observed, varies from 2 to 6 years depending on (1) the field of study and (2) the category of school. A 5-year term is standard for all university courses; in engineering schools the term of undergraduate instruction (varying from the more usual—and apparently the minimum—4 years and 10 months to 5½ years) may also be assumed to average 5 years, one year longer than in American colleges and universities.*

Although the term of study varies with the category of school, the yearly academic calendar is similar in all essential details for all academic institutions in the Soviet Union. The school year starts on September first and is divided into semesters which average about 17 weeks. The first semester runs from September 1 to the end of December and is followed by a 4-week examination session. After a 2-week

---

* It will be remembered, however, that Soviet students enter college after completing the ten-year school. As to the chronological age of students, the tenth grade in the Soviet system corresponds to the eleventh grade of the American high school. Nominally, therefore, Soviet freshmen are one year younger than their American counterparts, but the nominal age of students at graduation is about the same in the United States and the Soviet Union.

winter recess, the second semester starts early in February and continues through May or the first week of June. The final examinations for the year are held during the month of June (3 to 4 weeks), leaving only July and August for the summer vacation. Thus Soviet students spend about 41 weeks of every year in residence—some 8 weeks more per year than is typical for American students.*

Furthermore, a part of the Soviet student's summer vacation is periodically taken up by extracurricular but nevertheless compulsory activities such as training at military camps.

Over the entire 5-year course of study, the Soviet student will have spent some 50 per cent more time actually at school than is typically provided for in the 4-year undergraduate course of an American student. Or, to put it still another way, so far as total time spent in school is concerned, it would take over 6 years of residence in an American university to accumulate as much actual school time as is provided for in the 5-year curricula of Soviet schools. It is true that a considerable part of the Soviet school calendar is accounted for by the time-consuming oral examinations—up to 8 weeks per year versus approximately 3 weeks or less for examinations in American schools; but for the Soviet student, as for the American, examination weeks are very definitely a working part of the academic year. No significant change in the academic calendar has been proposed in the recent series of reforms.

The striking difference in the relative demand upon the student's time is only one factor in comparing Soviet undergraduate training with that in American schools. Much more important are other characteristics of the Soviet curricula and other elements of the Soviet educational process generally, some of which are considered under the separate subheadings in this chapter.

3. A PLAN FOR EVERY SPECIALTY

The point of departure in formulating new, or revising existing, *uchebnyi* plans is the currently designated list of specialties, that is, professional labels for each kind and type of college training. In the 1930's the number of specialties—and "specializations" within each specialty—was very large.† In subsequent years efforts were made to reduce the number of specialties and, somewhat correspondingly,

---

* At Massachusetts Institute of Technology, for instance, the scholastic year includes approximately 30 weeks of instruction and about 3 weeks of reading and examination sessions, leaving about 19 weeks for vacations.

† See Chapter 5.

to reduce the number of faculties and academic chairs (*kafedry*) within the separate faculties.* Considerable progress in that direction has been made since c. 1934, when the fields of study were fractionalized into innumerable specialties each with its own label—such as "Cold Working of Metal (Working by Cutting)," the graduate of this specialty having the title "Mechanical Engineer-Technologist of Cold Working of Metal." By 1953–1954 the number of specialties in higher education was reduced to 460; but 135 of these were further subdivided into 510 specializations. Thus a Soviet graduate of 1954 would have one of the 835 distinct labels then authorized.

No complete list of existing specialties and specializations appears to have been published recently, but the degree of fractionalization of the Soviet curricula can be judged indirectly and by a number of specific examples. For instance, there were 57 distinct faculties within the twenty-five engineering schools classified as "Polytechnic and Industrial Institutes"; and, on the average, each faculty embraced 3 specialties or a total of 171 distinct engineering curricula in all.† Even at the universities, where the combined number of variously designated faculties is only 30, there were 96 distinct specialties offered in 1955.‡ Of these specialties, however, only 25 specialties (listed in Table 43) were offered in five or more of the thirty-three universities, and 71 additional specialties (listed in Table 44, many of them in the minority languages) were taught in fewer than five of the universities.

There have been indications that under the reform initiated in 1954 the number of basic specialties and of "specializations" within them will be considerably reduced. One source states that eventually there will be only 280 basic curricula instead of 460.[10] The same source states that as of April 1955 the number of specializations (within the specialties) had already been reduced by 41 per cent. Some changes designed to translate the 1954 directives into practice were introduced on a limited scale in the 1954–1955 academic year. The revisions:

... on the whole, have been so far reflected only in the *uchebnyi* plans of the leading ... institutions of higher education, such as the

* See Tables 24 and 27 for the list of faculties in the universities, polytechnic institutes, and industrial institutes as of 1955.

† The number of formal fourth-year options at MIT for the selected fields of engineering was listed in its 1955–1956 Catalogue as follows: civil engineering 3, mechanical engineering 9, metallurgy 2, electrical engineering 1, chemical engineering 2, naval architecture and marine engineering 2, and aeronautical engineering 1.

‡ Some of the faculties, although distinct in name, embrace partly overlapping lists of specialties. See, for instance, Table 31 in Chapter 5, where the distribution of courses in mathematics, physics, mechanics, astronomy, and geophysics is given by four differently designated faculties.

TABLE 43. NUMBER OF UNIVERSITIES OFFERING REGULAR, CORRESPONDENCE, AND EVENING COURSES IN THE TWENTY-FIVE PRINCIPAL "SPECIALTIES" (MAJORS) OF THE SOVIET UNIVERSITY CURRICULA
USSR
1955

Note: The twenty-five specialties listed in this table are those which are offered by five or more of the thirty-three state universities of the USSR. Additional university specialties offered by fewer than five universities are listed in Table 44.

Name of Specialty (Major)	Number of Universities Offering Courses			
	Regular	Corre-spondence	Evening	Total
1. Mathematics	33	25	2	60
2. Physics	33	1	. . .	34
3. Zoology	32	17	. . .	49
4. Botany	32	18	. . .	50
5. Chemistry	29	. . .	. . .	29
6. Physical Geography	26	15	. . .	41
7. Economic Geography	19	10	. . .	29
8. Geologic Survey and Search for Useful Mineral Deposits	16	. . .	. . .	16
9. Geology and Exploration of Useful Mineral Deposits	16	. . .	. . .	16
10. Mechanics	13	. . .	. . .	13
11. Geology and Exploration of Oil and Gas Deposits	8	. . .	. . .	8
12. Geophysical Methods of Search for and Exploration of Useful Deposits	7	. . .	. . .	7
13. Hydrology and Engineering Geology	7	. . .	. . .	7
Subtotal, Science and Applied Science	271	86	2	359
14. Russian Language and Literature	33	26	1	60
15. History	32	22	1	55
16. Jurisprudence	16	10	1	27
17. Journalism	10	7	. . .	17
18. English Language and Literature	9	3	. . .	12
19. German Language and Literature	9	2	. . .	11
20. Ukrainian Language and Literature	7	7	. . .	14
21. Finance and Credit	7	3	. . .	10
22. Economics of Trade	7	3	. . .	10
23. Economics of Industry	7	1	. . .	8
24. Iranian Language and Literature	5	. . .	. . .	5
25. French Language and Literature	5	1	. . .	6
Subtotal, other than Science and Applied Science	147	85	3	235
Total for 25 majors (offered in 5 or more universities)	418	171	5	594
Total for additional 71 majors (offered in fewer than 5 universities, see Table 44)	116	22	5	143
Programs given in all 96 majors of the university curricula	534	193	10	737
Per cent	(72.4)	(26.2)	(1.4)	(100.0)

Source: Compiled from 1955 Handbook (*Spravochnik dlya postupayushchikh v vysshiye uchebnye zavedeniya SSSR v 1955 godu*) and Table 44.

TABLE 44. NUMBER OF UNIVERSITIES OFFERING REGULAR, CORRESPONDENCE,
AND EVENING COURSES IN THE SEVENTY-ONE "SPECIALTIES" (MAJORS),
EACH OF WHICH IS OFFERED IN FEWER THAN FIVE OF THE
THIRTY-THREE STATE UNIVERSITIES
USSR
1955

Note: See Table 43 for other majors provided for in the Soviet university curricula.

Name of Specialty (Major)*	Number of Universities Offering Courses			
	Regular	Corre-spondence	Evening	Total
1. Geochemistry (16) (17) (19) (27)	4	...	...	4
2. Agronomy (11) (27) (33)	3	...	...	3
3. Astronomy (12) (16) (19)	3	...	...	3
4. Human and Animal Physiology (1) (16) (19)	3	...	...	3
5. Hydrology of Land and Oceanography (4) (19) (23)	3	...	...	3
6. Medical Practice [*lechebnoye delo*] (3) (25) (29)	3	...	...	3
7. Plant Physiology (1) (16) (19)	3	...	...	3
8. Geophysics (16) (19)	2	...	...	2
9. Meteorology and Climatology (16) (19)	2	...	...	2
10. Soil Science and Agrochemistry	2	...	...	2
11. Anthropology (19)	1	...	...	1
12. Architecture (15)	1	...	...	1
13. Cartography (19)	1	...	...	1
14. Chemical Technology of Wood Pulp (15)	1	...	...	1
15. Electric Power Plants, Networks, and Systems (15)	1	...	1	2
16. Electrification of Industrial Enterprises and Plants (15)	1	...	...	1
17. Equipment for and Technology of Thermal Processing of Metals (18)	1	...	...	1
18. Forestry Engineering Practice (11)	1	...	...	1
19. Industrial and Civil Construction (15)	1	...	1	2
20. Pharmacy (25)	1	...	...	1
21. Stomatology (25)	1	...	...	1
22. Technology of Inorganic Substances (18)	1	...	...	1
23. Technology of Machine Construction, Metal Cutting Machine Tools, and Tools (15)	1	...	1	2
24. Technology of Silicates (15)	1	...	...	1
25. Zootechnics (11)	1	...	...	1
Subtotal, Science and Applied Science	43	...	3	46
26. Bookkeeping-Accounting (7) (10) (13) (26)	4	...	...	4
27. Philosophy (12) (16) (19) (26)	4	3	...	7
28. Economics of Agriculture (13) (15) (24)	3	1	...	4
29. Library Science and Bibliography (1) (3)(25)	3	3	...	6
30. Planning of State Economy (7) (10) (15)	3	...	...	3
31. Political Economy (12) (16) (19)	3	3	...	6
32. Psychology (12) (19) (26)	3	...	...	3
33. Manchu-Evenki Studies (16)	1	...	...	1
34. Physical Education (25)	1	...	...	1
35. Semitics (26)	1	...	...	1
36. Egyptology (16)	1	...	...	1
Language and Literature				
37. Armenian (7)	1	...	...	1

TABLE 44 (continued)

Name of Specialty (Major)*	Number of Universities Offering Courses			
	Regular	Corre-spondence	Evening	Total
38. Azerbaidzhan (1)	1	1	...	2
39. Buryat-Mongolian (8)	1	...	...	1
40. Byelorussian (2)	1	1	...	2
41. Chinese (16)	1	...	...	1
42. Czech (16) (17)	2	...	...	2
43. Danish (16)	1	...	...	1
44. Estonian (25)	1	1	...	2
45. Finnish (11)	1	1	...	2
46. Georgian (26)	1	...	...	1
47. Greek [classical] (17) (19)	2	...	...	2
48. Indian Languages and Literature (16) (23)	2	...	...	2
49. Italian (16)	1	...	...	1
50. Japanese (16)	1	...	...	1
51. Kazakh (10)	1	1	...	2
52. Kirgiz (13)	1	1	...	2
53. Latin (17) (19)	2	...	...	2
54. Latvian (15)	1	1	1	3
55. Lithuanian (3)	1	1	...	2
56. Malayan (16)	1	...	...	1
57. Moldavian (14)	1	...	...	1
58. Norwegian (16)	1	...	...	1
59. Polish (16) (17)	2	...	...	2
60. Romano-Germanic Languages and Literature (21)	1	...	...	1
61. Spanish (16)	1	...	...	1
62. Swedish (16)	1	...	...	1
63. Tadzhik (24)	1	1	...	2
64. Tatar (9)	1	1	...	2
65. Tibetan (16)	1	...	...	1
66. Turkic Languages and Literature (19) (26)	2	...	...	2
67. Turkish (1)	1	...	...	1
68. Turkmen (28)	1	1	1	3
69. Uigug (23)	1	...	...	1
70. Uzbek (23) (30)	2	1	...	3
71. Vietnamese (16)	1	...	...	1
Subtotal, other than Science and Applied Science	69	22	2	93
Unspecified	4			4
Total number of programs offered in majors listed in this table	116	22	5	143

Source: Compiled from 1955 Handbook (*Spravochnik dlya postupayushchikh v vysshiye uchebnye zavedeniya SSSR v 1955 godu*).
* Figures in parentheses designate the university or universities which offer the named program; see Table 30 for the list of universities.

Moscow Power Institute, Bauman Moscow Higher Technical School, Leningrad Polytechnic Institute, and certain other schools.[11]

In the following year new *uchebnyi* plans were introduced in the first 3 years of all university curricula and, apparently, in the majority of institutes.[12]   Under the new plans the number of specialties was reduced and certain specializations abolished altogether, including all the previously prescribed undergraduate specializations in mathematics, mechanics, astronomy, and geophysics.   Similarly, a number of narrow engineering specialties were consolidated into new specialties of "broad profile"; for instance, the following formerly separate specialties were consolidated into one:

Technology of Machine Construction.
Metal Cutting Machine Tools.
Metal Cutting Tools.[13]

Nevertheless, even with these changes, the number of individual *uchebnyi* plans within the majority of fields in science and especially of engineering remains large.

4. THE "ELECTIVE" COURSE SUBJECTS

Although no two *uchebnyi* plans are alike in every particular of their organization, a number of features are common to all.   One such feature of the Soviet curricula is the almost complete absence of elective subjects.   Some subjects listed in the Soviet curricula—the so-called "faculty" (*fakul'tativnye*) subjects—are optional with the student; but, if they are offered at all, in most cases the student can take them only *in addition* to his prescribed load.

Up to the present [1955–1956] time, the faculty ["elective"] subjects have not as a rule occupied a significant place in the *uchebnyi* plans of the institutions of higher education.   Of the total number of hours which are fixed by the plans, only an insignificant fraction is given to instruction on a faculty ["elective"] basis.   One can even cite not a few such cases in which the elective subjects formally designated by the plan are not offered at all.   There are also cases in which even this formality is not observed and *uchebnyi* plans provide for no elective subjects whatsoever.[14]

In American curricula the approved electives are given academic credit and constitute a substantial part of the total course.   To take an MIT course in mechanical engineering as an example of American diversification, up to 39 per cent of the academic load of the senior year is selected by the student himself from a number of subjects appropriate to the chosen area of specialization and to the student's particular interest.
Soviet practice has been to prescribe a very large number of specialized curricula with the content fixed minutely for each specialty.

American curricula of professional undergraduate training in leading schools, although broadly oriented, provide a wide choice of subjects in which the student may eventually specialize. In a purely statistical sense, therefore, the number of final "options" an American student may take within his field via the electives of the senior year can equal or exceed the fixed number of standard and rigidly defined corresponding "specialties" recognized by the Soviet educational system. An MIT student taking a course in mechanical engineering (Course II) has only six senior options: power, aircraft propulsion, air conditioning and refrigeration, internal combustion engines, materials and material processing, and design; but, as mentioned above, more than 30 per cent of the year's load, or, on the average, about four subjects, can be selected from 22 subjects in mechanical engineering alone. In fact, the additional subjects may be any choices approved by the Registration Officer and may include two humanities subjects. The important difference is that the American student makes his choice after 3 years of study within the general field, whereas for the Soviet engineering student the choice in many cases is made at the time he applies for admission.

It is not altogether clear to what extent the role of the Soviet "faculty" courses has been recently modified. One source states that in the curricula of the universities, where elective subjects have apparently always played a significant role, the number of hours previously allotted to the elective subjects (and seminars) has been considerably reduced.[15] The same source notes that the relatively large number of these subjects provided in the old *uchebnyi* plans had encouraged in some instances too narrow a specialization by the university graduates.

In the engineering institutes a substantial number of previously compulsory course subjects has apparently been given "faculty" status and some new elective subjects have been added since 1955. It is not completely clear whether any of these subjects can be taken for credit. The following comment, however, suggests that, as heretofore, the electives under the new plans are not credited as part of the required load:

> . . . in the old *uchebnyi* plans, as is known, all course subjects were usually compulsory. This [condition] necessarily led to overloading the students. An altogether different situation is developing at the present time when the inclusion of a faculty subject into a *uchebnyi* plan does not lead to additional examinations, does not demand compulsory attendance, and so forth.[16]

The same writer, incidentally, suggests that the "faculty" course subjects which may be given in conjunction with any one *uchebnyi* plan should vary from institution to institution in order to take advantage of the "individual peculiarities of teachers" in a given school; he adds:

> As to the choice [of such course subjects] it is most urgent that all schools be afforded a certain degree of freedom. One should support and encourage their initiative and not hamper it by petty concern and useless control.

In this connection it is important that at least the universities in 1955

> ... have been given the right yearly to establish the names and the scope of the "faculty" course subjects and seminars (within the time limits provided in the *uchebnyi* plan) and also to consider and to establish syllabi for these courses.

5. Courses Divided into Many Subjects

Another conspicuous feature of Soviet curricula generally is the large number of separate subjects of instruction included in a given course. There appears to be a definite and direct relationship between the number of existing academic chairs (*kafedry*) and the number of separate subjects into which a given discipline is divided in the curriculum. This relationship, it might be noted, is similar to a rough correspondence between the number of faculties and the number of recognized specialties. As the number of distinct specialties increased in the 1930's, the degree of specialization and the number of faculties also increased—and, with them, the number of both the component academic chairs and the separate subjects of instruction. In other words, the large number of course subjects which characterize Soviet curricula is but a reflection of a general policy initiated in the 1930's.

Leaving aside the difficulties which must arise in coordinating many closely related but separately taught subjects, one result of this policy is that the Soviet student has had to take a correspondingly large number of tests, of which there are two types: the regular, graded final examinations and the so-called *zachety*—ungraded final examinations conducted either orally or by inspection of written work to verify that the student has satisfactorily met such requirements as laboratory reports or reading. A (prewar) curriculum for one of the engineering specialties at the Dnepropetrovsk Mining Institute, which had 65 distinctly titled subjects,[17] called for 62 final examinations and for 32 *zachety*—94 promotional tests in all. At an agricultural institute the 1953–1954 plan called for a total of 89 tests, of which, apparently, 41 were examinations and 48 *zachety*.[18] Again:

To what extent students are overloaded by examinations and *zachety* can be judged by factual data from the experience of the construction engineering and transport institutes. At the Moscow Construction Engineering Institute [1954 and earlier], for instance, in a number of specialties the third-year students had 7 examinations, 9 or 10 *zachety,* and 3 or 4 term projects and computation and graphic assignments per semester.[19]

Soviet educators have complained perennially of duplications in the "fractionalized courses,"* particularly in the specialized course subjects in engineering curricula.

If, for instance, one compares the syllabi in physics and in heat engineering for technical higher schools, one can see that certain sections are repeated verbatim; the same should be said about the syllabi in electrotechnics and theoretical mechanics, and also many specialized subjects. Thus the topics in electric welding are almost identically formulated in the syllabi of "Construction Materials," "Construction Work and Machinery," and "Roadway Work and Machinery." Means for the pumping of water are mentioned (at times in identical expressions) in the syllabi of the course subjects, "Construction Work and Machinery," "Hydraulics and Water Supply," and "Footings and Foundations."[20]

Similarly, in the syllabi for one of the metallurgical specialties, we find that fuel, combustion calculations, and the kinetics of combustion are dealt with in three separate course subjects: "Metallurgical Furnaces," "The Theory of Metallurgical Processes," and "Metallurgy of Cast Iron." The total time allotted in the curricula for "Metallurgical Furnaces" is only 112 hours (50 hours for lectures, 52 hours for laboratory, and 10 hours for the term project), the broad scope and the nature of material to be covered in this relatively short time being indicated by the main subheads of the syllabus:

Fuel and Computation of Combustion.
Construction Materials for Furnaces.
Mechanics of Gases.
The Theory of Similarity and of Modeling.
Heat Transfer.
The Heating, Melting, and Cooling of Metals.
Equipment and Construction of Furnaces.
Fuel Economics of Metallurgical Plants.
Furnaces for Ferrous Metallurgical Plants.

* The content of each course subject is outlined in the officially approved syllabi (*programmy*) of the Ministry of Higher Education.

It would appear that at least some of the topics within these categories must be covered in a most superficial manner—only to be repeated, presumably also in summary fashion, as a part of another course subject.[21]

One of the specific objectives of the current efforts to improve academic plans is to eliminate needless duplication. Some improvements in that direction have been made, but even after the changes introduced in 1955–1956 it was said:

> . . . in a number of courses there exists wholly unjustifiable parallelism. Certain sections and topics are repeated with only small variations, and sometimes without significant differences, in several disciplines. The elimination of useless repetitions can provide the required time for the presentation of the latest material and the raising of the theoretical level in the training of engineers.[22]

6. Heavy Class Schedules

By far the most outstanding characteristic shared by all *uchebnyi* plans is the very large proportion of total time allotted to *scheduled,* i.e., compulsory, class attendance. Six scheduled hours per day, 36 hours per week (not counting the time given to military training) appear to be standard, at least for the freshman year, in all Soviet schools:

> In recent years the curricula [*uchebnye plany*] have been so structured as to provide, according to the schedule, 36 hours of required attendance per week in all semesters. Formerly, the plan, which unfortunately remained in effect for only one year, called for a different number of hours . . . [diminishing each year down to 24 hours in the fifth year].[23]

In comparison, the MIT freshman schedule, for instance, calls for about 24 hours of classroom and laboratory attendance, *including* Military Science (3 hours per week).* Thus a Soviet student has approximately 70 per cent more scheduled class hours in his freshman year than his American counterpart at MIT:

				Hours per Year	Index
MIT	(30 weeks)	(24 hours)	=	720	100
Soviet	(34 weeks)	(36 hours)	=	1,224	170

If one considers that, on the average, the number of class hours in American universities and colleges is about 20 hours per academic

---

* The normal student schedule at MIT is considered to be 50 hours per week, including class and laboratory attendance *and preparation.*

week, the score of the Soviet freshman on required attendance is just about double the American average. Furthermore, 36 scheduled hours per week has not been the maximum in Soviet curricula. The 1953 schedule for the seventh semester in all specialties at the Moscow Steel Institute was reported at 43 required hours per week.[24]

Whatever the variations from semester to semester, the total number of scheduled hours for the entire term of instruction and the yearly averages in all Soviet *uchebnyi* plans are very much higher than can be found in an American course schedule. At MIT, for instance, for a student taking Course II (Mechanical Engineering), Group 6 (Design), the total number of required and scheduled hours is 2,610 or about 652 hours per year; at the Bauman Moscow Higher Technical School (one of the outstanding engineering schools in the Soviet Union) the 1954–1955 plan for the specialty of "Material Handling Machinery and Equipment" called for some 4,886 hours or, on the average, 977 scheduled hours per academic year.[25] It seems inevitable that such heavy class schedules and the pressure of other compulsory work must leave the Soviet student little time for independent study and extra-curricular activities.

In addition to the heavy class schedule, and especially in the engineering schools, Soviet curricula call for numerous compulsory home assignments:

> The number of various assignments which the [engineering] student must complete per semester ranges from 45 to 65; further-more, during the first two years he is expected independently to solve 600 to 800 problems. Because of shortage of time these assignments not infrequently are carried out only partly, at times mechanically, without a creative approach to their solution.[26]

No other single feature of the *uchebnyi* plans as they have developed under the present system has been commented upon so frequently and so critically by Soviet educators as the size of the scheduled load carried by the student. The Ministry itself, as if the responsibility for the condition lay elsewhere, pointed out in 1954 that "excessive overload of students was [unfavorably] reflected in the results of the winter examinations."[27] Its editorial gave a specific example:

> According to the estimate made by the Committee on Instruction of the Moscow City Potemkin Pedagogical Institute, the students of its physics-mathematics faculty must spend not less than 18 hours per day to carry out their *uchebnyi* plan. It is not surprising that this faculty placed the lowest in the record of the winter examina-tion session: of the 606 students enrolled in this faculty, 136 have

not completed the *uchebnyi* plan, 26 received two unsatisfactory grades in the examinations, and 13 students received three non-passing grades each.

Under the reform initiated in 1954, one of the many proposed organizational changes was to reduce the scheduled load of the students. The new plans were said to envision not more than 30 hours in the senior year. Some reduction in hours was apparently made in the 1954–1955 schedules and more generally in the *uchebnyi* plans established in 1955. The reduction, however, has not been very significant, particularly if one considers that under the new plans some of the "electives" are in fact compulsory although they are not reflected in the formal time schedule. With reference to the *uchebnyi* plans in effect during the 1955–1956 academic year, the director of the Kaunas Polytechnic Institute stated that:

> For the majority of specialties the total load of the students, for the entire term of study [c. 5 years], has been lowered by approximately 150–250 hours, that is, by 3–5 per cent of the total number of hours prescribed in the former *uchebnyi* plans. In the meantime both the teachers and the students expected that the load would be reduced by at least 15 per cent. Only then could one talk about effective changes in the students' working conditions.[28]

Thus even in 1955–1956 the scheduled overload had not been materially reduced, despite the fact that in the past Soviet commentators have blamed most of the admitted academic ills of the Soviet educational system on the excessively heavy burden placed upon the student and the disproportionately high allocation of hours to compulsory work.

7. Organization of the Course

A given *uchebnyi* plan specifies the distribution of calendar time for the entire course. Taking, for example, the 5½ year course of instruction provided for one engineering specialty at the Bauman Moscow Higher Technical School (MVTU) according to the plan current as of 1955, the distribution of time by (typical) categories in weeks was as follows:*

* The example here cited is based on the *uchebnyi* plan, "Technology of Machine Construction, Metal Cutting, Machine Tools, and Tools," the complete translation of which is given in Cenis Translation Series No. 55–24. Although MVTU operates on special *uchebnyi* plans (*Vestnik vysshei shkoly*, No. 8, August 1955, p. 55), this sample curriculum most nearly corresponds to the recently consolidated three courses which were formerly given in this specialty at the specialized institutes.

Allocated for	Weeks	Per Cent
Academic Instruction	153	53.5
Industrial Practice	24	8.4
(Including: General—16 weeks		
Prediploma—8 weeks)		
Promotional Examinations	37	12.9
Diploma Project and Its Defense	21	7.4
Subtotal, in school	235	82.2
Vacations	51	17.8
Total, weeks	286	100.0

The time allotted to academic instruction is specified in the *uchebnyi* plans in hours—per subject, per week, per semester, and for the entire course—that is, the scheduled hours discussed in the preceding sections of this chapter. By type of instruction the hours are allocated to (1) lectures, (2) laboratory work, (3) "practice work, seminars, exercises, and similar," and (4) term projects and term papers.[29] The allocation of time among these four categories varies considerably with the type of institution and somewhat with the specialty. Judging by the few actual examples which we were able to obtain in the course of this study, the distribution in per cent may be roughly as follows:*

Per Cent of Hours Scheduled for	University (science)		Mechanical Engineering	
	Average	Range	Average	Range
Lectures	46	40 to 52	55	52 to 58
Laboratory	15	5 to 25	13	12 to 14
Practice Work	35	32 to 38	25	23 to 27
Term Projects	4	2 to 6	7	6 to 8
Per Cent	100	...	100	...

The periods allotted to industrial or other types of field practice and to the preparation of the diploma project, which culminates the course in all engineering institutes, are specified in weeks. The num-

---

* An attempt was made to obtain *uchebnyi* plans for this study from a number of representative institutions in the Soviet Union on the catalogue exchange basis. In the fall of 1954 Harvard University catalogues were mailed to 32 Soviet universities and MIT catalogues to 24 selected engineering institutes, with covering letters requesting comparable information on the Soviet curricula. Only six replies were received (the last one in May 1955), none including the information which was asked for; two of the correspondence-type institutes (Leningrad Industrial and All-Union Polytechnic), however, did send their prospectuses (*spravochniki*) giving general information on the admission rules and the choice of courses. It is obvious that the only place where a comprehensive selection of *uchebnyi* plans can be obtained is the Soviet Ministry of Higher Education.

ber of weeks allotted to industrial practice varies considerably from institution to institution and from specialty to specialty. As of c. 1952 the range was said to be as follows:[30]

Kind of School	Weeks of Practice
Engineering Institutes	16–38
Universities	6–16

Twenty-four weeks of industrial practice, starting with the third year in school, appear to be the most usual provision for engineering students. The last period of their industrial practice, lasting 6 to 8 weeks, immediately precedes the preparation of the diploma project and is called "diploma practice." In theory, it is directly related to the topic chosen for the student's diploma project.

A diploma project is required of every engineering student and its successful defense culminates the engineer's undergraduate training. In universities, where no comparable thesis is required, a comprehensive examination (called "state examination") is held at the end of the 5-year course. Upon completion of the course and after having successfully defended his diploma project or passed the state examination, the Soviet student receives a title corresponding to his specialty but receives no academic degree such as the bachelor's degree conferred by American universities and colleges. The title of an engineering graduate identifies the branch of engineering (e.g., mechanical) and the specialty (e.g., "Technology of Machine Construction, Metal Cutting Machine Tools, and Tools").* Beginning with 1955, all university graduates were to be identified by their major (e.g., physics) and their formal qualifications: "Teacher of ——— in Secondary Schools." A graduate of a pedagogical institute (normal school) is given the title of teacher in secondary schools with a designated specialty, e.g., mathematics. The curricular content of these three chosen examples of professional training will be examined in the next chapter after a comment on the category of subjects which is common to all Soviet curricula of higher education.

8. Course Subjects Found in Every Soviet Curriculum

Excluding military training, for which no hours are shown in the recent *uchebnyi* plans examined in the course of this study, all Soviet curricula provide for instruction in (1) physical education, (2) foreign language, and (3) social sciences—as defined.

* As of c. 1953 there were more than 200 distinct engineering specialities. (*BSE*, 2nd Ed., Vol. 18, 1953, p. 153.)

Physical Education

"Physical Nurture and Sport" (to give a literal translation), first introduced into Soviet curricula of higher education in c. 1929, must be taken by all students 2 hours per week during the first four semesters (134 hours in all). It is supposed to be integrated into the "union-wide complex of physical culture" known as "Ready for Work and for Defense of the USSR."* After the compulsory two years, physical education is offered as an elective. In 1955 it was said that about 10 per cent of the students (throughout the system) regularly continued some form of physical training on that basis.[31]

Foreign Languages

Until recently, when official emphasis was placed on the importance of foreign languages for physical scientists and engineers, the language requirements of the Soviet college curricula, although compulsory, had not been particularly demanding. In 1948, for instance, an article stated that:

> The teaching of foreign languages in the majority of institutions of higher technical training up to the present time is practically indistinguishable from that of the secondary schools.

In 1953 it was said that the former ineffectual organization of teaching foreign languages was being replaced by new methods based on the "classical work of I. V. Stalin, 'Marxism and the Question of Linguistics.' "[32] Subsequently published comments, however, would indicate that both the quality and the level of language teaching either deteriorated or, at best, remained at the former low level. The hours allotted to compulsory language study were progressively reduced from 270 hours (4 hours per week, first and second year) in 1950–1951 to 2 hours per week in most engineering schools and science faculties of the universities by 1954.[33]

Since the 1954 Party directives, the importance of foreign languages, especially to scientists and engineers, has been strongly emphasized as part of the Soviet effort to improve the quality of scientific and engineering training. A conference on the teaching of foreign languages was held in March 1955. Its proceedings[34] dealt extensively with shortcomings in the organization of language teaching in both secondary and higher schools. Shortage of qualified teachers, laxity in standards,

---

* "Gotov k trudu i oborone SSSR" abbreviated as GTO—1st stage, 2nd stage, and a special category, "Be Ready for. . . ." Each category has norms ("technical indexes") formally established for different ages and by sex.

absence of teaching aids, and particularly the general curricular overload were blamed for the admittedly low level of achievement:

> It is obvious to everyone that as far as the practical mastery of
> foreign languages is concerned the situation as it stands is clearly
> unfortunate. To a considerable extent it results from errors in the
> methodology of teaching and also from the inadequate qualifica-
> tions of teachers, particularly in the outlying institutions. Never-
> theless, the organizational defects and particularly the very tight
> time budget are exerting a not inconsiderable influence.[35]

Much more was said and published on the teaching of foreign languages in the months following this conference. In September one
letter to the editors of *Izvestiya* referred to the March conference in
part as follows:

> ... the Conference proposed a number of measures directed toward
> a radical improvement in the teaching of foreign languages in the
> secondary and higher schools. But the solution of the problems
> depends upon the ministries. ... We, the teachers, have not yet
> experienced any change in the attention given to the teaching of
> foreign languages.[36]

Toward the end of 1955, formal changes in the *uchebnyi* plans with
respect to language instruction were announced by the Ministry. The
announcement stated that the Ministry of Higher Education "has
worked out a number of measures, the adoption of which should [or
must] bring about a sharp change in the teaching of foreign languages
at institutions of higher learning."[37] Whether these measures have
already been introduced or are merely scheduled for a future adoption
is not clear.

The new provisions allot from 240 to 270 hours (first and second year,
$3\frac{1}{2}$ to 4 hours per week) for the study of foreign languages in the
science faculties of the universities and engineering schools and in all
other schools not less than 140 hours (2 hours per week). After the first
2 years of compulsory study, further class attendance (2 hours per
week) is optional with the student, who is, nevertheless, subject to
zachety and examinations, typically as follows:

Five *zachety* (after the first, second, third, sixth, and seventh
semesters).

Two graded examinations (after the fourth and eighth semesters).

The directors of institutions and heads of the language departments
were instructed:

> ... not to permit duplication of the [secondary] school course in
> a foreign language at the college level, [but] to raise the level of

demand and determinedly do away with liberalism in evaluating the student's achievement in foreign languages.[38]

Similar categorical injunctions were issued on a number of methodological points, such as the assignment of articles for translation in the field of a student's work, the formation of language clubs, the preparation of new textbooks to be published in 1956–1958, and the establishment of 3- to 6-month refresher courses to increase the qualifications of language teachers. Beginning with 1955–1956, provisions were to be made in the faculties of foreign languages in universities and pedagogical institutes to teach certain theoretical subjects in foreign languages.

The objectives have been set high. It is obvious, however, that several academic cycles will have to be completed before the average level of competency in foreign languages among the science and engineering students can be significantly raised.* Nevertheless, the fact remains that *every* student in the Soviet institutions of higher learning studies at least one foreign language.

What languages are being taught in the Soviet schools? At the college level the average student (excluding language specialists) studies English, German, or French—apparently in that order of frequency. The importance of English for engineers and scientists has been repeatedly emphasized in Soviet literature. Professor P. B. Terent'yev, for instance, recently published an article in which he advanced the view that "German is important for the study of the history of science and English for the study of its present status of development."[39] He supported his view by reference to an article published in *Science,* "The Languages of the Language of Science," in which it was shown that 45.5 per cent of some 34.7 thousand mathematical papers accounted for in a certain study were written in English.[40] He also cited the fact that at the Leningrad Public Library some 500 calls for [scientific or technical] English journals are made daily. His own count of 35,020 titles of papers in biology showed that 39.2 per cent were written in English. Among 727 titles listed in a few issues of the Soviet bibliographical publication "New Foreign Books" [natural sciences, technical, medical, and agriculture] the author found that 69.9 per cent were in English. He concluded that:

English should be considered the first and unconditionally necessary language for students; knowledge of English will give them the

* We would emphasize that these comments refer to students other than those who *specialize* in foreign languages *per se.* There are 19 pedagogical institutes and 72 faculties within other institutions which specialize in teaching foreign languages.

means of access to 40 or 50 per cent of the world's foreign [scientific and technical] literature.

Social Sciences

Approximately 7 per cent of the Soviet student's scheduled time in all schools is assigned for the study of the Foundations of Marxism-Leninism and Political Economy, these subjects together forming a category officially labeled "Social-Political" (in universities) and "Social-Economic" (in engineering schools). A closely related subject, Dialectic and Historical Materialism, usually listed as philosophy, is given in universities only.*   Including philosophy, the proportion of time given to instruction in Soviet dogma at the science faculties of universities, e.g., physics faculty, amounts to nearly 13 per cent of the total. The 1956 formulation of the social science content of the university and engineering school curricula prescribed the following courses:

Semesters	Subject	Hours
(1) (2) (3)	History of the Communist Party	160
(3) (4) (5) (6)	Political Economy	160
(7) (8)	Dialectic and Historical Materialism	70

The instruction in these subjects is conducted either by separate departments (*kafedra*) of similar name or jointly with the Department of Marxism-Leninism.[41]

The Soviet school generally "proceeds from the well-known Leninist thesis that the whole matter of education, nurture [*vospitaniye*], and teaching of modern youth should be the inculcation in it of communist ethics."[42]   At the secondary school level the task of bringing up the youth in accordance with Party objectives (which are reflected throughout the secondary school curriculum) is assigned to all teachers. At the college level the academic part of this task is allotted largely to the teachers of social sciences: ". . . the teachers of social sciences must nurture in the students the spirit of devotion to the tasks of the Party, the spirit of Soviet patriotism, friendship among peoples, and proletarian internationalism."[43]   Of these objectives, the spirit of devotion to Party tasks, that is, to the Party line, is presumably rated by the Party as far above the others; all other virtues are meant to derive automatically from devotion to the Party line. As the Party line shifts, so Soviet social science teachers change their emphasis and interpre-

---

* The 1956 designations are (1) History of the Communist Party of the Soviet Union, (2) Political Economy, and (3) Dialectic and Historic Materialism; all three subjects were included in every 1956–1957 curriculum without exception, but the syllabic content of these courses is said to vary somewhat with the category of school. (*Pravda*, July 7, 1956, p. 3.)

tations, obediently and passively following the path of the latest detour; and the teachers are obediently, accurately, and passively echoed by their students on the examinations.

The organization and content of courses in Soviet social sciences for university and engineering students are outside the scope of this survey. We would merely note that, leaving aside any direct consequences of the intense if not always effectual indoctrination, the spoon-fed dicta of Soviet social science effectively fill the time that might otherwise permit an engineering or science student to engage in genuinely humanistic reflections and study.

Some of the Subjects Not Found in Any Soviet Curriculum

A conspicuous feature of Soviet science and engineering curricula is the absence of any "make-up" courses in elementary mathematics or in any of the other subjects included in the curricula of the ten-year school. In contrast, a recent study has shown that among American colleges:

1. Sixty-two per cent offer remedial courses in high school algebra.
2. Some institutions among those which do not offer remedial courses require the deficient student to take night school or extension courses.
3. Of those students who would normally take college algebra, 34 per cent are taking a *remedial* algebra course.[44]

Except for physical sciences, mathematics, and a foreign language, no subjects taught in the secondary school are continued at college level by Soviet engineering or science students. There are no offerings comparable to the English composition, literature, history, or any other humanities found in American engineering and scientific curricula. The formal general education of the Soviet science or engineering student ends with his graduation from the ten-year school; in college, except for the Soviet "social sciences," his work is limited to training in professional subjects and skills.

NOTES TO CHAPTER 7

[1] M. G. Uroyev, "Novoye v uchebnykh planakh universitetov" (The New University Curricula), *Vestnik vysshei shkoly*, No. 11, November 1955, p. 28.

[2] *Vestnik vysshei shkoly*, No. 9, September 1953, p. 36.

[3] *Vestnik vysshei shkoly*, No. 11, November 1951, pp. 29 f.

[4] K. A. Potresov, "Nekotorye mysli ob uluchshenii uchebnovo protsessa" (Some Reflections on the Improvement of the Academic Process), *Vestnik vysshei shkoly*, No. 10, October 1953, p. 28.

5 *Ibid.*

6 K. A. Ivanovich, "Bol'she printsipial'nosti i trebovatel'nosti v nauchno-peda-gogicheskoi rabote" (Greater Adherence to Principles and Demands in the Work of Pedagogical Science), *Vestnik vysshei shkoly,* No. 10, October 1954, p. 45.

7 *Vestnik vysshei shkoly,* No. 11, November 1953, p. 4.

8 *Vestnik vysshei shkoly,* No. 5, May 1955, p. 58.

9 K. Ya. Shaposhnikov (Director of the Taganrog Radiotechnical Institute), in *Vestnik vysshei shkoly,* No. 2, February 1956.

10 G. P. Golovinskii, "Novoye v uchebnykh planakh i programmakh vtuzov" (What Is New in the Academic Plans and Syllabi of the Higher Technical Schools), *Vestnik vysshei shkoly,* No. 5, May 1955, pp. 19 and 21.

11 *Ibid.,* p. 24.

12 M. G. Uroyev, *op. cit.,* p. 28. Also an editorial in *Vestnik vysshei shkoly,* No. 7, July 1955, p. 1.

13 M. P. Ivanov, "Gotovit' inzhenerov stankostroitelei s shirokim tekhnicheskim krugozorom" (To Train Machine Construction Engineers with a Wide Technical Horizon), *Vestnik vysshei shkoly,* No. 1, January 1956, p. 5.

14 M. P. Vukalovich and L. Z. Fradkin, "O fakul'tativnykh predmetakh" (On the Elective Subjects), *Vestnik vysshei shkoly,* No. 10, October 1955, p. 4.

15 M. G. Uroyev, *op. cit.,* p. 30.

16 *Vestnik vysshei shkoly,* No. 10, October 1955, p. 7.

Nevertheless, judging by a later comment *(Vestnik vysshei shkoly,* No. 2, February 1956, p. 15), the new plans provide also for another type of "faculty" subjects, those that officially are optional with the student but in fact are required. The source states directly: ". . . there are course subjects which are not listed in the time schedule but which in practice are absolutely compulsory." The author mentions "physical training" as an example of such a course, referring to it as *"fizicheskaya podgotovka"* rather than the usual *fizicheskoye vospitaniye* (physical education), a course subject normally listed for the first two years (136 hours in all).

17 Cenis Source Memorandum No. 15.

18 P. I. Podgornyi, "O nedostatkakh vysshevo sel'skokhozyaistvennove obrazo-vaniya" (On the Shortcomings of Higher Education in Agriculture), *Vestnik vysshei shkoly,* No. 10, October 1953, p. 19. The author suggests a change in certain prac-tices which, in his opinion, have led to ". . . a condition under which *zachety* are being transformed into virtual examinations."

19 *Vestnik vysshei shkoly,* No. 10, October 1954, p. 3.

20 *Ibid.*

21 I. M. Galemin, "Reshitel'no ustranyat' dublirovaniye v prepodavanii" (Deci-sively to Eliminate Duplications in Teaching), *Vestnik vysshei shkoly,* No. 11, November 1954, p. 37.

22 A. M. Soifer, "Vospityvat' inzhenerov-novatorov" (To Nurture Engineers-Innovators), *Vestnik vysshei shkoly,* No. 10, October 1955, p. 15.

23 G. K. Borkhvardt, "Razvivat' samostoyatel'nost v uchebnoi rabote studentov" (Develop Self-Reliance in the Work of the Students), *Vestnik vysshei shkoly,* No. 9, September 1953, p. 37.

24 *Vestnik vysshei shkoly,* No. 4, April 1954, p. 3.

25 Cenis Translation Series 55–38. Other examples:

Moscow State Pedagogical Institute (Normal School, 4-year term) 4,103 hours
(*Vestnik vysshei shkoly,* No. 9, September 1953)
Machine Construction Institutes (5-year term?) 5,375 hours
(*Vestnik vysshei shkoly,* No. 4, April 1954)

Bauman School, "Technology of Machine Construction . . ." 4,848 hours
(Cenis Translation Series 55–24)
Moscow Higher Technical School (MVTU) Named after Bauman was established
in c. 1830 (as Moscow Trade School) and is perhaps the best engineering school in
the Soviet Union. Its 5½ year term of instruction is not typical of all the technical
institutes in Soviet Russia. For many engineering courses the term is 4 years and 10
months, and the average term perhaps does not exceed 5 years; the yearly load
and distribution of time, however, is approximately the same in all engineering
schools and universities.

26 *Vestnik vysshei shkoly*, No. 4, April 1954, p. 48.

27 *Ibid.*, p. 3.

28 K. M. Barshauskas, "Prodolzhat' sovershenstvovaniye uchebnykh planov" (Continue to Perfect Academic Plans), *Vestnik vysshei shkoly*, No. 2, February 1956, p. 15.

29 According to E. N. Medynskii, *Narodnoye obrazovaniye v SSSR*, p. 174, lectures on the average occupy 50 per cent of the scheduled time.

30 *Ibid.*

Agricultural Institutes	40–52 weeks
Normal Schools	12 weeks average
Medical Schools	16 weeks

31 *Vestnik vysshei shkoly*, No. 1, January 1955, p. 31.
This issue contains a number of articles on the question of physical education
in higher schools, pp. 28–38. For an article on the athletic achievements among
students see *Vestnik vysshei shkoly*, No. 9, September 1953, pp. 55 ff.

32 A review of articles on this topic is given in *Vestnik vysshei shkoly*, No. 8,
August 1953, pp. 20–23.

33 *Izvestiya*, September 15, 1955; letter to the editors.

34 *Vestnik vysshei shkoly*, No. 5, May 1955, pp. 47–56.

35 *Ibid.*, p. 54.

36 *Izvestiya*, September 15, 1955.

37 "Vooruzhit' studentov prochnymi znaniyami" (Arm the Students with Firm
Knowledge), *Vestnik vysshei shkoly*, No. 12, December 1955, pp. 53 f.

38 *Vestnik vysshei shkoly*, No. 12, December 1955, p. 54.

39 "Obyazatel'noye usloviye uspeshnoi podgotovki kadrov" (The Necessary Conditions for the Successful Training of Cadres), *Vestnik vysshei shkoly*, No. 12,
December 1955, p. 50.

40 R. Howerton and Ch. Diss, *Science*, No. 3041, 1953, pp. 391–392.

41 *Vestnik vysshei shkoly*, No. 7, July 1956, p. 46.

42 *Uchitel'skaya gazeta*, April 16, 1955.

43 S. V. Kaftanov, "Zadachi kafedr obshchestvennykh nauk v novom uchebnom
godu" (The Tasks of the Teachers of Social Science in the New Academic Year),
Vestnik vysshei shkoly, No. 10, October 1955, p. 4.

44 W. L. Williams, "What the Colleges Are Doing About the Poorly Prepared
Student," *Amer. Math. Monthly*, February 1954, pp. 86–88, cited in *A Survey of
Mathematical Education*, Educational Testing Service, October 1955 (draft for
interoffice circulation).

8

SOVIET HIGHER EDUCATION:

SAMPLE CURRICULA AT AN ENGINEERING

SCHOOL (ME), A UNIVERSITY (PHYSICS),

AND A PEDAGOGICAL INSTITUTE (MATHEMATICS)

1. A CURRICULUM IN MECHANICAL ENGINEERING

General Provisions

The specific curriculum presented here as a sample of a Soviet course in mechanical engineering represents perhaps the most advanced Soviet plan of training engineers in the specialty defined as "Technology of Machine Construction, Metal Cutting Machine Tools, and Tools."[1] It appears that until 1955 this specialty, very broad by Soviet standards, was taught only at the Bauman Higher Technical School.* In other engineering schools this field of mechanical engineering was divided into three distinct specialties, each with a different curriculum, as follows:

Technology of Machine Construction.
Metal Cutting Machine Tools.
Metal Cutting Tools.

In 1955 the Ministry of Higher Education decreed the consolidation of these formerly separate undergraduate programs in all engineering institutes offering training in machine and instrument construction specialties.† Consequently, the curriculum summarized and commented upon below refers to a very significant branch of training in

* Since c. 1945, when this broader specialty was first established.
† Among the various specialties recognized in this general category of mechanical engineering (somewhat comparable to MIT's single option [Design] in Course II

mechanical engineering and the one which is likely to be currently emphasized and expanded:

> In the machine and instrument construction industries the needs for highly qualified cadres in such basic specialties as "Technology of Machine Construction," "Metal Cutting Machine Tools," and "Metal Cutting Tools" . . . have not been completely satisfied now for a long time. For instance, last year [1955] the industry's demand for engineers in the enumerated specialties was only 50 per cent met.[2]

The curriculum for training "Mechanical Engineers in Technology of Machine Construction, Metal Cutting Machine Tools, and Tools" at the Bauman Higher Technical School provides for 4,848 scheduled class hours of instruction distributed within a 5-year course approximately as follows:*

	Scheduled Class Hours	
Year of the Course	MVTU	MIT*
First	1,222	660
Second	1,105	750
Third	973	615
Fourth	768	585
4 years	4,068	2,610
Fifth	780	
Total, 5 years, MVTU class hours	4,848	
Estimated preparation time for an average student†		3,180
Total, 4 years, MIT, including outside preparation		5,790

* Course II (Mechanical Engineering), Group 6 (Design).

† At MIT the credit hours associated with a given subject indicate the total hours per week required in class and laboratory *and estimated outside preparation.*

[Mechanical Engineering]) are "Peat Machinery," "Forestry and Forest Industries Machinery and Mechanisms," "Railroad Car Construction," "Machinery and Technology of the Foundry Industries," and others, including until recently "Metal Cutting Machine Tools," and "Metal Cutting Tools." *Vestnik vysshei shkoly,* No. 1, January 1956, p. 7.

* The total term of instruction for this specialty at MVTU is 5½ years as against typically 4 years 10 months in other engineering schools, the difference partly accounted for by a longer time allowed for industrial practice. Some of the differences between the MVTU curriculum cited here and similar curricula in other schools are as follows:

	MVTU	Other Schools
Total term	5½ years	c. 5 years
Total scheduled hours	4,848	4,886
Lecture hours	2,632	2,519
Diploma project preparation, weeks	21	17

This tabulation shows a very fundamental difference between the relative weights given to the scheduled hours in the Soviet plan and at MIT—to cite a typical schedule of an American engineering school.* Assuming that about 48 hours per week is the average practical limit of a student's effective application (the hours expected at MIT), the Soviet student in his first 4 years would have only one-third of his time available for independent preparation—against more than one-half (55 per cent) in the case of MIT undergraduates.

The total time of the MVTU curricula is allocated by types of instruction, as follows:

	Hours[3]	Per Cent
Lectures	2,632	54.3
Laboratory work	595	12.3
Practical work, seminars, exercises, and similar	1,303	26.9
Term projects and papers	318	6.5
Total	4,848	100.0

No direct and meaningful comparison of this distribution with practices in American schools (or at MIT specifically) can readily be made because of differences in the definitions and in the organization of work. At MIT, for instance, the gross categories in the most nearly comparable curriculum (Course II, Group 6) are approximately as follows:

	Hours	Per Cent
Lectures and recitations	1,935	74
Drawing and laboratory	675	26

The more or less corresponding divisions of time in the MVTU curriculum (with drafting and the term project time added to the laboratory hours) would show approximately 69 and 31 per cent, respectively.

Course Content, MVTU versus MIT

Table 45 presents a comparison between the major features of the selected MVTU curriculum and its nearest equivalent among the MIT curricula in mechanical engineering, the design option. The table is arranged in two parts. Part One lists the subjects of instruction, scheduled hours, and per cent of total scheduled time per subject in both the MVTU and MIT curricula. Insofar as possible, subjects

---

* With reference to scheduled hours the contrast between Soviet and European practice, where compulsory attendance is seldom required, is even greater.

identical in name, similar in content, or closely related in the two curricula are listed opposite each other to facilitate direct comparison of hours and coverage within a given category of subjects. Part Two lists class schedules semester by semester, permitting direct comparison of the sequence in which subjects are taught, thus indicating the degree of integration of separate disciplines in the two curricula.

The comparative listing of subjects (Part One of the table) graphically points up the Soviet emphasis on specialization and on extensive and intensive training in what appear to be largely vocational and industrially-oriented knowledge and techniques. The reader will note, for instance, three subjects in metallurgy and technology of metals (253 hours) in the MVTU curriculum, versus one required course, engineering metals (90 hours), at MIT. Even a more striking contrast is provided by the fact that the MVTU curriculum includes a large number of subjects dealing with various types of tools and equipment for which there are no counterparts in the basic curricula of mechanical engineering at MIT, including the majority of the MVTU subjects of the "present art" type, such as "Material Handling Machinery and Mechanisms." As to the specialized but fundamental engineering subjects which are included in the MVTU curriculum but do not appear in the MIT list, it should be noted that a large number of elective subjects is available to the American engineering senior, permitting him to begin specialization in any one area within his general field during the last year of undergraduate work.

TABLE 45. SOVIET MVTU[1] CURRICULUM IN MECHANICAL ENGINEERING, "TECHNOLOGY OF MACHINE CONSTRUCTION, METAL CUTTING MACHINE TOOLS, AND TOOLS," COMPARED WITH MIT CURRICULUM OF COURSE II (MECHANICAL ENGINEERING), GROUP 6 (DESIGN)

Summary	MVTU	MIT
Course of instruction, years	5[2]	4
Weeks of class instruction	153	120
Scheduled class hours	4,848	2,610
Class hours/week, average	31.7	21.7
Industrial practice, weeks	24	[3]

Part One: Subjects of Instruction, Scheduled Hours of Instruction, and Per Cent of Total Scheduled Load

MVTU			MIT		
Subject	Hours	Per Cent	Subject	Hours	Per Cent
Higher Mathematics[4]	388	8.0	Calculus	135	5.2
			Differential Equations	45	1.7
Physics[5]	245	5.0	Physics	300	11.5
Chemistry, General	120	2.5	Chemistry, General	180	6.9
Theoretical Mechanics	214	4.4	Applied Mechanics	150	5.8
			Fluid Mechanics	60	2.3
Heat Engineering, Gen'l	78	1.6	Heat Engineering	105	4.0
Descriptive Geometry	90	1.9	(Freshman elective, 60 hours)		
Machine Drawing	188	3.9	Machine Drawing	90	3.4
Strength of Materials	232	4.8	Strength of Materials	45	1.7
			Mechanical Behavior of Materials	60	2.3
Theory of Mechanisms and Machines	198	4.1	Machine Design	195	7.5
Machine Details	215	4.4			
Hydraulics and Hydraulic Machinery	84	1.7	Industrial Hydraulic Machinery (Design)	75	2.9
General Electrotechniques and Measurement of Nonelectric Magnitudes	190	3.9	Electrical Engineering, Foundations	60	2.3
			Engineering Laboratory	60	2.3

Note: MVTU data are from the 1955 curriculum in Cenis Translation Series 55-24; the MIT data are from MIT *Catalogue Issue for 1955–1956 Session.*

TABLE 45, Part One (continued)

MVTU			MIT		
Subject	Hours	Per Cent	Subject	Hours	Per Cent
Physical Metallurgy and Thermal Treatment of Metals	84	1.7	Engineering Metals	90	3.5
Technology of Metals (Metallurgy and Hot Fabrication)	118	2.4			
Thermal Treatment of [Machine] Details	39	0.8			
Shop Training	204	4.2	Machine Tools, Introduction[6]	60	2.3
Metal Cutting Machine Tools and Automatics	337	7.0			
Hydraulic Equipment in Machine Tools	56	1.2			
Electric Equipment in Machine Tools	65	1.3			
Machine Construction Technology	208	4.3			
Construction of Mechanical Equipment	39	0.8			
Interchangeability and Technical Measurement	68	1.4			
Material Handling Machinery and Mechanisms	116	2.4			
Metal Cutting	80	1.6	Machine Tool Fundamentals	45	1.7
Metal Cutting Tools	221	4.6			
Planning of Machine Building Shops and Elements of Structural Engineering	65	1.3			
Automation of Industrial Processes	65	1.3			
Industrial Economics, Organization and Planning of Enterprises	91	1.9			
Safety and Fire Protection Engineering	39	0.8			

Table 45, Part One (concluded)

MVTU			MIT		
Subject	Hours	Per Cent	Subject	Hours	Per Cent
History of Engineering	39	0.8			
			Mechanical Engineering Problems	45	1.7
			Humanities	360	13.8
Marxism-Leninism	252	5.2			
Political Economy	140	2.9			
Foreign Language	134	2.8			
Electives (for credit)			Electives (for credit)	270	10.3
Physical Education	134	2.8	Physical Education	7	
Military Training	8		Military Science	180	6.9
Total, hours	4,848	100.0	Total, hours	2,610	100.0

[1] Moscow Higher Technical School Named after Bauman.

[2] The total course of instruction is 5.5 years but there are no classes scheduled beyond the fifth year.

[3] None required. Six months or at least one summer of industrial employment before graduation is recommended; students enrolled in the Cooperative Course (Course II-B) spend approximately 6 months as regularly paid employees of co-operating concerns.

[4] Syllabus in Cenis Translation Series 55-37.

[5] Syllabus in Cenis Translation Series 55-17.

[6] At MIT shop training is incidental to topical subjects and is not given *per se*.

[7] Required. The requirement, equivalent to one year of physical education, can be met in a variety of ways during the first two years.

[8] Time allotment unknown.

TABLE 45 (continued)

Part Two: Subjects and Hours per Week by Semesters

First Semester
(First Year, First Term)

I. Subjects of Instruction	Hours per Week	
	MVTU	MIT
Foundations of Marxism-Leninism	4^9	
Foreign Language	2^9	
Higher Mathematics	8^{10}	3
General Chemistry	$4^{9,10}$	6
Descriptive Geometry	5^{10}	
Machine Drafting and Drawing	5^9	
Technology of Metals	2^9	
Shop Training	4^9	
Physical Education	2	11
Physics		5
Western Civilization, Foundations		3
Military Science		3
Elective		4
Total, first semester	36	24

MVTU: Examinations   3
             Zachety   6

II. Other Subjects

MVTU "Faculty" Subjects (optional, in addition to the prescribed load):
Physical Education and Sports   3 hr/wk

MIT Electives (taken for credit): One of fourteen approved subjects, including science, graphics, and language subjects. Can be taken either in the 1st or 2nd semester.

[9] Followed by a zachet.
[10] Followed by an examination.
[11] Required.

TABLE 45, Part Two (continued)

Second Semester
(First Year, Second Term)

I. Subjects of Instruction	Hours per Week MVTU	MIT
Foundations of Marxism-Leninism	3^{10}	
Foreign Language	2^9	
Higher Mathematics	8^{10}	3
Physics	$6^{9,10}$	5
General Chemistry	$3^{9,10}$	6
Machine Drafting and Drawing	2^9	
Theoretical Mechanics	3^{10}	
Technology of Metals	3	
Shop Training	4^9	
Physical Education and Sports	2^9	11
Western Civilization, Foundations		3
Military Science		3
Total, second semester	36	20

MVTU: Examinations   5
          Zachety   6

II. Other Subjects

MVTU "Faculty" Subjects (optional, in addition to the prescribed load):
Physical Education and
Sports   3 hr/wk
Machine Drafting   1 hr/wk

MIT Electives (taken for credit):
One of sixteen approved subjects or none if the student has taken his elective in the first semester.

[9] Followed by a *zachet*.
[10] Followed by an examination.
[11] Required.

TABLE 45, Part Two (continued)

Third Semester
(Second Year, First Term)

	Hours per Week	
I. Subjects of Instruction	MVTU	MIT
Foundations of Marxism-Leninism	4^9	
Foreign Language	2^9	
Higher Mathematics	4^{10}	3
Physics	$5^{9,10}$	5
Machine Drafting and Drawing	2^9	6
Mechanics[12]	6^{10}	3
Strength of Materials	$6^{9,10}$	
Technology of Metals	2^{10}	
Physical Education and Sports	2	11
Machine Tools, Introduction		4
Humanities		3
Military Science		3
Total, third semester	33	27

MVTU:	Examinations	5
	Zachety	5

II. Other Subjects

MVTU "Faculty" Subjects (optional, in addition to the prescribed load):

MIT Electives (taken for credit): None

Physical Education and Sports	3 hr/wk
Machine Drafting	1 hr/wk

[9] Followed by a *zachet*.
[10] Followed by an examination.
[11] Required.
[12] At MIT "Applied Mechanics"; at MVTU "Theoretical Mechanics."

TABLE 45, Part Two (continued)

Fourth Semester
(Second Year, Second Term)

I. Subjects of Instruction	Hours per Week	
	MVTU	MIT
Foundations of Marxism-Leninism	4^{10}	
Foreign Language	2^{10}	
Higher Mathematics	3^{9}	3
Physics	$4^{9,10}$	5
Machine Drafting and Drawing	2^{9}	
Mechanics[12]	4^{10}	3
Strength of Materials	$6^{9,10}$	
Theory of Mechanisms and Machines	$7^{9,13}$	
Physical Education and Sports	2^{9}	11
Engineering Metals		6
Humanities		3
Military Science		3
Total, fourth semester	34	23

MVTU: Examinations   5
           Zachety   6
           Term Projects   1

II. Other Subjects

MVTU "Faculty" Subjects (optional, in addition to the prescribed load):

MIT Electives (taken for credit): None

Physical Education and Sports   3 hr/wk
Machine Drafting   1 hr/wk

[9] Followed by a *zachet*.
[10] Followed by an examination.
[11] Required.
[12] At MIT "Applied Mechanics"; at MVTU "Theoretical Mechanics."
[13] Includes a term project.

TABLE 45, Part Two (continued)

Fifth Semester
(Third Year, First Term)

Hours per Week

I. Subjects of Instruction	MVTU	MIT
Political Economy	2^9	
Strength of Materials	2^9	
Theory of Mechanisms and Machines	$5^{9,10,13}$	
Machine Details (at MIT–Design)	7^{10}	4
Shop Training	4^9	
Interchangeability and Technical Measurements	4^{10}	
Machine Tools	$5^{9,10}$	
Theoretical Mechanics		4
Heat Engineering		4
Electrical Engineering, Foundations		4
Humanities		3
Total, fifth semester	29	19

MVTU: Examinations   4
       Zachety   5
       Term Projects 1

II. Other Subjects

MVTU "Faculty" Subjects (optional,   MIT Electives (taken for credit):
in addition to the prescribed load):   None

Physical Education and
Sports   3 hr/wk
Foreign Language   30 hr/sem

[9] Followed by a *zachet*.
[10] Followed by an examination.
[13] Includes a term project.

TABLE 45, Part Two (continued)

Sixth Semester
(Third Year, Second Term)

	Hours per Week	
I. Subjects of Instruction	MVTU	MIT
Political Economy	3^{10}	
Machine Details (at MIT–Design)	$6^{9,13}$	5
Electrical Engineering[14]	$5^{9,10}$	
Physical Metallurgy and Heat Treatment	$6^{9,10}$	
Material Handling Machinery and Mechanisms	2^{9}	
Machine Tools	3	3
Metal Cutting	$5^{9,10}$	
Fluid Mechanics		4
Mechanical Behavior of Materials		4
Heat Engineering		3
Humanities		3
Total, sixth semester	30	22

MVTU: Examinations   4
              Zachety   5
              Term Projects   1

II. After the Sixth Semester at MVTU:

"1st Technological Practice"   4 weeks

III. Other Subjects

MVTU "Faculty" Subjects (optional, in addition to the prescribed load):

MIT Electives (taken for credit): None

Physical Education and
Sports   3 hr/wk
Foreign Language
(subject to a *zachet*)   30 hr/sem
Nomography   25 hr/sem
Machine Design   50 hr/sem

[9] Followed by a *zachet*.
[10] Followed by an examination.
[13] Includes a term project.
[14] At MVTU: "Electrotechniques and Measurement of Nonelectric Magnitudes."

TABLE 45, Part Two (continued)

Seventh Semester
(Fourth Year, First Term)

	Hours per Week	
I. Subjects of Instruction	MVTU	MIT
Political Economy	2^9	
Electrical Engineering	$6^{9,10}$	
Hydraulics and Hydraulic Machinery	$6^{9,10}$	
Material Handling Machinery and Mechanisms	$6^{9,13}$	
Machine Tools	$3^{9,10}$	
Hydraulic Equipment in Machine Tools	$4^{9,10}$	
Strength of Materials		3
Machine Design		4
Humanities		3
Additional subjects (as selected), estimated		10
Total, seventh semester	27	20

MVTU: Examinations   4
Zachety   6
Term Projects   1

II. After the Seventh Semester at MVTU:

"2nd Technological Practice"   4 weeks

III. Other Subjects

MVTU "Faculty" Subjects (optional, in addition to the prescribed load):

Physical Education and
Sports   3 hr/wk
Foreign Language   30 hr/sem
Differential Geometry   25 hr/sem
Machine Design   50 hr/sem

MIT Electives (taken for credit): Additional topics (approximately 10 hours of scheduled instruction) selected from a large number of subjects representing various fields of endeavor

[9] Followed by a *zachet*.
[10] Followed by an examination.
[13] Includes a term project.

TABLE 45, Part Two (continued)

Eighth Semester
(Fourth Year, Second Term)

	Hours per Week	
I. Subjects of Instruction	MVTU	MIT
Political Economy	3^{10}	
Machine Tools	$12^{9,10,13,9}$	
Electrical Equipment in Machine Tools	$5^{9,10}$	
Metal Cutting Tools	6	
Machine Construction Technology	4	
Foreign Language	9	
Mechanical Engineering Problems		3
Engineering Laboratory		4
Industrial Hydraulic Machinery, Design		5
Humanities		3
Additional subject (as selected), estimated		4
		Thesis[15]
Total, eighth semester	30	19

MVTU: Examinations 3
Zachety 4
Term Projects 1

II. After the Eighth Semester at MVTU:

"2nd Technological Practice" (continued)   4 weeks

III. Other Subjects

MVTU "Faculty" Subjects (optional, in addition to the prescribed load):

Physical Education and
Sports 3 hr/wk
Foreign Language
(subject to a zachet) 30 hr/sem
Machine Design 50 hr/sem
Feed Mechanisms 25 hr/sem

MIT Electives (taken for credit):
Additional subject selected in the student's field of major interest

[9] Followed by a zachet.
[10] Followed by an examination.
[13] Includes a term project.
[15] Bachelor's thesis, estimated 8 hours per week or approximately 120 hours total time.

TABLE 45, Part Two (continued)

Ninth Semester
(Fifth Year, First Term)

Hours per Week

I. Subjects of Instruction	MVTU	MIT
Heat Engineering	$6^{9,10}$	
Metal Cutting Tools	$4^{9,10,13}$	
Machine Construction Technology	$7^{9,10}$	
Construction of [Mechanical] Devices	3^{10}	
Industrial Economics, Organization, and Planning of Enterprises	4^9	
History of Engineering	3^9	
Safety and Fire Protection Engineering	3^{10}	
Total, ninth semester	30	

	MVTU:	Examinations	5
		Zachety	5
		Term Projects	1

II. After the Ninth Semester at MVTU:

　　　"3rd Technological Practice"　　4 weeks

III. Other Subjects

MVTU "Faculty" Subjects (optional, in addition to the prescribed load):
　　Progressive Methods of Metal Fabrication　　25 hr /sem

[9] Followed by a *zachet*.
[10] Followed by an examination.
[13] Includes a term project.

TABLE 45, Part Two (concluded)

Tenth Semester
(Fifth Year, Second Term)

	Hours per Week	
I. Subjects of Instruction	MVTU	MIT
Electrical Engineering	2^9	
Machine Tools	$7^{9,10}$	
Machine Construction Technology	$5^{9,10,13}$	
Planning of Machine Building Shops and Elements of Structural Engineering	5^{10}	
Thermal Treatment of Details	3^9	
Automation of Industrial Processes	$5^{9,10}$	
Industrial Economics, Organization and Planning of Enterprises	3^{10}	
Total, tenth semester	30	

MVTU: Examinations   5
             Zachety   5
             Term Projects   1

II. After the Tenth Semester at **MVTU**:

     Prediploma Industrial Practice   8 weeks[16]
     Diploma Project and Defense   21 weeks

III. Other Subjects

MVTU "Faculty" Subjects (optional, in addition to the prescribed load):
     Assembly and Testing of Machinery   25 hr /sem
     Special Topics in Welded Construction   25 hr /sem

[9] Followed by a *zachet*.
[10] Followed by an examination.
[13] Includes a term project.
[16] At MIT: "All students of the Mechanical Engineering Department are urged to obtain 6 months, or at least one summer, of practical experience in some industrial activity of their own choice before graduation." Students enrolled in the Cooperative Course (ME II-B) spend approximately 6 months in actual practical work as regularly paid employees of the cooperating industrial concerns.

The single purposiveness of engineering training in the Soviet Union is reflected in the sequence of the (vocational) subjects directly related to the "profile" of a given specialty. The progression of specialized training directed toward immediate usefulness in industry is shown in Table 46.

At MVTU these specialized subjects take up 1,149 hours of instruction, that is, over 45 per cent of the scheduled time in the last 3 years of instruction; at MIT and in other accredited American schools of engineering these subjects, if given at all, are usually elective in the design options of mechanical engineering curricula. The explanation of this large difference in emphasis on technological and "practical" training is to be found not so much in the dissimilarities of educational theories as in the fundamental differences between the industrial structures and basic objectives of engineering schools in the two countries. In the Soviet Union, under central allocation of functions and responsibilities, the school is charged with the detailed preparation of specialists for specific industrial careers. The established trend in American engineering education (as distinct from the training of technicians) is away from narrowly vocational specialization at the undergraduate level. Soviet practice, in attempting to combine preparation in basic science, engineering theory, and fundamentals with training in specific applied skills, partly accounts for both the longer term of undergraduate instruction and the intensive pace at which instruction is carried on.

It is impossible categorically to say to what extent quality in Soviet preparation in science and in fundamentals of engineering theory is sacrificed in favor of "immediately useful" knowledge of existing technological practices, machinery, and materials. The Soviet student's scheduled load in mathematics, physics, chemistry, mechanics, and thermodynamics combined is 1,045 hours as against 975 hours for these subjects at MIT; but on a per cent basis (which we believe more realistically reflects the basic orientation of the curricula) the Soviet student's share of scheduled time for these fundamental subjects is only 21.5 per cent as against 37.4 in the MIT curriculum. Except for mathematics and theoretical mechanics the scheduled hours of instruction in basic subjects are *fewer* at MVTU than they are at MIT. In physics, for instance, the hours are 245 at MVTU as against 300 hours at MIT. Nevertheless, judging by the official syllabus and the prescribed textbooks, the expected *coverage* of the course in Soviet higher educational institutions is fully as comprehensive as and much more detailed and encyclopedic than that provided in a typical American physics curricu-

TABLE 46. SELECTED SPECIALIZED SUBJECTS OF INSTRUCTION IN A SOVIET
CURRICULUM FOR TRAINING MECHANICAL ENGINEERS IN "TECHNOLOGY OF
MACHINE CONSTRUCTION, METAL CUTTING MACHINE TOOLS, AND TOOLS"
USSR
c. 1955

Subject of Instruction	Hours per Semester						Total	
	V	VI	VII	VIII	IX	X	Hours	Per Cent
Total scheduled hours	493	480	378	390	390	390	2,521	100.0
Interchangeability and Measurements	68						68	2.7
Machine Tools:								
(a) General Survey	85						85	3.4
(b) Design and Construction		48	48	78			174	6.9
(c) Automatic Machine Tools				78			78	3.1
Hydraulic Equipment in Machine Tools			56				56	2.2
Electrical Equipment in Machine Tools				65			65	2.6
Material Handling Machinery		32	84				116	4.6
Machine Construction Technology:								
(a) Fundamentals				52	91		143	5.7
(b) Production Technology						65	65	2.6
Construction of Equipment					39		39	1.5
Metal Cutting Tools				78	52	91	221	8.8
Thermal Treatment of Details						39	39	1.5
Subtotal	153	80	188	351	182	195	1,149	45.6

Source: Table 45 and Cenis Translation Series 55-24 (breakdown of topics
under Machine Tools and Machine Construction Technology).

lum for engineers.* There is every reason to assume, therefore, that,
because of the excessive pressure of the scheduled load and the exten-

* The Soviet physics syllabus for higher technical schools is given in Cenis
Translation Series 55-17. This syllabus has been examined by a number of
physicists and professors of engineering at MIT. Their consensus is that this
syllabus is very complete and thorough and that it suggests a sound preparation for
specialized courses in any branch of engineering and provides for a comprehensive
presentation of physics for nonphysicists.

siveness of prescribed material, depth is somewhat sacrificed for coverage in the teaching of physics and other basic subjects of the Soviet engineering curricula. Thus the Soviet engineering student in some cases may be *exposed* to more instruction in basic science and theory than his counterpart in an accredited American engineering school; but, considering all other factors in his training program, he is more likely to acquire mere knowledge of or familiarity with basic principles than an understanding of them, and to acquire undue dependence on ready-made solutions and techniques in the approach to engineering problems.

Another characteristic of Soviet-trained engineers is reflected in the emphasis given to mathematics (388 hours at MVTU versus 180 hours at MIT). Many observers have pointed out the predilection of Soviet engineers to use formal mathematical analysis at high levels of refinement in dealing with phenomena and problems where their Western-trained counterparts are likely to depend largely on experimentally derived data and solutions.* Soviet textbooks in various branches of engineering theory as a rule give great emphasis to the analytical approach versus, for instance, the usually simpler and equally satisfactory graphic techniques. On the other hand, the many "present art"-type specialized engineering subjects appear to be largely descriptive, highly detailed, and burdened with too many specific examples of existing types of construction and design. Unfortunately, since no syllabi for any of the specialized engineering courses have been located among the available sources, the content of these subjects of instruction can be surmised only indirectly, largely from examination of textbooks and from references in Soviet publications. Without knowing the syllabus nor the extent to which a given textbook is in fact applicable and required, it is impossible categorically to pass qualitative judgment on many of the specialized courses for which only the name is known. Thus, for instance, the subject entitled Automation of Industrial Processes (Table 45) may be presented either on a highly advanced theoretical level or be largely descriptive, dealing mainly with established practices and devices.

In general, the curriculum here examined is aimed to provide for a thorough training in both basic science and engineering theory and

---

* The Soviet syllabus in higher mathematics for technological specialties is given in Cenis Translation Series 55-37.

The syllabus compares favorably with the subject matter included in the American freshman and sophomore courses in mathematics offered in the best engineering schools. Its content suggests a very thorough preparation for any theoretical course in engineering.

in specific industrial applications and practices within a major branch of the machine construction industry. Until 1955–1956 this curriculum apparently represented one of the few engineering curricula broadly structured by Soviet standards. The adoption of this or a very similar curriculum in the fall of 1955 to replace the formerly separate courses (Machine Construction, Machine Tools, and Metal Cutting Tools) represents the current drive to "broaden the profile" of engineers and to enlarge the area of their undergraduate specialization. The new policy must eventually be reflected in the organization and division of engineering responsibilities within the industry. The original reorganization of engineering curricula in the 1930's was made with a view toward satisfying the immediate needs of the key industries; and in general all the central decisions in the field of engineering education since that time have been similarly directed. It would seem that the planners have been attempting to train future engineers and technologists largely in terms of existing industrial arts and technology.

The current Soviet drive is to improve the quality of engineering training, and the adoption of broader curricula—such as the one examined here—is one step in that direction. With reference to the new curricula introduced in the fall of 1955 one Soviet educator stated:

> As is known, the profile of a specialist is determined by the *uchebnyi* plan. The overwhelming majority of the new *uchebnyi* plans were received by educators with satisfaction. It was noted that the new plans have eliminated many large defects of the academic process and have assured a transition to broader specialization.[4]

It is significant that some concern already has been expressed by the leaders of Soviet *industry* over the new approach. For instance, the wisdom of consolidating the areas of specialization which have been discussed in this chapter has been questioned:

> The curriculum of the new, consolidated specialty, "Technology of Machine Construction, Metal Cutting Tools, and Tools," under the existing term of instruction in the majority of higher institutions of technical education, four years and ten months, in our opinion cannot guarantee to the future machine builder (as a constructor) the necessary specialized knowledge in the area of computation for and design of hydraulic systems for metal cutting machine tools, the design of automatic machine tools, lines, shops, and factories. If, furthermore, one keeps in mind the substantial reduction of academic time for a number of subjects (for instance, the time allowed for such an important subject as "electrical equipment in machine tools" is reduced almost by 50 per cent) and the reduction of time given to practical studies, then it can be seen that the elimination of the specialty "Metal Cutting Machine Tools"

may lead to the lowering of quality in training engineer-machine tool constructors. The same thing can be said with reference to the specialty "Metal Cutting Tools."[5]

This comment suggests the persistence of the dilemma inherent in the Soviet approach to engineering training. The conflict between the longer-range and slower-paced view of the educator and the crash demands of the Party for industrial achievement at any cost has been resolved heretofore in favor of the immediate needs of industry.

2. A UNIVERSITY CURRICULUM IN PHYSICS

The reader will recall that under the Soviet system of higher education science *per se* is taught only at the universities; in engineering schools, physics, chemistry, other basic sciences, and mathematics are included only as service courses. The physics curriculum to be outlined in this section is typical of the physics course in all universities in the Soviet Union.

In a significant sense the development of Soviet physics, confined mainly to the universities and research institutes of the USSR Academy of Sciences, proceeded somewhat in isolation from engineering, largely because of the organizational barriers created in the 1930's between scientific education and research and the narrowly oriented training of engineers. For some years now efforts have been made by Soviet educational authorities to break down these barriers, and the reforms initiated since 1954 particularly aim at bridging the apparent gap between Soviet science and engineering.

The place of physics in engineering education has been discussed extensively both in Soviet educational literature and among American scientists.* Much of the debate in the two countries, despite the profound differences between the two educational systems, has dealt with the problems which derive from the same fact: the greatly accelerated expansion of scientific frontiers generally and the concomitant technological advances in new and revolutionary directions. The nature of the problems seen by scientists and educators can be equally well illustrated by quotations from either Soviet or American academic discussion. For instance, Professor Nathaniel H. Frank, head of the Physics Department at MIT, has stated:

*Many articles on the role of physics and the problems of teaching physics to engineers are to be found in *Vestnik vysshei shkoly,* for example, in the following issues: January 1949, March 1949, October 1951, November 1951, December 1951, January 1952, March 1952. For a translation of an article on this subject by a Soviet physicist, A. F. Ioffe, see Cenis Source Memorandum No. 5.

The problem of reassessing the role of physics in engineering education has come to be a matter of considerable urgency and significance
primarily because of the rapidly changing character and expanding
scope of both engineering and physics.[6]

Professor Frank's counterpart at the Ural Polytechnic Institute wrote
similarly of the Soviet educational philosophy:

> The question of arming young engineers graduating from insti-
> tutions of higher technical learning with knowledge in the field of
> physics is an extraordinarily important question. The role of physics
> in modern engineering is very great at the present time; undoubt-
> edly its importance will be increasing in the future. It is not simply
> a matter of quantitative growth in the number of technical appli-
> cations of achievements in physics but of a qualitatively new phe-
> nomenon: the emergence of whole new branches of technology.[7]

Professor Frank, in the address to which we referred, brought out the
dual role of physics in engineering education, that of a humanity and
that of a technical base of engineering science. He said:

> First, physics plays the role of one of the great humanities, and as
> such it follows that physics should be taught as a pure science. I
> feel that physics, along with mathematics, represents one of the
> greatest intellectual achievements of mankind, and the impact of the
> growth of science on social and political ideas has been such that a
> proper understanding of our present day culture and problems is
> difficult to attain without an adequate scientific background. This
> role of physics as a humanity fits in admirably with the growing
> emphasis on humanities in all engineering curricula.
> Secondly, there is the more traditional role of physics as a tech-
> nical base for engineering science subjects. In the past this has been
> almost exclusively the reason for the existence of physics in engi-
> neering curricula and as such the teaching of physics more often
> than not assumed the form of introductory engineering. I need
> hardly remind you that such limited objectives for physics are no
> longer adequate.

The dual role and significance of physics in the education of engineers are also recognized and commented upon—in the approved idiom
of the Party—by Soviet educators. Some of them see the teaching of
physics as providing "good opportunities for the scientific-atheistic
upbringing of the student."[8] Whatever interpretation they may put
on the humanities aspect of science, Soviet educators are, nevertheless,
clear and realistic in assessing the role of physics as the base for technical progress. The eminent Russian physicist, A. F. Ioffe, for
instance, in his article "On the Teaching of Physics in Higher Technical Schools" pointed out:

Physics is a reservoir from which new technical ideas and new technology are drawn. At a given stage of development, research in physics transmutes into important technical achievements.[9]

In this article Ioffe traces a number of revolutionary and important technological developments which have stemmed from the various branches of "pure" physics—such as luminescence (television, fluorescent lamps), semi-conductors (solar batteries, transistors), and many others. On the basis of his analysis he concludes:

... higher education must assure for the future engineer not only the knowledge of modern industries and their technology, but must also equip him with a knowledge of physics (particularly of those branches which are nearest his specialty) at such a level as will permit him to introduce into industry new, more progressive methods whenever they are ready for engineering application.[10]

Furthermore, according to Ioffe:

... higher education must arm the engineer with a clear understanding of the physical processes upon which production is based and with a sufficiently broad horizon to permit his selecting tools suitable for his purposes from the rich arsenal of physics. For that purpose the course in physics must convey not a number of disconnected bits of information but a harmonious system of knowledge. . . .*

On the basis of his conclusions Ioffe made a number of specific recommendations—"musts," in his words—among them, insofar as the curriculum is concerned, the following:

1. The teaching of physics should be a basic element of technical education, and not only an element of general education. That is why both the syllabi and the textbooks must be tailored to the profile of a given technical school.
Five or six distinct textbooks should be developed corresponding to the most important types of engineering institute. . . .
2. The courses in physics and in technical thermodynamics should be coordinated to assure that these courses give a broad treatment of energetics, an understanding of free energy, the role of irreversible processes, the place of atomic nuclear energy.
Sufficient room should be provided within the general course in physics for those fields which are connected with the most progressive directions of technology, namely, radio, semi-conductors, plastics, electronics, luminescence, and, of course, the atomic nucleus.
3. . . . the scornful attitude toward the secondary schools ought to be abandoned; the knowledge of elementary laws, which is important for the students in schools of higher technical education,

* ". . . steeped in dialectic materialism. Like the course in Marxism-Leninism, the course in physics must shape the engineer's concept of the world."

should be assured by clearly defined requirements in the entrance examinations and in physics *praktikum.** There is no need to encumber the lectures with this type of material.

4. In addition to a general course in physics in the first years of instruction, a special course of from thirty to forty hours (depending on the type of school) should be introduced for the fourth-year students. The content of these lectures should be strictly coordinated with the specific objectives of a given school and the areas of research conducted by the department (chair) of physics. One should hope that such lectures would be attended not only by the students but also by the teachers who would thus develop greater interest and knowledge in physics.

These (and many more) recommendations, made in 1951, were reinforced, modified, endorsed, and expanded by other articles and comments on the subject of physics in engineering education published in response to Ioffe's article.†

The discussion initiated by Ioffe's article was not the first on record. A. K. Kikoin, head of the physics department at the Ural Polytechnic Institute, wrote:

The problems of teaching physics in higher schools of technical education have been debated in the press and among educators on many occasions in the last few years. Unfortunately, no organizational consequences have been so far derived from these rather concrete discussions. It can be asserted that in 1951 the physics course [in schools of engineering] is structured approximately as it was fifteen years ago, and in certain of its sections is hardly distinguishable from the course as it was offered to students even in earlier times.[11]

* Recitation, drill, or review sections; more fully defined in one Soviet dictionary as follows: "A special type of learning activity which aims at a practical acquisition of the basic propositions of a certain subject, practical studies within a given subject primarily in an institution of higher learning."

† Ioffe's article (Cenis Source Memorandum No. 5), published in the USSR Ministry of Higher Education journal *(Vestnik vysshei shkoly)*, initiated an extensive debate on the role of physics and the problems of teaching physics to engineers which took the form of articles and comments published in that journal in the October, November, and December 1951 issues. Among other articles on the same or related topics published in this journal were:

"On a Physics Course for Higher Technical Schools" (No. 1, 1949).

"Problems Arising in Teaching Physics at Higher Technical Schools" (No. 3, 1949).

"On the Teaching of Physics in Higher Technical Schools" (No. 1, 1952).

"On Teaching Physics in the Higher Technical Schools: Necessity for a New Program" (No. 3, 1952).

"On Results of Considerations of Problems of Teaching Physics in Higher Technical Schools" (No. 5, 1952).

To the extent that it can be judged from the latest available references to the Soviet engineering curricula, including the one detailed in the preceding section, and to the approved physics textbooks, no significant changes have taken place in the organization of the physics course in engineering schools since the discussion of 1951 and prior to 1955. In the universities, however, the physics curriculum, far from being static, appears to have been constantly brought up to date.

The 1954–1955 Soviet university physics curriculum is summarized in Table 47.* It covers an undergraduate course in the physics "specialty" given under Physics-Mathematics, Mechanics-Mathematics, Physics, or Natural Science-Mathematics faculties.

The Soviet 5-year curriculum in physics is shown in Table 47 side by side with a comparable listing of subjects (and scheduled hours) included in the MIT (4-year) undergraduate physics course (MIT Course VIII).† It will be noted at once that the two curricula are more nearly comparable to each other than are the engineering curricula considered in the preceding section. Even with respect to the number of scheduled hours—a good index of the relative weight given to the independent work of the student—the two curricula, as can be seen from the following tabulation, are not so far apart as the engineering schedules:

	Soviet		MIT	
Field of Training	Hours	Index	Hours	Index
Engineering	4,848	186	2,610	100
Physics	4,290	150	2,865	100

Considering also the fact that the Soviet physics curriculum covers 9 semesters of scheduled work (versus 8 at MIT), the average number of hours per semester in the class schedule of Soviet physics students is only 33 per cent greater than that in the MIT curriculum; in the case of engineering courses the corresponding figure is over 48 per cent. It is significant also that the last (tenth) semester of the Soviet physics course has no scheduled hours, the entire time being available for

---

* A more detailed outline of the Soviet university course in physics is given in Cenis Translation Series 55-26.

† It should be noted that MIT occupies a rather significant place in the training of scientists, and particularly of physicists; in recent years, for instance, by one measure (eventual physics doctorates) MIT has ranked second (Harvard University being first) among American institutions of higher learning. ("Baccalaureate Origins of Science Doctorates Awarded in the United States, 1936–1950," Publication 382 of the National Academy of Sciences, 1955, cited by Professor E. H. Huntress in an abstract made for the Office of the Graduate School, MIT.)

TABLE 47. SOVIET UNIVERSITY CURRICULUM IN PHYSICS COMPARED
WITH THE MIT COURSE VIII (PHYSICS)

Summary	Soviet	MIT
Term of instruction, years	4.5*	4
Weeks of class instruction	140	120
Scheduled class hours	4,290	2,865 (approx.)
Class hours per week, average	30.6	23.9
Field practice†	unstated	. . .

Note: Soviet data are from the 1954–1955 curriculum of the Kharkov State University in Cenis Translation Series 55-26; the MIT data are from the MIT *Catalogue Issue for 1955–1956 Session.*

Part One: Subjects of Instruction, Scheduled Hours of Instruction, and Per Cent of Total Scheduled Load

Soviet University			MIT Course VIII		
Subjects	Hours	Per Cent	Subjects	Hours	Per Cent
Higher Mathematics	584	13.6	Higher Mathematics	270	11.2
			Chemistry, General Elective (e.g., Physical Chemistry)	180 45	
General Chemistry	100	2.3		225	9.3
Physics Core program Depending on the selected major‡	1,560 804	36.3 18.8	Physics Core program As elected (approx.)	870 300	36.0 12.8
	2,364	55.1		1,170	48.4
Radio Engineering, Fundamentals	36	0.8	Electronic Circuits	105	4.3
Electrodynamics	120	2.8	Electric Circuit Theory, Elementary	60	2.5
Marxism-Leninism	250	5.8			
Political Economy	140	3.3			
Philosophy	140	3.3			
Drafting	52	1.2			
Foreign Language	240	5.6			
Pedagogy	68	1.6			
Methodology of Teaching Physics	60	1.4			
Physical Education and Sports	136	3.2		§	

Table 47, Part One (continued)

Soviet University			MIT Course VIII		
Subjects	Hours	Per Cent	Subjects	Hours	Per Cent
			Humanities	360	14.9
Military Science	?		Military Science	180	7.5
			Freshman Elective	45	1.9
Two term projects (6th and 8th semesters)			Bachelor's Thesis		
State Examination					
Total, Soviet	4,290	100.0	Total, MIT (approx.)	2,415	100.0

* The total term of instruction is 5 years, but there are no classes scheduled for the last semester, which is apparently taken up largely by the preparation of a thesis and the final State Examinations.

† Soviet university curricula generally provide for a minimum of 6 weeks (and up to 16 in some specialties) of field practice.

‡ The Soviet Physics curriculum provides for ten options (specialties) as listed on pages 267–268.

§ Required. The requirement, equivalent to one year of physical education, can be met in a variety of ways during the first 2 years.

Table 47 (continued)

Part Two: Subjects and Hours per Week by Semesters

First Semester
(First Year, First Term)

	Hours per Week	
Subject of Instruction	Soviet	MIT
Marxism-Leninism, Foundations	4¶	
Foreign Language	4¶	
Physical Education and Sports	2¶	1
General Chemistry	2‖	6
Drafting	2	
Higher Mathematics	10‖·¶	3
General Physics	4‖·¶	
Physics Laboratory	4¶	} 5
Western Civilization, Foundations		3
Military Science		3
Elective Subject		3
Total, first semester	32	23

Soviet: Examinations   3
         Zachety   6

TABLE 47, Part Two (continued)

Second Semester
(First Year, Second Term)

Subject of Instruction	Hours per Week	
	Soviet	MIT
Marxism-Leninism, Foundations	3‖	
Foreign Language	4‖	
Physical Education and Sports	2¶	1
General Chemistry	4¶	6
Drafting	1¶	
Higher Mathematics	8‖·¶	3
General Physics	6‖·¶	5
Physics Laboratory	4¶	
Western Civilization, Foundations		3
Military Science		3
Total, second semester	32	20

Soviet: Examinations   4
Zachety   6

Third Semester
(Second Year, First Term)

Subject of Instruction	Hours per Week	
	Soviet	MIT
Marxism-Leninism, Foundations	4¶	
Foreign Language	4‖	
Physical Education and Sports	2¶	1
Higher Mathematics	10‖·¶	3
General Physics	6‖·¶	5
Physics Laboratory	4¶	
Humanities		3
Military Science		3
Elective Subjects (approximately)		7
Total, third semester	30	21

Soviet: Examinations   3
Zachety   5

TABLE 47, Part Two (continued)

Fourth Semester
(Second Year, Second Term)

Subject of Instruction	Hours per Week Soviet	MIT
Marxism-Leninism, Foundations	4‖	
Foreign Language	2¶	
Physical Education and Sports	2¶	1
Higher Mathematics	6‖·¶	3
General Physics	6‖·¶	
Physics Laboratory	4¶	} 5
Theoretical Mechanics	4‖	
Pedagogy	2	
Electric Circuit Theory, Elementary		4
Humanities		3
Military Science		3
Elective Subjects (approximately)		4
Total, fourth semester	30	22

Soviet: Examinations 4
          Zachety   5

Fifth Semester
(Third Year, First Term)

Subject of Instruction	Hours per Week Soviet	MIT
Political Economy	3¶	
Methods of Mathematical Physics	5‖	
General Physics	4‖·¶	4[2]
Physics Laboratory	6¶	
Theoretical Mechanics	4‖	
Thermodynamics and Statistical Physics	4‖	
Pedagogy	2‖	
Methodology of Teaching Physics and the Techniques of Physical Experiments	2	
Electronics		4
Experimental Atomic Physics		6
Advanced Calculus for Engineering		3
Humanities		3
Total, fifth semester	30	20

Soviet: Examinations 5
          Zachety   3

TABLE 47, Part Two (continued)

Sixth Semester
(Third Year, Second Term)

Subject of Instruction	Hours per Week	
	Soviet	MIT
Political Economy	2‖	
Methods of Mathematical Physics	5‖	
Physics Laboratory	6¶	4²
Thermodynamics and Statistical Physics	4‖	
Electrodynamics	4‖,⁵	
Fundamentals of Radio Engineering	3¶	
Selected Subjects³	4¶	
Methodology of Teaching Physics and the Techniques of Physical Experiments	2¶	
Foreign Language⁴	...¶	
Electronic Circuits		7
Experimental Atomic Physics II		4
Advanced Calculus for Engineering		3
Humanities		3
Total, sixth semester	30	21

	Soviet:	Examinations	4
		Zachety	5
		Term Papers	1

Seventh Semester
(Fourth Year, First Term)

Subject of Instruction	Hours per Week	
	Soviet	MIT
Political Economy	2¶	
Methods of Mathematical Physics	5‖	
Electrodynamics	4‖	
Quantum Mechanics	4¶	
Selected Subjects³	6‖,¶	7
Laboratory in Selected Subjects	8	
Experimental Physics		8
Introduction to Theoretical Physics		4
Humanities		3
Total, seventh semester	29	22

	Soviet:	Examinations	3
		Zachety	3

At MIT: Work on bachelor's thesis, per semester   15 hr.

Table 47, Part Two (concluded)

Eighth Semester
(Fourth Year, Second Term)

Subject of Instruction	Hours per Week	
	Soviet	MIT
Political Economy	2‖	
Philosophy	5‖	
Quantum Mechanics	4‖	
Selected Subjects[3]	8‖·¶,5	3
Laboratory in Selected Subjects	10¶	
Foreign Language[4]	... ¶	
Thermodynamics and Statistical Mechanics		4
Introduction to Theoretical Physics		4
Humanities		3
Total, eighth semester	29	14

Soviet: Examinations 4
Zachety 3
Term Papers 1
At MIT: Bachelor's thesis, per semester 180 hr.

Ninth Semester
(Fifth Year, First Term)

Subject of Instruction	Hours per Week	
	Soviet	MIT
Philosophy	5‖	
History of Physics	3‖	
Selected Subjects[3]	8‖·¶	
Laboratory in Selected Subjects	10¶	
Total, ninth semester	26	

Soviet: Examinations 3
Zachety 2

Tenth Semester

Preparation of the "diploma" project (thesis) and for the State Examinations.

‖ Followed by an examination.
¶ Followed by a *zachet*.
[1] Required.
[2] Atomic, Molecular, and Nuclear I.
[3] See list of Soviet specialties on pages 267–268.
[4] Attendance is optional but a *zachet* is required.
[5] Includes a term paper.

independent work (including research) in the selected field of specialization and in preparation for the State Examination.

Table 47 shows that there are few significant differences in the subjects and the per cent allocation of time among the various fields of instruction common to both. The somewhat greater emphasis on mathematics in the Soviet curriculum, the relatively small allocation of time to chemistry, and a drafting course stand in sharpest contrast with the MIT plan. It is to be noted, nevertheless, that the total relative allocation of time for science and mathematics is about the same in both curricula: 74.6 per cent in the Soviet schedule versus 77.6 at MIT.

The Soviet curriculum provides for ten areas of specialization beginning with the sixth semester (third year, second term). This provision is less significant than it may appear on the surface. Although at MIT, for instance, no similar areas of specialization are formally recognized, the elective subjects offered at MIT during the senior year can in fact lead, via one year of graduate work, toward any degree of specialization, including specialization in any of the fields listed in the Soviet curricula. In this respect the American system of electives is far more flexible and more capable of satisfying the specific interests and abilities of the student. The ten recognized areas of specialization in the Soviet undergraduate physics curriculum are as follows:

   I. Mathematical Physics
      1. Quantitative Methods in Differential Equations
      2. Theory of Functions of Real Variables
      3. Integral Equations
      4. Differential Equations of Partial Derivatives
  II. Theoretical Physics
      1. Theory of Solid State
      2. Special Course in Higher Mathematics
      3. Integral Equations
      4. Mathematical Methods of Modern Theoretical Physics
      5. Nuclear and Elementary Particles Theory
      6. Quantum Statistical Physics
      7. Quantum Electrodynamics
      8. General Theory of Relativity
 III. Low-Temperature Physics
      1. Low-Temperature Measurement Techniques
      2. Special Problems of Low-Temperature Physics
      3. Special Courses in Low-Temperature Physics
 IV. Molecular Physics
      1. Molecular and Kinetic Bases of the Condensed Media Theory
      2. Physics of Combustion and Explosion
      3. Gas Dynamics
      4. Molecular Structure
      5. Structure of Liquids and of High Polymers

6. Quantum Theory of Molecular Forces
7. Acoustical Methods of Study in Molecular Physics
V. Optics
  1. Applied Optics
  2. Electromagnetic Theory of Light
  3. Theory of Radiation
  4. Luminescence
  5. Theoretical Optics
  6. Atomic Spectroscopy
  7. Molecular Spectroscopy
  8. Gas Discharge Physics
  9. Physical Optics
VI. X-Ray Physics and Physics of Metals
  1. X-Ray Physics
  2. X-Ray Analysis
  3. Solid State Physics
  4. X-Ray Metallurgy [*Rentgenografiya metallov*]
  5. Technology of Metals
  6. Physical Metallurgy
  7. The Electron Theory of Metals
  8. Physics of Metals
  9. Electronography
VII. Magnetism
  1. Alternating Currents
  2. Electrical and Magnetic Measurements
  3. Ferromagnetism
  4. Physico-Chemical Analysis
  5. Fundamentals of Magnetic Analysis
  6. Quantum Ferromagnetism
  7. Quantum Theory of Metals
VIII. Solid State Physics
  1. Physics of Metals
  2. Physics of Semi-Conductors
  3. Physics of Dielectrics
  4. Crystal Physics
  5. Crystallography
  6. Metallography
IX. Physical Electronics
  1. Vacuum Physics and Techniques
  2. Electron Emission
  3. Electronic Semi-Conductors
  4. Electrons
X. Astrophysics
  1. General Course in Astrophysics
  2. Theoretical Astrophysics
  3. Celestial Mechanics
  4. Theory of Internal Structure of Stars

The new plan introduced as of September 1, 1955 (affecting students graduating in 1957 and thereafter) provides for the following physics specialties:

I. Theoretical Physics
II. Low-Temperature Physics
III. Molecular Physics
IV. Optics
V. X-Ray and Physics of Metals
VI. Magnetism
VII. Solid State Physics
VIII. Electrophysics
IX. Structure of Matter
X. Radiophysics

If, for the sake of quantitative comparison, one equates Soviet social science with the humanities included in the MIT physics course, it will be seen that about the same proportion of time is allotted for these subjects in the Soviet and MIT curricula—12.4 per cent and 14.9, respectively. But, as Professor Trilling surmised, "the content of the MIT humanities courses constitutes more nourishing intellectual fare than the indoctrination courses taught mainly by rote in all Soviet schools."[12]

The education subjects of the Soviet physics curricula have no counterpart in the MIT physics course summarized in Table 47.* The time allotted to the education courses in the Soviet physics (and other university) curricula has been increased since 1955–1956. Courses in pedagogy, psychology, and teaching methods, as well as actual teaching practice, have been added or expanded in the university curricula corresponding to the fields of instruction in the secondary schools, such as physics, mathematics, chemistry, geography, and others. The 1955–1956 university curricula in these fields include up to a total of 650 hours of instruction in education subjects and teaching practice.[13] In the prereform physics curriculum described here the education subjects took up only 128 class hours.

The physicists at MIT who have examined the Soviet physics curriculum (and related material, such as the syllabi listed in the bibliography) agree in characterizing it as extremely comprehensive, excessively overburdened, but in terms of its science content most favorably comparable with the best American curricula for physicists. As one MIT physicist said, "It definitely provides for and suggests a first-class physics training program—but all depends upon what they really *do* in their courses." In this connection it is pertinent to note that, whereas engineering training since the early days of the Bolshevik regime has been constantly interfered with and shaped by the Party's

---

* As noted in Chapter 7, Soviet university graduates since 1955 have been formally rated as *teachers* of their specialty in the secondary schools.

striving for immediate tangible results, the universities were allowed
for a time to continue largely in the pre-Revolutionary European tradition of scholarship. And today, after the comparative neglect of the
1930's, the university has emerged in academic prestige at the fore-
front of Soviet schools of higher scientific education. It is significant
also that the teaching process and its organization at the universities
have not been subject to such criticism by Soviet educators and scientists as has engineering training, especially in the narrowly specialized industrial institutes. The Party spokesmen, however, for instance
in the 1954 directives, have accused the universities of both too narrow
a specialization of the graduates* and the failure to prepare graduates
for practical work.[14] The introduction of education courses in the
1955–1956 university science curricula is one of the steps designed to
overcome this last objection:

> During the last two years the objectives of the physics faculties at
> our [Soviet] universities have changed considerably. The physics
> faculties, in addition to training physicists for research institutes and
> industrial enterprises, are also producing highly qualified teachers
> of physics who must in full measure meet the demands arising from
> the forthcoming transition to universal polytechnic instruction [in
> the secondary schools].[15]

Although the latest (but not the first) campaign to instill "polytechnic" orientation throughout the school system was initiated in
c. 1952, not until 1955 were any changes introduced in the university
physics curriculum designed to prepare future teachers for the task of
"polytechnic" teaching of physics in secondary schools. To indicate
the nature of changes in the physics curriculum of the Soviet universities, we quote an excerpt from a description of how one Soviet university sees the problem.[16]

> Having decided to help students of the physics department firmly
> master basic phenomena, concepts, laws, and quantitative data (con-
> stants, equivalents, etc.), the Department of Physics at Tartu Univer-
> sity first of all worked out a special list of questions the correct
> answers to which would show the student's knowledge of the sec-
> ondary school course in physics. We have reproduced this list and
> every students gets a copy in order that, by referring to the list, he
> may check his knowledge in this area and make up the existing
> deficiencies.

The same writer, reporting on the efforts of this university to modify
the teaching of physics in line with the Party-postulated vocationaliza-
tion of all secondary schools, points out that the curriculum is defec-

* Prior to the recent reform, for instance, there were 27 chemical specialties
taught at the universities; the new plan provides for only 5 chemistry options.

tive inasmuch as it fails to provide, for instance, practical instruction in woodworking and metalworking. This university, the author states:

> . . . was able to make up for this omission. Beginning with the current academic year [1955–1956] students enrolled in the course of physics regularly work during the third semester two hours per week in the school workshop. During that time they manage to become practically acquainted with the basic elements of cardboard craft, plywood, wood, and metalwork (materials, tools, basic methods of cutting, drilling, soldering, gluing, turning, painting, etc.).

The author further points out that the curriculum no longer includes the former 68-hour course, "Foundations of Engineering Mechanics," which, he believes, is very important for the education of a physics teacher and which the author suggests "must by all means" be added to the university curriculum. His university:

> . . . without waiting for the solution of the problem in the formal way . . . attempted to eliminate this defect by its own effort. Two disused trucks were obtained from a motor pool and . . . [the Physics faculty] engaged in organizing a course of practical instruction in the construction and operation of automobiles.

To what extent and for how long the present drive for "polytechnization" of science will affect the formal curricula of Soviet universities cannot be categorically forecast. The sense of the present Party-sponsored campaign would suggest that, paradoxically, the Party lends encouragement to science and research in engineering training while demanding vocational emphasis in the education of scientists at the universities.

3. Pedagogical Institute Curriculum in Mathematics

Soviet teachers of secondary schools are trained in universities and pedagogical institutes (*pedagogicheskie instituty*).* Prior to the reforms initiated following the 1954 Party directive, pedagogical institute and university graduates assigned to teach in secondary schools

---

* As of January 1955 there were 206 resident schools and 4 correspondence schools of this category. (See Table 25, Chapter 5.) About five times as many secondary school teachers are trained by these schools as by the universities. The total number of university graduates in 1956 was probably not much in excess of 20,000, of which number, it can be assumed, some 12,000 (60 per cent) may have been assigned to teaching in secondary schools. The 1955–1956 enrollment in the 4-year pedagogical institutes may have been as large as 300,000 ("2.5 times the 1940 enrollment in 1954–1955," *Vestnik vysshei shkoly*, No. 4, April 1955, p. 7; the planned 1941 fall enrollment was 76,000); the 1956 graduating class may be estimated

taught only in the upper grades (VIII through X). Beginning with the 1955–1956 academic year it was announced that: "The recruitment of [secondary school] teachers for grades V through X shall be from among those who have completed higher education."[17] It was also stated that, in addition to those graduating from the pedagogical institutes, university graduates of certain specialties would be assigned to teach in the secondary schools in increased numbers.

> Not fewer than 80 per cent of those graduating from the [university] faculties of Philology, History, Geography, and Biology; and not fewer than 60 per cent of the graduates of the Physics, Mathematics, and Chemistry faculties shall be directed to teach in secondary schools.

Inasmuch as both the university and the pedagogical institute train for teaching in secondary schools, we are including (Table 48) a comparison between the two curricula, taking for our example the mathematics curricula.* Table 48 lists all individual subjects of instruction and scheduled hours in the following categories arranged by us:

Category of Subjects	Pedagogical Institute		University	
	Hours	Per Cent	Hours	Per Cent
Political	504	13.2	504	12.8
General	260	6.8	406	10.3
Education	513	13.4	194	4.9
General Science	564	14.8	634	16.0
Mathematics	1,975	51.8	2,210	56.0
Total	3,816	100.0	3,948	100.0

at approximately 60,000. In 1954–1955 there were approximately 62,000 students enrolled in the 2-year teacher institutes. Consequently, the total 1956 output of teachers is likely to have been as follows:

University graduates (5-year term)	12,000
4-year Pedagogical Institute graduates	60,000
2-year Teachers Institute graduates	30,000
	102,000

comprising somewhere near 6 per cent of the total number of school teachers in the USSR (1.73 million) reported for the 1955–1956 academic year.

* Until 1954 the training of secondary school teachers of physics and mathematics (i.e., those enrolled in the Physics-Mathematics faculties) was organized jointly with two major specialties:

1. Physics Teacher, with the right also to teach mathematics.
2. Mathematics Teacher, with the right also to teach physics.

Since 1954 the two specialties have been made distinct and exclusive; specialization *begins with the first year of study.*

Table 48. A COMPARISON OF THE SOVIET MATHEMATICS CURRICULA
IN PEDAGOGICAL INSTITUTES AND UNIVERSITIES

I. Subjects and Scheduled Hours

Subject of Instruction	Pedagogical Institutes		University	
	Hours	Per Cent	Hours	Per Cent
Group I Political				
Marxism-Leninism, Fundamentals	224		224	
Political Economy	140		140	
Dialectical Materialism	140			
Philosophy			140	
Subtotal	504	13.2	504	12.8
Group II General				
Physical Education and Sports	130		136	
Foreign Language	130		270	
Subtotal	260	6.8	406	10.3
Group III Education				
Psychology	68		. . .	
Pedagogy	119		64	
History of Pedagogy	72		. . .	
Methods of Teaching Mathematics	188		70	
Special Preparation	48			
Pedagogical Practice			60	
School Hygiene	18			
Subtotal	513	13.4	194	4.9
Group IV General Science				
General Physics	378		340	
Theoretical Mechanics	106		240	
Astronomy	80		54	
Subtotal	564	14.8	634	16.0
Group V Mathematics				
Analytical Geometry	178		188	
Mathematical Analysis	437		476	
Higher Algebra	216		174	
Differential Geometry	65		100	
Foundations of Geometry	56		64	
Theory of Numbers			30	
Theory of Numbers and Theoretical Arithmetic	87			
Theory of Functions of Real and Complex Variables	116			
Theory of Functions of Complex Variables			100	

TABLE 48 (continued)

Subject of Instruction	Pedagogical Institute		University	
	Hours	Per Cent	Hours	Per Cent
Theory of Functions of Real Variables and Functional Analysis			86	
Differential Equations			136	
Equations of Mathematical Physics			100	
Integral Equations			36	
Variational Calculus			30	
Theory of Probability			54	
Elementary Mathematics	412		70	
Drafting and Fundamentals of Descriptive Geometry			68	
Projective and Descriptive Geometry	106			
Drafting	64			
Electives			328	
Mathematical *praktikum*	98		170	
Special Mathematics Seminar	100			
History of Mathematics	40			
Subtotal	1,975	51.8	2,210	56.0
Total hours	3,816	100.0	3,948	100.0

II. Other Data   Pedagogical Institute   University
Term of Study   4 years   5 years*
Distribution of Hours:†

Lectures	1,954	2,054
Laboratory	309	208
Practical studies, seminars, exercises, etc.	1,553	1,506
Other	...	180
Total hours	3,816	3,948

Number of Tests

Examinations (graded)	34	32
Zachety (ungraded)	40	34

Source: Copies of c. 1955 mathematics curricula (Kharkov State University), Cenis Translation Series 55-41; pedagogical institute (Rostov *Pedagogicheskii Institut*) curriculum, Cenis Translation Series 56-2.

* Of which the last semester has no scheduled class hours, the entire time being available for work in preparation for the State Examination.
† Not including teaching practice.

It will be noted that both the science (physics, theoretical mechanics, and astronomy) and the mathematics content are nearly equal in these curricula; a pedagogical institute student specializing to teach mathematics in grades V through X (age 12 through 17) is expected to spend nearly as much time in the study of mathematics as a future professional mathematician pursuing university training in his preparation for advanced work. It will be noted also that, with the exception of a few advanced topics (differential equations, equations of mathematical physics, integral equations, variational calculus, and theory of probability) which in the university curriculum take up in the aggregate 356 hours, the list of subjects is similar in both curricula. Thus for the mathematical subjects which are common to both curricula (including the theory of functions of real and complex variables) the pedagogical institute student spends even more time than the university mathematics student—1,975 hours versus 1,844 hours for these subjects in the university curriculum.

Both the scope and the quantity of instruction in mathematics stipulated for the Soviet student preparing to teach secondary school mathematics (arithmetic, algebra, geometry, and trigonometry) are as impressive as they are demanding. The effectiveness and quality of training achieved by the pedagogical institutes in recent years, however, may well be strongly questioned if only on the grounds of the extreme overload and excessive regimentation of the student's time. Prior to 1957 the pedagogical institute curriculum provided for only 4 years of instruction, resulting in a very crowded weekly schedule of classwork, as follows:

Semester	Hours per Week*
1st	36
2nd	36
3rd	36
4th	36
5th	30
6th	30
7th	30
8th	26

Furthermore, in addition to the scheduled class hours Soviet peda-

---

* The university term, by comparison, is 5 years, with an average scheduled load of less than 30 hours per week during the first seven semesters, 24 hours per week in the eighth semester, and only 16 hours per week during the ninth semester. The last (tenth semester) has no scheduled classes.

gogical institute curricula provide for from 612 to 1,524 hours of teaching and field practice, including 3 weeks of work at a Pioneer Camp at the end of the second year. The entire scheduled load under the mathematics teachers curriculum, as compared with the university mathematics curriculum, prior to 1957 was as follows:

	Scheduled Hours	
	Pedagogical Institute (4-yr. Term)	University (5-yr. Term)
Class hours (Table 48)	3,816	3,948
Teaching and field practice	612	248
Total load	4,428	4,196
Hours per year, average	1,107	839
Index	140	100

In 1949 the major criticisms of the plans for teacher training were directed against the overloaded curricula and syllabi;[18] the plans were revised in 1951, but the curricula remained nearly as crowded as before.* *Uchebnyi* plans were again revised in 1954, the mathematics curricula here presented being a sample of the revised plan. The overload remained as excessive as before, and, as one Soviet commentator has said with reference to the 1955 curricula: "It is clear that the students of pedagogical institutes are obviously short of time for independent work."[19] We have already noted (see Chapter 2) that in 1956, rather than replace the number of scheduled hours in the pedagogical institute curricula, the Ministry of Higher Education announced that the term of study in pedagogical institutes was to be increased from 4 to 5 years. It remains to be seen whether the scheduled load per unit of time will be proportionally or somewhat reduced.

4. Uchebnyi Plan versus Academic Realities

The three sample curricula commented upon in the preceding pages are representative of three great segments within the educational sys-

* The 1951 mathematics curriculum provided:

Class hours	3,927
Practice	500
Total	4,427

tem of the Soviet Union: teacher training, engineering education, and education in science. Soviet curricula in all specialties of these fields and many others have undergone considerable, sometimes radical, changes since 1954, and the process is far from complete. The former 460 distinct curricula for professional training were to be replaced by 280 specifications for undergraduate specialties of "broad profile." In this respect, the present Soviet efforts follow the same line of reasoning and the same philosophy which has conditioned the evolution of engineering education at its best in the United States.

The formal part of the present Soviet task of revising curricula is in itself very great; but a much larger and a much more difficult part of the proposed reform is the translation of objectives implied by the 1954 ukase into realities of the educational process in a system which has for so many years been dominated by the pressures of industrial expediencies. It is no simple process to make the transition from a policy of multiple undergraduate options aimed at training men to be useful to specific industries to a policy of training "that would make engineers continually useful as science advances."[20]

The complexity of the academic reorganization involved may be illustrated by the history of a recent curricular reform in the electrical engineering course at MIT.[21] For some years prior to 1952–1953 electrical engineering students could choose among several professional options during their sophomore year. In that year a major curricular change deferred the undergraduate choice of field until the senior year. The curriculum of the class of 1954 provided only three options: Electric Power, Electrical Communications, and Electronic Applications. In the following (1954–1955) year even this small choice of options was eliminated in the curriculum, which, however, retained a wide choice of electives in the senior year. This reorientation of the curriculum involved profound changes in the choice of subjects of instruction, in laboratory facilities and practices, and in the entire approach to the educational plan. Writing in 1955 Professor Brown said: "The work on the program has just begun."[22]

The magnitude of the task faced by the Soviet educational system in attempting effectively and sharply to reduce the number of basic curricula becomes apparent in the light of the example just cited. Moreover, it is compounded by the fact that in Soviet practice a given curriculum is compulsory for all schools in the relevant category. It is significant that exceptions have already been made and that some of the more radical curricular changes have been introduced so far only in a few schools. A policy of differentiation could lead to the development of curricular practices similar to those of American accredited institutions.*

In this country the representatives of accrediting agencies, such as the American Society for Engineering Education, critically study curricula, syllabi, and examination papers in a cooperative effort of the Society and schools to maintain the standards of instruction at a generally acceptable professional level; but this control is not restrictive in any sense of the word. The structuring of curricula is an autonomous process in every American school and, to a large extent, even autonomous in the separate departments within a given institution. Furthermore, an individual instructor, guided by the departmentally drafted general syllabus, has a large degree of freedom in the actual presentation of material. How to coordinate the coverage of topics in interrelated subjects, how to integrate the content, methods, and techniques of separate disciplines, and how to avoid unnecessary duplication—these problems are (or are not) solved in American schools as often in the course of personal and professional communication among fellow teachers as by means of formal planning of details, let alone by fiat of a supra-institutional authority.

These unregimented means of horizontal communication—within each institution and beyond—are of course also available to the faculty members of Soviet universities and colleges. There is no doubt that agreements and understanding informally arrived at among the teachers of a given Soviet faculty have helped in many individual instances and help now to circumvent some of the formal provisions of the curricula. The general climate of the Soviet Union, however, does not promote effective horizontal communication or agreements at any intermediate level of authority.

In the United States decisions on curricula, however reached, apply only to the institution in question. In the Soviet Union, with rare exceptions, a given curriculum is mandatory for all institutions giving instruction in the particular specialty.† In a formal way Soviet practice provides a minimum standard below which no institution rated as an institution of higher learning may fall. No such floor formally exists in the educational system of the United States. On the other hand, the centrally established curricula and other provisions included

---

* There are approximately 150 accredited schools of engineering in the United States.

† Certain select schools, such as the Bauman Higher Technical School in Moscow, and presumably all the military schools operate according to a special curricula established for them alone by the Ministry. See, e.g., *Vestnik vysshei shkoly*, No. 8, August 1955, p. 55.

in the Soviet *uchebnyi plan* impose upon all schools a number of rigid conditions which in the Soviet's own appraisal have been detrimental to the quality of instruction. As a concluding comment on this topic, we quote from an MIT report:

No single rule can apply generally to such a great variety of educational activity as we now have at MIT. In fact, we are suspicious of all fixed patterns and rules in education that impose uniformity and stifle spontaneity.[23]

NOTES TO CHAPTER 8

[1] All curricular data for this section are taken from Cenis Translation Series 55-24, "Curriculum for the Major in Technology of Machine Construction, Metal Cutting Machine Tools, and Tools" at the Bauman Higher Technical School of Moscow (MVTU).

[2] M. P. Ivanov (Deputy Minister, Machine and Instrument Building Industry) in *Vestnik vysshei shkoly*, No. 1, January 1956, p. 4.

[3] Cenis Translation Series 55-24 shows (as in the original) lectures, 582 hours and practical work, etc., 1,310 hours; correct totals are 595 and 1,303 hours respectively.

[4] A. M. Soifer (assistant professor at the Kuibyshev Aviation Institute), "Vospityvat' inzhenerov-novatorov" (To Nurture Engineers—Innovators), *Vestnik vysshei shkoly*, No. 10, October 1955, p. 13.

[5] Ivanov, *op. cit.*, p. 6.

[6] Address given by Professor Frank at the Annual Meeting of the American Society for Engineering Education at Urbana, Illinois, on June 15, 1954.

[7] *Vestnik vysshei shkoly*, No. 12, December 1951, p. 18.

[8] *Vestnik vysshei shkoly*, No. 3, March 1955, p. 23.

[9] *Vestnik vysshei shkoly*, No. 10, October 1951; translation given in Cenis Source Memorandum No. 5.

[10] *Ibid.*

[11] *Vestnik vysshei shkoly*, No. 12, December 1951, p. 18.

[12] Leon Trilling, *Soviet Education in Aeronautics: A Case Study*, Cambridge: Center for International Studies, Massachusetts Institute of Technology, 1956 (mimeographed), p. 34.

[13] *Vestnik vysshei shkoly*, No. 4, April 1955, p. 9.

[14] See, for instance, B. Koval', "Vazhneishiye zadachi vysshei shkoly" (The Most Important Tasks of Higher Education), *Pravda Ukrainy*, November 20, 1955, p. 3.

[15] *Vestnik vysshei shkoly*, No. 4, April 1956, p. 34.

[16] *Ibid.*, p. 35.

[17] "Svoyevremenno zavershit' podgotovku k novomu uchebnomu godu" (Timely to Complete Preparations for the New Academic Year), *Vestnik vysshei shkoly*, No. 7, July 1955, p. 2.

[18] E.g., K. I. L'vov, "O dal'neishem uluchshenii professional'noi podgotovki studentov v vysshykh pedagogicheskikh uchebnykh zavedeniyakh" (On the Further Improvement of Professional Preparation of Students in the Institutions of Higher Pedagogical Education), *Sovetskaya pedagogika*, No. 10, October 1949, p. 24.

[19] N. P. Suvorov, "Novye uchebnye plany pedagogicheskikh institutov" (New Curricula of Pedagogical Institutes), *Sovetskaya pedagogika,* No. 3, 1955, p. 86.

[20] Gordon S. Brown, "Educating Electrical Engineers to Exploit Science," *Electrical Engineering,* February 1955.

[21] *Ibid.;* also "The Modern Engineer Should be Educated as a Scientist," *Journal of Engineering Education,* Vol. 43, No. 4, December 1952; "Integration versus Options in Electrical Engineering," *Engineering,* Vol. 72, July 1953, pp. 595–597.

[22] Brown, "Educating Electrical Engineers to Exploit Science," *op. cit.*

[23] *Report of the Committee on Educational Survey to the Faculty of the Massachusetts Institute of Technology,* Cambridge: The Technology Press. 1949.

CHAPTER

9

SOVIET HIGHER EDUCATION:

TEACHERS, TEXTBOOKS, AND FACILITIES

The preceding chapters have outlined some of the major instruments of centralized control over the Soviet system of higher education, including *uchebnyi* plans, of which three specific examples have been given in Chapter 8. These plans, supplemented by directives and injunctions, minutely detailed rules and regulations, and methodological instructions of the central authorities, unquestionably serve as major determinants of the academic process. In the end, of course, carrying out the assigned academic tasks must depend heavily upon the collective effort and performance of university administrators, faculty members, and the student body. Indirectly, the ability of the system to carry out its objectives according to the prescribed model depends also on the performance of the entire Soviet economy, from which the educational system derives its standard of life, its physical plant, and, most importantly, its qualitative and quantitative share of the professionally trained talent of the nation: its teaching staff. In practice the written rules of the central authorities are considerably modified. The present chapter comments on the major factors involved in carrying out the central academic plans: the teaching staff, physical facilities, and textbooks.

1. THE TEACHING STAFF

Ranks and Qualifications

The senior academic category, comparable to the group which in the United States includes professors, associate professors, and assistant professors, in the Soviet Union includes only two ranks: professor and docent. The junior members in Soviet faculties are the assistants, senior instructors, and instructors.* The title (*zvaniye*) of professor and of docent are normally given to the holders of an advanced academic degree (*stepen'*), Doctor of Science and Candidate of Science, respectively.† Not all Soviet professors and docents, however, possess these normally minimum formal academic qualifications. Furthermore, in Soviet usage a distinction is made between the *position* (*dolzhnost'*) of professor (or docent) and the (lifetime) academic *title* (*zvaniye*) of professor (or docent); thus a professorship (*dolzhnost'*) is not necessarily held by a professor (*zvaniye*). The pre-Revolutionary graduate degrees (master and doctor of science) were abolished by the Soviet regime and not re-established until 1934, as *kandidat* (instead of master) and *doktor* of sciences.[1] At that time and in subsequent years a large number of degrees were awarded on the basis of current status and not, as is normally the case, after defense of a dissertation. At one time (1934–1937) the right to grant academic degrees was held by several organizations in addition to the USSR Higher Attestation Commission (VAK), such as the USSR and other Soviet Academies of Sciences, the Communist Academy, and a number of specially formed qualifying commissions. Many professors in the years following 1934 were given the degree appropriate to their rank by these various accrediting agencies. A. Ya. Sinetskii, Soviet author of a 1950 study, stated:

> The greatest number of those certified for the academic degree of Doctor of Science without defense of a dissertation (48.8 per cent [of all so certified during the entire period, 1934–1946]) were certified during 1937–1939. This development is connected with the establishment in 1937 of staff positions and salaries for professional and instruction personnel.[2]

From the roundabout indexes and other disconnected data given in the Sinetskii study one would conclude that as of 1947 perhaps as many as 25 per cent of the 5,370 professors then teaching at Soviet institutions of higher learning obtained their degree without having defended a dissertation. Furthermore, not all professors necessarily have the degree

* The title of "senior instructor" (*starshyi prepodavatel'*), which was apparently established specifically for teachers of Marxism-Leninism, etc., is disappearing. This title is not mentioned in the draft for a new basic charter for schools of higher education. (An outline of this draft is given, e.g., in *Vestnik vysshei shkoly*, No. 4, April 1955, pp. 16–21.)

† In Russian *doktor nauk* and *kandidat nauk*. See Chapter 10.

of doctor: professor-*kandidat* is a frequently mentioned category.* As of January 1, 1947 the distribution by academic *degrees* of those holding academic *titles* was on a per cent basis as follows:

Academic Title	Number (100%)	Per cent holding the degree of:		
		Doctor	Candidate	No Degree
Professors	5,370	67.8	11.0	21.2
Docents	13,863	1.5	77.1	21.4
Others	47,890	0.3	9.4	90.3
Total Staff	67,123	5.9	23.6	70.5

Source: A. Ya. Sinetskii (Table 30), cited in Table 51, q.v.

Data on the number and composition of the teaching personnel as of October 1, 1955 are summarized in Table 49. In comparison with 1946–1947, the total number on the teaching staff increased by 78 per cent (from 67,123 to 119,059); the number of professors by 14 per cent (from 5,370 to 6,119); and the number of docents by 87 per cent (from 13,863 to 25,828). But the 1955 resident enrollment was nearly 90 per cent greater than it was in 1946–1947 and the total enrollment more than 110 per cent greater if correspondent students are included.

Appointment and Tenure

The academic titles of professors and docents are granted only by the Higher Attestation Commission (VAK) of the Ministry of Higher Education.† The title of *assistent* (who may be a graduate student or a *kandidat*) is given by the director or rector of the institution on the recommendation of the Academic Council. Appointments to the *positions* of professor and docent are initiated by each institution. When a position becomes open the university or institute may publish an announcement of the vacancy in a periodical such as *Uchebnye novosti* (News of the Teaching World) or in the daily press.‡

Qualified persons are invited to compete for the position. For this purpose the applicant is required to submit a statement on his life history and background, his academic career, research work, and publications; a record of his Party career, if any; and recommendations

* This distinction, moreover, is pointedly suggested by the fact that professors with a doctor's degree so preface their names in publications: "Professor-Doctor" versus simply "Professor."

† An excerpt from the regulations on the academic titles (*zvaniya*) is given in Appendix K.

‡ A few examples of such announcements are given in Appendix L.

TABLE 49. TEACHING PERSONNEL IN SCHOOLS OF HIGHER EDUCATION AND DISTRIBUTION BY ACADEMIC DEGREES AND TITLES

USSR

October 1, 1955

Academic Titles	Distribution by Academic Degrees				
	Doctors	Candidates	Degree Holders	No Degrees	All Categories
Professors	5,070	342	5,412	717	6,119
Per cent	82.8	5.6	88.4	11.6	100.0
Docents	37*	23,147†	23,184	2,644‡	25,828
Per cent	0.1	89.6	89.7	10.3	100.0
Assistants	...	1,864§	1,864	4,170‖	6,034
Per cent		30.9	30.9	69.1	100.0
Title holders	5,107	25,353	30,460	7,531	37,991
Per cent	13.4	66.7	80.1	19.9	100.0
No titles	440	18,097	18,537	62,531	81,068
Per cent	0.5	22.3	22.8	77.2	100.0
Total number	5,547	43,450	48,997	70,062	119,059
Per cent	4.7	36.5	41.2	58.8	100.0

Source: Kul'turnoye stroitel'stvo SSSR, 1956, p. 249.
* "Senior Research Associates" (see Appendix K for explanation).
† Includes 647 Senior Research Associates.
‡ Includes 64 Senior Research Associates.
§ Includes 73 Senior Research Associates.
‖ Includes 244 Junior Research Associates.

from his supervisors and local Party authorities. A small committee (two or three persons) appointed by the director reviews all applications and presents recommendations to the Academic Council, whose simple majority vote in favor of the proposed individual (provided at least two-thirds of the members are voting) constitutes its recommendation to the higher authorities. The final decision rests with the Ministry.

It is safe to surmise that both Party considerations and academic record influence the Ministry's choice, but there is also the closely related consideration of the personnel needs for research and development. The group within the Ministry which finally passes on the proposed appointments is made up of individuals who represent not the interests of education *per se* but education for the purposes and objectives of the state. Thus the freedom of the individual university or institute to select its staff is subordinated to the centrally formulated allocations of scientific talent between research institutes and the institutions of higher education. The opening or expansion of a research laboratory or a research group may set off a series of shifts in academic appointments. Such a shift was observed, for instance, when the Central Aero- and Hydrodynamic Institute (TsAGI) was temporarily transferred in 1941 to Siberia. Such occasions suggest that in many instances the outcome of the ostensibly open competition for senior appointments is resolved in advance at the highest level.

Soviet faculty appointment policy is necessarily a compromise between academic independence—a strong tradition of Russian universities still respected by the older senior professors—and the fact that all academic personnel are civil servants. The principles of Soviet faculty appointment are not very different from those of other countries with a national university system; but the application of these principles in the Soviet Union is complicated by the shortage of highly qualified and competent personnel relative to the manpower requirements of research programs deemed to be of national importance and the demand for senior educators. The appointment policy is also influenced by efforts to strengthen the teaching staffs of provincial institutions by recruiting bright young graduates. More serious is the fact that considerations of political conformity or at least of political passivity are always given weight in any appointment. In general, then, it is clear that the freedom of a given institution to select and change its faculty is very small; even an exchange of faculty members which may be negotiated by the directors of any two institutions is subject to approval from above.

The duration of Soviet academic appointments is not clearly defined, nor is there a rule of tenure even for senior positions. Formally, all academic positions are open to competition every 5 years. The practice of periodically reopening the established academic posts to competition was established, or formalized, by an order of the Minister of Higher Education in March 1953.

A number of instructions and directives followed, including a set issued in February 1954 explaining how these periodic competitions were to be conducted. The new plan has not been very widely discussed in the educational press, and the few comments which have been published are rather general. In 1955, for instance, the Deputy Minister of Higher Education wrote:

> As is known, by the government decision competitions are conducted regularly at the institutions of higher education for appointments to all academic positions. As yet we use this lever but little for ridding the institutions of higher learning of teachers who are

not willing or are not able to work properly. The competition system, if it is used correctly, provides one of the best methods for assembling scientific teaching cadres who are called upon not only to organize the academic process successfully but also to participate actively in the promotion of technical progress.[3]

The same year two Soviet engineering school professors who are among the few educators to comment on the new system and its rationale wrote:

> Among the measures directed toward raising qualifications in the scientific cadres, the periodic check of their academic growth occupies an important place. It is known that we still have instances when a scientific worker, having defended his dissertation, considers the attainment of an academic degree as the limit of his achievements and thereupon relaxes. The system of periodic competitions introduced in 1954 for all faculty members in the institutions of higher education is an indispensable measure for raising the scientific and pedagogical qualifications of the higher school workers, assuming that such competitions are correctly conducted.[4]

Many questions have arisen in connection with these competitions. Appendix M cites a few statements published by the Ministry, presumably in response to (unpublished) questions, on implementing the new plan. But additional rules and regulations will not solve the problems.*

Even if the competition is "used correctly," as both quoted sources say it must be to be effective, such factors as the existing relative manpower shortage, the existing scale of priorities established by the state, and the method of administrative and economic control are all incompatible with the proposed system. Its application under Soviet conditions is likely simply to reinforce the already pronounced tendency to concentrate the best academic talent in the relatively few outstanding schools and the most desirable geographic areas of the Soviet Union.

There is considerable evidence to suggest inbreeding of the faculty of a given institution through the retention of its own graduate students—a phenomenon common enough in Western Europe and in the United States. In 1955 two American visitors to the Soviet Union, Homer L. and Norton T. Dodge, observed that:

> ... many of the teachers at the University [of Rostov] had been students there and had worked their way up through the academic ranks at the one institution. The Rector and Assistant Rector were

---

* The draft of a new charter for the institutions of higher education (under consideration since c. February 1955) confirms the method of periodic competition for appointments and apparently aims to give greater authority to the director of each institution in making final determinations.

Rostov men. The Physics Dean, the Biology Dean, and one other were local products. Only two of the eight men sitting around the table were not graduates of Rostov University—the psychology and the geography professors.

When visiting the Bauman Higher Technical School in Moscow, these visitors were met by five individuals, four of whom, the director, two assistant directors, and a department head, were Bauman graduates.

Obviously, when a new institution is opened the faculty members must be recruited from various places, as, for instance, was done for the Stalingrad Institute of City Economy established in 1952. But in 1955 the director of that Institute expected that

> . . . soon they will be training their own cadres at the Institute. Young people will be prepared for teaching through their work in departmental research projects and work on advanced degrees.[5]

Shortage of Senior Staff Members

The theoretically desirable composition of the faculties by academic ranks, as the Soviet Ministry of Higher Education might see it, is suggested by the proposed staff schedule mentioned in a 1938 Soviet article. For that year the aim was for the teaching staff of all institutions combined to include:

Rank	Persons	Per Cent
Professors	8,680	20.2
Docents	13,144	30.5
Subtotal, senior staff	21,824	50.7
Assistenty	15,000	34.9
Senior teachers	2,213	5.1
Teachers	4,000	9.3
Subtotal, junior staff	21,213	49.3
Total[6]	43,037	100.0

Assuming that the percentages shown above (50 per cent senior staff, with two professors for every three docents) continue to be held as a guide, the actual composition of Soviet faculties as to ranks has never even approximated the presumably desired proportions. For the USSR as a whole in 1940–1941 the senior staff members accounted for only 36 per cent of the total, and in 1947–1948 for 28.7. In 1955–1956 the proportion of senior members fell to approximately 27 per cent (see Table 49), and the ratio of professors to docents fell apparently

to the postwar low of one professor for every four docents, instead of
the two to three ratio aimed at in 1938. It should be noted also that,
as shown in Table 50, the rank composition of the faculty varies greatly
from institution to institution. Thus, for instance, at the University
of Kiev professors account for over 20 per cent of the entire academic
staff while the national average is less than 9 per cent. Such data as
are shown in Table 50 are not extensive enough to permit a detailed
analysis, but it is clear that Soviet universities, in comparison with
other types of civilian schools, have by far the highest per cent of
senior members on their faculties. Soviet military schools of higher
education may have an equal or even greater concentration of senior
members, but no conclusive data have been encountered to confirm
this general impression.

TABLE 50. COMPOSITION OF TEACHING STAFF OF SOVIET INSTITUTIONS OF
HIGHER EDUCATION BY ACADEMIC RANK IN SELECTED
YEARS AND CATEGORIES

(Number and Per Cent of Total; figures for the USSR are in thousands)

Description	Professors		Docents		Others		Total
	No.	%	No.	%	No.	%	100%
1. USSR, 1955–1956	6.1	5.1	25.8	21.7	87.1	73.2	119,059
2. USSR, 1947–1948	5.4	8.0	13.9	20.7	47.9	71.3	67,123
3. USSR, 1940–1941	5.0	10.0	13.0	26.0	32.0	64.0	50,000
4. Moscow University Fall of 1955, persons	400	16.3	550	22.4	1,500	61.3	2,450
5. Kharkov University 1954–1955, persons	50	14.2	150	42.9	150	42.9	350
6. Kiev University 1954–1955, persons	113	20.2	373	66.6	74	13.2	560
7. Universities, Economics and Law Schools, 1954–1955	1,000	6.3	7,000	43.7	8,000	50.0	16,000
8. Bauman MVTU (Engineering) 1955–1956	50	6.5	295	38.8	415	54.7	760
9. Leningrad Industrial (Extension) 1954–1955	17	9.9	75	43.6	80	46.5	172

Sources:
1. Table 49. Other sources state:
Vestnik vysshei shkoly, No. 3, March 1956, p. 3 (". . . more than 100,000 professors, teachers, and scientific workers. . . .").
Vestnik vysshei shkoly, No. 8, August 1955, p. 1 (". . . about 40,000 . . . with
academic degrees, i.e., one-half of all doctors, candidates, professors, and docents
of the country.").
Literaturnaya gazeta, January 14, 1956 (". . . there are 100,000 professors,
docents, and teachers in VUZY."). (As of March 1955, *Vestnik vysshei shkoly* [No. 3,

1955], p. 3, stated "There are now 86,000 professors, docents, and teachers in the institutions of higher learning.")
    2. Table 51.
    3. *BSE*, Volume on the USSR, 1947, p. 1240; data as of January 1, 1947.
    4. *Moskovskii gosudarstvennyi universitet imeni M. V. Lomonosova*, a pamphlet, Moscow, 1955, p. 14.
    5. Homer L. and Norton T. Dodge, field notes; *Vestnik vysshei shkoly*, No. 4, April 1955, p. 51, gives 328 as the total number on the faculty.
    6. *Ibid.*, p. 63. Of 113 listed under Professors, 83 had *doktor nauk* degrees and 30 had *kandidat* degrees.
    7. An officially designated administrative category, including (as of January 1, 1955):
        33 universities
        25 economics institutes
        6 law institutes
The data given in the table are from *Vestnik vysshei shkoly*, No. 4, April 1955, pp. 6 and 11.
    8. *Vestnik vysshei shkoly*, No. 9, September 1955, p. 8.
    9. *Vestnik vysshei shkoly*, No. 11, November 1954, pp. 9 f.

What is certain, however, is not only that the rank composition is extremely uneven from one category of schools to another (universities have the highest per cent of senior members; normal schools, the lowest) but also that within each category there are significant geographic differences, especially as to the relative number of "professors-doctors." For instance, one Soviet source states that as of 1954–1955 in the entire city of Minsk there were only "1,164 professors and teachers, of whom 396 were candidates of science and *seven were doctors of science*";[7] yet there are eleven institutions of higher education in Minsk, including a university, a polytechnic institute, and a medical school. The entire Byelorussian SSR (of which Minsk is the capital), with its population of some eight million according to the 1955 official data, had only 125 doctors of science, that is, only 16 per million of population as against the USSR average of approximately 47 per million.*

It should be emphasized, however, that a Soviet doctorate is a higher degree than an American Ph.D. and is more nearly comparable to the British or Swedish D.Sc. or the German *habilitation*. Similarly, in comparing academic ranks it should be noted that the age distribution of Soviet junior-rank teaching staff members (with a large number in the 30 to 49 age bracket) implies considerable teaching experience. A Soviet *assistent*, therefore, in training and teaching experience is

* So far as higher education is concerned, Byelorussian SSR appears to be among the least advanced republics of the Soviet Union. In 1955–1956 its total college enrollment accounted for only 0.6 per cent of the population as compared with the USSR average of 0.9 per cent and a high of 1.2 per cent in the Armenian SSR.

more nearly comparable to an American assistant professor; and the rather exclusive ranks of professor and docent in the Soviet Union correspond to full and associate professorships in the United States. Therefore, the members of the Soviet teaching staff may not be as inexperienced as the data given in Table 50 at first suggest.

Age Distribution of Teachers

There are no recent data on the age distribution of Soviet teachers, but some statistics were published in 1950 giving the age-group distribution as of January 1, 1947. At that time, as shown in Table 51, there were on the teaching staffs of Soviet universities and other schools of higher education 67,000 persons, of whom some 42,000, or 62 per cent, were 40 years of age or older. Of the 5,370 professors then on the faculties nearly 70 per cent were 50 years of age or older; and none were younger than 30 years of age. From the same source we learn, as these figures suggest, that the median age for professors was 55.4 years and that in 1947 more than 45 per cent of the professors had completed their undergraduate training before 1918. But of the entire body of instructors teaching in 1947 only about 12 per cent completed undergraduate work before the Revolution and 6 per cent during the early years of the Soviet regime (1918–1923); thus approximately 82 per cent even then were Soviet trained. The proportion of Soviet graduates among the faculty members has greatly increased in the last 10 years and is now rapidly approaching 100 per cent. The living links to pre-Bolshevik educational philosophy and practices have all but disappeared.

The source cited in Table 51 provides a detailed statistical analysis of the age structure and years of educational experience for the various categories of Soviet teaching personnel. Although—to emphasize again—the data refer to the situation as it was in 1947, some additional highlights of these findings can be used to illustrate the differences in distribution and in level of qualification among teachers in several branches of science and fields of learning. These data are shown in Table 52. The table shows a relatively high proportion of instructors in technological schools (28.1 per cent) and in teacher training (32.4 per cent). This last category includes university teachers. As a crude index the table also shows the proportion of teachers with less than 10 years of experience. For the Soviet Union as a whole, 54 per cent of the teachers were in that category in 1947, but in schools of industrial and construction engineering only 49 per cent.

In the teacher training schools 61 per cent of the instructors are shown to have had less than 10 years of experience. It is almost certain that the percentage of the relatively inexperienced teachers in universities is very much smaller than in the normal schools—if only because of the greater per cent of senior teaching personnel in the university faculties, for, as shown in Table 52, relatively few professors and

TABLE 51. AGE DISTRIBUTION OF MEMBERS OF THE TEACHING STAFF
AT SOVIET INSTITUTIONS OF HIGHER EDUCATION
BY ACADEMIC RANKS*
USSR
January 1, 1947

Age Group	Professors		Docents		Others		Total	
	No.	%	No.	%	No.	%	No.	%
Through 29	...	...	33	0.3	6,591	13.8	6,624	9.9
30–39	171	3.2	2,372	17.1	16,322	34.1	18,865	28.1
40–49	1,470	27.4	6,933	50.0	16,029	33.5	24,432	36.4
50–59	1,932	36.0	3,299	23.8	6,670	13.9	11,901	17.7
60 and over	1,797	33.4	1,226	8.8	2,278	4.7	5,301	7.9
Total	5,370	100.0	13,863	100.0	47,890	100.0	67,123	100.0
Per Cent	8.0		20.7		71.3		100.0	

Source: A. Ya. Sinetskii, *Professorsko-prepodavatel'skiye kadry vysshei shkoly SSSR* (Professorial-Teaching Personnel in the USSR Schools of Higher Education), Moscow: "Sovetskaya Nauka," 1950. Part III, Table No. 24 (abstracted).

* As a rule professors and docents hold advanced academic degrees (*doktor* and *kandidat* of science, respectively); "others" include *assistenty*, some of whom have *kandidat* degrees.

docents (3 and 16.7 per cent, respectively) have had less than 10 years of teaching experience. The senior component of Soviet faculties has been and remains relatively small; but proportionally the largest share of the available senior instructors is to be found in universities rather than in the specialized institutes.

A numerically small elite category of the teaching staff is that of the academicians—elected members or corresponding members of the USSR and other Academies of Sciences of the Soviet Union. In 1947 there were only 157 academicians on the teaching staffs, of whom 31 were on the faculty of Moscow University. In 1955 Moscow University had 122 academicians on its faculties: 30 members of the USSR Academy of Sciences, 59 corresponding members, and 33 members of other than the USSR Academy of Sciences. Only 6 academicians of the total number were listed in 1947 as having had less than 10 years of "academic experience."

TABLE 52. NUMBER OF TEACHERS IN SOVIET SCHOOLS OF HIGHER EDUCATION AND PER CENT WITH LESS THAN TEN YEARS OF TEACHING EXPERIENCE BY SELECTED CATEGORIES

January 1947

Category	Teachers		Per Cent with Less than Ten Years of Teaching Experience
	Thousands	%	
All higher schools, total for the USSR	67.3	100.0	54.2
By fields of teaching:			
Technological (VTUZ)	18.9	28.1	49.0
of which			
Industrial and Construction	16.4	24.4	48.6
Transportation and Communication	2.5	3.7	51.9
Teacher Training	21.8	32.4	61.2
of which			
Normal Schools	11.3	16.8	(Probably much greater than 61.2)
Universities	10.5	15.6	(Probably much smaller than 61.2)
By Academic Rank			
Professors	5.4	8.0	3.0
Docents	13.9	20.7	16.7
Others	48.0	71.3	70.0

Source: A. Ya. Sinetskii (See Table 51), Part III, *passim.*

Party Affiliations

As would be expected, Party membership is most heavily represented among Soviet instructors of "social sciences"—Marxism-Leninism, political economy, and philosophy. The only surprising fact is that the proportion of Party membership varies among different categories of teachers as much as it does. In 1947 the per cent in selected groups of teachers was as follows:[8]

Field of Science	Per Cent of Teachers Who Are Members of the Party
Teachers in all fields	34.4
"Socio-political and philosophical"	91.5
Physical-mathematics	26.9
Technological	31.5

The per cent of *professors* in any given field who were Party members as of 1947 is considerably lower than the average of all teaching personnel in that field. For instance, only 17 per cent of the professors of engineering were members of the Communist Party.

Women Teachers

As early as 1940, nearly 50 per cent of the undergraduate and more than 40 per cent of the graduate students in Soviet institutions of higher learning were women; and, as of 1947, 35 per cent of the instructors (as compared with approximately 24 per cent in the United States) were women:

Teachers	All Ranks	Professors	Docents	Others
Total number	67,280	5,370	13,863	47,890
Women	23,514	256	2,253	21,005
Per cent women	35.0	4.8	16.3	43.8

Women teachers in the Soviet Union are very unevenly distributed by fields, 68 per cent of them being the teachers of education subjects. Nevertheless, even in engineering and technology women accounted (in 1947) for 10 per cent of the teaching staff; and about 24 per cent of the faculty members of all engineering schools (VTUZY) generally were women. Although later figures are not available, it is safe to assume that the proportion of women teachers in Soviet higher education is even greater now because of the tremendous male deficit in the Soviet population which resulted from World War II losses of life and other causes.*

Student-Teacher Ratio

As we have already noted, because of the rapidly expanded student enrollment (including correspondence students) in the last few years and the failure to train (or to allocate) more teachers, the Soviet student-teacher ratio has increased somewhat in comparison with earlier years. In 1946–1947, for instance, with a total resident enrollment of 649.5 thousand and 67,280 persons on the teaching staff, the ratio was 9.6 students per staff member. The 1955–1956 resident enrollment was nearly 90 per cent larger, but during the intervening years the instruction staff had increased by less than 80 per cent, resulting in a

* As of October 1, 1955, according to official Soviet data, 45 per cent of all workers and employees (*not counting those engaged in kolkhoz agriculture*) were women. For example:

Occupation	Per Cent Women
Public health	85
Public catering	83
Education	68
Industry	41
Construction	31

ratio of 10.3 resident students to 1 teacher and 15.7 students if the correspondence enrollment is also considered.

It would not be meaningful to compare these average Soviet ratios with any similarly computed figures for American universities and colleges. In the United States the student-teacher ratio has been averaging somewhat less than 12 students per *full-time* teacher, but the ratios in individual schools vary so widely that an unweighted average ratio is almost meaningless.* For instance, among American institutions one may cite Harvard University with a 10.4 thousand enrollment and 3,164 on the teaching staff (3.3 to 1 ratio) or the University of California with 40.3 thousand students and 5,290 instructors (7.7 to 1) or a junior college where the ratio may run as high as 100 to 1 or higher.

Although the Soviet student-teacher ratio varies from school to school and by category of schools, the range—as would be expected under the Soviet system of control—is much narrower than in the United States. Table 53 shows a few examples of the student-teacher ratios in Soviet institutions of higher learning. Although the number of individual examples is small, it is possible nevertheless to derive some generalizations from these and other available data. Among the three categories of schools with which we are here concerned the best staffed are universities, the second best are engineering schools, and the least well staffed are teacher training institutions. If only the resident students are considered, the Soviet (administrative) category of schools ("[33] Universities, [22] Economics Institutes, and [6] Law Institutes") has a student-teacher ratio (10 to 1) almost identical with the average ratio for 129 American universities (10.5 to 1). Among Soviet universities Moscow University (resident enrollment 16,000) has perhaps the lowest student-teacher ratio (6.6 resident students to 1). This ratio is greater than the ratios which obtain in a number of American universities (e.g., Harvard: enrollment of over 10,000, ratio of 3.3 to 1; University of Illinois: 25,000 students, ratio

* In 1949–1950 the ratio was 12.6 to 1; in 1951–1952 about 11.6 to 1 (counting only resident full-time students versus *full-time* equivalent number on the faculties). By categories of schools the 1951–1952 ratios were as follows:

129 Universities	10.5 to 1
688 Liberal arts colleges	12.9 to 1
205 Teachers colleges	13.5 to 1
506 Junior colleges	16.7 to 1
304 Miscellaneous	10.0 to 1

Source: Biennial Survey of Education in the United States, Chapter 4, Section 1, *Statistics of Higher Education: Faculty, Students, and Degrees, 1950–1952,* Washington, D.C.: Office of Education, 1955. Computed from Table 2, pp. 46–47.

TABLE 53. EXAMPLES OF THE AVERAGE NUMBER OF STUDENTS PER TEACHER
OF THE PROFESSOR-DOCENT RANK, PER TEACHER OF LOWER THAN
PROFESSOR-DOCENT RANK, AND PER MEMBER OF THE ENTIRE
TEACHING STAFF IN A NUMBER OF SOVIET SCHOOLS
OF HIGHER EDUCATION

Kind of School, Date and Enrollment		Number of Students per Teacher		
		Professors-Docents	Lower Ranks	Entire Staff
1. All schools of higher education				
Students: Resident	1,228,000	38.4	14.1	10.3
Correspondence	639,000	20.0	7.3	5.4
1955–1956 Total:	1,867,000	58.4	21.4	15.7
2. Universities, economics, law				
Students: Resident	160,000	20.0	20.0	10.0
Correspondence	85,000	10.6	10.6	5.3
1954–1955 Total:	245,000	30.6	30.6	15.3
3. Moscow University				
Students: Resident	16,080	16.9	10.7	6.6
Correspondence	5,920	6.2	3.9	2.4
1954–1955 Total:	22,000	23.1	14.6	9.0
4. Bauman MVTU				
1955–1956 students:	8,600	24.9	20.7	11.3
5. Novocherkassk Polytechnic				
1953–1954 students:	5,000	50.0	?	?
6. Tiraspol' Pedagogical				
1955–1956 students:	3,000	150.0	37.5	30.0

Sources:
1. Same as Table 50, Item 1.
2. Same as Table 50, Item 7.
3. Same as Table 50, Item 4.
4. Same as Table 50, Item 9.
5. *Vestnik vysshei shkoly*, No. 8, August 1953, p. 26.
6. *Vestnik vysshei shkoly*, No. 4, April 1956, p. 47.

5.4 to 1) but is smaller than in the majority of American universities (for example, Yale—8.6 to 1; Cornell, University of California, Princeton—7.7 to 1; University of Denver, University of Houston—20 to 1).

For the Soviet engineering schools (not shown in the table) the over-all ratio, considering only the resident students and the total faculty of approximately 25,000, the student-teacher ratio is about 18 to 1 (counting correspondence students the ratio would be about 26 to 1). The Moscow Higher Technical School (MVTU), presumably the leading engineering school in the Soviet Union, has eleven students per member of the faculty staff—close to the Soviet national average. This ratio is considerably higher than in a number of leading American schools. At MIT, for instance, the over-all ratio runs about 4 to 1, and the student-*professor* (including associate and assistant) ratio is about 7 to 1, compared with MVTU, which has nearly 25 students per professor-docent member on the faculty.

In general, therefore, it may be noted that in the Soviet Union the over-all student-teacher ratio varies among the categories of schools here considered much more than it does from school to school within any one category. In the United States the reverse is true; the variations from school to school within each category are much greater than among the averages for the separate kinds of schools.

In connection with the data just considered, it should be mentioned that the number of graduate students in Soviet institutions of higher learning is extremely small in comparison with that in the United States.*

The difference between the percentage of total enrollment represented by graduate students in the Soviet Union and that in the United States can be seen from the following approximate figures:

Description	Enrollment		Per Cent of Graduate Students
	Total	Graduate	
USSR total in 1955–1956, thousands†	1,867.0	16.8	0.9
US total in 1951–1952	2,302.0	233.3	10.1
University of Moscow, 1955–1956	22.0	1.9	8.6
Bauman MVTU, c. 1954–1955	8.6	0.25	2.9
Harvard University, fall of 1954	10.4	5.9	56.7
California Institute of Technology	1.0	0.4	40.0
MIT, fall of 1954	5.4	1.9	35.2

* In the Soviet Union graduate training (largely for careers in research and development) is also given in the research institutes of the USSR Academy of Sciences and others. In 1955–1956 the total Soviet graduate enrollment was distributed as follows:

Institutions of Higher Education	16.8 thousand
Research Institutes	12.6 thousand

See Chapter 11.

† Including correspondence school graduate and undergraduate enrollment, approximately as follows:

Enrollment (1955–1956) in thousands

	Total	Graduate	Per Cent
Resident	1,228	13.4	1.1
Correspondence	639	3.4	0.5

Because of the great difference in the proportion of graduate students, a direct comparison of the student-teacher ratios for some institutions must be correspondingly judged. For instance, California Institute of Technology's student-teacher ratio is of the order of 1.7 to 1, but 40 per cent of its students are at the graduate level; at the University of Moscow, with its low (by Soviet standards) resident student-teacher ratio of 6.6 to 1, the graduate enrollment is less than 9 per cent of the total. Consequently, so far as Soviet graduate students are concerned, the student-teacher ratios may not be as low as the over-all ratios would imply.

"Sovmestitel'stvo"—Multiple Job-Holding

The practice of holding two or more academic positions simultaneously has been widespread in the Soviet Union. This "multiple hat" system, as Professor Trilling referred to it, was the rule rather than exception in the 1930's, and it remains a significant phenomenon at the present time.[9] The shortage of qualified men relative to the mushrooming demands of the state and the meagerness of real income per unit of effort have combined to perpetuate this officially frowned-upon practice. Although various measures have been taken in the past to reduce the extent of plurality of appointments, the "multiple hat" practice at high academic levels continues to play an important corrective role in unifying the otherwise circumscribed and functionally isolated elements of research, development, training, and engineering within selected key fields of industry or research into a coordinated campaign or a longer-range undertaking. To quote Professor Trilling:

> This "multiple hat" system in which leading academic personnel carry several responsibilities appears, from the available testimony, to operate with flexibility and effectiveness. Scientists engaged in fundamental research which underlies the whole problem . . . [here specifically of air flight] do their work both at the universities and at the Academy-sponsored research institutes.[10]

But, while in research and development the "multiple hat" system may permit effective mobilization of scientific manpower into a task force for a particular problem, the effect of this practice on the teaching process is not necessarily as salutary. The duties performed simultaneously by the Soviet educator do not necessarily combine teaching in one institution and research (or consultation) in another.* In the majority of cases *sovmestitel'stvo* appears to mean simply full-time

---

* It might be noted here that according to an editorial in *Pravda* (October 5, 1955): "Hardly one-fifth of the teachers of the institutions of higher learning take part in carrying out research."

teaching at one institution, half-time (or less) teaching at another, and possibly some teaching at even a third. In the 1930's many a Soviet educator might have held, according to numerous and reliable reports, four, five, and even six jobs, some of them wholly unrelated to either teaching or research. In many instances one person held two jobs in the same institution—each in some cases on a full-time basis.[11]

The practice of *sovmestitel'stvo* was so widespread as to call forth many rules and regulations attempting to set a limit, usually in terms of the additional pay for the second job as a per cent (up to 50 per cent) of the base pay for the regular staff position. Sinetskii's study, previously referred to, gives some statistics on *sovmestitel'stvo* as of c. 1947. He states that in addition to the 67.3 thousand teachers on the regular staff there were 7.1 thousand part-time teachers who were presumably full-time employees of industrial enterprises. Among the full-time staff members of the faculties about 21 thousand (31 per cent) held additional jobs elsewhere. Thus, of the total number of persons engaged in teaching (74.4 thousand), some 38 per cent (7.1 thousand plus 21,000) were *sovmestiteli*. This source also gives some data on the distribution of multiple job-holders by certain categories from which one may compute, for example, the per cent of multiple job-holders in engineering schools for industry and construction. In 1947 the composition of the teaching force in these schools was as follows:

	Sovmestiteli	One Job	Total
Regular teaching staff	4,990	11,377	16,367
Others (part-time)	2,221	..	2,221
Total number, individuals	7,211	11,377	18,588
Per Cent	38.8	61.2	100.0

Some data are also given by Sinetskii on the number, by cities and by a few specific universities and institutes, of persons holding academic appointments who also held other positions. There is a pronounced direct correlation between the relative academic and scientific importance of the cities as a whole (and of specific institutions) and the proportion of staff members who are *sovmestiteli*. Thus, for instance, in Moscow 38.8 per cent of the academic *staff members* also held other positions, versus only 22.7 in Tomsk; at Moscow University 44.2 per cent of the faculty members were *sovmestiteli,* and approximately the same per cent of multiple job-holders were on the university faculties in Kiev and Kharkov. Among the engineering schools, the faculty of Moscow Higher Technical School (MVTU) had the highest proportion of *sovmestiteli*—43.8 per cent, as contrasted, for instance, with 13 per

cent at the Ural Industrial Institute or 11.5 per cent at the Novocherkassk Industrial Institute. On the whole, Sinetskii's data show that
of all the *sovmestiteli* who had academic staff appointments (that is,
not including part-time teachers) about 40 per cent also held positions
in other schools and 60 per cent held additional positions in other
than academic capacities—for instance, as practicing engineers. At the
present time a certain number of engineers unquestionably combine
part-time teaching with their full-time work in a plant or a design
bureau, but apparently such instances are in the minority.

In June 1955 a Corresponding Member of the USSR Academy of
Sciences, Deputy USSR Minister of Higher Education V. A. Kirillin,
commenting on the problems of quality in higher education, wrote
that among other factors:

> Plural   job-holding   [*sovmestitel'stvo*]—the   practice   excessively
> common among the workers in schools of higher education—is also
> a major obstacle [to quality of instruction]. If the combining of
> work in industry with teaching in an institution of higher education
> is, for certain isolated, highly-qualified workers, a sensible and useful
> arrangement, then the practice of teaching simultaneously in two
> institutions of higher education—and with us it is specifically this
> type of *sovmestitel'stvo* that constitutes the majority of cases—is
> unconditionally harmful and cannot be justified by any reasoning.[12]

In November of the same year the Minister of Higher Education of
the recently created Ukrainian SSR Ministry, echoing his Moscow
counterpart in almost identical concluding words, also gave some
statistics:

> The simultaneous holding of several appointments [*sovmestitel'-
> stvo*], which has lately gained impermissibly wide proportions, has
> a detrimental effect upon academic process and research. Twenty
> per cent of the professorial-teaching staff of Kiev University hold
> multiple appointments. In the Polytechnic Institute of Kiev 108
> teachers hold more than one position; of them, 58 are staff members
> of the Institute and 50 are staff members of other institutions of
> higher education or of scientific establishments. The directors of
> certain institutes permit multiple job-holding even by teachers
> of low qualification. Such practice cannot be justified by any reason-
> ing. It is the duty of the directors duly to take care of this matter.[13]

Even if the economic factor which necessitated *sovmestitel'stvo* in
past years is no longer acute, the relative shortage of qualified personnel
remains. Moreover, the allocation of personnel resources is still made
by the central authorities according to priorities which are not determined by the Soviet academic world. It is doubtful that the directors
can "duly take care of this matter" unless either allocation of national

resources becomes decentralized or the supply of trained manpower qualitatively and quantitatively reaches a balance with the demands of the state.

The Teaching Load

By regulations issued in 1937, when monthly salaries were established by the Soviet government instead of the former hourly basis of compensation for university teaching, a 6-hour workday, 6 days per week, was set for the members of the teaching staff, with an annual paid vacation of 8 weeks in the summer. These basic provisions apparently are still in effect.

The regulations distinguish between duties involving direct teaching work and duties of other types, including research and administration, and specify that part of the total working time to be given to teaching. The teaching load, as defined, includes lectures, seminars, and laboratory sessions; supervision of undergraduate theses (*diploma* projects) and industrial practice; the checking and review of papers written by the correspondence students; participation in the state examinations; and other contacts with undergraduate and graduate students. The time allotment for all such duties depends on academic rank, as follows:

	Hours per Day		Hours per Year*	
Academic Rank	Min.	Max.	Min.	Max.
Professor, Head of Department	2.25	2.75	540	660
Professor or Docent	2.75	3.25	660	780
Others†	3.00	3.50	720	840

On the average, therefore, about one-half of the Soviet professor's time is spent in teaching and one-half in other work, including in some cases research, administrative duties of the department and laboratories, lecture planning and preparation, correcting students' homework and industrial practice reports, and other similar duties. In addition to the duties of the regular staff appointment, for which 6 hours of work per day is prescribed, half-time (or less) work in another capacity (by way of intra-institutional *sovmestitel'stvo*) may be—and, apparently in a very large number of cases, is—carried at half the regular pay (or less). Such additional work may include special research contracted for by an industrial organization of the state, as distinct from any research of the department done in the normal course of academic duties and supported by funds allocated by the state for this

---

* Six days per week, 40 working weeks in the academic year.
† Assistants, Senior Teachers, and Teachers.

purpose to the school directly. The time spent by way of *sovmestitel'-stvo*, according to the regulations, must be over and above the 6-hour norm of the regular work. This provision is apparently carefully observed, at least for the record.

Elaborate timekeeping procedures are provided for both budgetary and payroll purposes, and time norms for certain elements of academic work are prescribed. A set of regulations established in 1941 and at least until recently still in effect provides the standards for the computation of the total authorized staff-load of an institution (and therefore the composition of the teaching staff and salary budget) for a given enrollment of students.[14] The regulations prescribe, for instance, the following time norms:

1. Consultation with students—up to 15 per cent of scheduled lecture hours per "basic study group (25 to 30 students)."

2. Promotional examinations—from one-third to one-half of the academic hour per student; for a *zachet,* an ungraded examination —from one-quarter to one-third of an hour.

3. Term projects—2 to 3 hours per project per student.

4. Supervision, consultation, examination, and certification in connection with a *diploma* project—35 teacher-hours per student.

As to the actual distribution of staff time, none of such minutiae appears to be observed in practice. In 1953, for instance, K. A. Potresov of Dnepropetrovsk Engineering Construction Institute wrote:

> One may say that the problem of norms in the work of teachers is not satisfactorily formulated. The data on the expenditure of a teacher's time in various types of work established 15 years ago are still being used as the basis. These data naturally do not reflect the changes which have taken place in the requirements for carrying out many types of tasks (both as to the method and as to the scope and content). Furthermore, the data are not specific enough: for the supervision of a term project from two to three hours are allotted; for an examination—from one-third to one-half hour; for student consultation—"up to 15 per cent of the number of lecture hours," and so forth. Explanatory instructions with reference to these norms are not sufficiently detailed and therefore they permit arbitrary interpretations.[15]

These individual norms may not be as restrictive in actual practice as they appear to be on paper; but each teacher is nevertheless obligated to carry a standard teaching load—18 hours per week on the average. The fact that the designated teaching loads are not adjusted with respect to, for instance, the research load of a given instructor, or with respect to the level and content of a given subject, must on the whole be detrimental to the academic advancement of the faculty members. It is not surprising that many of the various recent suggestions by Soviet educators on improving the status of higher education touch upon the need to revise the existing workload provisions. A docent of the Taganrog Radio Engineering Institute, K. Ya. Shaposhnikov, pointing out the need (and the Party's injunction) to strengthen research at institutions of higher education, stated that, in his opinion:

> . . . it is necessary first of all to solve the problem of the excessive teaching load. . . . The only solution is to determine the minimum and the maximum teaching loads of professors, docents, and assistants depending on whether they are or are not engaged in research.[16]

The existing "labor norms," via the budgetary pressures they must necessarily exert, apparently tend to perpetuate such long-condemned features of Soviet higher education as the fractionalization of courses into many separate and frequently overlapping subjects of instruction (*"mnogopredmetnost'"*—"multi-subjectness") and the generally excessive number of scheduled hours provided by the *uchebnyi* plans. Although these plans, in the final analysis, are established by the Ministry, they are based on the representations and recommendations of the teachers. As one Soviet professor noted:

> It is well known that every teacher as a rule is convinced that it is precisely his subject which is most important for the training of specialists, and consequently, in the formulation of *uchebnyi* plans, he sees it as his objective to succeed in expanding the number of hours for his department. This unhealthy pursuit of hours is largely explainable by the fact that in reality the existing system of compensation in the institutions of higher education is not on the basis of monthly salaries [*shtatno-okladnaya*]. The system as it actually works takes into account the hours for lectures, supervision of term projects, exercises; if a teacher finds himself short of the number of hours officially designated for his position, such a situation leads to a change in the staff of the department. To sum up, the share given to one or another lecture course [in the *uchebnyi* plan] frequently is determined not so much by the real need [for such a course] as it is by the necessity fully to load up the teachers with hours that count, although these hours could be spent far more profitably for the cause [of education] in consultation, research, and so forth.[17]

The above was written in 1951. In 1955, in connection with the drive to improve the quality of Soviet textbooks and to eliminate irregularities in supply, "it was decided to include the compilation of textbooks within the research load of the teachers, to grant the authors creative leaves of absences, and to release from their regular load the most deserving scientists."[18] Beyond this, apparently no changes of any significance occurred in the Soviet system of work-load allocation until the summer of 1956. Details of the new system are unknown to this writer, but the nature of the recent change is indicated in an article by V. P. Yelutin, the USSR Minister of Higher Education, published in July 1956, which reads in part:

> The liquidation of the existing system of work norms for teachers and the introduction of fixed [faculty] staff will have an important role in correctly organizing research and in improving the quality of the training of specialists. Beginning with the next [1956–1957] academic year the size of the professorial-teaching staff at the institutions of higher learning will be determined on the basis of the average number of students per teacher.
>
> *Sovmestitel'stvo* of teachers shall be sharply limited. Teaching by way of *sovmestitel'stvo* in other institutions of higher education may be permitted in exceptional cases only for the purpose of improving the educational process.[19]

What average student-teacher ratio shall be taken as a basis, Yelutin did not state in this article.

Teachers' Salaries

The method now used for compensating the teaching personnel in Soviet institutions of higher education, based on a monthly salary but with a stipulated division of work time between teaching and other duties, was introduced in 1937. The directive of that year included a schedule of salaries graduated by academic rank and by length of professional experience. This schedule, showing the salaries then established for both the teaching and auxiliary or supporting personnel, is reproduced in Table 54. In absolute figures the table is out of date. Because of the wartime inflation and many adjustments in salary scales before and following a drastic postwar devaluation, the 1956 salaries in rubles were about $2\frac{1}{2}$ times those shown in Table 54.

What is significant, however, is the relative structure of the original salary schedule and thus the relative valuations associated with academic positions, degrees, and titles. If the lowest salary in the schedule (that of a junior laboratory assistant) is taken as a unit of comparison, the senior personnel salaries, it will be noted, run up to 15 times that minimum. It is certain that no comparable spread in base salaries can be found in American colleges. The sharply progressive Soviet scale of base compensation according to recognized academic levels remains in effect, as far as we know, up to the present time. If one were to consider additional earnings of the senior staff among Soviet educators (and scientists generally) through the widespread

TABLE 54. SCHEDULE OF BASE MONTHLY SALARIES ESTABLISHED IN 1937
FOR THE TEACHING AND SUPPORTING PERSONNEL IN SOVIET INSTITUTIONS
OF HIGHER EDUCATION

(As amended to 1942 and apparently in effect as late as 1945 or later)

| Staff Position, Academic Degree or Education* | If Professional Experience is† | | | |
| | Less than 5 years | | More than 10 years | |
	Rubles	Index‡	Rubles	Index‡
1. Professor,				
(a) Department Head,				
if doctor degree	1,700	11.33	2,300	15.35
if no doctor degree	1,300	8.66	1,800	12.00
(b) Not a Department Head,				
if doctor degree	1,500	10.00	2,000	13.33
if no doctor degree	1,200	8.00	1,500	10.00
2. Docent; Senior Teacher,				
if candidate degree	1,050	7.00	1,400	9.33
if no degree	800	5.33	1,100	7.33
3. *Assistent*; Teacher,				
if candidate degree	900	6.00	1,200	8.00
if no degree	700	4.66	900	6.00
4. Senior Laboratory Technician§	450	3.00	550	3.66
5. Laboratory Technician,				
(a) with specialized secondary education	350	2.33	450	3.00
(b) with general secondary education	225	1.50	325	2.16
6. Senior Laboratory Assistant‖	225	1.50	325	2.16
7. Junior Laboratory Assistant	150	1.00	200	1.33

Source: Vysshaya shkola, compiled by M. I. Movshovich, p. 296.

* The academic degrees identified as "doctor" and "candidate" are in Russian *doktor nauk* and *kandidat nauk*, respectively.

† The intermediate (from 5 to 10 years) range is omitted. In practically all cases the salary in the 5- to 10-year range is the average of those shown.

‡ The starting salary for a Junior Laboratory Assistant is taken as 1.00.

§ In Russian: (Senior) *laborant.*

‖ In Russian: (Senior) *preparator.*

sovmestitel'stvo, certain overtime and special fee payments and the author's royalties, the average money income of a Soviet professor or docent would stand in even greater contrast to the lowest salaries on the scale.* To our knowledge no official schedules of academic salaries

* The relative earnings of scientists of comparable rank are even greater for those on the staff of the Academy of Sciences or industrial research institutes, especially those engaged in military research.

have been published recently in the Soviet press. Some official figures, however, are available or can be estimated. It was recently (1955) stated, for instance, that for the purposes of computing academic pensions (40 per cent of the last staff salary: for men—at age 60 and after 25 years of qualifying teaching; for women—at age 55 and after 20 years of staff work) no actual monthly salary in excess of the following limits would be used:

	Rubles per Month
Academicians and corresponding members of the academies	6,000
Professors and doctors of science	4,000
Docents and candidates of science	2,000
Others (on the teaching staff)	1,000

An example is given, as follows:

> . . . if a docent had held a full-time appointment at an institution of higher education and his salary was 3,200 rubles (the maximum salary for a docent-candidate with more than 10 years of staff experience [stazh]), the size of his pension shall be computed on the basis of 2,000 and not 3,200 rubles. . . .[20]

Comparing the salary listed for a docent-candidate (1,400 rubles) in Table 54 with the 1955 salary of 3,200 we may assume that other salaries listed in the table have been increased in the same proportion—by some 130 per cent. If that is the case, the present maximum base salaries may be approximately as follows:

	Rubles per Month
Professor-doctor	5,000
Professor, not a doctor	3,500
Docent-candidate	3,200
Docent, not a candidate	2,500

If, however, we assume that the pension base limits were set at 62.5 per cent of the maximum base salary for all categories, the estimate of the 1955 maximum salaries (10 or more years of experience) would be, in round figures, as follows:

	Rubles per Month
Professor-doctor	6,400
Docent-candiate	3,200

These rough estimates are well within the range of examples of the 1955 and even more recent Soviet salaries cited in the accounts of visitors to the Soviet Union.

We quote here some of the recently reported academic and other salaries, without further documentation; unless otherwise noted the data are as of c. 1955:

	Rubles per month
Professor	
Academic rank not stated	5,000
In charge of a *kafedra* (department)	6,000
Academic rank not stated	5,500
In a research institute, leader	6,000
Docent	
Kafedra (department) head, degree not stated	3,200
Minimum	2,500
Upper level	3,200
Secondary school teacher	
Grade unspecified (1954)	700
Beginner (depending on hours, etc.)	800 to 1,200
Beginner	1,000 to 1,200
Examples of nonacademic salaries	
Truck driver (1954)	700
Laborer (1954)	300
Street cleaner	250

These admittedly sketchy data are sufficient to show a very great spread of salaries in the listed categories of what in fact is the Soviet civil service.*

One more category could be added to this list, that of academicians, the elite body of scientists elected members of the USSR and other Soviet academies of sciences.† A regular member of the USSR Academy of Sciences, in addition to his usual "professor-doctor" salary—reportedly 6,000 rubles per month at the present time—receives

* Compare the United States schedule of compensations for civil service employees under the Classification Act of 1949 as amended June 1955 and reflecting changes made in 1956 (Public Law 854, Eighty-Fourth Congress) whereby G.S. 18 salary was changed from $14,800 to $16,000 as shown:

Grade	Basic Salary	Grade	Basic Salary
GS–1	$2,690	GS–10	$ 5,915
GS–2	2,960	GS–11	6,390
GS–3	3,175	GS–12	7,570
GS–4	3,415	GS–13	8,990
GS–5	3,670	GS–14	10,320
GS–6	4,080	GS–15	11,610
GS–7	4,525	GS–16	12,900
GS–8	4,970	GS–17	13,975
GS–9	5,440	GS–18	16,000

The ratio of the new highest salary to the lowest is less than 6 to 1.

† On the USSR Academy of Sciences, see Alexander Vucinich, *The Soviet Academy of Sciences*, Stanford: Stanford University Press, January 1956.

an honorarium said to equal about one-half the amount of his regular salary or more—plus many tangible and intangible fringe benefits, such as allowances for the purchase of foreign books and provisions for individual medical care. A Corresponding Member of the USSR Academy of Sciences receives an honorarium of about one-half the amount paid the member. An academician's money income, therefore, can run to 10, 12, and more thousands of rubles per month.

It is of course extremely misleading and inappropriate to translate the relatively high compensations of Soviet educators and scientists into dollars—whether at the assumed purchasing power parity rate (of perhaps 10 to 1) or, much worse, at the Soviet-proclaimed ratio of four rubles to one dollar. In any case, the absolute level of income, however expressed, for any occupation in a given society versus a similar or identical occupation in another society is not a very meaningful measure of relative status. What is far more significant for any comparative assessment of social trends in a money economy is the relative scale of monetary values placed by a given society upon the productive duties of its members in various occupational categories. In the Soviet Union, where virtually the entire urban labor force is on the civil list, and where relative wages and salaries reflect a deliberately formulated and enforced scale of priorities among the objectives of the state, the highly trained scientist employed in education and research has rated high.

Whether his salary position relative to other occupational categories of workers in the Soviet Union will remain as high as it has been until now depends, of course, on many factors—among them, whether the sole power to allocate national resources remains in the hands of the central government. But even under the present form of government some change is likely to take place. The number of persons with higher professional education in the Soviet Union is steadily increasing; the growing need to improve the productivity and thus the earnings of the long depressed worker and peasant may also have a somewhat equalizing effect on salaries. Only recently it was announced that the minimum wage of workers has been raised to 350 rubles per month.[21] Even more significant is the fact that the "fairness" of the Soviet academic salary scale itself was questioned in *Komsomol'skaya pravda,* March 20, 1956. The article, entitled "The System of Pay for Scholars and Scientists Must Be Changed," was signed by a group of distinguished authors, including two professor-doctors of technical sciences and three academicians.[22] The following excerpts are indicative of the issues involved:

. . . how can it be explained that for the same kind of work, such as, for example, having charge of a department (*kafedra*), a professor with a Doctor of Science degree receives twice the monthly salary of a docent with the degree of Candidate of Science; and an engineer without a degree who [nevertheless] is in charge of a department receives even less? The existing system of salaries for scientists transforms the graduate thesis, written some time in the past to satisfy requirements for an academic degree, into a sort of annuity, a life income.

Can it be considered normal that a professor or a *kandidat nauk* ["Ph.D."] engaged in teaching or research receives two or three times the salary of, for example, a chief engineer in a factory who is in charge of many thousands of people engaged in producing goods of tremendous material value and who bears immense responsibility for exceptionally important work?

If the question [of quality of research] is to be solved at the core, there must be a basic change in the pay system for scientists.

We must eliminate the striking disparity between the salaries of scientists engaged in education and research and the salaries of scientists in other enterprises and institutions of our country.

Attention must be drawn, finally, to the disproportion between the wages of production workers and those of workers in educational and research institutes.*

* In contrast stands a recent American study by Beardsley Ruml and Sidney G. Tickton, *Teaching Salaries Then and Now*, Bulletin No. 1, The Fund for the Advancement of Education 1955, which is a 50-year comparison of teaching salaries with earnings in other occupations and industries. One finding: "The deterioration at the top [highest professional ranks in education] is so great that it affects the attractiveness of the academic career as compared to other professions and occupations" (p. 19). Their figures, for instance, show that in current dollars for twenty-seven selected occupations in 1953 the yearly earnings before taxes varied from the lowest of $2,709 to the highest of $16,500, a range of 1 to 6.1, including the examples given below. The relative status in terms of "real" purchasing power (earnings after Federal income and social security taxes and deflation) is shown in the column designated "Real Purchasing Power," with the total range of 1 to 4.9.

	Average Yearly Earnings	Index	
		Current Dollars	"Real" Purchasing Power
Tobacco manufacturing workers	$ 2,709	100	100
Elementary school teacher, large city	4,817	178	163
Railroad fireman	6,180	228	204
High school teacher, large city	5,526	204	184
Railroad conductor	6,676	246	219
Associate professor, large state university	5,600	207	186
Professor, large state university	7,000	258	229
University president	16,500	609	490

Whether the article from which we have just quoted was written and published for some particular purpose of official policy or to forecast an impending change, or whether it represents an independent objective analysis of the authors, it points up both the disproportions within the academic scale and between academic and industrial salaries and wages. We do not know whether any changes were made following the publication of this article or whether changes are contemplated in the immediate future. In any case, the level and the structure of Soviet academic salaries would have to be changed considerably if the present internal inequalities and the inequalities vis-à-vis other occupational groups are to be materially reduced.

It is beyond the scope of this study to attempt a statistically valid analysis of the Soviet wage scale in relevant categories—even if the data were freely available—or, still more, to develop a methodologically rigorous comparison of such a scale with that of the American economy. Nevertheless, merely to indicate the order of magnitude which a detailed comparison of selected wage relatives in the Soviet Union and in the United States would show, we submit a rough estimate based on the available Soviet data and a number of sources consulted with reference to the American counterparts of the Soviet employees in the synthetic occupational categories listed below. For both the United States and the Soviet Union the earnings of a "laborer" are taken as the unit and all other earnings are expressed as multiples of the laborer's monthly wage:

Category	USA[23]	USSR
Laborer	1.0	1.0
Truck driver	1.3	2.3
School teacher	1.6	3.3
Professor	2.5	16.0

2. THE TEXTBOOKS

In "The Role of Physics in Engineering Education," an address at the 1954 annual meeting of the American Society for Engineering Education, Professor Nathaniel H. Frank, Head of the Department of Physics at the Massachusetts Institute of Technology, having first outlined his views on the changing pattern of requirements in engineering education and the means for meeting them insofar as physics is concerned, said:

In the last analysis, the only really effective means of communication of new ideas and patterns of education are provided by the textbooks used by the teachers throughout the country.

More than one hundred Soviet textbooks have been examined in the course of this study by members of the faculty at MIT. An attempt was made to collect as representative a set of textbooks as could be obtained for various levels of Soviet training in the two fields selected for examination: physics and mechanical engineering. In some instances a very detailed examination and evaluation of the available text suggested itself; to name only a few, a highly advanced text in theoretical physics, *Quantum Electrodynamics* by Akhiyezer and Berestetskii (Moscow, 1953), was examined by Sidney D. Drell, Assistant Professor of Physics;* an engineering textbook, *Applied Gas Dynamics* by G. N. Abramovich (Moscow, 1953), was analyzed by Ascher H. Shapiro, Professor of Mechanical Engineering, and jointly by Robert C. Dean, Jr., and Alan H. Stenning, Assistant Professors of Mechanical Engineering;† Ya. I. Frenkel's *Introduction to the Theory of Metals,* a textbook for fifth-year engineering students, was examined by John T. Norton, Professor of Metallurgy, Michael B. Bever, Associate Professor of Metallurgy, and Dr. George W. Pratt, Jr., Lincoln Laboratory. Professors of Physics William P. Allis, Philip M. Morse, and Nathaniel H. Frank, Head of the Department of Physics, examined a large number of Soviet textbooks not only in general physics, such as the three-volume course in general physics by Frish and Timoreva (*Kurs obshcheyi fiziki*),‡ but also in modern physics at advanced levels and in other fields of science, in mathematical analysis, engineering theory, and application. Among the engineering textbooks examined by both physicists and members of the engineering faculties (including John A. Hrones, Professor of Mechanical Engineering; Frank A. McClintock, Assistant Professor of Mechanical Engineering; Walter McKay, Associate Professor of Aeronautical Engineering; Norman C. Dahl, Associate Professor of Mechanical Engineering; Thomas P. Goodman, Assistant Professor of Mechanical Engineering; Milton C. Shaw, Professor of Mechanical Engineering; and others) were a few texts corresponding to the subjects included in the engineering curriculum discussed in the preceding chapter, such as Artobolevskii's *Theory of Mechanisms and Machines.*[24] A number of texts in other branches of engineering were also examined; Appendix N is an evaluation of A. Voronov's *Elementary Theory of Automatic Regulation* made by Myron A. Hoffman, Assistant Professor of Aero-

* Dr. Drell's evaluation, brief excerpts, and the table of contents of this book are incorporated in Cenis Source Memorandum No. 17.

† The table of contents and comments on this textbook are given in Cenis Source Memorandum No. 14.

‡ A translation of the table of contents is given in Cenis Source Memorandum No. 16.

nautical Engineering. Finally, a selection of several textbooks related to aeronautical science and engineering were evaluated by Leon Trilling, Assistant Professor of Aeronautical Engineering, and commented upon in detail in his *Soviet Education in Aeronautics: A Case Study.*

The consensus which emerged from these and other evaluations by faculty members of MIT, aside from judgments of quality which, naturally, range widely from the highest level down to routine and lower depending on the particular textbook, singles out a number of characteristics which appear to apply to Soviet textbooks generally. Typically, a Soviet textbook is likely to be distinguished by one or more of the following features: (1) extremely comprehensive and detailed exposition of the subject (". . . mania for encyclopedic completeness," ". . . as if written under a morbid fear of omitting anything"); (2) as a rule, thorough familiarity with foreign, and particularly older German and current English, texts on the same subject ("Pattern of organization, topics, presentation similar to American textbooks—as if at one time much of the traditional material was copied"); (3) engineering texts, frequently overloaded with examples and elaborate detailing of applications (". . . much of the material covered in the Soviet engineering texts is assumed to be self-evident and does not deserve extensive classroom presentation"); (4) specialized engineering texts, e.g., on internal combustion engines and other types of machinery, are almost wholly descriptive (". . . completely 'present art' type—not even the performance curves are included.* This type of text would not be used at MIT at all"; ". . . cookbook engineering"); (5) a tendency to overemphasize mathematical analysis and solutions of engineering problems even where simpler graphic methods, for instance, would be equally satisfactory.

By other criteria—as reference books or monographs comprehensively embracing material in a given field of science or engineering—many of the advanced Soviet texts are in no way inferior to the best produced elsewhere, and some are uniquely valuable in content and in thoroughness of presentation in highly specialized areas for which no counterpart texts are available in Western literature. The fact that many Soviet texts in science and mathematics have been translated into foreign languages, including English, speaks for itself.[25]

---

* E.g., V. T. Tsetkov, *Dvigateli vnutrennevo sgoraniya* (Internal Combustion Engines), Moscow: Mashgiz, 1953. A reference text for schools of higher technical education, 530 pp.

The Soviet textbook fund seen as a whole, however, appears in a less favorable light. In addition to the characteristics already listed, one finds that Soviet textbooks, especially engineering texts, reflect the general organization of Soviet curricula; they are narrowly specialized, vocationally oriented, geared to specific industries, and follow correspondingly a pyramidal organization of material pointed to some fractionalized specialty. Much overlap and duplication necessarily results. For example, there is apparently no generally available textbook embracing foundry processes; but there are many textbooks in this field dealing with separate elements of technology such as cast iron castings, steel castings, nonferrous metal castings, moulding materials, and mould technology.[26] Each of such texts is typically detailed and bulky. The entire assortment of prescribed textbooks for a course in foundry engineering or technology would fill a small library. The sheer bulk and the excessive factual content of Soviet textbooks is, in fact, a feature most frequently complained about in the current educational press in the Soviet Union. The "multi-subjectness" ("mnogopredmetnost'") of the Soviet curricula—plus the influence, perhaps largely psychological, of the Soviet social and political climate—has contributed to the progressive swelling of the individual texts. As one Soviet bibliographer, L. L. Grif, wrote (in 1953):

> Quite clearly, a tendency toward a further increase in the size of textbooks and reference texts has been in evidence of late; the publication of books with 700–800 pages has become a usual and widespread phenomenon. Republished textbooks, as a rule, appear as an enlarged version.

The bulk of many of the prescribed texts is totally out of proportion to the time allotted to its study in the *uchebnyi* plan:

> Really, how can one count upon the student to master in depth a three-volume textbook of nearly 1,600 pages on the subject "The Surveying for and Planning of Railroads" in the 200 academic hours allotted to this subject by the *uchebnyi* plan.[27]

Corresponding Member of the USSR Academy of Sciences and Deputy Minister of Higher Education, V. A. Kirillin, wrote in 1954:

> ... perhaps the main defect of teaching manuals for students in the institutions of higher technical education is their excessively large compass. Thus the students who specialize in steam boilers are still being offered today as the basic teaching aid a two-volume text, *Boiler Installations,* published in 1941 and 1946. Outstanding specialists participated in the creation of this text, and the text is, as it were, an encyclopedia on boiler installations. But the two

volumes of the text contain more than 120 printing sheets [approximately 2,000 pages], precluding, for practical reasons, any extensive use of the text by the students.[28]

Docent I. M. Galemin of Dneprodzerzhinski Metallurgical Evening Institute, discussing the problem of excessive duplication in a number of metallurgical subjects, pointed out also:

> . . . the basic defect of many textbooks used in the institutions of higher education is their "pudginess," which more often than not is the result of excessive theorization on the details in the course. At times the theorizing reaches such a degree that the student cannot get the idea of rather simple processes and phenomena, and is at a loss to find what is important. A student may find himself in this predicament if he addresses himself, for instance, to the textbook *Hydraulics, Pumps, and Air Blowing Machines* by B. V. Kantorovich, which has 540 pages of text with illustrations and drawings, whereas the lecture course is planned for only 20 hours. The same can be said about N. M. Belyaev's *Strength of Materials*—a text of 817 pages for a 50-hour lecture course.[29]

Many other similar examples can be cited, not only from recent sources but also from the much earlier warnings voiced—apparently without effect—by some Soviet scholars against the approach to education which has been largely responsible for the overlapping organization, bulkiness, and encyclopedic character of Soviet textbooks, especially the engineering texts. One such earlier example, an article published in a journal of the USSR Academy of Sciences in 1941 by Academician A. N. Krylov (b. 1863), was cited elsewhere in 1953 as follows:

> An outstanding scientist and teacher, Academician A. N. Krylov . . . came out with a sharp but just criticism of those specialists who "have a tendency to deal with their subject 'in its full scope,' forgetting, as it were, that they themselves have spent perhaps ten, fifteen, twenty-five, or more years in studying the subject during the course of their teaching experience, whereas the student can devote only a small part of a year, or a semester, to the same subject. . . ."
>
> A. N. Krylov ridiculed the all-embracing syllabi and textbooks which are fed to the students, forcing them to occupy themselves not in the study of science but in a passive cramming on an immense quantity of very tenuously connected facts.
>
> "In the old days [wrote Krylov] the Moscow merchants never failed to fatten up fowl for Christmas—geese on soaked peas, and turkeys on boiled chestnuts. For this purpose the fowl would be hung sewed up to the neck in a bag, and stuffed with food—growing fat to the limit of the merchant's taste and stomach. So the students often are similarly treated: they are stuffed with knowledge . . . but are not allowed sufficient time for thinking through, digesting, and really studying the subject."[30]

The original reorganization of the educational process in the 1930's influenced the development of Soviet engineering textbook literature into separate industrial categories corresponding to the vertically integrated monopolies of the Soviet economy. The originally narrow fractionalization of engineering fields necessitated a corresponding multiplicity of textbooks, largely of "cookbook" type, designed to provide rapid results,* in the process of industrial and technological growth, each textbook category multiplied in number, and each textbook tended to expand in size. Perhaps another factor has contributed to the phenomenon of size: the authors have been paid on a piece-work basis. According to the rates in effect as of July 1944, the royalty for the first edition of college-level textbooks ranged from 1,500 to 2,000 rubles per "author's sheet."[31] At this rate, such a textbook as, for instance, *Steel Casting*, by Yu. A. Nekhendzi, rated at 69.5 author sheets, should bring anywhere from 104,250 to 139,000 rubles to the author.[32] Obviously, writing textbooks, particularly large ones, has been a very remunerative part of academic activity. It may be noted, in passing, that the textbook taken for this example was published in an edition of 10,000 copies and priced at 34 rubles each.

No such voluminous texts as some Soviet engineering curricula require can be used as textbooks in the accepted sense; and, in fact, not all the approved texts are designated "textbooks" (*uchebniki*), some, usually the more detailed, comprehensive texts, being designated "reference texts" (*uchebnye posobiya*). In theory, the student is responsible for the material presented in the textbook (*uchebnik*) which is supposed to follow closely the established syllabus. The reference texts are intended for supplementary reading. In practice, however, the distinction is not necessarily as sharp, and in some cases reference texts are used as textbooks.

At the present time [1954] the concepts *uchebnik* and *uchebnoye posobiye* are not rigorously distinguished. . . . It is not unusual for a text which cannot be accepted as a stabilized *uchebnik* to be stamped "Approved as a reference text" but to be nevertheless used as a "textbook" because no other is available.[33]

For some years, for instance, a 784-page reference text, *Detali mashin* (Machine Details) published in 1951, was used as a textbook, there being no alternative text.[34]

---

*In 1954: "the method still remaining in the textbooks, that of recipe-like instructions on how this or another process is to be carried out, is a great evil; this method habituates conformity, encourages the student's tendency to memorize material mechanically, to master it by memory not by reasoning." Professor-Doctor N. I. Sus, in *Vestnik vysshei shkoly,* No. 21, December 1954.

The inevitable result of disproportion between the available time and the volume of required texts is the widespread use of lecture notes—the *konspekty*:

> Very frequently lecture notes made by the student become all but the basic source of knowledge. Furthermore, it also happens that the student uses someone else's notes.[35]

The use of lecture notes—a practice not limited to Soviet schools—provides perhaps the only means for all but the most talented students to reconcile the formal demands of Soviet curricula with academic realities:

> If our students make little use of [textbook] literature and study largely lecture notes, it is not a consequence of their unfavorable attitude toward books; the explanation is in the tight time budget and a difficult situation with our textbook literature.[36]

By "difficult situation" the author of this observation means not only that many of the available texts are inappropriate as textbooks but also that in some areas of study textbooks are in short supply. Two types of shortages seem to have persisted, at least until recent times: shortages arising from uneven distribution of textbooks geographically and by subjects. It is frequently said, for instance, that correspondence students who live in small cities and towns experience difficulty in obtaining textbooks locally. More significant is the complaint of shortages for specific subjects of study. It is not surprising that there should be a shortage or even absence of textbooks in such areas of study as economics or the humanities, but, according to many recent statements, shortages because of obsolescence and other reasons are experienced in other fields as well. It was stated at one time, for instance, that no textbooks and reference texts were available for approximately one-third of the 327 basic subjects of the curricula at the universities, economic institutes, and law institutes taken as a group.[37] On the basis of our sampling of textbooks, however, it would appear that texts in physical science, applied science, and especially in mathematics are not lacking; the reported shortages in the textbook fund of these schools, therefore, are likely to be concentrated in subjects such as Darwinism which raise ideological problems.

Production factors may have contributed periodically to shortages or at least to delays in the output of textbooks, as for example prolonged spot shortages of paper in the hands of the printing establishment or improper assortment of delivered stock (enough printing grades but a shortage of binding paper, or the other way around).[38] One factor which places an undue burden on book publishing in the

Soviet Union—even if it may not directly interfere with the production of technical books—is that not only people but books also have to be purged, necessitating at times the withdrawal of entire editions, replacing sections of books, or at least blocking out a name such as Beria in the text of published books.* No college-level *technical* texts, however, have to our knowledge been suddenly withdrawn as part of the Soviet process of rewriting history.

In engineering schools the textbook shortage is more difficult to explain, considering the emphasis given to engineering training in the Soviet Union. Nevertheless, V. A. Kirillin's 1954 article on higher technical education, to which we have previously referred, includes a categorical statement on the textbook problem:

> Suffice it to say that for approximately 40 per cent of the subjects studied in the institutions of higher technical education there are no modern textbooks and reference texts recommended [i.e., approved] by the Ministry of Higher Education. Among such subjects, to name a few, are "Fundamentals of Electronics," "Fundamentals of Automatic Control," "Technology of Electrical Instrument Construction," "Piston Pumps and Piston Compressors," the majority of industrial economics subjects, and many others.

The 1954 Party directives on measures for improving higher and secondary professional education single out as one of the important tasks the need to expand the supply and improve the quality of textbooks:†

> The USSR Council of Ministers and the Central Committee of the Communist Party have obligated the Ministry of Higher Education and other ministries who have jurisdiction over institutions of higher education to assure in the next three or four years the preparation of high-quality textbooks and reference texts for the basic subjects of instruction in the higher schools.[39]

The plan for revising existing textbooks and writing new texts visualizes both individual contributions and joint authorship by specialists working as a committee. As we have noted, the writing of textbooks has been recently classified as an acceptable part of the normal workload of scientists engaged in teaching; but the author's royalty will apparently no longer be directly related to the *size* of a work accepted for publication, a reduction in the size of college texts

---

* E.g., an article on Beria in the Great Soviet Encyclopedia in Volume 5 *(BSE,* 2nd Ed.) was replaced by an article on the Bering Sea; see *The New York Times,* August 19, 1953. Recently the publishers of this encyclopedia distributed another "replacement," this time pages 213–214 for the tenth volume, which had been given to a laudatory article on Kao Kang, the purged Chinese Communist leader.

† See Appendix I.

being one of the major specific objectives of the new plan. Other objectives include better coordination of material in related subjects, greater emphasis on theory and fundamentals, and updating of textbooks to conform with advances in science and technology at home and abroad. Engineering textbooks may well present, as heretofore, the greatest difficulty. The objectives are, on the one hand, to extend the length of time during which they will remain useful—in Soviet terminology, to "stabilize" them—and, on the other, to bring them up to date in terms of actual industrial practices, design techniques, and applications. The traditional Soviet approach to engineering education created the continuing problem that textbooks became rapidly obsolescent.

In 1955 an editorial of the Ministry of Higher Education, whose responsibility it is to see that the textbook reform is carried forward, stated:

> The publication of [new] stabilized textbooks for all the basic courses and a radical revision of the existing textbook literature must be completed in the next 3 to 4 years, as this was specified in the decision of the USSR Council of Ministers and the Central Committee of the Communist Party.
>
> Despite certain successes in publishing textbooks and reference texts, there are still no textbooks for nearly one-third of the subjects studied in the higher school. High quality textbooks are lacking for certain complex subjects such as, for instance, the physics course for schools of engineering, or a course in the technology of metals for nonmachine-design specialties—and no working groups of authors have been formed for the creation of such textbooks.[40]

The problem involved in the current Soviet campaign to improve its fund of engineering textbooks is, of course, only a part of the very complex task of improving the quality and changing the character of engineering training generally. The training of Soviet engineers has been conditioned by and has consistently reflected the vertical organization and management of the Soviet industrial and economic complex. It may be assumed that in the course of industrial reorganization initiated in the summer of 1957 efforts will be made to diversify and to balance the output of engineering graduates also on a regional basis. Any progress in that direction will necessarily be slow, requiring, as it will, relocation of some facilities and personnel and development of new curricula, and, at least temporarily, making for even a greater shortage of suitable textbooks.

3. FACILITIES

Since many university buildings and facilities in the occupied areas of the European part of the USSR were destroyed or damaged during the war, the Soviet school system faced a very large reconstruction task after 1945. The physical plant, especially the facilities needed for training and internal research in science and technology, has been expanding ever since that time at an impressive rate—if unevenly from institution to institution.

The most outstanding addition to educational and university research facilities in the postwar period has been the highly publicized new plant of Moscow University (MGU). The construction of the new MGU buildings was started in c. 1948 and largely completed by September 1, 1953. The Great Soviet Encyclopedia (BSE, 2nd Ed., Vol. 28, 1954) describes the new facilities, in part, as follows:

> . . . the new buildings house 168 lecture halls, 1,700 laboratories, reading rooms with some 1.2 million books, and so forth. The laboratories and workrooms are provided with electronic equipment, special optical devices, X-ray apparatus, and other specialized equipment of many types corresponding to the modern demands of science for teaching and for research in mechanics, physics, astronomy, chemistry, biology, geology, and geography.

No detailed first-hand accounts of the laboratory facilities in the new MGU buildings appear to have been published, but the general reports brought by many foreign visitors suggest that these facilities are lavish in scale and high in quality. The new plant totals thirty-seven buildings, including a 32-story main building, and houses the physics, chemistry, mechanics-mathematics, geological, and geographic faculties of the University, including all instruction laboratories, shops, and research facilities in these branches of science. Some details of the scientific equipment selected for the new plant of Moscow University are given in an article which was published at the time the new buildings were officially opened but apparently very much in advance of the actual delivery and installation of facilities in their entirety.[41] According to this account, all (or nearly all) the scientific equipment was to be of domestic manufacture; more than 500 enterprises within the jurisdiction of some thirty-three industrial ministries participated in the design and manufacture of equipment, much of it apparently made for the first time in the Soviet Union. The article specifically mentions the following two categories of items among those which had been previously imported:

Horological instruments—"first-class clocks for time keeping," "clocks with quartz stabilization, printing chronographs, and interval timing devices of original design."

Electrical measurement apparatus—"including thermometric bridges, low-resistance potentiometers, and other devices needed for precise calorimetric measurements."

Much of the equipment, the article states, was manufactured to new specifications and designs which were worked out by the University's scientists in cooperation with the manufacturing enterprises. The final selection of standard and special items was made by a central commission organized for that purpose in 1949 under the chairmanship of Professor A. S. Predvoditelev. Several committees were formed, including thirty-six groups charged with the selection of scientific equipment, approval of specifications, and placement of orders. The area of responsibility of a few committees among the thirty-six appointed for this task is briefly described in the article, which also names some of the major items of equiment by categories:

Spectrographic optics, Professor V. M. Tatevskii in charge—"spectrographs and spectrometers of high resolving power through the entire range of spectral frequencies," including "vacuum spectrographs and spectrometers; spectrographs with a rapid action for the registration of high-speed processes; spectrographs with diffraction screens."

Electrical measurements apparatus, Professor R. V. Telesnin in charge—"many new types of apparatus of high sensitivity and great accuracy," "mirror galvanometers with sensitivity to the current of 1.10^{-11} ampere; our having mastered the manufacture of mirror galvanometers of high sensitivity ended the monopoly of certain foreign firms."

Radiophysical apparatus, Docent P. A. Petrov in charge—"electronic devices and high-voltage apparatus," "generators, receivers, amplifiers, and radiotechnical measuring devices."

Electronics and power apparatus, Professor N. A. Kaptsov in charge—"cathode oscillographs, electron microscopes of high resolving power, various electronic devices which will permit numerous high-vacuum arrangements; X-ray apparatus, including the specially valuable portable apparatus."

Cryogenic apparatus, Docent N. A. Bril'yantov and Professor A. I. Shal'nikov in charge—"equipment for instruction and low-temperature research (liquid nitrogen, oxygen, and helium)," also equipment for the manufacture of "liquid nitrogen and oxygen."

Computing and calculating devices, Professor B. M. Shchigolev in charge—"special machines which combine certain computing-analytical devices; complex computing machines, including integrators of various types for the solution of systems of linear equations with constant coefficients and of differential equations with partial derivatives; simple calculating machines: automatic calculators, full keyboard machines, ten-key calculators, ten-key printing calculators, and hand-operated adding machines; graphics devices: planimeters of various constructions, integrators, and harmonic analyzers."

Heating equipment and thermostats, Candidate of Chemical Sciences A. V. Bilevich in charge—"high-temperature vacuum ovens, thermostats, multiple thermostats, and temperature regulation equipment," equipment in this category "shall permit" research in physicochemical processes "at temperatures up to 2,500°C and, among others, the determinations of pressure of saturated steam and of specific heat of evaporation of heat-resisting substances."

Other types of scientific equipment assembled by 1953 or to be assembled thereafter at Moscow University included the following:

General laboratory equipment.
Microscopy and geodesy apparatus.
Geophysical apparatus.
Photographic equipment.
Expedition equipment.
Machine tools.

The article particularly emphasized as a special achievement the design and manufacture of optical equipment, including special, not mass-produced apparatus, adding:

The specifications for special apparatus of all types were developed with a view toward the future utilization of identical equipment in research institutions and other institutions of higher education. Thus the placement of this order should serve as a stimulus for further developing the optical industries and enriching Soviet science with new types of scientific equipment.

Many of the optical and other instruments and devices mentioned in these excerpts were still at the manufacturing stage at the time of the formal opening of the new facilities. Nevertheless, Professor J. D. Bernal, a British physicist,[*] who was apparently present at the opening ceremonies, in a private conversation 2 years later said that he was at the time very much impressed by both the quantity and the quality of equipment.[42] On their return trip from the Soviet Union in 1955 the Dodges stopped off in Sweden, England, and Denmark, visiting a number of scientific institutions, including the Bohr Institute in Denmark. Dr. A. O. Gunnar Källen, a Swedish scientist who in April of 1955 had attended a Field Theory Conference in Moscow and was working at the Bohr Institute, told the Dodges about his visit to the new 6-story physics building of Moscow University:

* Incidentally, a Marxist and a member of the British Communist Party.

He found the equipment for student experiments to be very good. Student laboratories seemed to occupy the first three floors. He would classify the equipment as being above normal in quality and quantity. He found it better than the equipment at Lund, which is about the same sort of equipment one would find at Uppsala, Sweden's other leading university. However, in spectroscopy he felt that Lund had better equipment, but he granted that this perhaps was due to a particularly capable and well-known spectroscopist at Lund. Hence, his standards in judging spectroscopy in Russia were perhaps too high. He was particularly impressed by the fact that the Frank-Hertz experiment was performed by all students in the physics faculty. This equipment, which is quite complicated, was set up permanently for the students to perform measurements.[43]

A number of similarly favorable accounts and impressions of the availability of scientific laboratory equipment at Soviet institutions of higher education also mention other universities, notably the University of Leningrad, which has generally a very high reputation. An important observation which emerges from the available accounts is that, whereas prior to c. 1945 most of the scientific equipment in Soviet universities and research institutes was of foreign make, more and more scientific apparatus of domestic manufacture has become available in the last few years. The Dodges, for instance, in May 1955 saw a great collection of scientific equipment at the University of Kharkov:

> All of the equipment looked excellent and new, and we were amazed to find so much fine new equipment crowded into this room and inquired how it happened to be there. We learned that they had only recently received it from an optical plant in Leningrad.*

Soviet war reparations extracted from Germany and elsewhere in Eastern Europe—whole plants, scientific and manufacturing equipment, and the services of highly skilled personnel—may have added materially to Soviet productive capacity in the field of scientific apparatus and precision manufacture. The industrial effort mobilized to produce standard and special equipment for the new Moscow Univer-

---

* The development of optics and the manufacture of optical equipment in the Soviet Union is strongly associated with the work of a Russian physicist D. C. Rozhdestvenskii (1876–1940): graduated from Leningrad University (1900), research work abroad, University of Leipzig (1901–1902), University of Paris (1907–1910). In 1918, at his initiative, an optical institute was organized in Leningrad—State Optical Institute (GOI). The Leningrad Institute of Precision Mechanics and Optics, a school of higher education, was organized in 1930. The institute has (1953) four faculties: precision mechanics, optical-mechanical, electromechanical, and radiotechnical.

sity must have materially increased the rate at which new equipment of the type theretofore in short supply could be made available in the future to the institutions of higher education. Nevertheless, specific shortages are certain to persist, as current comments in the Soviet press indicate. An insufficient "material base" of laboratory and research equipment, training shops and maintenance shops, and an insufficient flow of supplies to operate these facilities, are sources of weakness which the directives of 1954 and subsequent measures aim to eliminate.

The degree of physical and material deficiency varies from school to school. It is certain, for instance, that military schools of engineering, such as Zhukovskii Military Air Academy, lack no facilities and equipment of either foreign or domestic manufacture deemed desirable to fulfill their objectives.[44] Among civilian schools the plant facilities seem to be allocated most unequally. No resources were apparently spared in the attempt to create in the new Moscow University a complex of educational and research facilities second to none; in contrast, one reads that, at the same time the new University was opened in Moscow, the rate of capital construction of facilities for an agricultural engineering school at Novocherkassk was such that "the completion of the planned classroom buildings and student dormitories would take twenty years."[45]

The entire program of higher school building construction was reported in 1953 to have lagged materially behind the plan.[46] In 1955:

> The construction of buildings for institutions of higher education is still being carried out unsatisfactorily; the plans established on the scope of work to be done and on the time of completion for individual units have not been fulfilled year after year. A substantial part of the funds allocated for construction purposes have not been used.[47]

In February 1956 the director of the Central Asia Polytechnic Institute wrote:

> The extremely crowded conditions do not permit the institute to provide the many laboratories, shops, demonstration rooms, and exhibits which are necessary to carry out academic work. There is a shortage of classrooms, there is no satisfactory club room, no drafting room, no gymnasium. Classes are held in three shifts. The student dormitories are as crowded as ever.[48]

Student housing normally reflects the general shortage of "living space" in the Soviet Union (urban floor space per capita was 41 square feet in 1950). The new Moscow University building, which provides 5,755 individual well-furnished rooms of approximately 70 sq. ft. each and has ample communal facilities, is an exception to the general rule.

About 40 sq. ft. (10 sq. m.) of dormitory space per student is apparently considered to be satisfactory in most institutions, although that standard is by no means always met. At Ashkhabad, to take an extreme, "frequently the most elementary conveniences are lacking" in the crowded student dormitories:

> The supply of drinking water in the tubs filled each morning is as a rule exhausted before the day is over and students are forced to trot along to the faucet with a cup.
>
> . . . . . .
>
> Repairs have been completed, but the dormitory is nevertheless hardly ready for the winter. Many windows lack window panes. Last winter the rooms were poorly heated, and it is still not clear how the steam heat will work this winter.
>
> . . . . . .
>
> The dormitory has no shower room, no laundry, and no kitchen.
>
> . . . . . .
>
> Students wash at the faucet in the yard.[49]

The conditions suggested by these selected excerpts represent perhaps the lowest end of the scale and may not be typical; but those at the new Moscow University are also certain to be unrepresentative of the Soviet civilian student's average living standard.[50] The average—insofar as housing provided by the schools is concerned—perhaps approaches the level suggested by the following information on the dormitory facilities at Kharkov University which the Rector of that University gave in 1955 to the Dodges:

> Living in a dormitory costs 12 rubles a month, including bedding, etc. Food is extra, but cheap. In the *new* [our emphasis] dormitory students will be four to a room, or six to a slightly larger room. The Rector, in commenting on these, said, "They are good enough for a student." He was not making any claims for their being luxurious.

The over-all problem of student housing is summed up in the fact that the expansion of building space for the system as a whole has lagged materially behind the expansion of enrollment. Whereas the resident enrollment in Soviet schools of higher education in 1955–1956 was 110 per cent larger than the enrollment in 1940 (having increased from 585 to 1,228 thousand), the floor area of the school buildings increased only by 37 per cent and the student dormitory area only by 20 per cent of the area available in 1940.[51]

As far as equipment is concerned, particularly at the universities and engineering institutes—the present concern centers on the recently (since c. 1954) initiated campaign *to intensify the rate, expand the scope, and raise the quality of internal research,* that is, research done at the institutions of higher education as distinct from the industrial

research institutes or those under the academies of sciences. As will
be more fully commented upon in Chapter 11, research at the institutions of higher technical education and even at the universities of
the Soviet Union heretofore has been conducted on a relatively small
scale. Whether abundant laboratory and other scientific equipment
could in itself rapidly transform a typical narrowly specialized engineering school into an effective research institution is questionable;
in any case, the inadequacy of equipment and facilities throughout
the system as a whole is being pointed to as a major detriment to the
desired scale and quality of research and instruction. It will be remembered that the 1954 directives called for the improvement of engineering and scientific education both in fundamental theory and in
practical up-to-date industrial knowledge.

> The fund of equipment in the laboratories of many institutions of
> higher education, among them our [polytechnic] institute, is not
> up to the level of contemporary science and engineering; and in
> part the [existing] equipment is completely obsolete and worn out.
> Such a condition of the school laboratory base cannot help but lower
> the quality of instruction and of research.[52]

Similar comments on general or specific shortages could be quoted
at length from earlier and current Soviet sources; that such comments
do not greatly, if at all, exaggerate the average material conditions of
the Soviet higher educational system would seem to be amply confirmed by the top-level official pronouncements and directives aimed
at the elimination of material deficiencies. Nevertheless, it is also
perfectly clear that the leading institutions, the military schools of
higher education, the best universities, and the foremost engineering
schools, such as the Moscow Higher Technical School or Leningrad
Polytechnic Institute, as well as engineering schools in the metropolitan
centers generally, are well supplied with laboratory and other scientific
and technical equipment, except perhaps for the heavier and more
expensive items for which both the industrial research institutes and
those of the Academy of Sciences unquestionably enjoy a higher
priority.

NOTES TO CHAPTER 9

[1] Reference to the applicable legislation can be found, for instance, in *Vysshaya shkola*, compiled by M. I. Movshovich, pp. 245 ff.

[2] A. Ya. Sinetskii, *Professorsko-prepodavatel'skiye kadry vysshei shkoly SSSR* (Professorial-Teaching Personnel in the USSR Schools of Higher Education), Moscow: "Sovetskaya Nauka," 1950, Part III, Chapter 6.

3 V. A. Kirillin, "Tekhnicheskii progress i vysshaya shkola" (Technical Progress and the Higher School), *Vestnik vysshei shkoly*, No. 6, June 1955, p. 6.

4 V. V. Bolotov and A. A. Melent'ev in an untitled article, *Vestnik vysshei shkoly*, No. 8, August 1955, p. 16.

5 Quoted from notes made available to this author by Homer L. and Norton T. Dodge.

6 S. Kaftanov, "Vysshaya shkola i podgotovka sovetskikh spetsialistov" (The Higher School and the Training of Soviet Specialists), *Bol'shevik*, No. 16, 1938, pp. 11–27.

7 Our emphasis. N. Shavel'skaya, "Podgotovka professorsko-prepodavatel'skikh i nauchnykh kadrov v Belorussii" (The Training of the Professorial-Teaching Personnel in Byelorussia), *Sovetskaya Belorussiya*, January 5, 1955, p. 2.

8 Sinetskii, *op. cit.*, Part III, Chapter 3.

9 On the "multiple hat" system see Trilling, *Soviet Education in Aeronautics: A Case Study*, Cambridge: Center for International Studies, Massachusetts Institute of Technology, 1956 (mimeographed), particularly Chapter V, pp. 46–57.

10 *Ibid.*, p. 46.

11 "A check has established that certain directors of institutions of higher learning permit intra-institutional *sovmestitel'stvo* without the permission of . . . [the central authorities] and at times up to the limit of full-time salary," *Vysshaya shkola*, compiled by M. I. Movshovich, p. 307.

12 V. A. Kirillin, "Tekhnicheskii progress i vysshaya shkola" (Technical Progress and the Higher School), *op. cit.*, p. 6.

13 "Vazhnye zadachi vysshei shkoly" (Important Tasks of the Higher School), *Pravda Ukrainy*, November 20, 1955, p. 3.

14 "Ukazaniya k raschetu shtatov professorskovo—prepodavatel'skovo i uchebno-vspomogatel'novo personala vuzov na 1941/1942 uchebnyi god" (Directives for the Computation of the Professorial-Teaching and Supporting Personnel Staff Requirements of the Institutions of Higher Education for the 1941–1942 Academic Year), *Vysshaya shkola*, compiled by M. I. Movshovich, p. 304. The source states that these directives were still in effect at the time of publication (August 1945).

15 *Vestnik vysshei shkoly*, No. 10, October 1953, p. 30.

16 "Bol'she initsiativy i samostoyatel'nosti" (For Greater Initiative and Self-Reliance), *Vestnik vysshei shkoly*, No. 2, February 1956, p. 10.

17 I. G. Ivanov-Dyatlov, in *Vestnik vysshei shkoly*, No. 11, November 1951, p. 29.

18 *Vestnik vysshei shkoly*, No. 3, March 1955, p. 5.

19 V. P. Yelutin, "Vysshuyu shkolu—na uroven' sovremennykh zadach" (To Lift the Higher School to the Level of Contemporary Objectives), *Pravda*, July 7, 1956, p. 2.

20 *Vestnik vysshei shkoly*, No. 3, March 1955, p. 55.

21 Moscow dateline September 8, 1956, *New York Herald Tribune*, September 9, 1956.

22 A condensed text of this article is given in *CDSP*, Vol. VIII, No. 13, May 9, 1956, pp. 4–5.

23 Among the sources consulted in making this rough estimate were the following: U.S. Department of Labor, "Wages in 17 Labor Markets, 1953–1954," August 13, 1954.

American Federation of Teachers, "A Survey of Current Teachers Salary Schedules in 893 U.S. Cities of Population of 10,000 and Over," January 26, 1955.

Beardsley Ruml and Sidney G. Tickton, *Teaching Salaries Then and Now*, Bulletin No. 1, The Fund for the Advancement of Education 1955.

Union Wages and Hours: Motortruck Drivers and Helpers, July 1, 1955, Bulletin No. 1195, Bureau of Labor Statistics, U.S. Department of Labor.

Occupational Wage Rate Survey, National Industrial Conference Board, Inc., August 1953.

1952 National Survey of Professional Scientific Salaries, Los Alamos Scientific Laboratory of the University of California.

[24] I. I. Artobolevskii, *Teoriya mekhanizmov i mashin,* 3rd Ed., Moscow: Gosudarstvennoye izdatel'stvo tekhniko-teoreticheskoi literatury, 1953, 712 pp.

[25] Among others:

Andronov, A. A., and Chaikin, C. E., *Theory of Oscillations.* English edition edited under the direction of Solomon Lefschetz. Princeton: Princeton University Press, 1949.

Frankl, F. I., and Karpovich, E. A., *Gas Dynamics of Thin Bodies.* Translated by M. D. Friedman. New York: Interscience Publishers, Inc., 1954.

Gnedenko, B. V., *Theory of Probability.* Translated by K. L. Chung. Cambridge: Addison-Wesley Press, 1954.

Krylov, Nikolai M., and Bogoliubov, N. N., *Introduction to Nonlinear Mechanics.* A free translation by Solomon Lefschetz of excerpts from two Russian monographs (Annals of Mathematics Studies, No. 11). Princeton: Princeton University Press, 1943.

Khinchin, A. I., *Three Pearls of Number Theory.* Translated from the second, 1948, revised Russian edition by F. Bagemihl and others. Rochester, N. Y.: Greylock Press, 1952.

Khinchin, A. I., *Mathematical Foundations of Statistical Mechanics.* Translated by G. Gamov. New York: Dover Publications, 1949.

Landau, L. D., and Lifshitz, E., *Classical Theory of Fields.* Translated by Morton Hamermesh. Cambridge: Addison-Wesley Press, 1951.

Landau, L. D., and Lifshitz, E., *Quantum Mechanics,* 1938. A new English edition is now being published by the Pergamon Press, London.

Pontryagin, L. S., *Foundations of Combinatorial Topology.* Translated from the first, 1947, Russian edition by F. Bagemihl, H. Komm, and W. Seidel. Rochester N. Y.: Greylock Press, 1952.

Vinogrodov, I. M., *The Method of Trigonometrical Sums in the Theory of Numbers.* Translated, revised, and annotated by K. F. Roth and A. Davenport. New York: Interscience Publishers, Inc., 1954.

[26] *Vestnik vysshei shkoly,* No. 9, September 1953, p. 31.

[27] An editorial of the Ministry of Higher Education, *Vestnik vysshei shkoly,* No. 10, October 1954, p. 4.

[28] V. A. Kirillin, "Nekotorye voprosy raboty tekhnicheskikh vuzov" (Certain Problems in the Work of the Technological Schools of Higher Education), *Vestnik vysshei shkoly,* No. 12, December 1954, p. 6.

[29] *Vestnik vysshei shkoly,* No. 11, November 1954, pp. 39 f.

[30] L. L. Grif, "Za sokrashcheniye ob'ema uchebnikov" (To Reduce the Size of Textbooks), *Vestnik vysshei shkoly,* No. 11, November 1953, p. 57, quoting from *Vestnik akademii nauk SSSR,* No. 11, 1941, p. 77.

[31] *Vysshaya shkola,* compiled by M. I. Movshovich, p. 330. An "author's sheet" is defined as "40,000 letters" which would be equivalent, depending on the size of type, to approximately 14 to 16 pages of a typical 6″ by 9″ book. The 40,000-letter equivalent measure is usually shown in every book as so-many "uch.-izd. l.," that is, "accounting-publishing sheets."

32 Yu. A. Nekhendzi, *Stal'noye lit'yo*, approved as a textbook in the metallurgical and polytechnic institutes, Moscow: State Scientific-Technical Publications of Literature on Ferrous and Nonferrous Metallurgy, 1948, 766 pp.

33 M. M. Arkhangel'skii, "Sootnosheniye uchebnika i lektsionnovo kursa" (The Relationship Between the Textbook and the Lecture Course), *Vestnik vysshei shkoly*, No. 12, December 1954, p. 29.

34 *Vestnik vysshei shkoly*, No. 11, November 1953, p. 58.

35 *Vestnik vysshei shkoly*, No. 11, November 1951, p 30.

36 Arkhangel'skii, *op. cit.*, p. 27.

37 *Vestnik vysshei shkoly*, No. 4, April 1955, p. 13.

38 See, e.g., *Literaturnaya gazeta*, September 28, 1954, p. 1; in *CDSP*, Vol. VI, No. 44, p. 14.

39 Kirillin, "Nekotorye voprosy raboty . . . ," *op. cit.*, p. 6.

40 An editorial of the Ministry of Higher Education, *Vestnik vysshei shkoly*, No. 3, March 1955, p. 5.

41 N. L. Pokrovskii, "Uchenye universiteta—aktivnye uchastniki stroitel'stva i oborudovaniya novykh zdanii" (The Scientists of the University—Active Participants in the Design of Structure and Equipment of the New Buildings), *Vestnik vysshei shkoly*, No. 9, September 1953, pp. 9–17.

42 Cited in a memorandum prepared for the Center for International Studies by Norton T. Dodge.

43 *Ibid.*

44 On military air academies see Trilling, *op. cit.*, pp. 40–45.

45 *Vestnik vysshei shkoly*, No. 11, November 1953.

46 *Vestnik vysshei shkoly*, No. 8, August 1953, p. 39.

47 *Vestnik vysshei shkoly*, No. 7, July 1955, p. 11.

48 *Vestnik vysshei shkoly*, No. 2, February 1956, pp. 11 f.
Pravda (July 9, 1956) gives additional details, such as: ". . . the floor area [of the entire institute] at the present time is not more than three square meters [per student]. . . . Two-thirds of the teaching personnel have no working space of their own."

49 Z. Ioffe, "Zabotit'sya o byte studentov" (The Student's Standard of Life Must Be Taken Care Of), *Turkmenskaiya iskra*, October 20, 1955.

50 See, e.g., "Bol'she zaboty o byte studentov" (The Living Standard of Students Needs Greater Attention), *Vestnik vysshei shkoly*, No. 10, October 1953, pp. 44–45 This article cites both good conditions (". . . dining room, barber shop, tailor shop a bathhouse, a storage room. Fuel is on hand for the entire winter.") and unsatisfactory ones (". . . the lodgers of some dormitories are denied the most elementary provisions").

51 The per cent of increase is mentioned in *Vestnik vysshei shkoly*, No. 6, June 1956, p. 10.

52 *Vestnik vysshei shkoly*, No. 2, February 1956, p. 12.

CHAPTER

— 10

SOVIET HIGHER EDUCATION:

THE TEACHING PROCESS

Many of the elements of the Soviet teaching process—lectures, laboratory work, seminars, and practice exercises—are so nearly identical organizationally with similar divisions of the student's class time everywhere that they need not be examined here in detail. This chapter, therefore, is in the main a discussion of some of the less familiar elements of the Soviet educational process—promotional examinations, *zachety*, term papers, industrial training practice, and, finally, the diploma project which culminates Soviet undergraduate engineering training.

1. Lectures and Teaching Practice

A directive issued by the Soviet government and the Party in 1936, restoring the traditional organization of instruction, specified the following forms of supervised (contact) instruction:

(a) lectures conducted by professors and docents;
(b) practical studies in laboratories, shops, clinics, and so forth under the guidance of professors, docents, and assistants;
(c) industrial practice, to be carried out in accordance with the *uchebnyi* plan, under the guidance of supervisors appointed by the departments for one or another type of practice.[1]

This directive, and particularly the reinstatement of lectures as a principal form of instruction, in Professor I. I. Agroskin's words, ended:

... the notorious "laboratory-brigade method" [of instruction] under cover of which the right opportunists and the benders to the "left"

328

attempted to bury the heritage accumulated by the progressive Russian pedagogy.[2]

The present Soviet 5-year course in undergraduate engineering or science provides about as many hours for lectures alone as an American 4-year curriculum prescribes for scheduled work of all types: seminars, drafting, shop work, laboratory, recitation, and lectures.

The major determinant of the content and organization of lecture material is the syllabus, *programma*—a highly detailed prescription of ingredients issued by the Ministry for every lecture course in the curricula. The relationship between the syllabi and lectures has been perennially discussed in Soviet literature, with a notable lack of unanimity. On the one extreme stands, for instance, a proposal which Professor Ya. I. Frenkel' (b. 1894), one of the outstanding Soviet physicists of world-wide reputation, made in 1945 to limit lectures to the most essential and fundamental topics of the course so that the lecture would be seen:

> . . . not as a basic but as a supplementary method for informing students on the indispensable knowledge of theory, a method which supplements the printed manual and does not duplicate it.[3]

The Frenkel' proposal implied many conditions of university life which had not in fact been fostered under the Soviet system—among them, highly qualified teachers who combine teaching with research and students who are accustomed to and have time for independent study. Officially, research combined with teaching and independent work by the student had both been held to be indispensable if the quality of Soviet scientific and engineering education were to be improved; but the actual administration, philosophy, and organization of the educational system provided only limited opportunities for resident research (except at the universities) and neither encouragement nor time for independent work by the student.

In striking contrast to Professor Frenkel's view on the role of lectures stands the practice whereby:

> . . . the lectures of many teachers are transformed into an exhaustive exposition of the syllabus, including every detail, and factual data which obscure the basic scientific core of the discipline.

Judging by the many similar comments and criticisms, it would appear that such practice is widespread. The Dodges, while visiting Kharkov Polytechnic Institute, were told that:

> In the actual teaching of a subject within the established curriculum the professor can teach as he pleases *as long as he follows the syllabus* [our emphasis].

They were also told that the professor:

> ... can recommend additional reading, comment on the suggested reading, etc. Professors of the same discipline may lecture very differently. The more advanced the work, the greater the freedom enjoyed.

When the question of lectures versus the official syllabus was raised by the Dodges on their visit to Kharkov State University, the Rector and the Dean told the Dodges:

> ... that syllabi are not absolute. A specialist in a particular discipline many change a syllabus or add to it, expressing his individuality or his own point of view.

Such claims of academic freedom appear totally in conflict with all other evidence. Not even the university itself—let alone an individual professor—can change the syllabus of any course except as the change may be authorized by the Ministry. We would also add that the Soviet academic and general social climate has hardly been conducive to expressing one's own point of view. In fact, the impression one derives from the Rector's statement paraphrased above is significantly modified by a further explanation given to the Dodges. An official syllabus, they were told:

> ... insures that the professor will cover the entire course, not leaving out any parts. A professor of optics cannot omit any section of the syllabus in optics, but within the various sections he can place emphasis where he wishes and present his own views freely. He must also observe the order of subjects [topics] required by the syllabus.

In connection with general teaching practices, it is worth noting at this point that Soviet educational literature devotes much space to discussion of graphic aids, motion pictures, slides, and other types of projection material for classroom instruction. Directives have been periodically issued by the Ministry of Higher Education about the production, selection, and wider school use of motion pictures and other visual aids; and articles and reports appear from time to time describing experience with visual aids and discussing various techniques in using them.

Central control of planning, production, and distribution of educational motion pictures is exercised by the Ministry's Central Film Laboratory (TsKL). It not only places special orders but also selects from the currently available output of the USSR Administration of Popular and Training Scientific Films (and of the motion picture studios at universities) such material as it deems suitable for wider distribution. The role of TsKL of the Ministry and of the Methodological Administration is said to include the long-range development of motion picture aids for engineering students in such subjects as strength of materials, theory of mechanisms and machines, and machine details; and for universities, biology, physics, and inorganic chemistry. In c. 1954 a special "five-year plan" to develop suitable material for these and other courses was formulated by TsKL.[4]

Although extensive lecture-room use of motion pictures has been advocated in the Soviet Union since the 1930's and much work has gone into building up a fund of training films, their actual use seems to be on a moderate and uneven scale. In a period of 15 months (1953 and the first quarter of 1954) the Ministry of Higher Education distributed only some 2,000 copies of educational films—an average of fewer than three copies per school. At certain institutions, however, fairly extensive use of films is now and then reported. At Moscow University, which is said to have extensive facilities for making scientific motion pictures and for projecting films in its lecture rooms, "848 teaching films" (different subjects or different showings?) were used in 1952. At Bauman Higher Technical School in 1952–1953 some "900 lectures were illustrated by motion pictures or slides"[5]—apparently mostly slides, since in the following academic year only "up to 300 lectures and seminars were illustrated with motion pictures."[6] Considering the variety of courses and great multiplicity of subjects taught at the Bauman School, the reported number of film showings is not very significant. It is reported that at the Leningrad Polytechnic Institute, one of the top-level Soviet engineering schools, motion pictures are used not only in conjunction with lectures but also during laboratory and shop sessions and as a part of "pre-examination consultations." Among the topics presented on films the source mentioned "The movement of liquids through capillary tubes," "The study of sandy soils under vibration," and "Atomization of liquid fuel."[7]

The expanding use of motion picture photography in Soviet research is counted upon to accelerate the development of training films. Moscow University and apparently a number of other Soviet universities have departments (*kafedry*) of Training and Scientific Cinematography equipped with motion picture studios and processing laboratories which work in cooperation with various research projects on the development of special techniques and processes for scientific photography. Cuttings from research films are utilized in the compilation of training sequences. It might also be noted that in a number of normal schools chairs of Training and Scientific Cinematography have been established within the last few years and that special courses such as "Training-Educational Films" are included in the curricula of a few normal schools.[8]

In general, it appears that some progress has been made by the Soviet Union in developing training and scientific motion pictures but that their use is still confined to relatively few institutions. Elsewhere the much emphasized employment of visual aids is still limited to rather primitive, largely hand-drawn lantern slides which frequently simply duplicate diagrams and other data in the textbooks.[9]

For several years now, especially since 1954, the need to improve the quality of lectures has been emphasized over and over in Soviet educational literature: descriptive and textbook material must be reduced, theory and fundamentals emphasized. In conjunction with the reforms initiated by the 1954 Party directive and the curricular and other changes introduced for the 1955–1956 academic year, an editorial in the Ministry's official journal said that in the course of the campaign to broaden the theoretical base of professional training:

> ... attention must first of all be given to the lecture courses; their conceptual and scientific-technical level must be raised. The departments (*kafedry*) should critically approach the content of lectures, eliminate material which has no scientific value, move from the exposition of innumerable quantities of similar facts to broad scientific generalizations.
>
> The descriptive material—with which the student can familiarize himself in laboratories, in field practice, in excursions, and, finally, through textbooks and handbooks—should be sharply reduced in lectures. It would be far more useful for the lecturer to examine more deeply the particularly important questions of the course and to acquaint the listeners with the latest achievements of domestic and foreign science and engineering.

At this point, apparently not having had enough time to work out a detailed set of regulations, the Ministry added:

> One should not wait for instructions from the Ministry on the introduction of new material into the lecture courses; the departments of the institutions of higher education *in this respect* [our emphasis] must show initiative and self-reliance.[10]

It is easy, of course, for the Ministry suddenly to shift the responsibility to the teacher, but few Soviet educators in 1955 could have been anywhere near ready to exercise in this or any other respect the initiative called for. The new policy, it should be pointed out, is related to the consolidation of specialties and elimination of many fractionalized individual subjects of instruction. It is not likely that an instructor who until 1955 lectured, let us say, on "Pumps and Ventilators" and who himself was narrowly trained can effectively lead a fundamental course in machine design. A substantial number of highly specialized subjects of instruction apparently were eliminated in 1955–1956, and more are presumably scheduled for consolidation into broader entities. Correspondingly, the faculties and individual instructors will have to reorient themselves and broaden their outlook—necessarily a slow process and one which depends on a number of other factors, among them a corresponding revision of textbooks.

Dr. Leon Trilling, on the basis of his study of Soviet education in aeronautics, analyzed the relationship between Soviet textbooks and teaching staff qualifications thus:

> The deliberate effort to produce encyclopedic textbooks may be the consequence of a teaching staff short in numbers and, except in Moscow, uneven in quality.
>
> . . . . .
>
> An elaborate textbook may be considered as the most efficient method for enabling a small number of excellent part-time teachers to mass-produce engineers, the larger number of younger or less skilled docents being employed as a mere transmission belt.[11]

This hypothesis seems to be amply confirmed. For instance, apropos of a new and greatly condensed edition of a textbook for the normal schools on the theory of functions of a real variable, an article published in a journal of the USSR Academy of Sciences pointed out that the new text would be suitable if the course were given by a first-rate teacher:

> The trouble, however, is that at the normal schools, scattered all over the great expanse of the Soviet Union, in actual fact the course in the theory of functions is at times given also by persons who do not possess solid theoretical preparation. . . .[12]

The relative shortage of highly qualified teachers, coupled with the uniform and highly demanding curricula, which in engineering courses embrace extensive and detailed coverage of both fundamental theory and applied techniques, unquestionably has tended to make the Soviet school lecture an instrument for transmitting facts rather than ideas and broad concepts. The extreme cases, frequently reported as being much in evidence, include "lectures" *read* from the prescribed textbook or dictated from notes for students to *record verbatim*. But we would most emphatically note that the descending scale of quality in Soviet university lectures is inversely related to the degree of political and moral implications of a given course and therefore the degree of ideological interference of Party dogma; Soviet lectures in the social sciences—wholly independent of the teacher as to content, interpretation, and emphasis—are inevitably at the lowest possible qualitative level.* We would also expect that even a very able instructor in specialized engineering courses would be highly restricted by the encyclopedic syllabi which he must cover. There are enough references in Soviet literature to confirm this general impression. But neither ideological limitations nor those imposed by the need to cover large quantities of technological details apply in the same degree, if at all, to the lecturer in mathematics, theoretical physics, theoretical mechanics, and other fundamental disciplines.

From these considerations, negative as they are, we conclude that the quality of Soviet lectures in mathematics and in the theory of physical sciences generally depends upon the competence, ability, and motivation of the teacher as much, or nearly as much, as it does in any educational system. Russia has long been known for a high level of achievement in mathematics and in many branches of theoretical science. As Eric Ashby, author of *Scientist in Russia* (1947), has concluded:

> The ideals of university life have survived the iconoclasm of the revolution and are still surviving the schoolboy regimentation of the Soviet student.

We would add, however, that the degree of survival must vary considerably—for instance, in the realm of mathematics or theoretical physics as compared with that of economics, history, or philosophy.

2. Laboratory, Drafting, and Shop Work

The differences in the quality and availability of laboratory equipment and facilities which we have noted inevitably affect the quality of laboratory instruction given to Soviet undergraduates. Docent A. M. Soifer, who teaches at one of the elite schools, Kuibyshev Aviation Institute, commenting on the fact that some laboratory work is conducted on a group basis, wrote:

> The shortage of laboratory equipment frequently necessitates allocating five or six students to each setup. Under such conditions it is difficult to talk of genuinely independent work by the student and of any research aspect of such work.[13]

* Example of a typical Soviet comment: "Dogmatism and parrot-like repetition of formulas exist not only in university lectures delivered by teachers of various disciplines and first of all of social sciences; at times they also invade research papers and dissertations which emerge as collections of quotations and do not contain a single individual idea of the author. Such propaganda of the Marxist-Leninist theory the Party justly has characterized as political fireworks and meaningless rattle." *Vestnik vysshei shkoly*, No. 4, April 1956, p. 4.

We do not know whether Docent Soifer was referring to a specific situation at his (aviation) Institute or to Soviet engineering school laboratories generally.

In theory, at least, Soviet schools have the potential organizational advantage of an enrollment controlled as to size and categories whereby, for instance, the size of their freshman and sophomore classes need not be as large relative to the upper classes as is frequently the case in American institutions. The President of Massachusetts Institute of Technology, James R. Killian, Jr., noting a considerable proportional increase of enrollment in some fields (notably electrical engineering and physics) and an imminent increase in the freshman enrollment generally, pointed out in 1955 that the number of students attracted to these fields at MIT is "embarrassingly large as measured by the demands on our staff and facilities (but not large measured by demand for graduates)." With reference to the first two years of the undergradute program generally, President Killian stated:

> We are limited by the capacity of our class and lecture rooms and of our physics and chemistry laboratories. Increased enrollment in the first two years must be accompanied either by expansion of classroom and laboratory facilities or by lower standards of education.[14]

The theoretical advantage of the Soviet plan for matching staff and facilities in advance of any prescribed increase in the enrollment is, as has been shown, not always realized in practice. On the contrary, the sudden shifts in the plan for the production of specialists have at times required individual institutions to start courses of instruction for which neither staff nor laboratory facilities were available. Nevertheless, in the Soviet system an increase in the number of applicants tends to raise the standards of admission. Since such an increase does not necessarily lead to a proportional or any increase in the enrollment, it can serve to raise the academic quality of the student body. In the United States, for the educational system as a whole, the comparable general trend—that is, an influx of applicants— is certain to mean a nearly proportional increase in enrollment. Under some conditions and in some fields the now imminent rapid increase in the United States college enrollment could adversely affect standards of instruction—unless facility limitations are overcome.

Although detailed data on the Soviet conduct of laboratory work are lacking, a few generalizations may perhaps be ventured. It appears, for instance, that the laboratory work of the undergraduate student, except perhaps in his senior year, is standardized and reduced to his performing a sequence of outlined operations with equipment and apparatus pre-set for each experiment. That was the impression of the Dodges when they visited the physics laboratory of the Bauman Higher Technical School in Moscow:

> The physics laboratories at Bauman were the largest and pleasantest we saw anywhere. They were well equipped. Judging from the experimental setups we saw, the work would be like that covered in our own intermediate and advanced undergraduate courses. The students work from instructions and write up the reports outside. We were under the impression that the instructions are more cut and dried than in this country and that the students have less responsibility for setting up the apparatus and solving the problems of making it work.

After a conversation with Dr. A. O. Gunnar Källen, a Swedish scientist who visited the physics laboratories at the University of Moscow, Dr. Norton T. Dodge recorded Dr. Källen's observation:

> Källen said that [in the physics laboratory] an instruction book went with the experiments and that the students were supposed to read this in advance so that they would be prepared for the experiment. The setup of experiments was similar to that which he was acquainted with in Sweden, where most of the equipment was set up in advance. The student largely performed operations and measurements with the equipment. He said more experiments were performed by the students at Moscow University than at Lund.

Soviet university physics curricula allocate more than one-fifth of the total scheduled hours of instruction to laboratory work. In the sample curriculum shown in Chapter 8 (4,290 total scheduled hours) 992 hours, or 23 per cent, are distributed as follows:

Subject and Semester in Which Given	Total Hours (100 per cent)	Laboratory Work	
		Hours	Per Cent
All subjects, 5-year course	4,290	992	23
General Chemistry 1	100	50	50
General Physics 1, 2, 3, 4, 5, 6	896	452	51
Thermodynamics and Statistical Physics 5, 6	120	20	17
Electrodynamics 6, 7	120	20	17
Advanced Topics 7, 8, 9	804	424	53
Methods of Teaching 5, 6	60	36	60
All subjects with laboratory work	2,100	1,002	48

The laboratory work in the engineering curricula accounts for from 10 to 15 per cent of the total class time. In the sample engineering curriculum for training specialists in the "Technology of Machine Construction, Metal Cutting Machine Tools, and Tools" laboratory work is prescribed for the following subjects of instruction:

Subjects and Semester in Which Given	Total Hours (100 per cent)	Laboratory Work	
		Hours	Per Cent
All subjects, 5½-year course	4,848	595	12
Physics 2, 3, 4	245	98	40
Chemistry 1, 2	120	50	42
Strength of Materials 3, 4, 5	232	40	17
Mechanisms and Machines 4, 5	198	20	10
Machine Details 5, 6	215	17	8
Electrical Technology 6, 7	190	34	18
Heat Engineering 9	78	13	17
Hydraulics and Mechanics 7	84	14	17
Metallurgy and Heat Treatment 6	96	32	33
Interchangeability and Measurments 5	68	28	41
Machine Tools 5, 6, 7, 8	337	63	19
Hydraulic Equipment for Machine Tools 7	56	16	29
Electrical Equipment for Machine Tools 8	65	15	23
Metal Cutting 6	80	25	31
Metal Cutting Tools 8, 9, 10	221	50	23
Machine Construction Technology 8, 9, 10	208	30	14
Thermal Treatment of Details 10	39	13	33
Automation of Industrial Processes 10	65	15	23
Industrial Economics 9, 10	91	13	14
Safety Engineering and Fire Protection 9	39	9	23
All subjects with laboratory work	2,727	595	22

It will be noted, therefore, that the proportion of laboratory time in the physics curriculum (23 per cent of total) is nearly twice as large as that in the engineering curriculum. Furthermore, the average amount of time allocated for laboratory work, counting only such subjects as require it, in the physics curriculum is more than twice that of engineering subjects (48 per cent versus 22 per cent).

Drafting (first 4 semesters, total of 188 hours) and shop training (first 2 and the fifth semester, 204 hours) are counted in the same category of the engineering curricula, "Practice Studies, Seminars, Exercises, and Similar," as physical training (134 hours). It may be noted that graphics and drafting techniques are given a considerable emphasis in the Soviet training of engineers; for all engineers descriptive geometry, apparently, is a must, and their drafting courses include much detail work, including inking on tracing cloth—a practice which has been largely abandoned in American schools. Even the physics majors at Soviet universities take drafting for 2 semesters.

Shop training, for which a considerable part of class time is allocated in the engineering curricula, in the majority of schools has been handicapped by lack of equipment and for other reasons. Thus, for instance, Docent V. S. Sominskii (Leningrad Technological Institute), pointing out the importance of shop training in the preparation of engineers for work in industry, in 1955 commented:

> . . . students in mechanical engineering must learn in the shop the elementary techniques of metal bench work and of basic machine tool operations; chemical engineering students, technologists, textile engineering students [must learn] to operate typical equipment and machines in their specialty.
>
> In their present state, the majority of the training-production shops of the institutions of higher education cannot cope with the tasks required of them. This condition is due to at least two causes, namely: inadequate equipment and the excessive burden of work assignments which have nothing to do with the training process.[15]

Because of the unsatisfactory distribution and the general shortages of spare parts, components, and maintenance items in the civilian economy and trade of the Soviet Union, university shops are depended upon to manufacture what they can for the institution's own needs. Furthermore, it appears that various industrial and other (nonacademic) establishments contract with university shops to make spare parts and perform other work: " . . . the shop superintendents accept orders from outside organizations and hire workmen for this purpose —thereby pushing the training of students into the background."[16] On the whole, it is the regularly scheduled outside industrial practice of students, rather than school shop training, which has been relied upon to acquaint the students with operational skills.

3. TERM PAPERS

The nearest a Soviet engineering student normally comes to independent work in all but his last semester of residence is in the preparation of term projects prescribed for the most important applied subjects of his course. The curriculum in mechanical engineering, which we have taken as a specific example,* calls for a total of seven term projects for which the time allotment varies from subject to subject as follows:

Number of Term Projects	Subject and Semesters	Number of Hours Allotted for Projects
2	Theory of Mechanisms and Machines (4) (5)	60
1	Machine Details (6)	96
1	Material Handling Machinery and Mechanisms (7)	84
1	Machine Tools (8)	78
1	Metal Cutting Tools (9)	. . .
1	Machine Construction Technology (10)	. . .
7	Term Projects	318 hours

We do not know why no hours are specified for the last two listed assignments; perhaps the hours for the preparation of these senior-year projects or papers are included in the time allotted for laboratory work: 50 hours in metal cutting tools, and 30 hours in machine construction technology.†

It should be noted that the curriculum from which we quote represents perhaps the most advanced type of engineering training in the Soviet Union at one of the oldest and best schools among its nearly 200 technical institutes. In the curricula of other engineering schools individual term projects are apparently structured on a smaller scale, with only 10 to 20 hours allotted to each project; but, instead of only seven or so such projects, some engineering curricula may call for as many as eighteen design projects and layout exercises in the last five semesters of the 5-year course.[17]

Docent G. N. Ustinov (Novosibirsk Construction Institute) stated in 1955 that in actual experience the student must spend 50 to 70 hours on a project for which 10 to 20 hours is supposed to be the

* Chapter 8; also Cenis Translation Series 55-24.

† Similarly, no hours are allotted in the physics curriculum (Chapter 8; also Cenis Translation Series 55-26) for either one of the two term projects (or papers) called for:

Electrodynamics	6th semester
"Elective" subject	8th semester

It may be noted that, beginning with the 1955–1956 academic year, the number of term projects in the university curricula generally has been increased. *Vestnik vysshei shkoly*, No. 11, November 1955, p. 31.

norm. Other sources also confirm the impression that Soviet term projects are extremely time consuming, apparently requiring a very considerable amount of graphic work and routine computations. As to the Soviet term projects providing an effective means of introducing students to creative engineering and an independent approach to problems, the evidence would strongly suggest that despite the large amount of time the project requires these objectives are not generally realized.

> A term project could constitute one of the rewarding forms of independent work, of work which contains elements of research. The instructors are allowed [that is, are credited with a total of] three hours for the supervision of each term project—clearly an insufficient time. Conscientious instructors (and they are in the majority) provide consultation without counting the hours, but difficulty frequently arises on other grounds: in the departments where the largest proportion of the staff load consists of the hours allotted to project consultation, there are at times 70 or 80 students per instructor, which condition denies him the possibility of guiding the development of term projects along the path of research.[18]

In addition to this problem of giving enough supervision under the existing method of determining the staff load, we would also recall the general condition of overload under which Soviet students work and, more specifically, the lack of opportunity for the Soviet student during the highly regimented secondary schooling and thereafter to develop the self-reliance and initiative required for independent work. Other factors which seem unfavorably to condition the character and educational value of the Soviet term projects, a potentially useful and effective means of instruction, will be mentioned in connection with a similar but much more important responsibility of Soviet seniors, the diploma project. Here we cite a typical Soviet comment on how the unreasonable paper requirements of the term projects are sometimes reconciled with the realities of the *uchebnyi* plan:

> Under existing conditions, inasmuch as students have little time for independent work, one cannot demand that they work exhaustively and seriously on the term projects. That is why the departments [*kafedry*] follow the road toward simplifying and standardizing term projects—with the entire group of students [being assigned] to solve [one and the same] standard problem.[19]

4. Promotional Examinations

In the section on "Attrition and the Rate of Graduation" in Chapter 6 we discussed what appears to be the remarkably high "success ratio" of the Soviet student: it seems that well over 80 per cent of those who enter as freshmen graduate 5 years later.* We have suggested that the Soviet planned rate of graduation may perhaps serve as a parameter to which other elements of the academic process, including promotional examinations, must under Soviet conditions adjust themselves. In contrast with the usual Soviet practice, the promotional examinations (and *zachety*) are not subject to any well-defined qualitative norms. On the contrary, the method of administration (oral) and the arrangement (face to face with the instructor) would imply total flexibility of standards.

Even the customary duration of promotional examinations is not fixed. Here, for instance, is a comment on examinations excerpted from an editorial of the Ministry itself, complete with the names of the professors involved:

> In the winter session of examinations in Strength of Materials at the Leningrad Polytechnic Institute 8 students in the metallurgy group being examined by Docent Solyanik received unsatisfactory grades, 6 were just passing, 3 good, and 2 excellent; the group of radio engineering students examined by Docent Kushelev received one unsatisfactory grade, 80—good, and 5—excellent. It would not be correct to explain these results only by the difference in quality of the students' work or in the examiners' standard of requirement. An important role, in this respect, is played by the methodology of conducting the examination—the examiner's skill in guiding the student's ideas, in helping the student, when he is lost, to pick up the thread of consecutive argumentation. That is what Docent Kushelev had done, and each student was detained by him but a short time whereas some of the students examined by Docent Solyanik were kept at the blackboard up to 4 to 4½ hours.[20]

More important, many comments in the Soviet press condemn the practice of grading promotional examinations with undue leniency and accepting as a *zachet* other evidence of satisfactory work such as term papers and laboratory reports. Similar accusations leveled at such practices in secondary schools and in the graduate schools distinctly imply that teachers are influenced by the necessity to meet the Plan. At the undergraduate level, however, they suggest a pressure of a different nature, namely, the reluctance of the professors to disqualify a student from receiving his scholarship:

> It is no secret to anyone that many instructors permit liberalism in the evaluation of a student's knowledge and, being unwilling to

* It should be noted, however, that this estimate is based on gross figures in which the graduation data may include graduates of special short-term emergency programs and others who did not enter 5 years previously as freshmen.

deprive the student of his scholarship, not always deservedly give the grade "good."[21]

There is no evidence, however, that examinations are held lightly by the student, with a passing grade taken for granted. On the contrary, it appears that intense review and drill for the examinations is the rule, and that the 3-week examination sessions place a severe strain on the students. During such sessions, in addition to a student's personal review, group consultations on each subject are conducted, not merely to "cram" the student for the examination, we are told, but to clarify questions which may arise during the preparation for the test.[22]

There is some recent evidence that examination grades are becoming of less influence than before in awarding scholarships. The new regulations were described in *Komsomol'skaya pravda* in part as follows:

> Previously grants were awarded only to students who received "good" or "excellent" marks at examination sessions. The new decision establishes that progress will also be a deciding factor; it also provides that a student's material resources will be taken into account. In individual cases a student who needs state aid will be given a grant even though his mark is merely fair.[23]

The criteria and level of achievement as tested by Soviet examinations must necessarily reflect the general Soviet philosophy of education. We may be sure that the result of an examination in the History of the Communist Party is determined wholly by the student's ability to repeat verbatim the current set of slogans; in contrast, a Soviet oral examination in physical sciences or mathematics can be a constructive part of professional training and an effective means for the timely recognition, guidance, and encouragement of the special aptitudes, interests, and capabilities of the student. The role of examinations in engineering subjects, especially in the so-called *otraslevye*—specific industry or branch of industry—institutes, appears to be more nearly parallel to the general preoccupation with facts, applications, and technological practices which distinguishes Soviet engineering curricula, syllabi, and textbooks. In this respect the nearest we can come to a generalization is to quote an appraisal of a Soviet educator. His comments are directed to the Soviet system of higher education generally, but they apply with particular force, we believe, to engineering training. Doctor A. V. Mirtov, a professor at Gorki State University, in 1955 stated the case as follows:

> At the present time it is held that the objective of the higher school is to see to it that students acquire a firm knowledge of the factual material—on the basis of established syllabi, many of which

are worked out in excessive detail and in a descriptive manner. A good knowledge of facts is of course necessary for every scientist, but such knowledge does not become deep and firm under the *memorization* method for the mastery of material which has prevailed in our secondary schools and now also prevails in schools of higher education. The method of intense memorization without a thorough reflection upon what is being studied is what has been long known in schools as *zubryoshka* [cramming by rote].

The raised examination requirements which presuppose knowledge of large quantities of disconnected facts, chronological data, enumeration of details, and so forth over some years has led our students to *zubryoshka*.[24]

5. INDUSTRIAL PRACTICE

Prescribed in every curriculum of the Soviet schools of higher education, industrial practice has been held particularly important in the training of engineers, from 16 to 38 weeks of the total time in residence being set aside for it. Such practice is intended to prepare the student for effective work in industry immediately upon graduation by introducing him to the organization of industrial processes, to operations, and to the utilization of skills in his specialty.

As has been mentioned in Chapter 7 and illustrated by examples given in Chapter 8, the time allotted to industrial practice is divided into three sessions. For a 4-year 10-month or a 5-year engineering curriculum it begins after the third year, taking up typically a total of 18 weeks in three separate sessions of 4 to 8 weeks each.[25] The first session takes place during or after the third year of study; the last and usually the longest session, called the "diploma practice," immediately precedes the final semester of the course.

We have not been able to locate the text of the "Directive on Industrial Practice"* referred to in Soviet literature. According to one typical reference, students were to be given during the practice sessions an opportunity " . . . to study broad areas of production and to acquire familiarity with its organization, management, and controls." Thus, as a Soviet commentator interpreted the directive,

. . . it is obvious that the practicing students first of all must be assigned the duties of engineers, inspectors, shop supervisors, and so forth. . . .

If he is correct, students must be assigned essentially to engineering duties rather than to learning manual skills; but the same commentator

* Unless the authors had reference to the 1938 regulations issued by the USSR SNK (cited in *Vysshaya shkola*, pp. 111 ff.).

cited another stipulation of the directive in effect in 1953 and earlier as follows:

> In accordance with the directive on industrial training of students at the USSR institutions of higher education, the students undergoing practice must be assigned a [definite] work station.[26]

This would certainly imply that the student must be assigned a place and the duties of a regular plant worker.

The same source sharply criticized the fact that in actual practice regular work stations were seldom assigned to the students (for instance, "only 100 of 536 students were given work stations at the Kharkov Tractor Plant") and pointed out a number of other defects in the practice sessions, among them the following:

> 1. Unrealistic plans—" . . . a two-month schedule for the fourth-year students of the radio engineering faculty, Leningrad Radio Technical Institute, provided for familiarization with all the shops and departments of one of the plants—allowing two days for each production section of the plant."
>
> 2. Lack of interest on the part of the school—the source names Leningrad Technological Institute, Kiev Polytechnic Insitute, and L'vov Polytechnic Institute among examples of institutions which failed to provide proper supervision.
>
> 3. Lack of interest on the part of students—"The students frequently shirk their work . . . aimlessly wander around the plant, sleep, go for a swim, play chess, break labor discipline."
>
> 4. Lack of interest on the part of the plants—"No definite programming for practice work has been established, no systematic allocation of facilities for practice. The question of how to pay plant workers for the supervision of the students' practice has not been solved; that is why the people at the plant frequently lack interest in working with the students."

More important, the article stated that, although industrial practice is intended to combine the learning of manual and operational procedures with the development of an engineering outlook, few students have in fact been exposed to a challenge of that nature: not a single student worked as "an assistant to a supervisor of a shop, a section, a subsection, or a bureau" at such key industrial plants as, for example, the Moscow Automobile Plant, Kirov [formerly Putilov] Plant, and Uralmashzavod. During the preceding 3 years, the article stated, only one suggestion for a "rationalization" of plant procedure had been advanced by engineering students who served their practice sessions at the Leningrad Metal Works (one of the largest Russian and now Soviet plants specializing primarily in the construction of steam and water turbines).

The article on which we have just drawn and other similarly critical comments foreshadowed, perhaps by intent, one phase of the educational reform ordered by the Party's directive of 1954. This now familiar directive, which mentioned all the major aspects of higher education, stipulated the drafting of new regulations covering student industrial practice—"within a two-month period,"[27] such regulations to be worked out jointly by representatives of the Ministry of Higher Education and of the industrial ministries having budgetary and administrative jurisdiction over one or another category of schools—a move no doubt designed to compel cooperation. We have not seen the text of the new regulations—if they have in fact been issued. The new emphasis, however, can perhaps be discerned from the numerous comments on the objectives and effectiveness of student industrial practice which have since appeared in the Soviet press.

Shortly after publication of the Party directives, the Ministry of Higher Education took up the cause pointing out what had been wrong with practical training. Its editorial of October 1954 stated:

> The organic tie of theoretical with practical training is one of the achievements of the Soviet higher school. But it would be incorrect to close one's eyes to the most glaring defects in industrial practice. Industrial practice is frequently organized in a formal manner and fails to give future specialists the necessary practical habits. It is not infrequently conducted in a primitive fashion, with an overtone of training in a trade. In many cases industrial practice has a contemplative, sight-seeing character: the student himself does not carry out this or that work assignment, as provided for in the syllabus, but [merely] observes how it is done by others.[28]

The Ministry's somewhat ambiguous comment would suggest that it is not enough simply to train in operational skills and that the student must himself perform the required work. Two months later the Deputy Minister of Higher Education, Corresponding Member of the USSR Academy of Sciences V. A. Kirillin, in a lead article devoted to the problems of higher technical education made a specific reference to industrial training which we quote in full:

> The final problem on which one must comment is the problem of the students' practical training. The students' industrial training at the present time [1954–1955] is organized badly: the shops and laboratories of the institutions of higher education are altogether insufficiently supplied with modern equipment and apparatus; during the practice at industrial plants the students as a rule do not work directly at the work stations. As a result, many engineers upon graduation reveal themselves to be poorly prepared for work in industry.

There is no need to debate on the exceptionally great importance of the students' practical training—this fact is known to all. The task of the professors and teachers is to raise the quality of practical training within the shortest possible time, to eliminate the now existing serious shortcomings in this phase of training. Altogether abnormal is the fact that in many cases the least qualified instructors supervise industrial practice. It happens also that persons who, because of their limited qualifications, would have difficulty in holding any teaching position, engage in the conduct of practical instruction. The leading professors, in contrast, very seldom show up at the plants during the practice sessions of the students.

Another great shortcoming is that students during

> . . . the industrial practice frequently have no specific assignments or, at best, familiarize themselves with the blueprints and other shop material while sitting around in the Red Corner of the shop, or watch the work as it is carried on by others. Seldom can one see a student who works directly at a work station, who studies the productive process not by blueprints and instruction manuals—one can do that without leaving the school building—but on the basis of personal experience.
>
> The criteria for giving the student a *zachet* for his industrial practice are frequently also altogether insufficient.[29]

Following the Minister's appraisal various educators spoke in behalf of particular institutions. A March 1955 article states that the difficulties (inability of the plants to accommodate a large enough number of students, reluctance to permit students to operate plant equipment, and shortage of supervisors) have been long realized at the Leningrad Forest Engineering Academy and that a solution was found (after 1953) by organizing the students into special work groups:

> Each team consists of approximately 20 to 25 trainees and is furnished with, for example, the following equipment: a portable electric generator, two saws, two knot-cutters, two tractors, an automobile, a winch or a crane for loading.
>
> The student work section was first organized in 1953. . . . The section was supervised by instructors A. A. Fedorov (Chair of Mechanical Traction) and G. A. Paustovskii (Chair of Mechanization of Forestry Work). During the time spent at the students' work section the students (a group of 20 persons) have met the requirements prescribed as the Technical Minimum and qualified themselves as tractor operators, winch operators, and operators of portable [electric] plants. In the spring of 1954 these students successfully defended their diploma projects. Those among the trainees who, having mastered the operation of [such] mechanisms, have also had [academic] instruction in the specialty of engineer-technologist were directed [after graduation] to work in the capacity of master mechanics.[30]

Simultaneously there appeared another extensive article dealing with practical training, by Docent V. S. Sominskii (Leningrad Technological Institute), pointing out several examples of successful conduct of training—for instance, at the Leningrad Mechanical Institute, where students work at the actual production stations of a plant such as that of a lathe or milling machine operator.[31] Other favorable examples were cited:

> Geology students, for instance, go through the practice sessions as full-fledged and responsible members of exploration parties; students of the transportation institutes drive locomotives, automobiles, and electric locomotives; students of the water transport institutes spend practice time not as passengers but as members of the crew on ocean-going or river vessels.

Nevertheless, the author concluded:

> . . . on the whole, as the Party and government justly pointed out in last year's [1954] directives on the higher and specialized schools, the industrial practice of students is organized unsatisfactorily.[32]

In support of this conclusion the author cited all the now familiar arguments and gave an illustration of the actual conduct of practice in what he claimed to be the words of a student:

> During our third year we visited the plant named after Lenin. We spent one month there, shifting from one department to another. In substance it was as if we were on an extended excursion. During the fourth year we hung around the fireman and the operator of a turbine. To get credit [for industrial practice] we were given an examination—but it was a pure formality: the fourth-year students had no difficulty in learning all the details of boiler operation from the [printed] operating rules. But we were not permitted actually to operate a boiler on our own. During the fifth year, in the course of the prediploma practice, we collected materials for the diploma project but very seldom entered the plant, and if so, only for short periods.[33]

Since the original airing of criticism of student practice training, which filled the Soviet educational press following the 1954 directives, various specific measures have been proposed to increase the effectiveness of the training programs. A 1956 survey of reports from various institutions, while citing instances of satisfactory practice training, points to a number of difficulties arising from the generally rigid planning of the educational process as a whole.[34] Like other elements of academic work, the duration, sequence, and locale for the students' practical training are prescribed from above. The mechanical allocation of nearby plants for industrial practice at times overlooks the fact that the "profiles" of the plant and of the school do not match.[35] A fundamental difficulty, the educators say, derives also from the fact that nearly all industrial practice is scheduled during the summer.

> This means that during these months a multitude of students gravitate to the leading enterprises which possess the latest techniques and perfected technology of the industrial process. Consequently, it is impossible to organize industrial training rapidly. There are not enough work stations, not enough supervisors, and difficulties arise in providing living quarters for the students. The students do not know how they should spend their time, conflicts arise with the administration of the enterprise, and industrial practice is transformed into a formality bringing no useful results.[36]

Individual institutions are not free to develop a staggered plan. The Leningrad Forest Technology Institute wanted to change the time of practice so as to eliminate a conflict with diploma project supervision and to allow the practice to coincide with the most active seasonal phase of plant operation:

> Repeated attempts of the Department of Forest Chemical Industries to change the periods for the conduct of practical training proved to be unsuccessful, although the academy's council passed a resolution to that effect. As it develops, no change can be made without special permission from the Ministry of Higher Education.[37]

These and many other similar instances of rather trivial organizational difficulties can be used as negative evidence for our assumption that in the key categories of professional training such obstacles are easily eliminated. The presumption is that whenever both the particular school and the enterprise, laboratory, or other operating unit suitable for training purposes are strongly dominated by one of the key ministries, no gross discrepancies in the over-all plan are allowed to interfere with the effectiveness of industrial practice. It may be noted, for instance, that at the Bauman Higher Technical School some practice training sessions are scheduled after the fall semester and none are scheduled from April through July. The practical training in Soviet military schools of engineering is presumably well integrated and coordinated with the plants of military importance and under military control. However, in the civilian sector of the Soviet engineering industries there appears to be a basic conflict at the operating level: plants have production plans to fulfill and are not interested in lending their resources to train outsiders—an activity for which plant directors receive no tangible credit.

As to the dual role assigned to the students' practice training—learning operational skills and introduction to a practical professional out-look—it appears that the first two sessions are devoted mainly to manual training, if possible by assignment to actual work stations, and the last, the diploma practice, is counted upon to provide the student his first opportunity for synthetizing his undergraduate academic training by working on a more or less complex engineering problem, his diploma design project.

6. THE DIPLOMA PROJECT

When the Soviet student begins his final, usually the tenth, semester of undergraduate work he finds himself, in one sense, in a strange academic climate: for once he is free of hour-to-hour regimentation. Having no classes to attend and no other compulsory sessions, he encounters for the first time the opportunity—or necessity—for independent work. A few of the students entering this final stage of undergraduate training, those particularly bright and talented and fortunate enough to have had capable and unharrassed teachers in their junior and senior years, may already have had limited experience in working on their own. Some may have participated in the depart-mental research which goes on at widely varying levels at all Soviet institutions of higher education. Some also may have taken part in one of the many but not well attended students' science clubs or study groups. An increasingly larger number, but still a small per cent of the total of last-semester students, may have had some independent work experience in industry. This is true especially of the employed students attending evening courses.[38] The great majority must experi-ence an abrupt transition from a high degree of regimentation to comparative freedom, accompanied by new and unfamiliar demands on originality and initiative. Such a transition, which is perhaps less abrupt for the university student who faces only a state examination in the key disciplines of his field, must be critical for the Soviet engi-neering student, who must now prepare and defend an original quali-fying design project.

A typical engineering diploma project is the designing of a machine or an installation or an important component—complete with draw-ings (anywhere up to 18 or even more sheets), design and cost com-putations, performance estimates, and other data (100 or more pages in all). Soviet educational literature understandably assigns a very important role to the diploma project, intended as it is to focus the student's theoretical knowledge upon an engineering problem in the specific field of his future work:

The work on the diploma project at the institutions of higher technical education is the concluding and the most significant phase in the preparation and shaping of Soviet engineers. It is in this period that the future specialist has the possibility of developing with particular intensity his capabilities for independent creative solution of the engineering problems which are presented to him.[39]

Unfortunately, no opportunity presented itself in the course of this study to examine samples of any diploma projects; we have, therefore, only Soviet comments on which to base judgment.

The titles and brief descriptions of diploma projects encountered in the Soviet press suggest that some of them are unrealistically ambitious. Here is, for instance, an entry outlining the graduating design project submitted jointly by two students of Moscow Higher Technical School in the spring of 1956:

> The graduating students . . . V. Shaikov and A. Stepanov have just successfully defended their diploma project, *Design of an Atomic 5,500 HP Freight Locomotive*. This work is a serious attempt to evaluate the possibilities of utilizing atomic energy for railroad transport.
>
> The greatest difficulty involved the choice of type and size of the reactor. Having studied many types of distinct schemes and their suitability in view of the demands of high economy and the limitations of railroad clearances, the designers selected the heterogeneous type of reactor with graphite moderator.
>
> The locomotive consists of two sections. The first contains the reactor and the boiler installation; the second, the steam turbine, the condenser, and the auxiliaries. The locomotive can travel 1,000 kilometers without having to replenish its supply of water. Its fuel supply is sufficient for 7,200 hours of work.
>
> The authors of the project have given considerable attention to protecting the locomotive crew from harmful radiation effects. For this purpose the working part of the reactor is surrounded by a graphite shield and the entire reactor covered by a housing made of lead and concrete.
>
> The state examination commission has rated this diploma project highly.[40]

For work on this project the students may have had 8 weeks for the prediploma industrial practice (say from August 10 to October 5, 1955), during which period they may have visited a number of plants collecting information and design data. Following the 8 weeks of field work, they had approximately 21 weeks (October 6, 1955 to March 1, 1956) in which to complete the project, submit it for approval, and finally to "defend" it—a more or less ceremonial formality once their report was approved. In the course of their work they were in consultation mainly with one professor specially appointed by the department to supervise their work and, because of the complexity of the project, perhaps also with professors of other departments. Officially the school staff-time budget allows only 35 staff-man-hours per student "for supervision, criticism, and consultation" and for the formal acceptance of the completed diploma project at the state examination.[41]

It may be assumed that, circumstances permitting, exceptionally promising students may receive much more help and supervision than the Soviet professor's time-card prescribes—particularly at Bauman Higher Technical School, one of the best in the Soviet Union. Here, as has been noted, the students had 22 weeks for their work on the design of an atomic-powered locomotive. Elsewhere the time allowed for the preparation of a diploma project, however ambitious, is typically only 15 or 16 weeks.

The scope of projects assigned in the more nearly typical (narrowly specialized) engineering schools appears to be, in many instances, equally extensive, if not as challenging as the one we have just cited. A 15-week diploma project requirement for a student specializing in rolled steel products technology, for instance, was described (to condense the original text) as follows:

1. Carry out technological computations for the manufacture of a number of shapes and design the required mill rolls, checking them for strength; select operating machinery and equipment; determine the rates of output for the given shapes; describe the problems of producing these shapes from steels of given types.
2. Design a heating oven and one of the major or auxiliary power units for the rolling mill.
3. Carry out economic computations to determine the labor requirements, cost of the rolling plant, cost of production, the turnover of operating funds, etc.[42]

These paragraphs apparently describe the minimum requirements. The author of the article stated:

In our institute [Donetskii Industrial], as is the case in other schools, the accepted practice is to assign design problems dealing not just with one shop but with the entire metallurgical plant. In such cases additional work is required to determine the type, the basic dimensions and number of blast and Martin furnaces, the requirements for raw materials, fuel, means of transportation and other data.

. . . . . .

Furthermore, a diploma project, as is known, also includes a special part: a qualitative analysis of the existing dimensional standards at the plant; recommendations on mechanization of the labor-intensive processes, on increasing the accuracy of the rolled products, and on means to reduce the proportion of defective goods.[43]

This last reference to the "special part" of the project suggests the likelihood of occasional friction between the operating personnel of the plant and the eager engineers-to-be. In recent years, for instance, the cost and productivity factor analysis in the diploma projects has been particularly emphasized—as it has been in the Soviet Union's economy generally; but, quite aside from the fundamental problem of dealing rationally with Soviet managed costs, the students working on diploma projects encounter difficulties in obtaining routine industrial and plant statistics. Even the students specializing in engineering economics, to point out a distinct anomaly, cannot obtain realistic data:

> The basic shortcoming is that certain plants by way of re-insurance* refuse to furnish students the most ordinary data on the fulfillment of the plans, on cost of production, and other data without which the student cannot analyze the performance of the shop and arrive at conclusions; he cannot even fulfill his practice assignment, let alone collect the material on the basis of which he is expected eventually to prepare his term or diploma project.[44]

In general, and particularly since 1954, in assigning diploma project topics to the student before he commences his diploma practice, the aim has been to select "a real problem" of the industry or the specific plant at which the senior serves his diploma practice and where he is likely to be sent to work after graduation. For this purpose, the cooperation of the industrial enterprises has been solicited by the schools, if it has not been ordered from above, following the 1954 directives. A recent article by a Soviet professor states that in the experience of his department (Technology of Machine Construction, Latvian University)† the plant management "have shown a cautious attitude toward the department's offer to organize realistic projects"; one objection was that it takes a long time for a diploma student to complete the work. The author, Docent B. A. Sak-Shak, states, however:

> ... the very first projects completed have shown that students can successfully solve significant problems and that the quality of treatment compensates for the long time [required to complete a project]—

3 to 4 months, according to the author.[45] It should be noted, however, that far from the design of an atomic-powered locomotive or the determination of basic specifications for a steel plant, this author

---

* *Perestrakhovka*—Soviet vernacular for "avoiding unnecessary risk."

† An exception to the rule, this University has an engineering department, retained from its non-Soviet organization as it existed prior to the Soviet occupation of Latvia in 1940.

refers to relatively modest assignments dealing directly with current production of a particular detail, subassembly, or unit in a given plant.

Whatever may be said of the educational value of the recently emphasized practical orientation of the diploma projects, the Soviet author last cited concluded that "carrying out realistic diploma projects increases the student's sense of responsibility." Another Soviet commentator described the effect of the student's experience on the diploma project in much stronger terms:

> One can cite many different evaluations of the diploma projects and of their authors. But one common element, present in all of them, can be expressed thus: during the diploma project work, when the students work on their own, with a sense of total responsibility for the task delegated to them, the majority become simply transformed. Many young specialists can cope with responsible production tasks after graduation thanks only to the experience gained in the process of working out their diploma design.[46]

From our limited knowledge we would assume that, regardless of the professional value of the diploma project, the Soviet engineering student finds this period of his career an unusual and stimulating experience. His diploma project has the aura of professional prestige, importance, and authority; his designs and proposals are not hampered by considerations of cost and practicability, or by the organizational limitations of the Soviet civilian industry and economy. Furthermore, having successfully reached the diploma stage, he can confidently look forward to graduation. The engineering student's diploma project may be rated "satisfactory," "good," or "excellent," and the desirability of the job to which he will later be assigned may be partly determined by his project mark; in any event he will henceforth rate as a "diploma engineer." Nevertheless, his first encounter with the realities of Soviet industrial life during the diploma period may also have a sobering effect on the student's vision of his future career.

However exhilarating the experience of work on the diploma project may ordinarily be for the Soviet engineering student, the training value of this introduction to professional life has been periodically criticized both by Soviet educators and by the Party and its planning authorities. In spite of many improvements, presumably introduced since 1954, designed to bring this phase of training closer to the current problems of the Soviet industrial economy, the 1956 summation of the Ministry of Higher Education emphasized the need for further improvement:

> The institutions of higher technical education must carry out a serious methodological study on the conduct of the term and diploma

projects. The July [1955] plenum and later the 20th Party Congress have pointed to the urgent need of improving the economic and technological preparation of the future engineers. The higher school has been subjected to criticism because these two most important elements of training given to the specialists have been pushed into the background. One must frankly recognize that to a considerable extent the fault lies with the teachers of specialized disciplines, who have failed to show interest in the problems of economics and technology. That is why we consider that, to eliminate defects in this area, it is with these instructors that the work must be begun—to inoculate them with a taste for economics and the technology of production.[47]

7. The Quality of Soviet Undergraduate Education

We have examined the major elements of Soviet undergraduate education, with emphasis on training in physical sciences and mechanical engineering. Before considering Soviet graduate training in these areas, it is relevant to attempt an answer to a general question, namely: how "good" is Soviet undergraduate training on the whole?

No simple answer to this question can be expected or given. We can only attempt to visualize how all the many unique elements of the Soviet educational process combine to give this or that kind of undergraduate training—in different types of schools, in different localities of the Soviet Union, in different selected fields of study—to students of every level of talent, motivation, and capability. Even if all the relevant data were available—and they are not—it would be difficult, if not impossible, to structure a set of concise, unqualified, and meaningful judgments; and the fact that our interest is limited primarily to the character and quality of Soviet training in physics and engineering does not greatly minimize the problem. However, certain general factors can be isolated and the direction of their qualitative influence noted in a more generalized manner than was possible on the basis of any one separate topic discussed in detail in the preceding chapters. The conditions, or factors, which stand out are not by themselves unique to the Soviet system; but their great capacity to influence the quality of education appears to be uniquely the property of the Soviet Union.

The location of the school is one of the important conditions of education in the Soviet Union which apply equally to all students. Other things being equal, the student residing in one of the few metropolitan or industrial centers of the Soviet Union is likely to be far better trained than his counterpart in a provincial town.

The institutional factor is even more important. In spite of the drastic reorganizations of the 1930's, it is the older schools or those splintered from the pre-Revolutionary universities and institutes which appear to have emerged with the greatest academic prestige. Furthermore, naming only the categories of schools which are relevant to this survey, we would decisively rank them in a sharply descending qualitative order: first, the university, the Soviet center of education in physical sciences; second, the polytechnic institute, which achieves cross-fertilization of engineering science; a poor third, the industrial, single-industry oriented, narrowly specialized engineering school; and finally, in our opinion the lowest ranking category, its elaborate curricula notwithstanding—the normal school.* The third institutional dimension which should be clearly kept in mind is the type of instruction. Resident students include two qualitatively distinct categories: full-time day students and part-time evening students. Students taking correspondence courses comprise qualitatively an altogether separate group. By types of instruction, we would rank Soviet schools in the order named: first, the full-time resident schools; poor second, the part-time evening schools and departments; and third, the correspondence schools. And, as we have noted, it is the extension type of training (evening and by correspondence) that has significantly added to the impressive growth of Soviet enrollment in schools of higher education in the postwar years. In engineering schools, for example, where the full-time resident enrollment by 1955–1956 had increased by some 62 per cent over the 1950 figure, the number of extension (evening and correspondence) students over the same period rose more than four times— from approximately 43,000 to about 200,000 in 1955–1956. It may be

* Approximate statistics on the number of schools and enrollment, here cited for round number reference, as of c. 1955–1956:

Type of Institution	Number of Schools	Resident Enrollment	
		Thousands	Per Cent
Universities	33	120	10
Polytechnic and industrial	23	100	8
Specialized engineering	165	450	36
Normal schools		320	26
4-year	225		
2-year	52		
All other higher schools	245	240	20
Total for the USSR	743	1,230	100

Note: No military or correspondence schools are included in this table. As of June 1956 the total number of higher schools for the USSR was said to be 798; this number includes 22 correspondence schools and may or may not include the military schools.

noted also that the 1956–1957 admission's quota for all schools of higher education was set at 225,000 new resident and 215,000 new correspondence students, the latter thus accounting for nearly 50 per cent of the total.

The history of the institution, its general category, and the method of instruction it provides are qualitatively important. Still one more distinction is vital, namely: whether a given (engineering) school is in the jurisdiction of a military or a civilian industrial ministry; and, within the latter category, how highly the represented ministry is rated in the scale of Soviet priorities. It makes a big difference whether an institute trains mechanical engineers for heavy machine building or for consumer goods production.

The last suggested variable more generally refers to those qualitative factors in Soviet education stemming from the nature of Soviet ideology which affect specific fields of training in varying degrees. The negative value of this complex of variables may be zero in the training of a Soviet theoretical physicist, but it may approach infinity in the training of a Soviet economist—to take perhaps the extremes in the range of variation attributable to the negative influence of dogma. More specifically, the same relationship obtains with reference to all the individual subjects of instruction. The character and quality of instruction a Soviet mechanical engineer gets in mathematics or theoretical mechanics are sharply distinct from what he is likely to find in his course in political economy.

There are many other dimensions in which the quality of Soviet professional training has varied and will continue to vary, among them the political cycles in Soviet life; but these are imponderables which, important as they are, lie outside the province of this examination. The first general observation to be made here, on the basis of factors already enumerated, is that, in spite of the ostensibly monolithic, uniform, and nondiscriminatory Soviet system of higher education, and aside from the most important, the human, variable, which is here taken for granted, the training provided by the Soviet system is qualitatively very uneven—not only generally but also within the fields which we have largely been examining, physics and mechanical engineering.

But, to complete, insofar as we can, the answer to our question, it is also clear that both in science and, to a lesser extent, in engineering, *under a set of circumstances which combines all or the majority of the possible favorable factors,* the quality of training provided within the Soviet system can be and is in its technical content comparable to the very best that is included in the undergraduate education of a comparable professional man in the United States and other nontotalitarian societies.

How do the levels of training achieved in the Soviet 5-year undergraduate course compare with those of American bachelors (with 4 years of college work) or masters (with 1 additional year of training)? The qualitative considerations already enumerated provide a part of the answer: the level of Soviet undergraduate training varies from field to field so much as to make an over-all direct comparison inappropriate. But, with reference to the fields of our special interest, physics and mechanical engineering, a direct comparison can be ventured as a rough, over-simplified approximation.

A Soviet physics undergraduate starts his course without any formal deficiencies from his secondary education; he pursues his highly concentrated, professionally oriented study for 5 long years; the university he attends, relative to other Soviet schools of higher education, has been least affected by the unhappy experimentation with curricula, methods, and objectives of training; his school commands relatively the best teachers, textbooks, and facilities. As to the level of professional training, therefore, we would conclude that the Soviet physics graduate is at par with, and in his particular area of specialization (one of ten options) perhaps at a higher level of professional preparation than, his American counterpart after 1 year of graduate training.

The problem of similarly comparing the level of engineering training reached by the Soviet engineering student after his 5-year course with that of the engineering bachelor or master in American schools is more difficult. The important fact to remember is that Soviet engineering schools are assigned a dual responsibility: to instruct in engineering subjects and to train for a specific job. The last-named function in the United States is associated largely with professional employment *after* graduation—the training on the job which continues throughout the years of professional experience. Further difficulty in any direct comparison arises from the fact that Soviet engineering schools include two categories: the (25) polytechnic institutes and (c. 165) specific industries' institutes. The level of training achieved in the schools of the last-named category varies greatly depending on the *industry* they are designated to serve.

Discounting the vocationally oriented store of precarious knowledge a Soviet engineering graduate possesses after his 5 years of training, we conclude that in terms of basic engineering preparation he does not achieve appreciably if at all a higher level of competency in his 5 years of training than his American counterpart does after a 4-year course.

Notes to Chapter 10

[1] June 23, 1936 SNK USSR and TsK VKP(b), "On the Work and Supervision of the Institutions of Higher Education," quoted in *Vestnik vysshei shkoly*, No. 3, March 1948, p. 17.

[2] *Ibid.*

[3] Ya. I. Frenkel', *Vestnik vysshei shkoly*, No. 4, April 1945, p. 35; cited in the same journal, No. 3, March 1948, pp. 17 f.

[4] *Vestnik vysshei shkoly*, No. 11, November 1954.

[5] *Vestnik vysshei shkoly*, No. 4, April 1954, p. 60.

[6] *Vestnik vysshei shkoly*, No. 11, November 1954, p. 41.

[7] *Ibid.*

[8] *Ibid.*

[9] E.g., "Ekranizatsiya graficheskikh elementov uchebnovo protsessa" (Projection of the Graphic Elements in the Teaching Process), *Vestnik vysshei shkoly*, No. 4, April 1954, p. 49.

[10] An editorial, *Vestnik vysshei shkoly*, No. 7, July 1955, p. 3.

[11] Leon Trilling, *Soviet Education in Aeronautics: A Case Study*, Cambridge: Center for International Studies, Massachusetts Institute of Technology, 1956 (mimeographed), p. 37.

[12] " . . . and, in some cases, by those who, while being sufficiently well grounded in theory, lack teaching experience (for instance those who have just completed graduate training)." F. D. Gakhov, *Uspekhi matematicheskikh nauk*, Vol. IX (1954), Issue 4/62, p. 280, a review of N. A. Frolov's *Theoriya funktsii deistvitel'novo peremennovo*.

[13] A. M. Soifer, "Vospityvat' inzhenerov-novatorov" (To Nurture Engineers-Innovators), *Vestnik vysshei shkoly*, No. 10, October 1955, p. 16.

[14] *Report of the President and of the Deans of the Schools for the Year Ending October 1, 1955*, Massachusetts Institute of Technology, pp. 21 f.

[15] V. S. Sominskii, "Vazhneishiye usloviya uluchsheniya proizvodstvennoi podgotovki studentov" (The Most Important Conditions for the Improvement of Industrial Training of Students), *Vestnik vysshei shkoly*, No. 3, March 1955, p. 29.

[16] *Ibid.*, p. 30.

[17] E.g., *Vestnik vysshei shkoly*, No. 3, March 1955, p. 34.

[18] Soifer, *op. cit.*, p. 16.

[19] G. K. Borkhvardt, "Razvivat' samostoyatel'nost' v uchebnoi rabote studentov" (Develop Self-Reliance in the Work of the Students), *Vestnik vysshei shkoly*, No. 9, September 1953, p. 37.

[20] *Vestnik vysshei shkoly*, No. 4, April 1954, p. 2.

[21] K. M. Barshauskas (Doctor of Physico-Mathematical Sciences, Professor, Director of Kaunas Polytechnic Institute), "Prodolzhat' sovershenstvovaniye uchebnykh planov" (Continue to Perfect the Academic Plans), *Vestnik vysshei shkoly*, No. 2, February 1956. ,

[22] *Vestnik vysshei shkoly*, No. 4, April 1954, p. 4.

[23] August 16, 1956; *CDSP* translation, Vol. VIII, No. 23, September 26, 1956, p. 24.

[24] A. V. Mirtov (Professor-Doctor, Gorki State University), "Zametki nauchnovo rukovoditel'ya" (Notes of an Educator), *Vestnik vysshei shkoly*, No. 10, October 1955, p. 30.

[25] M. A. Minkov (Docent, Leningrad Mechanical Institute), "Rashryryat, tekhno-

logicheskiye znaniya budushchikh inzhenerov" (To Broaden the Technological Knowledge of Future Engineers), *Vestnik vysshei shkoly*, No. 4, April 1956, p. 10.

26 M. Andreyev (Deputy-in-Charge, student section of the Komsomol Central Committee), "Proizvodstvennaya praktika studentov" (Production Practice of Students), *Molodoi kommunist*, No. 5, May 1954, pp. 79–85.

27 See Appendix I.

28 *Vestnik vysshei shkoly*, No. 10, October 1954, p. 4.

29 V. A. Kirillin, "Nekotorye voprosy raboty tekhnicheskikh vuzov" (Certain Problems in the Work of the Technological Schools of Higher Education), *Vestnik vysshei shkoly*, No. 12, December 1954, pp. 6 f.

30 A. V. Chirkov, "Iz opyta organizatsii proizvodstvennoi praktiki" (From Experience in Organizing Industrial Practice), *Vestnik vysshei shkoly*, No. 3, March 1955, p. 31.

31 Sominskii, *op. cit.*, p. 26.

32 *Ibid.*

33 *Ibid.*, p. 27.

34 *Vestnik vysshei shkoly*, No. 6, June 1956, pp. 45–49.

35 *Ibid.*, p. 46.

36 A. I. Donskoi (Moscow Power Institute), *Vestnik vysshei shkoly*, No. 11, November 1955, p. 37.

37 *Vestnik vysshei shkoly*, No. 6, June 1956.

38 See, e.g., V. I. Kuznetsov, "Razvivat' vecherneye vyssheye obrazovaniye" (Develop the Evening School System of Higher Education), *Vestnik vysshei shkoly*, No. 4, April 1954, an article describing the work of evening schools and particularly of the Evening Institute of Machine Construction in Moscow, pp. 34–39.

39 N. V. Vorob'yev (Doctor-Professor, Moscow Higher Technical School), "Nekotorye metodicheskiye soobrazheniya o diplomnom proektirovanii" (Certain Consideration of Methods in the Conduct of the Diploma Projects), *Vestnik vysshei shkoly*, No. 11, November 1948, p. 20.

40 *Vestnik vysshei shkoly*, No. 6, June 1956, p. 64.

41 *Vysshaya shkola*, compiled by M. I. Movshovich, p. 305. The "State Examining Board" includes the chairman representing the relevant industry appointed by the Ministry of Higher Education, the director of the school, dean of the particular faculty, chair professor, and "one or two specialists not on the staff of the institution in question." *Ibid.*, p. 148, citing 1938 regulations.

42 *Vestnik vysshei shkoly*, No. 2, February 1956, p. 43.

43 *Ibid.*

44 K. A. Shtets and L. M. Liberman (Docents, Kharkov Engineering Economics Institute), "Vnesti yasnost' v napravleniye podgotovki inzhenerov-ekonomistov" (To Clarify the Direction in Training Engineers-Economists), *Vestnik vysshei shkoly*, No. 11, November 1953.

45 *Vestnik vysshei shkoly*, No. 2, February 1956, p. 42.

46 Borkhvardt, *op. cit.*, p. 35.

47 An editorial, *Vestnik vysshei shkoly*, No. 6, June 1956.

SOVIET HIGHER EDUCATION:

THE GRADUATE TRAINING

$\mathbf{F}$rom the time of the reorganization of the Soviet educational system in the early 1930's through 1955 nearly 3 million students received undergraduate training.[1] During approximately the same period, and more specifically since 1934 when formal plans for *graduate* training were re-established, a total of some 80,000 Soviet students completed training at the graduate level.[2] Typically, therefore, about 3 per cent of Soviet college and university students have continued to the graduate level,* and some 97 per cent have entered state employment directly upon completion of undergraduate training. Although this concluding chapter on Soviet higher education is primarily

---

* In the United States, for the comparable period, the ratio of graduate degrees to the bachelor's was approximately as follows: master's or 2nd professional—15 per cent; doctor's or equivalent—1.8 per cent. This estimate is based on the following examples:

Earned Degrees Conferred, in Thousands

Year	Bachelor's	Master's	Doctor's
1929–30	122	15	2.2
1939–40	187	27	3.3
1947–48	271	42	4.2
1949–50	432	58	6.6
1951–52	329	64	7.7

(Biennial Survey of Education in the United States, Chapter 4, Section 1, *Statistics of Higher Education: Faculty, Students, and Degrees, 1950–1952*, Washington, D. C.: Office of Education, 1955, p. 44.)

In 1955 earned degrees conferred included bachelor's—287,401; master's—58,204; and doctor's—8,840 (master's, 20 per cent and doctor's 3 per cent of the number of bachelor's degrees earned in 1955).

concerned with the graduate training of Soviet specialists, it is appropriate first to comment on the career opportunities and alternatives open to a Soviet student just out of college. The basic alternatives, of course, are to continue resident study toward a graduate degree or to go directly to work. The student himself at this stage of his career has little to say about the choice: it is made for him by the appropriate authorities.

1. PLACEMENT AFTER GRADUATION

By statutory provisions which with some modifications apply to Soviet graduates at any level of specialized training—from trainees of labor reserve schools to postgraduate degree holders—a Soviet student upon graduation is obligated to accept any position designated by the authorities at any organization in any locality and to work in the assigned capacity for at least 3 years—an obligation which naturally and logically derives from the basic philosophy of Soviet social management.[3]

As far as the state is concerned, planned allocation of trained manpower is an indispensable part of the Soviet total design. It was introduced in the early 1930's and in principle has remained unchanged. Its administration and operational details, however, have undergone many changes aimed to correct perennial structural and administrative difficulties; and the general political climate has largely determined the pattern of distribution of manpower and the severity and inflexibility in the actual application of the stern legal provisions on work assignments. In 1940, for example, criminal liability was attached to any infraction of rules either by a student or by the persons responsible for his placement in accordance with a prearranged ministerial plan. In recent years, however, especially since Stalin's death, considerable flexibility has been permitted, officially or unofficially, in making postgraduate assignments. Formal changes in the rules were introduced in 1954 by a directive entitled "Regulations on the Personnel Distribution of Young Specialists upon Completion of the Higher and Specialized Secondary Educational Institutions." We have not seen the text of those regulations. It is obvious, however, that they include a number of liberalizing provisions designed to minimize individual dissatisfactions but continue to emphasize the overriding importance of meeting the needs of the state. An editorial, and therefore a quasi-official statement of the Ministry, published in February 1955 gives an indication of both the past difficulties in the administration of the Soviet appointment system and the renewed emphasis on the basic objectives it is intended to serve. We quote from this article selectively to illustrate the major points.

As the experience of the past years in the distribution of college graduates has shown, many shortcomings in this process have stemmed from the fact that the commissions on the allocation of graduates have at times adopted hasty, thoughtless decisions on the assignment of graduates to work, without taking into account the level of their preparation, the state of their health, and their marital status; whereas a thoughtful, attentive, sensitive attitude of the Commission toward the graduates, combined with a strict observance of the interests of the state, could have forestalled at the very outset many complications in the independent work of young specialists and could have assured the most fruitful utilization of their physical and spiritual forces in social production.

. . . . . .

The duty of the Commission on personnel allocation consists in assuring unconditional fulfillment of the plan for the allocation of young specialists, assigning them directly to production duties—in shops, machine-tractor stations, collective farms, state farms, and also hospitals, schools, and so forth.

. . . . . .

According to the "Regulations . . . ," young married specialists must be assigned upon graduation from the higher school to work in one and the same city or county (*raion*). The Commission must take all the necessary measures for the final solution in appointing young married specialists to work in accordance with the "Regulations. . . ."

. . . . . .

One of the serious shortcomings in the distribution of graduates is that the directors of institutions, responding to unwarranted requests from organizations or individuals, let a large number of graduates remain in big cities, where they are not especially needed, or make it possible for them to arrange for employment on their own. Such actions not only hurt the state but also harmfully affect the graduates themselves, leading them to a belief that they can get away with the neglect of their obligations to society, that they can sacrifice the interest of the state to personal interests.[4]

The major determinants for the distribution of graduates are, of course, set at the highest level of planning. Thus, for instance, under Malenkov in 1953 the Council of Ministers and the Central Committee of the Party ordered that 6,500 mechanical engineering graduates be assigned in 1954–1955 to work at the machine-tractor stations in a move designed rapidly to bolster agricultural production.[5] It was also announced that, beginning with 1955–1956, not less than 80 per cent of the university graduates from the faculties of philology, history, geography, and biology and not less than 60 per cent of those graduating from physics-mathematics and chemical faculties would be assigned to teach in the secondary schools.[6] In 1955 nearly 50 per cent of the 256 thousand Soviet college graduates were assigned to heavy industry, more than 24 per cent to agriculture, and only 4 per cent to consumer goods and food industries.[7] An unknown but relatively small per cent of the 1955 graduates (less than 3 per cent) were selected to continue study at the graduate level.

There were 7,367 new students enrolled in 1955 for graduate training in the Soviet Union, but not all of them were recruited from the 1955 graduates; as will be shown, prior work experience has become one of the major requirements in qualifying for admission to graduate standing.

2. ORGANIZATION AND FACILITIES OF GRADUATE STUDY

Several Types of Graduate Training

Soviet graduate training (*aspirantura,* leading to the *kandidat nauk* degree and, until recently, also *doktorantura,* leading to the highest, *doktor nauk* degree) is conducted not only at the universities and other institutions of higher education but also at many of the research organizations maintained by the Soviet academies of sciences and various industrial ministries.* Thus, for instance, of the approximately 7.4 thousand new graduate students enrolled in the fall of 1955, some 4.2 thousand or 57 per cent entered institutions of higher education, and the remaining 3.2 thousand or 43 per cent were accepted for training at the research institutes. Furthermore, the graduate enrollment in each institutional category is divided into full-time resident students and part-time correspondence students. Thus in 1955–1956 admissions to the first year of graduate study were distributed as follows:

	Full-time	Part-time	Total
Educational institutions	3,225	968	4,193
Per cent	77	23	100
Research institutes	2,159	1,015	3,174
Per cent	68	32	100
Total	5,384	1,983	7,367
Per cent	73	27	100

Soviet published statistics on enrollment, number of graduate stu-

* *"Kandidat nauk"* and *"doktor nauk"* will be hereafter referred to as "candidate" and "doctor," respectively.

dents in training, and number of graduate degrees awarded by field of training are scarce and not enlightening. Nevertheless, we quote here (in Table 55) the available official data for 1940, 1950, and 1955.* The following observations with reference to these statistics may be especially noted:

(1) A significant increase, both relative and absolute, in the number of graduate students earning the degree of candidate from *research* institutions. In 1940 the 506 research institute degree earners accounted for 26 per cent of the total number of new candidates; in 1955 the corresponding figures were 2,855 and 38 per cent. The trend is even more strongly indicated by the admissions figures for the research institutes versus the total number assigned to graduate training: in 1940—762 students or 22 per cent; in 1950—2,934 or 38 per cent; and in 1955—3,174 or 43 per cent of the total for the Soviet Union. And, it may be noted, the entire 1955 graduate enrollment of 12.6 thousands at the research institutes accounted also for 43 per cent of the total for the Soviet Union.

(2) The relatively faster growth of *correspondence* training leading to the candidate degree. In 1940 only 113 students, or 6 per cent, earned candidate degrees on a part-time basis; in 1955 their number was 1,071 or 14 per cent of the total number of new candidates. The current trend is even more significantly indicated by the number of new students admitted to graduate schools on a part-time basis: in 1950—1,340 or 17 per cent; in 1955—1,983 or 27 per cent.

(3) A markedly small number of correspondence graduate students complete their training. Table 55 shows that correspondence graduate enrollment in 1950 accounted for nearly 83 per cent of the total number of graduate students; but, as shown in (2) above, only 27 per cent of those completing graduate training in 1955 came from the correspondence schools.

The four categories of graduate training associated with the Soviet statistics shown in Table 55 (at schools versus research institutes and resident versus part-time, by correspondence) are qualitatively distinct; further differentiation within each category naturally arises, partly from the same factors which condition undergraduate training, and partly because of special provisions applicable only to graduate training.

Graduate Facilities

Not every Soviet institution of higher education and not every research organization has graduate training programs. The regulations issued in 1937 listed the names of the institutions (schools and

* The distribution of the 1955–1956 graduate enrollment by fields of study is given in Table 56.

TABLE 55. STATISTICS ON GRADUATE (*Aspirantura*) TRAINING AT SOVIET INSTITUTIONS OF HIGHER EDUCATION AND RESEARCH INSTITUTES 1940, 1950, and 1955

Explanation and Year	Number of Students in Graduate Facilities at								
	Schools of Higher Education			Research Institutes			Both, Schools and Research Institutes		
	Full-time	Part-time	Total	Full-time	Part-time	Total	Full-time	Part-time	Total
Completed graduate training in									
1940	1,411	61	1,472	454	52	506	1,865	113	1,978
1950	2,281	180	2,461	1,368	264	1,632	3,649	444	4,093
1955	4,263	489	4,752	2,273	582	2,855	6,536	1,071	7,607
Started graduate training in									
1940	2,223	545	2,768	559	203	762	2,782	748	3,530
1950	4,253	530	4,783	2,124	810	2,934	6,377	1,340	7,717
1955	3,225	968	4,193	2,159	1,015	3,174	5,384	1,983	7,367
Graduate enrollment, end of (in thousands)									
1940	1.7	11.5	13.2	0.8	2.9	3.7	2.5	14.4	16.9
1950	1.3	11.2	12.5	2.5	6.9	9.4	3.8	18.1	21.9
1955	3.6	13.2	16.8	4.4	8.2	12.6	8.0	21.4	29.4

Source: The National Economy of the USSR, 1956, p. 241, and Kul'turnoye stroitel'stvo SSSR, 1956, p. 255.

research institutes) which were then given the right of accepting either candidate or doctoral dissertations or both.[8]

A list with amendments to 1945 names 216 institutions which are authorized (1) to accept doctoral and candidate dissertations, (2) to recommend (to the Higher Attestation Commission) the granting of doctor's degrees, and (3) to grant candidate's degrees. Of the 216 institutions so authorized in 1945, 23 were under direct military control.* An additional 130 were authorized to conduct only the *aspirantura* training (and to grant candidates' degrees)—among them 15 institutions within the jurisdiction of the military. The total number of institutions accredited for graduate instruction at any level in 1945 was therefore 346, of which number approximately 132 were research institutes, 2 were Party schools, and 214 were regular educational institutions, including all the universities; and 38 of the 346 accredited establishments were under direct control of the military.†

At that time (1944–1945) the number of students enrolled in *aspirantura* was perhaps not larger than 9,000—only some 26 graduate students per institution authorized to conduct advanced training. The number of those who completed *aspirantura* training in 1945 was about 2,000, that is, an average of only 3 earned candidate's degrees per institution in that last of the war years. Although the graduate enrollment in the Soviet Union has greatly expanded from the 1945 low, even in 1955–1956, with the reported enrollment of 29.4 thousand, the average number per institution was still relatively small, perhaps about 50 students; and the average number of new degree earners in 1955 could not have exceeded 15 per accredited institution.

The apparent intention of the Soviet plan to restrict graduate instruction to the institutions which are best equipped for research and best staffed, and the relatively small number of graduate students, would lead one to assume that favorable conditions for advanced training could be normally maintained. However, the rapid rate of expansion in graduate enrollment and the relative shortage of highly qualified teachers have apparently made it necessary for the system to lower the standard somewhat insofar as supervision is concerned. The original regulations promulgated in 1939 provided as follows:

Every graduate student (*aspirant*) from his first year is attached to

* Ministries of Defense, Navy, Aviation, Munitions, and Armaments.

† As of 1945, for instance, the Bauman Higher Technical School in Moscow was listed under the USSR Ministry of Armament.

The number of accredited institutions may be compared with the approximately 800 schools of higher education and perhaps as many as 1,000 research establishments of different types then operating in the Soviet Union.

an academic adviser—a member of the faculty holding the academic rank of professor or the academic degree of doctor. As a rule not more than five graduate students are to be assigned to one supervisor.[9]

A year later an order was issued as follows:

> The assignment of more than five graduate students to one supervisor is to be forbidden. The appointment of persons who do not have the title of professor or the academic degree of doctor to serve as academic supervisors of graduate students is not to be permitted.[10]

In actual practice, with the establishment of additional graduate programs, candidate-docents have also served as faculty advisers; and it is likely that the official rules may have been at one time changed accordingly.[11] In any case, the training of "more than half" of the nearly 30 thousand graduate students in 1955–1956 was supervised by candidates of sciences,

> . . . who are naturally far from being always capable of giving adequate guidance in the training of qualified scientists.[12]

The original provision whereby the conduct of graduate programs was to be authorized only at institutions possesssing adequate research facilities and engaged in active research may also have been compromised as, under the pressure of the increased demand for graduate training, more and more institutions were added to the certified list. The directives designed to improve the quality of graduate training (initiated in August 1956) announced a reduction in the number of institutions accredited for graduate studies:

> It has been deemed appropriate to reduce the number of scientific institutions with the right to accept and to conduct the defense of dissertations, retaining among them only those [institutions in which the academic] councils are staffed with highly qualified specialists able to give a correct evaluation of the work submitted in defense.[13]

The number of accredited institutions, nevertheless, was said to be larger than it was in 1945:

Accredited to receive dissertations	1945	1956
Candidate's and doctor's	216	283
Candidate's only	130	250

As this is written, we have no information whether a new list applied in the 1956–1957 academic year. In the meantime it is clear that the basic approach to graduate training has been subjected to much criticism since Stalin's death and especially since the 20th Congress of the Party in February 1956. A subsequently issued directive, "On Measures to Improve the Training and the Certification of Scientific and Teaching Cadres,"[14] deals with every major phase of graduate training—the selection and admissions policy, scholarships, the conduct of training, the rules on dissertations and academic degrees, and the degree-certification procedure. Above all, recently introduced measures re-emphasize the importance of research as a part of graduate training. Before proceeding with a review of the major aspects of Soviet graduate education it is appropriate, therefore, to comment on research activities in the Soviet Union generally and particularly at the institutions of higher education.

Research in Soviet Schools of Higher Education

Scientific research in the Soviet Union is organized in three administratively distinct institutional complexes. By far the most important is the USSR Academy of Sciences and its thirteen sister academies of sciences at the republic level,* forming, in one observer's terms,

> . . . a gigantic enterprise, one which has no equal in the world in the scope of its scientific work, the versatility of its social functions, and the size of its staff.
> The world has never before seen a more elaborate system of coordinated and centralized research work in the natural sciences, in technology, and in the humanities.[15]

The second component of organized facilities for research and development is made up of the industrial and other research institutes which are maintained by the various ministries, such as the Ministry of Heavy Machine Building.[16] Finally, research work at the institutions of higher education is also conceived as a coordinate part of the Soviet scientific potential, although in practice it appears to be least effectively integrated within the total plans for centralized research.

The work of all Soviet scientific organizations, whether under the Academy of Sciences, under other economic and cultural agencies of the state, or at the institutions of higher education, is supposed to follow the over-all Soviet state plan for scientific and technological development. Detailed planning is done at the institutional levels and coordinated into master plans by the USSR Academy of Sciences, the ministries, and, for research work at the institutions of higher education, by the Ministry of Higher Education.[17]

* Including Ukrainian SSR, since 1919; Byelorussian SSR, since 1929; Latvian—1940; Lithuanian and Georgian—1941; Armenian and Uzbek—1943; Azerbaidzhan—1945; Kazakh and Estonian—1946; and the Kirgiz SSR Academy organized in c. 1954.

Following World War I and the Revolution, the years of "War Communism," the productive and cultural activities of Russia were all but extinguished. In the words of one contemporary scientist, "In the frozen laboratories of universities and institutes all scientific activities came to a standstill."[18] Research and development activities were revived largely in connection with the plans for industrialization. During the NEP period (1921–1928) the Scientific-Technical Section (NTO) was organized within the Supreme Soviet on the National Economy (VSNKh). In 1925 the Russian Academy of Sciences (founded in 1724) was given recognition as "the highest scientific organization of the Soviet Union" (its name was changed to the USSR Academy of Sciences). With the decision to industrialize, the introduction of the Five Year Plans, and the organization of the national economy by key sectors under state super-trusts (future ministries), it became necessary to establish specialized industrial research and development facilities, the future "branch of industry" (*otraslevye*) research institutes.

By 1935 the Ministry (then Commissariat) of Heavy Industry alone had 99 research and development institutes and 27 branch institutes.[19] The USSR Academy of Sciences was subordinated directly to the Council of Ministers, and, by a 1935 statute, the scope of its work was greatly expanded by the establishment of a new, industrially oriented Technical Department of the Academy.* But the revival and growth of research activities at universities and engineering schools proceeded slowly, impeded, for example, by the higher priority given to research institutions in the allocation of facilities, operating funds, and qualified personnel.

In 1936 the Council of Ministers (then Commissars) and the Central Committee of the Party declared that they condemned

> . . . the view, . . . widespread among certain officials of the [industrial] ministries and institutions of higher education, that the departments [*kafedry*] of the higher educational institutions need not engage in research work and [may or should] limit themselves only to teaching activities.[20]

Not until 1944, however, did the central government implement its earlier injunctions by a set of formal regulations and detailed instructions on the conduct of research at the institutions of higher education.[21] The point of departure for the policies enunciated in the 1944 regulations was defined in a statement cited from the 1936 declaration of the Party:

* A list of the Academy's major departments as of 1949 is given in Appendix O.

. . . the training of specialists up to the level of the demands made by modern science cannot be achieved, nor can the preparation of scientific-teaching personnel and the raising of their qualifications be conceived, unless the institutions of higher education engage in scientific research.

The directions in which internal research was to be channeled were designated as follows:

1. Experimental and theoretical scientific research generally
2. Solution of problems of importance to the national economy
3. Specific research assignments as may be designated by the various ministries
4. The writing of textbooks and monographs
5. Research in teaching methodology
6. Popularization of achievements in science and technology, via lectures, exhibits, conferences, and publications

The 1944 regulations have been supplemented or amplified from time to time, but the particular emphasis on the utilization of the research potential of universities and engineering schools for the solution of current industrial problems is of relatively recent origin: the 19th Party Congress (1952) declared for an increase in quantity, scope, and usefulness; the July 1955 Plenum of the Central Committee called upon scientists to engage in "solving problems of technical progress"; and in 1956 the 20th Congress of the Party specifically expressed the intention "to enroll the institutions of higher education in the carrying out of research for the national economy on a broader scale."

Organizationally, research work carried on by the departments (*kafedry*) of the faculties comes under two major budgetary categories: (1) the work done under the centrally allocated university research budget of the USSR, controlled and supervised by the Ministry of Higher Education, and (2) contract work financed by the economic (and other) ministries out of their own budgets.*

The first-named category, which embraces what we may call sustaining research, is the least regimented—although the work is supposed to follow a previously approved plan. Until 1955 the Ministry of Higher Education had a special planning, coordinating, and control section in charge of institutional research.† A letter by Professors

---

* In Soviet bureaucratic jargon, the two types are referred to as *"gosbyud-zhetnyi"* for "state-budgetary" and *"khozdogovornyi"* for "economic management-contractual."

† Department of Research Work at the Institutions of Higher Education, organized in 1944; disbanded sometime in 1955, its functions were distributed among the Ministry's departments in charge of one or another category of schools.

V. I. Atroshchenko and G. B. Kukolev (Kharkov Polytechnic Institute) comparing the organization of research in the Academy and industrial institutes with that at the educational institutions made the following typical comment on the effectiveness of planning:

> It is well known that within the powerful network of research institutes of the Academy of Sciences and the industrial ministries research work is successfully planned and coordinated; such planning at the institutions of higher education, substantively speaking, is not practiced; the choice of direction and the content of such work, especially that financed through the state budget, is usually determined only by the interest of the authors of the work or the individuals comprising the department (*kafedra*).[22]

The advantage of relative freedom from regimentation at institutions of higher education appears to be frequently limited to the opportunity to write textbooks and monographs. Soviet educators complain that the opportunity to conduct independent experimental and laboratory research has been restricted by budgetary limitations and, more important in the final analysis, by the excessive teaching and administrative loads of the university scientists.[23] Although it is said that sustained research allowances have been growing (e.g., " . . . in 1954 to four times that in 1946"),[24] the funds are earmarked in such a way that it is impossible to engage the needed

> . . . laboratory technicians, craftsmen, and skilled workers who are not [already] on the departmental staff for participation in such research projects; all supporting work on the state-financed research programs must be carried out only by the auxiliary personnel on the staff. But at the present time the staff members of the departments are, as a rule, unable to conduct fully meritorious research because every one of them is overloaded with teaching work.[25]

Similar budgetary restrictions apparently apply to a lesser degree or not at all to the contract projects financed by outside organizations. For such projects the departments are able to obtain outside help (engineers and technicians of the interested organization) and are permitted to spend some of the agreed sums for new laboratory and testing equipment. On the other hand, the planning and control procedures of the contracted research projects are much more cumbersome and wasteful. As an illustration of the process involved we may quote from the account of a deputy director of a food technology institute:

> The planning of the contract research topics (*khozdogovornye*) involves a series of complex, multi-stage coordinations. The Ministry of Higher Education demands the submission of the plan for research on the agreed topics—together with the obligatory copies

of contracts or letters of guarantee—by a strictly set date: the 10th of December. But the economic enterprises do not conclude agreements within the time limit, and do not issue guarantees, because they themselves do not know what funds will be allocated to them for research [during the following year].

After a series of prolonged negotiations with the industrial ministries and enterprises, the departments [of the faculties] begin to organize the work [presumably beginning on January 1 of a given year]. [Sometime] after the first quarter [of the year] the Ministry of Higher Education returns the list of contract research topics approved by it. The appropriation [may be] reduced (in our institute for the current year [1956] the amount was cut nearly in half); certain topics [may be] eliminated altogether. The institute suspends the work on such topics and annuls the agreements previously entered into.[26]

The author of the statement quoted above also describes other difficulties, ". . . at times unsurmountable," such as the difficulty in arranging the construction of special equipment. A given plant does not want to be bothered with special orders because "the output of such [special devices] cannot be counted in the producer's plan-fulfillment indexes."

We would doubt that such difficulties as those cited by the director of a food technology institute are encountered only in the consumer goods sector of the Soviet economic and administrative organization. But we would also note that, as is true of Soviet production generally, the usual bureaucratic rules—and costs—are disregarded where research and development of military importance are concerned.* Conse-

---

* We would cite here one of the many available testimonies of competent observers, former Soviet administrators. Lev Vasil'ev writes:

> One of the crash tasks of the Ammunition Ministry [c. 1940] was to expand production and, in this connection, to construct facilities designated by a code number, 359. It was on this project that I was to concentrate my basic attention. The flow of supply of all the necessary materials proceeded without a break. Any demand whatsoever was filled by the Ministry with remarkable speed.

> I could not help thinking of conditions in Vladivostok when in connection with construction steel or cement [for consumer industry construction] one had to bombard Moscow with scores of telegrams. Here the delivery of raw and other materials was never delayed and the work was financed to the limit of need.

>   . . . .

> The basic thing was to fulfill the plan—expenditure of material, human, or financial resources was not a matter of concern. The management was accountable for its action only to the ministry, and all the innumerable auditors from the side—such as the bank, the state control, or local Party organizations—were denied the right of interfering with the work of administration.

Puti sovetskovo imperializma (The Ways of Soviet Imperialism), New York: Chekhov Publishing House of the East European Fund, Inc., 1954, pp. 145 f.

quently, for reasons already enumerated in connection with the distribution of teaching personnel and facilities throughout the Soviet institutions of higher education, the quantity, scope, effectiveness, and quality of research at Soviet universities and engineering schools varies perhaps more than any other element of the academic process.*

The controlling fact to be emphasized here is that, generally speaking, research has occupied a relatively small and secondary part in the work of the Soviet system of higher education, significant Soviet research and development potential residing largely in the Academy and the specialized industrial institutes. The fact that in later years, and with an increasing sense of urgency since 1954, the Soviets have been trying to revitalize the role of research in advanced training suggests that the educational system was for many years progressively drained of scientific talent for the benefit of current industrial achievements in selected areas of military and political importance, with a consequent lowering of the quality of advanced training at the institutions of higher education.

To summarize, in organizing key industries for production and growth under the forced draft of central planning, the Soviet plan demanded and encouraged vertical integration by industries of all components needed to achieve the designated ends—including, as we have seen, specialized educational facilities and the research and development apparatus within each key industry. The Academy of Sciences and related research institutions, although they are not structured by industries but by fields of science and by areas of applied science and technology, have also been mobilized, especially since 1936, "to elevate the needs of the current Five Year Plan above all other types of intellectual activity."[27] This emphasis has had plainly visible effects on Soviet higher education. Relative to the greater and greater concentration of research and development personnel and facilities in the academies' and industries' research organizations, the research functions of engineering schools and even of universities (with some notable exceptions) have declined. For the educational system as a whole, according to a Soviet statement,

> The number of scientists at the institutions of higher education who are engaged in the solution of problems of importance to the national economy is not larger than 10 per cent. Others, as we have said, carry on minor investigations financed through the state budget

* Taking as our criteria the quality of physical and engineering science research, we would rate, as we did on the basis of all other criteria, the university first, the polytechnic institute second, and the specialized engineering schools third.

or contract assignments dealing in most cases with specific problems of production.[28]

V. A. Kirillin, the Deputy Minister of Higher Education, stated:

Even in our foremost institutions of higher technical education far from all the instructors (including the instructors of specialized technical departments) actively participate in the conduct of scientific research.[29]

The differentiation between research scientists and scientists-educators has become sharper; and the educational process has been much further divorced from research than the theoretical model for an effective organization of graduate training would call for. Academician M. N. Tikhomirov (Moscow University), for instance, concluded:

Two types of young scientific workers are thus being created: the scientist in the research organizations and the teacher in the institutions of higher education. The former is denied vital communion with the students; the latter teaches at the higher school but himself hardly carries on any research.[30]

As has been shown, the locus of Soviet graduate training has been shifting away from the university to the research organizations.

Although recently introduced legislation aims to improve conditions for graduate work at the universities and engineering schools, partly by stimulating the intensity and expanding the scope of research, the rationale of the present drive still emphasizes applied science and practical orientation of the universities' research work. Above all, the effectiveness and the long-range educational value of the current program would depend on mutuality of aims and horizontal cooperation between the institutions and the coordinate industrial and other agencies of the state—a condition which is not yet in evidence in the Soviet social system.

3. Aspirantura: Selection and Admission Standards

One fact should be kept in mind while considering Soviet graduate school admission policies: at the graduate level, qualitative considerations apart, Soviet rates of output numerically have been consistently below the planned rates. The discrepancy appears to derive not only from a larger than planned per cent of dropouts and the longer than stipulated actual time taken to complete formal graduate programs but also from the frequent failures to fill the admission quotas set by the Ministry for each institution each year.

The Factor of Prior Experience

The original rules of admission to graduate status (*aspirantura*) established in the 1930's drew a sharp distinction between the prospective full-time (resident) and part-time (correspondence) graduate students. Prior completion of undergraduate training was of course required of applicants in both categories, but two of the several qualifying factors, age and practical experience (*stazh*), were designated as follows:

	Resident Students	Correspondence Students
Age	Not over 40	No age limit
Practical experience	Not specifically required	3 years

Furthermore, the field of part-time graduate study by correspondence was limited to that of the applicant's undergraduate training and his current employment. The provisions on the field of prior training and practical experience have undergone an important change. In 1944 not less than 2 years of practical experience in a corresponding field became a requirement for full-time applicants seeking advanced training in "applied specialties."

> For persons who do not have practical experience exceptions may be permitted insofar as graduate training in these specialties is concerned only if the persons in question have graduated from an institution of higher education with distinction, have shown creative ability during their residence at school, and have references to that effect and recommendations from academic supervisors and institutions.[31]

Practical experience for full-time students in the applied fields, e.g., engineering and technology, continued to be emphasized in Soviet official and supporting pronouncements, but the rule established in 1944 apparently proved unworkable. In any event, in 1955 a professor at a mining-metallurgical institute, commenting on the defects in graduate training, said:

> At the present time, inasmuch as we do not demand of graduate students prior practical experience, the holders of the candidate's degree possess most diverse [levels] of scientific and technical experience.[32]

The text of the 1956 regulations was not available to us, but references to these rules in a number of Soviet publications make it clear that, despite past difficulties, the new directive again prescribed practical experience of 2 years as a minimum for *all* prospective graduate students except those who are to take graduate work "in theoretical disciplines, such as mathematics, physics, and certain others."[33]

This sharp differentiation between applied and theoretical training requirements somewhat reflects the character of Soviet undergraduate engineering training—the fact that the average undergraduate has had no opportunity to develop the habits and attitudes of self-sufficiency needed for fruitful work at advanced levels. According to Soviet sources, the graduate work records of students with prior practical experience are better than those of the engineering student who enters *aspirantura* without any experience and directly after the defense of his undergraduate diploma project.

Relative Shortage of Qualified Applicants

Why the failure to recruit a sufficient number of students with practical experience for graduate training? At an important polytechnic institute (Kharkov), for instance, only 25 per cent of the students accepted for graduate training during the period 1950–1955 had had prior practical experience.[34] One answer given with variations in the Soviet press runs, typically:

> . . . a paradoxical situation: the best qualified persons employed in production as a rule are deprived of the opportunity to enroll for graduate studies inasmuch as, being the leading production workers, they are needed by the enterprises.[35]

It appears, then, that the prospective graduate student cannot always obtain the required release from the employing ministry. Another problem, according to Soviet accounts, has been one of finances: a young engineer earning as much as 1,800 or 2,000 rubles per month after two years of employment following his graduation has had to think twice before embarking on a 3-year course of graduate work on the scholarship of 680 rubles per month offered apparently in the majority of cases, a discrepancy frequently commented upon in the Soviet press. A recent writer stated, for instance:

> To the extent that the graduate scholarships have been lower than the salaries received by the majority of specialists with higher education employed in production, the latter were little interested in entering graduate school because to do so meant a lowering of their earnings.[36]

We would doubt that the potential student's decision is made simply in terms of rubles per month now, as the author of this comment suggests; it is certain, for instance, that the experienced Soviet student's assessment of the future benefits of an advanced degree versus the immeasurably greater administrative responsibility and political risks it entails is another factor which enters into his decision.

In any event, under the 1956 regulations, graduate scholarships were to be *equal* to the industrial earnings received by the applicant (but not more than 1,000 rubles per month)—a situation not unlike the currently practiced underwriting of graduate training expense by many industrial companies in the United States.

As to the general mechanism of selection and admission procedure at the graduate level, the important detail is the one mentioned at the beginning of this section: each accredited institution has a plan to fulfill. In theory, admissions are on a competitive basis by examinations, but there is abundant evidence that for some years it has been difficult enough for Soviet institutions to fill the graduate admissions quotas at all, let alone competitively.[37] Generally speaking, the academic qualification of the student is not by itself a sufficient factor in the selection process; and for many fields of Soviet *aspirantura* it appears to be not even a categorically necessary factor. The future *kandidat* of historical or political sciences, for instance, is likely to have been accepted for graduate training on other than academic grounds, as is suggested in the following (1955) comment of Professor A. M. Ladyzhenskii (Moscow University):

> Individuals have often been designated [for graduate training] with the uppermost consideration being not their abilities and predisposition toward scientific work but other at times very valuable but not academic qualities.[38]

There is no reason to assume that the relative shortage of qualified applicants is uniformly distributed in the various fields of training; nor is there any evidence that in selecting students for graduate training in the physical sciences nonacademic considerations are uppermost. It is certain, nevertheless, that a politically suspect applicant would be disqualified.

Graduate Entrance Examinations

All individuals authorized to apply for admission to graduate schools* submit an application together with numerous documents, including the all-important autobiography and "political and work references." The applications are considered by a committee appointed by the director of the institution, which either rejects the applicant or authorizes him to appear for the qualifying examina-

---

* Persons who have just completed undergraduate education cannot apply for admission unless they are recommended for graduate study by the Academic Council.

tions in (1) the designated specialization, (2) a foreign language, and (3) "Foundations of Marxism-Leninism."*

On the basis of the data submitted by the applicant, including references to any work published by him, and the results of examinations, the committee forwards recommendations to the ministry having jurisdiction over the employment of the applicant. The ministry's decision is final. There are many indications, it should be added, that the ministries frequently reverse the negative findings of the committee and "attach" applicants of their own choice to graduate schools. We shall cite only one of many examples, this one involving the USSR Ministry of Higher Education which is concerned with the training of university teachers in sufficient numbers. A Soviet university professor writes:

> What is still worse [than the poor selection of graduate students], the Ministry is often guided by the mere fact that the case involves the training of a [potential] higher school teacher—therefore [the Ministry concludes] every applicant is suitable. . . . And, without considering our opinion, such persons have been "attached" to our institution [Kazan' University] for graduate instruction and the writing of a dissertation.[39]

Once formally accepted, all graduate students qualify for the graduate student scholarships, which have varied in amount from institution to institution† and which, since 1956–1957, as we have noted, have ranged up to 1,000 rubles per month.

4. Aspirantura: The Academic Plan

In contrast with the undergraduate procedures determined by fixed and uniform *uchebnyi* plans, Soviet *specialized* training at the graduate level is based on individual plans worked out for each student separately but in accordance with the requirements of a particular predesignated graduate specialty. In 1954, to cite some examples, the Engineering Physics Institute in Moscow accepted graduate students for training in the following specialties: computers, electronics, automation and telemechanics, experimental physics, and theoretical

* Since 1953 "persons who have demonstrated competency in scientific and practical work and who have published scientific works or hold certificates of invention" may be excused from having to take entrance examinations.

† For example:

	Rubles per month
1954–55 Ordzhonikidze Aviation Institute	780
1955–56 Estonian Academy (research) institutes	680
1943–44 USSR Academy (research) institutes	900
1943–44 Georgian Academy (research) institutes	700

physics; the Moscow Aviation Institute (MAI) accepted graduate students in all specialties of aeronautical engineering and, it should be noted, in a number of fields not specifically related to aeronautics, among them higher mathematics, physics, machine tools and cutting tools, and theory of mechanisms and machines; the Academy of Sciences Institute of Physical Problems offered graduate courses in theoretical physics, low-temperature physics, low-temperature techniques, structure of matter, molecular physics, and physics of magnetic phenomena. The fields of graduate specialization have been centrally designated for each institution from year to year, in some instances with total disregard of the available academic personnel and facilities.[40]

The 1955–1956 distribution of graduate students, by fields of study at the educational institutions and research institutes, is given in Table 56. It will be noted that, as at the undergraduate level, engineering, physical, and mathematical sciences are emphasized at the graduate level, with 41.6 per cent of *aspirantura* enrollment being in these categories of specialization.

The Term of Graduate Instruction

The normal term of *aspirantura* is 3 years, culminated by the defense of a dissertation leading to the degree of candidate of sciences. Depending apparently on the prior experience and achievement level of the student, advanced standing can be granted with a corresponding reduction of the term, usually to 2 years. There is also, however, a 1-year *aspirantura,* designed mainly for the upgrading of university instructors with prior teaching experience. "The Ministry of Higher Education is permitted," one source stated in 1954, "every year to assign 400 university assistants and instructors to *aspirantura* for a term up to 1 year for the writing of a candidate's dissertation."[41] The source, however, adds that in the period 1948–1953 only 1,169 persons were so assigned. Another source in 1953 stated that 425 students were enrolled each year in 1-year *aspirantura* courses designed to prepare for the teaching of "Foundations of Marxism-Leninism," "Political Economy," and "Philosophy" in institutions of higher education; 600 new *kandidat* degree holders were thus trained during 1948–1953.[42] Considering the relatively small Soviet total output of candidates, these figures are highly significant.

The Graduate Curriculum

A complete 3-year graduate course has included preparation for and passing examinations in a number of subjects which constitute the

TABLE 56. GRADUATE (*Aspirantura*) ENROLLMENT BEGINNING OF 1956
TOTAL NUMBER AND DISTRIBUTION BY BRANCHES OF SCIENCE
AND BY TWO TYPES OF GRADUATE TRAINING FACILITIES
USSR

Branch of Science	Enrolled in		Total Enrollment	
	Educational Institutions	Research Institutes	Students	Per Cent
Engineering	4,562	4,796	9,358	31.9
Physics-Mathematics	1,983	872	2,855	9.7
Subtotal	6,545	5,668	12,213	41.6
Agriculture and Veterinary Medicine	910	1,654	2,564	8.7
Philology	1,736	428	2,164	7.4
Medicine and Pharmaceutics	1,624	540	2,164	7.4
History and Philosophy	1,432	632	2,064	7.0
Economics	1,295	515	1,810	6.2
Biology	583	843	1,426	4.8
Chemistry	483	835	1,318	4.5
Geology-Mineralogy	504	756	1,260	4.3
Education	765	272	1,037	3.5
Arts	333	97	430	1.5
Law	274	93	367	1.3
Geography	212	147	359	1.2
Architecture	78	108	186	0.6
Total	16,774	12,588	29,362	100.0
Per Cent	57.1	42.9	100.0	

Total graduate enrollment includes:	Thousands	Per Cent
Full-time students	21.4	72.8
Part-time students	8.0	27.2

Source: Kul'turnoye stroitel'stvo SSSR, 1956, pp. 255–257.

so-called "candidate's minimum," and, until 1956–1957, the writing
and defense of a dissertation was obligatory.* The "candidate's minimum" in recent years has been limited to only two (instead of the
former five or six) professional subjects of instruction closely related
to the particular specialty and the more narrow area of specialization
of the student, one foreign language, and, whatever the major field of

* Since 1953, the directors of educational institutions—but apparently not of
the research institutes—have been authorized to permit qualified individuals to
meet the "candidate's minimum" requirements by examination at the time of entry
for a shortened term (up to two years) which is devoted to the writing of a
dissertation.

study, an extensive course of instruction and examination in Marxism-Leninism.

We need not comment here on graduate training in Marxism-Leninism except to note that, as in the undergraduate curricula, it takes up a very significant part of the student's time and that failure to pass the test in the context of the currently required orthodoxy is fatal.*

The graduate study of a foreign language formally calls for 60 hours of class instruction (in groups of five students) and, according to one source, oral and written translation of not less than 300 pages of text. In the Soviets' own evaluation, the average quality of instruction and the level of achievement attained by the student in foreign languages are not so impressive as one would expect on the basis of the time allotted in Soviet curricula to foreign languages.† Although nominally a candidate in some fields of study is apparently expected to demonstrate proficiency in two foreign languages, a 1955 Soviet source states that no definite standards for the study of a second language at the graduate level have been maintained:

> The absence of concrete directives on the number of hours to be devoted to the study of the second language and on the level of expected achievement complicates the organization of graduate work and frequently prevents the inclusion of the second language course in the student's individual schedule, even when the necessity for this course is dictated by the [student's] specialty and the topic [of his dissertation].[43]

The preparation for and the examinations in the foreign language or languages and "philosophy" take up the best part or all of the first graduate year. Up to about half a year, in the aggregate, is spent in the preliminaries and mechanical details of arranging the dissertation for defense. Thus the time normally available to the student for advanced work in the field of his specialization for the required teaching practice, for the laboratory and bibliographic research on the topic

* For one of the most outspoken Soviet articles which inadvertently reveals the character, quality, and role of "social science" in Soviet universities the reader is referred to an article by S. V. Kaftanov, "Zadachi kafedr obshchestvennykh nauk v novom uchebnom godu" (The Tasks of the Social Science Departments in the New Academic Year), *Vestnik vysshei shkoly*, No. 10, October 1953, in which the then Deputy Minister of Culture, USSR, gives an early warning on the forthcoming posthumous purge of Stalin. Example: " . . . there are departments of social sciences which as yet have not drawn conclusions from the latest directives of the Party . . . " (p. 9).

† Six years in the secondary schools, 4 years in college, and about a year in graduate school.

of his dissertation, and, finally, for the writing of the dissertation itself is approximately 1½ years.*

The topic of the dissertation is selected in the earliest stage of *aspirantura*. If, to use as an example the narrowly specialized engineering training at the graduate level, the selected topic is "The Application of Metal Spraying in Repairs on Tractors and Agricultural Machinery,"[44] the student's course work would include a specialized course in metallography, as a foundation for the specific technique under his study, and in "technology of repairs on tractors and agricultural machinery," the general area of his specialization, followed by examinations. Unless resident facilities are available, arrangements may be made for such a student to study experimental techniques and to conduct experiments (1 to 3 months) at an industrial research institute, such as the Technological Research Institute on the Repair and Operation of Tractors and Agricultural Machinery. His dissertation, accordingly, may have two parts, or chapters, such as "The Present Status of Techniques for the Restoration of Machine Parts and the Place of Metal Spraying in This Field of Technology" and "Metal Spraying as a Means of Restoring Worn Parts."†

One of the major criteria by which a Soviet engineering dissertation is rated is its relevance to current industrial or manufacturing problems. The Deputy Director of Kharkov Polytechnic Institute, for instance, criticized the quality of the institute's own candidate dissertations because few of them dealt with concrete problems:

> It suffices to say that only twenty-two among the one hundred dissertations defended by the graduate students of the Institute in 1950–1955 have yielded practical suggestions which were adopted by the industry and were published. . . .[45]

Judged by the criteria of immediate usefulness, the part-time graduate engineering students often have been credited with important contributions made in the course of their research and the writing of their dissertations, both of which bear directly on some technological problem of the employing organization. The term of part-time *aspirantura*, 3 years or less, is set for each student at the time of admission depending on the level of prior training and experience. Em-

---

* Graduate students may also be employed on an hourly or part-time basis in teaching or as research assistants—a very important factor, especially for the part-time graduate students professionally employed at the research institutes while also working toward an advanced degree.

† The titles and brief descriptions of defended dissertations are from time to time selectively published in various academic and scientific journals of the Soviet Union, e.g., *Izvestiya akademii nauk SSSR*.

ployed individuals qualified to apply for admission to institutions offering graduate training by correspondence are entitled to a 10-day leave of absence (without pay) for the purpose of taking the entrance examinations, and thereafter are given up to 30 days (plus travel time) per year for consultations, examinations, laboratory work, and, finally, the defense of the dissertation.

Although the dissertation is supposed to be completed and defended within the specified term of *aspirantura,* relatively few Soviet graduate students are able to meet this requirement; and a relatively large number drop out upon the expiration of the term or earlier without having even begun to write one. This last fact is difficult to explain, considering the apparent efforts on the part of everyone concerned to assist the graduate student in every step of his training, including the writing of the dissertation. In fact, Soviet comments suggest that altogether too much assistance is at times given, perhaps in the efforts to fulfill the Plan. As in the past, it is with reference to the conduct of graduate training in the social sciences that the recent criticisms have been the sharpest. Here is a very typical comment:

> Our [hypothetical] *kandidat* entered graduate study actually without any competition: it was necessary for the school to fulfill the plan of enrollment for graduate training—by whatever means.
>
> . . . . . .
>
> The grades received by our *kandidat* in the course examinations, including that in his major subject, political economy, were "passable." It was then the question could have been raised—and in fact was raised—whether he should not be detached from *aspirantura.* But the student's supervisor and the head of the department were told that the future *kandidat* must be helped with the dissertation, that a dropout must not be permitted.[46]

But such criticism has not been limited to graduate training in the social sciences. "You do not have to be a scientist, but you must get to be a *kandidat,*" is said to be a common academic quip in the Soviet Union. A physicist, Corresponding Member of the USSR Academy, V. D. Kuznetsov,* is only one of the many Soviet educators to admit the pressure of the Plan throughout the system; he said:

> The responsibility for the defense of the dissertation by a graduate student on time often is placed upon the supervisor. Such an approach to the question assumes that every graduate student must without fail become a scientific worker. . . .[47]

A similar comment may be quoted to point out—in the words of two

---

* Born 1887, professor (Tomsk University) since 1920, member of the Communist Party since 1945.

Soviet professors at schools of engineering—the effect of the pressures exerted by the Plan upon the quality of dissertations:

> As everyone knows, nowadays it is not the graduate student himself who first bears the responsibility for defending his dissertation on time but his thesis supervisor. Consequently, certain supervisors, wishing to avoid "unpleasantness," either pass the student with a poorly prepared dissertation or directly participate in the writing thereof.[48]

Academician M. N. Tikhomirov, Moscow University historian, writing in July 1956, concluded that the completion of a dissertation in the shortest possible time, rather than its quality, had become the major criterion: "The earlier a graduate student completes [his dissertation] the higher he and his supervisor are rated."[49] Still another Soviet university professor likened the present position of the graduate thesis supervisors to that of the Soviet secondary school teachers in an earlier period when "their work was judged by the students' grades."[50]

Nevertheless, the fact remains that relatively few Soviet *aspirantura* students are able to complete their dissertations on time. Thus, for instance, during a 7-year period (1948–1955) 6,757 students completed the prescribed term of Soviet *aspirantura* in "universities, economic institutes, and law schools," and of these only 28.5 per cent (1,925 students) defended their dissertations on time.[51] Imperfect as this index may be as a measure of quality, it could nevertheless serve as a very rough but objective indicator of the qualitative difference in Soviet graduate training by fields of study. The only set of comparative figures we can cite refers to the experience of a single important institution, Kazan State University (est. 1804). Mrs. E. I. Tikhvinskaya, Professor of Geology, gave the per cent of graduate students for the 11-year period (1944–1954) who failed to complete their dissertations on time, by categories, as follows:[52]

Broad Field of Graduate Work	Per Cent Failing to Complete on Time
Physics-mathematics	About 33 per cent
Natural sciences	35 to 50
(in certain disciplines	more than 50)
Humanities	
"Social sciences"	75
Literature, language, linguistics	83
Pedagogy	More than 83
History of the USSR	More than 83

The reader will at once note how closely the ranking suggested by these percentages corresponds to that indicated by many other factors heretofore considered, including those which condition Soviet training at the undergraduate level. The fact that the sweeping changes in the prerequisites for graduate training announced in August 1956 did not apply to students in physics-mathematical specialties would also indicate that Soviet graduate training in these fields has been much more effective than in others, including engineering. It appears that by all standards, including the quality of selection, Soviet graduate training in mathematics and physics, to take one extreme, should be rated very much higher than graduate training in History of the USSR, to take the other extreme.

Procedure in Awarding the Candidate's Degree

The Soviet administrative machinery which governs the graduate student from the time he completes his dissertation to the moment he may officially become a *kandidat* of sciences is complex, and its gears grind slowly. Once the dissertation is approved by the thesis supervisor, the author prepares a brief summary (*avtoreferat*) which is endorsed by his thesis supervisor and printed for distribution. A few copies are mailed automatically to the institutions of identical "profile" for reference and comments; the author of the dissertation distributes additional copies. It is said, however, that the effectiveness of these summaries as a means of obtaining evaluations and critical comments is very low, in most cases the distribution of *avtoreferaty* being a pure formality.

Much more important and in many cases decisive is the next stage—the preliminary and final evaluations of the dissertation by two or more officially appointed "opponents," one of whom must be a *doktor* of sciences. The preliminary evaluation by the opponents having been made, the seeker of the degree must submit that evaluation accompanied by a formal and extensively documented request for the privilege of defending the submitted dissertation. If his request is granted, the opponents' final role is to make a detailed analysis of the dissertation and determine whether it meets the official requirements whereby

> . . . the dissertation . . . must reveal general theoretical competence in the given discipline, specialized knowledge in the questions dealt with, and the ability to conduct independent scientific research which must be expressed by achieving in the dissertation a new scientific result.

The opponents' role is a difficult one inasmuch as they too must be aware of the Plan. A member of the Academy of Artillery Sciences,

Professor G. V. Zimelev, in an extensive (1948) article entitled "To Increase the Scientific Importance of Evaluations Made by the Official Opponents," analyzed the then existing practices in part as follows:

> In the beginning everything is as it should be: the work is subjected to real criticism. Its shortcomings are revealed, along with the positive qualities; the errors of theory are underscored; in short, an objective evaluation of the dissertation is given. But, finally, one arrives at the concluding paragraph; and here in most cases one resorts to well-standardized closing statements such as, for instance, "The indicated shortcomings not at all lower the over-all value . . . the author fully deserves to be granted an academic degree."[53]

The author of this quotation further suggests that in many instances the concluding paragraph is written, as it were, first, and that the body of the opponents' reports is taken up by a description rather than an analysis of the work. He also cites a few examples, including a half-page evaluation given at the Leningrad Institute of Railroad Engineering in which:

> . . . four lines were allotted to "scientific" criticism, as follows: "Certain hastiness in the exposition of the subject and some stylistic roughness could be considered as shortcomings of the dissertation; but neither the former nor the latter in any way lower the quality of this work."

The student's thesis supervisor, the opponents, and the author of the dissertation orally present their views at a meeting of the academic council, which, on the basis of a simple majority by secret ballot, decides whether or not to accept the dissertation and—with reference to *kandidat* dissertations—to award the corresponding academic degree. Doctoral dissertations are accepted (or rejected) provisionally, the academic council having the authority only to recommend the award of a doctor's degree by the Higher Attestation Commission (VAK) of the Ministry of Higher Education. Although in the published rules the decisions of the councils on the awards of *kandidat* degrees are referred to as "final," there is frequent mention of such decisions having been rescinded by VAK—the "finality" of the councils' decisions notwithstanding.[54]

VAK's apparently direct influence on the Ministry's policies in accrediting an institution for graduate work has also been used as a means to improve academic standards.[55] The August 1956 directive appointed seventy-seven individuals to serve as members of VAK under the chairmanship of the Minister of Higher Education and redefined the Commission's functions. With reference to dissertations, the subsequently issued rules provided for a review by the Commission of *all* dissertations defended at the institutions of higher education and at research institutes at both the candidate and doctoral levels. Furthermore, in the words of a Soviet reporter, the Commission was instructed

> . . . to suspend, for a period up to two years, the right to hear the defense of dissertations of those academic councils which should award an academic degree for a meritless dissertation or should allow gross infractions of the prescribed procedural rules for the defense of dissertations.[56]

Thus the policing power of VAK, which in 1955 was described as "a menacing and not infrequently unchallengeable power,"[57] had been increased—in the attempt, no doubt, to supplement or to substitute for the authority of the institutions themselves to maintain the desired academic standards.

A Candidate's Dissertation No Longer a Requirement

The directives issued in August 1956 also prescribe a fundamental change in the heretofore basic requirements of both candidate and doctoral formal training. The writing and defense of a dissertation is now optional with each graduate student working toward a degree of *kandidat nauk;* however, those students who complete *aspirantura* and defend a dissertation "shall have a privileged status in the [subsequent] assignment to fill the vacancies at research institutions, institutions of higher education, and industrial laboratories." In lieu of an obligatory dissertation, all graduate students must, as heretofore, pass the "candidate's minimum" examinations and must carry out a scholarly work project *(nauchnuyu rabotu),* reporting on it at the academic council of the institution or at a scientific conference. A noteworthy detail of the new provisions is that the graduate curriculum of *all students* at the institutions of higher education (versus research institutes) now includes apparently extensive teaching practice. The distinction thus made between the two categories of graduate facilities would suggest a further step toward specialization in research versus teaching, upon which we have already commented; yet such a tendency would conflict with other recently introduced measures designed to expand the role of research in Soviet higher education.

Formal Doctoral Training Abolished

The 1956 regulations also did away with the *doktorantura* type of postgraduate training which previously was the resident program leading to the highest Soviet academic degree, *doktor nauk*—doctor of sciences.*

Originally, when the institution of academic degrees was restored in the 1930's, the award of the doctor's degree was made normally contingent upon a successful defense of a doctoral dissertation by anyone holding a degree of *kandidat*. A doctoral dissertation was expected

> . . . to reveal independent research and work resulting in a solution or a theoretical generalization of scientific problems, or a scientifically valid formulation of new problems which represent considerable scientific interest.[58]

No prerequisite resident study or interim examinations were originally prescribed for those intending to write and defend a doctoral dissertation; and the original 1937 legislation on advanced training provided no organizational counterpart of *aspirantura* for training at the doctoral level. Some years later, however, a 2-year *doktorantura* was introduced in the attempt to increase the rate of doctoral training and thus to increase the proportion of senior members in the teaching staffs of the universities and institutes.

We are not certain for how many years and on how large a scale the *doktorantura* training had been conducted prior to its abandonment beginning with 1956–1957,[59] but in 1955 it was said that a significant proportion of the future doctors of sciences were enrolled in *doktorantura*. Apparently this type of training was not effective. In recent years, at least, the *doktorantura* has been consistently criticized as being incompatible with the level and character of achievement expected of the Soviet *doktor nauk*. In the 1955 Soviet discussions of the graduate school problems, *doktorantura* found few defenders:

> Rigid regimentation of the time allotted for doctoral training is altogether inadmissible. As is known, our [Soviet] doctor of sciences degree is awarded to fully mature scientists who have done original scientific work and who are independently developing one or another school of scientific thought. And yet *doktorantura*—as it is conducted in many cases—does not correspond to such demands and, at times, places the seeker of the doctor's degree in the same "hothouse" conditions as those [prevailing] in *aspirantura*.[60]

More specifically, it has been said that under the *doktorantura* plan

---

* Some examples are "doctor of physico-mathematical science," "doctor of technical science," "doctor of historical science," and so forth. Soviet *kandidat* degrees are similarly identified with one of the eighteen officially designated categories: physics-mathematics, chemistry, biology, geology-minerals, technical, agriculture, history, economics, philosophy, philology, geography, law, pedagogy, medicine, pharmaceutics, veterinary sciences, art, and architecture.

the postgraduate student, besides working under a regular thesis supervisor, had a number of formally designated consultants, each a specialist in the field of the student's research and dissertation. As in the case of *aspirantura* training, "the department conducting doctoral training and the administration of the institution were responsible for 'the timely fulfillment of the plan' for the doctoral training."[61]

It would appear that *doktorantura* was originally instituted as a consequence of bureaucratic pressures from above; and it may have helped slightly to increase the number of doctors among the faculty members in Soviet universities and other schools of higher education. Its qualitative effect, however, has been questioned at all levels of Soviet published opinion. Forecasting, no doubt, the official announcement whereby a month later this type of training was to be abolished, Professor A. D. Aleksandrov, Rector of Leningrad University, in July 1956 wrote:

> All hopes for the growth of scientific cadres are usually placed on *aspirantura* and *doktorantura;* inferentially, the individual guidance [of graduate students] is presumed to be the solution. Even the doctors of science, according to that point of view, must be "nursed along" under suitable guidance—a contradiction of the very concept of "doctor," that is, a scientist who has made a significant, independent, original contribution to science.
>
> Experience has shown that *doktorantura* is not a sufficiently effective method for the training of cadres because, as is known, only a minority of those who are assigned to *doktorantura* defend dissertations. In the meantime, at Leningrad University, for instance, the number to defend doctoral dissertations has grown from four in 1952 to fourteen in 1955, but not all to the credit of *doktorantura:* only two persons of the thirty-two who defended doctoral dissertations in 1951–1955 were *doktorantura* students.[62]

In any case, *doktorantura* has been recently abolished. As one Soviet source explains, the Central Committee of the Communist Party decided that

> . . . the preparation of a doctoral dissertation should be based on an active participation of scientific workers in research at scientific institutions, institutions of higher education, and industrial and agricultural enterprises.[63]

The new rules, incidentally, provide "a creative leave of absence"—up to 6 months, with pay—for the writing of doctoral dissertations for persons engaged in industry, agriculture, or teaching who may be recommended to do this by the academic councils of research or educational insitutions, or by scientific-technical councils of industrial and other ministries. Recent Party directives have also apparently slightly modified the criteria by which both the candidate and doctoral dissertations are henceforth to be judged. Our emphasis in the following quotation is added to show the new direction:

> Considerably higher requirements have been established for the dissertations. From now on, the candidate's dissertations must contain new scientific conclusions and *recommendations;* and the doctoral dissertations theoretical generalizations and solutions of new scientific problems which constitute a considerable contribution to science and *practical problems.*[64]

It will be some years before the implications and consequences of the 1956 changes in the organization and objectives of Soviet graduate training are clearly revealed.

5. Kandidat versus Ph.D.: A Postscript

American and other Western commentators have frequently been tempted to compare qualitatively the levels of training corresponding to the American Ph.D. and Master's degrees on the one hand and the Soviet *doktor* and *kandidat* of sciences on the other. But is there any single dimension or any combination of factors which make possible an objective and meaningful comparison of this nature? Even assuming that the American "Ph.D." and "Master" represent educational levels and degrees of quality which are definable within reasonably narrow limits—a highly unrealistic assumption—it is clear that the *kandidat*-through-*doktor* part of the Soviet academic spectrum encompasses too wide a qualitative range to be meaningfully defined in such terms.

There are, of course, certain variables which can be expressed with some precision for both systems of education, one of them being the chronological age at which individuals qualify for the degrees. A Soviet student is likely to be several years older when he becomes a *kandidat* than an American student when he receives his M.A. or M.S. after 1 or 2 years of graduate work; the Soviet *doktor* of sciences is distinctly in a much older age group than is the American Ph.D. at the time the respective degrees are awarded. The age variable alone, with what it implies as to experience, makes any direct comparison unrealistic.

Another variable is the time spent in formal training. The Soviet *doktor* (except for those who earned their degrees in the now abolished *doktorantura*) could not properly be included in any time comparison since, in theory and apparently in fact, the award of the doctor's degree in the Soviet Union has normally meant recognition of scientific *achievement* attained in the course of professional work and not simply the acquisition of formal academic *qualifications* which is generally signified by an American Ph.D. degree. By the time measure, the Soviet *kandidat* would appear to rate distinctly higher than the American M.S. One could make the following "computation":

Education after Age Seven	Years of Study	
	USSR	USA
Elementary, junior and secondary	10	11
Undergraduate	5	4
First graduate	3	1 or 2
Soviet *Kandidat*	18	
American M.S.		16 or 17

However, the very listing of the stages of education brings to the fore not only the many questions which have been dealt with in this study but also other equally important factors in Soviet education and the Soviet social system generally which are outside our scope and which, since they critically determine the net effect of professional training per unit of time spent in formal study, make any time comparison meaningless in itself.

At this point we feel compelled to point out that it is the factor of time which has been taken by many observers as the major basis for equating the Soviet *kandidat* with the American Ph.D.—categorically or with some qualifications. One American report published in 1955 concluded:

> In terms of formal requirements, which include three years of postgraduate study (or its equivalent in professional experience) and the defense of a dissertation, the Soviet degree of *kandidat* is the near equivalent of the American Ph.D. Qualified comparative evaluations of *kandidat* and Ph.D. degrees are too few either to confirm or to modify this provisional appraisal.[65]

Furthermore, the report from which the above is quoted includes two charts which at least inferentially suggest direct comparability between *kandidat* and Ph.D. science degrees.* Clearly, the implication of the

---

* One of these charts (Figure 5), entitled "US and USSR Higher Degrees in Science Awarded Annually," is a time series giving the estimated number of *kandidat* and the actual number of Ph.D. degrees awarded in science each year, 1930–1955. Another chart (Figure 6), entitled "US and USSR Persons Holding Higher Degrees in the Major Scientific Fields as of July 1954," gives the distribution of 64,000 Soviet candidates and 51,000 American Ph.D.'s. These data, in one form or another, have been extensively reproduced in American periodicals and the daily press.

quoted text and of the charts is that the American M.S. degree is totally outside the range considered—a position which we cannot wholly share.

In January 1956 Professor John Turkevich of Princeton University published an article in which he placed the *kandidat* level with greater precision and within the limits designated by American graduate degrees (M.S. and Ph.D.):

> The *kandidat* degree is of slightly lower standard than the American Ph.D. but definitely more advanced than our M.Sc.[66]

The tables accompanying Professor Turkevich's article give figures for the upper end of his scale showing statistics on the Soviet candidates and American Ph.D.'s—but *not* on the M.S. awards in the United States.* In March 1956 a shorter article by Professor Turkevich, "The Soviet's Scientific Elite" (*Saturday Review*, March 24, 1956), compared the *kandidat* degree with the American Ph.D., but without reference to the American M.S. degree in the text; and a pictograph shown on the adjacent page was entitled "The Battle of Ph.D.'s," implying equivalence of the Soviet *kandidat* and the American Ph.D.

If the comparison of degrees is limited to the physical sciences, a formula similar to that given by Professor Turkevich is perhaps as good as can be offered for a first approximation: the level of training a Soviet physical scientist reaches by the time he becomes a *kandidat* is higher than that corresponding to an American M.S. degree and is likely to be near or equal to that of the American Ph.D. Similar formulas (suitably modified depending on the field of training) which

---

* Table 2—Number of Ph.D. Degrees Granted in U.S. and *Kandidat* Degrees in USSR, 1952–1955; Table 4—Number of Individuals Holding Advanced Degrees in Science in USSR (*Kandidat*) and U.S. (Ph.D.).

The figures shown in Table 2 for the United States must refer only to some *part* of the total, although this fact is not noted either in the heading of the table or in the text. Table 2, for example, shows the following figures for 1955 (in thousands):

Degrees	1955
American Ph.D.	4.4
Soviet *Kandidat*	8.4

In 1955 the total number of Ph.D. degrees awarded in the United States was 8,840; the figure shown in the table (4.4 thousand) may refer to Ph.D. degrees in sciences (excluding social sciences, education, arts, and others). As to the Soviet *kandidat*, the total number of students who completed *aspirantura* in 1955 was 7,607—smaller than shown in the table; and obviously not all of them by far were in science—if that was the category the table was meant to illustrate.

Sources of our figures:

(1) U.S. Office of Education, Circular 461, "Earned Degrees Conferred . . . 1954–55."
(2) Table 55.

would attempt to define the levels of Soviet professional training in terms of American degree equivalents may be useful for a rough general orientation. But no such "table of equivalents" can possibly provide a factor by which the rates of training at advanced levels in the Soviet Union and the United States need only be "multiplied" in order to arrive at a numerical index of relative increment to scientific and technological manpower capabilities. Moreover, we would not wholly exclude either the American M.S. level of training or statistics on the American M.S. degrees from any computations calculated to consider realistically the American counterpart of the Soviet *kandidat* training—even in numbers alone.*

At the end of the preceding chapter we summed up and generalized our impressions on the relative level of professional preparation attained by undergraduates in the Soviet Union and the United States, taking for our examples a physicist and an engineer. We placed the Soviet undergraduate physicist at or near the level corresponding to one year of graduate work in physics in the United States—*with no significant differences in the kind of training*. We rated the hypothetical Soviet-trained engineer at or near the American undergraduate level—*with important and highly significant differences in the character of training* which make any direct comparison of doubtful value. We would express a similar judgment on the levels attained in the Soviet Union through the many types of *aspirantura* versus American graduate programs leading to the second-level degree and to the doctorate. No significant differences are apparent in the kind and level of professional preparation of a Soviet *kandidat* in physico-mathematical sciences and an American Ph.D. in comparable fields of specialization. As to mechanical engineering in particular, the differences between the kind and orientation of training a Soviet graduate student receives and American training are so significant that any direct comparison of Soviet graduate training with the American M.S. and Ph.D. levels of engineering education would be of little or no practical value.

It is certain that, by qualitative criteria, Soviet engineering training at all levels, including the graduate, has lagged materially behind the

---

* Without suggesting any specific direct equivalence, we would cite here for the reader's ready reference the aggregate statistics on graduations and advanced degrees awarded in 1955 in the Soviet Union and the United States:

Soviet Union		United States	
Graduates, including correspondence	250,000	First-level degree	287,401
Aspirantura, including correspondence	7,607	Second-level degree	58,204
Awarded *doktor nauk* (approx.)	500	Doctorate	8,840

training in physics and related branches of science. This is not, of course, uniquely or exclusively a Soviet problem, deriving as it does from the revolutionary advances in science and the greatly accelerated pace in the expansion of technological horizons everywhere. In the Soviet Union, however, the advancement in the quality of engineering training has been further hampered by a variety of institutional factors —such as the vertical organization of training facilities, curricula, and teaching personnel by industries—and other factors, many of which have been examined in this survey.

NOTES TO CHAPTER 11

[1] Soviet official figures, 1929–1955 graduates:

Type of Training	Thousands
Resident	2,565
Extension	378
Total number of graduates	2,943

The National Economy of the USSR, 1956, p. 235.

[2] "From the time academic degrees were re-established more than 9,000 doctoral and about 80,000 candidate dissertations have been defended in our country [the Soviet Union]," *Vestnik vysshei shkoly*, No. 3, March 1956, p. 7.

[3] Selected legislative documents on the job assignment of graduates are given in Chapter XIII, *Vysshaya shkola*, compiled by M. I. Movshovich, Moscow, 1945. There is also a 1948 edition. A letter to the editor (*Vestnik vysshei shkoly*, No. 1, January 1956) spoke of the need for an updated reissue of this reference book.

[4] *Vestnik vysshei shkoly*, No. 2, February 1955, pp. 2 f.

[5] *Vestnik vysshei shkoly*, No. 11, November 1953.

In this connection it may be noted that special 2-year courses were organized to train 700 agricultural technicians up to the engineers' level at five leading institutes for the mechanization of agriculture.

[6] *Vestnik vysshei shkoly*, No. 7, July 1955, p. 2.

[7] *Vestnik vysshei shkoly*, No. 10, October 1955, p. 2.

[8] Supplements No. 1 and 2, Decision of the SNK SSSR, March 20, 1937, No. 464, cited in *Vysshaya shkola*, compiled by M. I. Movshovich, Moscow, 1945, pp. 245 ff.

[9] *Ibid.*, p. 176.

[10] *Ibid.*, p. 185.

[11] See, for instance, *Spravochnik dlya postupayushchik v aspiranturu* (Handbook for Those Entering *Aspirantura*), Moscow: "Moskovskaya pravda," 1954, p. 5, paragraph 13a.

[12] V. Ryanzhin (Learned Secretary, Presidium, Estonian SSR Academy of Sciences), "Novoye v podgotovke nauchnykh kadrov" (What Is New on the Training of Scientific Manpower), *Sovetskaya Estoniya*, September 13, 1956, p. 3.

[13] V. Kirillin, "O podgotovke nauchnykh kadrov" (On the Training of Scientific Cadres), *Pravda*, August 29, 1956, p. 2.

[14] August 20, 1956, issued by the Central Committee of the Party and the Council of Ministers.

[15] Alexander Vucinich, *The Soviet Academy of Sciences,* Hoover Institute Studies, Stanford: Stanford University Press, January 1956, p. 1.

According to *BSE,* as of 1949 the Academy had 56 research institutes, 15 laboratories, 4 observatories, 7 museums, 5 field stations, and 51 committees or commissions engaged in research work. (*BSE,* 2nd Ed., Vol. I, 1949, p. 571.)

[16] The number of "scientific research institutes, their branches, and departments" in 1955 was said to be 1,180. This count, no doubt, includes the various research institutes under the academies of sciences. In 1955 "scientific institutions employed 96.5 thousand scientific workers" (versus 119.1 thousand in institutions of higher education and 8.3 thousand in "enterprises, administrative apparatus, and other institutions"). *The National Economy of the USSR, 1956,* p. 239.

[17] On the role and work of the USSR Academy of Sciences we refer the reader to the study already cited, Alexander Vucinich, *op. cit.*

The functioning of the industrial research institutes is illustrated and analyzed in *Soviet Education in Aeronautics: A Case Study,* by Leon Trilling; see particularly his Chapter VII, "Aeronautical Research Institutes and the Aircraft Industry."

[18] V. Ipat'ev, "Nauka v sovremennoi Rossii" (Science in Today's Russia), *Novyii zhurnal* (New York), No. 5, 1943, p. 294.

[19] Distributed as follows (number of branches shown in parentheses):

Physics	6	Nonferrous Metallurgy	5
Chemistry	27 (5)	Mining	4 (10)
Fuel	5 (2)	Geology-Geodesy	3 (2)
Power	7 (1)	Machine Building	14 (3)
Electrotechnics	6	Construction	12 (3)
Ferrous Metallurgy	6	Organization of Labor	4 (1)

Source: Cited by V. Ipat'ev, *ibid.,* p. 298, from *O nauchno-issledovatel'skikh institutakh* (On Science-Research Institutes), Commissariat of Heavy Industry, 1935.

[20] June 23, 1936, cited in *Vysshaya shkola,* compiled by M. I. Movshovich, 1945, p. 316.

[21] *Ibid.,* Decision No. 178, SNK SSSR, February 18, 1944.

[22] Letter to the editor, *Vestnik vysshei shkoly,* No. 10, October 1953, p. 62.

[23] E.g., *Vestnik vysshei shkoly,* No. 4, April 1956, p. 39.

[24] *Vestnik vysshei shkoly,* No. 6, June 1955, p. 4.

The statement, of course, tells nothing about the size or adequacy of allocation. The same source states that the expenditures for contract research during the same period "almost doubled"; but it should be remembered that prior to 1946 all engineering schools, except the polytechnic institutes, were under one or another ministry, and we do not know the 1946 reclassification of the budget, if any was made.

[25] N. G. Maksimovich (Director of the L'vov Polytechnic Institute), "Pervoocherednye voprosy organizatsii issledovatel'skoi raboty" (The Foremost Questions in the Organization of Research Work), *Vestnik vysshei shkoly,* No. 2, February 1956, p. 17.

[26] E. D. Kazakov (Doctor of Technical Sciences, Professor), "Uporyadochit planirovaniye khozdogovornoi tematiki" (To Bring Order into the Planning of Contract Research Topics), *Vestnik vysshei shkoly,* No. 2, February 1956, p. 24.

[27] Alexander Vucinich, *op. cit.,* p. 13.

[28] N. S. Arzhanikov (Professor, Chief of Administration, Polytechnic and Machine Construction Engineering Schools), "Shire ispol'zovat' nauchnye kadry vysshei

shkoly" (Broader Utilization of the Scientific Cadres of the Higher Schools), *Vestnik vysshei shkoly*, No. 9, September 1955, p. 8.

29 *Vestnik vysshei shkoly*, No. 12, December 1954, p. 3.

30 M. N. Tikhomirov, "O molodykh uchenykh i issledovatel'skoi rabote" (On Young Scientists and Research Work), *Vestnik vysshei shkoly*, No. 7, July 1956, p. 16.

(Academician Tikhomirov is an historian and he may refer specifically to research and education in his field; his conclusions, however, apply in varying degrees to other fields.)

31 Union Committee on the Higher School (VKVSh), January 2, 1944, Order No. 2, cited in *Vysshaya shkola*, compiled by M. I. Movshovich, 1945, p. 181.

32 E. D. Shlygin, "Prinimat' v aspiranturu proizvodstvennikov" (To Enroll Production Men into the Ranks of Graduate Students), *Vestnik vysshei shkoly*, No. 8, August 1955, p. 23.

33 Unless otherwise documented, our references to the latest directives on graduate training are from either "O podgotovke nauchnykh kadrov" (On the Training of Scientific Cadres), an article by V. Kirillin in *Pravda*, August 29, 1956, p. 2, or from "Novoye o podgotovke nauchnykh kadrov" (What Is New on the Training of Scientific Cadres), an article by V. Ryanzhin, in *Sovetskaya Estoniya*, September 13, 1956.

34 *Vestnik vysshei shkoly*, No. 3, March 1956, p. 45.

35 E. D. Shlygin, *op. cit.*

36 V. Ryanzhin, *op. cit.*

For an earlier similar comment see, e.g., *Vestnik vysshei shkoly*, No. 8, August 1955, p. 13.

37 For examples see *Vestnik vysshei shkoly*, such as No. 8, August 1955, pp. 2, 8, 31—to mention only a few.

38 *Vestnik vysshei shkoly*, No. 11, November 1955, p. 5.

39 *Vestnik vysshei shkoly*, No. 9, September 1955, p. 14.

40 E.g., Ural State University, *Vestnik vysshei shkoly*, No. 8, August 1955, p. 21.

41 *Vestnik vysshei shkoly*, No. 10, October 1954, p. 6.

42 *Vestnik vysshei shkoly*, No. 10, October 1953, p. 11.

43 M. I. Ainbinder and E. L. Shraiber, "Aspiranty dolzhny vladet' inostrannym yazykom" (Graduate Students Must Have Mastery of a Foreign Language), *Vestnik vysshei shkoly*, No. 8, August 1955, p. 45.

44 *Vestnik vysshei shkoly*, No. 10, October 1954, p. 10.

45 Doctor of Technical Sciences, Professor V. I. Atroshchenko, in *Vestnik vysshei shkoly*, No. 3, March 1956, p. 44.

46 A. I. Pilipenko (an economist) in *Vestnik vysshei shkoly*, No. 8, August 1955, p. 8.

47 *Vestnik vysshei shkoly*, No. 8, August 1955.

48 V. V. Bolotov (Leningrad Polytechnic Institute) and A. A. Melent'ev (Leningrad Engineering-Economics Institute), in *Vestnik vysshei shkoly*, No. 8, August 1955, p. 16. For similar admissions see, e.g., No. 11, November 1955, p. 11.

49 M. N. Tikhomirov, *op. cit.*, p. 15.

50 *Vestnik vysshei shkoly*, No. 8, August 1955, p. 20.

51 M. A. Prokof'ev (Deputy Minister of Higher Education) in *Vestnik vysshei shkoly*, No. 4, April 1955, p. 13.

Another example (Kazan University, 1944–1951):

44 per cent—completed their dissertations on time
31 per cent—were late, "some considerably late"
25 per cent—have not completed as of 1955.

Other sources (e.g., *Vestnik vysshei shkoly*, No. 8, August 1955, p. 20) suggest that the average for the USSR is about 30 per cent.

52 *Vestnik vysshei shkoly*, No. 8, August 1955, p. 25.

53 *Vestnik vysshei shkoly*, No. 3, March 1948, p. 24.

54 E.g., ". . . from 1948 to 1952 VAK rescinded the decisions of the councils involving nine doctoral and thirty-seven candidate dissertations [in social sciences]." (*Vestnik vysshei shkoly*, No. 10, October 1953.)

"In 1952–1953 . . . [VAK] rescinded 186 decisions of the councils . . . involving 65 on the award of the doctor's degree and 121—the candidate's degrees." (*Vestnik vysshei shkoly*, No. 9, 1953.)

55 In 1951–1952, for instance, VAK "for the last time warned [Kiev] University's Council that in the event similar errors [of granting a degree undeservedly] are made" the council of the particular faculty shall be denied the right to conduct defenses of the candidates' dissertations. (*Vestnik vysshei shkoly*, No. 11, November 1954, p. 56.)

56 V. Ryanzhin, *op. cit.*

57 Professor A. V. Mirtov (Gorkii University), in *Vestnik vysshei shkoly*, No. 10, October 1955, p. 33.

58 *Vysshaya shkola*, compiled by M. I. Movshovich, 1945, p. 245.

59 One source in 1955 refers to ". . . recently introduced *doktorantura* (on a full-time basis). . . ." (*Vestnik vysshei shkoly*, No. 9, September 1955, p. 14.)

60 V. V. Bolotov and A. A. Melent'ev, *op. cit.*, No. 8, August 1955, p. 17.

61 *Ibid.*

62 "Vazhneisheye sredstvo razvitiya nauchnovo tvorchestva" (The Most Important Means for the Development of Scientific Creativity), *Vestnik vysshei shkoly*, No. 7, July 1956, p. 25.

63 V. Ryanzhin, *op. cit.*

64 *Ibid.*

65 *Status and Trends in Soviet Scientific and Technical Manpower Resources* (mimeographed), May 4, 1955, Washington, D.C., 40 pp., p. 4.

66 John Turkevich, "Soviet Science in the Post-Stalin Era," *The Annals of the American Academy of Political and Social Science*, January 1956, p. 148.

CHAPTER

— 12

COMMENTS AND REFLECTIONS

Since we have limited our detailed analysis primarily to those aspects of the Soviet educational system which appear to be most directly related to the selection and training of engineers and scientists, the present volume has dealt with Soviet education in a highly restricted sense. Nevertheless, much of the material we have examined is equally applicable to the entire range of formal training—if not to education in the broadest sense of the term—in the Soviet Union. Moreover, the fundamentals of the Soviet philosophy of education and the main objectives of Soviet education also emerge clearly from the background and topical material examined in the preceding chapters; for the rationale and aims of Soviet education inevitably reflect the basic communist view of society and the place the individual occupies in it. We can, therefore, discern four all-embracing facts which set a context for reflections on the Soviet educational system as a whole.

The dominant feature of the communist state is the total control over political, economic, cultural, and social life exercised by a self-appointed and self-perpetuating Communist Party dictatorship. Its educational system, correspondingly, is an instrument designed solely to serve Communist Party interests; and the Communist Party dictatorship defines precisely what it wants of its educational system and what kinds of skills it needs at its command at any given time. It has a *proprietary* interest in training its subjects in whatever numbers and at whatever levels and categories of skill are needed for its designs and purposes. Thus two foundation facts of the Soviet educational system are the prescription of *national maximum* admissions quotas and the assurance that all designated vacancies are filled.

A third foundation fact stems from dictatorship's capacity to move by decree to adjust to changing circumstances and needs. As Cheops, in building his Great Pyramid, needed and used perhaps only one architect and a hundred thousand slaves, the Soviet dictatorship needed and used millions of inmates of "corrective labor" camps to dig the White Sea-Baltic Canal, to produce timber for export, to wash gold in the frozen Kolyma, to mine nickel in Noril'sk, coal in Vorkuta and Karaganda, and to build railroads, highways, and hydroelectric dams. But, if it was once rational for the Soviets, when they first launched the drive for industrialization, to dig a thousand-mile canal using only shovels and picks in the hands of 500,000 prisoners, the now enormously expanded Soviet industrial plant with its highly demanding technology and production calls for complex machinery, techniques, and processes and, therefore, an army of trained workers, technicians, engineers, and scientists. And so, ever since the formulation of the first Five Year Plan in 1928 and the adoption of the overriding objective to "catch up with and to outstrip" America—as if America could be measured exclusively in so many tons of coal and cast iron produced—technical training and other professional education in selected fields important to an industrial society have been energetically developed by the Soviets and are now conducted on a massive scale.

Fourth, and most important of all, although the history of education under Soviet dictatorship has not been static, although in the last few years radical alterations have been introduced in the organization, method, and plans for instruction throughout the system from the ten-year school to the postgraduate level, and although within the narrow limits of freedom set by the centralized control the means are publicly debated, experimented with, and frequently changed, the ends of Soviet education have not been modified since the inception of the regime 40 years ago. Accordingly, the organization and content of Soviet education reflect two dominant objectives: first, to inculcate a complete—and, if possible, devout and enthusiastic—commitment to the will and ways of the Communist Party; and second, to develop maximum technical competence for work in designated occupations and capacities. A good analogy could be drawn, it would seem, between the educational system of the Soviet Union as it has operated for 40 years and a military training program anywhere in *time of war*. The individual is subordinated, fields of training are prescribed and limited, with quotas in each category, and the best possible facilities and resources are mobilized for training in the most crucially needed fields.

It is with these four cardinal facts in mind that the following comments are made.

There is no doubt that Soviet education has achieved impressive gains in the quality of training since the early 1930's, when for a time standards were low indeed, especially in engineering. But, as the evidence examined by us conclusively shows, there is a wide variation in the quality of training afforded in the Soviet system, a condition not attributable so much to universal factors as to unique Soviet determinants, such as the importance of the ministry in behalf of which the training is conducted and the degree to which a given branch of knowledge is held to be incompatible with communist dogma.

The most spectacular achievement of the Soviet educational system— an achievement strongly emphasized by the Soviets, readily acknowledged by foreign observers, and endlessly cited by them in public speeches and the daily press—is the grand total of Soviet students. But total numbers should be considered in relation to some other magnitude by categories. It would be instructive, for instance, to have answers to a whole set of questions regarding Soviet schools. What per cent of the school-age children attend school—by age groups? How many tenth-grade students qualify for the Certificate of Maturity? How many apply for admission to colleges and universities in excess of the established quotas? What is the average actual school attendance versus the fall registration figures? How many among the undergraduate and graduate students are enrolled in the abbreviated emergency training programs? How many of the announced number of students—or how many not included in that number—are enrolled in the military schools; and how many in the Party schools? Answers to these and many other questions, which would permit us to see the quantitative dimensions of Soviet achievement in education in a clearer light, are not provided in Soviet statistics. But even the known, largely aggregate statistics and the derived figures which can be obtained from them clearly show that as to numbers the Soviet achievement in education is of somewhat less heroic proportions than the undifferentiated gross statistics imply.

As we have noted, for example, the great increases in Soviet college-level enrollment are largely attributable to the expansion of correspondence school education in recent years; but, since Soviet correspondence students form a distinct category, it is misleading to include their number at par with the resident students. Moreover, Soviet resident enrollment, including part-time evening students, in the last few years has been averaging less than one half the number of students enrolled in American universities and colleges. Relative to the population, the American resident college enrollment currently is close to 17 students per thousand of population and is rapidly growing; the corresponding figure for the Soviet Union is somewhat fewer than 7 per thousand.

However, if, instead of comparing the aggregate enrollment, we compare the number of engineering students, the (1956) ratio is approximately 2 to 1 in favor of the Soviets. Similarly, out of a smaller number of students in comparison with the American enrollment in secondary schools, junior colleges, normal schools, universities, and graduate schools, the Soviet educational system in the last few years has been training more students in science and technology and in certain other professional fields than American schools. The most conspicuous and significant example is in the ratio of engineering technicians in training, with the number of Soviet technicum graduates likely soon to approach approximately ten times the number of engineering technicians being trained in American technical institutes.

Whatever can be said of the numbers—and quality—in the Soviet educational system, the dimension that must above all be taken into account if we are to understand the nature of the Soviet educational system is the power of the Soviet dictatorship to allocate national resources, including intellectual resources, to its own ends. The degree of state control over manpower resources is exemplified by the obligation of every trained individual to work in a designated capacity and location for a number of years (in practical terms, indefinitely) after completing training.

Under Stalin, compliance with this requirement was substantially assured by the threat of direct punishment—a term in a forced labor camp. Under the "collective leadership," the harshness of enforcement has apparently been mitigated somewhat, with increased reliance being placed on exhortation and appeals to duty; and the many comments in the current Soviet press on the placement of graduates point to a considerable resistance on their part to accepting undesirable assignments. But graduates are still obligated to accept appointments. Despite Stalin's death and the subsequent relaxation of fear of police penalties, the statutory obligation of all graduates to take up designated work has been, to our knowledge, neither repealed nor modified; and it would be a mistake to believe—as Khrushchev would have the world believe—that the Soviet labor laws merely expressed Stalin's "cruelty." The need for compliance—if necessary under a threat of extreme punishment—arises not from the qualities of individual leaders but inevitably from the logic of communist philosophy and practice. The Soviet educational system must always be related to a basic problem of communist dictatorship: if the entire training program is controlled and organized for specific planned uses—as it is in the Soviet Union—can the distribution of trained manpower be left to chance?

A related problem, and one which is particularly important for the future course of Soviet education, is the problem of what to do with the ten-year school graduates. As far as we know, no statutory or "common law" provision exists whereby the ten-year school graduate is obligated to work in any designated or other capacity. In 1940, when Soviet labor laws were perfected to the ultimate of communist logic, the ten-year school graduates were not included in their strict provisions. At that time, since the number of ten-year school graduates was small, the majority were expected to enter institutions of higher education, and those who failed of admission were subject to military draft; there was thus no placement problem so far as the ten-year school graduates were concerned. But, as we have seen, from 1954 on, a surplus of ten-year school graduates has been accumulating. Whereas in 1950–1951 the total enrollment in the tenth grade was less than 300,000, barely large enough to make up the 1951 freshman class of full-time resident college students, in 1956 approximately 1.3 million graduated from the tenth grade. In the meantime, the rate of admission to resident schools of higher education in the Soviet Union has not increased. In 1956 only 222,000 resident freshmen were matriculated, and perhaps another 200,000 became correspondence students. Thus, some 900,000 ten-year school graduates in that year were to be syphoned off into industry directly or via short-term vocational training.

According to the Soviet press, many of the recent ten-year school graduates who failed of admission to higher education have been slow in entering the labor force voluntarily, and many remain unemployed. Traditionally, the expectation of the ten-year school graduates—until recently a highly selective group—and of their parents was that they would continue on to higher education. To reconcile the frustrated vision of privileged status of the ten-year school graduates who fail of admission to college with Soviet economic realities is one of the currently pressing Soviet sociological problems—one which will be aggravated if there continues to be an "overproduction" of ten-year school graduates aspiring to go on to college. It is not surprising, therefore, that the original 1952 plan of making ten-year school education universal by 1960 has been modified so that, beyond the seventh year of general education, any kind of training, such as in a labor reserve school, will count toward the universal minimum of education to age 17.

How realistic are these plans? If it were not for a large birth deficit during World War II and the resulting diminishing number of school-age children, the task of expanding facilities to provide schooling of any kind for every Soviet child to age 17 by 1960 would be wholly unattainable. So far as the *total* number of pupils is concerned, only a moderate expansion of Soviet school facilities would be needed—

statistically speaking—to house all those pupils who are now in school and who by *1960* will have reached grade VIII through X levels. But because of the present uneven distribution of enrollment, the pressure of numbers in the age 14 to 16 group will continue to grow until the fall of 1960 and will continue to overtax the existing facilities of grades VIII through X. If our estimate of the 1955–1956 distribution of Soviet school enrollment by grades as shown in Chart 1 is correct, and if all pupils then enrolled were to be allowed to continue on to age 17, Soviet facilities for schooling of one type or another at the tenth grade level would have to be about doubled by 1958. This could be accomplished only by a continual shift of the ten-year school teachers from the lower to the higher grades—unless in the meantime vocational (labor reserve) and technicum facilities could be greatly expanded to absorb an increasing share of the seven-year school graduates. Since it is obvious that the capacity of these vocational and technical training schools cannot be increased rapidly enough, the main burden of carrying out the plan for expanding universal education to age 17 must necessarily fall on the ten-year school. Its changing orientation away from college preparatory objectives and the resurrection in 1952 of the principle of "polytechnization"—that is, practicalization—of Soviet general education are presumably designed to solve the problem of designing one kind of education for all.

Progress in the new direction has been slow. It is doubtful that, pending the development of additional facilities for vocational training, rapid progress can be made toward universality of education to age 17 for some years to come. In the meantime, an increasing number of "surplus" ten-year school graduates will accumulate, to many of whom the impossibility of continuing their education is certain to be a disillusioning experience.

As significant as its exercise of power to employ the already available resources of trained manpower in desired directions is the apparent success of the Soviet system in inducing, on the part of the student, self-motivation toward higher education. In terms of status, prestige, and economic advantage there are no desirable alternatives to professional education in the Soviet Union (aside from a purely Party career). Consequently, the aspirations and energies of Soviet youth are automatically directed toward educational goals. Furthermore, the political climate of the Soviet Union tends to polarize the desire for formal education and the quest for enlightenment in a politically neutral direction—toward professional specialization in politically safe disciplines such as mathematics and the physical sciences.

Given a general drive on the part of the students to obtain a higher education, Soviet planners can direct this force into desired channels by manipulating admissions quotas and scholarships. The Soviet admissions barrier to higher education serves as a dam erected to contain the great and varied potential of the coming generations and to harness it to operate the power plant of the Communist Party. Manipulating the intake gates, the Ministry directs the flow of this potential energy into the designated fields of training at the levels and in the volume called for by the over-all plan. The overproduction of ten-year graduates in recent years has already lifted the level on the intake side of the dam beyond the limit for which the Soviet educational system was originally designed.

It is plain, then, that central control over the educational system is an inevitable and logical consequence of the Soviet rationale of education. That control explains both the major strengths and the major weaknesses of the system. Among the elements of strength deriving from centralized control—which include the power to enforce decisions, to allocate resources, and to coordinate the component parts of the educational ladder into a system—perhaps the most important from the qualitative standpoint is the mechanism for establishing a minimum standard, at least in a formal way, for schools at every level and of every kind throughout the Soviet Union. But to the extent that the intensification and effectiveness of central control may enhance the positive elements of the system, they also increase its deferred costs and liabilities. Among the negative consequences of centralized control—which include progressively increasing difficulties of accurate planning, a capacity for committing policy blunders all at once on a national scale, and the unprecedented growth of bureaucracy—the most significant is the progressive paralysis of individual initiative which has been spreading through the entire Soviet educational fabric.

As the power of decision has been more and more concentrated at the highest level of control, so the exercise of initiative even in relatively minor areas of educational policy necessarily has become the prerogative—and also the burden—only of those far above the operational level at which issues arise and normally should be resolved. In consequence, the top-level administrative organ, the Ministry of Higher Education, has to intervene and take the initiative in every last detail of administration and conduct of training although, whatever its advisory capacity, it has no authority to initiate broad policies, that authority being vested exclusively in the leadership of the Communist Party. Among the most notable developments in the Soviet Union since Stalin's death has been the growing pressure upon the educational system to decentralize many of the functions of the

Ministry, to expand the area of local autonomy, and to revive the role of individual initiative in improving the educational process.

The manifestations of this pressure so far show an uneasy compromise between conflicting objectives: on the part of Soviet leadership, to achieve greater efficiency, better results, and closer fulfillment of its unchanged educational aims; on the part of educators and students, however timidly asserted, to gain something in the direction of individual dignity and freedom from the humiliating tutelage of the Communist Party hacks and prophets. As we have seen, a number of measures have in fact been taken since Stalin's death to revitalize education by appeals to individual initiative; for instance, separate institutions now have some autonomy in the choice of elective (non-credit) courses. But the major instruments of control, such as the fundamental provision whereby the state determines the numbers to be trained both by fields and by total number and allocates them by institutions, have not been impaired; nor has the central authority relinquished any of its exclusive power to prescribe the content and scope of instruction at all levels. Further experiments toward decentralization of operational burdens, of day-to-day responsibility, and of authority within limits to select the means whereby the centrally dictated policy can be best carried out will no doubt be made. But there is no evidence to suggest any willingness or desire on the part of the Soviet leadership to decentralize the formation of educational policy and philosophy. Nor can any change in that direction be rationally expected, since such decentralization would inevitably undermine the very foundation of the power of the Communist Party dictatorship.

When we consider the possible future trends of Soviet educational policy, therefore, we must set the evidence against the background fact that, since indivisibility of control is a prerequisite for the maintenance of power in the communist state, it cannot be safely compromised—not even on grounds of economic expediency, and certainly not in response to any popular desire for a greater degree of individual self-determination in such a highly integrated and inflexible structure of controls as that which ties the entire educational system to the over-all objectives of central planning. It would be difficult and in some areas impossible to make substantial changes toward decentralization of authority in education without risking the collapse of the entire system of social controls.

Nevertheless, as has been demonstrated in the last few years, there can, within the essentially unaltered administrative and organizational setting, be vigorous, determined, and significant effort to improve the techniques and technical content of instruction and the quality of professional preparation generally. For instance, there are strong intentions to broaden the theoretical base of engineering training, to reduce the emphasis on already established engineering practices and existing technology, to encourage independent work by students, and otherwise to depart from the pattern of immediate and specific "usefulness" which was established with the vertical integration of key industries under the Five Year Plans. If such intentions are carried through, there may well be a substantial increase in the versatility and competency of the future generation of young Soviet engineers. We can expect unremitting Soviet efforts in this direction.

Even when we have examined the available facts of the operation and content of the Soviet educational system and have been thereby enabled to see some of its current trends, we have still not come to grips with its ultimate meaning. There remain questions to which we must attempt to find answers.

Have the measures so actively fostered and supported by the Soviet government in behalf of science and technology been measures to develop education or to develop training? Indeed, when we talk about the vast Soviet efforts in schools, colleges, and universities, are we talking about education as we Americans and the other free peoples conceive of education? Or are we talking about training, a far narrower concept? And what, then, emerges when we set the Soviet educational system against our own and attempt the inevitable comparisons?

"Education's real challenge," one authority has said, "is to produce men and women who know how to think; and knowing how, do it; and having done it, voice their opinions."[1]

Clarence Faust, President of the Fund for the Advancement of Education, speaking at a conference at Arden House said:

> It is the fundamental purpose of education to develop as fully as possible the range of this mysterious and amazing human capacity for reflecting upon sense experience, our own states of mind, our beliefs and ideals. Deprive a man or a society of these capacities and education becomes meaningless—indeed, impossible. At best, it becomes mere training—an unthinking channeling of instincts in obedience to some superior will. If the development of the human capacity for reflection is the essence of education and consequently the essential task of educational institutions, the mere accumulation of information is not education. Indoctrination in even the noblest ideas and ideals is not education. Nor is the mastering of vocational skill true education if all that it involves is the training of hands to perform a task efficiently.[2]

But indoctrination and training are the two goals which communist planners must designate for any educational system they control. For under communism the guidance of human destinies is the exclusive concern and prerogative of the political and ideological dictatorship. Assisted by its henchmen who make up the backbone of the Communist Party, the dictatorship sets moral and ethical standards, codes of human behavior, and patterns of social organization. It not only relieves its subjects from the necessity to think, providing the answers to all questions and absolving all who follow the prescribed path of any moral, civic, and social responsibility for their actions; it also pre-empts all loyalties to itself.

Thus the personal responsibilities of a Soviet citizen—whether a tractor driver, a teacher, or a high-energy physicist—are reduced to the acquisition and exercise of the maximal technical knowledge, vocational and professional skills, and diligence in the performance of designated duties. And when we consider Soviet education, we are considering a system of training originally structured and consistently operated in harmony with communist goals.

The emergence of the Soviet Union as a major industrial power is, to be sure, eloquent evidence of the massive accomplishment of that system of training. Moreover, there have been substantial advances by the Soviet Union in science and technology and in certain branches of industry, notably in military aircraft, nuclear weapons, and presumably in guided missiles. But these accomplishments of *training* are not adequate criteria for judging a system of education; and it is an unhappy commentary on the state of the Western mind in this era of cold war that we have often been tempted to make an illogical transition from the one to the other.

Western observers, impressed by such achievements as the H-bomb and more generally by the advanced level of Soviet research in physics and other branches of pure and applied science, have tended to generalize, actually or by implication, from the excellence of Soviet performance in selected fields of science and technology about the quality of Soviet education generally. With the greatly increased interest in Soviet education, facts or alleged facts have been copiously quoted in newspapers, articles, and public speeches. Moreover, it is significant that the implications of the frequently cited comparisons between the United States and the USSR of the formal content and amount of instruction in science and mathematics are usually unfavorable to the performance of the American educational system. Similarly, the comparative statistics which are frequently cited in attempts to measure the relative achievements of the two systems are not only often of uncomparable units; they also carry unwarranted implications—one of them being that the chief purpose of educational systems is to train engineers and physicists.

It was perhaps because of that subconscious assumption on the part of the reporter that an American educator was quoted—or misquoted— as having said that the Soviet Union has the "finest system of education in the world."[3] More specifically, with reference to Soviet education in science and engineering, Soviet gains have been underscored with alarm and concern and with pessimistic reflections on the ability of the American educational system even to match the Soviet record. An American educator and scientist was quoted in 1954 in part as follows:

> We have almost lost the battle for scientific manpower. . . . All the money we could pour into scientific education would not stop Russia from producing two or three times as many engineers as we do in the future.[4]

And more recently, in February 1957, an address of an American scientist delivered at the Air Force Association Conference on "Manpower and Education" was reported in part as follows:

> Today our leadership in science is being challenged by Russia . . . you will have to say that ten years from now the best scientists will be found in Russia.
>
> I am not saying that this will happen unless we take this or that measure, I am simply saying that it is going to happen.[5]

In general, it would appear that Western commentators have been bemused by the exercise of making purely numerical comparisons.

We grant that any thoughtful American reader encountering statistical data on Soviet education may instinctively compare them with the American counterparts and be tempted to use them as a gauge of American performance. But such comparisons, however valid in detail they may be, miss the very essence of the problem and obscure the fundamental noncomparability: the difference in the goals, the philosophy, the operating rationale, and the functions of education in the two systems and the magnitude of the tasks which the two systems respectively must fulfill to achieve their objectives. Only in such a frame of reference can the Soviet educational performance be seen in its proper scale as we have endeavored to show it in this survey.

In this connection, let no reader infer that because we have pointed to many shortcomings and defects of Soviet technical training we would imply the comforting suggestion that American education has nothing to worry about. On the contrary, we would submit that, when judged in terms of its own goals and needs, American education has a far greater and more complex task, and one that demands greater attention, dedication, and energy, than any task suggested by the allegation that the Soviet Union produces twice as many engineers per year as does the United States.

Can we make a rational comparison of Soviet and American education?

Although the survey presented in this volume is not a comparative study of the Soviet and American educational systems and methods, statistical and other references to the American educational scene and some direct comparisons have necessarily been made by way of presenting Soviet data against a familiar background. Many features of the Soviet educational process have appeared in sharp contrast with comparable aspects of education in the United States; some are unique to the Soviet system and wholly alien to the American educational setting. On the other hand, the majority of the operational variables discussed with reference to Soviet education, such as teachers, textbooks, facilities, cost of education, maintenance of standards, and curricula, are altogether too familiar to anyone who is concerned with education in the United States. It would seem, therefore, with so many elements in the educational process of the two systems common to both, that some direct qualitative comparisons could be made between Soviet and American education.

With that provisional assumption, we have in fact suggested a generalized comparison between Soviet and American trained physicists and engineers; and we have commented on the relative levels of academic and professional achievement indicated by the graduate degrees awarded in the Soviet Union and in the United States. In a strictly formal sense, such a comparison of the corresponding curricula and content of instruction by itself provides a basis for qualitative evaluation; but it is also obvious that any evaluation which would abstract technical achievement from the philosophy, objectives, and social and moral criteria of education cannot provide an adequate basis for determining the quality of Soviet education generally.

More specifically, such an evaluation could not provide a basis for direct comparison of the Soviet potential in trained manpower with that of the free world. For the sake of argument, however, we might assume the quality of specialized training in the Soviet Union as given and as being technically more or less comparable to that achieved in American schools. We might multiply this hypothetically comparable quality by numbers and thus estimate the trained manpower potential of the Soviet Union. Going further, we might assess the realizable capabilities of Soviet trained manpower and then examine and compare the entire Soviet political, economic, and social setting relative to that of the free world generally and to that of the United States. But, no matter what route we took, we would arrive at the one really crucial question: Capabilities for what? In other words, what are the Soviet objectives, requirements, and tasks which its educational system and its trained manpower are intended to serve?

The answer is provided by history. In the context of the war long ago declared by communism against the free democratic societies, but still not taken seriously enough by many of the intended victims, the Soviet Union has committed the major part of the productive effort, skill, and talent of its people to the maintenance and increase of communist capability for the aggressive expansion of communist power. It has mobilized a major share of the social and economic resources of the areas it controls to advance its technological means toward achieving this objective. It is this objective which the Soviet educational system is ultimately designed to serve.

We cannot emphasize too strongly, then, that if we are seeking for the deeper meanings of the nature of the Soviet educational system as set against our own, if we are seeking to find in a comparison of the two systems a measure of the challenge which confronts American education, then our comparison must be set in the broad context of communist and democratic objectives in their widest sense.

It is clear that in terms of such a comparison the American task is great and far reaching.

We must maintain and decisively increase our technological, industrial, and military lead—for self-defense in the last resort, but first of all in the hope that a superior weapons capability may effectively discourage any large-scale communist military aggression. But this negative task is overshadowed by the even larger tasks set by basic American objectives, moral commitments, and aspirations. At this juncture of history these constructive tasks urgently demand the allocation of an increasing share of the national effort and resources not only to the maintenance of the national and international gains already made but also to the continued advancement of social, economic, and moral progress. If American objectives are to be vigorously advanced and America's historic role as the champion of liberty and human dignity is to be effectively fulfilled on the international scene, our national task is without historic parallel—and infinitely greater and more difficult than that for which the Soviet communists would mobilize their resources.

Correspondingly, the task of American education is infinitely greater, more difficult, and more challenging than that of Soviet education. It is greater because, in addition to the training it must provide on a very large scale in the rapidly expanding fields of modern technology and increasingly specialized vocational, industrial, and professional skills, it is the goal of American education to afford enlightenment, to develop the independent individual intellectual and moral stature requisite for and compatible with the responsibilities of informed and mature citizenship in a free society, and to encourage the maximum realization of individual capabilities and satisfactions. The task of American education is more difficult because, unlike its Soviet counterpart, the American educational system has no vested central authority backed by police power and able to prescribe ready-made specific objectives, standards, norms, quotas, and categories. And related to this fact is perhaps the most important role of education in a free society: it is a major avenue of progress toward the development and refinement of a self-generated scale of moral, ethical, aesthetic, and social values as standards of personal and group behavior; toward the generation of a freely and maturely arrived-at choice of alternatives and a consensus as to political, economic, and social priorities; and toward informed and responsible popular choice and effective support of elected leadership in communal, national, and international affairs.

In contrast, such objectives are excluded from the philosophy of Soviet education. As the title of a recent article in *Leningrad pravda* puts it, "The Will of the Party Is the Law for Youth." Viewing the Soviet exclusive preoccupation with training in physical sciences, mathematics, and technology, we see that the question of whether other intellectual capabilities of the young generation may be thwarted and other social potentialities sacrificed could not even be raised in the context of the Soviet philosophy of education.

Thus the vital elements of American education have no place in the Soviet scheme and cannot have in any communist state. To the extent that such elements distinguish education from mere training, the greatest tragedy of this century may well ultimately be that for 40 years successive generations of the Russian peoples, living in a country with enormous potentials in natural resources and possessing vigor, talent, and a rich spiritual heritage, for all the training they have so eagerly and grimly undergone, have been denied the privilege of education.

Although indoctrination, along with training, is the overriding goal of the Soviet educational system, there is ample evidence that its success in formal training in literary and manual skills, technology, engineering, science, and, notably, in mathematics has not been matched by anywhere near equal success in communist indoctrination.

Since Stalin's death particularly, Soviet spokesmen have steadily denounced lapses of "communist morality"—identified as survivals of "alien," "bourgeois," and other unorthodox moods and attitudes—and the spread of "hooliganism" among students, manifestations which have apparently increased in frequency since the historic recasting of Stalin's image by Khrushchev in February 1956. It would be a mistake to assume, we believe, that unrest and dissatisfaction, including occasional open challenge of some official stand, among Soviet students reflect a newly emerged sense of disaffection with the regime. Rather, as we see it, the only new element is a diminished fear of publicly expressing resentments; the currently acknowledged ineffectiveness of indoctrination of Soviet students in communist *philosophy* is probably not much greater today than it has been for many years. We would venture a calculated guess that, so far as the teaching of Marxism-Leninism and similar required subjects comprising Soviet social science is concerned, the overwhelming proportion of both teachers and students have for many years now gone through the motions without any illusions as to the nature of the required ritual.

That is not to say that 40 years of indoctrination have left no mark on Soviet generations. One negative effect of intense indoctrination, ineffective as it may be *per se,* is that it leaves no individual free, or at least it limits his opportunities and incentives, to develop his own reasoned philosophy and outlook; for, whatever the individual response to indoctrination—boredom, resentment, or, the most likely outcome, cynicism and a profound distrust of any philosophy—it is hardly conducive to the development of realistic and clearly seen alternatives. But there is an equally important positive effect. Communist indoctrination includes very persuasive propaganda emphasis on the concrete achievements of the Soviet Union which are attributed to and identified exclusively with communism. The impressive gains symbolized in such monuments as the grandiose plant of Moscow University, the biggest high-energy accelerator, and even more impressive plans on paper are held up as models typical of the communist future. The mirage of the communist life to come is contrasted with a distorted view of the Western democracies; Soviet behavior in the international arena is exhibited as a proof of its world leadership; and the recently proclaimed era of cultural and scientific "cooperation" with the Western world has been explained by the image of the world knocking at the Soviet door. It is certain that this kind of indoctrination, supported by the facts of Soviet material growth and coupled with a steeply differentiated system of tangible rewards, has been a powerful factor in inducing a strong degree of self-motivation among Soviet students to strive hard to gain the highest possible professional status in any field the government desires to cultivate.

At this point we can recapitulate our evaluation of the Soviet educational system in terms of three major variables of Soviet technical and scientific education—quality, numbers, and motivation—in the following generalizations. The Soviet criteria of quality have rested on the emphasis given to specialized knowledge largely in its technical and manipulative aspects; in this solely technical sense, the quality of training at best has been very high, ranging all the way down the scale in accordance with designated priorities. As to numbers, a direct element of planning, the central fact is that the Soviet government trains only as many as it thinks it needs to train—not as many as desire training and are capable of advancement. Finally, as to motivation, if our analysis is correct, the significant elements from which it derives such strength as it has had are indoctrination and the inducements of a steeply progressing scale of rewards in terms of social status and purchasing power.

But any final evaluation, any attempt to seek ultimate meanings as we return to the inevitable questions which arise when we set the Soviet educational system against our own, brings us back to a single fact. It is the total Soviet government power of control over the allocation of all resources which alone concentrates educational resources in accordance with the government's scale of priorities.

In the Soviet planned economy there must be a balance between the functioning of the allocation mechanism and the functioning of the educational system if there are not to be upsetting repercussions throughout the entire economy. Under Stalin, that is, under a completely centralized control supported by unconcealed police power, the Soviet educational system, for all its costs and inefficiency, functioned well enough in relation to its objectives. Since Stalin's death, under the "collective"—and we would suggest competing—leadership, control over the allocation of resources has become more diffuse and the overt threat of police power has somewhat diminished. The educational system, as a result, may be subjected to certain strains.

The sum total of economic and status expectations of the greatly increased and growing number of professionally trained elite may readily become much too high to be easily satisfied except by depressing still lower the standard of living of workers and peasants or by very materially increasing the productivity of labor without a corresponding increase in wages. Either one of such alternatives would be difficult to carry out without the application of severe punitive sanctions—despite Khrushchev's reported statement (to 60,000 workers at a meeting called to hear him announce that the Soviet government had decided to suspend interest and freeze repayment of the Soviet equivalent of defense bonds) that Western capitalists "do not understand the soul of the Soviet people, . . . [they] never will believe that you are doing this of your own free will."[6] In this context, the current overproduction of ten-year school graduates is especially significant. It has already led to material changes in the education pattern at the precollege level and, for related and other reasons, to many precipitate changes in the organization of undergraduate and graduate training.

As we see it, the many post-Stalin educational changes, the net effect of which will not be ascertainable for many years, and which are officially represented as further steps in already proven directions, have been initiated largely in a renewed effort to compensate for the inherent long-range defects of the Soviet educational system as a whole. Whatever the case, the fact remains that the largest single school system in the world is under the control of the Communist Party, that it emphasizes science and technology more than any other educational system, and that, beyond a certain minimum of general education, it concentrates exclusively on specialized training at vocational, subprofessional, and professional levels.

What does this fact mean to Russia and her annexed neighbors and to the rest of the world? What does it mean to America?

Soviet education has been called a challenge—a defiant invitation to engage in a contest.* That it presents a challenge, few observers would deny. But one must be clear as to the direction in which the challenge lies. The conclusions derived from the evidence here examined would suggest that the nature of the Soviet challenge is not expressed in numbers, nor even in quality, but in the degree to which national education and training efforts and performance are consonant with national goals. The essence of the challenge for the United States, therefore, is not to permit the scale, character, flexibility, vigor, and quality of American education to lag behind its expanding goals and responsibilities. These are the criteria by which American education must be judged, not by reference to how many engineers are or are not trained in the Soviet Union.

Soviet education has also been called by many justifiably apprehen-

---

* For example, the title of a book by George S. Counts, *The Challenge of Soviet Education* (McGraw-Hill Book Company, Inc., 1957). In this work Dr. Counts deals comprehensively with Soviet education in the widest sense of the term, which includes the sum total of influences in and out of school to which the Soviet-raised generations have been exposed. Dr. Counts' study encompasses a much broader view of Soviet education than the present volume.

sive American observers a threat. The choice of terms, incongruously linking as it does the word "threat" with "education," is unfortunate, for its implication is false. The locus of the threat is not Soviet education but Soviet communism. For that matter, the threat derives in part from the fact that there is no true education under communism. Soviet education, with its emphasis on specialized training, has been transmuted into a threat to freedom only because Soviet scientific and technological capabilities are mobilized solely for the support and expansion of communist power. It is the employment of the accumulated resources of the Soviet Union and of its satellites to the ends of the Communist Party that constitutes the threat.

Soviet education has also been viewed as a weapon which will help eventually to destroy the very threat that some observers believe it poses. This view reflects an abiding faith in education as a means of social progress; it derives from the identification of moral values and social goals with educational advances. In the Western democracies this identification is taken for granted. Consciously or unconsciously we tend to endow any education with those ideals which are counted upon to contribute progressively to the well-being and quality of human society. Since we are convinced that democracy thrives and grows strong on education, it is easy to presume that an inverse relationship is equally valid—that education automatically leads to the formation of democratic values and strengths.

It would seem that the philosophy of Soviet education militates against such a presumption. Nevertheless, as Soviet indoctrination has produced disillusionment with communist dogma, so Soviet educational gains in science and technology may produce disaffection with the political and economic structure of communism, stimulating a desire for change. In consequence of the advances and the spread of knowledge, it is already difficult for the Soviet Union to keep its people in the dark on the status of the economic, scientific, and cultural progress of the Western industrial societies. In this sense Soviet education is a promise both to the people now under communism and to the rest of the world. It may not be fulfilled by any direct emergence among the educated elite in the Soviet Union of the democratic political and economic ideas we associate with liberal education, but it does imply a growing capacity of the Soviet people for political and economic changes which could destroy Soviet communism.

Whether such changes can come about gradually, which seems to us very doubtful, or in a series of rapidly evolving developments, the crucial issue which will decide the future meaning and role of Soviet education and thus the future quality of Soviet society is the control

over the allocation of its resources. When ultimately the Soviet people
gain a decisive voice in the allocation of their intellectual and physical
resources, Soviet educational philosophy and pattern will certainly
change. When that time comes, their schools will produce fewer but
better engineers. After decades of virtual captivity their scientists will
once again become members of the world's scientific community.
Their universities will produce perhaps fewer physicists and mathematicians, but their graduates will include economists, historians,
jurists, and philosophers. Science and technology will continue to
advance—but in the service of the people—and the creative genius of
the emancipated peoples will also find outlets in literature, the arts,
and the humanities.

The broad implications of what we have set down in this study are
clear. The free nations should know the direction in which lies the
real threat to their survival lest through inaction, compromise, or
short-sighted expediency they themselves should unwittingly help the
growth and expansion of communist power. In the long run the
threat of communism will be removed if the free peoples vigorously
continue—Soviet Union or no Soviet Union—to pursue their highest
social goals and to maintain their combined scientific, technological,
and moral superiority. But for the free nations to believe that they
can somehow achieve these goals while continuing to carry on their
educational efforts and all the other pursuits of life "as usual" is to
refuse to face the realities of the world scene at this junction of history.
If, in the face of the Soviets' superior power to allocate the resources
under their control, democracy and economic progress for all nations
are to prevail, and the freedom and dignity of every individual are to
be attained, we free peoples must find a way to release a larger share
of our aggregate resources and energy from nonessential material uses
and devote them to the service of indispensable goals.

Notes to Chapter 12

1 Henry Townley Heald, *The New York Times Magazine*, September 30, 1956,
p. 62.

2 "Our Secondary Schools and National Manpower Needs," an address by Clarence
Faust, in *Improving the Work Skills of the Nation*, National Manpower Council,
Proceedings of a Conference held April 27–May 1, 1955 at Arden House, Harriman
Campus of Columbia University, p. 33.

3 "Soviet Education System Held Finest," by the Associated Press, *Christian
Science Monitor*, November 10, 1956, reporting the address delivered by Dr. Homer
Dodge to the student body of Worcester Polytechnic Institute. On the following

day the *Christian Science Monitor* carried a follow-up statement by the Associated Press under the title, "Dodge Charges Talk Distorted on Red Schools," the first paragraph of which reads:

> Dr. Homer Dodge, former president of Norwich University, said last night a story of a speech he gave on Soviet Education Nov. 9 in Worcester, Mass., was reported "out of context and gave a completely distorted view" of his opinions.

4 *New York Times*, November 7, 1954, an article by Benjamin Fine quoting John R. Dunning, Dean of Columbia University's School of Engineering, p. 80.

5 *Ibid.*, February 16, 1957, an article by John W. Finney quoting Dr. Edward Teller, p. 8.

6 *Christian Science Monitor*, April 11, 1957, p. 7.

APPENDICES

LIST OF BASIC EQUIPMENT

FOR SHOP TRAINING

IN A SOVIET SECONDARY SCHOOL

Description	Quantity
1. Screw-cutting lathes with a set of attachments; 1.2 to 2.2 kw motors:	
RMTs 500–700 mm	1
VTs 120–170 mm	1
2. Drill presses, 8–12 mm capacity	2
3. Wood-turning lathes, simplified type, length of bed 500–700 mm, motor 0.3 to 0.5 kw	2
4. Bench grinder, 0.2 to 0.4 kw, and the following woodworking tools:	1
a. Motor-driven hand plane 100 mm	1
b. Electric jig saw	1
c. Circular saw	1
5. Work benches adapted for wood and metal work	20 (work spaces)*
6. Metalworking hand tools	20 sets*
a. Vise, 60 to 20 mm	
b. Machinist try square	
c. Scale, 300 mm	
d. Scriber	
e. Center punch	
f. Machinist hammer	
g. Files, assorted	
h. Metal shears	
i. Soldering iron	
j. Hacksaw	
k. Pliers, flat nose	
l. Pliers, round nose	
m. Cutting pliers	
n. Chisel	
o. Screwdrivers	

7. Woodworking tools　　　　　　　　　　　　　　　　20 sets*
   a. Carpenter's square
   b. Ruler
   c. Folding ruler
   d. Rough plane
   e. Hand plane
   f. Finishing plane
   g. Frame saw
   h. Chisels, assorted
   i. Gouges, assorted
   j. Claw
   k. Claw hammer
   l. Mallet
   m. Nippers
   n. Scribing gauge
8. Metalworking and woodworking tools for general use
   a. Hand drills　　　　　　　　　　　　　　　　　　2*
   b. Braces　　　　　　　　　　　　　　　　　　　　10*
   c. Hacksaws, assorted　　　　　　　　　　　　　　10*
   d. Frame saws, assorted　　　　　　　　　　　　　10*
   e. Compass, calipers, inside and outside, and beam
      compass　　　　　　　　　　　　　　　　　　10 sets
   f. Tap and die sets　　　　　　　　　　　　　　　2 sets
   g. Wrenches　　　　　　　　　　　　　　　　　　　5
   h. Gauge block　　　　　　　　　　　　　　　　　　1
   i. Rasps, files, and finishing files of assorted shapes　50
9. Grindstone (wheel)　　　　　　　　　　　　　　　　1*
  Grindstones (bars)　　　　　　　　　　　　　　　　5
  Whetstones, flat　　　　　　　　　　　　　　　　　5
  Holder for sharpening plane blades　　　　　　　　1
10. Metalworking vise 120 mm　　　　　　　　　　　　1
11. Switchboard with transformer, rectifier, and an assort-
    ment of instruments for electrical and radio setups
12. Lockers for storing work items in progress, tools, and
    certain materials　　　　　　　　　　　　　　　　3–4†
13. Blackboard　　　　　　　　　　　　　　　　　　　1
14. Table and chair for instructor　　　　　　　　　　1*
15. Stools　　　　　　　　　　　　　　　　　　　　　18*
16. First-aid kit　　　　　　　　　　　　　　　　　　1*

Source: Programmy srednei shkoly na 1954–1955 uchebnyi god. Prakticheskiye zanyatiya na uchebno-opytnom uchastke. Prakticheskiye zanyatiya v uchebnykh masterskikh. V klass (Syllabi of the Secondary School for the 1954–1955 School Year. Practical Work on Experimental Garden Plots. Practical Work in School Shops. Grade V), Moscow: Uchpedgiz, 1954, pp. 22–23.

* These items are needed to begin with.
† One locker is needed to begin with.

A SUMMARY OF THE SOVIET

SECONDARY SCHOOL MATHEMATICS SYLLABUS

FOR THE 1955–1956 SCHOOL YEAR

GRADES V THROUGH X

Only the major topic headings are listed in this summary. In the original syllabus the elements of each topic are enumerated in such detail that the material summarized here takes up twenty printed pages.*

Except for arithmetic in grades V and VI and algebra in grade VI, the 1955–1956 syllabus is identical with the 1952–1953 syllabus.†

Class hours (hours per week for each grade and total hours by topics) of 45 minutes duration correspond to the curriculum shown in Table 9 and Table 11 in Chapter 2.

Homework hours by topics are the officially assumed average listed in the syllabus as a guide in assigning home study.

Grade V (age 11–12). Mathematics: 6 hr/wk

Arithmetic (6 hr/wk)	Class Hours	Homework
1. Whole numbers	20	8
2. Divisibility of numbers	20	8
3. Common fractions	90	36
4. Decimal fractions	50	20
5. Practical studies	6	..
6. Review	12	6
Total	198	78

* *Programmy srednei shkoly na 1955–1956 uchebnyi god. Matematika* (Syllabi for the Secondary Schools, 1955–1956 School Year. Mathematics), Moscow: Uchpedgiz, 1955, Cenis Translation Series 56-2.

† 1952–1953 Soviet Syllabus in Mathematics, Cenis Translation Series 56-1.

Grade VI (age 12–13).   Mathematics: 6 hr/wk

Arithmetic (2 hr/wk)	Class Hours	Homework
1. Percentage*	20	10
2. Proportions. Direct and inverse proportionality	32	16
3. Review	14	7
Total	66	33

Algebra (2 hr/wk)	Class Hours	Homework
1. Algebraic expressions. Equations	15	8
2. Positive and negative numbers	20	10
3. Operations with whole algebraic expressions	31	16
Total	66	34

Geometry (2 hr/wk)	Class Hours	Homework
1. Introduction	10	5
2. Triangles	30	15
3. Parallel straight lines	26	13
Total	66	33

Grade VII (age 13–14).   Mathematics: 6 hr/wk

Algebra (4 hr/wk, 1st semester; 3 hr/wk, 2nd semester)	Class Hours	Homework
1. Algebraic fractions	24	12
2. Proportions and proportionality	6	4
3. Linear equations with one unknown	30	15
4. Systems of linear equations	18	9
5. Extraction of square roots	12	6
Total	90	46

Geometry (2 hr/wk, 1st semester; 3 hr/wk, 2nd semester)	Class Hours	Homework
1. Quadrangles	26	13
2. Circumference	32	16
3. Inscribed and circumscribed triangles and quadrangles	16	8
Total	74	37
Review (arithmetic, algebra, and geometry)	34	

* Prior to 1956 percentage was taught in Grade V.

Grade VIII (age 14–15). Mathematics: 6 hr/wk

Algebra (4 hr/wk, 1st semester; 3 hr/wk, 2nd semester)	Class Hours	Homework
1. Powers and roots	30	15
2. Quadratic equations and equations of higher powers reducible to quadratics	42	21
3. Functions and their graphs	10	5
4. System of 2nd degree equations with two unknowns	18	9
Total	100	50

Geometry (2 hr/wk, 1st semester; 3 hr/wk, 2nd semester)	Class Hours	Homework
1. Similar figures	30	15
2. Trigonometric functions of an acute angle	12	6
3. Metric relationships in a triangle and a circle	24	12
4. Areas of polygons	14	7
Total	80	40
Review	18	

Grade IX (age 15–16). Mathematics: 6 hr/wk

Algebra (2 hr/wk)	Class Hours	Homework
1. Numerical sequences	19	10
2. Generalization of the concept of exponents	8	4
3. Exponential functions and logarithms	36	18
Total	63	32

Geometry (2 hr/wk, first 3 quarters; 3 hr/wk, last quarter)	Class Hours	Homework
1. Regular polygons	12	6
2. Length of circumference and area of a circle	10	5
3. Straight lines and planes	43	22
Total	65	33

Trigonometry (2 hr/wk, first 3 quarters; 1 hr/wk, last quarter)	Class Hours	Homework
Total	56	28
Review	14	

Grade X (age 16–17).   Mathematics: 6 hr/wk

Algebra (2 hr/wk)	Class Hours	Homework
1. Combinations and the binomial theorem	12	6
2. Complex numbers	12	6
3. Inequalities	22	11
4. Equations of higher powers	12	6
Total	58	29

Geometry (2 hr/wk, 1st semester; 1 hr/wk, 2nd semester)	Class Hours	Homework
1. Polyhedrons	28	14
2. Solids of revolution	20	10
Total	48	24

Trigonometry (2 hr/wk, 1st semester; 3 hr/wk, 2nd semester)	Class Hours	Homework
1. Solution of oblique-angled triangles	18	9
2. Inverse trigonometric functions	14	7
3. Trigonometric equations	16	8
4. Review and problem solution	16	8
Total	64	32
Review	28	

Recapitulation

Mathematics in the last six grades of the Soviet ten-year school of general education (grades V through X, age 11 through 17).

Subject	Class Hours (45 minutes each)	Homework Hours (est.)
Arithmetic*	274	111
Algebra	389	191
Geometry	363	167
Trigonometry	162	60
Total, grades V–X	1,188	529

* In addition to the elementary school arithmetic taught in grades I through IV, 6 hr/wk. According to the syllabus of the elementary school (*Programmy nachal'noi shkoly*, Moscow, 1950, p. 47), upon completion of grade IV the pupil should have acquired:

1. A firm knowledge of the four arithmetic operations with numbers of any magnitude, a lasting skill in making oral and written computations, and the ability to use the abacus.

2. A firm knowledge of the metric system units and of units for measuring time and the ability to use them.

3. An elementary understanding of common fractions and per cent.

4. An elementary knowledge of visual geometry and the ability to apply such knowledge to practical tasks.

5. Ability to solve various arithmetic problems involving whole numbers.

LIST OF SELECTED SOVIET

SECONDARY SCHOOL TEXTBOOKS IN PHYSICS,

CHEMISTRY, AND MATHEMATICS

PHYSICS

Sokolov, I. I. *Kurs fiziki* (Physics). Part I: Mechanics. Textbook for grade VIII of the secondary school. 9th Ed. Moscow: Uchpedgiz, 1948. 254 pp.
Number of copies: 300,000
Table of Contents (major topics only):
Introduction to mechanics
I. Kinematics and dynamics of rectilinear motion
1. Simplest types of rectilinear motion
2. Newton's laws of motion
3. Addition of motions
4. Mechanical energy
II. Statics
1. Addition and resolution of forces
2. Center of gravity and stability
3. Moment of force
4. Conditions for an equilibrium of forces and the work law in simple mechanisms
III. Hydro- and aeromechanics
IV. Rotary motion
V. Law of universal gravity

Sokolov, I. I. *Kurs fiziki* (Physics). Part II: Oscillations and Waves. Heat. Textbook for grade IX of the secondary school. 11th Ed. Moscow: Uchpedgiz, 1950. 200 pp.
Number of copies: 300,000
Table of Contents (major topics only):
I. Oscillations and waves
II. Heat and molecular physics
1. Heat energy
2. Expansion of bodies in heating

428   **Soviet Education**

III. Molecular phenomena in gases, liquids, and solids
  1. Elements of the molecular kinetic theory
  2. Properties of gases
  3. Properties of liquids
  4. Properties of solids
IV. Changes of phase
  1. Fusion and solidification
  2. Vaporization
  3. Humidity of the air
V. Work of steam and gases

Sokolov, I. I. *Kurs fiziki* (Physics). Part III: Electricity. Optics. Textbook for grade X of the secondary school. 8th Ed. Moscow: Uchpedgiz, 1947. 302 pp. Number of copies: 155,000
Table of Contents (major topics only):
  Introduction
  I. Electric field
  II. Electric current laws
  III. Magnetic field
  IV. Electric current in liquids and gases
  V. Electromagnetic induction
  VI. Alternating current
  VII. Electromagnetic oscillations
    Optics
  Introduction
  I. Propagation of light
  II. The nature of light

Sokolov, I. I. *Kurs fiziki* (Physics). Part III: Electricity. Optics. Textbook for grade X of the secondary school. 11th Ed. Moscow: Uchpedgiz, 1950. 384 pp. The major topics are identical with those in the eighth edition except that under "Optics" a chapter entitled "Structure of the Atom" has been added.

Peryshkin, A. V., and Krauklis, V. V. *Kurs fiziki* (Physics). Part I: Mechanics. Textbook for grade VIII of the secondary school. 3rd Ed. Moscow: Uchpedgiz, 1956. 160 pp.
Number of copies: 1,500,000
Price: paper back 1.20 ruble; binding extra, with lettering—0.75 ruble, without—0.50 ruble
This text apparently is destined to replace the old standard text by Sokolov.

Znamenskii, P. A., and others. *Sbornik voprosov i zadach po fizike* (Questions and Problems in Physics). For grades VIII through X of the secondary school. 8th Ed. Moscow: Uchpedgiz, 1956. 192 pp.
A standard Soviet collection with 1,327 problems; includes table of physical constants.
Number of copies: 800,000
Price: paper back 1.50 ruble; binding 0.50 ruble extra

Volkova, K. A., and others. *Sbornik zadach po fizike* (Problems in Physics). For grades VIII through X in the secondary school. 13th Ed. Moscow: Uchpedgiz, 1947. 184 pp.

Number of copies: 310,000
Price: paper back 1.50 ruble; binding 0.60 ruble extra

Peryshkin, A. V., and Tret'yakov, N. P. *Fizika* (Physics). 2nd Ed., revised and enlarged. Approved as a reference text for schools of specialized secondary education by the USSR Ministry of Higher Education, Department of Specialized Secondary Schools. Moscow: All-Union Textbook Publishing House, "Trudrezervizdat," 1955. 436 pp.
Number of copies: 100,000
Price: 8.90 rubles
Note: This textbook is intended for the schools discussed in Chapter 4 (Technicums). The text is arranged in five sections: mechanics, molecular physics and heat, electricity, optics, and elements of the atomic theory. The last-named section (pp. 398–426) includes brief explanations and schematic diagrams on the construction of atomic and thermonuclear bombs.

CHEMISTRY

Levchenko, V. V., and others. *Khimiya* (Chemistry). Textbook for grades VIII through X of the secondary school. 3rd Ed. Professor S. A. Balezin, editor. Moscow: Uchpedgiz, 1950. 456 pp.
Other authors: M. A. Ivantsova, N. G. Solov'ev, and V. V. Fel'dt.
Number of copies: unstated
Price: paper back 4.80 rubles; binding extra; cardboard—0.90 ruble, cloth—1.80 ruble

Khodakov, Yu. V., and others. *Khimiya* (Chemistry). Textbook for grade VIII of the secondary school. 2nd Ed. Moscow: Uchpedgiz, 1956. 128 pp.
Number of copies: 900,000
Price: 1.00 ruble

Khodakov, Yu. V., and others. *Khimiya* (Chemistry). Textbook for grade X of the secondary school. Moscow: Uchpedgiz, 1956. 168 pp.
Number of copies: 1,400,000
Price: paper back 1.35 ruble; binding 0.75 ruble extra
This, apparently, is the first edition, perhaps intended to replace Levchenko's text.

Kiryushkin, D. M. *Khimiya* (Chemistry). Textbook for grade VII of the seven-year and secondary schools. 3rd Ed. Moscow: Uchpedgiz, 1951. 120 pp.
Number of copies: 500,000
Price: paper back 1.25 ruble; binding 0.50 ruble extra

ARITHMETIC

Pchelko, A. S., and Polyak, G. B. *Arifmetika* (Arithmetic). For grade IV. 2nd Ed. Moscow: Uchpedgiz, 1956. 160 pp.
Number of copies: 900,000
Price: paper back 0.75 ruble; binding extra, with lettering—0.75 ruble, without—0.50 ruble

Kiselev, A. P. *Arifmetika* (Arithmetic). For grades V and VI in the seven-year and secondary schools. Revised by Professor A. Ya. Khinchin in 1938. 17th Ed. Moscow: Uchpedgiz, 1955. 168 pp.
Number of copies: 1,200,000
Price: paper back 1.30 ruble; binding 0.50 ruble extra

ALGEBRA

Kiselev, A. P. *Algebra*. Part I. Textbook for grades VI through VIII of the seven-year and secondary schools. 28th Ed. Moscow: Uchpedgiz, 1954. 112 pp.
The 28th edition is said to be "unchanged from the preceding edition"—actually perhaps since c. 1935.
Number of copies: 2,100,000
Price: paper back 1.10 ruble; binding 0.50 ruble extra

Kiselev, A. P. *Algebra*. Part II. Textbook for grades VIII through X of the secondary school. 33rd Ed. Moscow: Uchpedgiz, 1956. 232 pp.
Judging by the publisher's note, this 33rd edition is identical with the last revised, 16th edition.
Number of copies: 800,000
Price: paper back 1.95 ruble; binding 0.75 ruble extra

Larichev, P. A. *Sbornik zadach po algebre* (Problems in Algebra). Part I: for grades VI and VII of the seven-year and secondary schools. 8th Ed. Moscow: Uchpedgiz, 1956. 240 pp.
A collection of 1,274 problems, some with answers
Number of copies: 1,200,000
Price: paper back 1.60 ruble; binding 0.75 ruble extra

Larichev, P. A. *Sbornik zadach po algebre* (Problems in Algebra). Part II: for grade VIII of the secondary school. 7th Ed., revised. Moscow: Uchpedgiz, 1956.
Some 685 problems arranged in groups corresponding to the 1956–1957 syllabus of eighth-grade algebra
Number of copies: 2,000,000
Price: paper back 1.05 ruble; binding 0.50 ruble extra
Table of contents:
  1. Problems for review and greater mastery of the earlier topics
  2. Powers and roots
  3. Quadratic equations and equations which can be reduced to quadratics
  4. Functions and their graphs. Trinomials of the second degree
  5. Systems of equations of the second degree with two unknowns
  6. Problems for review of eighth-grade material

Bradis, V. M. *Chetyrekhznachnye matematicheskiye tablitsy dlya srednei shkoly* (Four-Place Mathematical Tables for the Secondary Schools). 27th Ed. Moscow: Uchpedgiz, 1956. 64 pp.
Price: 0.65 ruble

GEOMETRY

Kiselev, A. P. *Geometriya* (Geometry). Part I: Plane geometry. Textbook for grades VI through IX of the secondary school. Under the editorship of and with supplements by Professor N. A. Glagolev. 16th Ed. Moscow: Uchpedgiz, 1955. 184 pp.

16th edition unchanged from the 15th (and, judging by the introduction dated February 20, 1938, without change since the original revision by Glagolev)

Number of copies: 1,600,000

Price: paper back 1.65 ruble; binding 0.50 ruble extra

Kiselev, A. P. *Geometriya* (Geometry). Part II: Solid geometry. Textbook for grades IX through X of the secondary school. Edited by and with supplements by Professor N. A. Glagolev. 18th Ed. Moscow: Uchpedgiz, 1956. 104 pp.

18th edition unchanged from the previous edition and apparently identical with the originally revised 1938 (1st Soviet) edition of the old Kiselev text. Glagolev's preface to the 18th edition is undated, but an identical preface, dated March 15, 1938 and entitled "Preface to the First Edition," was included in the 2nd (1939) edition.

Number of copies: 1,400,000

Price: paper back 0.90 ruble; binding 0.50 ruble extra

Nikitin, N. N., and Fetisov, A. I., *Geometriya* (Geometry). Part I: Textbook for grades VI through IX of the secondary school. Moscow: Uchpedgiz, 1956. 200 pp.

Apparently 1st edition; the new text may be intended to replace Kiselev's textbooks.

Number of copies: 2,000,000

Price: paper back 1.40 ruble; binding 0.74 ruble extra

Table of contents:

1. Basic concepts
2. Parallel straight lines
3. Triangles
4. Quadrangles
5. Circumference
6. Measurement of line segments. Ratio and proportion
7. Homothetic [figures] and similarity
8. Metric relationship in geometric figures
9. Areas of polygons
10. Regular polygons. Length of circumference and area of a circle

Rybkin, N. *Sbornik zadach po geometrii* (Problems in Geometry). Part I: Plane geometry, for grades VI through IX of the seven-year and secondary schools. 22nd Ed. Moscow: Uchpedgiz, 1956. 120 pp.

Number of copies: 500,000

Price: paper back 0.90 ruble; binding 0.50

TRIGONOMETRY

Rybkin, N. *Pryamolineinaya trigonometriya* (Plane Trigonometry). Textbook for grades IX and X of the secondary school. 32nd Ed. Moscow: Uchpedgiz, 1954. 116 pp.

32nd edition unchanged from the 31st.

Number of copies: 1,300,000
Price: paper back 0.75 ruble

Novoselov, S. I. *Trigonometriya* (Trigonometry). Textbook for grades IX and
X of the secondary school. Moscow: Uchpedgiz, 1956. 96 pp.
Apparently 1st edition, most likely intended to replace Rybkin's text.
Number of copies: 1,600,000
Price: paper back 0.70 ruble; binding 0.50 ruble extra
Contains the following chapters:
1. Angles and arcs; their measurement
2. Trigonometric functions
3. Theorems of addition and their corollaries
4. Basic properties of trigonometric functions
5. Computations using tables
6. Computation of elements in geometric figures
7. Trigonometric equations

Kozheurov, P. Ya. *Kurs trigonometrii dlya tekhnikumov* (Trigonometry for Technicums). 2nd Ed. Moscow: State Publications of Technical-Theoretical Literature, 1955. 296 pp.
Number of copies: 200,000
Price: 6.10 rubles
Note: This text on trigonometry with an emphasis on applications is intended for
the type of schools (technicums) discussed in Chapter 4.

DRAFTING

Abrikosov, A. A. *Chercheniye* (Drafting). Part II: A manual for grades VIII
through X of the secondary school. 2nd Ed. Moscow: Uchpedgiz, 1956. 272 pp.
Number of copies: 1,500,000
Price: paper back 2.20 rubles, cardboard binding 0.75 ruble, cloth binding 1.50
ruble
Table of Contents (major topics):

Chapter IV   Drawing objects of prismatic and of cylindrical shapes
            A. Regular prism
            B. Rectilinear isometric projection
            C. Regular cylinder
Chapter V   Sections and cross-hatching
Chapter VI   Tangencies and transitions
Chapter VII   Drawing objects having the shape of a pyramid or a cone
Chapter VIII   Drawing objects the shape of which includes a sphere or a cir-
            cular ring
Chapter IX   Drawing objects the shapes of which include prisms and cylin-
            ders sectioned by planes
Chapter X   Drawing objects the shapes of which include pyramids and cones
            sectioned by planes
Chapter XI   Drawing objects containing intersecting shapes
Appendices
1. Basic formats of drawings
2. Basic rules for making sketches of objects and fundamentals of assembly
drawings

AN ANALYSIS OF THE SOVIET TEN–YEAR SCHOOL

FINAL EXAMINATION IN ALGEBRA

This appendix contains a description of two analyses made by the Evaluation and Advisory staff of the Educational Testing Service, Princeton, New Jersey. In the first analysis the topics included in the 1955 Soviet (oral) examination questions (Center for International Studies, Translation Series 55-12) are classified in terms of College Board mathematics examinations. In the second analysis the topic coverage of the Soviet examination questions is compared with material taught in American schools.

The Russian terms *bilet* ("ticket") and plural *bilety* are used throughout to designate a particular set of questions (or all such sets) which a student draws, lottery fashion, when he comes up for examination.

ANALYSIS 1

Each *bilet* consisted of three questions. There were 21 *bilety* in all. Since in each case the second question* was marked only "problem or example," without indication as to its nature,† it was not considered here, thus making a total of 42 questions on which to base a comparison.

Because there is no indication given as to the level of response required of the Soviet examinees in order to achieve a perfect score, it seemed better to consider these "questions" as "topics" covered in a

---

* The second question in each *bilet* is evidently selected by teachers in individual schools upon approval by the principal.

† The only specification is that these problems or examples be selected "so as to cover all the topics of the course comprised by the *bilety*."

433

curriculum. Thus, whatever comparison is made here is on the safer basis of topic coverage rather than actual achievement.

In this analysis it was decided in which College Board examination each topic normally appears. Before discussing the results, a brief description of College Board mathematics examinations is in order:*

1. SAT-Mathematics: an aptitude examination which any candidate for a College Board college, regardless of training, can and probably must take. It is based on the arithmetic, intuitive algebra, and informal geometry normally taken by the end of the eighth grade.

2. Intermediate Mathematics: an achievement examination which is based on 1½ years of high school algebra and 1 year of plane geometry.

3. Advanced Mathematics: an achievement examination which is based on 4 years of high school mathematics. (The usual sequence in such a 4-year course is beginning algebra, plane geometry, intermediate algebra, trigonometry, solid geometry, and, perhaps, some advanced alegbra.)

4. Advanced Placement Mathematics: an achievement examination which is based on the year of analytic geometry and calculus normally given to college freshmen. Students taking this examination have had an accelerated program in mathematics in high school and hope to score high enough to be permitted to take sophomore mathematics in their freshman year.

The result of this classification of the topics indicated by the 42 questions is exhibited in Table 1.

TABLE 1. CLASSIFICATION OF TOPICS IN *Bilety* IN TERMS OF COLLEGE BOARD ENTRANCE TESTS IN MATHEMATICS

Examination	Number	Per Cent
Advanced Mathematics	23	55
Intermediate Mathematics	10	24
College Level-		
Advanced Placement	6	14
SAT-Mathematics	2	5
Unclassifiable	1	2

Note that more than half of these topics fall within the purview of

* For further description of these examinations, see the following pamphlets:

College Board Tests, Bulletin of Information 1955–1956, published by the College Entrance Examination Board, P. O. Box 592, Princeton, New Jersey.

College Admission with Advanced Standing, an announcement published by the College Entrance Examination Board, P. O. Box 592, Princeton, New Jersey, January 1954.

the College Board Advanced Mathematics Examination. *On this basis, plus the fact that 29 per cent fall below* (Intermediate Mathematics plus SAT) *and 14 per cent fall above* (Advanced Placement) *the Advanced Mathematics level, it is concluded that in topic coverage in algebra the Russian examination involved is roughly equivalent to the College Board Advanced Mathematics Examination.* Thus it appears that the graduates of American high schools who probably intend to take engineering or the sciences in College Board colleges are examined on approximately the same topics in algebra as are the graduates of the Soviet ten-year schools.

However, to avoid any possible false inferences from these statements, several words of warning seem in order:

1. Only about 10 per cent of the twelfth-grade students in the United States take the mathematics courses on which the Advanced Mathematics Examination is based.*

2. Not all of this 10 per cent actually take the Advanced Mathematics Examination, since there are probably many such students who do not apply for entrance to College Board colleges.

3. Many American high school graduates admitted to college, some to major in engineering and science, have deficiencies in beginning algebra and plane geometry.†

These facts must be balanced with whatever knowledge the MIT Center for International Studies has about the percentages of Soviet students covering the material indicated by the examination at hand. Thus nothing can be said here about equal percentages of American and Soviet students having had equivalent training resulting in equivalent achievement. Even if the percentages were approximately equal, no comparison can be made as to relative training and achievement until information is gained as to the administration, scoring, and score distributions of the *bilety*.

Finally, it should be noted that at least 50 per cent of the material in the College Board Advanced Mathematics Examination consists of trigonometry and solid geometry. Although there are indications in some of the *bilety* (e.g., *Bilet* No. 9, Question 1) that the Soviet students have studied trigonometry, there is no indication of whether or not they have studied any solid geometry. This raises the questions:

---

* Kenneth E. Brown, *Mathematics in Public High Schools,* Bulletin 1953, No. 5. Washington, D. C.: U. S. Dept. of Health, Education, and Welfare, Office of Education, 1953.

† W. L. Williams, "What the colleges are doing about the poorly prepared student," *Amer. Math. Monthly,* February 1954, *61,* 86–88.

1. When do Soviet students study trigonometry and plane, solid, and coordinate geometry?

2. When are they tested on this material?

ANALYSIS 2

Simultaneously with Analysis 1 above, a tabulation of the subject matter covered by all questions was made. The results are as follows:

TABLE 2. DISTRIBUTION OF TOPICS IN *Bilety*

Topic	Frequency	Topic	Frequency
Percentage	2	Arithmetic progressions	2
Ratio and proportion	4	Geometric progressions	2
Combinations and		Quadratic equations	5
permutations	2	Linear ıunction (graph)	2
Special products	1	System of linear equa-	
Factoring	1	tions	1
Complex numbers (in-		Inequalities	3
cluding DeMoivre's		Solutions of inequalities	2
theorem)	4	Equations of degree	
Exponential functions	1	greater than two	2
Logarithmic functions	1	Bézout theorem	1
Logarithms	4	Binomial theorem	2

1. This is a good distribution of algebraic topics—one that could be used and would be desirable to achieve in assembling the algebra part of the College Board Advanced Mathematics Examination. It is a distribution which, with the exceptions noted below, includes topics that American students cover in taking the 2½ years of algebra that is a part of the 4-year sequence in high school mathematics.

2. There are some topics *not* in the 21 *bilety* which are studied by most American students taking a full quota of high school algebra. Among the more important of such topics are coordinate geometry, limits, statistics, probability, and absolute value. It should be noted, however, that none of these topics presently plays a fundamentally important part in American high school algebra; also, they are only lightly covered in the present College Board Advanced Mathematics Examination.

3. However, there are influential movements now afoot in the United States that are likely to recommend a more comprehensive coverage of these topics and other more modern aspects of mathematics. (These movements include the Commission on Mathematics of the College Board, the University of Illinois Committee on School Mathematics,

and a Curriculum Committtee of the National Council of Teachers of Mathematics.) If the forthcoming recommendations of these groups are implemented, then American students who take 4 years of mathematics will be even further ahead of the Soviet students in these respects (assuming, of course, that the Soviet examination under consideration is typical of those given every year).

The above distribution indicates that there are a few subject matter topics studied by Soviet students which all American students taking 4 years of mathematics do not study. These include:

(a) Solution of inequality relationships.

(b) Equations of degree greater than two.

(c) Logarithmic and exponential functions.

Some American high schools do cover these topics lightly, but the subject matter involved is primarily a part of a college freshman course. With the exception of an occasional question that might be considered in the realm of these three topics, the College Board Advanced Mathematics Examination normally does not include this material. However, the College Board Advanced Placement Examination does cover this subject matter thoroughly.

Note: In the opinion of the curriculum groups mentioned under (3) above, these topics should be a part of the high school curriculum.

4. Because of the lottery system used for these *bilety*, it seems fair to assume that all Soviet students who take this examination have studied all of the topics indicated in Table 2 in some fashion or another.

This brings us to a matter of extreme speculation, yet a necessary consideration when one considers topic coverage—how much about each topic is the Soviet student expected to know? The phrasing of each question in each *bilet* is equivalent to a section heading, sometimes even a chapter heading in a textbook. Although it is impossible to determine from the material at hand what kind of response is to be considered correct, there is the possibility that the Soviet examinee is expected to develop his answer to the fullest extent. This would require considerable knowledge of each topic and perhaps be more than is required of the student taking the Advanced Mathematics Examination.

Still in the speculative realm, it should be noted that the manner in which each question is phrased gives some indications that the response required is more theoretical than that required by Advanced Mathematics questions. If this is true, and if there has been no rote memorization of subject matter, then one would have to conclude that the

Soviet examination requires a more advanced and theoretical concept of algebra than the American examinations and, possibly, American teaching. These "ifs" are all important, particularly in view of the statement on page 5 of Translation Series 55-12 that "upon receipt of the *bilety* teachers may acquaint the students with their contents. . . ."

AN ANALYSIS OF THE SOVIET TEN–YEAR SCHOOL
FINAL EXAMINATION IN PHYSICS

This appendix contains a description of two analyses made by the Evaluation and Advisory staff of the Educational Testing Service, Princeton, New Jersey. In the first analysis the topics of the 1955 Soviet (oral) examination questions (Center for International Studies, Translation Series 55-12) are classified in terms of College Board physics examinations. In the second analysis the topic coverage of the Soviet examination questions is compared with material taught in American schools.

The Russian terms *bilet* ("ticket") and plural *bilety* are used throughout to designate a particular set of questions (or all such sets) which a student draws, lottery fashion, when he comes up for examination.

ANALYSIS 1

Each *bilet* consists of three questions. There were 33 *bilety* in all, thus giving a total of 99 questions on which to base a comparison. The candidate draws one *bilet* for his examination.

Because there is no indication as to the level of response required to achieve a perfect score, the questions are compared as "topics" both as to subject matter and as to the type of question, whether theoretical, a problem, or a laboratory demonstration.

Before discussing the results a brief description of College Board physics examinations is in order:*

* For a further description of these examinations, see the following pamphlets: *College Board Tests*, Bulletin of Information 1955–1956, published by the College Entrance Examination Board, P. O. Box 592, Princeton, New Jersey and *College Admission with Advanced Standing*, an announcement published by the College Entrance Examination Board, P. O. Box 592, Princeton, New Jersey.

1. CEEB Achievement Physics: an achievement examination which is based on 3 years of high school science. (The usual sequence is 1 year of general science, 1 year of biology, and 1 year of chemistry or physics, though some students may take both.)

2. CEEB Advanced Placement Physics: an achievement examination based upon 50 per cent more physics than in (1) and correspondingly more mathematics preparation. Students taking this examination have had an accelerated program in physics in high school and hope to score high enough to be permitted to obtain credit for first-year physics. As of 1955 the Advanced Placement Test was just becoming known and the number of candidates was only 1 to 2 per cent of those who took the Achievement Test.

Subject Matter

The results of this classification of the subject matter areas are exhibited in Table 1.

TABLE 1

Subject Matter	CEEB 1956 Achievement Committee Recommendation Per Cent	CEEB 1956 Advanced Placement Test (33 questions) Per Cent	Soviet 1955 Obtained on Basis of 33 *Bilety* Per Cent
Mechanics	40	43	32
Heat	20	9	19
Sound	5	0	3
Light	10	15	12
Electricity	22	18	23
Modern physics	3	15	11
	100	100	100

The relative weighting of subject matter areas is broadly the same. However, note that:

1. The *bilety* have a lower percentage of mechanics and a larger percentage of electricity and modern physics. This arises partly because the Soviet examination is given at the end of the high school year and the CEEB Achievement Test mainly in March, before most candidates have completed the electricity part of the course.

2. The *bilety* seem to devote more time to modern physics, which is again partly explained by the above. In this respect the CEEB Advanced Placement Test is given in May at the end of the year and contains more modern physics material than the *bilety*.

Type of Question

Classification of the type of question is shown in Table 2.

TABLE 2

Type of Question	CEEB 1956 Achievement Test (108 questions) Per Cent	CEEB 1956 Advanced Placement Test (33 questions) Per Cent	Soviet 1955 Obtained on Basis of 33 *Bilety* Per Cent
Laboratory demonstration	0	0	8
Laboratory subject	10	6	0
Problems	11	50	25.5
Average number of lines of computation required for solution	3	12	9

Note here that:

1. No experimental laboratory work is given in the CEEB tests, though the question is under discussion for the future. The translated statement pertaining to the *bilety* is: "Laboratory demonstration: determination of. . . ." This may or may not mean that the student actually has to perform an experiment. However, in view of the statement on page 3, line 15, of Translation Series 55-12 that the candidate "must show . . . ability . . . to solve problems and conduct experiments," the percentage of such questions is listed as being performed experiments in Table 2. In the American tests questions probing knowledge of laboratory techniques have been developed in recent years and are listed under the College Board columns. None of these appeared in the *bilety*.

2. The percentage of problems that the candidate is required to solve according to the *bilety* is about double that in the 1956 College Board Achievement Test and about half that of the Advanced Placement Test (the latter reaching 50 per cent). However, questions are asked in the Achievement Test to an extent equal to the *bilety* 25 per cent which measure the candidate's ability to reason quantitatively, even though not so many mathematical problems are posed for solution.

3. An attempt has been made to estimate the difficulty level of the actual problems given in the *bilety* and the College Board tests. This is a very speculative comparison since it involves:

   a. The average number of lines of mathematical computation required to reach a solution with all the solutions given, including the *bilety*. (The same person, the author, using the same methods, took all three tests.)

b. The requirement of the USSR *bilety* that the candidates take into consideration such factors as:

(1) friction effects

(2) efficiency of practical operation

(3) internal resistance of a battery

(4) the resistance of wiring

(5) numbers which are not rounded off

In general, factors 1 through 4 are neglected, and the numbers are usually rounded off in the Achievement Tests (but not in the Advanced Placement Tests).

As seen in Table 2, the *bilety* have problems which, in regard to average length of computation, are close to the Advanced Placement Test, though subjectively it is thought they are not quite so difficult. It is to be noted also that no constants, properties, coefficients, or units needed to solve the problems are given in the *bilety,* and whether the candidate must know all these or has the use of a handbook of tables in the examination is not known. In the College Board tests any outside information required is usually given in the questions.

ANALYSIS 2

Simultaneously with Analysis 1 above, a tabulation of the topics covered by all questions was made. It has to be recognized that the comparison is with the final examination given to those graduating from Soviet secondary schools and not necessarily with that for admission to college. The results are as follows:

TABLE 3. DISTRIBUTION OF TOPICS IN *Bilety* IN PHYSICS

Topic	Question	Problem	Laboratory
	Frequency		
Mechanics			
Acceleration	2	2	...
Newton's laws	5	2	...
Center of gravity	1	1	...
Resolution of forces and movements	2	1	...
Circular motion	1	...	...
Bernoulli and Pascal	2	...	...
Laws of the lever	...	1	...
Efficiency	...	...	1
Specific gravity (Archimedes)	...	1	1
Pressure (Boyle's Law)	1	1	1
Capillarity and surface tension	2	...	1
Momentum	...	1	...
Kinetic and potential energy	1	...	...
Hooke's Law	1	...	...
Heat			
Mechanical equivalent	1	2	...
Fuel heat	...	2	...
Expansion and absolute temperature	2	1	...
Specific heat	...	1	...
Elevation boiling point and depression of freezing point	1	...	...
Saturated and unsaturated steam	1	...	...
Humidity	1	...	...
Heat engines	2	...	...
Kinetic theory (Brownian Motion)	4	...	...
Sound			
Vibrations and formation of waves	1	...	...
Wavelength	1	...	...
Pendulum	1	..	...
Light			
Illumination	1	1	...
Refractive index	1	..	1
Lens power and focal length	1	1	1
Magnification	...	1	...
Microscope and telescope	1	...	...
Interference and diffraction	1	...	...
Spectroscope and dispersion	2	...	...
Photo luminescence	...	...	1
Electricity			
Charge	2	1	...
Intensity of electric field	2	...	...
Intensity of magnetic field	2	...	...

TABLE 3 (continued)

Topic	Frequency		
	Question	Problem	Laboratory
Capacitance	1	...	...
Internal resistance	2	1	2
Ohm's Law	1	2	...
Faraday's Laws	1	1	...
Motors	1	...	...
Heat and work effects	1	1	...
Lenz's Law	1	...	...
Modern Physics			
Oscillograph	2	...	...
Generation of alternating current and phases	2	...	...
Rectification, feedback and radio	3	...	...
X-rays	1	...	...
Quanta and photoelectricity	1	...	...
Structure of the atom	1	...	...
Structure of the nucleus and fission	1	...	...

This is a good distribution of physics topics and corresponds roughly with most of what is taught in American schools and contains extra topics as shown below. The bold statement of what is taught in American schools is a very subjective estimation.

The topics appearing in the *bilety* which are not taught in most American schools are shown in Table 4. All these are required, however, for the Advanced Placement Test.

TABLE 4.   TOPICS IN *Bilety not* TAUGHT IN MOST
AMERICAN SCHOOLS

Subject Matter	*Bilet* No., Question No., Topic No.	Topic
Mechanics	(1, 2, 6)	1. Derivation of the path equation for motion with constant acceleration
	(6, 3, 1)	2. Surface tension coefficient of water (laboratory demonstration)
	(7, 2, 1)	3. Motion of a body projected at an angle to the horizon
Heat	(30, 2, 1)	1. Saturated and unsaturated steam
	(30, 2, 2)	2. Relation between the volume and pressure of a steam at constant temperature
	(32, 2, 1)	3. Conditions necessary for the functioning of heat engines
	(32, 2, 2)	4. Efficiency of heat engines

TABLE 4 (continued)

Subject Matter	*Bilet* No., Question No., Topic No.	Topic
	(33, 2, 1)	5. Methods of increasing the efficiency of heat engines (steam engine, internal combustion engine)
Light	(24, 1, 2)	1. Derivation of the lens formula
	(31, 1, 1)	2. Photo luminescence and its application
	(31, 1, 2)	3. The pressure of light
Electricity	(1, 1, 3)	1. Coulomb's Law
	(1, 1, 4)	2. Units of quantity of electricity
	(2, 1, 3)	3. Homogeneous electric field
	(4, 1, 1)	4. The work of a charge transfer in a homogeneous electric field
	(4, 1, 3)	5. Units of the difference of potentials
	(5, 1, 2)	6. Units of capacitance
	(12, 1, 4)	7. Magnetic flux
	(16, 1, 2)	8. Period, frequency, phase of an alternating current
	(16, 1, 3)	9. A-c generators
	(17, 1, 2)	10. Working principle of a three-phase motor
	(17, 1, 1)	11. The principle of a three-phase current
	(20, 1, 1)	12. Oscillatory circuit
	(20, 1, 2)	13. Transformation of energy in oscillatory circuit
	(20, 1, 3)	14. Generation of undamped oscillations
	(20, 1, 4)	15. Electrical resonance
Modern Physics	(30, 1, 3)	1. The concept of quanta
	(32, 1, 2)	2. Emission and absorption of energy by an atom

1. In addition to the above there are four topics which the American student would not be expected to know, as follows:

Subject Matter	*Bilet* No., Question No., Topic No.	Topic
Mechanics	(16, 2, 3)	1. N. E. Zhukovskii's work in the field of aviation
Electricity	(19, 1, 3)	1. Progress of electrification of the USSR
Modern Physics	(21, 1, 1)	1. Invention of the radio by Popov
	(30, 1, 2)	2. Stoletov's work on photoelectric effect

2. Percentagewise the number of topics not taught in most American schools is 32 out of 148 topics appearing in the *bilety,* or about 22 per cent. It is not possible to say whether these are taught by giving extra time to the subject or whether other physics topics are left out. One can say that all 32 extra topics are regarded as more difficult

concepts to grasp than the other topics which are taught in American schools.

3. There is heavy emphasis on applications of physics principles in engineering in the *bilety*, whereas in the United States the tendency is more towards a pure attitude to physics.

4. Considerable attention seems to be paid to heat from various kinds of fuel, oil, kerosene, and firewood, and the snow melting box, which is not done much in the United States.

All the above relate to the actual questions in the *bilety* and not to the syllabus since it is so vague and one cannot know how much is taught. Similarly, the comparison deals with topics taught in American schools, tempered with the knowledge of what has been put in College Board tests over the last 3 years. The *bilety*, however, are for graduation from high school and not for entrance to college.

It seems that the *bilety* system, which allows the *bilety* topics to be published, enables the candidate to know in advance what questions he will be asked and, further, to study only the material of such questions. The College Board system, requiring the candidate to attempt all of somewhat over one hundred questions which are not published beforehand, would seem to require a broader, surer knowledge, even if it does not go quite so deep.

EXAMPLES OF PROBLEMS USED IN SOVIET MATHEMATIC "OLYMPIC GAMES," THAT IS, PUBLIC CONTESTS IN SOLVING MATHEMATICAL PROBLEMS ORGANIZED FOR STUDENTS OF SECONDARY SCHOOLS

The study of mathematics is particularly emphasized and encouraged in Soviet schools. One means of promoting students' interest in mathematics has been the holding of public contests—citywide, regional, and national. Dr. Philip Franklin, Professor of Mathematics at the Massachusetts Institute of Technology, examined a number of Soviet contest problems in mathematics, including the problems reproduced below. We quote Professor Franklin's comment:

These sample questions from prize contests for secondary school students are well suited for the exceptionally able student. Although about half have some similarity to problems found in textbooks, all are above-average difficulty and many show the originality and ingenuity of the examiner. Without going beyond secondary school material, they test the ability to apply and combine basic ideas in novel situations.

PROBLEMS

1. Factor this expression: $x^5 + x + 1$

Leningrad, 1951, grade VIII

2. Factor this expression: $a^{10} + a^5 + 1$

Lvov, 1946, grades IX–X

3. Solve this system of equations:

$$xy(x + y) = 30$$
$$x^3 + y^3 = 35$$

Leningrad, 1951, grade IX

4. Two regular tetrahedrons are placed within a cube in such a manner that four apexes of the cube are also apexes of one of the tetrahedrons and the remaining four apexes of the cube are the apexes of the second tetrahedron. What part of the cube's volume is occupied by the volume of the part common to both tetrahedrons?

Ivanovo, 1951, grades IX–X

5. A space quadrangle is circumscribed about a sphere. Prove that the points of tangency are in one plane.

Moscow, 1950, grades IX–X

6. Prove that the sum of the distances from any point within a regular tetrahedron to its faces is a constant.

Stalingrad, 1950, grade X

7. Prove that the straight lines from the mid-point of the altitude of a regular tetrahedron to the apexes of its base are mutually perpendicular.

Kazan', 1947, grades IX–X

8. 500 boxes contain apples. It is known that no box can hold more than 240 apples. Prove that at least 3 boxes each contain the same number of apples.

Kiev, 1950, grades VII–VIII

9. How many zeros are there in $50! = 1 \cdot 2 \cdot 3 \cdot 4 \cdots 49 \cdot 50$?

Lvov, 1950, grades VII–VIII

10. How many times in twenty-four hours are the pointers of a clock perpendicular to each other?

Kiev, 1950, grades VII–VIII

11. What is the largest possible number of acute angles that a convex polygon with n sides can have?

Kiev, 1949, grades IX–X

12. Prove that a 13-sided convex polygon cannot be divided into parallelograms.

Moscow, 1947, grades VII–VIII

13. Prove that, if a is any whole number, $a^7 - a$ is divisible by 42.

Stalingrad, 1950, grade X

14. Show that a complex number

$$a + ib$$

(where $i = \sqrt{1}$; a and b are real), the absolute value of which is equal to unity and $b \neq 0$, can be represented in the form:

$$a + ib = \frac{c + i}{c - i},$$

where c is a real number.

Kazan', 1947, grade X

15. Numbers 1, 2, 3, ..., 101 (altogether 101 numbers) are placed in a series of unknown order. Show that 90 of these numbers can be struck out so that the remaining integers will occur either in descending or ascending order of magnitude.

Moscow, 1950, grades IX–X

16. Prove that there can be no seven-edged polyhedron.

Kiev, 1952, grades IX–X

17. Prove that

$$\frac{n}{12} + \frac{n^2}{8} + \frac{n^3}{24}$$

is a whole number if n is an even number.

Republican Olympics of Latvian SSR, 1952, grades VIII–IX

18. Solve this system of fifteen equations with fifteen unknowns:

$$1 - x_1 x_2 = 0$$
$$1 - x_2 x_3 = 0$$
$$1 - x_3 x_4 = 0$$
$$\ldots\ldots\ldots\ldots$$
$$1 - x_{14} x_{15} = 0$$
$$1 - x_{15} x_1 = 0$$

Moscow, 1952, grade VII

19. Prove that if $n > 1$ then

$$2 < \left(1 + \frac{1}{n}\right)^n < 3$$

Ordzhonikidze, 1953, grade X

Source: The sample problems quoted in this Appendix were taken from A. N. Kolmogorov, *O professii matematika* (On the Profession of a Mathematician), 2nd Ed., enlarged. Moscow: "Sovetskaya Nauka," 1954.

Professor Kolmogorov, one of the best known mathematicians in the Soviet Union, is Dean of the Mechanics-Mathematics Faculty, Moscow University, and a member of the USSR Academy of Sciences.

APPENDIX

— G ————————————————————————

THIRD ANNUAL [AMERICAN] ENGINEERING

TECHNICIAN SURVEY OF ENROLLMENTS

AND GRADUATES*

1955–1956

This annual survey of engineering technician enrollments and estimated graduates for 1955–1956 shows a continued increase of both. Data for 148 schools are included, 29 of which have curricula accredited by ECPD.

Enrollments, Table I, in full-time programs are up 12% to 32,664 while part-time enrollments are up somewhat more, 14%, due to reports from 5 schools which last year included small or no part-time enrollments. This gives a total enrollment of 64,722.

* We are indebted to the American Society for Engineering Education and to Donald C. Metz, Director, Technical Institute, University of Dayton, under whose chairmanship this survey was made, for permission to publish this material here.

TABLE I. ENGINEERING TECHNICIAN ENROLLMENTS

Institutions with ECPD Accredited Technical Institute Programs*

	1954–1955		1955–1956	
	Students	Institutions	Students	Institutions
Full-time	11,649	29	13,179	29
Part-time	7,857	15	11,558	28
Total	19,506	29	24,737	29

Institutions with No ECPD Accredited Technical Institute Programs

	1954–1955		1955–1956	
	Students	Institutions	Students	Institutions
Full-time	17,553	110	19,485	108
Part-time	20,339	64	20,500	67
Total	37,892	119	39,985	119

All Institutions

	1954–1955		1955–1956	
	Students	Institutions	Students	Institutions
Full-time	29,202	139	32,664	137
Part-time	28,196	79	32,058	85
Total	57,398	148	64,722	148

* Enrollments in both accredited and non-accredited programs.

The number of graduates, Table II, increased 8% to 15,314, with graduates from full-time programs accounting for 11,403 or 74% of the total. Since the part-time graduates are fully employed while attending school, many of them will not affect the available engineering technician supply.

TABLE II. ENGINEERING TECHNICIAN GRADUATES

Institutions with ECPD Accredited Technical Institute Programs*

	1954–1955		1955–1956	
	Graduates	Institutions	Estimated Graduates	Institutions
Full-time	4,370	29	4,461	29
Part-time	969	14	1,038	15
Total	5,339	29	5,499	29

Institutions with No ECPD Accredited Technical Institute Programs

	1954–1955		1955–1956	
	Graduates	Institutions	Estimated Graduates	Institutions
Full-time	6,145	102	6,942	101
Part-time	2,669	48	2,873	53
Total	8,814	119	9,815	119

All Institutions

	1954–1955		1955–1956	
	Graduates	Institutions	Estimated Graduates	Institutions
Full-time	10,515	131	11,403	130
Part-time	3,638	62	3,911	68
Total	14,153	148	15,314	148

* Graduates from both accredited and non-accredited programs.

It is currently estimated that the annual demand for engineering technicians is approximately 40,000 to 50,000, or nearly five times the number graduating from full-time programs. If it is assumed that the part-time graduates are employees seeking up-grading, they serve to increase the supply during their schooling, before graduation. This would still indicate an increase of three times the current number. To meet this demand for graduates, enrollments would have to increase to between 150,000 and 200,000.

From evidence available, it is believed there are between 175 and 200 schools offering programs for training engineering technicians. Many industries are providing their own training programs. Persons are also enterng the field who have completed only part of their engineering or scientific education. Still, if the need is to be met, a great increase in the number and quality of schools is required.

Donald C. Metz, Chairman
Manpower Studies
Technical Institute Division
American Society for Engineering Education

EXAMPLES OF PROBLEMS ASSIGNED

IN A WRITTEN ENTRANCE EXAMINATION GIVEN

TO THE APPLICANTS FOR ADMISSION

TO THE MECHANICS–MATHEMATICS FACULTY,

MOSCOW UNIVERSITY IN 1953

The following six problems constitute one of the sets assigned in the written entrance test in mathematics. It is not known how much time was allowed for this particular examination; two hours is the duration usually mentioned in Soviet sources with reference to the written tests.

1. Within a hexagon the side of which is equal a, place a square of the largest possible size. Find the side of this square.

2. It is known that $\sin \beta = 4/5$. What is the value of this ratio:

$$\frac{\sqrt{3} \sin (\alpha + \beta) - 2 \sec \frac{\pi}{6} \cos (\alpha + \beta)}{\sin \alpha} = ?$$

(Consider β being both an acute and an obtuse angle.)

3. Two spheres are placed within a regular pyramid with a hexagonal base. The first sphere touches the base and all the six sides; the second sphere rests upon the first sphere and also touches all the sides of the pyramid. Find the ratio of the volumes of the two spheres.

4. Two factories received an order for an identical number of machines. The first factory started 20 days earlier and finished the work 5 days earlier than the second factory. At the moment when the number of machines made by both factories taken together was equal to one-third of the total number on order, the number of machines made by the first factory was four times the number produced by the second.

The first factory worked on the order altogether x days, producing m machines per day; the second factory worked y days, producing n machines per day. Find those of the quantities x, y, m, and n, and those of ratios $x:y$ and $m:n$ which can be determined from the data given in the problem.

5. Which values of x fulfill the inequality

$$\frac{1}{x} < \frac{1}{x-1} - \frac{1}{2}?$$

6. How many six-cipher numbers are there is which three ciphers are even numbers and three are uneven?

Note: A zero is an even number; it is understood that a zero is not to be used as the first cipher of a six-cipher number.

Source: A. N. Kolmogorov, *O professii matematika* (On the Profession of a Mathematician), 2nd Ed., enlarged. Moscow: "Sovetskaya Nauka," 1954.

(Additional examples of examination problems from this source are cited in Cenis Translation Series 55-43.)

TRANSLATION OF A SOVIET ARTICLE

ON THE EDUCATIONAL REFORMS

DECREED IN 1954*

In connection with the decision of the USSR Council of Ministers and the Central Committee of the KPSS on improving the training, distribution, and utilization of specialists with higher education, the Minister of Higher Education in his order of September 9, 1954 directed the main administrations, administrations, and departments of the Ministry to undertake steps toward the realization of measures called for by the Party and the government.

The Administration in charge of plans for the preparation and distribution of young specialists and the Planning-Financial Administration have been directed to develop within a month a plan for measures toward improvement in the planning of the training of specialists.

Main administrations, the Planning-Financial, and the Methodological Administrations have been directed to review within a two-month period the composition of faculties and specialties in the institutions of higher education with a view to their most rational redistribution by economic regions and to liquidating parallelism in the training of specialists.

The Administration of the Secondary Specialized Schools [technicums] has been directed to develop within a two-month period a plan for measures toward the realization of the directive to expand considerably the number of admissions to the specialized secondary schools, drawing upon those who have completed a ten-year school. In 1955–1956 the proportion of such students must be not less than 60 per cent of the total number admitted to the specialized secondary schools.

In harmony with the task of training specialists of broad profile, the Methodological Administration, together with the main administrations, must within a four-month period develop and coordinate with the USSR GOSPLAN and the relevant ministries and agencies a plan for the consolidation of the academic chairs and faculties in the institutions of higher education.

* Source: Vestnik vysshei shkoly, No. 10, October 1954, section entitled, "At the Ministry of Higher Education," p. 54, entire text.

The Methodological Administration also has been directed to submit within a month for approval a plan for the revision of the higher education curricula and syllabi in accordance with the new list of specialties; and also [to submit] a procedural plan for broadening the existing specializations within the specialties and establishing a list of specialties in the new technologies.

The Administration of the Specialized Secondary Schools has been entrusted to develop, also within a two-month period, a list of specialties for the specialized secondary schools and to re-examine the curricula and syllabi so that the training of cadres in the new specialties can be started on September 1, 1955.

The Textbook Department has been instructed, in cooperation with the main administrations, to investigate within a month the adequacy of the supply of textbooks and reference texts in the basic subjects at the institutions within the jurisdiction of the Ministry. The Textbook Department has also been given the responsibility, jointly with the Main, the Methodological, and the Planning-Financial Administrations, to work out within a two-month period a draft proposal on competitions in writing the best textbook and to draft suggestions on [the determination of] the author's royalty for writing a textbook [to be made] independent of the number of printing sheets.

The Main Department of Procurement [Glavsnab], together with the main administrations and the Planning-Financial Administration, is to work out within a three-month period a plan for the establishment during 1954–1957 of machine shops for training purposes at all the institutions of higher technical education and at the institutes and faculties of mechanization of agriculture.

The Methodological Administration jointly with the main administrations within a two-month period has been assigned to the drafting of a new set of regulations on the industrial training of students.

The Minister has given a number of instructions to the main administrations, administrations, and departments on the problems of further development of research and methodological work, on the allocation of funds for the construction of experimental models [mock-ups], sample machines, [and] laboratory testing stands.

The Main Administration of Universities and Institutions of Higher Education in Economics and in Law, the Methodological and Planning-Financial Administrations, and the Administration for the Planning of Training and Distribution of Young Specialists have been directed to re-examine within a two-month period university curricula with the view of bringing the university training of specialists closer to the demands within the sectors of the national economy, culture, and education; and also to effect necessary changes in the composition of the student body in the universities to make it correspond with the demands of the national economy and culture for the following specialties: astronomy, geophysics, geomorphology, Slavic and classical philology, fine arts studies, and others in which the number of graduating specialists yearly exceeds the demand for them.

The Minister also has obligated the Main, the Methodological, and the Planning-Financial Administrations, and the Administration of Specialized Secondary Schools within a month to explore steps for a further development of higher education by correspondence and in the evening courses.

SOVIET REFERENCES

TO THE AMERICAN SYSTEM

OF HIGHER TECHNICAL EDUCATION

(1934–1935 Debate on the Need for Educational Reform)*

It is of interest that in the discussion of 1934–1935, during which the entire system of Soviet higher technical education was reviewed, Soviet writers studied and referred to the practices of higher technical education in the United States.

The contributors to the debate were careful to qualify their references to American technical education. Thus, for instance, engineers Gurtovoi and Deshalit preface a new list of specialties proposed by them with the following statement:

To raise a question about training broadly qualified engineers is by no means an attempt, as some people interpret the issue, blindly to copy the practices of Western European countries and particularly of the United States.†

Nevertheless, having noted "the peculiarities of socialist conditions," the authors conclude that the Soviets should profit by American practices in higher technical education:

Naturally we have no intention of denying ourselves the benefit of the experience of the capitalist countries and particularly of America, but we should, and we must, adopt it critically.

In the reviews of the then existing lists of engineering specialties this "experience of capitalist countries and particularly of America" emerged as an extremely telling argument for consolidating related fields of engineering training and rejecting narrow specialization.

* This is a condensed translation of an appendix to a working memorandum written by Dr. Barbara Tschirwa, Harvard University, for the Center for International Studies, Massachusetts Institute of Technology.

† *Vysshaya tekhnicheskaya shkola*, 1935, No. 8, p. 20.

The system of higher technical education in the United States was discussed in a large number of articles. In most cases specific references were made to the Massachusetts Institute of Technology, but arguments were generalized to apply to all engineering schools in the United States, as in the following:

> The curricular content and methodology of instruction in other higher technical schools of the United States are comparable to those cited inasmuch as MIT is one of the leading schools of higher technical education in America.

In an article entitled "The Curricular Content of Engineering Training in the USA," a Soviet engineer, N. I. Barabashev, presents a detailed analysis of the MIT curricula. The author points out that the Institute [MIT] graduates specialists of broad qualifications:

> The task of training at MIT is to prepare students for work in *any* branch of mechanical specialties, be it the construction of internal combustion engines, machine construction, locomotive construction, steam engines, power stations, or others.*

In this article the author included MIT course schedules for all eight semesters. In commenting on the programs under which MIT trains engineers of broad competency, the author suggested that "the rational organization of the academic process in the USA" should be made use of in the Soviet schools.

During the discussion of Soviet technical education and its policy of narrow specialization there developed a particular interest in the professional designations used in American technical schools. In an article, "New Era in Engineering Education," it was pointed out that MIT,

> . . . the largest engineering school in the USA, limits its *uchebnyi* plans in the basic specialties to four categories: chemical, construction, electrical engineering, and mechanical.

The author adds that, in his opinion, in the Soviet system of technical training,

> . . . these four branches, with the addition of mining and metallurgy and perhaps in certain schools one or two others, should be at the present time sufficient for the basic *uchebnyi* plans; the various specializations should be more correctly considered to be branches rather than coordinate main stems [of training]; and they should be achieved after graduation from higher schools and not necessarily via the graduate courses of study.†

The fact that four broad specialties [in American technical education] suffice to prepare engineers for work in 337 professional categories appears to have been extremely significant to the Soviet commentators.‡

* *Vysshaya tekhnicheskaya shkola,* 1935, No. 11, p. 92.

† G. Vil'yams, *Vysshaya tekhnicheskaya shkola,* 1935, No. 13, p. 877.

‡ *Vysshaya tekhnicheskaya shkola,* 1935, No. 4, p. 135, cites figures in translation of an American article by Hoover (Herbert Hoover?), "Specializing in Engineering Professions."

Comparisons with the American system of technical education provided much material for the formulation and solution of a whole series of questions which were raised in the Soviet Union during the discussion of 1934–1935. Thus, in the proposals for a new list of specialties, it was argued that the relative importance of elective course subjects should be increased: "The relative weight of these subjects must be increased by two or three times."*
In the articles devoted to American technical education published during this period the desirability of introducing elective subjects was mentioned quite frequently. It was stated that at MIT the students could select any two subjects among the following specialized subjects: "airplanes, automatic tools, fire protection, locomotives, steam turbines, heat engineering measurements, and the mechanical equipment of buildings."†

In an article on the importance of training engineers of broad qualifications the MIT curricula was cited as a model:

> The institute [MIT] proposes to graduate specialists of broad range in mechanical engineering. Preparation is divided into three successive stages: (1) general theoretical preparation, 1st and 2nd years; (2) general engineering preparation, 3rd year; and (3) narrower specialization during the 4th year.‡

Although Soviet investigators reiterated that the "purposes of American training are different from those of the Soviet Union," the examination of American higher technical education made by them in the 1930's led to a number of constructive conclusions.

* *Vysshaya tekhnicheskaya shkola,* 1935, No. 8, p. 19.
† *Vysshaya tekhnicheskaya shkola,* 1935, No. 11, pp. 96–97.
‡ *Vysshaya tekhnicheskaya shkola,* 1935, No. 11, p. 92.

EXCERPT FROM "INSTRUCTION

ON THE APPLICATION OF THE DECISIONS

OF THE COUNCIL OF PEOPLE'S

COMMISSARS USSR OF MARCH 20, 1937

AND APRIL 26, 1938 ENTITLED

'ON ACADEMIC DEGREES AND TITLES',"

WITH AMENDMENTS TO MAY 22, 1954*

26. The title of *Assistent* (Junior Research Associate)† may be given to persons who have completed higher education, who have sufficient qualifications for teaching and research, and who conduct such activities under the supervision of a professor or a docent (senior research associate). The title of *Assistent* (Junior Research Associate) is granted, upon recommendation of a department [*kafedra*] head (professor), by order of the director of the institution of higher education (research institute) in confirmation of the [learned] council's decision.

27. The academic title of Docent is given by the Higher Attestation Commission to persons who have the academic degree of *kandidat nauk* and who have been elected competitively to the position of docent

The academic title of Senior Research Associate is given to persons who have the academic degree *kandidat nauk* and who have held a staff position of senior research associate [in a research institute] for not less than one year.

28. The academic title of Professor is given by the Higher Attestation Commission to persons who have the academic degree of *doktor nauk* and who have been confirmed by VKVSh [now the Ministry of Higher Education] in the position of a department [*kafedra*] head or who, on a competitive basis,

* *Source: Vysshaya shkola,* compiled by M. I. Movshovich, pp. 263 f.

† *Assistent* is a teaching rank, and "junior research associate" is a rank of equal level given to research workers at the institutes of the USSR Academy of Sciences

have been elected by the council of the institute to the position of professor
and have been confirmed for such a position by the *narkomat* [now ministry]
and who have had one year of successful teaching activity in the capacity of
professor.

Persons who have the academic degree of *doktor nauk* and who work in
research institutions are given the academic title of Professor by the Higher
Attestation Commission if those persons for not less than one year have had
charge of work as research leaders at the head of a research section or
a laboratory.

29. The Higher Attestation Commission may grant academic titles to
persons who hold no academic degrees but who are highly qualified specialists with extensive practical experience in industry, transport, or agriculture
or in the field of the arts, and who have been enlisted to teach in the institutions of higher education . . . upon their having been elected on a competitive basis to the position of professor or docent, but only after one year of
successful teaching in a given institution of higher education from the day
of their appointment on a competitive basis to such a vacancy.

30. The right to nominate candidates for an academic title is given to the
academic councils of all institutions of higher education (including those of
correspondence education) and to the councils of research institutions.

31. The decisions of the councils on the granting of the academic titles of
Professor, Docent (Senior Research Associate), and *Assistent* (Junior Research
Associate) are arrived at by secret balloting in accordance with the procedure
described in paragraph 21 of this instruction.

and others. Similar distinction applies to other pairs of titles mentioned in this
excerpt, except that the rank of Professor is both a teaching and a research rank.

EXAMPLES OF ANNOUNCEMENTS PUBLISHED

BY SOVIET INSTITUTIONS OF HIGHER EDUCATION

INVITING APPLICATIONS TO COMPETE

FOR ACADEMIC APPOINTMENTS

Example I. *Source: Kazakhstanskaya pravda,* April 29, 1955, p. 4.

Kazakh State University Named after S. M. Kirov, of the USSR Ministry of Higher Education, announces a competition for the following vacant positions:

Department Heads, professors or docents: general physics, higher algebra, physical chemistry, Russian language, foreign languages, history of the USSR, psychology and pedagogy, physical education and sports, foundations of Marxism-Leninism, philosophy, industrial economics, general history, higher geometry, and oil and gas geology;

Docents and Senior Teachers in the Departments of general physics, higher algebra, physical chemistry, Russian language, foreign languages, history of the USSR, psychology and pedagogy, physical education and sports, foundations of Marxism-Leninism, philosophy, optics and spectroscopy, differential equations, theoretical mechanics, economic geography, physical geography, petrography, general geology, oil and gas geology, Russian literature, general history (medieval and ancient), economic statistics, finances and credit, bookkeeping-accounting, organization of Soviet trade, and commodities study;

Assistants and Teachers in the Departments of: general physics, physical chemistry, Russian language, foreign languages, physical education and sports, foundations of Marxism-Leninism.

Example II. *Source: Kommunist,* April 7, 1955, p. 4.

USSR Ministry of Higher Education, Erivan' Polytechnic Institute announces competition for the following vacant positions:

Geology Department Head: professor or docent.

Docents for the Departments of: geodesy, descriptive geometry, technology of electrochemical manufactures, heat engineering and thermodynamics, electric power stations, electric distribution networks and systems, technology of machine construction, mining, and utilization of water power.

Example III. *Source: Zarya vostoka,* March 26, 1955, p. 4.
Announcement of the Georgia Polytechnic Institute in Tbilisi:

1. Department Heads:
   Technology of silicates
   Theory of mechanisms and machines
   Automation of production processes
   Mining electrotechniques
   Mine ventilation and safety engineering
   Technology of inorganic substances
   Construction [material] manufacture
   Structural constructions
   Physics
2. Docents and Assistants for the Departments:
   Mineralogy, petrography, and crystallography
   Automotive highways
   Central electric power plants
   Automotive repairs and operation
   Technology of electrochemical manufactures

ON THE CONDUCT OF COMPETITIONS

IN FILLING PROFESSORIAL–TEACHING

POSITIONS AT THE SOVIET

INSTITUTIONS OF HIGHER EDUCATION

(Excerpts from "Replies to Questions from the Readers,"
Vestnik vysshei shkoly, No. 2, February 1955.)

In the carrying out of competitions to fill professorial-teaching vacancies the names of all individuals who participated in the competition—whether the individuals received positive or negative recommendations from the Committee on Competitions—must be included in the lists submitted for secret balloting. The question of electing an applicant to a professorial-teaching position is decided by the council of the institution by a secret ballot.

An individual may compete for a position at only one institution at a time, because to participate in competition at several schools may result in a disruption of the academic process in the event a person should be elected to two or more schools.

An instructor who does not participate in the announced competition for the position held by him up to that time, and provided that another person is elected to hold that position, is dismissed without severance pay, not having participated in the competition.

If an instructor participates in a competition for the position up to that time held by him and if, as a result of such competition, another person is elected, said instructor is dismissed with the entry in his labor book "Dismissed as a Consequence of Competition." Under this condition professors or teachers are given severance pay only in the event no prior two-week notice of dismissal, as provided by the regulations, had been given.

Individuals who desire to participate in competitions conducted by the institutions of higher education for the positions of docent, professor, and department chairman . . . have the right to demand from the administration [present employing organization] the [written] evaluations which are required for participation in the announced competitions. In such an event the administration is obligated to give to such persons its objective evaluations. [Successful applicants in this (docent, professor, department head) category] must be released from positions held prior to the election [by competition].

The rule indicated above does not extend to individuals who wish to participate in a competition for teaching positions of teacher [*prepodavatel'*], *assistent,* and senior teacher. In their case a transfer to an institution of higher education, in the event they are elected, can take place only with the consent of the administration at the place of their employment.

APPENDIX
— N

A. A. VORONOV, *ELEMENTY TEORII AVTOMATICHESKOVO REGULIROVANIYA* (1954)

A. EVALUATION BY PROFESSOR MYRON A. HOFFMAN, MIT

In attempting to evaluate the contents of A. A. Voronov's book *Elementary Theory of Automatic Regulation* (1954), I have based my conclusions on a comparison with similar texts currently in use in this country. These include *Servomechanisms and Regulating System Design*, Vol. 1, by H. Chestnut and R. W. Mayer (1951) and *Principles of Automatic Controls* by F. E. Nixon (1953). These texts are quite comparable in number of pages and coverage of the subject.

The Russian text covers material suitable for a one-term senior course if the seniors have adequate preparation in mathematics, including elementary complex variable theory and operational calculus. Our seniors at MIT generally have the necessary background. As a third-year subject it would probably take one and a half to two terms for adequate coverage (as it would in this country).

The treatment in the Russian text of the introductory material on present-day applications and the components commonly found in automatic control systems appears quite comparable to ours.

The fundamental subject of system stability is covered in a somewhat different manner than in our first texts. While our elementary texts stress simple graphical techniques for evaluating system stability, the Russian text emphasizes the more complicated analytical approach.

The important subject of frequency response analysis is covered in some detail in Voronov's book. However, there seems to be much less discussion of synthesis techniques than in our texts. That is to say, the major portions of the American texts I used for comparison are devoted to discussions of various techniques for obtaining the desired system performance and methods for including special compensation devices. This appears to be touched on only briefly in the Russian text.

Finally, the Russian text makes no mention of the root-locus technique, another very useful graphical technique for system analysis and design.

In summary I would say that the text is more comparable to the earlier book by G. S. Brown and D. P. Campbell, *Principles of Servomechanisms*, published in 1948. Even when compared to this early text (which was a pioneer work in the field), the Russian text reveals a lack of emphasis on the important graphical tools and techniques which enable designers to *shortcut* much laborious calculation. (However, they are presented with enough analytical tools to obtain comparable answers.)

B. EXCERPTS:

From the Introduction, p. 3.

The basic material utilized in writing this book was given by the author in 1948-1952 in lectures at the MVTU for the aspirants and research workers and at the Moscow Power Institute (Molotov) for the undergraduate students.

In revising this text the author attempted to bring it closer to the syllabus in the theory of automatic regulation for the specialty of "Automatic and Measuring Devices" in the polytechnic power and industrial VUZY approved by the Ministry of Higher Education USSR, August 10, 1951.

From page 23.

The introduction of automation into the separate industrial processes in the capitalist countries leads to throwing masses of workers out into the street. The remaining workers are, even to a greater extent, enslaved by the machine, becoming merely its appurtenances. The development of science in the field of automation reflects the contradictions which are tearing capitalist society asunder. An enormous quantity of effort and time is given to thinking up various superfluous ingenuities to the harm of scientific and technological rationality for the sole purpose of overcoming the patent restriction established by competitors. In contrast with the drive of Soviet engineering toward the creation of basic solutions, normalization, and unification of means for automation, capitalist automation is characterized by diversity and superfluity of many types of automatic devices brought into being because of the same patent situation.

. . . .

The so-called cybernetics has become a fashionable novelty in foreign countries lately.

The basic objective of cybernetics is to replace the man by a machine and, as to his intellectual activity, the creation of "thinking" machines—thinking in the direction needed by the imperialists. Cyberneticians assure us that this problem will be solved if a computing machine is created in which the number of sensitive cells will be equal to the number of cells in a human brain.

. . . .

A rational and harmonious development of automation is impossible in the capitalist world. Only in socialist society where automation serves the entire people is powerful and harmonious development possible.

— O

A NOTE ON THE USSR ACADEMY OF SCIENCES

As of 1949 the USSR Academy of Sciences engaged the work of over 6,000 scientists, of whom 918 had doctor's and 2,455 candidate's degrees, in its eight major departments, namely:

(1) Physics-Mathematics Sciences, of which the main units were:
Steklov Mathematics Institute
Lebedev Physics Institute
Physico-Technical Institute
Institute of Physical Problems
Crystallography Institute
Geophysics Institute
Institute of Marine Hydrophysics
Main Astronomical Observatory
Crimean Astrophysical Observatory
Institute of Theoretical Astronomy
Astronomical Council
(2) Chemical Sciences, with eight major institutes
(3) Geological-Geographical Sciences—six major units
(4) Biological Sciences—eleven major units
(5) Technical Sciences, including:
Krzhizhanovski Energetics Institute
Institute of Mineral Fuels
Oil Institute
Metallurgical Institute
Institute of Mining
Institute of Machine Studies
Mechanics Institute
Institute of Precision Mechanics and of Computational Techniques
Automation and Telemechanics Institute
(6) History and Philosophy
(7) Economics and Law
(8) Literature and Languages

A SELECTIVE BIBLIOGRAPHY ON THE

SOVIET EDUCATIONAL SYSTEM

This bibliography is arranged in three parts. Part One lists representative books, articles, and reference material in English. Part Two lists a number of source memoranda and translations which were made by the Center for International Studies in the course of the original study upon which this volume is based. Part Three is limited to the Russian-language sources, including both the Soviet and émigré publications, which are most readily available in American libraries.

PART ONE

Books and Pamphlets

Academic Freedom under the Soviet Regime. A symposium of refugee scholars and scientists who have escaped from the USSR. Munich: The Institute for the Study of the USSR, 1954.

Ashby, Eric. *Scientist in Russia.* New York and London: Penguin Books, Ltd., 1947.

British Students Visit the Soviet Union. A report of a delegation of the National Union of Students of the universities and colleges of England, Wales, and Northern Ireland. London: K-H Services, Ltd., May 1951.

Counts, George S. *The Challenge of Soviet Education.* New York: McGraw-Hill Book Company, 1957.

Counts, George S., and Nucia P. Lodge. *The Country of the Blind.* Boston: Houghton Mifflin Company, 1949.

DeWitt, Nicholas. *Soviet Professional Manpower.* Washington, D.C.: National Science Foundation, 1955.

Efron, Alexander. *The Teaching of Physical Sciences in the Secondary Schools of the United States, France, and Soviet Russia.* New York: Teachers College, Columbia University, 1937.

Engineering Education in the Soviet Union. Report of a team of engineers who visited Russia in the autumn of 1956. The Institution of Civil Engineers, the

Institution of Mechanical Engineers, and the Institution of Electrical Engineers. London: Unwin Brothers, Ltd., 1957.

Ignatiev, Paul N., Dimitry M. Odinetz, and Paul J. Novgorotsev. *Russian Schools and Universities in the World War.* New Haven: Yale University Press, 1929.

Recent Trends in Soviet Schools. Intelligence Report No. 6685. Washington, D.C.: Department of State, Office of Intelligence Research, September 10, 1954.

The Soviet Educational System: A Basic Outline. London: British Foreign Office, May 1950.

Soviet Science. A symposium presented on December 27, 1951 at the Philadelphia meeting of the American Association for the Advancement of Science. Arranged by Conway Zirkle and Howard A. Meyerhoff. Washington, D.C.: American Association for the Advancement of Science, 1952.

Tokaev, G. A. *Betrayal of an Ideal.* London: The Harvill Press, 1954.

Trilling, Leon. *Soviet Education in Aeronautics: A Case Study.* Cambridge: Center for International Studies, Massachusetts Institute of Technology, 1956 (mimeographed).

Vucinich, Alexander. *The Soviet Academy of Sciences.* Hoover Institute Studies, Series E: Institutions, No. 3. Stanford: Stanford University Press, 1956.

Articles

Ashby, Eric, "Soviet Science *Is* a Challenge to Us," *New York Times Magazine,* April 18, 1954.

"British Scientists' Visit to Russia: New Links of Learning," *Times Educational Supplement* (London), No. 1576, July 14, 1945.

"Delegation to Russia: Questions Answered," *Times Educational Supplement* (London), No. 1953, October 3, 1952.

Fine, Benjamin, "Russia Is Overtaking U.S. in Training of Technicians," *New York Times,* November 7, 1954.

Frayn, Michael, "Cambridge Goes to Moscow," *Everybody's,* February 9, 1957.

Gnedenko, B. V. "Mathematical Education in the USSR," *The American Mathematical Monthly,* Vol. 64, No. 6, June–July 1957. (Translation of an article written for publication in the United States by a Soviet Professor of Mathematics, Kiev University, Member of the Academy of Sciences of the Ukrainian SSR.)

"Information on Russian Schools," *Times Educational Supplement* (London), No. 1824, April 14, 1950.

"Technology in the Soviet Schools," *Times Educational Supplement* (London), No. 1959, November 14, 1952.

Tolpin, J. G., "Engineering Education in the Soviet Union," *Journal of Engineering Education* (Pittsburgh, Pa.), Vol. 34, October 1943.

Turkevich, John, "Soviet Science in the Post-Stalin Era," *The Annals of the American Academy of Political and Social Science,* January 1956.

————, "The Soviet's Scientific Elite," *Saturday Review,* March 24, 1956.

"University Life in Russia: for the Privileged," *Times Educational Supplement* (London), No. 1851, October 20, 1950.

Reference and Other Material

The Current Digest of the Soviet Press. Published weekly by the Joint Committee on Slavic Studies, American Council of Learned Societies and Social Science Research Council, New York.

Gorokhoff, Boris I. "Materials for the Study of Soviet Specialized Education." Unpublished mimeographed report. Washington, D.C.: National Research Council, Office of Scientific Personnel, 1952.

The National Economy of the USSR, a Statistical Compilation, issued by the Central Statistical Administration, USSR Council of Ministers, Moscow, 1956. Mimeographed translation published by the U.S. Government. Original title, *Narodnoye khozyaistvo SSSR,* is listed in Part Three.

Rosow, Irving. *Aspects of Soviet Education.* Project on the Soviet Social System, AF No. 33(038)–12909. Cambridge: Russian Research Center, Harvard University, March 1953.

Selections from the Soviet Press. Published several times a week since January 1957 by the Department of State, Division of Acquisition and Distribution, Washington, D.C.

"The Soviet Union as Reported by Former Soviet Citizens." A series of reports released through the Department of State, Office of Intelligence Research, Washington, D.C.

Widmayer, Ruth Carol. "The Communist Party and the Soviet School—1917–1937." Unpublished Ph.D. thesis, Department of Government, Radcliffe College, Harvard University, August 1954.

World Survey of Education, Handbook of Educational Organizations and Statistics. Paris: UNESCO, 1955.

PART TWO

Source memoranda and translations made by the Center for International Studies in the course of the original study, some of which contain material not heretofore readily available either in the original Russian or in translation. It should be emphasized that these are working drafts.

Background Information

Source Memorandum No. 12, 14 pp.

Excerpts and summaries with reference to primary and secondary education from E. N. Medynskii, *Public Education in the USSR,* Moscow, 1952, first 160 pages. Original title, *Narodnoye obrazovaniye v SSSR,* is listed in Part Three.

Source Memorandum No. 3, 15 pp.

Excerpts and summaries with reference to higher education, teacher training, and research in pedagogy from E. N. Medynskii, *Public Education in the USSR,* Moscow, 1952, pages 161–218.

The publication summarized in Source Memoranda No. 12 and No. 3 is among the best secondary Soviet sources of information on the *de jure* status and operation of the Soviet educational system as of c. 1952.

Source Memorandum No. 28, 39 pp.

Summary of information given in an official handbook on technicums, *Specialized Secondary Schools of the USSR (Technicums and Other Schools),* Moscow, 1948, 503 pages.

This memorandum gives (a) the distribution of 3,425 technicums by 23 categories of training corresponding to the various branches of the economy (such as fuel industry technicums, agricultural technicums, and others) and, within each category, by the specific ministries operating these schools; (b) the 1948 rules for admission to the specialized schools at the technicum level; and (c) a list of some 285 major "basic profiles" (that is, kinds of training) given in the technicums.

Translation Series 55-42, 9 pp.

Rules of Admission to the *Specialized Secondary Schools of the USSR,* 1954, as approved by the USSR Ministry of Culture, January 5, 1954. (The 1948 rules of admission are given in Source Memorandum No. 28.)

Source Memorandum No. 31, 21 pp.

Excerpts, summaries, and comments on a special 1954 publication, *Where to Obtain a Specialty, a Handbook for Those Who Have Completed Secondary Education,* RSFSR Ministry of Education and the Main Administration of Labor Reserve, USSR Council of Ministers, Moscow, 1954, 100 pages.

The original source of the information summarized and commented upon in this memorandum is apparently the first publication of its kind, listing vocational training facilities open to graduates of the ten-year schools of general education, including the schools of technical trades *(tekhnicheskiya uchilishcha),* first organized in 1954 (249 schools), and more than 700 other trade schools or training programs.

Source Memorandum No. 2, 23 pp.

Summaries of selected chapters on Moscow University and complete translations of sections with reference to Departments of Physics, Chemistry, and Mechanics-Mathematics and the table of contents from *Handbook for Those Entering Moscow University in 1954,* 137 pages.

Source Memorandum No. 11, 9 pp.

Brief summary of selected rules and regulations with reference to graduate training in [three-year] *Graduate Program in the Institutions of Higher Learning of the USSR. A Handbook,* USSR Ministry of Higher Education; data as of July 1, 1948. Moscow: "*Sovetskaya Nauka,*" 1949, 276 pages. Original title, *Aspirantura vysshikh uchebnykh zavedenii SSSR. Spravochnik,* is listed in Part Three.

This memorandum includes the count of institutions (by categories) which are authorized to conduct graduate programs and to receive academic dissertations.

Source Memorandum No. 8, 1 p.

Complete translation of "Machine Construction Research Institute of the USSR Academy of Sciences," an article in *BSE* (Great Soviet Encyclopedia), 2nd Ed., Vol. 18, 1953, p. 227.

Source Memorandum No. 4, 3 pp.

Excerpts from S. L. Sobolev, "On Scientific Criticism, Innovation, and Dogmatism," *Pravda,* July 2, 1954.

Source Memorandum No. 5, 12 pp.

Complete translation of A. F. Ioffe, "On the Teaching of Physics in Higher Technical Schools," *Vestnik vysshei shkoly* (Herald of the Higher School), No. 10, 1951.

This source publication is an official journal of the USSR Ministry of Higher Education. The editors, with the publication of this article, opened "a discussion on the problems of teaching physics in the institutions of higher learning," inviting readers to take part.

Examinations

Translation Series 55-12, 32 pp.
Explanatory notes with reference to examinations and the content of *final* examinations leading to the certificate of graduation from a ten-year school, 1954–1955.
This translation gives the complete text of the explanatory introduction and the sets of examination topics in algebra, physics, and chemistry prescribed for the final ten-year school examinations published in pamphlet form by the Ministry of Public Education. Typical examination problems in mathematics have been added from another source. The text of questions in literature and history (given in the original source) was omitted in this translation.

Translation Series 55-43, 7 pp.
Selection of questions from written *entrance* examinations for admission to the Mechanics-Mathematics Department of Moscow University, 1950–1952, 1953.
Five sets of problems in algebra and five sets in geometry (and trigonometry) are included. These examples were taken from a pamphlet entitled *O professii matematika* (On the Profession of a Mathematician), 2nd Ed., 1954, by the Dean of the Mechanics-Mathematics Faculty of Moscow University, Academician A. N. Kolmogorov.

Translation Series 55-40, 12 pp.
Syllabi of the entrance examination in physics for admission to the USSR institutions of higher learning in 1954 and in 1955.

Curricula

The memoranda included in this category give detailed examples of the curricula, organization of courses, and academic calendar (in Russian jointly referred to as *uchebnyi plan*).

Source Memorandum No. 15, 15 pp.
Description of Electro-Mechanical Faculty, academic calendar, and curriculum of the Electrical Engineering option at the Dnepropetrovsk Mining Institute in the 1930's and other information drafted from notes and memory by a man who studied and taught there.
This memorandum describes the subjects taught under the specific curriculum, gives the number of class hours and their allocation to different types of instruction, and outlines the organizational structure of Dnepropetrovsk Mining Institute before and after 1927.

Translation Series 55-38, 4 pp.
Translation (from a longhand copy) of the official 1954–1955 curriculum at Bauman Higher Technical School prescribed for students majoring in "Material Handling Machinery and Equipment" in the Faculty of Transport Machinery.

Translation Series 55-24, 6 pp.
The 1955 curriculum and the academic calendar at Bauman Higher Technical School prescribed for students in Mechanical Engineering majoring in Technology of Machine Construction, Metal Cutting Machine Tools, and Tools.

Translation Series 55-26, 7 pp.
Part of the curriculum at Kharkov State University for students majoring in Physics under the Physics-Mathematics Faculty.

Textbooks

The memoranda included in this category give the tables of contents, selected passages, and in some cases comments on a number of officially approved textbooks (*uchebniki*) and reference texts (*uchebnye posobiya*) used in the Soviet Union.

Source Memorandum No. 16, 13 pp.

The table of contents from S. E. Frish and A. V. Timoreva, *Course of General Physics*, a textbook for state universities, in 3 volumes, as follows:

Volume I—Physical Basis of Mechanics. Molecular Physics. Oscillations and Waves. 4th Ed., 1952.

Volume II—Electric and Electromagnetic Phenomena. 4th Ed., 1952.

Volume III—Optics. Atomic Physics. 2nd Ed., revised, 1952.

Source Memorandum No. 20, 3 pp.

Table of contents and comments on S. P. Strelkov, I. A. El'tzin, and I. A. Yakovlev, *A Collection of Problems for a General Course in Physics*, 1949, a reference text for state universities and pedagogical institutes.

Source Memorandum No. 17, 18 pp.

Evaluation and comments on A. I. Akhiyezer and V. B. Berestetskii, *Quantum Electrodynamics*, 1953.

Source Memorandum No. 14, 6 pp.

Table of contents and foreword of G. N. Abramovich, *Applied Gas Dynamics*, 1953, a textbook for higher technical schools.

Source Memorandum No. 22, 6 pp.

Table of contents and foreword of V. S. Zhukovskii, *Engineering Thermodynamics*, 3rd Ed., 1952, a reference text for schools of higher technical education.

Source Memorandum No. 23, 11 pp.

Evaluation and comments on Ya. I. Frenkel', *Introduction to the Theory of Metals*, 1950, based on the translation of the table of contents and forewords to the first and second editions, which are included.

Source Memorandum No. 24, 3 pp.

Flyleaf, foreword, and table of contents of S. O. Dobrogurskii, *Computation-Solving Mechanisms*, 1950, a textbook for schools of higher technical education.

Source Memorandum No. 10, 5 pp.

Brief abstracts and table of contents of S. A. Ginzburg, I. Ya. Lekhtman, and V. S. Malov, *Fundamentals of Automatic and Remote Controls*, 1953, a textbook for technicums.

Syllabi

The documents included in this category are draft translations of the official "*programmy,*" that is, "programs" or syllabi, for a number of subjects.

Translation Series 56-1, 47 pp.

Mathematics for grades V through X in Soviet ten-year schools, 1952. Syllabus and methodological instructions with reference to the teaching of mathematics in these grades.

Translation Series 55-17, 15 pp.

Physics for higher technical schools, 1954.

Translation Series 55-11, 9 pp.
Theoretical Mechanics, 1954. Major: Chemical Engineering and Economic Engineering.
Translation Series 55-37, 11 pp.
Higher Mathematics, 1954. Technological Specialties.
Translation Series 55-28, 12 pp.
Higher Mathematics, 1954.
Translation Series 55-32, 4 pp.
Differential Equations, 1953. Major: Mathematics, Mechanics, and Astronomy.
Translation Series 55-30, 7 pp.
Mathematical Analysis, 1953. Major: Astronomy.
Translation Series 55-31, 6 pp.
Mathematical Analysis, 1953. Major: Mathematics and Mechanics.
Translation Series 55-20, 3 pp.
Foundations of Geometry, 1952.
Translation Series 55-27, 7 pp.
Higher Algebra, 1954. Major: Mathematics and Mechanics.
Translation Series 55-4, 3 pp.
Theory of the Functions of a Real Variable, 1954 (with elements of functional analysis). Major: Mathematics.
Translation Series 55-3, 3 pp.
Theory of the Functions of a Complex Variable, 1953. Major: Mathematics and Mechanics.
Translation Series 55-29, 2 pp.
Variational Calculus, 1952. Major: Astronomy.
Translation Series 55-5, 3 pp.
Theory of Numbers, 1953. Major: Mathematics.
Translation Series 55-13, 3 pp.
Equations of Mathematical Physics, 1954. Major: Mathematics.
Translation Series 55-21, 3 pp.
Equations of Mathematical Physics, 1953. Major: Mechanics and Astronomy.
Translation Series 55-36, 16 pp.
History of Mathematics, 1952. Major: Mathematics.
Translation Series 55-34, 10 pp.
Physics, 1954. Major: Mechanics and Mathematics.
Translation Series 55-1, 12 pp.
General Physics, 1952 and 1953. Major: Physics.
Translation Series 55-8, 12 pp.
General Physics Laboratory Practices. Major: Physics and Geophysics.
Translation Series 55-9, 9 pp.
Theoretical Mechanics, 1953 and 1954. Major: Mechanics and Astronomy.
Translation Series 55-33, 5 pp.
Theoretical Mechanics, 1953. Major: Physics.
Translation Series 55-19, 6 pp.
Methods of Mathematical Physics, 1953 and 1954. Major: Physics.
Translation Series 55-14, 5 pp.
Statistical Physics, 1953. Major: Physics.
Translation Series 55-18, 5 pp.
Thermodynamics, 1953. Major: Physics.

Translation Series 55-2, 10 pp.
Electrodynamics, 1953. Major: Physics.
Translation Series 55-22, 11 pp.
Electrodynamics, 1952. Major: Physics.
Translation Series 55-23, 5 pp.
Fundamentals of Electrotechniques and Radiotechniques, 1952. Major: Physics.
Translation Series 55-10, 15 pp.
History of Physics, 1953.

PART THREE

Soviet Reference Publications

Bilety dlya ekzamenov na attestat zrelosti za kurs srednei shkoly (Tickets for the Secondary School Certificate of Maturity Examinations), published each year by *Uchpedgiz.* See Translation Series 55-12 in Part Two.

Bogdanov, I. M. *Statistika shkol'novo obrazovaniya* (School Statistics). Moscow: State Statistical Publications, 1954.

Direktivy VKP(b) i postanovleniya sovetskovo pravitel'stva o narodnom obrazovanii; sbornik dokumentov za 1917–1947 gg. (Directives of the Communist Party and Acts of the Soviet Government on Public Education; a Collection of Documents from 1917–1947). 2 Vols. Moscow-Leningrad: RSFSR Academy of Pedagogical Sciences, 1947.

Finansirovaniye prosveshcheniya; sbornik zakonodatel'nykh materialov (Financing Education; a Collection of Legal Documents). Compiled by P. I. Zubok, N. A. Pomanskiy, and F. A. Gal'perina. Moscow: Gosfinizdat, 1946.

Gosudarstvennyi plan razvitiya narodnovo khozyaistva SSSR na 1941 god (State Plan for the Development of the USSR Economy in 1941), American Council of Learned Societies Reprints, Russian Series No. 30.

Kul'turnoye stroitel'stvo SSSR, statisticheskii sbornik (Cultural Progress of the USSR, a Statistical Compilation). Moscow: State Statistical Publications, 1956.

Narodnoye khozyaistvo SSSR, statisticheskii sbornik (The National Economy of the USSR, a Statistical Compilation). Moscow: State Statistical Publications, 1956.

Narodnoye obrazovaniye; osnovnyye postanovleniya, prikazy, i instruktsii (Public Education; Basic Decisions, Orders, and Instructions). Compiled by A. M. Danev. Moscow: Uchpedgiz, 1948.

Pravila priyoma i programmy priyomnykh ekzaminov dlya postupayushchikh v sredniye spetsial'nye uchebnye zavedeniya (tekhnikumy, uchilishcha, shkoly) v 1955 g. [Admission Rules and Syllabi of Entrance Examinations for Those Entering Institutions of Secondary Specialized Education (Technicums and Other Schools) in 1955]. Moscow: "Sovetskaya Nauka," 1955.

Pravila priyoma i programmy priyomnykh ekzaminov dlya postupayushchikh v vysshiye uchebnye zavedeniya v 1955 g. (Admission Rules and Syllabi of Entrance Examinations for Those Entering Institutions of Higher Education in 1955). Moscow: "Sovetskaya Nauka," 1955.

Sbornik rukovodyashchikh materialov o shkole (A Collection of Rules, Regulations, and Other Material on the Schools). Edited by N. I. Boldyrev. Moscow: RSFSR Academy of Pedagogical Sciences, 1952.

Spravochniki (Handbooks)

The USSR Ministry of Higher Education, ministries of public education, and other agencies concerned with education and training in the Soviet Union publish every year handbooks listing institutions in various categories for the USSR as a whole or by regions. A typical *spravochnik* includes the admission rules, the outlines (*programmy*) of required entrance examinations, and a list of institutions. Each institutional entry lists the departments (*fakultety*) and the options (*spetsial'nosti* and *spetsializatsii*) offered by each department. A few typical handbooks on Soviet educational institutions are listed below. (See also Source Memoranda Nos. 28, 31, 2, and 11 and Translation Series No. 55-42 in Part Two.)

A. GRADUATE SCHOOLS

Aspirantura vysshikh uchebnykh zavedenii SSSR. Spravochnik (Graduate Program in the Institutions of Higher Learning of the USSR. A Handbook). Moscow: *"Sovetskaya Nauka,"* 1949.

Spravochnik dlya postupayushchikh v aspiranturu (Handbook for Those Entering Graduate Training). Moscow: *"Moskovskaya Pravda,"* 1954.

B. UNDERGRADUATE SCHOOLS

Spravochnik dlya postupayushchikh v moskovskii universitet v 1955 g. (Handbook for Those Entering Moscow University in 1955). Moscow: *Izdatel'stvo moskovskovo universiteta,* 1955.

Spravochnik dlya postupayushchikh v moskovskiye vysshiye uchebnye zavedeniya v 1954 godu (Handbook for Those Entering Moscow Institutions of Higher Education in 1954). Moscow: *"Moskovskaya Pravda,"* 1954.

Spravochnik dlya postupayushchikh v vysshiye uchebnye zavedeniya v 1955 godu (Handbook for Those Entering Institutions of Higher Education in 1955). Moscow: *"Sovetskaya Nauka,"* 1955.

C. SPECIALIZED SECONDARY SCHOOLS (TECHNICUMS AND OTHERS)

Spravochnik dlya okonchivshikh sredniye shkoly (Handbook for the Graduates of the Secondary Schools). Moscow: *Uchpedgiz,* 1955.

Spravochnik dlya postupayushchikh v sredniye spetsial'nye uchebnye zavedeniya (tekhnikumy, uchilishcha, shkoly) v 1954 g. [Handbook for Those Entering Secondary Specialized Educational Institutions (Technicums and Other Schools) in 1954]. Moscow: *"Sovetskaya Nauka,"* 1954.

Spravochnik dlya postupayushchikh v tekhnikumy (Handbook for Those Entering Technicums). Moscow: *"Moskovskaya Pravda,"* 1954.

Spravochnik direktora shkoly (Handbook for the School Director). Moscow: *Uchpedgiz,* 1954.

Tekhnikumy (sredniye spetsial'nye uchebnye zavedeniya); postanovleniya i prikazy [Technicums (Specialized Secondary Educational Institutions); Resolutions and Decrees]. Compiled by M. I. Movshovich. Moscow: *"Sovetskaya Nauka,"* 1947.

Vysshaya shkola; osnovnye postanovleniya, prikazy, i instruktsii (The Higher School; Basic Regulations, Orders, and Instructions). Compiled by M. I. Movshovich. Moscow: *"Sovetskaya Nauka,"* 1945.

Soviet Books and Pamphlets

Alpatov, N. I. *Vneklassnaya rabota v srednei shkole* (Extracurricular Activities in Secondary Schools). Moscow: *Uchpedgiz*, 1949.

Boldyreva, N. I. *Klassnyi rukovoditel'* (Class Adviser). A manual for class advisers in secondary schools. Moscow: RSFSR Academy of Pedagogical Sciences, 1954.

Bradis, V. M. *Metodika prepodavaniya matematiki v srednei shkole* (Methods of Teaching Mathematics in Secondary Schools). 3rd Ed. Moscow: *Uchpedgiz*, 1954.

Goncharov, N. K. *Puti dostizheniya vysokoi uspevayemosti v shkole* (Ways Toward High Achievement in Schools). Moscow: RSFSR Academy of Pedagogical Sciences, 1954.

Kaftanov, S. V. *Vyssheye obrazovaniye v SSSR* (Higher Education in the USSR). Moscow: *"Molodaya Gvardiya,"* 1950.

Kayrov, I. A. *Pedagogika* (Pedagogy). 2nd Ed. Moscow: *Uchpedgiz*, 1948.

Kirsanov, A. N., and I. A. Kudinov. *Inspektirovaniye eksamenov v shkole* (The Inspection of Examinations in Schools). Moscow: *Uchpedgiz*, 1950.

Kolmogorov, A. N. *O professii matematika* (On the Profession of a Mathematician). 2nd Ed., enlarged. Moscow: *"Sovetskaya Nauka,"* 1954. See Translation Series 55-43 in Part Two.

Lyasnikov, I. A. *Podgotovka spetsialistov promyshlennosti SSSR* (The Training of Specialists for the Industry of the USSR). Moscow: *Gospolitizdat,* 1954.

Medynskii, E. N. *Narodnoye obrazovaniye v SSSR* (Public Education in the USSR). Moscow: RSFSR Academy of Pedagogical Sciences, 1952. See Source Memoranda Nos. 12 and 3 in Part Two.

Perovskii, E. I. *Ekzameny v sovetskoi shkole* (Examinations in Soviet Schools). Moscow: *Uchpedgiz,* 1948.

Petukhov, N. N. *Soderzhaniye i formy raboty komsomol'skoi organizatsii v shkole* (Content and Form of the Work of the Komsomol Organization in Schools). Leningrad: *Vsesoyuznoye obshchestvo po rasprostraneniyu politicheskikh i nauchnykh znanii,* 1954.

Politekhnicheskoye obucheniye v obshcheobrazovatel'noi shkole (Polytechnic Instruction in Schools of General Education). Edited by M. A. Mel'nikov and M. N. Skatkin. Moscow: RSFSR Academy of Pedagogical Sciences, 1953.

Programmy srednei shkoly (Syllabi for the Secondary Schools). Every year the RSFSR Ministry of Public Education publishes a series of syllabi for secondary (and elementary) school subjects. The general title of these series, published by *Uchpedgiz*, is: *Programmy srednei shkoly na —— uchebnyi god* (Syllabi for the Secondary Schools for —— Academic Year). Separate pamphlets under this general title are subtitled by one or more subjects of instruction and (sometimes) by grade, for example:

    Chercheniye (Drafting).

    Fizika. Astronomiya (Physics. Astronomy).

    Matematika (Mathematics).

    Prakticheskiye zanyatiya na uchebno-opytnom uchastke. Prakticheskiye zanyatiya v uchebnykh masterskikh. V klass (Practical Work on Experimental Garden Plots. Practical Work in School Shops. Grade V).

Sinetskii, A. Ya. *Professorsko-prepodavatel'skiye kadry vysshei shkoly SSSR* (Professorial-Teaching Personnel in the USSR Schools of Higher Education). Moscow: *"Sovetskaya Nauka,"* 1950.

Soviet Periodicals

Articles on education can be found in many Soviet journals not specifically devoted to education, such as:
Kommunist
Kul'turno-prosvetitel'naya rabota
Molodoi kommunist
Partiinaya zhizn'

Journals listed below deal exclusively with problems of education:

Doshkol'noye vospitaniye (Preschool Education), 12 issues per year.
Fizika v shkole (Physics in Schools), 6 issues per year.
Geografiya v shkole (Geography in Schools), 6 issues per year.
Inostrannye yazyki v shkole (Foreign Languages in Schools), 6 issues per year.
Khimiya v shkole (Chemistry in Schools), 6 issues per year.
Literatura v shkole (Literature in Schools), 6 issues per year.
Matematika v shkole (Mathematics in Schools), 6 issues per year.
Nachal'naya shkola (Elementary School), 12 issues per year.
Narodnoye obrazovaniye (Public Education), 12 issues per year.
Prepodavaniye istorii v shkole (The Teaching of History in Schools), 6 issues per year.
Professional'no-tekhnicheskoye obrazovaniye ("Professional" [i.e., subprofessional, such as in technicums] Technical Education), 12 issues per year.
Russkii yazyk v shkole (Russian in Schools), 6 issues per year.
Sem'ya i shkola (Family and School), 12 issues per year.
Sovetskaya pedagogika (Soviet Pedagogy), 12 issues per year.
Vestnik vysshei shkoly (Herald of the Higher School), 12 issues per year.
Yestestvoznaniye v shkole (Natural Science in Schools), 6 issues per year.

In the spring of 1957 the USSR Ministry of Higher Education announced its plans to publish the following journals:

Nauchnye doklady vysshei shkoly (Reports on Scientific Work at the Institutions of Higher Education).

Izvestiya vysshikh uchebnykh zavedenii (News of the Institutions of Higher Education).

In addition to the Soviet newspapers of general circulation, among them, *Pravda*, *Izvestiya*, *Literaturnaya gazeta*, *Krasnaya zvezda*, *Pionerskaya pravda*, and other metropolitan and provincial daily papers, articles on education frequently appear in trade papers, such as *Gudok* (a railroad trade paper), *Trud* (Labor), and *Vodnyi transport* (Water Transport).

Uchitel'skaya gazeta (Teachers' Gazette), as the name implies, deals almost exclusively with education through the secondary level.

Emigré Publications

Institute for the Study of the USSR, Munich:

Marchenko, V. *Planirovaniye nauchnoi raboty v SSSR* (The Planning of Scientific Research in the USSR), mimeographed, 1953.

Mishalov, Yu. *O podgotovke i usloviyakh raboty prepodavatelei sovetskoi shkoly* (Training and Working Conditions of Soviet School Teachers), mimeographed, 1955.

Lazarevich, I. and N. *Narodnoye obrazovaniye v SSSR (Nachal'naya i srednyaya shkola)* (Public Education in the USSR; The Elementary and Secondary School), mimeographed, 1956.

Also, by the same authors, in French: *L'Ecole soviétique (enseignements primaire et secondaire)*. Paris: Les Iles d'Or, 1954.

Skorodumov, V. *Struktura rukovodstva sovetskoi shkoloi* (The Structure of Soviet School Administration), mimeographed, 1955.

Research Program on the USSR, New York:

Budanow, Jakow. *Technical Institutes in the USSR,* Mimeographed Series No. 26, 1952, in Russian.

Ivanov, Nicolay. *Higher Technical Training in the USSR,* Mimeographed Series No. 42, 1953, in Russian.

Taskin, George A. *Geographic Studies in Soviet Universities and Teachers' Colleges,* Mimeographed Series No. 64, 1954, in Russian.

Periodicals and Newspapers:

Novoye Russkoye Slovo (New York), published daily.

Novyi zhurnal (New York), published quarterly.

Posev (Frankfurt am Main), published weekly.

Sotsialisticheskii vestnik (New York–Paris), published monthly.

Svoboda (Munich), published monthly.

Vestnik instituta po izucheniye SSSR (Munich), published quarterly.

Also, in English, *Bulletin,* published monthly.

INDEX OF SOURCES

GENERAL INDEX

Academic appointments:
administrative, 150, 152, 154
competition for, 283, 285–286, 464–
465
faculty, 149, 283–290
see also Sovmestitel'stvo
Academic chairs (*kafedry*):
definition of, 153
rule on designation of, 149
specialization by, 221
Academic degrees:
central control in conferring, 150
distribution of faculty members by,
284
examples of designations, 388 n.
Learned Council and, 164
Soviet vs. American, 390–394
titles vs., 282 f.
see also Candidate of Sciences; Doctor
of Sciences
Academic (Learned) Council:
composition and functions of, 163–165
faculty appointments and, 283–284
graduate enrollment and, 377 n.
Academic mortality:
correspondence student, 197–201
undergraduate resident student, 194 f.,
340 f.
"Academic plan" (*uchebnyi plan*):
aspirantura, 378–379
broader specialization and, 255
definition of, 209
elective subjects and, 219–221
fields of specialization and, 214, 219
for graduate students, 378–379

"Academic plan" (*uchebnyi plan*):
formulation of, 210–213, 302
recent trends and, 276 f.
textbooks and, 312 f.
see also Class hours; Curricula
Academic positions (*dolzhnosti*):
competition for, 464–465
titles and, 282
Academic titles (*zvaniya*):
advanced degrees and, 282
distribution of teaching personnel by,
283
regulations on, 460–461
selection for, 164
teaching positions and, 282
Academicians:
earnings of, 306 f.
on the teaching staff, 291
Academies of sciences:
other than USSR, 368 n.
see also Academy of Sciences, USSR
Academy of Armored-Tank and Mechanized Troops:
cited, 141
Academy of Artillery Sciences:
cited, 141
Academy of Pedagogical Sciences,
RSFSR:
polytechnic instruction and, 31
publications of, 28, 35
school syllabi and, 69, 73
Academy of Sciences, USSR:
earnings by members of, 306 f.
Five Year Plans and, 373
graduate training and, 296

Date Due